HYPNOSIS

Modern Applications of Psychology
under the editorship of
Joseph D. Matarazzo

HYPNOSIS
Research Developments
and Perspectives

EDITED BY

Erika Fromm
University of Chicago

Ronald E. Shor
University of New Hampshire

ALDINE PUBLISHING COMPANY   Chicago

The Editors

Erika Fromm is Professor of Psychology at the University of Chicago; she is President of the American Board of Psychological Hypnosis, and the Clinical Editor of the International Journal of Clinical and Experimental Hypnosis.
Ronald E. Shor is Associate Professor of Psychology at the University of New Hampshire, and Vice-Chairman of the Education and Research Foundation of the American Society of Clinical Hypnosis.

First published 1972
Aldine Publishing Company
529 South Wabash Avenue
Chicago, Illinois 60605

ISBN 0–202–25070–9
Library of Congress Catalog Number 70–182910

Printed in the United States of America

Second Printing, 1973

to the memory
of our friend
ARTHUR SHAPIRO

Preface

There are times when it is good to pause for a moment and ask ourselves: Whence have we come? Where do we stand now? Where are we going? This book attempts to answer these questions for the field of hypnosis research. The book was conceived when its senior editor, as program chairman for the Twentieth Annual Convention of the Society for Clinical and Experimental Hypnosis, organized a symposium on research in experimental hypnosis. Later, in order to secure representation for all the major experimental viewpoints in hypnosis research, other scholars were also invited to prepare chapters.

Describing the status of the field involves three tasks: earmarking the obstacles that have stood in the way of the study of hypnosis as a science, presenting the current state of knowledge concerning hypnosis, and pointing the way toward future study.

The first two chapters of the book set the stage. Chapter 1 establishes the theoretical base, and Chapter 2 sketches the historical background. The final chapter surveys predicted future trends. The other 17 chapters focus directly on key aspects of present-day hypnosis research.

We sought contributions of three types:

Surveys of broad topic areas

Descriptions in depth of individual investigators' programmatic lines of research

Reports on research within specific areas, especially those representing new viewpoints and promise for programmatic developments.

We solicited a number of papers in the third category in order to capture the excitement investigators experience as they get new ideas and eagerly pursue them. As the chapters developed and were revised, the lines of demarcation between the three types of papers became blurred, but in the main the basic structure held.

The majority of currently active investigators in experimental hypnosis are contributors to this volume. Inevitably there is overlapping when the same material is reviewed from divergent perspectives. Where we felt the overlap was simply redundant we worked to reduce it; where it provided an opportunity to see divergent viewpoints we retained it. Brief biographies of the contributors preface each chapter.

None of the chapters have been published elsewhere. Where authors reviewed their own previously published work, they updated and substantially expanded their materials.

All of the chapters have been written so that experimental researchers, clinicians, and students can read them with profit. Obviously readers with extensive backgrounds in the field will see wider implications and appreciate challenging subtleties.

As editors we sought to encourage diversity, and so the chapters vary considerably in length. We discussed length with authors in terms of scope and function, not pages. Each contributor was instructed to use no more space than was necessary to make his material challenging to new investigators and helpful to his colleagues. Given this mission some chapters became long, others short. One contributor whose viewpoint differs substantially from the rest felt that he needed a long chapter to present his dissent. So also the paper on hypnotic amnesia, for example, had to be long in order to help the new investigator who wishes to do research in this area avoid spending most of his time falling into old pitfalls.

This volume is devoted mainly to experimental research, but also addresses itself to clinicians. For clinicians can be good clinicians only if they keep abreast of research developments and modify their techniques in accordance with unfolding relevant research findings. The editors hope that bringing together these papers on current research efforts, young laboratory and clinical researchers will be stimulated to search out and examine facts about hypnosis so far ignored, ask questions not yet posed, and test ideas as yet untested.

The editors wish to express their appreciation to the contributors for their splendid cooperation in bringing this collaborative volume into being.

Doris Gruenewald, Louis Gottschalk, Sebastian P. Grossman, and Randolph Easton read chapters of this book; we thank them for their helpful comments. We also wish to thank Joseph Litchman and Kay Levensky Shanks for compiling the index.

Acknowledgments

We are grateful to the following for permission to reproduce material: *International Journal of Clinical and Experimental Hypnosis* for quotes, tables and figures from April, 1970 issue, copyrighted by the Society for Clinical and Experimental Hypnosis, 1970. *Journal of Transpersonal Psychology* for a figure from Vol. 2, No. 1, 1970; copyright by *Journal of Transpersonal Psychology*. Reprinted by permission. Andre M. Weitzenhoffer and Ernest R. Hilgard, *Stanford Hypnotic Susceptibility Scale, Form C*. Palo Alto: Consulting Psychologists Press, 1962, © 1962 by the Board of Trustees of the Leland Stanford Junior University. Calvin S. Hall and Robert L. Van de Castle, *The Content Analysis of Dreams,* New York: Appleton-Century-Crofts, 1966. Copyright 1966 by Meredith Publishing Company. University of Chicago Press for tables and figures from *Personality and Hypnosis: A Study of Imaginative Involvement* by Josephine R. Hilgard, © 1970 by the University of Chicago. *Behavioral Science* for tables from Vol. 13, 1968 issue. *The Psychological Record* for tables from Vol. 14, 1964. *Psychological Reports* for tables from Barber, T.X., Measuring "hypnotic like" suggestibility with and without "hypnotic induction." *Psychological Reports,* 1965, *16,* 809–844, Tables 3 and 5. *Psychosomatic Medicine* for table data from Vol. 25, 1963. *Psychological Bulletin* for table data from Vol. 63, 1965. *Journal of Consulting Psychology* for table data from Vol. 25, 1961. University Microfilms, Inc. for table and figure from Plapp, J. M., Hypnosis, conditioning, and physiological responses, 1967. *Journal of Abnormal Psychology* for figure from Vol. 70, 1965. *American Journal of Clinical Hypnosis* for figures from Vol. 11, 1968.; copyright 1968 by the American Society of Clinical Hypnosis. *Journal of Nervous and Mental Disease* for tables from Vol. 148, 1969; © 1969 by The Williams & Wilkins Co., Baltimore, Md. 21202, U.S.A.

Contents

V. Anticipations for Future Research

I

Theoretical and Historical Perspectives

1

Underlying Theoretical Issues: An Introduction

ERIKA FROMM AND RONALD E. SHOR

Scientific research on hypnosis began two centuries ago with Mesmer's first "magnetic" treatments in 1774. Hypnosis had been known and practiced for thousands of years, but Mesmer was the first to seek a scientific explanation for the powerful psychological forces he had learned to control. In the two centuries since then, research on hypnosis has been vigorous. While cycles of greater or lesser activity have occurred, research has gone on more or less continuously. Often researchers have drawn unwarranted conclusions; often their work has seemed to be demolished by the polemics of their critics. Nonetheless, the fabric of interest was never torn for long. For hypnosis was a phenomenon that would not go away, even though it was sometimes roundly misconceptualized and encountered resourceful enemies.

Hypnosis was an area of psychological research long before the phenomenon was recognized as primarily psychological and more than a century before the emergence of psychology as a separate discipline with the founding of Wundt's laboratory in 1879. In fact, research in hypnosis was a major influence in the development of the psychologies of motivation, the unconscious, and social influence. A number of historically important persons, known primarily for their work in other areas, have made significant contributions to the study of hypnosis: Jean Charcot, Wilhelm Wundt, Sigmund Freud, Alfred Binet, Charles Féré, Ivan Pavlov, Vladimir Bechterev, Pierre Janet, Henri Bergson, Auguste Forel, Richard von Krafft-Ebing, Frederick Myers, Théodule Ribot, Charles Richet, Morton Prince, Sandor Ferenczi, William James, Eugen Bleuler, William McDougall, Vittorrio Benussi, Paul Schilder, Clark Hull, and Henry Murray.

Despite such credentials in the way of background, manpower, and impact, the study of hypnosis has not yet reached an advanced stage of scien-

3

tific development. In terms of clinical skill and practical application we know a great deal about hypnosis, but the art of its application is far ahead of its scientific elucidation. The situation is analogous to the scientific study of humor. Everyone has an intuitive grasp of humor, and comedians and writers of comic drama have practiced their craft for many centuries. This fund of practical know-how does not, however, help to build a psychology of humor, because that practical knowledge is not in a form amenable to direct use by the scientist. The scientist must tread his own paths and he must put findings into his own forms.

We believe it will be useful to begin this book by summarizing and highlighting the underlying theoretical issues that have divided and united our contributors. We will not attempt to tally votes; but will be content simply to sensitize the reader to important issues—scientific truth is not arrived at by poll taking. Nor do we emphasize those areas where there is general agreement; such areas might be called solved issues, or nonissues. For example, our contributors generally would agree that, at its best, hypnosis is a method of tapping potent psychological forces. Yet the day is not far behind us when this statement would have been hotly debated.

In our view, the key issues fall into the following categories:

- the role of unconscious mentation in hypnosis;
- phenomenological versus behavioristic aspects of hypnosis—with special emphasis on the confusion of metatheories with scientific methodology;
- continuity and discontinuity between waking and hypnotic states; and
- physiological changes and psychological behaviors distinguishing hypnosis from the waking state.

Altogether 12 key issues are presented. Usually two alternatives are set forth. However, presenting these alternatives is not intended to deny that some of the contributors may have taken intermediary positions, or that others may be unconcerned with certain issues.

These key items are expressed in various levels of generality. In some instances, redefinitions or elaborations of a particular item merit development through subquestions, or even the rewriting of the item in the form of an additional one.

The Role of Unconscious Mentation in Hypnosis

The first four items concern themselves with the nature of hypnosis, broadly stated.

ITEM 1

> *In any complete theory of hypnosis the concept of unconscious mental functioning (more or less in the psychoanalytic sense) will be found to be necessary and important;*

or, alternatively,

will be found to be unnecessary and unimportant.

While most of the contributors feel that the concept of the unconscious is indispensible to their thinking about hypnosis, a small minority take pains not to use it in their formulations.

ITEM 2

In any complete theory of hypnosis the concept of usually unavailable modes of mentation will be found necessary and important;

or, alternatively,

will be found to be unnecessary and unimportant.

To investigators who use the concept of the unconscious, Item 2 would seem to be almost a derivative of Item 1. Those who start with the concept of the unconscious also view hypnosis as a way of tapping usually unavailable modes of mentation. Many terms are used to describe these modes of mentation: primary process, regression, primitive, dreamlike, nonrational thinking, trance logic, utilization of nonconscious resources, wellsprings of buried human potentialities, retrieval of fantasy residues, and so forth.

We decided to list Item 2 separately because investigators can refer to usually unavailable mentation without necessarily subscribing to the concept of the unconscious, and some do. Thus two contributors theorize that subjects have usually unavailable experiences as a function of intensive organismic involvement in the hypnotic role, and deny the need to invoke the concept of unconscious mental functioning.

ITEM 3

At its best hypnosis is something more than merely a profoundly compelling imaginal fantasy;

or, alternatively,

hypnosis is nothing but a profoundly compelling imaginal fantasy.

To our contributors Item 3 may appear to be a nonissue. All of them would agree with the second alternative. Perhaps such agreement is possible today because we have reached a stage in the development of psychology where we can readily acknowledge the power of the processes of imagination. But what are the processes of imagination? That issue would now merit attention.

ITEM 4

Learning to be a good hypnotic subject basically involves the development of a cognitive skill, of increasing one's capacities for cognitive control;

or, alternatively,

it involves succumbing to the control of others, decreasing one's capacities for cognitive control.

Again, this appears to be a non-issue today. All our contributors would agree that the first alternative applies to their own work. However, some clinicians would urge keeping open the possibility that an unscrupulous hypnotist might be able to use hypnosis to take advantage of his subjects (see Kline, 1970). But no one doubts that, in responsible hands, hypnosis involves learning a cognitive skill.

Phenomenological versus Behavioristic Aspects of Hypnosis: Metatheories versus the Scientific Method

The next six items (Items 5–11) focus on major theoretical issues that are still unsolved and hotly debated. In our view, this lack of resolution is at least partly due to the so far neglected task of separating metatheories from systems of scientific inquiry. Item 5 raises this issue.

ITEM 5

> The ultimate issue to be explained with regard to hypnosis is the subject's inner subjective experience;

or, alternatively,

> the ultimate issue is the subject's outward, observable, behavior.

This item poses the issue that is central to the classic dispute between phenomenology and behaviorism. The phenomenological position is that the subjective experience of hypnosis is the fundamental fact to be explained, and that it provides the primary defining datum of hypnosis. Phenomenologists contend that outward behavior is a meaningful index of hypnosis only to the extent that it accurately reflects the primary subjective events. The behavioristic position is that behaviors observable by an outsider are the fundamental indices, and that reports of subjective experience are simply one form of behavior—verbal behavior. The behaviorist thinks it is irrelevant to discuss whether people have subjective experiences; he flatly states that unless such experiences are translated into observable behavior they have no place within the scientific system.

Two examples help to clarify these two positions. Let us suppose that an investigator initially became interested in hypnosis because he himself had had profound subjective hypnotic experiences; no amount of rational argument could shake his conviction of the reality of these experiences. These subjective experiences have become the fundamental puzzle he wants to explain; they are the reason why he is willing to devote his professional energies to the study of hypnosis. Nothing will convince him that outward behavior is more real, or more fundamental, than his own subjective experiences. He will argue that if science is not big enough to encompass and explain these primary subjective events, then the conception of science must be broadened. If these experiences do not fit into the scientific test tube, he will insist science needs a bigger test tube.

However, a second investigator, also initially interested in hypnosis because of compelling subjective hypnotic experiences, may arrive at a radically different conception of the kind of science that should be developed to explain hypnotic experiences. He may conclude that it is folly to try to pursue subjective events in their own terms, and that the only way to build a fruitful, coherent science is on the basis of observed behavior. In his view, if science is broadened to include pure mentalisms, inevitably it will become pseudoscience. He will insist that men have no direct pipeline to mentalisms, and that the sooner they acknowledge this fact and get on with the business of building a solid behavioral science, the better off the discipline will be.

These issues have not been resolved since the battle lines were drawn by J. B. Watson in the 1920s; it is obvious that they will not be resolved in the confines of this volume.

In our judgment, allegiance to the phenomenological or to the behavioristic position is basically a matter of philosophy of science, not science; it is a philosophic commitment, not a scientific decision. However, once such a philosophic commitment has been made one way or the other, it determines the kind of scientific system that can unfold within it.

In our view science does not begin in a vacuum. Prior to the scientific enterprise all science begins with a set of philosophic assumptions, a philosophic metatheory, a bedrock of unassailable "givens" that are axiomatically assumed to be true. While, by selected criteria, one scientific system may prove more fruitful than another, the philosophic metatheories themselves are not amenable to scientific proof or disproof within the scientific systems that arise out of them. Metaphorically speaking, these metatheories create "elbow room," the context of definition and outlook within which the scientist can set about doing his work. We believe that many of the current controversies among hypnosis researchers have their origin in the philosophic commitment to either a fundamentally phenomenological or a fundamentally behavioristic metatheory. To so assert is not to resolve the differences between the two views; but it is useful to put them on the table where they can be seen more clearly.

The controversy between these two points of view has often been phrased in terms of "inner subjective experience of the hypnotic effects" on the one hand, and "outwardly observable behavior" on the other. These phrasings carefully avoid specifying the nature of the subjective or the behavioral events—except to say that they are somehow hypnotic. A variety of scientific theories can flow from both philosophic positions. Scientific theories and philosophical commitments, however, are in different realms of discourse. We believe that it is important to try to separate scientific theoretical formulations from metatheories. This can best be done by asking two series of questions, one from the phenomenological position, and the other from the behavioristic position.

Key Questions from the Phenomenological Point of View

Eleven questions should be raised from the phenomenological point of view.
1. Do the subjective events in hypnosis involve some kind of alteration or change in the organism?
2. Assuming a Yes answer to the above question, is it meaningful to say that this change is a change in the *state* of the organism?
3. Do the subjective changes in hypnosis involve some kind of change in consciousness?
4. Do the subjective changes in hypnosis represent a fundamental discontinuum from nonhypnotic subjective events?
5. Assuming Yes answers to questions 2 and 4, do the subjective changes in hypnosis involve a fundamentally discontinuous change in the state of the organism?
6. Assuming Yes answers to questions 2, 3, and 4, do the subjective changes in hypnosis involve a fundamentally discontinuous change in the state of consciousness?
7. Are the subjective changes in hypnosis somehow responsible for (the cause, the explanation, the mediating event for) hypnotic phenomena?
8. Assuming Yes answers to questions 2 and 3, is the altered state of consciousness an intrinsic element in all hypnosis or does it occur only some of the time?
9. Assuming a Yes answer to question 7 and to the first alternative in question 8, is the altered state of consciousness somehow responsible for (the cause, the explanation, the mediating agent for) hypnotic phenomena?
10. Under what circumstances can objective behavioral responses be trusted to be meaningful reflections of the primary subjective events?
11. Is behavioral responsiveness to test suggestions (suggestibility) an invariant defining characteristic of hypnosis or can there be hypnosis without suggestibility?

Key Questions from the Behavioristic Point of View

The second set of questions, posed from the behavioristic point of view, involves fewer issues, and they follow each other more obviously. This may be a tribute to the greater parsimony of the behavioristic position—or a sign of its limitations.
1. Do the behavioral events in hypnosis refer to the subject's observable responses (muscular and verbal) to such suggestions as "your arm is growing heavy"?

2. Assuming a Yes answer to question 1, is there a certain basal level of responsiveness to test suggestions in nonhypnotized subjects?
3. Assuming a Yes answer to the two preceding questions, are the behavioral events that define hypnosis indexed by the *increase* in responsiveness to test suggestions beyond this basal level?
4. Assuming a Yes answer to questions 1 through 3, is it necessary to posit some kind of a special hypnotic agency to account for the increased responsiveness to test suggestions? Or is such a notion merely excess conceptual baggage—superfluous, circular, misleading?
5. How and under what circumstances can reports of subjective experiences be trusted as reliable behavioral data?

These 16 questions concerning the phenomenological and behavioristic positions all could have been translated into separate items with alternative formulations; however, such treatment would have taken the spotlight away from what we see as the six major points of controversy. Five of these six points are involved in the phenomenology versus behaviorism debate; these are Items 6 through 10.

ITEM 6

Altered states of consciousness are valid psychological phenomena worthy of scientific study in their own right. Whether they cause, mediate, predict, or correlate with responsiveness to test suggestions are separate issues;

or, alternatively,

altered states of consciousness can be considered valid psychological phenomena worthy of scientific study only if some kind of independent, nontautological, noncircular behavioral criterion can be found for them.

This item clearly reflects the dispute between the phenomenological and behavioristic positions in regard to the concept of the altered state of consciousness.

ITEM 7

In any complete theory of hypnosis the concept of an altered state of consciousness will be found necessary and important;

or, alternatively,

will be found unnecessary and unimportant.

This item must be kept separate from the preceding one because an investigator can believe that the concept of altered states is valid in its own terms yet feel that it is unnecessary or unimportant in explaining hypnosis.

ITEM 8

In any complete theory of hypnosis all of the concepts used to explain hypnosis will be part of the fabric of psychology in general;

or, alternatively,

> *at least one aspect of the explanation must be special and unique to hypnosis.*

On first glance this appears to be a nonissue. All of our contributors would say that they want to integrate the study of hypnosis into the framework of general psychology. Indeed, they would assert that if hypnosis were only a unique and circumscribed phenomenon—a foreign body standing apart from other psychological processes—they would lose interest in it and turn their attention to more important matters. Dissenters would argue, however, that those investigators who adhere to the traditional hypnotic trance state viewpoint have in fact selected the second alternative, whether they realize it or not. The heart of the matter is expressed in the next item.

ITEM 9

> *In any complete theory of hypnosis the concept of a special mediating agent unique to hypnosis will be found to be necessary and important;*

or, alternatively,

> *will be found unnecessary and unimportant.*

Interpretation of this issue depends on what precisely is meant by "special mediating agent" and "unique to hypnosis." While these are subtle matters it is the stance of the dissenters that they can explain hypnosis without having to invoke a concept of a unique mediating agency but that those who hold to the traditional hypnotic trance state position have no choice but to do so.

ITEM 10

> *Suggestibility (responsiveness to test suggestions) is an invariant, irreducible, defining feature of hypnosis;*

or, alternatively,

> *suggestibility is nonintrinsic to hypnosis.*

This issue is mentioned explicitly only in one paper in regard to expectancies arising historically from Puységur's observations, but it arises implicitly wherever hypnosis is somehow equated to, or explained by, suggestibility, or where hypnotic depth is measured by amount of responsiveness to test suggestions.

Continuity versus Discontinuity Between Hypnosis and Waking State

Item 11 involves the sixth key issue in the behaviorism versus phenomenology controversy. It has been set off from the preceding five key points in order to emphasize its importance in the struggle of metatheoretical stances. This item is concerned with the issue of continuity versus discontinuity between hypnosis and waking states. Three questions (4, 5, and 6) in the section on the phenomenological point of view also dealt with this issue.

ITEM 11

> *There is a quantitative continuity between the usual waking state of everyday life and deep hypnosis;*

or, alternatively,

> *there is a fundamental qualitative discontinuity between them.*

Item 11 would seem a nonissue. All of the contributors hold that hypnotic depth is a quantitative continuum along one or more dimensions of depth. However, at least one contributor insists that it is still an issue. The assertion is that a fundamental, qualitative discontinuity between hypnosis and the usual waking state is implicit in the traditional hypnotic trance state paradigm.

In the hope of helping to clarify the problem, let us draw the following analogy: the dissent expressed is that, according to the traditional paradigm, being in hypnosis is something like the issue of whether or not a woman is pregnant. To be pregnant is fundamentally, qualitatively different from not being pregnant. A woman cannot be a little bit pregnant. Whether in early or late pregnancy, she is totally pregnant. In regard to hypnosis the dissenting view is that the traditional hypnotic trance state paradigm implies that a special altered state causes or mediates increased responsiveness to suggestion. In this context depth of hypnosis refers to the extensiveness of the altered state. The altered state, like pregnancy, is defined as fundamentally discontinuous from the usual waking state regardless of its extent. The dissenter usually comes across to readers as if he vigorously were demonstrating and believing that there is no such thing as hypnosis—which de facto is not his position at all.

Physiological Changes and Psychological Behaviors Distinguishing Hypnosis from the Waking State

Another significant group of issues centers on the extent to which changes in physiological and psychological behavior in hypnosis differ from those that can be produced in the waking state. These are the issues of transcendence of normal volitional capacities.

ITEM 12

> *There is convincing evidence that deeply hypnotized subjects can produce certain observable behaviors and physiological changes that even highly motivated nonhypnotized subjects in the usual waking state are unwilling or unable to produce or unable to mimic;*

or, alternatively,

   there is no such convincing evidence.

This item focuses on the issue of transcendence of normal volitional capacities and it should be reiterated that it refers to outward behaviors and physiological changes only, not to subjective events. Most of our contributors have been concerned with this issue in one form or another; several have developed specialized methodologies for dealing with it. The item encompasses the issues of sensitivity to subtle demand characteristic, discernment of experimental deception, ability to fool the experimenter, antisocial and self-destructive behavior, and the ability to figure out what a deeply hypnotized person would do.

Most of the contributors would agree with the second alternative: there is at present no *convincing* evidence. The hard fact is that in the last decade of research in hypnosis all claims made for the unique behavioral and physiological effects of hypnosis have proved unconvincing when subjected to careful experimental scrutiny. Two of our contributors, however, believe that they have discovered several typical psychological hypnotic behaviors that simulators are not able to figure out.

Item 12 completes this roster of key issues. Doubtless the list is incomplete. But posing it may help to alert the reader to a number of underlying themes reflected throughout the volume in a variety of ways.

Ronald E. Shor *is an Associate Professor of Psychology at the University of New Hampshire. He received his Ph.D. from Brandeis University in 1960, and joined the staff of the Studies in Hypnosis Project at the Massachusetts Mental Health Center and Harvard Medical School, becoming Associate Director in 1963. He continued in that role when the laboratory became the Unit for Experimental Psychiatry at the University of Pennsylvania. Shifting to a greater commitment in teaching, he joined the staff of La Salle College in 1966, and moved to the University of New Hampshire the following year. He has co-edited* The nature of hypnosis: Selected basic readings *with Martin Orne. His major interests are a cognitive approach to the study of alterations in conscious experiencing, concept identification, and skill in symbol use.*

Shor *argues that there are two intertwined—and fundamental—dangers in hypnosis research: not maintaining the disciplined skepticism of the scientist, and not maintaining the confident persuasiveness of the hypnotist. The more the scientist-hypnotist tries to avoid one of these two dangers, the more likely it is that he will succumb to the other. In the first part of his chapter Shor surveys the major events in the history of hypnosis. He shows how the fundamental problem has been manifested at different times in ways that differ only superficially. In the second part he presents an exposition of this fundamental problem as it has emerged from its historic background.*

2

The Fundamental Problem in Hypnosis Research as Viewed from Historic Perspectives

RONALD E. SHOR

> On one side of the narrow strait lay Scylla, a treacherous rock; on the
> other side lay an equal danger, Charybdis, a dreadful whirlpool. The only
> safe passage was to sail the narrow course in between. Sailing to either
> one side or the other brought unfailing disaster. The only method for
> avoiding either of these two dangers was therefore to take the terrible risk
> of succumbing to its counterpart danger. The more leeway the navigator
> allowed himself in avoiding the danger to port meant just that much less
> leeway in avoiding the reciprocal danger to starboard. These two entirely
> distinct and separate dangers of rock and whirlpool were
> thus so situated that unavoidably they had to be faced together,
> as if one single, unitary problem.
> The Straits of Messina

The fundamental problem in hypnosis research is that it is faced with two dangers, which, like the rock and whirlpool of Scylla and Charybdis, are so situated that they must be encountered together, as if they were one. The two inextricable dangers are the danger of not providing sufficient disciplined skepticism, and the danger of not providing sufficient positive catalyst. The investigator of hypnosis is always faced with the extremely difficult task of maintaining both caution and conviction at one and the same time, that is, maintaining both the disciplined skepticism of the scientist and the confident persuasiveness of the hypnotist. Fulfilling the two roles of scientist and hypnotist simultaneously is a slippery task, beset with many

15

subtle difficulties. The more the scientist-hypnotist tries to avoid one of the two dangers, the more likely it becomes that he will succumb to the other.

The fundamental problem has emerged repeatedly throughout the two centuries since Mesmer's first "magnetic" treatments. The specific forms it has taken have been as superficially different in every era as is the antelope from the whale, but with proper background the underlying uniformity can be discerned.

I. Survey of Major Historic Events

From time immemorial men in the most diverse cultures have discovered how to use hypnotic and suggestive phenomena with immense pragmatic effectiveness for faith healing and for magico-religious and other purposes. But it was during the ultrarational Age of Enlightenment in the late eighteenth century, as fundamentalist religion was waning and the physical sciences were emerging, that a physician faith healer, Franz Anton Mesmer, devoted his life to the development of a scientific understanding of the powerful therapeutic forces which he had learned to control. Mesmer's theories have been proved untenable, but the insights they contained initiated and provoked a continuing scientific development (see Figure 2.1).

The history of hypnotism from Mesmer to the present day may conveniently be divided into four periods, representing stages of scientific sophistication. These four stages are: Presomnambulistic Mesmerism, Somnambulistic Mesmerism (later renamed Hypnotism), the Early Psychological Period, and the Later Psychological or Modern Period. In the first stage mesmeric-hypnotic phenomena were brought within the general boundaries of science; in the second stage attention was recentered on artificial somnambulism as the pivotal event; in the third stage many inaccurate, prepsychological interpretations were eliminated in favor of more accurate, psychological interpretations; in the present, fourth stage the insights of psychodynamics and precise quantitative methods have been and are being incorporated. The chief events in this development have been summarized in Table 2.1. The four stages are, of course, interpretive classifications rather than entities or events. Once stated, however, they are assumed valid and will be referred to throughout as guideposts to the historic development. (For further reading the following secondary sources are recommended: Ackerknecht, 1948; Boring, 1950; Bromberg, 1959; Conn, 1957; Ellenberger, 1970; Galdston, 1948A; Marks, 1947; Murphy, 1949; Pattie, 1967; Podmore, 1909; Rosen, 1948, 1963; Sarbin, 1962; Shor, 1968; Tinterow, 1970; Watson, 1971; Williams, 1952; Zilboorg & Henry, 1941; Zweig, 1922).

PRESOMNAMBULISTIC MESMERISM

There was little if any historic novelty in Mesmer's therapeutic successes nor in the theoretical pseudology he derived to account for them. His contribu-

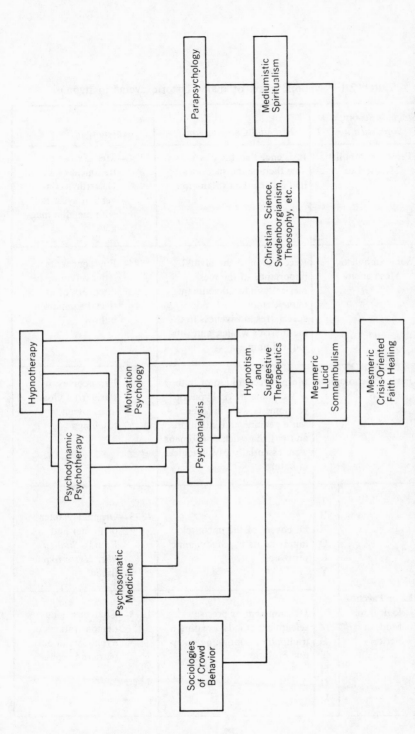

FIGURE 2.1. *Mesmer's intellectual progeny. (Height indicates rough chronology and is not an evaluation of relative importance. Mesmerism's precursors are not indicated, nor are the other roots contributing to the development of the various offshoots.)*

TABLE 2.1   Synoptic chart of major historic events in hypnosis

Stage of Scientific Sophistication		Essential Contribution	Beginning of Period
1. Presomnambulistic Mesmerism		Insistence that the observable therapeutic successes had a scientific explanation	1774—Mesmer begins treatment of F. Oesterlin's conversion hysteria with metallic magnets
2. Somnambulistic Mesmerism		Recognition of the pivotal importance of the mesmerically-induced somnambulistic state with lucid speech, responsiveness to the mesmerist's wishes, and subsequent amnesia	1784—Puységur writes letter outlining his discovery of artificial somnambulism
3. Early Psychological Period		Merged recognition of both (*a*) that mesmeric-hypnotic phenomena were in some sense genuine and important, and (*b*) that such phenomena were essentially psychological in nature	1814—Faria comes to Paris from Goa and expounds teachings
4. Later Psychological, or Modern Period	T H E O R Y	Discovery of the unconscious mind and its psychodynamic processes	1893—Original chapters of Breuer and Freud's *Studien über Hysterie* published
	M E T H O D	Development of precise scientific methods, creating a tradition of continuing scientific evolution	1878—Charcot begins demonstrations of hypnotism at Salpêtrière hospital

Major Contributor		Entrance into History of Hypnosis	
Name	Life Span	Year	Event
Mesmer, F. A.	1734–1815		
Puységur, A. Marquis de	1751–1825		
Elliotson, J.	1791–1868	1837	Begins magnetic experiments at University Hospital
Braid, J. (early)	1795–1860	1843	Publishes *Neurypnology*
Charcot, J. M. (theory)	1825–1893	1882	Gives nosological description to Academy of Sciences
Faria, J. C. di	1756–1819		
Bertrand, A. J. F.	1795(?)–1831	1823	Publishes *Traité du somnambulisme. . .*
Braid, J. (later)	(above)	1847	Advances psychological view
Liébeault, A. A.	1823–1904	1866	Publishes *Du sommeil. . .*
Bernheim, H. M.	1837–1919	1884	Publishes *De la suggestion. . .*
Freud, S.	1856–1939		
Erickson, M. H.	1901–	1933	Publishes *Hypnosis and*
Charcot, J. M. (method)	(above)		
Hull, C. L.	1884–1952	1933	Publishes *Hypnosis and Suggestibility*

tion lay not in originality but in his insistence that the observable therapeutic effects had a scientific explanation.

Mesmer's therapy and theory were minor variants of the teachings of many other faith healers throughout history. His therapy was a combination of the ancient procedure of laying-on-of-hands with a disguised version of medieval demonic exorcism. His theory was a combination of ancient astrological concepts, medieval mysticism, and seventeenth century vitalism. But Mesmer viewed himself as a thorough-going mechanist, and thus garbed his teachings in the terminology of eighteenth century physical science, particularly of magnetism and electricity.

Health to Mesmer was the harmonious distribution in mind and body of an impalpable, ethereal fluid that permeated the universe; disease was fluidic imbalance. To some extent the cosmic fluid could be controlled by the human Will, and even stored in inanimate objects. Mesmer's clinical investigations soon led him to observe extreme agitation, convulsive seizure, and other temporarily deteriorated behavior in his patients after therapeutic manipulations.[1] From these observations he concluded that an indispensable first step in treatment was to cause some of his own stored cosmic fluid to flow into a receptive patient to provoke thereby an even more severe fluidic imbalance. The patient's behavior would then deteriorate into a violent convulsive seizure, meaning that the malady had reached a head or crisis, after which equilibrium would tend to become restored.

These convulsive crises became the pivotal event in Mesmer's therapeutic system. We know today that they were purely artifacts of mutually shared expectations. But Mesmer, his disciples, and his patients became convinced that the crises were indispensable preliminaries to cure. And just so long as these beliefs were firmly shared, it remained (thereby) pragmatically true that mesmerized patients did not derive therapeutic benefit without first experiencing this type of crisis. The necessity and therapeutic effectiveness of the interposed crisis thus was repeatedly verified clinically, strengthening the conviction even more.

Mesmer's was an age of fanatic ultrarationalism and emotive alienation of the doctor from the folk culture, but the orthodox physicians had little. to offer sufferers of functional ailments beyond impersonalized faith healing rationalized in the form of potions, bleeding, and purges. Mesmer's brand of faith healing on the other hand was a credo that enlisted enthusiastic belief and high expectancy of cure; it was emotionally comprehensible and sensitively attuned to the emotive needs of the multitudes. While untenable from

1. These original agitated reactions were probably due to three factors: expectations deriving from medieval demonic exorcism rites, the dancing manias (St. Vitus's Dance, for example), and possibly epilepsy; a probable aftereffect of anxiety release after direct symptom suppression (see particularly the case of Maria Theresa von Paradis in Mesmer's *Mémoire*. . ., first published in 1774); a derivation of the *vapeurs,* the hysterical fainting and nervous fits fashionable among society women at that time.

the standpoint of objective scientific truth, Mesmer's powerful therapeutic theories were functionally, pragmatically true.

Mesmer did not fail to note that unless his patients were cooperative and sincerely wished to be cured they would not allow themselves to become receptive to the physician's healing influences. In other words, although his physicalistic theoretical interpretations were incorrect, as a clinical practitioner Mesmer had an astute working knowledge of the importance of a favorable doctor-patient relationship.

He also evolved highly successful methods of group treatment by using the storage condenser principle of accumulating the cosmic fluid in inanimate objects, later to supply quantities of the fluid to large numbers of persons at a time. In addition, by enlisting the credulous yearnings of the populace in mystic ceremonials, Mesmer and his disciple d'Eslon developed to a fine theoretical art the heightening of expectancy of the crisis and cure.

But these important insights were ignored in the controversy over whether the cosmic fluid, whose effect on living organisms was called Animal Magnetism, was a physical entity, and thus a legitimate object of scientific study, or mere imagination, and thus nothing but fraud and collusion, with overtones of danger to morality.

Mesmer, although disheartened eventually by ceaseless vitriolic rebuff from official quarters, had defenders who were both eloquent and incisive; but the French Revolution and the Napoleonic Wars soon scattered the protagonists. Presomnambulistic mesmerism, with the convulsive crisis as the pivotal event, disappeared from the center of the historic stage. (Recommended primary and secondary sources are Bailly et al., 1784a, 1785, 1784b; Barbarin, 1786; Bergasse, 1784; Bonnefoy, 1784; Darnton, 1968; Eslon, 1780, 1784; Galdston, 1948b; Goldsmith, 1934; Grimm & Diderot, 1784; Jussieu, 1784; Ludwig, 1964; Mesmer, 1774, 1785, 1814; Pattie, 1956b; Poissonnier et al., 1784; Sernan, 1784; Wydenbruck, 1947).

SOMNAMBULISTIC MESMERISM

In 1784, the same year that the Royal Commissioners disaffirmed the existence and value of Animal Magnetism, one of Mesmer's many layman disciples, Armand Chastenet, Marquis de Puységur, wrote a letter to a colleague outlining his discovery of artificial somnambulism. Later that same year Puységur expanded on his findings in the first edition of his *Mémoires*. To Puységur belongs the credit for the first clear recognition of the pivotal importance of mesmerically-induced sleepwalking, in which strange, mysticlike events seemed to occur. With this recentering of concern on artificial somnambulism, and away from the convulsive crises, mesmerism entered its second stage of scientific sophistication.

Puységur and his followers discovered that in this special entranced, sleeplike state, the mesmerized subjects could speak lucidly, open their eyes and walk about, respond to the mesmerist's wishes and commands, and sub-

sequently forget their experiences when aroused. They also discovered that
crises were not indispensable to cure, and thus the crises slowly slipped into
historic obscurity, less and less expected and thus less and less seen.

While it is true that Puységur independently discovered mesmeric somnambulism, Mesmer and others had witnessed it earlier. But as this sleeplike
condition was irrelevant to the production of the convulsive crises, these
earlier observers had viewed somnambulism only as an unfortunate interruption to their therapeutic process.[2]

Puységur's reorientation in outlook could come only under conditions
where people were far less convinced that the crisis was the dominating
event in therapy. At Puységur's provincial estate, peasants and villagers
were treated who were far removed from the sophisticated Parisian gossip
about what to expect during mesmeric treatments. Dispensing with somber
surroundings and mystic ceremonials, Puységur adopted the less theatrical,
simpler methods that Mesmer had evolved earlier, such as accumulating
Animal Magnetism in a tree, under the open sky.

Inordinate responsiveness

To the peasants and artisans of Puységur's province it was assuredly a
gratifying event to have the prestigious marquis show profound concern for
their welfare by mesmerizing them, and these humble folk basked in his
aristocratic presence. It is hardly surprising that Puységur discovered that
his somnambulists were inordinately responsive to his directions, and were
trying very hard to please him.

Recall that Mesmer's initial observations on agitated reactions soon led
him to conceptualize and instill firm expectations of crises, which then precipitated these crises just so long as the expectations remained shared. Perhaps similarly, an inordinate responsiveness is not intrinsic to artificial
somnambulism either, but is demonstrably true so long as the shared expectations—fabricated from Puységur's initial observations—remain to make it
functionally true. Such shared expectations of increased responsiveness
when entranced persist into our own day[3] (see especially Ellenberger,
1965b; Puységur, 1784a, 1784b, 1807, 1811, 1837).

2. Some historians have held that Mesmer suppressed knowledge of mesmeric
   somnambulism because of its unwelcome resemblance to sorcery. Also prior to
   Puységur's discovery, the Chevalier de Barbarin and his devotees had routinely
   induced somnambulism, but their zealous animistic interpretations likewise
   blocked clear recognition of its pivotal importance.
3. Although theoretical interpretations differ, this same observation of inordinate
   responsiveness finds expression in the later concepts of remarkable docility,
   hypersuggestibility, increased motivation, role-taking, and increased responsiveness to test suggestions. Ellenberger (1965b) has pointed out that the kind of authoritarian relationship between the magnetizer and his somnambulist became
   transformed as a function of the change from an aristocratic to a bourgeoisie
   dominated society. In Puységur's day the type of relationship between the noble-

The Doctrine of Will Power

The discovery of the somnambulist's inordinate responsiveness to the wishes and commands of the mesmerist initiated two concomitant theoretical developments. The first was a shift away from Mesmer's view of man as some kind of animal "magnet" who could to some extent willfully control a physical, external, impersonal cosmic fluid. The second was a concomitant shift toward the highly personalized doctrine of Will Power.

To Puységur and his followers the curative fluid was secreted by the mesmerist's brain and passed along his nerves to the peripheral organs in response to his Will. The manufacture and transmission of the vital fluid depends on the mesmerist's exuberant faith and unaltering self-confidence in his own dominating powers. Albeit an easy vehicle for the expression of the mesmerist's egoistic fantasies, the doctrine of Will Power nonetheless represented an advance in translating the interpersonal aspects of the mesmeric process into psychological terms.

The discovery of this mesmerically-induced trance state in which wondrous phenomena seemed to occur led to widespread and enthusiastic experimentation by Puységur and his followers. This experimentation in turn soon led to the clear recognition of just about all of the major mesmeric-hypnotic phenomena acknowledged today: the motor automatisms and catalepsies, amnesias, anesthesias, positive and negative hallucinations, posthypnotic phenomena, and individual differences in susceptibility.

Credulous excess

But inextricably confounded with the genuine observations there grew up a tangle of wild pseudologizing and extravagant, mystic claims of paranormal powers conferred in the special state: clairvoyance, transposability of the senses, somnambulistic medical diagnosis, foretelling of the future, spiritualistic mediumship, and so forth. These credulous excesses were inevitable both because they fit the mood of nineteenth century Romanticism and because at a nonconscious (if not also conscious) level the mesmerized somnambulist was strongly impelled to produce the phenomena that he perceived were expected of him.

Because mesmeric phenomena are initiated by enthusiasm and expectancy, credulous excess tends to augment the phenomena and scientific skep-

---

man and his peasant was manifested as a kind of "bargaining therapy," with the personality of the somnambulist more brilliant than usual. This was replaced during the nineteenth century by forms of treatment based on hypnotic command and direct suggestion, with the subject a mere automation in the style of the relationship between the bourgeois master and his servant. In our own day, the enormous psychological and social distance supportive of the authoritarian hypnotic relationship has faded, but the concept of suggestibility and its variant expressions remain.

ticism (doubt) tends to attenuate them. Thus investigators with cooler heads were often at a disadvantage, whereas those with wilder fantasies and blinder resolve were more readily able to produce striking effects. There was consequently a natural selection in the direction of extravagance.

Thus each mesmerist would tend to see his expectancies and as yet unformulated speculations repeatedly proved true by the behavior of his trained somnambulists, and the more outspoken his position became, the clearer was the proof engendered. While apparently utilizing a process roughly akin to hypothetic-deductive scientific method—by hypothesis, experimental test, verification, reformulation, etc.—many of the mesmerists evolved the most extravagant, mutually contradictory pseudologies.

But the very multiplicity of the mesmerists' divergent doctrines served to undermine the plausibility of any one of them, and thus, in a negative fashion, helped prepare the advent of more sedate theories. Despite the jibberish and nonsense, too many genuine and startling effects had been uncovered not to lead some wiser minds to recognize that there was something important in mesmerism to be explained. And once thoughtful men sought to encompass what seemed genuine in mesmerism within the conservative framework of existing physical and physiological science, a psychological interpretation became inevitable.

But even in the mid-1820s, when at least two men, José Faria and Alexandre Bertrand, had already arrived at the third stage of sophistication, the issues were nonetheless still being misstated at the prepsychological, second stage when the French Academy reopened its inquiry into mesmerism. The investigators were primarily interested in whether there were psychical phenomena in somnambulism, such as clairvoyance, which were beyond the bounds of ordinary science. Since under careful scrutiny no such miracles were forthcoming, mesmerism was again officially rejected. (Recommended sources are Bennett, 1851; Binet and Féré, 1886; Burdin & Dubois, 1841; Carlson, 1960; Colquhoun, 1844; Deleuze, 1819, 1825; Hall, 1845; Husson et al., 1833; Kerner, 1847; Lafontaine, 1860; Leger, 1846; Macchi, 1858; Poe, 1837; Reichenbach, 1850; Schneck, 1959.)

Braid's early theory

Nothing substantive prevented the formulation of conservative theories at the second stage of sophistication, however. One such second-stage theory of considerable historic importance was advanced by James Braid in his book *Neurypnology* (1843). Braid recognized that certain mesmeric phenomena were genuine but rejected all mesmeric theories of external influences. Taking as his starting point the eye fixation induction technique that he had observed in demonstrations by the mesmerist Lafontaine, Braid advanced a naturalistic physiological explanation. He theorized that staring fixedly at a bright object for a protracted period induces fatigue of the levator muscles of the eyelids, which in turn promotes a general exhaustion or derangement of the nerve centers. Or, stated more broadly, by deliberately fixing attention on a single, continuous, monotonous stimulation, a special nervous sleep or stupor results, in which the functional activity of the central nervous system is decreased. This condition Braid termed neuro-hypnotism.

A few years later, in 1847, Braid revised his thinking to give preeminence to psychological factors and somewhat minimized the physiological; thus he advanced to the third stage. At that point he regretted his general use of the term neuro-hypnotism, because the nervous sleep had become for him only a special case of the more fundamental principle of exclusively concentrated attention (monoideism, that is, single-idea-ism). But the very change from one misnomer to another, from mesmerism to hypnotism, helped to alter mesmerism's public and professional image. And because the age found that the new name had the proper antimesmeric and physiological ring to it, the phenomena could more easily be brought within the bounds of cautious, respectable science. The change in name thus helped transform the spirit of investigation from credulous excess to naturalistic science.

Charcot's neurological theory

Three decades later, in 1878, Jean Martin Charcot, the eminent clinical neurologist, began his demonstrations of hypnotism at the Salpêtrière Hospital in Paris. Charcot offered precise scientific descriptions based on the meticulous empiricist methodology of the neurological examination. In 1882, he presented his neurological theory of hypnosis to the French Academy of Sciences. In a precise nosologic classification, hypnotism was described as three distinct sequential physiological reflex stages in hysterically predisposed individuals. These three stages were induced and terminated by certain definite physical stimuli.

We know today that Charcot's theory of hypnotism was for the most part a disguised return to many of the old mesmeric errors, phrased in advanced neurological terminology. As a theorist, Charcot was deluded by procedural artifacts introduced by the very nature of the meticulous scientific methodology he adopted. These delusions were the same errors and pitfalls that the practicing clinicians of that period, Liébeault, Bernheim, and others, had so successfully learned to recognize and avoid. In other words, Charcot's theory was a blind insistence on a naive, prepsychological explanation at a time when practicing clinicians had clearly advanced to the third, more sophisticated level of understanding.

But despite the objective weakness of Charcot's theoretical views, his eminence as one of the world's leading neurologists, his rigorous methodology, and his precise nosological descriptions removed any lingering doubts in the medical profession about the scientific respectability of studying hypnotism. Although from the standpoint of theory, Charcot's rigorous approach was a hindrance that led him to repeat many of the old second-stage mistakes, his work paradoxically represents a methodological advance to the fourth stage of sophistication, if only because of what he was trying to accomplish. This paradox in the work of Charcot foreshadows a disparity in the fourth stage between theory and method, which will be discussed later in more detail (Charcot, 1882a, 1882b, 1893; Ellenberger, 1965a; Schneck, 1952, 1961a, 1961b).

EARLY PSYCHOLOGICAL PERIOD

The third stage of sophistication was marked by the concurrent recognition of two basic insights: that mesmeric-hypnotic phenomena are in some sense genuine and important, and that mesmeric-hypnotic phenomena are essentially psychological in nature. These two basic insights then fused to produce a third, derivative insight: that the psychological processes underlying mesmeric-hypnotic phenomena—imagination, expectancy, belief, enthusiasm, receptivity, attention, attitude, monoideism, ideoexpressive tendency, suggestion, hypersuggestion, motivation, etc.—are scientifically valid and important.

The validity of either the first basic insight or of the second had been recognized by every interested observer from the time of Mesmer's first cases in Vienna. But the intellectual climate was such that to accept either one seemed tantamount to rejecting the other.

The mesmerists clearly recognized the therapeutic potency and scientific importance of their procedures. But despite their astute clinical acumen in manipulating psychological variables, they had at best only a defensive inkling that the source of their influence was imagination and not a physical agency. Mesmer's detractors on the other hand had realized that the agent was primarily psychological, but for them this realization constituted more than ample proof of trickery and unworthiness.

Faria's notion of lucid sleep

Although in the early periods someone occasionally caught a fleeting glimpse of both basic insights together, the first person to do so seriously was the abbot José Custodi di Faria, who in 1814 arrived in Paris from Goa, a Portugese colony in India. Faria rejected mesmeric theories of special agencies and stressed that lucid sleep (somnambulism) was produced solely by the subject's heightened expectations and receptive attitude.

Mesmer had clearly recognized the value of heightened expectancy and the indispensable importance of the patient's receptive attitude; later workers like Puységur and Deleuze further stressed these factors. But in Mesmer's theoretical view expectant receptivity had meant only something like completing electric circuits and the willful opening or closing of hydraulic-like valves to receive or impede the flow of cosmic fluid; Puységur and Deleuze also adhered to a fluidic formulation. In a sense, Faria merely saw what is now obvious: that the elaborate mesmeric pseudologies had pragmatic value in helping to initiate psychological processes within the subject, but had no validity independent of that consequence.

One expression of Faria's new psychological outlook was the use in his induction procedure of verbal suggestion, both soothing and commanding. Mesmer's induction procedures had been based on direct physical contacts that were designed to promote the flow of cosmic fluid into the receptive patient. Puységur and his followers had elaborated these procedures to include waving movements of the hands without direct physical contact, in order to radiate the nervous fluid from a distance. Another second-stage elaboration was talking to the entranced somnambulist, but the induction procedure as such remained nonverbal. Only when it was recognized that the mesmeric influences lay within the subject himself did words become important elements in the process of induction.

In 1823, and again in 1826, Alexandre Bertrand, originally an orthodox mesmerist, published works vigorously expounding and developing Faria's psychological point of view (Bertrand, 1823, 1826a, 1826b; Faria, 1906).

Braid's later theory

In his theory of 1847, Braid's interest shifted away from the rather mechanical physiological changes of exhausted nervous centers, and toward events at the psychological level of analysis. The psychological concept of monoideism now became central for Braid, but he continued to maintain that it resulted in definite physiological changes in the subject.

In monoideism the mental attention becomes so engrossed in a single idea, a single train of thought, that for the time being the attention is thereby rendered insensible and indifferent to all other considerations and influences. One active train of ideation becomes extraordinarily intense and subjectively real to the subject because all of his attention is exclusively concentrated on it, rather than diffused and distracted into a multitude of competing ideas and impressions. All of the various mesmeric, hypnotic, and verbal suggestive induction procedures have only one objective: to help promote this state of single-mindedness, of exclusively concentrated attention, letting other ideas pass into torpid oblivion. Because the monoideized attention has heightened the intensity of the one focal or dominant idea, the power of the imagination on mind and body is considerably greater than in the ordinary waking state, and thus suggestions are likely to initiate correspondingly greater influences.

Monoideism became for Braid the central unifying concept, of which neuro-hypnotism was but a subconcept, designating a special, extreme state characterized by oblivious nervous sleep with subsequent amnesia until again hypnotized. Braid said that this rare state was achieved by only about one-tenth of his subjects. The majority showed no loss of consciousness. Moreover, some subjects immediately passed into an alert, active somnambulistic state with eyes open the very first time they were hypnotized, without previously passing through a condition in any way resembling the nervous sleep (Braid, 1846, 1852; Bramwell, 1896–97a, 1896–97b, 1903).

Liébeault and the Nancy Practitioner's tradition

In France, Braid's third-stage theory did not become known until it was published in a condensed version along with the first French translation of *Neurypnology* in 1883. But as early as 1859, Braid's earlier views began to be publicized by a number of French physicians.

We have already seen how, from a modern perspective, Braid's prepsychological, second-stage theory from its earliest inception was only a hair's breadth away from the third stage. That decisive step was independently taken in France by Ambroise Auguste Liébeault, a kindly and unassuming country doctor who settled in Nancy in 1864. Liébeault's vigorously psychological viewpoint was presented in his book *Du sommeil. . .*, first published in 1866. The book was ignored for 20 years until Hippolyte Marie Bernheim, then professor of medicine at Strasbourg, "discovered" Liébeault, and championed his viewpoint. Bernheim soon succeeded in drawing worldwide attention to the importance of mental therapeutics based on verbal suggestion.

Liébeault and Bernheim were essentially clinical practitioners, interested mainly in curing and teaching how to cure. They were far less seriously concerned with developing a systematic theory of hypnosis for its own sake than had been Mesmer or Braid.

Outgrowths of Liébeault's and Bernheim's teachings revolved about the doctrine of suggestion, which became both the fundamental description and the unifying explanation of hypnosis and related events. From today's advanced orientation, it is difficult to comprehend the style of thinking in that earlier era, except as a random collection of pragmatic teachings. But the underlying internal coherence of their views must be grasped, because even now, long after the theoretical substrate of these teachings has withered from view, its product—the doctrine of suggestion—remains deeply infused in modern thinking about hypnosis in many subtle and unanalyzed ways.

The doctrine of suggestion

At that time, ideas were understood to be atomic entities swarming in the arena of the mind. By a kind of mental chemistry—by combination, permutation, closeness, and distance between ideas—was created the panoply of waking rationality, waking suggestibility, sleep, monoideism, indirect suggestion, reverie, and hypnosis. Each separate idea possessed some quantity of energy that blindly, automatically pressed toward translation into its motoric and sensory equivalents. The ideoexpressive energies of all of the ideas in the mind's arena were seen to enhance and complement one another as well as to compete and inhibit. The net effect of this complex interaction was that the blind, automatic ideoexpressive energies of each idea were held in check by the ideoexpressive energies of all of the many other ideas. Waking suggestibility was seen as the state of mind where a dominant idea became relatively stronger than competing ideas. Hypnosis was seen as an extension of suggestibility that began by having the subject focus on the idea of sleep. During the ensuing sleep the idea of the hypnotist was retained within the sleeper's awareness. Thus the sleeper was in rapport with the hypnotist. Since the critical faculties—that is, the swarm of competing ideas—were in abeyance during sleep, the result was a state of heightened suggestibility. The hypnotized subject had to obey without volition ideas implanted by the hypnotist, as would an automaton.

In sum, ordinary waking suggestibility and hypnotic heightened suggestibility were both seen to result from a temporary weakening of the usual critical faculties. But it was also possible to slip ideas past the intact critical faculties by indirection, thus circumventing rationality. This latter process was called indirect suggestion.

Theoretical deficiencies

The doctrine of suggestion provided many useful insights, but also missed and obscured other important factors. The ideoexpressive principle did provide an organized account of the continuity from ordinary waking rationality to waking suggestion and then to hypnosis, but its stress on debilitated functioning, automatism, "will-less" obedience, and exclusive rapport, overlooked the assertive, alert, active, and productive capacities of the hypnotized individual. The stress on sleep shaped the outward appearance of hypnotic behavior from that time through our own; it also obscured the fact, noted so clearly by Braid, that some subjects could enter a highly active somnambulistic state without at any time passing through a condition resembling sleep in any way, even the first time hypnotized.

The doctrine of suggestibility was especially weak in illuminating the factors of enthusiastic credence and firm expectation. The central feature of Mesmer's method of faith healing was, for example, more sensibly viewed as a matter of enlisting rational belief than of releasing ideoexpressive energies. Mesmer's main emphasis was not placed on causing the critical faculties of his patients to become temporarily suspended that is, it was not a matter of waking or hypnotic suggestion. Nor did Mesmer stealthily try to slip ideas past his patients' intact critical faculties unbeknown to them—that is, he did not practice indirect suggestion. Instead, Mesmer tried to enlist the critical faculties of his patients in the most direct manner possible. Mesmer was himself convinced, and tried hard to convince his patients, of the truth and potency of his scientific doctrines at the level of full critical rationality, and not at all in spite of it.

A second example of the importance of expectant belief is John Elliotson's observation that, as the crest of popular enthusiasm and credence in mesmerism waned in London, and was replaced more and more by widespread scorn and skepticism, mesmeric anesthesia seemed to lose its power to remove pain.

> I believe I was not wrong; I believe that in what I originally saw, mesmerism played the parts precisely that I claimed for it. It is a wicked error to suppose that I was a party to a deception, or to a whole series of deceptions, if you like; but I candidly say. . . that mesmerism, at the present moment, has no power to remove pain. It is a mystery; it had power, and I once saw a leg painlessly removed under its influence; but we are now in another cycle, and it seems to me that there are special periods only in which mesmeric phenomena can be induced. (Quoted in Rosen, 1948.)

The kinds of variables illustrated in these two examples are not fully expressed by the concepts of ordinary suggestion and indirect suggestion, and are only slightly embodied by the even later concept of prestige suggestion. Far richer and more accurate characterizations are terms such as enthusiastic credence, exalted confidence, intense emotive excitement, firm expectancy of influence, faith healing, and charismatic personality, which imply a good deal more than the often tacit, limited, mechanical, and perfunctory suggestion influence. Rather, they refer to emotionally highly-charged beliefs giving expression to core energies of the personality.

By maintaining the generic term "suggestion," concepts such as indirect suggestion, prestige suggestion, and the other later accretions seemed to preserve the single-principle explanatory character of the doctrine of suggestibility, but in actuality psychological processes quite different in character were thereby obscured.

As a conceptual tool, the single-principle doctrine of suggestion was useful in discrediting a number of then current physical and physiological second-stage theories. The doctrine disavowed all but a parsimonious description of events at the psychological level of analysis. The doctrine found its most cogent expression in the extended polemic controversy between the clinical practitioners led by Bernheim at Nancy and the puristic scientists led by Charcot at the Salpêtrière Hospital in Paris. The eventual victory of the more accurate Nancy suggestionist viewpoint unfortunately tended to obscure the recognition that a psychological analysis is not in any sense inherently antagonistic to a concern with underlying physiology, as Braid had earlier come to recognize so clearly. (Recommended sources are Baudouin, 1922; Benussi, 1927; Bleuler, 1907; Dessoir, 1888, 1890; Elliotson, 1846, 1848–49; Esdaile, 1846, 1852; Forel, 1907; Hart, 1898; Heidenhain, 1888; James & Carnochan, 1885–89; LeBon, 1895, 1911; Marmer, 1956; Moll, 1898; Rand, 1925; Richet, 1881; Rosen, 1936, 1946; Sarbin & Kroger, 1963; Schneck, 1956; Sidis, 1898; Solomons & Stein, 1896; Tarde, 1907.)

LATER PSYCHOLOGICAL OR MODERN PERIOD

Because we are presently living in the fourth stage of scientific sophistication about hypnosis, we cannot yet know where it will eventually lead. But the beginning of the fourth stage is characterized by two important intellectual contributions and their ongoing elaborations. One of these contributions relates to theory, the other to method. That relating to theory was Sigmund Freud's charting of the unconscious mind and of psychodynamic processes. The contribution relating to method was Charcot's fundamental commitment to an extremely precise and purified scientific method, which established a tradition of a continuing scientific evolution.

These two contributions have been and remain somewhat incompatible. Although some day it would seem that they must fuse into one, there is as yet no clear alternative to describing the fourth stage as two separate lines of development. Perhaps the fifth stage will emerge only after these two lines fuse, or perhaps the fifth stage will itself be their fusion.

CONTRIBUTION RELATING TO THEORY

Hypnotic therapy in the Nancy tradition consisted essentially of induction of the state of heightened suggestibility, and then verbal suggestion of general well-being and direct symptom disappearance in a tone of authority and confidence.[4] This overly mechanical approach allowed for little concern with the causal etiology of the symptoms. Pierre Janet, Morton Prince, Frederick Myers, and some others soon began to think in terms of multiple systems of consciousness where serious attention was given to underlying dynamics, but these developments were soon overshadowed by the contribution of Sigmund Freud and his psychoanalytic movement.

It was while visiting the clinic of Liébeault and Bernheim in Nancy that Freud made the fundamental observation that determined the direction of his life's work. Freud observed that a suggestion given during hypnosis often would not be available to recall upon awakening. The forgotten suggestion was nonetheless carried out posthypnotically, with the patient readily able to rationalize pseudoreasons for his unconsciously motivated act.

> [Visiting Nancy in 1889] I witnessed the moving spectacle of old Liébeault working among the women and children of the laboring classes. I was a spectator of Bernheim's astonishing experiments upon his hospital patients; and I received the profoundest impression of the possibility that there could be powerful mental processes that nevertheless remained hidden from the consciousness of men.   (1925, 1952 trans.)

4. Braid's therapeutic practice was substantially the same. In his theoretical view, however, suggestion always remained only a procedure and never an explanation. Unlike the lengthy induction procedures common today, Liébeault usually allotted only a couple of minutes, telling his subjects simply to close their eyes and go to sleep.

Here was Freud's first impressive inkling that beneath the conscious mind lay a hidden, seething cauldron of immense unconscious forces which were the primary determinants of human affairs.

In the meantime, Josef Breuer, an older colleague of Freud, had discovered that the root causes of hysteric symptoms were painful memories and pent-up emotions, buried below consciousness. The hysteric symptoms could be eliminated in an indirect manner by encouraging spontaneous verbalizations by patients under hypnosis, to evoke a free venting or catharsis of the bottled-up energies causing the symptoms. Freud collaborated with Breuer in pursuing this discovery. Versions of the first chapters of their *Studien über Hysterie* were published in 1893.

Breuer chose not to pursue the matter further, but for Freud the discovery of a positive etiology of hysteria was only the first step in his exploration of the unconscious mind and his learning to speak its special language.

Freud was neither the first nor the only man to discern the existence of unconscious mental processes, in the sense of a subterranean region of the mind with its own laws, contents, and dynamic forces. But he was the first to chart this region systematically, and his discoveries revolutionized man's conception of himself.

Freud's development of psychoanalysis began somewhat paradoxically with his rejection of hypnotism as his scientific and therapeutic method—but he never lost interest in developing a theoretical understanding of hypnosis. Freud turned instead to free association and the analysis of dreams as his royal road to the unconscious, but hypnotism is properly recognized as the treasure map that sent him forth on his journey.

Freud's abandonment of hypnosis as a therapeutic method was a wise decision if not historic necessity, since the authority and obedience brand of hypnotism that dominated his era was too unwieldy, artifact-laden, and encrusted with transference and countertransference problems to allow the slow, painstaking, detached exploration of the hidden inner world which was needed. Hypnotism, moreover, allowed access to certain repressed contents too quickly; it suppressed symptoms too easily, yet often without permanence; and the hypnotized individual's responses were too readily swayed by what he perceived the hypnotist wanted. Hypnotism was thus a swampy terrain that Freud as a pioneer explorer did well to avoid. Later investigators, however, had far less cause for such trepidation (Breuer & Freud, 1883a, 1883b; Burchard, 1958; Chertok, 1967; Freud, 1925; Gurney, 1884; Janet, 1919; Kline, 1958; Myers, 1886–87, 1891–92; M. Prince, 1920; Schilder & Kauders, 1927; Schneck, 1954b, 1963a).

Renaissance

The revolutionary discoveries of one generation become the basic axioms of following generations. From the light of the psychodynamic insights provided by the Freudian heritage it was inevitable that therapists would evaluate the potentialities of hypnotism afresh. Thus there occurred a renaissance of interest in hypnotism, but now from a broader point of view, a fourth stage of sophistication.

Milton H. Erickson was probably the first, and certainly the boldest, most ingenious, and influential of these new fourth-stage hypnotists. In 1923, while still an undergraduate and medical student at the University of Wisconsin, Erickson gave, at Clark Hull's request, a graduate seminar on his intriguing informal researches on hypnotism. Not only were these events the beginnings of Erickson's productive career, but in all likelihood they helped spark Hull's contributions to hypnotism as well.

Stated concisely, Erickson's therapeutic approach emphasizes brevity and limited goals without insight. Figuratively speaking, Erickson enters the world of the patient's neurosis with him, and, with clinical artistry and intuitive understanding of nonrational dynamics, rearranges definitions and symptoms to make the neurosis more successfully adaptive.

In broader terms, modern hypnotherapy takes the form of a developing relationship between the therapist and his patient, who is in an altered state of responsiveness, in which repressed materials are often more readily available than in the usual waking state. Although hypnosis now is sometimes used as a tool in the context of long-term conventional psychotherapy and psychoanalysis, the emphasis is usually on brevity. Times of war have given special impetus to the development of brief hypnotherapies to deal with soldiers emotionally traumatized by battle conditions (Erickson, 1939b, 1941, 1960, 1964a, 1967b).

CONTRIBUTION RELATING TO METHOD

The clinical practitioner's prime objective in using hypnotic techniques is to cure the patient, if possible, here and now. The pure scientist's prime objective is to accumulate and generalize from present findings succinctly and in a form that helps lay the groundwork for a continuing process of skeptical reappraisal, now and in the future. Knowledge about hypnosis in the clinical tradition is established mainly in terms of pragmatic effectiveness, clinical experience, sensitivity, skill, general plausibility, and the consensus of authoritative opinion. While a valuable wealth of knowledge has been provided by this authority-based clinical tradition of pragmatic teachings, the practitioner's knowledge has generally not taken the form most readily useful to the method-oriented pure scientist.

The end-product of knowledge—the facts—are quite reasonably what matter most to the practitioner, oriented as he is toward cure. But of equal importance to the scientist are the conditions under which the facts were gathered. The conditions must be specified precisely so that procedures can be closely replicated and systematically varied in continuing research. The scientific method, in other words, requires that knowledge be formulated in terms amenable to minute scrutiny of all phases of the knowledge-generating process.

Charcot's contribution to method

Charcot's rigorous empiricism derived from an unswerving commitment to precise scientific method as his fundamental concern. This commitment created a point of departure for a continuing scientific evolution. As noted earlier, however, the very nature of Charcot's farsighted puristic methodology led him to adopt a rather inaccurate second-stage, prepsychological theory, at a time when the practitioners in the Nancy tradition had already advanced to a more accurate third-stage, psychological formulation.

The aim of the scientific method is the cautious accumulation and purification of verifiable knowledge. The merit of the scientific method is that it is a self-correcting process. All knowledge is considered tentative, a springboard for disciplined skepticism. Even when, as with Charcot, purified methodology leads to an inaccurate theory, it nonetheless embodies the logical machinery for a perpetual reappraisal. Accuracy as such, particularly in the first stages of an inductive scientific development, is thus far less important to the working scientist than is verifiability and fruitfulness. Irrespective of its accuracy, to be scientific, knowledge must be in a form that provides the basis for further advancement. The scientist's exposition of the procedures he has used to reach his conclusions must be so explicit as to provide other scientists with the means to disprove and transcend them. It is thus no denial of Charcot's important contribution to realize that his findings were soon critically reappraised and rejected.

It would be of some cogency to argue that the first clear advancement to the fourth stage of sophistication in terms of method should be ascribed to Braid rather than to Charcot. There is no doubt that Braid, and indeed some others, went beyond discursive clinical observation to carry out painstaking experimentation, much as Charcot was later to do. But scientific method as such did not become their central allegiance as it did for Charcot.

There are several illuminating parallels between the contributions of Charcot and Mesmer. Both developed theories that were later found to be quite inaccurate and confounded with procedural artifacts. Both developed theories that were restatements of formulations advanced by earlier workers —of Mead, Paracelsus, and others in the case of Mesmer; of Du Potet and others in the case of Charcot. Both created traditions of continuing scientific development—insistent belief that his therapeutic method was subject to scientific explanation in the case of Mesmer; allegiance to rigorous scientific method in the case of Charcot. For his work, however, Mesmer frequently has been judged as a charlatan, a simpleton, and a plagiarist. For the most part, Charcot has been spared similar accusations, perhaps because of his undeniably brilliant and original contributions in other areas.

Hull's contribution to method

The next important step in the application of scientific method to the study of hypnosis was made possible when mathematicians developed the powerful Null Hypothesis statistical model that provided a procedure for dealing in a systematic and quantitative fashion with the otherwise confusing variability inherent in human responses. This Null Hypothesis model enabled the experimenter to estimate precisely the probable differences in the distributions of responses in experimental and control groups. Thus the new statistical technique made it possible to design more exact and sensitive control experiments than even the most conscientious and ingenious of the earlier experimenters had been able to attain.

The Null Hypothesis model was first used in hypnosis research by Clark L. Hull, around 1930. Hull and his students carried out a broad program of intensive research, which still stands today as a paradigm and foundation for much of the current psychological experimentation in hypnosis.

Statistical techniques were also available at this time for describing the degree of linear correlation between variables in precise quantitative terms. These correlation techniques were used by various workers in conjunction with scales of hypnotic depth to ascertain the psychometric correlates of hypnotic responsiveness, again in a more precise manner than had been achieved earlier. The observation of individual differences in mesmeric-hypnotic responsiveness had been made by everyone from Mesmer onward, but it became the object of serious theoretical attention only after it had been made the chief item of dispute in the Nancy-Salpêtrière controversy. Scientists in the Salpêtrière tradition held that hypnosis was pathological because they believed that only persons with hysterical predispositions could be hypnotized. Practitioners in the Nancy tradition held that hypnosis was a normal process because they believed that virtually everyone under appropriate circumstances would manifest some degree of suggestibility.

To codify their viewpoint, the practitioners evolved scales in which various suggestibility phenomena were arranged by observed order of difficulty, from the simplest induced relaxation to the most profound amnesias and visual hallucinations. These graded scales enabled the skilled examiner to ascertain the depth of hypnosis in any given hypnotized individual. This clinical tradition for measuring hypnotic depth has continued with minor modifications into the present day.

Around 1930, various investigators began to develop standardized objective procedures for rating hypnotic depth in terms of outwardly observable behavioral criteria that minimized the role of the examiner's diagnostic judgment. This second, or behavioral, tradition for measuring hypnotic depth has also continued, with various psychometric improvements, into the present day (Barry et al., 1931; Hull, 1929, 1930, 1931, 1933; M. White, 1930; Williams, 1953; P. Young, 1925).

II. The Fundamental Problem in Hypnosis Research

The fundamental problem in hypnosis research is the necessity of maintaining at the same time both caution and conviction. As Hull's adoption of the Null Hypothesis probability model marks the beginning of modern experimentation in hypnosis, the discussion can be introduced by stating how the fundamental problem manifested itself in Hull's contribution.

HULL'S METHODOLOGICAL CONTRIBUTION

To understand Hull's contribution to scientific method, the paradox inherent in Charcot's contribution should be recalled. Charcot advanced to the fourth stage of sophistication in terms of scientific method, but the very nature of his advanced methodology introduced unrecognized procedural artifacts that grossly distorted the hypnotic phenomena he produced. Hull's contribution manifests a similar paradox. His adoption of the Null Hypothesis probability model provided a marked increase in experimental precision, but the very nature of his laudable scientific objectivity tended subtly to destroy the hypnotic phenomena under investigation. Hull and other method-oriented academic experimentalists failed to realize that the experimenter's job is directly opposed to the hypnotist's job. The experimenter's job is to maintain an attitude of questioning skepticism; the hypnotist's job is to maintain the opposite attitude of assured optimism. Whereas the experimenter must keep himself impartial and neutral regarding the outcome of his investigation, the hypnotist must commit himself with an avowed partisanship to making his induction procedures "come true" for the subject.

Although no experimenter is ever disinterested in his experimental results, his role as scientist requires that he keep his normal enthusiasm and partisanship in abeyance, that he adopt the somewhat unnatural stance of skeptical objectivity in order to prevent prejudgments and unknown factors from confounding his results. Many investigators have succeeded so well in this laudable sterilization of procedure that they have thereby unwittingly tended to inhibit the fullest unfolding of the hypnotic processes supposedly under investigation. The posture of impartial neutrality simply does not evoke in subjects the enthusiastic expectancies and deep emotional commitments that mobilize and sustain the hypnotic processes.

PSYCHOLOGICAL CATALYST

A useful analogy can be drawn here to the well-known concept of catalysis as used in chemistry. Many chemical reactions take place rapidly and fully only in the presence of certain chemical substances, called catalysts, that are not themselves permanently altered in the chemical transformations they augment. Other chemical substances, called negative catalysts, impede the rate of certain chemical reactions.

Likewise, hypnotic processes are set into motion within the subject, strengthened, and brought to their fruition only when the positive psychological catalysts of assured confidence, expectant enthusiasm, and persuasive authority are present in notable concentrations. When these positive psychological catalysts are absent, insufficient, or offset by the negative psychological catalysts of skepticism, discouragement, and the impression of possible failure, then only diluted and incompleted versions of the hypnotic phenomena can generally be produced.

Whereas contemporary experimentalists often tend to provide insufficient positive catalyst, in earlier periods the problem was typically apparent as a contest between positive and negative factors. By way of illustration, for both John Elliotson and his critics in the 1830s the efficacy of mesmeric procedures signified either the existence of some unknown physical agency or outright fraud. With battle lines thus drawn, Elliotson explored the pragmatic usefulness of the unknown agency with little concern for its underlying nature; his critics hounded his efforts with vitriolic denunciation. This bitter and unrelenting opposition soon forced Elliotson and his band of loyal devotees to drift in the direction of cultism. Inasmuch as the mesmeric-hypnotic processes require for their fruition a marked superiority of positive catalysts, this drifting was necessary to generate the indispensable enthusiastic expectancies and deep emotional commitments from subjects. To be effective as mesmerists, Elliotson and his circle had to infuse their procedures with ever more evangelistic zeal to counteract the corrosive currents of skepticism and scorn gathering about them. But the increased fervor of their catalytic appeals itself provided more fuel for the polemics of their critics, augmenting even further the level of skepticism and scorn. By this spiral process, Elliotson's mesmeric structure was extended so far that it eventually collapsed, leaving behind the unwarranted residue of absurdity and charlatanism.[5]

THE VALIDATING TENDENCY

From an even broader perspective, however, the generic problem of relative catalyst is only one manifestation of the basic fact that hypnotized individuals tend to produce the responses that they believe are expected from them. At least since Puységur this tendency to conform to expectations has typically been described as a tenacious compulsion extending far beyond ordinary rational compliance; it is best characterized by terms such as inordinate responsiveness, remarkable docility, and hypersuggestibility. Whether these expectations stem from the verbal communications of the hypnotist while the subject is hypnotized, from cues implicit in the hypnotic situation, or from beliefs existing prior to hypnosis is irrelevant, as Braid for one so

5. A similar drifting toward cultism characterized the Societies of Harmony (patterned after Freemasonry), organized by Mesmer's disciples for the promulgation of his teachings.

clearly noted. For example, Mesmer's nonverbal faith-healing procedures and the complex behavior they engendered were predicated in large measure on belief systems inculcated prior to induction.

This impulsion to produce the expected responses obviously can not yield what is physically impossible. For example, in response to a hypnotist's directions to sprout wings and to fly, the subject, of course, will not develop a wingspan measurable by any material yardstick. But in response to such unrealizable hypnotic directions the proficient subject can secretly arrange at a nonconscious level to delude himself into believing with the fullest subjective conviction and sincerity that he has indeed grown wings and flown. In the most detailed and compelling subjective fantasy the proficient subject can spin a wondrous tale for himself and for his listeners.

Few observers would believe that a subject is flying when they see that he is not. But when a subject is given an impossible task that the hypnotist believes is possible, the subject can again secretly arrange with himself at a nonconscious level to find devious and clever methods of cheating in order to gratify the hypnotist with an outwardly convincing performance. Although in subtler guises the phenomenon of nonconscious deception is just as prevalent today, it was most blatant during the nineteenth century when the mesmerists believed that the somnambulist was endowed with clairvoyance and other paranormal powers. Before the inception of stringent controls, such as specially designed blindfolds, proficient somnambulists were able to give striking demonstrations of clairvoyance. But even when subjects were caught cheating, the allegations of fraud were sincerely denied since the subject's secret arrangement with himself had been to delude his own subjective experience as well as to convince observers.

The hypnotized subject's impulsion to produce expected responses, which even incorporates his own subjective conviction, may also be described as the subject's impulsion to validate what he believes the hypnotist expects. Moreover, this tendency to validate the shared expectations is quite independent of the contents of these beliefs.

It will be recalled that it was this same tendency toward automatic validation that built the edifice of nineteenth century mesmeric extravagance. We noted earlier how each mesmerist was able to see his expectancies and as yet unformulated speculations repeatedly proved true before his eyes by his subjects' responses. The more the mesmerist's beliefs became trenchant and outspoken, the more unequivocally were they proved in the corresponding responses of his enthusiastic and committed subjects. Thus there was a natural selection in the direction of extravagance because the more reasonable and sober-minded mesmerists tended to exude weaker catalysts than investigators with wilder fantasies and blinder resolve. Thus the mesmerist was inexorably drawn down into the vortex of a conceptual whirlpool in which his expectations and unstated speculations were repeatedly validated by the responses of subjects strongly impelled to do so. This validation, of course crystalized the shared expectations even further. Since each mesmerist tended to evolve his own variant belief-system, and since each belief-system —quite irrespective of its contents—would tend to be validated, it was inevitable that the whole wildly sprouting mesmeric edifice would eventually have to crumble under the weight of its own grossly unresolvable contradictions.

From a contemporary point of view, mesmerism is merely the quaint relic of a bygone era. In the more subdued tones of modern terminology, however, investigators are still being seductively lured into pseudologies by this same double-vectored process in which the hypnotist is trying his best to make the hypnotic procedures come true for his subjects, and the subjects in return are trying their best to make the hypnotist's fondest theoretical dreams come true—even if to comply sometimes requires that they secretly arrange to cheat and delude themselves. Under these mutually bewitching circumstances of trying to make shared expectations become functionally true for each other, wishes easily are made to appear as if so, and arbitrary artifices are easily made to appear as if they were natural law.

No investigator is such a paragon of scientific objectivity that he completely escapes blinding emotional commitment to his favorite hypotheses. Even the most brilliant and cautious of men have a sizable talent for intellectual self-delusion. When, however, as in the investigation of hypnosis, this penchant to self-delusion is harnessed to the hypnotized subject's validating tendency, it is extremely difficult—unless the most rigorous experimental controls are applied—for *any* investigator to avoid being drawn into the vortex of pseudology.

THE TWO GENERIC DANGERS

But as we have already seen, the moment an investigator tries to apply these necessary scientific controls he thereby leaves himself open to the danger of dashing his study against the rock of failing to give sufficient catalyst to subjects' enthusiasms and commitments. There are, to reiterate, two generic methodological dangers in hypnosis research, which, like Scylla and Charybdis, are inextricable: the first is the danger of not providing sufficient disciplined skepticism, and the second is the danger of not providing sufficient positive catalyst. The more an investigator tries to avoid one of these two separate and distinct dangers, the more likely it becomes that he will succumb to the other.

In practical terms, the attitude of disciplined skepticism, so essential for building a realistic science, must not become such a blinding preoccupation that the investigator thereby becomes an inept hypnotist. But equally important, the hypnotist's exuding of confident persuasiveness, so essential for properly catalyzing the hypnotic processes, must not become such a blinding preoccupation that the investigator thereby loses his scientific objectivity. Thus, taking the "magic" out of hypnosis debilitates the phenomena but taking the "magic" too seriously deludes the investigator.

Investigators in the academic experimentalist's tradition have generally been most vulnerable to the danger of insufficient catalyst; investigators in the clinical practitioner's tradition have generally been most vulnerable to the danger of insufficient skepticism. The experimentalists have been mainly concerned with rigorous method and the practitioners mainly with improving their clinical skill and effectiveness. Attempts to understand and share each other's objectives and points of view unfortunately have frequently been hampered by clannish loyalties and polemics. This itself is another manifestation of the fundamental problem.

Postscript

In keeping with the aim of providing historic perspectives, this chapter is limited to discussing events sufficiently in the past to see their historic impact. Recent and current developments are consequently not reviewed. (See the remainder of this book and also Barber, 1969b; Brenman & Gill, 1947; Chertok, 1959, 1966; Gordon, 1967; Gormly, 1961; Hilgard, 1965b; Jenness, 1944; Kaufman, 1961; Marcuse, 1964; Pattie, 1958; R. Prince, 1968; Shor & Orne, 1965; Stukát, 1958; Szasz, 1963; Tart, 1969; Weitzenhoffer, 1953; Wolberg, 1945, 1948).

The questions that emerge from the past need to be pondered in relation to the present and future. How well have modern investigators learned to sail between Scylla and Charybdis? To what extent will modern viewpoints be seen through time as true advances—perhaps to a fifth stage of sophistication—and to what extent merely as changes to culturally more acceptable misnomers and disguised returns to old mistakes?

I shall not try to answer these questions because, regrettably, I do not know the answers. To try to speak with authority about the long-range impact of our present era would be premature. I can neither see into the future nor adopt the same degree of impartiality and objectivity toward the contemporary scene, in which I have deep personal commitments and hopes, as I can toward the more distant past. This chapter thus serves to raise questions; answers will inevitably come as the verdict of our posterity.

II

Surveys of Broad Areas

FREDERICK J. EVANS *is a full-time member of the Unit for Experimental Psychiatry, Institute of the Pennsylvania Hospital and an Associate Professor of Psychology in Psychiatry at the University of Pennsylvania. He was born in Australia, where he completed his formal education. He completed his Ph.D. at the University of Sydney, Australia, working with A. Gordon Hammer. As a graduate student he worked with Martin T. Orne, who visited the University of Sydney for three months in 1961. As a result, he joined the Studies in Hypnosis Project, Massachusetts Mental Health Center, and Harvard Medical School, in 1963. He remained with Martin T. Orne when the research group moved to Philadelphia in 1964. While pursuing his work on hypnosis and sleep, he is also conducting research on pain and on the placebo response. His interest in special states of consciousness and the problem of subjective experience has been responsible for a continuing concern about methodology and the social psychology of the psychological experiment.*

Evans *deals with three broad issues. The first is the extent to which there are similarities between hypnosis and sleep. After reviewing behavioral and phenomenological similarities, he concerns himself particularly with EEG and other physiological measures. He finds that sleep and hypnosis EEGs are basically different, and that there is no convincing evidence of physiological similarities between the two states. Secondly, he asks whether hypnotic techniques can influence specific sleep characteristics such as dream content, length of sleep, and parameters of the sleep cycle. While hypnosis cannot be used as an effective substitute for sleep, Evans finds provocative pilot study evidence of hypnotic manipulations of sleep functions. Finally, he investigates to what extent there can be cognitive and behavioral interaction between the sleeper and the external environment. Techniques for exploring cognitive activity during sleep are reviewed. He discusses investigations in which hypnosis was used as a model for studying suggestions administered and tested during sleep.*

3

Hypnosis and Sleep: Techniques for Exploring Cognitive Activity During Sleep

FREDERICK J. EVANS

Introduction: Hypnosis and Sleep

Interest in hypnosis as a potential research tool in the study of sleep has been sparked by the compelling similarities between the two states. In this report, an attempt will be made to evaluate three broad issues. First, to what extent is there any physiological similarity between hypnosis and sleep? Second, to what extent could hypnotic techniques be useful in influencing the course and nature of specific sleep characteristics? Third, to what extent

The preparation of this review, as well as the substantive research conducted at the Unit for Experimental Psychiatry, was supported in part by a grant from the Institute for Experimental Psychiatry, in part by grant #AF-AFOSR-707-67 from the Air Force Office of Scientific Research (AFSC), United States Air Force, and in part by grant #MH 19156–01 from the National Institute of Mental Health, Public Health Service.

Many people have contributed substantially to the completion of this review. I would like to thank several colleagues for their valuable comments, particularly Harvey D. Cohen, Mary R. Cook, Charles Graham, A. Gordon Hammer, Emily Carota Orne, Martin T. Orne, David A. Paskewitz, and John W. Powell. Several of the reported studies completed at the Unit for Experimental Psychiatry were conducted with the active collaboration of these colleagues, and also with Jeremy Cobb, Lawrence A. Gustafson, Ulric Neisser, Donald N. O'Connell, William A. Orchard, Campbell W. Perry, and Ronald E. Shor. I wish to thank Lillian R. Brazin, Eileen F. Grabiec, Maribeth A. Miller, Lani L. Pyles, David S. Roby, Susan Jo Russell, Deborah E. Seeley, Neal A. Shore, and Mae C. Weglarski for their invaluable assistance in such important matters as finding references, making suggestions about style and format, typing, and proofreading.

could hypnosis provide a useful model for studying cognitive activity that occurs during sleep, and the interaction between the sleeping S with his external environment?

PHENOMENOLOGICAL SIMILARITIES BETWEEN HYPNOSIS AND SLEEP

If he had not witnessed the induction procedure, the casual observer might well characterize a typical hypnotized S as being asleep. It was this sleeplike appearance that led Braid (1852) to coin the terms "hypnosis" from the Greek *hypnos* [to sleep] and "somnambulist" from the Latin *somnus* [sleep] and *ambulae* [walk], to describe the deeply hypnotized person. According to Braid, hypnosis was an artificially induced state of somnambulism.

There are many parallels between sleep and hypnosis. The hypnotized person often appears to be asleep, and he typically describes the experience as sleeplike. When awaking from either condition, the person remembers little of what has transpired. Like the sleepwalking somnambulist, the hypnotized person may move about and talk, and he maintains contact with selected aspects of the external world. Some parallels exist in cognitive processes. Vivid dreams may occur in both states. The sleepwalker avoids obstacles; the hypnotized subject avoids colliding with a chair he is negatively hallucinating. The long historical association between hypnosis and sleep is still reflected in many of the standard induction suggestions that S should enter into a deep, relaxed, restful sleep.

The relationship between hypnosis and sleep has intrigued scientists throughout the history of hypnosis. The interest in the interrelationship between the two conditions reached its culmination in Pavlov's theoretical position, which is particularly influential in Eastern Europe. Sleep is considered by Pavlovian theorists as a state of cortical inhibition, while hypnosis is more or less halfway between sleeping and waking, a state of partial excitation surrounded by cortically irradiating inhibition. This viewpoint has been reviewed and evaluated recently by Edmonston (1967; see also Chapter 10 of this book).

The phenomenological similarities between sleep and hypnosis raise many interesting theoretical and methodological questions. Phenomena that appear similar may indeed have many different qualities. Hypnosis has a chameleonlike character that precludes easy determination of its essential features. The somnambulistic state studied by Braid was already quite different in appearance from animal magnetism as practiced by Mesmer. For Mesmer, sleep was an aftereffect of the crises, or hysterical seizures, of his patients. Many effects that have temporarily gained vogue as invariant characteristics of hypnosis can be attributed to the influence of culturally determined factors and the expectations of the hypnotized S. New phenomena of hypnosis have been "invented" by subtle manipulations of S's expectations.

Orne's (1959) demonstration of catalepsy of the dominant hand provides a dramatic example of the "discovery" of an apparently new hypnotic phenomenon. In spite of the elusive nature of the hypnotic state and the difficulty of establishing its invariant effects, its existence as a phenomenon has been challenged by only a few modern investigators.

The relationships between sleep and hypnosis have been further obscured by the apparent interchangeability of the two states.[1] If the hypnotized S is left alone, or if specific suggestions are given, he may pass into a natural sleep. Similarly, in the context of hypnotic research, it appears that a sleeping S may sometimes awake directly into a hypnotic state rather than into a normal waking state, particularly if he has been instructed to do so before falling asleep. Whether the individual is in a sleep, hypnotic, or normal state at a given time may depend upon how he perceives what he is expected to do. The precise state in which an individual exists at any given time is extremely difficult to evaluate by objective methods. Although there are several objective behavioral and physiological characteristics that help identify S's present state, S's verbal description of the subjective aspects of his experiences ultimately provides the main criterion for determining his state.

CHARACTERISTICS OF THE WAKING-SLEEP CYCLE

Behaviorally, sleep is easily recognized. The behavioral evidence for sleep includes the person's general appearance, physical relaxation, lack of communication with and response to the external world, and special manifestations such as snoring. The sleeping S is prone and relaxed, his breathing is slow and even, and autonomic functions are depressed. Sleep can be confirmed post hoc by the person's subjective experience. The S reports he has not been particularly aware of anything, he usually has a poor sense of elapsed time, and he may include in his description reports of dreaming. The subjective awareness of sleep is a universal experience, and is easily described. Following the development of electroencephalographic (EEG) technology, physiological indices were developed that allowed a more stringent definition of sleep. A variety of physiological and biochemical changes during sleep have been studied extensively. The behavioral, subjective, and physiological signs of sleep are usually, although not always, in close agreement (Dittborn & O'Connell, 1967).

Sleep has commonly been considered a relatively homogeneous experience. Both subjectively and behaviorally, sleep seems to be much the same throughout a typical eight-hour night. The EEG evidence, however, shows

1. In this chapter the term "state" is intended primarily as a convenient descriptive term. With some possible exceptions in the last section of the paper, this usage should not affect any conclusions drawn by those who prefer not to conceptualize hypnosis as an altered state of consciousness. The author's position regarding the controversy about state and motivational or interpersonal theories of hypnosis has been made explicit elsewhere (Evans, 1968).

clearly that sleep is complex, consisting of two or more separate states that occur in predictable cycles both in humans and in many species of animals. These stages are quite different physiologically, and the accompanying behavioral and cognitive activity associated with them may be different. The salient characteristics of human sleep stages (Rechtschaffen & Kales, 1968) are described below. The discussion of EEG patterns during waking and sleep (and during hypnosis) requires that special attention be paid to one particular EEG rhythm—alpha activity of 7-13 cycles per second (Hz.). Illustrative samples of occipital and frontal EEG recordings and horizontal eye movement recordings are presented in Figure 3.1.

Waking (eyes closed). The EEG will usually show alpha activity intermixed with low-voltage, mixed frequency activity. During on-line recording, alpha occurs predominantly in the occipital regions. It may occur continuously for many seconds or intermittently in "waves" or "envelopes" of a few seconds' duration. Some individuals rarely generate alpha; some do so almost continuously. Under relatively controlled, optimal conditions, the distribution of the amount of alpha (density) in a homogeneous sample is approximately normal. When alpha is present, its density within a given individual varies considerably over time, depending, in part, on what *S* is doing. Alpha is most likely to occur when the person is relaxed, with his eyes closed, and when he is not engaging in any particular mental activity. Complex cognitive activity blocks alpha. Alpha also disappears as the person becomes drowsy. The paradox of alpha activity is that its density decreases both with drowsiness and with heightened arousal or difficult cognitive tasks. In both instances it is replaced by similar, mixed, low-voltage fast activity. The sudden appearance of alpha activity in an otherwise "flat" random record may indicate arousal if the person has been asleep, or it may indicate the onset of drowsiness if the individual has been engaged in an attentive task.

Changes in alpha density must be interpreted cautiously and only when it is known what *S* has been doing. If the waking EEG does not contain alpha, it is indistinguishable from the EEG during sleep stage 1 and stage REM, described below. For those individuals who show little or no alpha even under optimal waking conditions, there is no way to discriminate from the EEG alone whether the person is aroused, relaxed, drowsy, or in stage 1 or stage REM sleep. If *S*s without waking alpha are not excluded from samples, critical determinations of *S*s' position on the arousal (and sleep) continuum cannot be made. It has not always been reported whether samples contain some nonalpha generators.

Stage 1. Within the limits of his optimal waking alpha density, as *S* falls asleep alpha becomes intermittent and lower in amplitude, until it disappears. Desynchronized fast activity dominates the EEG record, which is

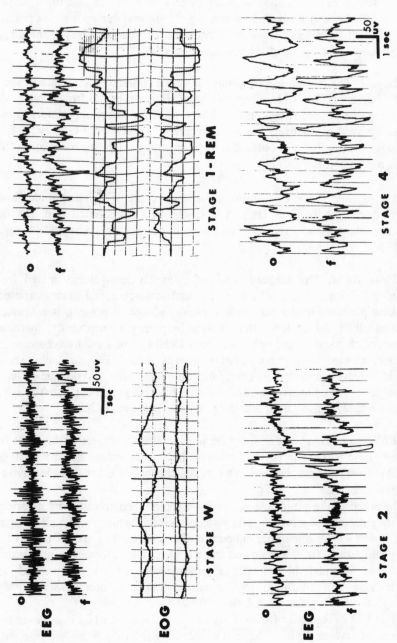

FIGURE 3.1. *Electrophysiological recordings of sleep stages. Occipital and frontal EEG and horizontal eye movements (EOG) are shown for waking and stage REM. For stages 2 and 4, only the EEG is shown.*

similar to the activated waking record. Slow, rolling eye movements (SEM) are usually observed. This descending stage 1 recurs during the night whenever *S* falls back to sleep after awakening. If aroused during this descending stage, he often denies he was asleep, typically reporting that he was thinking, daydreaming, or engaging in hypnogogic reverie.

Stage 2. The stage 1 record changes into one containing a mixture of sporadic bursts of 12–14 Hz. sleep spindles (primarily in the frontal regions) with high amplitude K-complexes. These wave forms are superimposed on a background of relatively low-voltage, mixed frequency EEG activity. Although it accounts for about half of total sleep time, this stage has attracted little research attention.

Stages 3 and 4. The EEG during these stages contains high amplitude, slow wave delta activity (1–3 Hz.). The stages are differentiated primarily by the density of delta. Stages 2, 3, and 4 combined are sometimes called stage NREM.

Stage REM. This stage consists of relatively low-voltage, mixed frequency EEG activity, similar to that found in stage 1 and during aroused waking periods. Alpha activity is generally absent; if present, it is sparse, and usually 1–2 Hz. slower than waking frequency. Concurrently, sporadic bursts of conjugate rapid eye movements (REM) and a relative decrease in submental electromyogram (EMG) activity occur. Paradoxically, stage REM involves activated and irregular autonomic and physiological functions (such as penile erection, and irregular breathing and heart rate) in spite of the relaxed musculature and the general appearance of *S*.

EEG diagnosis of sleep: Some limitations. For the objective diagnosis of sleep, these EEG criteria, supplemented by eye movement activity in stage REM, have been emphasized, often at the expense of other reliable physiological changes.

In practice, the simple classification of stages is complicated by a variety of irregularities observed in many sleep records. While the NREM stages (2, 3, and 4) are sometimes difficult to differentiate, they are relatively easily distinguished from waking and stage 1. Delta waves, however, may occur in awake *S*s under the influence of barbiturates, and irregularities such as these may add confusion to the interpretation of otherwise relatively straightforward studies (Beh & Barratt, 1965).

The EEG diagnosis of sleep stages is most accurate when made over intervals of several minutes. When it is necessary to evaluate on-line segments of a few seconds' duration, particularly during stage REM, the task becomes difficult and arbitrary (O'Connell, Gustafson, Evans, Orne, & Shor, 1965).

The occurrence of transient alpha is particularly perplexing in this context. Short bursts of alpha are not uncommon in stage REM, particularly with *S*s who generate a great amount of alpha when awake. Such intermittent alpha does not necessarily indicate transient awakening. In the absence of other evidence, however, alpha during sleep is best considered as indicating consciousness or arousal. Certainly, when *S* awakens fully, alpha appears in the EEG. The meaning of intermittent alpha is particularly difficult to evaluate when attempts are made to distinguish between waking and sleep (and hypnosis) using EEG criteria alone, or when attempts are made to present stimuli to sleeping individuals.

The sleep cycle. As *S* falls asleep, alpha activity becomes desynchronized and intermittent. After a short time in stage 1, *S* typically passes through stages 2, 3, and 4, sometimes alternating between them for 90 minutes to 2 hours. Then stage REM emerges for the first time. This cycle of stages is repeated several times during the night. Stage 4 occurs almost exclusively in the first part of the night. Stage REM returns about every 90 minutes and becomes progressively longer (from a few minutes to over half an hour), dominating the second half of the night. Slightly less than a quarter of an average night's sleep is spent in stage REM. However, if stage REM is prevented from occurring (because of shortened sleep, drugs, experimental awakenings, or other factors), time in stage REM will increase on subsequent nights until at least some of the lost stage REM is recovered.

Perhaps the most significant recent discovery in sleep research was reported by Aserinsky and Kleitman (1953). They observed that awakening *S* during a REM period almost always led to vivid reports of dreams, but waking *S* from NREM sleep did not usually lead to dream reports.[2] The association between stage REM and dreaming stimulated considerable interest in sleep research. Several excellent reviews of the many sleep studies completed since 1953 are available (for example, Foulkes, 1966; Kales, 1969; and Oswald, 1962).

EVALUATION OF HYPNOSIS

Several general issues in hypnosis research require some brief comments so that studies reviewed below can be interpreted meaningfully. These issues are concerned with the measurement of hypnosis and methodological problems arising in this kind of research.

2. Frequency of dream reports from abrupt stage REM awakenings have been reported by many investigators, and is typically above 80 per cent. For comparable NREM awakenings, the incidence of content reports varies in several studies, but is typically about 20 per cent. Content reports from REM and NREM awakenings can be reliably discriminated by blind judges. Unfortunately, REM and NREM reports have not typically been collected "blind": *E* has remained aware of the stage of sleep from which *S* has awakened.

The measurement of hypnosis. There is no single criterion that can be used to indicate reliably the presence of hypnosis or its depth. Several standardized scales of hypnotic susceptibility and hypnotic depth are available that objectively measure susceptibility to hypnosis. These scales have satisfactory psychometric properties. They include the Stanford Hypnotic Susceptibility Scale, Forms A, B, and C (SHSS:A, SHSS:B, SHSS:C) of Weitzenhoffer and Hilgard (1959, 1962) and the Harvard Group Scale of Hypnotic Susceptibility (HGSHS:A) of Shor and E. Orne (1962), a group-administered adaptation of SHSS:A. Except for the first time S is hypnotized, these scales correlate highly with each other (typically .75 and above) and with diagnostic ratings of hypnotizability made by experienced clinicians (Orne & O'Connell, 1967).

Assessments of hypnotizability based on the administration of only one such scale should be evaluated cautiously. Differences in the adequacy of establishing rapport and easing S's apprehensions arising from his expectations and misconceptions about hypnosis may affect scores. Because hypnosis is a new experience for him, S may not know what to expect nor how to behave appropriately. Striving to please E is not restricted to the good hypnotic S (Orne, 1959, 1969). The problems are particularly acute when group hypnosis evaluations are made. The correlation between an initial HGSHS:A and a subsequent SHSS:C is only about .6. This lower correlation is due in part to some Ss being influenced by the performance of neighboring Ss: for these Ss, HGSHS:A correlated only .49 with SHSS:C, while a correlation of .74 was obtained for those Ss who did not conform to their neighbors' performance.[3]

While combinations of standard scales are adequate for evaluating susceptibility to hypnosis for many purposes, these scales should be supplemented by thorough clinical evaluations (Orne & O'Connell, 1967) if the aim is to select those excellent hypnotic Ss that come from the extreme of the susceptibility distribution. The standardized scales do not always discriminate adequately in the upper ranges of hypnotic depth, and there is still no adequate substitute for diagnostic ratings when attempting to select (as is often the case) classical somnambulist Ss.

Recent evidence has shown that the phenomena traditionally associated with hypnosis can be meaningfully conceptualized in terms of relatively independent clusters or dimensions, including one concerned with passive motor suggestions, one consisting of challenged motor suggestions (rigidities and inhibitions of movement), one with hallucinatory (imagery) experiences, and one, tentatively labeled "dissociation," consisting of such phenom-

---

3. These comments do not reflect on the value and adequacy of HGSHS:A if it is used, as originally intended, as an economical screening device in conjunction with other assessment methods, and as a first exposure to scientific hypnosis, but not as the only measure of hypnotic susceptibility used (Evans & Mitchell, unpublished manuscript).

ena as posthypnotic suggestion and amnesia (Evans, 1965; Hammer, Evans, & Bartlett, 1963; Hilgard, 1965b). Relationships may exist between sleeping behavior and only one of these aspects of hypnosis. Separate consideration of these hypnotic clusters may clarify the meaning of obtained relationships that might be obscured by a complex, multidetermined global hypnosis rating.

Methodological considerations. The effects of *S*'s expectations and attempts to conform to his perceptions of the hypothesis being tested are subtle, but have been amply documented (Orne, 1959, 1962b, 1969). If, for example, eye movement electrodes are applied, and it is then suggested to *S* during hypnosis that he hallucinate a visual, moving scene, then it is not too difficult for *S* to realize that eye movements are anticipated during the hallucination. It is necessary and often difficult to evaluate whether it is hypnosis or *S*'s expectation that is the causal variable. Similarly, if it is suggested hypnotically that *S* respond during sleep (by dreaming, for example), special techniques are required to determine whether *S* responds while asleep, whether he temporarily awakens (or reenters hypnosis) to respond, or even whether other techniques such as waking suggestion or a pep talk would achieve similar results. While the EEG is most helpful in this regard (and, generally, only sleep studies using EEG techniques will be considered), it is difficult to determine from the EEG alone whether *S* is awake, hypnotized, or even in stage REM sleep. It is naive to assume that if a suggestion given during hypnosis works, then it worked because of hypnosis. Because adequate control techniques such as those introduced by London and Fuhrer (1961), or the use of Orne's simulating *S*s (1959, 1969), have not been used, many of the studies reviewed below are inconclusive.

Physiological Similarities Between Hypnosis and Sleep

If hypnosis and sleep share common mechanisms, then it should be possible to document physiological parameters that are similar under both conditions. Most studies have used the EEG; some have investigated specific variables such as the electrodermal response.

EEG PATTERNS DURING SLEEP AND HYPNOSIS

The EEG during hypnosis appears to be quite different from the basic EEG patterns of sleep stages 2, 3, and 4. Some investigators have reported that spindle and slow delta activity is occasionally found in the EEG of hypnotized *S*s (Barker & Burgwin, 1949; Marenina, 1955; Schwarz, Bickford, & Rasmussen, 1955). These investigators have not been able to communicate verbally with such *S*s until a waking or alpha pattern had been elicited.

Hypnotic "somnambulism" (or deep hypnosis) and sleep somnambulism appear to be different phenomena. The symptoms of sleep somnambulism

—sleep talking and sleepwalking—occur primarily in stage 4 sleep (Jacobson & Kales, 1967). Stage 4 delta waves do not occur during hypnosis, even when the induction emphasizes suggestions of sleep. The frequently assumed relationship between susceptibility to hypnosis and the incidence of sleep somnambulism has not been investigated in the sleep laboratory, although Sutcliffe (1958) reported that a questionnaire measure of the frequency of sleepwalking and sleep talking correlated significantly with hypnotizability.

Several studies have found hints of similarities between hypnosis and specific aspects of EEG activity. These studies raise many questions that cannot be resolved, and they have been reviewed adequately by Barber (1969b), Chertok and Kramarz (1959), Domhoff (1964), Gorton (1962), Kratochvil (1970), and Tart (1965a). Similarly, several studies (reviewed by Chertok & Kramarz, 1959, and by Tart, 1965a) have indicated similarities between the EEG of hypnosis and that of "light sleep," or the descending stage 1 *transitional* sleep. Similarities between hypnosis and drowsiness, light sleep, and stage 1 sleep may be attributed to the difficulties in using the EEG as a criterion. The EEGs of aroused and relaxed waking, drowsiness, and stages 1 and REM are comprised of various mixtures of intermittent alpha and desynchronized low-voltage fast activity. The EEG is not sufficiently sensitive to discriminate between these conditions.

Even if drowsiness could be discriminated reliably from hypnosis by the EEG, paradoxical similarities between hypnosis and drowsiness could occur in the EEG of hypnotized Ss. Many investigators have used hypnotic induction techniques that include suggestions of relaxation and sleep. These inductions are often long, repetitive, and perhaps, to a very hypnotizable S, somewhat boring, particularly as he is implicitly restricted in activity. The suggestions to sleep may be taken literally and S may fall asleep briefly. In the induction procedures of the standardized scales we have observed Ss who appear to nap briefly during the relatively long, monotonous induction. These Ss may not recognize their transient napping because of the repetitiveness of the suggestions. When Ss are aware of napping, they may become confused, attributing the sleepiness to hypnosis.

When a suggestion is given, some Ss can respond even while remaining asleep (Evans, Gustafson, O'Connell, Orne, & Shor, 1969). The S may never realize he has napped if, for example, E gradually raises his voice, subtly changes his intonation, or, as part of a suggestion, unobtrusively raises S's arm, thereby "reawakening" him. If E's actions are carried out carefully, in a plausible hypnotic context in which the break in continuity is not apparent, S will not be aware that anything special has happened. The hypnotist may remain unaware of S's light sleep as these "awakening" techniques are part of his natural technique during the transition between inducing hypnosis and testing its effects. Alpha desynchronizes in this transitional sleep, but it is a phenomenon of a tired S rather than of hypnosis. The tendency for hypnotizable Ss to nap during hypnosis is supported by recent evidence that hypnotizable Ss fall asleep in the laboratory more quickly than insusceptible Ss (Evans et al., 1969).

Most authors agree that the EEG during hypnosis is similar to waking EEG patterns consisting of desynchronized fast activity and alpha activity. The available evidence suggests that there is no similarity between hypnosis and sleep in the EEG, although without independent criteria of both hypnosis and the relevant sleep stage, any hypothesized similarity is difficult to evaluate conclusively. However, a more meaningful, related question has been investigated. What is the relationship between hypnosis and specific EEG patterns?

EEG ALPHA ACTIVITY AND HYPNOSIS

Investigations of specific EEG patterns during hypnosis have primarily involved the alpha rhythm (7–13 Hz.). Renewed interest in the alpha rhythm has been stimulated by Kamiya's (1969) claim that alpha can be operantly shaped and brought under voluntary control. The paradox of alpha activity, discussed above, is that it becomes desynchronized and disappears with both drowsiness and with heightened arousal or difficult cognitive tasks. It appears to be related to attentional processes in a U-shaped fashion. Currently, sophisticated computer techniques are being employed to investigate the EEG in ways that could not be achieved by simple on-line visual scanning and manual scoring. Most of the studies reviewed below have not employed sophisticated instrumentation, and the findings should be interpreted with reservations.

The relationship between EEG alpha activity and hypnosis may be explored in two ways: (1) Do Ss who are highly susceptible to hypnosis have different (waking) brain wave patterns from those Ss who are insusceptible to hypnosis? (2) Does hypnosis alter brain wave activity? Are there any changes in alpha activity after hypnosis has been induced, particularly in deeply hypnotized Ss?

EEG alpha and susceptibility to hypnosis. London, Hart, and Leibovitz (1968) recently presented evidence that, in a sample of 125 volunteers for a "brain waves and hypnosis" study, highly susceptible Ss generated more waking alpha than other Ss. The HGSHS:A was completed, with some imagery tests, and alpha was measured one week later. While 8 Ss who scored the maximum of 12 points on HGSHS:A generated alpha for a mean of 42.3 seconds per minute during eyes-closed, awake, resting periods, 25 Ss who scored 4 or less generated alpha for only 24.0 seconds per minute ($p < .005$).

From unpublished data collected at the Unit for Experimental Psychiatry, a sample of 139 volunteer students, who had participated in hypnosis experiments and for whom resting alpha baseline measures were available, was examined. Sessions recording alpha were always presented to S as being independent of the previously completed hypnosis sessions. These Ss, who had originally volunteered for "hypnosis experiments," had been given HGSHS:A and SHSS:C. Individual clinical diagnostic ratings (Orne & O'Connell, 1967) were also available for 111 of the 139 Ss. The distribution of alpha density during 2-minute rest periods for Ss classified according to their hypnotic susceptibility is presented in Table 3.1. The hypnotic susceptibility categories used by London, Hart, and Leibovitz (1968) were chosen, and the two samples are compared. In addition, Ss are reclassified according to SHSS:C scores, a more reliable estimate of hypnotic susceptibility. In Table 3.2, correlations between alpha density and HGSHS:A, SHSS:C, and diagnostic ratings, respectively, are reported. In addition, for a sample of 60 of these Ss, alpha frequency and amplitude were measured, and correlations between these measures and hypnotic susceptibility are also reported.

Examination of the data initially appeared to confirm the exciting results of London, Hart, and Leibovitz. They reported that their 8 Ss who scored 12 on HGSHS:A generated almost continuous alpha (70 per cent of the 2-minute period). The 3 Ss in our sample who scored 12 on HGSHS:A also generated continuous alpha (90 per cent of 2 minutes). However, 40 insusceptible Ss displayed considerably more alpha (for a mean of 65 per cent of the rest period) than the 25 similarly selected insusceptible Ss (37 per cent alpha during rest) reported by London, Hart, and Leibovitz. When Ss of medium susceptibility are included in both samples, no overall relationship between alpha density and hypnotic susceptibility is apparent in either sample.

Because of the earlier cautions about assessing hypnotic susceptibility by a single group measure, we examined our Ss' scores on SHSS:C. The 3 Ss who had scored 12 on HGSHS:A (and who had continuous alpha) subsequently scored 9, 12, and 12, respectively, on the individual SHSS:C. An

TABLE 3.1   Mean per cent alpha generated during 2 minutes rest for Ss differing in susceptibility to hypnosis

	London, Hart, & Leibovitz, 1968 HGSHS:A		Evans [a] HGSHS:A		SHSS:C	
Hypnosis Score	N	$\overline{X}$ per cent alpha	N	$\overline{X}$ per cent alpha	N	$\overline{X}$ per cent alpha
0–4	25	37	40	65	46	46
4–7	25	56	43	40	25	39
7–11	67	42	49	45	58	46
12	8	70	3	90	10	40
Total N	125		135		139	

a. Evans (unpublished data). All Ss received both HGSHS:A and SHSS:C (4 Ss who received SHSS:A instead of the group version eliminated).

TABLE 3.2   Correlations between alpha activity characteristics and susceptibility to hypnosis

Hypnosis	N	Frequency	Amplitude	Density	N	Density
HGSHS:A	60	−.19	.04	.02	135	−.08
SHSS:C	60	−.01	.03	−.02	139	−.02
Diagnostic	40	−.05	−.02	.13	111	.12

NOTE: All correlations insignificant ($p > .10$).

additional 8 Ss scored the maximum of 12 on SHSS:C (they had averaged 8.6 on HGSHS:A). Of these, 5 Ss had less than 80 per cent (continuous) waking alpha and 3 Ss generated virtually no alpha (less than 20 per cent).

The lack of relationship between hypnotic susceptibility and alpha frequency, amplitude, and density is apparent in Table 3.2. No significant correlations were found between the alpha parameters and either HGSHS:A, SHSS:C, or clinical diagnostic ratings.

Several studies involving smaller samples have reported correlations between alpha density and susceptibility to hypnosis. Galbraith et al. (1970) administered HGSHS:A to 80 volunteer students. Two weeks later, 59 of these Ss were invited to participate in an independent "study of brain waves." The criteria for selecting the subsample are not reported. Using a complex procedure, auto- and cross-spectral frequency analyses were carried out for several EEG leads, and these results were submitted to a stepwise multiple linear regression analysis to determine the particular EEG parameters most related to hypnotic susceptibility. The density of theta activity correlated with hypnotizability, but, as theta appears in drowsiness when alpha desynchronizes, this result must be interpreted cautiously. Variables from the alpha range did not increase the predictive relationship with HGSHS:A scores. The first-order correlations between hypnosis and specific frequencies are not reported. The apparent lack of a relationship between alpha frequencies and hypnotizability is not discussed, even though it appears to be inconsistent with the previous results from the same laboratory (London, Hart, & Leibovitz, 1968).

A third study from the same laboratory was conducted by Engstrom (1970). The HGSHS:A was administered to 180 Ss, and for the two-thirds of the sample scoring 7 or less (medium and low susceptible Ss) baseline alpha was subsequently recorded. From this pool, 30 Ss fulfilled the second selection criterion of less than 50 per cent alpha in a 4-minute baseline period. For this specially selected sample of 30 Ss with both low alpha and low hypnotic susceptibility, the correlation between alpha density and HGSHS:A was 0.56 ($p < .01$). This result is difficult to interpret. About 120 Ss met the HGSHS:A criterion of 7 or less. From several sources, including the results in Table 3.1, it appears that alpha density is approximately normally distributed, with a mean and median of about 50 per cent.

Even if there were a zero correlation in the total sample, mathematically it would be expected that about 60 Ss should score below the dichotomy scores of 7 and 50 per cent (two-thirds of 180 multiplied by one-half of 180, divided by N). If alpha and hypnotizability were correlated in the total sample, the number of Ss scoring low in both alpha and hypnotizability would be correspondingly higher. However, only 30 such Ss were obtained by Engstrom. It would appear, therefore, that some unknown variable has also influenced the availability of Ss in his specially selected subsample, and that the reported correlation of .56 is only representative of a special subsample accidentally selected using unknown criteria.

The data for the Ss whose results are presented in Table 3.1 was reexamined. A subsample was selected using the same criteria as that applied by Engstrom. For the 48 Ss selected (46 would have been expected by chance), the correlation between HGSHS:A and alpha density was .26 ($p < .05$). Using the same special selection criteria, Engstrom's results are confirmed, even though the correlation between HGSHS:A and alpha in the complete sample was insignificant ($-.02$). It appears that there may be no inherent relationship between alpha and hypnotizability, but rather there may be special situational factors that may result in some Ss scoring low on an initial hypnosis scale, as well as producing little alpha. This possibility is further supported when the relationship between HGSHS:A and alpha density is examined for those Ss whose HGSHS:A scores are not accurate assessments of hypnotizability. For those 8 Ss who decrease in hypnotizability (between HGSHS:A and SHSS:C) by at least 4 points, HGSHS:A and alpha correlate $-.62$, whereas for those 15 Ss who increase in hypnotizability by at least 4 points, the correlation is .43. The two correlations differ significantly ($p = .02$).[4] In contrast, for those 63 Ss whose hypnotizability scores differ by no more than one point, the correlation between HGSHS:A and alpha density is $-.04$. It appears that the apparent relationship between alpha and hypnosis may be in part a function of the instability of a single criterion of hypnosis, and particularly of those Ss whose first hypnosis score is significantly depressed.

Engstrom then showed that for these Ss, operantly increasing alpha density, using a combination of auditory feedback and photic driving, increased scores on SHSS:B. Because of the special nature of his sample and the apparent statistical regression effects, the generality of these interesting findings requires further evaluation.

Using 28 Ss selected on undefined variables, Hartnett, Nowlis, and Svorad (1969) found an insignificant correlation of $-.27$ between alpha density and SHSS:C. The mean SHSS:C score of 8.0 obtained by these Ss is

---

4. These correlations capitalize on regression effects to some extent. The correlations between HGSHS:A and alpha for Ss who show any subsequent decrease in hypnosis is $-.21$ ($N = 46$), and for Ss who show any subsequent increase, is .22 ($N = 57$). Even with this less stringent criterion of instability, the two correlations differ significantly ($p < .05$, two-tailed).

very high. However, a rank order correlation of .69 between alpha and SHSS:C was obtained for a subsample of 14 of the original 28 *S*s (mean SHSS:C, 7.9). No comments were made about how these *S*s were selected. A similar rank correlation of .70 was obtained by Nowlis and Rhead (1968) between waking alpha and the sum of HGSHS:A and SHSS:C scores. Again, it is not reported how the small sample of 21 *S*s was selected. Nowlis and Rhead published a scatterplot depicting the relationship between alpha density and hypnotic susceptibility. Examination of this scatterplot clarifies the interpretation of their results. Most of their *S*s were highly susceptible, as 11 of the 21 had combined scores of at least 16 on the two scales. From the scales' normative data, in an unselected sample the mean and median would be about 11 out of a maximum of 24 points. For those susceptible *S*s scoring 11 and above, the rank order correlation between alpha density and hypnotizability was calculated by this author to be .16 (insignificant). For the 9 insusceptible *S*s, however, the correlation between alpha density and hypnotizability was .79 ($p < .05$).

What, then, can be said about the correlation between alpha density and hypnosis? The studies reviewed are often contradictory. From one laboratory, a positive correlation (London, Hart, & Leibovitz, 1968), no apparent correlation (Galbraith et al., 1970), and a positive correlation among *S*s specially selected in a manner suggesting a lack of correlation in the larger sample (Engstrom, 1970) have all been reported. Three issues are worth raising. First, in the two studies in which *S*s did not know that the psychophysiological session was related to the hypnosis experiments (Galbraith et al., 1970; Evans, unpublished study), no relationship was found between the two measures. In the studies finding positive relationships, *S*s apparently knew that the two sets of measures were being related. This possibility suggests that problems of bias or demand characteristics (*S*s' expectations) may exist in these studies. Second, it was implicit in the study by Engstrom (1970), and demonstrable in the study by Nowlis and Rhead (1968), that the positive correlation between alpha and hypnosis may hold only for *S*s who are insusceptible to hypnosis.

These observations lead to a third point concerning the mechanisms underlying these findings. The inconsistencies in these results may arise in part from the tendency for both standard scale scores and baseline physiology to be affected by situational variables, even though both susceptibility to hypnosis and basal alpha production are stable characteristics of the individual. For example, earlier reports by O'Connell and Orne (1962, 1968) suggested that there were initial differences in basal skin potential (SP) level in susceptible and insusceptible *S*s. Later results have shown, as was implied by O'Connell and Orne, that the apparent physiological index of hypnotic depth was an artifact of relaxation (Evans, 1970). The correlation held only if baseline SP were measured during initial physiological recording sessions. However, when insusceptible *S*s were thoroughly acclimated to the laboratory over several sessions, basal SP did not differ from the lower levels of susceptible Ss. Base level continued to drop at the beginning of each session, the magnitude of the changes being positively correlated with anxiety. In addition, SP levels changed during hypnosis, but equally for susceptible and insusceptible Ss. The magnitude of change was positively correlated with the imagery-reverie-relaxation cluster of hypnotic items. This correlation is presumably determined situationally, particularly as initial differences between Ss no longer occur in later sessions.

Baseline alpha may be similarly affected by situational variables and indeed may not be as stable as it has been hitherto considered (Paskewitz & Orne, 1970). An adequate study to resolve these questions would involve repeated measures until a stable plateau is reached for both alpha and hypnosis.

I would predict that situational anxiety, adequacy of the initial session rapport, and degree of relaxation would correlate in moderator-variable fashion with several measures, including such physiological variables as SP and alpha density and conformity-prone initial group assessments of hypnotizability. Apparent correlations between single hypnosis measures and psychophysiological variables may arise because similar situational variables are operating in both conditions.

No data are available to test this prediction, but a preliminary attempt was made to test the correlation between alpha density and the hallucination-reverie cluster of hypnotic performance. The correlations between alpha density and total SHSS:C, motor suggestibility, and dissociation factors derived from SHSS:C were respectively $-.02$, $+.01$, and $-.06$. However, the correlation between alpha density and the imagery cluster (defined by the SHSS:C dream, taste, fly, and boxes items) was in the predicted direction of $+.17$, but insignificant ($N = 33$). The tetrachoric correlation was .50, indicating a more complex nonlinear relationship. In fact, Ss who had good "imagery" never had poor alpha, but predictions about alpha density could not be made if S scored low on the imagery cluster. This "imagery" factor correlates well with Ss' rated ability to relax during hypnosis (Evans, 1967), although it does *not* typically discriminate between good and poor hypnotic Ss. The imagery measure also correlates significantly with the speed of falling asleep at night, and with S's ability to respond during sleep (Evans et al., 1969).

A poorly defined picture emerges of an anxious S, perhaps initially apprehensive about hypnosis, whose SP will change as he becomes less tense, and who does not generate a great deal of alpha initially. As he becomes less apprehensive in the experimental situation over time, he relaxes, SP decreases (lowered arousal), alpha becomes disinhibited and increases in density, he feels sufficiently comfortable to "accept" his (limited) hypnotic experiences, thereby being willing to let himself go along with the situation to have new experiences. Thus, the relationship between physiological measures and susceptibility to hypnosis may be situationally determined, and once stable baselines of both physiology and hypnotizability are determined, these apparent relationships no longer exist.

In spite of conflicting results, it is concluded that waking alpha frequency, density, and amplitude are probably not correlated with susceptibility to hypnosis.

Changes in alpha during hypnosis. Marenina (1955), and others subsequently, reported decreases in alpha amplitude and density during hypnosis. The problems inherent in determining if this is a function of hypnosis, or of *S*s' napping during the hypnotic session, have been discussed. Decreases in alpha density and amplitude would be more convincingly attributed to hypnosis than to sleep if frequency did not simultaneously slow down.

Brady and Rosner (1966) reported anecdotally that some deeply hypnotized *S*s showed greater alpha amplitude than they did in the waking state. We recall one *S* who had shown no alpha in two 2-hour sessions. He was relaxed, at ease, and deeply hypnotized. No waking alpha was found. In a mildly stressful hypnotic situation, he suddenly began to show continuous large amplitude alpha for several minutes.

A definitive study would require that the relevant alpha parameter change under hypnosis from the waking level (recorded under similar conditions), and that a comparable change does *not* occur in insusceptible *S*s appropriately motivated to experience hypnosis as well as they can. Two methodological techniques allow adequate exploration of these questions: the motivated insusceptible *S*s paradigm of London and Fuhrer (1961), and the simulation model proposed by Orne (1959, 1969). Definitive studies do not exist, but some preliminary data are available from a study involving simulating *S*s.

Table 3.3 reports mean frequency, amplitude, and density of alpha for hypnotized and simulating *S*s tested by a "blind" *E*. Waking and hypnotic rest periods were presented identically by a tape recording, and were scored

TABLE 3.3 Mean alpha characteristics for hypnotized *S*s and simulating *S*s before and after induction of hypnosis

Group	Session	Frequency	Amplitude	Density (per cent)
Hypnosis	Waking	10.16	7.89	27
(*N* = 12)	Hypnosis	10.43	7.98	17
Simulator	Waking	10.33	8.72	52
(*N* = 12)	"Hypnosis"	10.20	9.21	45
F: Real versus Simulator[a]		—	3.22*	13.15***
F: Waking versus Hypnosis[a]		—	1.20	8.08**

NOTE: *p < .10; ** p < .01; ***p < .001.
a. All interactions insignificant.

blind. Means are reported for both normal waking and deeply hypnotized (or simulating) conditions of eyes closed. Each mean is the average of three passive 2-minute rest periods.

There was a tendency ($p < .10$) for simulators to have higher alpha amplitude than hypnotized Ss, both in the normal waking state and when they were simulating hypnosis. Simulating Ss generated significantly more alpha than hypnotized Ss both when awake and when simulating hypnosis (about 65 percent alpha for simulators; about 25 per cent for hypnotized Ss, $p < .001$). All Ss generated less alpha during hypnosis (or while simulating hypnosis) than during waking ($p < .01$). None of the analysis of variance interactions was significant. It is surprising that the supposedly highly alert simulating Ss generated alpha so readily during "hypnosis," more readily than supposedly relaxed hypnotized Ss. These results suggest, however, that merely being in a hypnotic trance does not alter frequency, amplitude, or density of alpha.

Alpha and hypnosis: conclusions. Alpha activity does not appear to predict hypnotizability, nor does it change during hypnosis. Reported correlations or changes are probably mediated by situationally determined factors not related to hypnosis per se. It appears that EEG alpha activity is unrelated to hypnosis.

Hypnotic Manipulation of Sleep

The apparent ease with which hypnosis has been used to control and influence behavior, the historical association between sleep and hypnosis, and concepts such as dissociated and altered states of consciousness have each contributed to the hope that hypnotic manipulations could influence special characteristics of sleep. Many studies have focused on hypnotically induced dreams. The use of hypnosis in attempts to influence dream content directly has important theoretical implications, particularly if sleep dreams and hypnotically induced dreams are similar or functionally equivalent.

HYPNOTIC DREAMS AND SLEEP DREAMS

Hypnotically induced dreams. Even Ss of only medium susceptibility to hypnosis can respond successfully to suggestions to dream during hypnosis. Hypnotically induced dreams are important for two different reasons. Any demonstration of the similarity or equivalence of hypnotic and sleep dreams would provide sophisticated evidence regarding the similarity of the two states in which the dreams are obtained. In emphasizing the importance of the interpretation of dreams, Freud (1900) stressed their symbolic meaning as a technique for evaluating unconscious mental processes. Largely on the assumption of equivalence, the hypnotic dream became, for some theorists, a method for exploring the unconscious, as it did not suffer from the effects of forgetting and time decay that plagued the collection of night dreams.

The revolution in dream research following Aserinsky and Kleitman's discovery (1953) of the relationship between rapid eye movement bursts (REM) and dream recall has been amply documented. As dreaming seems to occur throughout stage REM, about two hours are spent dreaming each night. In contrast, when dreams are collected at home or in the psychiatrist's office, recall is relatively sparse. The possibility that hypnosis could be used to increase the amount of dream material was appealing (Fisher, 1965; Jones, 1962).

Some studies have demonstrated that the content of REM awakening and home-recalled dreams are qualitatively different in several ways (Perry, 1965; Foulkes, 1966). That there are significant content differences between hypnotic and sleep dreams is not altogether surprising. Several excellent reviews of these data are available (Domhoff, 1964; Gill & Brenman, 1959; Moss, 1967; Tart, 1965a, 1966a).

Hypnotically influencing dream content. The content of sleep dreams is determined by a multiplicity of factors. Waking suggestion, direct stimulation of the sleeping *S* (in all modalities, but preferably tactile), day residues, emotional states, films of traumatic events, films of neutral travelogues, the sex of the experimenter, pictures transmitted by ESP, social isolation, spoken neutral names, spoken friends' names, details of experimental environments, drugs, as well as hypnosis, are among the experimentally manipulated variables that have allegedly become incorporated in dreams (see Tart, 1965b and Witkin, 1969, for careful reviews).

Numerous studies, both without EEG technology (such as Nachmansohn, 1925; Schroetter, 1912) and with sophisticated EEG and REM awakening techniques (Barber, 1969b; Schiff, Bunney, & Freedman, 1961; Stoyva, 1965; Tart, 1965b), have demonstrated that a posthypnotically suggested topic will appear directly or indirectly in *S*'s verbally reported dreams. These studies have been reviewed elsewhere (Barber, 1962d; Moss, 1967; Tart, 1965a). Tart concludes: "At present, then, posthypnotic suggestion seems to be the most powerful and precise method for affecting dream content, although its use is restricted to a minority of [good] subjects" (1965b, p. 85). Not surprisingly, Barber (1962d, 1969b) concludes that the results depend upon how the suggestions are administered. Stoyva's study (1965), reviewed below, is the first of its kind to use objective EEG evidence of sleep and REM, and is the only one using adequate waking controls for comparison with the posthypnotic manipulation.

A word of caution is required for the researcher who would proceed to use hypnosis as a means of influencing dream content. Dream content can be affected easily by a variety of manipulations other than hypnosis. The Freudian analyst elicits psychoanalytic dreams from his patient; the Jungian analyst obtains dreams of an entirely different kind. The first year psychiatric resident may elicit higher proportions of dreams with manifest sexual content because he tends to "reinforce" the patient for such interesting, relevant material.[5] The researcher is dependent upon S's verbal report (and memory) to evaluate the success of his manipulation. While subjective report is not inherently untrustworthy if it is carefully evaluated, Tart (1964) has shown, for example, that hypnotic and sleep dreams differ in quality even though S reports them to be similar kinds of experience. In addition, there is no objective means of knowing whether the hypnotically suggested dream actually occurs in REM sleep or whether S awakens, either normally or in hypnosis, and produces waking or hypnotic fantasy instead of a dream. Complicated research designs, such as simulating Ss, will be required to control the obvious demand characteristics of this kind of procedure.

Hypnotic and sleep dreams and REM. It has already been shown that except for some special limiting cases, the EEG of the hypnotized S is that of a waking person rather than of a sleeping one. This is true even when it is suggested to the hypnotized S that he should sleep and dream. Similarly, Tart (1964) demonstrated that both basal level and nonspecific random activity of the GSR during hypnotic dreams were more similar to that of a waking than to that of a sleeping S. Such physiological data provide compelling evidence for the dissimilarity of sleep and hypnotic dreams. The only physiological parameter on which clear similarities between the two types of dreams have been shown is in eye movement patterns (Brady & Rosner, 1966; Schiff, Bunney, & Freedman, 1961; Tart, 1964).

Dreams are primarily visual, and when the association between REM and dreaming was discovered it was quickly hypothesized that the eye movements represented scanning of the visual scene. Like many plausible hypotheses this one has led a vigorous existence. The fortuitous early emphasis on eye movement correlates of the sleep stage, rather than any of the many concomitant physiological changes during stage REM, has been the primary stimulus, and a major hindrance, to sleep research over the past 15 years. The visual scanning hypothesis is properly losing favor with many investigators due to a lack of supporting evidence. The REMs are saccadic in nature and difficult to relate to specific content scenes. Pursuit movements normally involved in the perception of motion are rarely seen during sleep dreams, even though motion is often a characteristic of dream reports. Saccadic eye

5. M. T. Orne, personal communication.

movements may occur not only in conjunction with specific visual scenes, but also often related to arousal and attention (Amadeo & Shagass, 1963; Antrobus, Antrobus & Singer, 1964) and to meditative, contemplative, and daydreaming incidents (Singer, 1966).

While the scanning role of REM is open to question, the observation by Tart (1964), the detailed case study by Schiff, Bunney, and Freedman (1961), and the careful experiments by Brady and Rosner (1966), indicate that REM may occur when deeply hypnotized Ss are asked to dream. In each study, the investigation of REM during hypnotic dreams was the primary focus of the investigation. Eye-movement recording electrodes were applied to Ss carefully selected for hypnotizability, and the Ss were asked to dream. Popular magazines have widely publicized the REM-dream phenomena and the purpose of the study must have been readily apparent (even explicit) to Ss, although no control procedures were adopted to evaluate the effects of such powerful demand characteristics.

In an unpublished study employing EEG, EOG, SP, and other physiological measures, a suggested hypnotic dream was one short, incidental, item embedded in two 2-hour sessions. Testing 14 deeply hypnotized and 14 simulating Ss, REM was not found in any S during the suggested dream. In contrast, under appropriate circumstances some Ss can quickly learn to establish delicate control over their eye movements. Some Ss were able to produce optokinetic nystagmus voluntarily, a much more specific reflexive pattern of minute movements than that of REM saccades. Such control was not a function of either hypnosis, vivid and real hallucinations, or vividness of imagery (Evans, Reich, & Orne, 1972). The nonspecific saccades of REM would be much easier to produce when Ss are confronted with the demand characteristics of justifying one's ability as a good hypnotic S. Because of the ability of some Ss to control delicate eye movements it does not seem surprising that REM was found during dreams. Unfortunately, no quantitative analyses of the eye movements comparing sleep and hypnotic dreams were conducted. The occurrence of stage REM eye movement patterns during the hypnotic dream has not been established conclusively.

INFLUENCING SLEEP FUNCTIONS BY HYPNOTIC TECHNIQUES

Relatively few studies have used hypnotic techniques to influence and alter specific characteristics of sleep and the sleep cycle. Attempts to use hypnosis in sleep learning studies, and to explore cognitive functioning and response to suggestions during sleep, will be discussed separately in the final section.

Direct suggestions have successfully been given that Ss should awaken at a presuggested time (Tart, 1970a). It has also been suggested directly that Ss would be able to discriminate between REM and nonREM sleep (Antrobus & Antrobus, 1967). Three exploratory studies are especially important because their focus is not on the nature of hypnosis, but rather on the use of hypnosis as a special technique or tool, just as the EEG is used as a tool, to study the functions of sleep.

A study by Arkin, Hastey, and Reiser (1966) explored the use of hypnosis and posthypnotic suggestion to induce sleep talking. One hypnotizable S who had a long history of sleep talking was studied over many nights. Following appropriate posthypnotic suggestions to talk during sleep, and during stage REM dreams, the incidence of sleep vocalization rose from 1 per night prehypnosis to 8 and 13 times per night respectively. However, baseline nights without hypnosis near the end of the series yielded a comparable incidence of 8 episodes, similar to the posthypnotically stimulated incidence. Thus it is not clear whether hypnosis was instrumental in affecting the incidence of sleep talking. However, sleep vocalizations were less likely to occur during REM (28 per cent and 42 per cent pre- and postbaselines) than were the hypnotically induced incidents (64 per cent). The authors report frequent occurrence of low-voltage fast EEG activity (typically found in both waking and stage REM), alpha (indicative of awakening), and "sawtooth" waves (indicative of sleep) during vocalization. They conclude that the sleep talking incidents contain characteristics of both sleep and the hypnotic state.

Two interesting attempts have been made to explore the function of stage REM sleep by the use of hypnosis. It has been well documented that when a person is deprived of stage REM sleep over a series of nights and is subsequently allowed to sleep normally, a greater occurrence of REM sleep is observed during the following "recovery nights." This REM-rebound effect has led investigators to postulate that dreaming involves an essential need system and that long-term REM deprivation (such as that induced by many drugs) may be deleterious to psychological health. After depriving three Ss of REM sleep for two consecutive nights, Halper, Pivik, and Dement (1969) allowed Ss, who had high scores on SHSS:A, two 2½-hour periods of hypnotic hallucinations and dreaming. If there were any functional equivalence between hypnotic and sleep hallucinations (dreams), they hypothesized that no REM rebound would occur on recovery nights: Ss had an opportunity to "make up" by hypnosis what they had lost during deprivation. This ingenious hypothesis was not confirmed—the normal REM-rebound effect occurred for these REM-deprived Ss.

Using deeply hypnotizable Ss, Stoyva (1965) gave posthypnotic suggestions, with amnesia, that Ss would dream about specified topics during sleep. He employed standard REM-awakening techniques. Although the dream reports from REM awakenings were not rated blind, Stoyva divided Ss into two groups: a "successful" group who dreamed about the suggested topic in over 70 per cent (mean of 85 per cent) of their average 19.4 awakenings, and an "unsuccessful" group who reported dreaming correctly on less than 60 per cent of their average of 5.6 awakenings. Stoyva tested the "need to dream" hypothesis by arguing that those Ss who successfully dreamed about the suggested topic would do so during their early stage REM periods and, having quickly disposed of the "business of dreaming," would consequently have shorter REM duration than those who did not successfully dream about the topic (and implicitly did not dream well). His hypothesis was confirmed: successful dreamers had a total uninterrupted REM time of 26.6 minutes, which was 6.6 minutes less than for baseline nights and 7 minutes less than the REM time of unsuccessfully stimulated Ss. It was also tentatively found that posthypnotic suggestions for more complex dreams led to a further reduction in REM time. NREM awakenings did not typically yield reports of dreams about the suggestion.

These three ingenious studies could serve as prototypes for ways in which hypnosis may be used as a technique to study characteristics and parameters of sleep. No particular conclusions are possible from these pilot studies; they should be replicated and extended. It is hoped that similar studies will be conducted more frequently.

Hypnosis as a Model for Sleep-Induced Behavior

A different set of questions has been explored recently concerning the sleeping individual's ability to interact with his environment. Hypnosis has provided both a model for studying interactions with the sleeping person and a means of exploring cognitive functioning during sleep.

Anecdotal examples support the notion that, in addition to dreaming, complex cognitive behavior can occur during sleep, particularly if an appropriate set has been established before sleep. One rarely falls out of bed, for example, even though a great deal of gross bodily activity occurs throughout the night. Loud noises that are repetitive or familiar are less likely to wake the sleeping person than softer strange noises. Mothers can sleep through conditions of high ambient noise but are easily awakened by soft familiar cries from their babies—the so-called "mother's cry" phenomenon. Some people claim they can wake regularly at a preselected time. Similar phenomena have been studied in the laboratory. For example, when appropriate waking instructions had been given, sleeping Ss woke up only when specified names of friends were spoken (Oswald, 1962). Conditioned responses and discrimination among auditory stimuli may be elicited during sleep if a waking response tendency has been established (Beh & Barratt, 1965; Granda & Hammack, 1961; McDonald, 1966; Weinberg, 1966; Williams, Morlock, & Morlock, 1966; Zung & Wilson, 1961).

Historically, it has been recognized that if a hypnotized S is given a specific suggestion, or even if he is left alone for a long period of time, he may fall asleep without passing through a natural awake state. Dittborn has been able to induce sleep by repetitive suggestion (Dittborn, Munoz, & Aristeguieta, 1963). Although the occurrence of suggested sleep was confirmed by the EEG, the ease of falling asleep following suggestions was not related to hypnotizability (Dittborn & O'Connell, 1967). Dittborn and O'Connell showed a kind of dissociation between behavioral and physiological sleep with hypnotizable Ss who, by discontinuing a repetitive response, appeared asleep behaviorally even though they were not asleep physiologically. Kratochvil (1970) has also suggested that sleep and hypnosis may be superimposed, although such combined states are difficult to demonstrate operationally.

A controversial claim has been that hypnotic-like suggestions can be given successfully during sleep (Bernheim, 1889; Bertrand, 1826b; Fresacher, 1951; Gill & Brenman, 1959; Schilder & Kauders, 1927). Barber (1956) whispered hypnotic-like suggestions to 22 Ss who were asleep in their rooms. Some Ss responded to the suggestions; physiological and EEG criteria were not employed to monitor sleep.

RESPONSE TO SUGGESTIONS DURING SLEEP

Our background and experience with hypnosis both provoked our interest in cognitive awareness during sleep and also provided insight into how to explore the complexity of behavior that could be induced during sleep. With the intial Ss we tested, we were tentatively exploring parallels between hypnosis and responses to suggestions we supposed might be induced successfully during sleep (Cobb et al., 1965). The general procedures were the same as in later studies and will be outlined below.

Four observations were particularly interesting: (1) Some Ss could respond, while remaining asleep, to simple hypnotic-like suggestions administered during stage REM sleep. (2) When awakened, Ss did not recall these suggestions. However, the analogy with posthypnotic amnesia was superficial, as, unlike posthypnotic amnesia, the postsleep amnesia could not be reversed. The Ss seemed to remain unaware of their sleeping activity. (3) When given the same cue after sleep that had elicited the suggested response during sleep, Ss did not respond behaviorally while awake. The sleep-induced cue was not analogous to a posthypnotic cue for S to respond to the associated suggestion. Sleep-induced behavior was at best only superficially related to hypnotic behavior. (4) The Ss' ability to respond to suggestions during sleep did appear to be related to hypnotic susceptibility. Four Ss responded to suggestions during sleep; each was a deeply hypnotizable S who had worked with E in several previous experiments. The four insusceptible Ss did not respond at all to sleep suggestions.

The implied relationship between susceptibility to hypnosis and sleep-induced response must be interpreted with caution. The susceptible and insusceptible Ss had quite different background experiences with hypnosis. Repeated failure by insusceptible Ss to respond to hypnotic suggestions may have changed the interpersonal relationship between S and E. The Ss' expectations, rather than their susceptibility to hypnosis, could have been a critical determinant of their responsivity during sleep. In addition, *E* administering the sleep suggestions was the same *E* who had evaluated *S*'s hypnotic susceptibility; as he was quite aware of each *S*'s susceptibility during sleep testing, the possible influence of *E*'s biases on the predicted outcome cannot be overlooked. Nevertheless, the interrelationship between hypnosis and the sleep suggestions that were induced and tested during stage REM sleep seemed worthy of detailed exploration. A more elaborate study was designed (Evans et al., 1969, 1970). Susceptibility to hypnosis was not evaluated until after the completion of all sleep sessions, and was evaluated by hypnotists who were unaware of *S*s' performance during the sleep sessions. Differences in rapport and the interpersonal factors arising in the hypnotic relationship were not present during the sleep sessions.

Procedure.[6] Nineteen male student nurses slept for two nights. Standard EEG sleep-monitoring techniques were used. During on-line visual diagnosis of alpha-free stage REM sleep, suggestions were presented verbally to *S*. Typical suggestions were: "Whenever I say the word 'itch,' your nose will feel itchy until you scratch it"; "Whenever I say the word 'pillow,' your pillow will feel uncomfortable until you move it." The suggestion was tested by saying the cue word ("itch" or "pillow") once. An attempt was made to test each cue word on at least two separate occasions during the same stage REM period in which the suggestion was given *(immediate)*, during all subsequent stage REM periods that night *(delayed)*, and during stage REM periods of the second night *(carry-over)*. The suggestion itself was not re-administered on the second night. Suggestions were not repeated after their initial presentation. Two new suggestions were presented each night whenever possible. Suggestions were administered and cues were tested only during stage REM. At least 120 seconds of alpha-free stage REM were required between cue word presentations. It was conservatively assumed that visually-detected alpha indicated arousal (O'Connell et al., 1965). Only *S*s who displayed an alpha density exceeding 40 per cent of an eyes-closed waking-rest trial were included in the study.

The *S*'s behavior was observed by *E*, who was in the same room. When *S* awakened in the morning, memory for the session was tested directly and indirectly during an interview and by administering the cue words in the context of a word association test. Any behavioral response to the critical cue word was observed. When *S* awakened after night 2, a more detailed inquiry evaluated memory for the sleep events.

The *S* was not told before either session that suggestions would be given, but he was told that sleep cycles were being studied. Thus, any specific wak-

6. A detailed description of the procedures and results discussed below has been given elsewhere (Evans et al., 1969, 1970).

ing "set" indicating what was being tested during sleep was avoided. He was not told that he would be invited back later to participate in a hypnosis experiment.

About a month after the completion of the sleep experiment, HGSHS:A and SHSS:C were administered to these Ss by "blind" Es. Five subscores were derived from HGSHS:A and SHSS:C: waking motor suggestion, hypnotic motor suggestion, challenge suggestion, hallucinatory-reverie, and posthypnotic-dissociative.[7]

Characteristics of sleep induced behavior. A detailed parametric description of the important characteristics of sleep-induced behavior are presented elsewhere (Evans et al., 1969, 1970) and are only summarized now. During the two nights, 416 cue words were presented during sleep, and 89 correct responses were observed. On the average, the 19 Ss responded to a mean of 21.2 per cent of all cue words: the highest response rate by a S was 48 per cent.

Uninterrupted stage REM sleep continued for at least 30 seconds for 71 per cent of all cues administered, that is, alpha activity did not occur before or while the cue word was administered. Many responses were obtained without eliciting alpha activity during the suggestion, after the cue words were administered, or before and after the response. When alpha followed a successful response, it was signficantly slower than waking alpha frequency, but it was not significantly different from the slowed frequency occurring spontaneously during unstimulated stage REM sleep.

After S awakened, he did not remember the verbally presented material, nor could he remember responding. No difference was found between the latency of word associate cue words and latency of control word associates. This lack of recall involved amnesia rather than forgetting, because the material was still available for future responding during sleep. When S returned to sleep the next night (or, in some of the cases described below, even 5 months later), the mere repetition of the relevant cue word (without repetition of the suggestion itself) was sufficient to elicit the appropriate response. The behavioral response appeared to be specific to sleep in spite of the intervening amnesia.

7. These clusters were derived by summing scores on SHSS:C items as follows. *Hypnotic motor suggestion:* items 1 and 2, hand lowering and moving hands apart. *Challenge suggestion:* items 5 and 8, arm rigidity and arm immobilization. *Hallucinatory-reverie:* items 6 and 11, dream and negative visual hallucination. *Posthypnotic-dissociative:* item 12, posthypnotic amnesia, and item 11 from HGSHS:A, posthypnotic suggestion. The *waking motor suggestion* consisted of item 1 of HGSHS:A, head falling. These clusters do not necessarily represent the underlying dimensions adequately, particularly the hallucination and dissociative ones (Evans, 1966). Although the underlying dimensions may be unrelated, the estimated scores are moderately correlated. The highest correlation ($r = .51$) is between the hallucination and posthypnotic clusters.

The response could not be elicited by repeating the cue word in the waking state. As in the preliminary study, behavior analogous to posthypnotic suggestion was not elicited.

A successful response tendency was mobilized slowly. The average response latency was 32 seconds. Latency increased as the temporal dissocation between the administration of the suggestion and the cue word increased. For example, latencies for immediate and carry-over responses were 19 and 59 seconds, respectively. In contrast, a similar suggestion given during hypnosis would be responded to immediately: even if tested posthypnotically the response latency is typically only a few seconds.

A subsequent study (Perry et al., in press) has confirmed these characteristics, although a lower response rate and even longer response latencies were found. Three additional findings confirmed that the motor behavior during sleep was not random, but was directly elicited by the suggestions and associated cue words. (1) Correct responses could be discriminated from random body movement behavior when videotaped responses were rated by blind raters. (2) Interspersed dummy cue words not associated with any suggestion that had been administered did not elicit behavioral responses appropriate to any suggestion that had been given. (3) If a cue word was presented before the suggestion had been given, the cue word was not sufficient by itself to elicit the specific behavioral response that was to be later on associated with the suggestion.

SLEEP RESPONSE AND SUSCEPTIBILITY TO HYPNOSIS

Based on individual percentage response rates for the two nights combined, a post hoc dichotomy was made between *responsive* ($N = 9$) and *unresponsive* ($N = 10$) Ss. Mean HGSHS:A and SHSS:C scores for responsive and unresponsive Ss are presented in Table 3.4. Those Ss who respond most frequently to sleep-induced suggestions are more susceptible to hypnosis. Pearson correlations between susceptibility to hypnosis and frequencies of cue administration, response, and response rate are presented in Table 3.5. The correlations are positive and consistent for the several measures, indicating that sleep-induced response and susceptibility to hypnosis are related

TABLE 3.4   Susceptibility to hypnosis and response to suggestion during sleep

| | | Hypnosis Scale | | | |
| | | HGSHS:A | | SHSS:C | |
		$\overline{X}$	SD	$\overline{X}$	SD
Responsive Ss	($N = 9$)	7.6	3.5	9.5	2.1
Unresponsive Ss	($N = 10$)	5.5	2.8	5.5	2.4
Mann-Whitney U		28.5	(insig.)	8.5	($p < .01$)
t		1.41	($p < .20$)	3.93	($p < .005$)

SOURCE: Evans et al., 1969.

TABLE 3.5   Correlations between sleep response and susceptibility to hypnosis

Hypnosis[a] Measure	Response Frequency	Cue Word Frequency	Per Cent Response	Delay Between Suggestion-Cue		
				immediate response	delayed response	carry-over response
HGSHS:A	.48*	.63**	.42	.23	.32	.64**
SHSS:C	.56*	.68**	.39	.38	.43	.60**
Suggestion:						
Waking	−.15	−.21	−.19	.11	−.42	.06
Passive	.32	.23	.32	.05	.40	.41
Challenge	.26	.47*	.22	.33	.08	.44
Hallucinatory-reverie	.54**	.61**	.43	.35	.42	.52**
Posthypnotic-Dissociative	.46*	.64**	.17	.23	.30	.58**

SOURCE: Evans et al., 1969.
NOTE: * $p < .05$; ** $p < .01$ (two-tailed values).
a. The clusters of hypnotic items are derived from SHSS:C. See text footnote 7.

in some manner. The relationship is, however, complex, and several factors influence the interpretation of these correlations.

Response frequency. The correlations between susceptibility to hypnosis and response to sleep-induced suggestions are, then, positive and significant (see Table 3.5). However, susceptible Ss responded more often, at least in part, because they were administered more cue words. Hypnotizable Ss were found to awaken following stimulation less frequently than insusceptible Ss. Consequently they slept longer, and more cues were inadvertently tested. The correlations between response-rate percentage (which effectively controls the difference in the frequency of cue administrations) and both HGSHS:A and SHSS:C are of borderline significance (.42, $p < .10$; and .39 $p < .10$, respectively, two-tailed values).[8] However, the relationship between sleep responsivity and hypnosis depends on two factors: the delay in time between administering the suggestion and testing with the cue word; and the aspect of hypnosis (factor or cluster score) being considered.

Hypnosis and temporal dissociation of sleep response. Table 3.5 summarizes the correlations between hypnotizability and the three categories of response: immediate, delayed, and carry-over. The correlations with susceptibility to hypnosis are higher for percentage rate of delayed response than for percentage rate of immediate response. Susceptibility to hypnosis more successfully predicts ability to respond to sleep-induced suggestion when there is a temporal dissociation between the administration of the suggestion

8. The number of times S awakened during the 2 nights correlated −.49 ($p < .05$) with HGSHS:A and − .29 ($p > .05$) with SHSS:C.

and the cue word, that is, when the response is elicited during the second night to a suggestion that has been administered only during the first night. The correlations between the carry-over response rate with HGSHS:A and SHSS:C are .64 ($p < .01$ and .60 ($p < .01$) respectively.

Sleep response and type of hypnotic performance. Correlations between the sleep-induced response and factors of hypnotic behavior are summarized in Table 3.5. These results should be interpreted with considerable caution. Neither the frequency of cues nor the frequency of responses correlates with waking suggestibility, hypnotic motor suggestibility, or challenge suggestibility. This is surprising, because the sleep behaviors suggested involved motor responses. The correlations with the hallucinatory-reverie and posthypnotic-dissociative clusters are significant for the percentage rate of carry-over (dissociative) response ($r = .52$, $p < .01$ and $r = .58$, $p < .01$, respectively), but not for the immediate responses. These two hypnotic clusters include phenomena experienced only by the very few *S*s who can be deeply hypnotized.

Sleep patterns, hypnosis, and sleep response. We were surprised to find that the more hypnotizable *S*s fell asleep faster, and were less likely to be awakened during the night. This prompted us to examine *S*s' subjective sleep patterns. At the beginning of their first night, a questionnaire was administered to *S*s inquiring about their ability to sleep well without being disturbed. Several items from this questionnaire discriminated significantly between responding and nonresponding *S*s. A combined score, including items reflecting objective measures of sleeping well during the study (Evans et al., 1969) correlated .55 ($p < .02$) with response frequency. Combining the predictive criteria, the multiple correlation between percentage response frequency and the combination of the questionnaire and SHSS:C was .48 ($p < .05$). The multiple correlations predicting the carry-over responses were .69, and .68, and .62 ($p < .01$) when the questionnaire was combined with SHSS:C, and the dissociation and hallucinatory factors, respectively.

Hypnotizability and sleep induced responsivity. Subjects who were able to remain asleep while responding to verbal suggestions administered during sleep were more susceptible to hypnosis and slept more soundly than *S*s who did not respond. This joint relationship reflects the hypnotizable responder's ability to sleep well, in terms of both his verbal claims about his sleeping habits and his ability to sleep without awakening in the experimental situation. By waking more often, both spontaneously and following stimulation, the unresponsive *S* provided himself with less opportunity to respond because fewer cue word administrations were possible.

This result clarifies the perfect association between responding and hypnotizability observed by Cobb et al. (1965). Then, as in the present study, insusceptible Ss tended to awaken whenever there was any verbal stimulation. The interesting theoretical question is not so much the extent to which sleep suggestion is analogous to hypnotic phenomena, but rather why the hypnotizable S sleeps better than the more easily aroused insusceptible S. Ranking Ss by all available hypnosis scores, the 6 Ss who were least susceptible to hypnosis accounted for 48 per cent of all awakenings occurring during the two experimental nights. In contrast, the 6 Ss who were most hypnotizable accounted for only 26 per cent of the total awakenings.

The paradigm adopted for administering the suggestions during sleep was similar to that regularly used with passive motor suggestions during waking or hypnosis. The sleep response was not, however, a simple manifestation of motor or primary suggestibility as the concept is usually applied to waking and hypnotic conditions (Evans, 1967). Frequency of sleep response did not correlate with score clusters derived from the hypnosis scales measuring the various aspects of motor suggestion. Instead, sleep response frequency was related to the clusters consisting of phenomena typically obtained with somnambulistic hypnosis: hallucinations and posthypnotic effects.

The correlation between sleep-induced response to suggestion and susceptibility to hypnosis was statistically significant only when the carry-over responses (responses during night 2 to suggestions administered during night 1) were considered. The relationship between response and hypnotic susceptibility was most apparent when there was a dissociative temporal gap between the administration of the suggestion and the related cue eliciting the response. A common mechanism may exist in both the hypnotic and sleep situations, although it takes a different form in each state. This speculative interpretation is supported by the significant correlation between the post-hypnotic-dissociative cluster of items in the hypnosis scales and the frequency of carry-over or dissociated responses. In the spirit of this kind of speculation, the correlation between the hallucinatory-reverie cluster of items and sleep response is possibly consistent with data indicating that when a successful response occurs the cue word may be incorporated into ongoing dream activity (Evans et al., 1970). Some kind of facility to control imagery and ideational content seems necessary to experience convincing hypnotic hallucinations and to manipulate ongoing dream content. It is also interesting that there are some Ss who experience posthypnotic amnesia, who respond during sleep in spite of intervening waking amnesia, and who claim they do not recall dreams when they awaken.

The assumed selective attention of the hypnotized S during trance and his ability to discriminate between relevant and irrelevant stimuli have often been stressed. If this is a general characteristic of the susceptible S, then he may maintain this advantage during some stages of sleep. He is able to attend selectively and to process incoming information in a way that allows discrimination as to whether it is "necessary" for him to arouse himself and process the information at a more integrated waking level. On some occasions this processing can be completed without arousal. Because of his lack of selective attention the insusceptible *S* has to awaken to process similar incoming information. From this point of view the relationship between susceptibility to hypnosis and sleep-induced response does not imply any similarity or interchangeability of trance and sleep states. Rather, the evidence seems to indicate that ability to have dissociative mental processes leading to a selective attention to external stimulation is common to both phenomena.

Alternatively, some *S*s may be able to shift from one state of consciousness to another with relative ease. A fluidity, or perhaps a blurring of the boundaries between different states, occurs. There may be people who can be hypnotized readily, who can fluctuate between a variety of dissociated states, whether while awake or asleep, and who can fall asleep readily, yet be able to alert themselves quickly to process incoming stimuli, sometimes responding while remaining asleep. The common mechanism may be a fluidity or interchangeability of state boundaries rather than any specific features of any of these dissociated states.

FURTHER EXPLORATIONS OF DISSOCIATED SLEEP RESPONSES

Several important questions remained unanswered. What are the limits of the carry-over responses? Was the cue word sufficiently strong to elicit a sleep response even after several months of intervening amnesia? Was it possible to increase the response rate during sleep by appropriate sets or instructions in the waking or hypnotic conditions prior to sleep? Were there any means available, such as presleep sets or the use of hypnotic techniques after sleep, to recover memory for the sleep experiences in the waking state? While these questions have not been answered satisfactorily as yet, an attempt was made to explore some of these issues in a pilot study by making additional observations with some of the *S*s already tested.

About five months after the completion of the study described above, 7 of the 19 *S*s were invited to sleep another night in the laboratory. In general, the procedures already described were used. Specific procedures, which differed from *S* to *S*, and the main results are summarized in Table 3.6. The hypnotizability rankings are based both on standardized scale scores and individual diagnostic ratings that had been administered shortly after completion of the original two nights.

An attempt was made to hypnotize each *S* at the beginning of the sleep session. No special suggestions regarding responding or recall were given to five *S*s. One of these *S*s was allowed to fall asleep while hypnotized. The remaining two *S*s were given strong suggestions to respond during sleep and to recall when awake. During sleep, several cue words were administered that were appropriate to the suggestions of the two nights from five months previously. New suggestions were also given. Waking recall was tested as before, but each *S* was hypnotized in an attempt to elicit further recall. When *S* was finally awakened from sleep, recall was tested as before. A va-

TABLE 3.6 Relationships between hypnosis, sleep induced response and subsequent waking recall for Ss sleeping several months after initial sessions

S	Hypnosis[a]		Use of Hypnosis on Night 3[b]	Response Per Cent		Recall[c]	
	level	rank		nights 1 & 2	night 3	waking	added by hypnosis
1	High	1	\	31	55	Nil	Nil
2	High	4	No suggestion to	42	43	Some	Some
3	Med.	5	respond	25	14	Poor	Nil
4	Low	7	/	20	0	Nil	Some
5	High	2	No suggestion, fell asleep in hypnosis	5	9	Nil	Nil
6	High	3	) Suggest response,	8	39	Much	Some
7	Med.	6	) recall	48	63	Some	Much

a. High, medium, or low susceptibility to hypnosis based on HGSHS:A, SHSS:C, and diagnostic ratings. Rankings of hypnotizability based on all available evidence.

b. See text for description.

c. Crude rating scale of nil, poor, some, much, or complete recall of sleep suggestions and responses.

riety of hypnotic techniques, including regression, were used with the more hypnotizable Ss in an attempt to reverse the amnesia for the sleep experiences.

The main results are summarized in Table 3.6. Because of the exploratory nature of these sessions conclusions are not justified. Some Ss responded much more frequently than they had during the original two nights. Under special conditions, response rates approached the initial response rates reported by Cobb et al. (1965). While the induction of hypnosis and the hypnotic experience gained since the original nights may have contributed to these increases, the evidence indicates that neither hypnotic depth nor the interpersonal variables could account for all of the increases. Specific presleep suggestions aimed at increasing sleep responsivity may have been helpful, but it cannot be judged whether the increased response rate is due to hypnosis per se or is a generalized, nonspecific response due to E's convincing S that high response rates could plausibly be expected. Certainly such influences did not merely affect new suggestions. Many responses were obtained to cue words associated with suggestions that had not been repeated, nor apparently recalled, since the first night some five to six months before.

Similar problems of interpretation recurred when attempts were made to utilize hypnosis, either before or after the sleep session, to obtain recall of the sleep events. Hypnosis helped, but again the results were not a direct function of hypnotic depth. Some hitherto unrecalled old suggestions were recalled while using hypnotic techniques. This result may indicate that the techniques originally used to probe morning recall were insufficiently sensitive. Perhaps our *S*s may have deceived us. On the other hand, the possible timeless or contextless effects of hypnosis have been documented by the work on source amnesia (Evans & Thorn, 1966; Evans, 1968). The investigator working in this area may find hypnosis important, if not essential, in improving recall and response rates, but whether hypnosis per se is a causal variable requires additional sophisticated research.

SLEEP RESPONSE—THREE CASE STUDIES

Case study summaries of three *S*s who participated for three nights are presented below. These summaries will invite speculation without providing answers. They will also serve to give some insight into the dramatic quality of the sleep suggestion response that is not apparent in sterile statistical description.

Subject 1. This *S* was an exceptionally good hypnotic *S,* scoring 12 on both HGSHS:A and SHSS:C, with several 5+ diagnostic ratings (Orne & O'Connell, 1967). Before the third session he was easily and deeply hypnotized, displaying all major hypnotic phenomena.

He had responded to 11 of 36 cues (31 per cent response rate) on the first two nights. He had recalled more than any other *S* about the two nights. He remembered the cue "itch," and said he deduced that he had been given suggestions. He felt that two other cue words ("pillow," "blanket") during the second night word association test were in some way significant. Thus, he had partial recall of three of the five suggestions that were used. In no case could details be elaborated. Of his 11 responses, 7 were to the three cue words that were recalled.

This *S*'s sleep behavior during the first two nights seemed both purposeful and emotional. After he had been presented with the cue word "itch," he scratched his nose for several seconds, adjusted his "pillow" by pushing it into a new shape with both hands, pulled his "blanket" above his head, and kicked with his "leg," pausing each time between the successive movements. There was no EEG evidence of arousal. He had been given these four suggestions separately, but in this sequence, during the previous two nights. Repetition of any of the four cue words failed to elicit further response. When the next stage REM period occurred, presentation of any one of the four cue words again elicited the same sequence of responses, but no more responses could be elicited with another cue word. In the final stage REM period, the same sequence occurred again. This time *S* repeatedly thrashed his left leg with considerable violence. By responding in sequence to all suggestions, then failing to "acknowledge" further stimulation, he obtained a deceptively low response rate. (This kind of sequential "response chaining" was observed with at least two other *S*s.)

During the third night he did not respond to a new suggestion. The old cue word "leg" was administered three times. The first time he raised his left leg to almost a vertical position and held it there for several seconds. He responded again to the second repetition. On the third time, with little delay, he lifted his left leg and put it down, repeating the lifting sequence three times, each time more aggressively. This suggestion had not been given since the first night five months previously: he had responded to it then but did not recall it. He responded to two of four additional cues, the last of which involved another response chain, followed by arousal. He could not fall asleep again. He responded to five of nine cues (55 per cent). He could not recall anything under some pressure while awake nor while hypnotized.

Subject 2. The *S* slept well and responded well. In all, he responded 14 times to 33 cues (42 per cent response rate). He responded 6 times on the second night to the 8 testings of first night cue words. Neither recall nor dreams were elicited. He scored 11 and 10 on HGSHS:A and SHSS:C respectively, and, although diagnostic ratings could not be made, he appeared to be a very susceptible *S*. On the third night he was hypnotized, displaying all standard hypnotic phenomena.

During the third night he responded to 2 of the 7 old cues and to 4 of 7 new cues (43 per cent). Once, when the old cue word "pillow" was given, he moved his pillow and, with a significant pause each time between movements, he then scratched his nose, moved his right leg, and appeared to brush something from his chin. These were very precise, specific movements. They were appropriate responses to all of the suggestions that had been administered during the two original nights, in correct order. This response chaining occurred several times with him.

He responded twice, as he had on night 2, to a verbal command to raise his left arm on the cue "arm." Unlike the suggestions, this command did not have any specific subjective experience associated with it. He continued to hold his arm up until he was told to let it drop (in one case, after about 5 minutes). (Maintaining responses to a command until told to stop was observed with other *S*s.) Suggestions were then given that he would dream about the experiment and that he would be able to recall the experiment, his responses, and his dreams in detail.

Upon awakening he reported one of the most vivid dreams we obtained. He was studying for an examination (not true in real life) and he was very excited, disturbed, and annoyed because he was being interrupted. During the 15 word associates test he inappropriately moved both legs twice (to the neutral words "night" and "head"), he then correctly moved his right leg to "leg" and momentarily lifted his left arm to "arm." This was the first evidence of a sleep state analog of a posthypnotic response.

When questioned about the night, he spontaneously recalled that he had been asked to move his leg, but could not recall any details. He was then hypnotized and, in response to suggestions of recall, he was able to elaborate upon the dream and recall the exact details of the leg suggestion and his response to it, both during sleep and during his word associate response. He could recall nothing about any other suggestions used.

In general, this *S* did not behave very differently in this session than in his previous sessions. It is possible that the sleep and hypnotic suggestions stimulated some recall. Any differences in "rapport" variables added by the hypnotic evaluations did not result (as hypothesized by Cobb et al., 1965) in a greater response rate.

Subject 6. This *S* scored 6 and 9 respectively on HGSHS:A and SHSS:C and received two clinical hypnotic ratings of 5. At the beginning of the third session he had no memory for the previous suggestions. He was easily hypnotized before he slept. He was given emphatic suggestions that he would respond to any suggestions given during sleep and recall them when awake.

He had previously tended to awaken when suggestions were administered (three of seven attempts), and had been classified as a nonresponder. He responded only twice to 25 cues. One of these responses occurred on the second night to a first night suggestion. On the third night he responded to 7 out of 18 cues, a change from 8 per cent to 39 per cent response rate following the hypnotically induced "set" to respond. These statistics, however, do not capture the quality of his performance. He was tested unsuccessfully seven times during his first stage REM period. During this time a new suggestion that "when I say the word 'blanket,' you will feel cold and pull the blanket up over you," failed to elicit a response. In the remaining stage REM periods the cue words "itch" and "leg" were given a total of three times unsuccessfully. These cue words had not elicited any response during the first two sessions either, perhaps implying a failure of stimulus registration.

The "blanket" and "pillow" suggestions were then readministered, again with no signs of arousal (alpha) in the record. The *S* then responded to each of the three "pillow" cues and to three of the four "blanket" cues. (Following the fourth "blanket" cue, a partial movement of the arm was made below the covers, but could not have been considered a clear response.) It is possible that *S* suddenly began "hearing" or "understanding" what was being said for the first time. It is not possible to tell, of course, if hypnosis was instrumental in this dramatic change in response rate from almost 0 to almost 100 per cent.

Later, upon waking, *S* knew *E* had been in the room talking several times —about five times. He knew *E* had used the word "itch." He remembered this because one of the electrodes made him itchy. (He had not responded to this cue since his only night 1 response five months ago.) Gradually he recalled that he had been restless, particularly with the pillow. He then recalled that *E* said it was lumpy, and this is why he wanted to move it. Then he said, "Oh, another word was 'blanket.' I can recall curling into a ball under the blanket—it was rather cool. You told me I was gonna be cool, and I would pull it up all around me." He described these things as occurring in a nonwaking state, more like sleeping than waking, but more like hypnosis than sleep. He also recalled the word "leg," and that he had lifted his right leg up into the air and held it there, but he thought he woke up. He recalled that these events occurred before the "blanket" suggestion (which had been administered early in the second stage REM period). He commented that he had been surprised to see his leg up in the air and also was surprised to see E leaving the room. Although E had made no notes about a response to "leg," about 90 seconds after the last cue of the first stage REM period the technician had signaled to E that S seemed to be awakening. The E left the room immediately. The cue word at that time was "leg," and apparently S had responded, possibly while awakening, as E left the room. The S also recalled the cue word "arm," and remembered that he lifted his left arm and that this response had been suggested. In fact, this suggestion was administered only during the first night six months previously, and he had responded to it during the second night. It was not tested during this third night.

This S was able to recall most of what happened during the session. He had been given a presleep hypnotic suggestion that he would be able to remember everything that occurred during the night. Some of the memories were of complete suggestions given *only* in the previous sessions for which amnesia had not been successfully broken, either by direct interviewing or by subtler word association latencies and responses. Whatever the role of hypnosis in this session, it did not simply give S the "set" to recall only future happenings. Rather, hypnosis may have acted in a "timeless," dissociated, or contextless way to help retrieve events that *had* transpired as well as those which *were to* transpire.

HYPNOSIS AND SLEEP LEARNING

Since the carefully controlled EEG studies by Simon and Emmons (1956), learning during sleep has not been seriously considered. They reported that stimulus material presented during sleep was not recalled later when S awakened unless alpha activity occurred simultaneously with the stimulus material. As alpha during sleep indicates arousal, they felt that any learning occurred in a waking state. In sleep learning studies, lack of retention upon awakening has been considered as evidence that registration or acquisition did not occur during sleep. However, we have shown that retention (response to cue words) occurs during sleep, demonstrating that registration and acquisition have occurred during sleep. Not only can S respond to sleep-induced suggestions while remaining asleep, but he can also respond on subsequent nights without repetition of the suggestion and without any apparent waking memory of the suggestions or his response to them. The problem remaining unsolved is that of the retrieval of sleep-acquired material. In this sense, the problem of retrieval of sleep-acquired material is similar to the problem of the retrieval of dreams when *S* awakens in the morning.

In Soviet countries hypnopaedia or sleep learning is widely practiced. Not only do individuals apparently learn languages during sleep, but it has even been claimed that whole villages have been taught languages by radio at night. These studies have been adequately reviewed (Hoskovek, 1966; Rubin, 1968). Although some studies use EEG techniques, the written and translated reports are unclear as to what the EEG shows during stimulus presentation. Nevertheless, other evidence, such as a lack of any symptoms of sleep deprivation, points to the possibility that not all *S*s were really awake during stimulation. The concept of hypnopaedia implies hypnosis, and it is typically claimed that learning occurs only with "suggestible" *S*s. It is not clear whether "suggestible" implies hypnotizability or whether a strong waking "set" is induced to convince the person that sleep learning is possible. Simon and Emmons (1956) did not induce such a set. The case studies summarized above support the notion that hypnosis may be implicated in the waking recall of sleep behavior.

In an unpublished study an attempt was made to maximize the possibility of sleep learning. In order to obtain waking recall of sleep-acquired material it was felt that four conditions would have to be fulfilled: (1) Subjects were chosen who could respond during sleep to sleep-administered suggestion, using the procedures already discussed. (2) Some *S*s were included who were highly susceptible to hypnosis. (3) Any stimulus presented that was accompanied simultaneously by alpha was not included or scored. It was, therefore, not possible to replicate the findings by Simon and Emmons (1956); acquisition during arousal was ruled out by eliminating stimuli presented during alpha. (4) A strong waking set was established that sleep learning was possible. The sleep-induced responses were described, and *S*s were told about their own sleep-induced responses during the first sleep session. Soviet hypnopaedia claims were reviewed extensively, and *S* was motivated both by the competitive aim to duplicate Russian studies and by his special qualifications as a likely candidate for successful sleep learning.

Procedure

Nine *S*s were tested who could respond, while remaining asleep, to suggestions presented during sleep, without a presleep "set." The *S*s had had no subsequent waking recall of these suggestions. An appropriate presleep "set" was then established before the sleep learning session. The *S*s slept for about 6 hours. Several *S*s were included who did not receive this "set," although *E* was not blind.

Material in the form of "A is for Apple," "P is for Palace," etc., was presented during sleep stages REM, 2, and 4, defined by standard EEG criteria. Waking recall was tested by asking *S* to check any familiar word on a

list of 10 words beginning with "A," and again from 10 words beginning
with "P," etc. Eight stimulus words, each beginning with a different letter,
were presented twice to each S. Where possible, at least two different letter-word pairs were presented during each stage. After awakening, S received the eight appropriate 10-word lists, and two similar "dummy" lists
containing letter-word pairs not used during sleep. Thus, conservative prob-
abilities of checking one correct word by guessing was .10 for each of the
eight relevant lists. In addition, S was asked to rate on a five point scale
whether he was certain or uncertain that he had heard that word or letter.

Results

The number of words correctly recognized is presented in Table 3.7.
While recall was partial, it exceeded conservatively estimated chance recall
(in fact none of the "dummy" lists were ever checked). Of the letter-word
combinations administered during stage REM, 28 per cent of the administered words were correctly checked. In addition, S was able to select with
certainty the correct letter (without specifying a word) in an additional 17
per cent of all lists. Only those letters were counted that S was quite certain he
heard. In fact, Ss did not guess a letter unless they were convinced it had
been spoken. Although words were rarely recalled from stages 2 and 4, S
could often recognize letters from these stages. The incidence of guessing,
that is, incorrectly recalled words or letters, was virtually zero. No control S
(without presleep "set") recalled any words correctly.

A secondary result is important theoretically. Although none of the words
were presented simultaneously with alpha activity, whenever words presented during stage REM were subsequently recalled, transient alpha had
been evoked within 30 seconds after the presentation of the stimuli during
sleep. During sleep stimulation, evoked alpha for words successfully recalled
was significantly ($p < .01$) slower in frequency (9.64 Hz.) than waking
alpha (10.25 Hz.) and slower than alpha during sleep which was evoked by
nonrecalled stimuli. Alpha evoked by recalled stimuli was the same fre-

TABLE 3.7   Waking recognition of material learned during sleep with 9 sleep-
responsive Ss with presleep set to learn

Sleep Stage	Total Words Presented	Percentage Recall	
		correct word	addit. correct letters
1	29	28	17
2	20	10	40
4	13	0	39
All stages	62	16	29

NOTE: Words checked incorrectly: 0%; additional letters checked incorrectly: 10%.

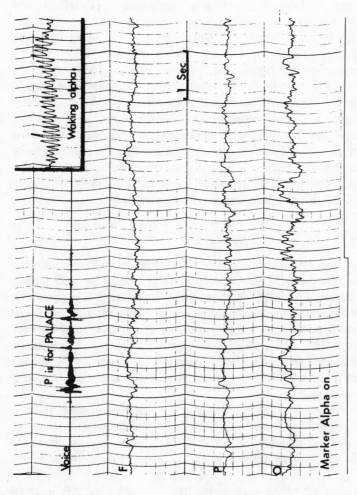

FIGURE 3.2. *EEG record showing presentation of a stimulus during stage REM sleep which was learned and subsequently recalled the next morning when S was awake.*

VOICE: Stimulus-activated voice-key marking administration of "P is for palace." "Palace" was successfully recognized next morning from a list of 10 words beginning with P. F, F, P, O: Frontal, parietal, and occipital monopolar EEG recording. Compare occipital EEG during stage REM sleep and during waking (inset). MARKER: Used by technician to signal possible onset of alpha. Note typical slowed onset of alpha. Alpha was later recalled when S was awake.

quency as spontaneous alpha during sleep (9.61 Hz.). An example of the EEG during the presentation of a word that was subsequently recalled is presented in Figure 3.2. The rate of alpha following to-be-recalled stimuli is difficult to explain. Perhaps alpha activity, even of a slower frequency (lower arousal?), may be required for consolidation: perhaps an altered EEG pattern in general is required for memory consolidation.

A third important finding of this study confirms some of the Russian claims. Of the nine Ss, seven had been administered HGSHS:A and SHSS:C, and had at least two clinical diagnostic ratings of hypnotizability. The correlations between the total (all stages) recall of words and HGSHS:A, SHSS:C, and diagnostic rating were .69, .42, and .52 respectively. The respective rank correlations with stage REM recall were .41, .49, and .49. While the results of the correlational analysis on a small sample are equivocal, they are consistent with some of the case study evidence cited above, as well as with the Soviet "hypnopaedia" results.

It would seem that under optimal conditions in the laboratory, sleep learning can occur with subsequent waking recall. While the relative effects of set and susceptibility to hypnosis were not separated in this study, hypnosis would seem to play a role in further explorations of the theoretically exciting but practically limited phenomenon of sleep learning.

Summary

What use, then, does the sleep researcher have for hypnosis? It seems clear that there is no interchangeability of sleep and hypnosis. The EEG during hypnosis and sleep are basically different. For this reason, it is perhaps not surprising that hypnosis cannot be used as an effective substitute for sleep. For example, the hypnotic dream is not a functional substitute for dream activity during stage REM sleep. Visual hallucinatory activity during hypnosis cannot be substituted for sleep and REM deprivation. Hypnotic techniques will be of limited value to the sleep researcher in studying the parametric characteristics of sleep.

For the researcher interested in examining the functions of sleep and the limits of cognition during sleep, hypnosis may be an adjunct as a technical aid. It may be possible to influence and affect such things as dream content, length of sleep, and ease of falling asleep, although more evidence is required.

Hypnosis is clearly relevant to exploring the sleeping individual's interaction with his environment. Hypnotic techniques may be used to explore and facilitate sleep-induced behavior, and the subsequent recall of sleep experiences, whether they involve learned material, suggestions, commands of motor and cognitive activity, or perhaps even the recall of dreams. Possibly because of common dissociative mechanisms, susceptibility to hypnosis may be useful for selecting *S*s in studies involving sleep-induced response and learning, and even for selecting *S*s who will sleep well, relatively undisturbed by distracting and arousing stimuli. While these may be the practical uses of hypnotic methods in sleep research, the provocative studies using hypnosis as a model for sleep-induced cognition, behavior, and functioning are most likely to be rewarding because of their exciting theoretical significance.

Eugene E. Levitt *is Professor of Clinical Psychology at Indiana University Medical School and Director of the Section of Psychology of the Department of Psychiatry at the Indiana University Medical Center since 1957. He received his Ph.D. from Columbia University in 1952, was research Assistant Professor at the Child Welfare Research Station of the University of Iowa (1952–1955), and Director of Research, Institute for Juvenile Research in Chicago (1955–1957). Of his five books, the most relevant to hypnosis research is* The hypnotic induction of anxiety: A psycho-endocrine investigation, *with Harold Persky and John Paul Brady. He holds diplomas in clinical psychology from the American Board of Professional Psychology, and in experimental hypnosis from the American Board of Examiners in Psychological Hypnosis.*

Rosalie Hennessy Chapman *is a consultant psychologist at Riley Child Guidance Clinic at Indiana University Medical Center, and Instructor in Clinical Psychology, Department of Psychiatry at Indiana University School of Medicine. She received her Ph.D. in 1970 from Case Western Reserve University and completed a year of postdoctoral study in child clinical psychology at Indiana University School of Medicine.*

Levitt and Chapman *consider the use of hypnosis as a method for the experimental investigation of phenomena other than hypnosis itself. The authors have three main objectives: to discuss the advantages and disadvantages of using hypnosis as a research tool, to compare specific methodological strategies, and to evaluate the overall effectiveness of this research tool. Hypnosis is used as a tool whenever the researcher clearly intends to use hypnosis to induce a replica of a naturally occurring phenomenon, such as an emotion or a dream, as a way of getting useful information about the naturally occurring phenomenon. The authors conclude that hypnosis is a satisfactory method for creating usable facsimiles of a number of naturally occurring conditions, but that other claimed advantages of hypnosis as a research tool remain debatable. The chapter is intended as an evaluation of methodological issues rather than as a comprehensive review of substantive findings.*

4

Hypnosis as a Research Method

EUGENE E. LEVITT AND
ROSALIE HENNESSY CHAPMAN

Introduction

Popular knowledge of hypnosis derives from its clinical applications, such as analgesia, hypnotherapy, and various forms of personal improvement. Most professional persons interested in the area are aware that there is also a considerable body of research into the nature of hypnosis and the hypnotic trance. The least known use of hypnosis is as a research tool, as a method for the experimental investigation of content areas other than hypnosis itself. The researcher seeks to exploit the trance state to induce in an experimental subject a replica of a naturally occurring state or phenomenon, such as an emotion or a dream, thus enabling study of that state or phenomenon.

This chapter deals with this relatively neglected use of hypnosis, but we do not propose to review substantive findings in the various content areas. A number of such reviews have already appeared (Barber, 1965b; Blum, 1967; Deckert & West, 1963; Gordon, 1967; Levitt & Brady, 1963; Reyher, 1967), and the contribution of still another is dubious. Rather, the purpose of this chapter is to discuss the advantages and disadvantages of hypnosis as a research method, to compare specific methodological strategies falling within the framework of hypnosis as a research method, and to evaluate the overall effectiveness of the technique.

Since no attempt will be made to review the literature, references will be illustrative rather than comprehensive. Even with this limitation, the selection of reports for inclusion in the chapter was no simple matter. It is often

The authors acknowledge with utmost gratitude the efforts of Kathryn N. DeWitt and Lynn Boudreaux in the preparation of this paper.

difficult to determine whether or not hypnosis has actually been used to investigate another content area. In a sense, the hypnotic state is always a research technique. Any investigation of hypnotic analgesia also has some bearing on the pain phenomenon. A study of hypnotically induced amnesia may be relevant to memory and attention. Hypnotically induced hallucinations may have something to do with the normal perceptual process. Any experimental study of the hypnotic trance may furnish data that are relevant to general methodological considerations such as demand characteristics and experimenter effects. Almost the entire literature of hypnosis could conceivably find its way into this chapter.

It appeared to us that an evaluation of hypnosis as a research method must be based on experiments in which the connection between the technique and substantive findings was unequivocal. There must be no question about the relevance of the findings to an independent content area. This can be done invariably only when the experimenter clearly intended to use hypnosis as an investigative method. Therefore, only investigations of this type are included in this chapter.

POTENTIAL ADVANTAGES OF HYPNOSIS AS A RESEARCH METHOD

Claims for administrative and technical advantages of hypnosis over other research techniques are based on allegedly unique properties of the trance state. Most of these properties have not been verified by experimentation, and remain debatable. Levitt, Persky, & Brady (1964) suggest five advantages:

1. Artificial states can be induced and terminated rapidly. In addition to being a convenience experimentally, this maximizes control over their duration.

2. Amnesia for the experience may be induced by a hypnotic suggestion to that effect. This manipulation can prove valuable for both experimental and administrative reasons.

3. By a careful formulation of the stimulus, relatively "pure" states can be induced.

4. The induced state may be prolonged, intensified, or diminished by appropriate suggestions in the course of the experiment as the experimental situation and design demand.

5. The experimental procedure can be repeated with the same subjects, making possible tests of the reproducibility of the phenomenon. In addition, the effects of new experimental variables may be studied in the same subjects by the use of an own-control experimental design.

Gidro-Frank and Bull (1950) propose additional advantages: simplicity of the experimental setting, narrowing of the subjects' focus of attention, and absence of self-consciousness in the subjects.

The subject's ability to focus his attention was suggested long ago by Leuba (1941) and recently by White et al. (1968) as a unique feature of hypnosis as a research method. Despite some positive experimental findings, this phenomenon is still not clearly verified.

A reduced diffidence in the hypnotized subject is often reported by practitioners. Increased accessibility of thoughts and feelings in hypnotherapy is thought to be a consequence of this phenomenon. Shameful, embarrassing, or guilt-ridden verbalizations are more fluently emitted by the patient who believes that he is being forced to expose himself. The phenomenon was first reported in hypnosis research by Nachmansohn (Rapaport, 1951) more than 40 years ago. He found that some of his subjects felt awkward when they were asked to dream in the waking state, but were more comfortable and hence more productive under hypnosis. The Nachmansohn effect can possibly be produced in an experimental sample by careful subject selection, or by exhorting instructions.

Another apparent advantage that has special relevance for the induction of states of negative affect is that the subject who has been stressed under hypnosis appears less likely to suffer any permanent effect, and rarely seems to experience postexperiment resentment toward the investigator. Debriefing the subject under hypnosis after the experiment presents no greater difficulty than inducing the artificial state. The subject is easily convinced that he is completely normal again, and that he will suffer no ill effects. He seems almost to *expect* to be deceived in some way by the hypnotist during the experiment; the severest manipulations do not prevent him from volunteering for future hypnosis studies. In contrast, a normal, volunteer subject who has been convinced in the waking state by the experimenters that he has a previously undiagnosed cardiac problem (Bogdonoff et al., 1959) may never be completely debriefed.

Flexibility is yet another potential advantage. The technology of the artificial induction of natural states is chronically underdeveloped. A majority of effort has focused on two emotions that seem simplest to evoke: anxiety and hostility. Other conditions rarely have been reproduced in the laboratory. Hypnosis is the only technique that has a broad, general potential for artificially creating a wide range of naturally occurring conditions in the experimental subject.

POSSIBLE DEFICIENCIES OF HYPNOSIS AS A RESEARCH TECHNIQUE

The experimental use of hypnosis also has a few serious shortcomings. The most important is an unknown, but probably fairly high, possibility of sampling bias. Most investigations necessarily employ volunteer subjects. Relevant data are scanty, but a study by Lubin, Brady, & Levitt, (1962) hints at the existence of at least a few personality differences between volunteers and nonvolunteers for hypnosis experiments. The best available current estimates are that among volunteers, fewer than half will demonstrate sufficient hypnotizability to qualify for most experiments (Hilgard, 1967). A common practice is to accept only volunteers attaining scores of 10 or higher on the Stanford Hypnotic Susceptibility Scale (SHSS), Forms A or B. Using this criterion, only about 15 per cent of the volunteers will qualify (Weitzenhoffer & Hilgard, 1959). It is difficult to counter the argument that the final distillate of the subject selection procedures is a sample that is unrepresentative of any large population.

The investigator may attempt to circumvent the problem of sampling bias by lowering the cutoff point. Using a score of 5 on the SHSS as the lower limit for qualification, for example, would permit inclusion of about 55 per cent of the volunteers. But this introduces a fresh problem. A number of response measurements have been demonstrated to be correlated with the hypnotic capacity of the subject as determined by a standard scale (see, for examples, Hepps & Brady, 1967; Hilgard, 1967; Tart, 1966a). Responses of subjects will be determined to varying degrees by factors other than the dependent variables of the study, that is, by those that influence hypnotizability. It is conceivable, though not inevitable, that such an effect could confound experimental results.

THE POWER OF HYPNOSIS AS A RESEARCH TECHNIQUE

A relevant issue is posed by Hilgard's (1969b) postulate that "if a legitimate psychological question can be answered better by using hypnosis than by some other approach, then hypnosis should be used (p. 132)." One needs then to inquire whether hypnosis is indeed the superior method. But perhaps Hilgard has oversimplified the issue. There can be more than one fruitful approach to the investigation of a particular content area. Perhaps it is only necessary to demonstrate that the hypnotic state offers a mechanism whereby valuable information can be obtained. In most instances the use of hypnosis as a research strategy may be dictated by its methodological advantages, but in some cases, it may be complementary to other experimental avenues.

The issue raised by Hilgard is what might be called the "power" of hypnosis, its capacity to induce usable facsimiles of naturally occurring conditions of the human organism. The significance of any experiment employing the hypnotic method would seem to depend heavily on the degree of similarity between the natural and hypnotically induced conditions. It is unlikely that the two states need to be identical, but it is obvious that some minimum degree of resemblance is required. Specifying this minimum in stimulus terms is extremely slippery. One of the perennial traps in hypnosis research is the credulous belief that the subject invariably is able to carry out the experimenter's suggestions with strict literality. It is certain, for instance, that the hypnotic suggestion, "to have a dream," does *not* guarantee the subsequent behavior of all subjects.

The problem of defining experimental stimuli pervades behavioral science research far beyond studies using the hypnotic method. Dependent variables provide the best basis for gauging the success of the experimental operations. If the aim is to stress the subject and he gives no stress responses, then the stimulus must be judged to be improperly defined. If the subject does give stress responses, then the stimulus has been successful in reproducing a natural event, for whatever reason. Thus, all experiments that seek to artificially induce naturally occurring conditions in the subject have a distinct, construct validity aspect.

In general, most laboratory methods for inducing naturally occurring conditions, especially states of arousal, are weak. Artificial methods of inducing anxiety, for example, usually fail to evoke reactions of the range and intensity found in naturally occurring situations (Levitt, 1967). We are unaware of any experiments in which the power of an hypnotic induction and a conventional laboratory technique have been compared. There are, however, a number of reports of a very particular comparison that is indigenous to the hypnosis experiment: the hypnotic subject versus the simulator control subject.

SIMULATOR VERSUS HYPNOTIC SUBJECT

Since the publication of Orne's (1959) classic study, investigators into the nature of hypnosis have been aware of the necessity for including a simulator control. Behavior that can be successfully simulated by an unhypnotized individual is evidently not of the essence of the trance state. The contrast of simulator and hypnotic subject has sometimes been misconstrued as a test of the genuineness of hypnotically induced behavior. Is the behavior *induced* by hypnotic suggestion in the classical sense that implies a force beyond the subject's control, or is it merely "requested," and the subject complies voluntarily as he might do if he were not hypnotized? The implication is that an adequate replica of the natural condition must be induced, and cannot be produced voluntarily.

This is a debatable assumption. Simulation is potentially a powerful method of bringing about temporary changes in the individual. It actually is another, though neglected, technique for artificially inducing natural states. Many individuals are capable of self-inducing, by voluntary fantasy, autonomic changes that clearly resemble the physiological concomitants of a naturally occurring emotion. This should not be surprising; emotions like anxiety and elation are often caused by anticipation or recollection, which are mental activities akin to fantasy, if not, indeed, indistinguishable from it.

Successful simulation hardly impeaches the genuineness of hypnotic behavior, any more than accurate imitations of drunkenness should be interpreted to mean that alcoholic intoxication is a myth. It does, however, question the value of hypnosis as a research strategy. Why bother to screen and train subjects if a simpler, equally effective technique is easily available? It is therefore relevant to an evaluation of hypnosis as a method to compare its effects with those of simulation.

Investigations in which hypnotized subjects and simulating controls have been compared have yielded conflicting and sometimes contradictory results. Some indicate that simulators are less convincing than, or behave differently from, hypnotic subjects (Brady & Levitt, 1964, 1966; Brady & Rosner, 1966; Dudley, Holmes, & Ripley, 1967; Evans, 1966a; Graham & Kunish, 1965; Gruenewald & Fromm, 1967; Hepps & Brady, 1967; Kehoe & Ironside, 1963; Vanderhoof & Clancy, 1962; Wiseman, 1962). Other studies suggest that simulators perform at least as credibly as hypnotized subjects, if not more so (Barber, 1965c; Barber, Chancey, & Winer, 1964; Barber & Hahn, 1964; Damaser, Shor, & Orne, 1963; Helfman, Shor, & Orne, 1960; May & Edmonston, 1966; Orzeck, 1962; Sheehan, 1969).

THE "OVERPLAY" PHENOMENON

Several comparative studies whose findings appear to suggest superior performances by simulators turn out to be, on closer analysis, peculiarly suggestive. Branca and Podolnick (1961) administered the MMPI to a group of hypnotized college students to whom an anxiety state had been directly suggested, and again in the waking state with instructions to fake anxiety. The mean MMPI subscale scores are shown in Table 4.1 along with the customary MMPI dissimulation index, F-K. Hypnotic anxiety produced modest, statistically significant increases in F, Pa, Sc, Si, and A, Welsh's

TABLE 4.1 A comparison of subjects in hypnotically induced anxiety and simulating anxiety on the MMPI

	Normal State	Hypnotic Anxiety	Simulated Anxiety
F	3	6+	25*
K	58	51+	43*
F − K	−14	−7	+17
Hs	52	50	71*
D	48	56	79*
Hy	56	55	71*
Pd	54	59	81*
Mf	42	46	50
Pa	49	60+	87*
Pt	54	61	85*
Sc	55	65+	99*
Ma	61	64	72
Si	50	55+	72*
A	44	55+	73*

NOTE: F is given in raw score units, K in T-scores. The corresponding raw score K's are approximated.
A is the Welsh Anxiety Index (Welsh, 1952).
+ Significantly different from normal state.
* Significantly different from hypnotic anxiety state and the normal state.
SOURCE: Data from the study by Branca and Podolnick (1961).

anxiety index (Welsh, 1952), and a small, significant decrease in K. The simulators, in marked contrast, produced diffuse elevation on all clinical scales except Ma. While neither profile resembles the classic 2-7 anxiety state, it is important to note that instructions to fake anxiety had a drastically different effect on MMPI scores than did hypnotically induced anxiety.

The most significant finding concerns the dissimulation index. The data in Table 4.1 bear a striking resemblance to certain F-K norms provided by Gough (1950). College students obtained a mean of -13.84, almost precisely like Branca and Podolnick's subjects in the normal state. A group of students faking psychopathology deliberately obtained an average index of $+17.19$, again practically identical with Branca and Podolnick's subjects in the faking state. The index in hypnotically induced anxiety is reasonably close to that provided by female university hospital psychiatric patients (-8.70). In terms of the dissimulation index, one could conclude that Branca and Podolnick's subjects were normal college students on one test-taking occasion, simulating psychopathology on another, and experiencing it in some form on a third.

The data in Table 4.2 are condensed from a report by Damaser, Shor, & Orne (1963). At first glance, they appear to indicate that the simulators have had more intense physiological responses than the hypnotized subjects. This is true for heart rate and forehead muscle reaction. The hypnotized subjects manifested somewhat greater change in electrical skin potential, the most difficult of the three behaviors to control voluntarily. The muscle data for the simulators suggest an overreaction analogous to the anxiety simulators of Branca and Podolnick. Striped musculature would be, of course, the easiest system to alter voluntarily.

TABLE 4.2   A comparison of hypnotized subjects and simulators on three physiological variables in induced states of anxiety and calmness

	Anxiety	Calmness
Heart Rate (beats per minute)		
Hypnotized	87	77
Simulating	106	86
Skin Potential (millivolts)		
Hypnotized	27.8	23.2
Simulating	22.3	19.9
Muscle Reaction (No. constant voltage spikes)		
Hypnotized	18	8
Simulating	73	11

SOURCE: Data from Damaser et al. (1963).

The heart rate data may also reflect an overreaction by the simulators, though this is not nearly so clear as in the case of the muscle reaction. As a side issue, heart rate findings of Damaser, Shor, and Orne are the opposite of those obtained by Hepps and Brady (1967).

In addition, Damaser, Shor, and Orne found that data furnished by a number of the simulators showed an interaction between the requested emotion and the state of the subject. The statistical interpretation is that some of the simulators produced higher scores in the waking state on some emotions, and higher scores in the simulated hypnotic state on others. No such interactions were produced by the hypnotized subjects whose reactions were evidently more consistent across emotions and states. No substantive interpretation is apparent, but the important fact is the existence of another difference between performances of hypnotized subjects and simulators.

Reyher (1969b) interprets the exaggerated data as evidence of the simulator's "unusual and high motivation." This cannot be a complete explanation of the overplay phenomenon. There is no sound reason why eagerness to comply with experimental instructions should impel the subject to do poorly. Theoretically, high motivation should improve, not impair, performance. An added ingredient in the explanation must be that the simulator is *unaware* of his poor performance, and actually believes that he is doing well. The simulator performs on a totally cognitive level. He plays the role as he thinks it ought to be played. There is no feedback to advise him to modify an overplayed role or to step up an underplayed one. The hypnotic subject, in contrast, is able to give a more realistic performance because he is emotionally affected, or deceived or induced, if you will, to a higher degree than is the simulator. He *feels* his role rather than develops it cognitively. The overplay phenomenon is an excellent argument in favor of the power of hypnotic suggestion.

Accuracy of the portrayal of an induced state in the trance is probably affected by many experimental factors. Several well-executed experiments (Brady & Rosner, 1966; Hilgard, 1967; Tart, 1966a) suggest that an important factor, if not the paramount one, is the subject's hypnotic capacity. Other possible influential variables are the nature of the experimental situation, the attitude and ability of the experimenter, and the relationship between experimenter and subjects.

Dudley, Holmes, & Ripley (1967) suggest that simulators will perform as well as hypnotic subjects under certain optimal conditions, but that these optimal conditions rarely occur in the laboratory. On the other hand, it is also likely there is a minimal level of experimental circumstances below which the performances of hypnotized subjects will not exceed those of simulators.

Artificial Induction of Natural States

The most frequent experimental use of hypnosis is in the artificial induction of naturally occurring conditions, primarily emotions and psychopathological symptoms. The desired state is suggested directly or indirectly to the subject. The stimulus suggestion itself may be totally concocted, or it may be "real" or "natural" in the sense that it describes an actual earlier experience of the subject, which he is directed to remember or "relive" in the trance.

Theoretically, all combinations are possible; either a contrived or a "natural" suggestion could be given directly or indirectly. In experimental practice, the bulk of the indirect approach experiments have made use of paramnesias. The stimulus in studies using direct suggestion is usually a simple description of the required state. The suggestion of an earlier experience is relatively rare, and does not warrant discussion under a separate heading. An ingenious union of early experience and indirect suggestion was pioneered by Blum (1961) and his students. Its uniqueness warrants a separate discussion along with the two major headings, direct suggestion and paramnesia.

DIRECT SUGGESTION

Suggesting the desired state directly is the most commonly used technique for inducing states, especially emotions. Direct suggestion stimuli vary greatly in length and complexity. Ikemi et al. (1959) used a simple word or term ("sadness," "resentment," "gastric disturbance"), presumably preceded by some sort of instructions that are not specified. Gidro-Frank and Bull (1950) also used single words, set in the following context:

> In a little while I shall count to five. Immediately afterward I shall say a word which denotes an emotion or state of mind. When you hear the word you will feel this emotion, experience the state of mind strongly. You will show this in your outward behavior in a natural manner. You may do anything you like, open your eyes or leave them closed, remain seated or get up, lie down on the couch or walk about—anything at all. . . (P. 92)

This technique or a variant of it has been used by Eichhorn and Tracktir (1955a, 1955b) and Kehoe and Ironside (1963) in studies of the effect of emotions on gastric functioning. Levine, Grassi, & Gerson (1943) employed a variant of this method in which depression was induced by repeating three times the words "sad," "blue," and "low in spirit."

Another approach is to suggest a series of symptoms of the required state:

> You will have a pronounced feeling of sadness, discouragement, and futility. This sadness will give you a feeling of constant unpleasant tenseness. You will want to be left alone. Each new experience will cause you mental pain, and it will seem to you like you have an inability to think. You won't have any pep. It will be difficult to make decisions. Your dejection and hopelessness will be so great that you will have ideas of personal worthlessness and self-accusation. (Sweetland, 1948, p. 93)

Direct suggestion of symptoms is confounding when a verbal inventory or interview is used as a measure of the dependent variables. The fact that

Sweetland's (1948) subjects obtained elevated scores on the MMPI Depression scale is an unconvincing demonstration; the experimenter, in suggesting depression, directly instructed the subjects how to respond to about a dozen D scale items.

Whitehorn et al. (1930) and Martin and Grosz (1964) used a few simple sentences as an inducing suggestion. The latter's stimulus is a condensation of the passage formulated by Levitt, den Breeijen, and Persky (1960). Damaser, Shor, and Orne (1963) introduced the subject to the experiment by describing each emotion briefly ("happiness—giddy joy, you feel wonderful"), urging the subject to "try to *feel* the emotions," and suggesting that emotions are also felt with the body. A single word such as happiness or anxiety directed the subject's behavior in the experiment proper. Another variation was used by Pattie (1954) who told his subjects that they would "feel very hostile, aggressive, and angry" toward the experimenter in the posthypnotic phase.

On purely lyrico-dramatic grounds, the most effective stimuli are passages used by Fisher and Marrow (1933-34):

> Just as soon as you are awake the most wonderful happiness will come over you that you have ever experienced. With each minute you will grow happier and happier. Everything will be sunshine and happiness. All of the most happy moments of your life will descend upon you. All your cares will be forgotten; you will know nothing but happiness, just pure unadulterated happiness. Even the saddest thing in your life will have a happy side for you. In a few moments I will awaken you; as soon as you are awake you will bubble like a mountain brook with sheer happiness. Happiness will well up within you; it will descend from all sides upon you; you will be the happiest person in the whole world; no one will be half as happy as you. As soon as you are awake you are going to experience the most undreamed of happiness. You are already beginning to grow happy. All of your worries and cares are already beginning to leave you. The wave of happiness is already descending upon you. (Pp. 202–3)

> Just as soon as you are awake the most terrible depression you have ever experienced will begin to descend upon you. This terrible depression will completely engulf you; sunshine will appear as shadows and shadows will become the most despairing hopelessness. All of the unhappiness of your past life will take possession of you. There will be absolutely nothing gay or happy in life for you; everything will have but one side, a dark side, and not even a glimmer of happiness will filter into your dark despondency. In a few minutes I will wake you up, and as soon as you are awake you will feel miserable and depressed. Depression and unhappiness will engulf you; darkness will pervade your soul and everything will seem utterly futile and empty. The wave of depression is already descending upon you. You are already growing despondent and everything is growing grey and devoid of joy. Unhappiness is creeping through you; you are already growing unhappy and despondent. (P. 203)

These suggestions are general and require no special knowledge of the subject. Occasionally, stimuli are derived from anamnestic examination of the subject (Erickson, 1944; True & Stephenson, 1951). The approach is apt to be discouraging because of the additional time involved in probing the subjects. The suggestion that Erickson (1944) used for his subject was a thousand-word narrative, so complex that the subject must be hard-pressed to digest and assimilate it, let alone to respond.

Comparative experimental studies of the effectiveness of different direct suggestions are lacking. On the basis of "clinical observation, logical analysis, and practical considerations," Levitt, den Breeijen, and Persky (1960) proposed that the formulation of a direct suggestion should follow these guidelines:

1. Content of the suggestion should not be based on the subject's personal experiences. An event in an individual's life may have been exceedingly anxiety producing, but it is also likely to have facets which evoke other emotional responses, or otherwise complicate the subject's reaction. Our early trial runs indicated that it is difficult to obtain a "pure" reaction when the suggestion is based on the subject's personal experience.

2. A number of synonyms should be employed in the suggestion. A single word like "fear" may evoke quite different psychophysiological reactions from different individuals depending on idiosyncratic interpretations. The use of a number of synonyms, or words with similar general meaning, maximizes the possibility that the meaning of the stimulus suggestion will have at least some common elements among the subjects.

3. The suggestion itself should not be lengthy. The hypnotized subject must understand clearly what is being suggested. His capacity to retain a suggestion will hence have some effect on his reaction. If a stimulus is, for example, several thousand words long, it is likely that the subject will not remember a considerable portion of it.

4. Key words and expressions should be repeated and paraphrased. This maximizes the probability of both comprehension and retention of the stimulus suggestion.

5. Nothing in the stimulus suggestion should lead the subject to believe that he is in an artificial situation. The transference which often exists between the subject and the hypnotist appears to incline the former to the attitude that the latter will protect him from harm while he is hypnotized. Such a belief may vitiate the effectiveness of a suggestion intended to produce a painful emotional state. The subject's belief in the protectiveness of the hypnotist seems likely to be enhanced if he is reminded in some way that he is actually in an artificial experimental situation which is obviously under the control of the hypnotist. Of course, this is not to suggest that the subject is not at least in some way aware of this consideration in any event. None the less, it appears prudent not to emphasize the point.

A sixth adjuration could be appended. The stimulus should specify the subject's reaction as minimally as possible.

The anxiety-inducing suggestion employed by Levitt and his coworkers (1960) is reproduced below in toto. It was used in experiments by Brady, Levitt, and Lubin, (1961), Ferster et al. (1961), Levitt et al. (1961, 1963), and Levitt and Persky (1960), among others. A similar version was used in studies of Persky et al. (1959), Grosz and Levitt (1959), Levitt and Grosz (1960), and Grosz (1961).

In a moment you will begin to experience a feeling of anxiety, of fear. (Pause, 5 seconds). You are now becoming afraid, very afraid. You are experiencing a strong feeling of apprehension and anxiety, as if you knew that some dreadful thing was going to happen to you. But you do not know what this awful thing is. You do not know what makes you so fearful every moment. You are becoming more and more anxious and afraid all the time, yet you have no idea what you are afraid of. You are certain that some dreadful thing is going to happen to you, perhaps something more horrible than you can possibly imagine. Your feeling of dread and fear increases with each passing second, and it will continue to increase, no matter what you try to do to stop it. You are so obsessed by this horrible fear that you cannot get it off your mind even for a moment. All that you can think of is that some dreadful thing is going to happen to you, and you are helpless to prevent it from happening. The dread is so unbearable that you cannot conceal it. No matter what you do, your feeling of fear, of anxiety, of dread, will continue to become stronger and more vivid every moment. In a very few minutes, you will find yourself on the verge of panic. (P. 209)

AN EARLY EXPERIENCE INDIRECTLY SUGGESTED

The following technique was developed by Blum (1961, 1967) and his students.[1] The procedure is essentially this: an occurrence in the subject's past that had evoked the desired state is determined, often by means of the Blacky Pictures (Blum, 1950), or by an interview. The subject is then made to "relive" this experience under hypnosis. Simple cues that can be used to evoke the desired state posthypnotically are then associated with the experience. In some studies (Benyamini, 1963; Hedegard, 1968) the subject is trained under hypnosis to respond to systematically varied cues with proportionate intensities of the desired state. For example, posthypnotic presentation of the numbers 0, 40, 70, and 100 evoke proportionate degrees of anxiety in the subject.

The specific contents of the subject's state-evoking experience are then dissociated by suggestion from the state itself, leaving the latter in a "free-floating" condition. Amnesia is induced for the experimental procedures to that point, and the subject is then considered to be "programmed" for the experiment proper. Theoretically, this approach could be used to produce any kind of condition. Blum's students have been guided largely by psy-

---

1. Recent research by Blum and his students is presented in Chapter 13 of this book.

choanalytic theory in which anxiety holds a central place. Hence, most of their experiments have sought to induce anxiety (Benyamini, 1963; Ehrlich, 1965; Hedegard, 1968; Lohr, 1967; Mendelsohn, 1960). A study by Gei-witz (1966), in which boredom was evoked, illustrates the flexibility of the technique.

PARAMNESIA

Paramnesia is used in the specific sense of a false memory, a recollection of occurrences that did not happen, rather than in the general sense of mne-monic abnormality. The usual purpose of the paramnesia is to produce a conflict within the subject so that he will react in some desired fashion. In practice, the independent variables of the investigation are measured post-hypnotically, but there is no reason why response measurements could not be made at any time after implanting the paramnesia. The technique was first used—apparently with considerable success—in the 1920s by the Rus-sian psychologist, A. R. Luria. He describes his method as follows:

> We suggested to the person under test, while in a sufficiently deep hypnotic state, a certain situation, more often a disagreeable one, in which he was playing a role irreconcilable with his habits and contrary to his usual behavior. We made those suggestions imperatively, and forced the person under hypnotism to feel the situation suggested with sufficient painfulness; we thus obtained an actual and rather sharply expressed acute affect. After awakening the person under test and following the awakening by amnesia (a suggested one or a natural one), we had a subject who was "loaded" with certain definite af-fective complexes, which mostly remained unknown to himself, but which were recorded by us in almost all important details. (1932, p. 130)

A more concise, less dramatic explanation is offered by Eisenbud (1939).

> The method consists essentially in inducing a deep state of hypnosis in a suitable subject, and then introducing an artificial "complex" by causing the subject to live through a trumped up emotional experience. . . . the subject finally is awakened from hypnosis with a command for complete posthypnotic amnesia. (P. 377)

Some of Luria's "trumped up" events were based on personal attributes of the subject, others on general, psychosocial considerations. The latter type, illustrated below, has been the model for later experimenters employ-ing the technique.

> You are in great need of money. You go to a friend in order to borrow from him; he is not at home. You decide to wait in his room and suddenly notice on his bureau a fat wallet with money. You open it and find many five ruble notes. You make a decision; you quickly take the wallet and conceal it on your person. You cautiously go outside and look around to see if you are

detected. You have stolen money and now you are afraid that there will be a search in your home and that they will discover you. (Luria, 1932, p. 140)

In the 25 years following the publication of Luria's book, the paramnesia technique was used occasionally in studies of repression (Eisenbud, 1939; Bobbitt, 1958), psychosis (Brickner & Kubie, 1936), conflict (Huston, Shakow, & Erickson, 1934), psychosomatic effects (Erickson, 1943), hostility (Eisenbud, 1937; Counts & Mensh, 1950); psychotherapy (Kesner, 1954; Gordon, 1957, 1967), and in a repetition of the celebrated Bruner-Goodman (1947) study of the effect of economic states on estimated sizes of coins (Ashley, Harper, & Runyon, 1951). In the Ashley study, a brief, "artificial life history," which led the subject to believe that he had been brought up either in poverty or in wealth, was implanted.

REYHER'S PARADIGM

The principal developer and exponent of the paramnestic technique in recent years has been Reyher. Unlike his predecessors, Reyher (1962) believes that it is the *only* valid hypnotic method of studying emotions and psychopathology and, presumably, other induced conditions.

According to Reyher (1967) there are five principles that should be used to formulate experiments employing hypnotic induction of emotion or psychopathology.

1. Indirect induction: Hypnotic suggestion should be used only to *induce* a process that, under certain specifiable conditions, is theoretically capable of *producing* pathogenic psychodynamics and psychopathology. This is the sine qua non of what Reyher calls his "paradigm."

2. The above process must be entirely devoid of specific cues that might suggest to the subject how the experimenter wishes him to behave in the experiment proper.

3. Some of the responses that are indirectly induced must "satisfy criteria for the identification of manifestations of psychopathology (p. 112)," especially physiological reactions because they seem to be involuntary.

4. An attempt must be made to assess the demand characteristics of the experiment by using a faking control group. Presumably, only subject behavior beyond that called forth by the demand characteristics is truly hypnotically induced.

5. The experimental subject should never be directed to carry out suggestions. He should be told, always in a "passive voice," that "he will be acted upon by something or that he is going to experience something (p. 112)."

Another indirect technique for inducing a state is to distort the subject's perception of his immediate environment. To induce anxiety, it may be suggested to him that he is teetering on the top of a tall building, or is about to face a poisonous snake, or a maniac armed with an ax. The suggestion of the loss of a loved one, or a severe blow of a more general sort, could be used to induce depression. Like the Luria technique, the induced misperception can be based on general, psychosocial considerations, or on a personal knowledge of the subject. Berman, Simonson, and Heron (1954) provide an example of the former type: "The subject was told that he was incarcerated in a hotel room during a fire that was destroying the building, and this situation was further elaborated" (p. 89). The perceptual distortion may also incorporate specific suggestions. For example, the suggestion that the subject was climbing an interminable hill in the teeth of a rising wind and falling snow, with the gradual development of constricting, penetrating, severe pain in the chest radiating to the left arm, was reported in the same study.

A COMPARISON OF STATE INDUCTION METHODS

The use of a paramnesia has a notable drawback when the experiment seeks to examine a single emotion or symptom in isolation. An implanted conflict does not lead invariably to the required emotion or symptom. Or, it may evoke an admixture of emotions. A notable exception has been found in the investigation of hostility. This exception illustrates the ubiquitous association that is necessary in order to use a paramnesia in the study of a single emotion. Most people, if they are led to believe that they have been wantonly mistreated, completely without cause, are likely to respond by becoming hostile. It is significant that most of the hypnosis research based on Reyher's paradigm has dealt with hostility in some form (Moore, 1964; Perkins, 1965; Pruesse, 1967; Sommerschield, 1965; Veenstra, 1969). The invention of conflicts that will consistently lead to other isolated conditions or emotional states in most individuals presents a formidable challenge to the hypnosis experimenter.

If the purpose of the investigation is to study conflict for its own sake, or to reproduce naturally occurring, gross psychopathology, such as a "miniature psychotic storm" (Brickner & Kubie, 1936) or a "miniature neurosis" (Gordon, 1967), then paramnesia is the method of choice.

Induced, posthypnotic amnesia is a fundament of any indirect method, and hence the effectiveness of the latter depends heavily on the validity of the former. It is either stated openly or is implicit that posthypnotic amnesia is an experimental analog of repression, the defense mechanism that is the cornerstone of psychoanalytic theory. Indeed, there is a marked, structural resemblance. Both have a relatively sudden onset in contrast to normal memory decay. In both, the loss of recall is actively induced, rather than simply a submerging under the weight of fresher, competing recollections. And the forgotten material is theoretically recoverable. The analogy is complete if the amnesia is applied to a stressful or unpleasant occurrence or thought.

Luria, the pioneer of the paramnestic technique, was a Pavlovian, not a Freudian. He was aware that the amnesia he induced, or which occurred spontaneously in his subjects, required an explanation, but he conceptualized in neurodynamic, not psychodynamic, terms. The amnesia was a parabiosis (temporary loss of neural conductivity), rather than a defense mechanism. It remained for those more familiar with psychoanalytic theory to propose the repression analogy. "When the subject finally is awakened from hypnosis with a command for complete posthypnotic amnesia, a factor tantamount to repression has been introduced" (Eisenbud, 1939, p. 377).

This is the theoretical position adopted by several other investigators into the nature of repression as well as by Eisenbud (Bobbitt, 1958; Gordon, 1957; Imm, 1965), and in a number of psychotherapy analog studies (Gordon, 1967). Experimental support for the analogy comes from Levitt et al. (1961), Hilgard and Hommel (1961), and Clemes (1964). Reyher (1967) takes a somewhat different view.

Reyher formulated paramnesias whose intent was to create intense, hostile feelings in the subject. He carefully separated the paramnesia from the associated affect, directing the posthypnotic amnesia at the former only: "After I awaken you, you will not be able to remember anything about this session. However, anything that comes into your mind that is associated with [a class of words related to the paramnesia] will stir up overwhelming feelings of hate. If these feelings break into consciousness, you will realize that it is the person who owns these papers that you hate, and you will experience an overwhelming urge to tear them up" (1967, p. 120).

Most of the subjects failed to carry out the posthypnotic suggestion directing them to act out their hostility destructively. Reyher's view is that these failures are the consequence of repression. The conflict-inducing suggestion arouses anxiety in the subject and is hence naturally repressed. Earlier, Reyher (1961b) had theorized that in the few subjects who did tear up the paper, the hostile impulse was so strong that guilt feelings were repressed so that acting out could occur.

While the analogy between repression and induced amnesia is striking, few theorists would posit an identity. Repression, as Cooper (see Chapter 7 of this book) rightfully points out, falls short as a *complete* explanation of hypnotic amnesia. The significance of the analogy for the experimental use of hypnosis is that it points to a consideration that is relevant to evaluation of the paramnestic method—the validity of hypnotically-induced amnesia itself.

The impact of an implanted paramnesia depends on the subject's lack of awareness of its existence, that is, on the dissociation of fabulated event and present state. Hypnotic amnesia must actually function tantamount to naturally occurring repression. If amnesia is a sham, what inference should be drawn from the subject's subsequent, disturbed behavior? He must know that he has not stolen any money. He must be aware that hostile feelings toward someone or other have merely been suggested to him and do not actually exist. Nothing more than the demand aspects of the experiment could be motivating him. Indirect techniques would be vulnerable to the same logical criticisms leveled at direct suggestion by Reyher (1962).

The validity of hypnotically induced amnesia is another debated issue among hypnosis researchers. The view that hypnotic amnesia is a real memory loss in some sense is represented by Hilgard (1965b, 1969b) and others. The opposing position is manned by Barber (1969b), who contends that the experimental evidence is either negative or based on equivocal tests, and that "the burden of proof is upon those who claim that suggestions of amnesia at times produce actual amnesia" (p. 216).

Cooper (see Chapter 7 of this book), after a comprehensive review, concludes that there is a flavor of genuineness to hypnotic amnesia that cannot be explained by recourse to demand characteristics, subject expectations, and similar aspects of the experimental situation. Surprisingly, no one refers to the paramnesia research as relevant evidence, not as a possible method for studying hypnotic amnesia. Most of the paramnesia research, especially Reyher's work, seems to support the validity of hypnotic amnesia, and the technique appears to be ideal for investigating the phenomenon.

No one denies that suggestions to forget, in the absence of an hypnotic induction, also produce considerable reported amnesia (see, for example, Cooper's review). This parallel is significant for the investigator who wishes to employ a paramnestic technique. Again, why bother with what may be an unnecessary step in the experimental procedure? The contention of Hilgard, Cooper, and others, that hypnotic amnesia offers something beyond requested forgetting, remains to be demonstrated.

The natural event technique and direct suggestion are both suitable for the investigation of an isolated emotion or symptom. The former would seem the more powerful of the two on the simplistic grounds that natural is usually superior to artificial. Unfortunately, there has never been an experimental comparison of the power of the two approaches, so the alleged superiority of the natural event technique remains hypothetical.

Use of the natural event technique also has certain disadvantages. There is an obvious connection between the event and the emotion that may be undesirable in the context of the experiment. If the investigator, for example, wishes to induce free-floating anxiety, additional experimental manipulations such as those used by Benyamini (1963) are necessary in order to dissociate the experimental emotional state from the natural past experience.

It is possible that a previous event that is recalled or "relived" in the hypnotic state will not lead to the emotion that it had evoked originally. In one of our studies (Levitt, 1963), natural occurrences that had been anxiety evoking brought about depression or hostility upon recall in hypnosis. Perhaps the subject actually experiences an admixture of emotions, recalls one of them as having been prominent at the time, but experiences another when he "relives" the original experience.

People do not always respond identically to similar happenings over time. An event that may have evoked anxiety some years ago may produce a different reaction currently because of developments in personality or changes in life situation. That the experimenter can circumvent this contingency by requiring the subject to "relive" the event has not yet been demonstrated clearly.

These disadvantages of Blum's technique are merely possibilities. In a given experiment, the technique may function effectively, depending upon the particular subjects, the skill of the experimenter, and the nature of the experiment. Technical shortcomings are unlikely to appear if the purpose of the experiment requires a replica of naturally occurring psychopathology rather than an isolated symptom. Again, there is no direct comparison of the effectiveness of Blum's method and paramnesia in evoking a "miniature neurosis."

Finally, it seems logical, if not demonstrated, that the natural technique presents a greater threat to the postexperimental well-being of the volunteer subject than does direct suggestion. At one time in our research, we felt it necessary to make the subjects amnesic for the directly suggested anxiety experience. Subsequent follow-up data, however, indicated that there were no untoward reactions or other undesirable sequelae even in the occasional subject who remembered the experiment (Levitt, Persky, & Brady, 1964). Without exception, those who remembered stated that they felt perfectly comfortable after the experiment because of the realization that the anxiety had been directly suggested by the hypnotist, and thus did not represent a threat to the current adjustment. The subject seldom confuses the artificial laboratory situation with a naturally occurring situation. This may not be invariably true when the anxiety stimulus represents an actual, earlier event in the subject's life. It seems unlikely, but possible, that the fantasied event may occasionally become confused with a natural occurrence, leading to postexperimental upset.

Reyher (1962) has severely criticized the direct suggestion method, primarily on the grounds that the stimulus is not distinctly separate from the response. The subject may merely be seeking to please the hypnotist by conforming to his evident wish, that is, to the demand characteristics of the experiment. The method does not furnish evidence that the subject has been affected by the hypnotic state itself. To deny this possibility would be highly imprudent; the urge to please the experimenter appears throughout behavioral science research. But to assume that the hypnotized individual experiences nothing more than a desire to please the hypnotist would be equally incautious.

It is possible to contend also that the paramnesic subject is experiencing neither amnesia nor a distorted recollection. The posthypnotic interviewer may not at all remind the subject of the teacher he hates. The subject may clearly remember the attempt to implant this artificial conflict in the trance state. However, he may wish to please the experimenter and may be perfectly capable of discerning that he is supposed to react hostilely in the post-hypnotic interviews. Sheehan's (1969) findings mildly suggest this possibility.

In laboratory research, defining an intervening condition of the subject by stimulus operations is unwise, especially when hypnosis is used. The safest approach is to lean heavily on response data. Reyher apparently agrees. He emphasizes physiological response measurement: "There is little doubt that the obtained psychopathology is genuine with many of the symptoms (such as skin disturbances, tics, tremors, sweating and changes in skin color) being objective and autonomically controlled and, therefore, outside the realm of simulation for most subjects" (1969a).

In this respect, direct suggestion has been at least as successful as the indirect techniques. Barber, a notoriously cautious appraiser, wrote in summing up a dozen experiments employing direct suggestion: "In summary, the experiments reviewed in this section indicate that suggestions designed to evoke emotional responses are at times effective in producing alterations in heart rate, skin conductance, respiration, gastric secretions, and other physiological variables" (1965b, p. 218).

The review of pre-Reyher research by Deckert and West (1963) is cited by Reyher in support of his attack on the direct suggestion method. These reviewers, according to Reyher (1967), "also have noted a general deficiency in experimental design and recognized the problem of assessing the significance and generality of the reported results" (p. 111). Deckert and West also list 11 studies as exceptions to their generally dismal appraisal of the field. Among these are such direct-suggestion experiments as Branca and Podolnick (1961), Eichhorn and Tracktir (1955a, 1955b), and Persky et al. (1959).

The intervening mechanism whereby direct suggestion evokes emotional reactions is not known, just as the essence of the hypnotic state itself is neither known nor understood. It may be that a majority of hypnotized subjects potentiate direct suggestion by deliberately fantasying a past event in order to carry out the experimental direction. An example would be the subjects who responded to a suggestion of change in heart rate by imagining anxiety-evoking experiences (Solovey & Milechnin, 1957). The mechanism has relevance for the investigator whose interest lies in the nature of hypnosis. It has scant importance for the experimenter who is employing hypnosis as a research method, whose requisite is to induce a state by whatever means.

In summary, it appears that there is no sound, consistent evidence that one method of hypnotically inducing a natural state is superior to others. The experimenter's choice should depend primarily on the intent of his investigation.

The Study of Dreams

The earliest research use of hypnosis was the investigation of the sleep dream.[2] In 1911, Schroetter attempted to verify Freud's system of symbols

2. The dream, like an emotion or symptom, is a naturally occurring phenomenon, and as such could have been discussed in the previous section. Its singular nature warrants separate treatment.

using hypnotically induced dreams (Rapaport, 1951). A dream study by Nachmansohn in 1925 (Rapaport, 1951) must be the first reported use of a waking control in an hypnosis investigation. The literature on the hypnotic study of dreams has been reviewed with varying degrees of comprehensiveness and criticality by Barber (1962), Tart (1964, 1965a), Moss (1967), and Stross and Shevrin (1969). A number of the early reports were collected by Rapaport (1951), and a judicious selection of 12 studies is reprinted in Moss's book (1967). There are about 50 reports in all, characterized by much variability in method and results.

The value of the data contained in these reports seems to depend on the veridicality of the parallelism of the hypnotic dream and the sleep dream. This is a highly controversial issue. It is no problem at all to obtain some sort of narrative from the hypnotized individual in response to the suggestion to have a dream. Nearly half of unexhorted subjects will give such verbalizations, but the response has one of the lowest item correlations with total scale scores on the Stanford Hypnotic Susceptibility Scale, Form C (Weitzenhoffer & Hilgard, 1962). This means that it occurs more often than other responses among those with low total scores. A verbal response by the subject following the suggestion to dream is a meager, insufficient bit of evidence linking hypnotic and sleep dreams.

SIMILARITY OF THE HYPNOTIC AND SLEEP DREAM: SOME EXPERT OPINIONS

The controversy over the natural dream–hypnotic dream parallel is epitomized by a recent survey. Of a group of diplomates of the American Board of Examiners in Psychological Hypnosis, Moss (1967) found that 56 per cent regarded hypnotically induced and sleep dreams similar in essential respects, while 22 per cent disagreed with this position, and another 22 per cent were uncertain or had no opinion.

According to Tart (1965a), 10, or 28 per cent, of the 36 articles that he reviewed assumed or concluded that the hypnotic dream and the sleep dream were equivalent. Four, or 11 per cent (including Tart, 1964), drew the contrary inference, and the remaining 61 per cent made no assumption or conclusion at all. All but two of the studies assuming equivalence were published prior to 1960, while three of the four contrary investigations were reported in the last decade.

The trichotomy reflects differences in views among practitioners and researchers. The equivalence hypothesis is accepted by many clinicians. For example: My acceptance of the dream under hypnosis as *equivalent* (not necessarily identical) to the dream during natural sleep represents an equivalence in *psychological, intellectual, and emotional,* not necessarily in physiological terms (Sacerdote, 1967, p. 39). "It is my impression that hypnotic dreams differ in certain ways from spontaneous nocturnal dreams in regard to function. . . . I do feel that with allowance for comparisons of spontaneous nocturnal and hypnotic dreams derived from the same subjects and patients, that the structure of such dreams is apparently essentially similar" (Schneck, 1963, p. 98).

Barber (1962) takes the opposing position that the hypnotic and natural dream differ in *every* essential respect. Most of the experimentally-inclined workers in hypnosis have adopted various intermediate postures that acknowledge an essential dissimilarity but maintain that an intriguing similarity remains.

Hypnotic dreams and spontaneous dreams are sufficiently similar in the employment of symbolism to allow crossgeneralization. (Moss, 1961, p. 109)

Although hypnotic dreams are not night dreams, the two dream categories overlap and they undoubtedly have much in common. (Hilgard, 1965b, p. 163)

There is a wide range of response to the hypnotic suggestion to "dream," the average production having a structure which seems intermediate between the daydream and the spontaneous night dream, in that primary processes are used more than is common in waking thought, but less than in the typical night dream. (Brenman, 1949, p. 465)

Thought processes in hypnosis seem to follow the primary process mode of organization. In this respect, cognitive processes in hypnosis may resemble dream thinking more closely than the predominant mode of thinking that governs the waking state. (Stross & Shevrin, 1967, p. 69)

Tart represents the substantial group who are as yet uncommitted to any position in the controversy, preferring to wait for definitive data. "The general picture is that of a very large number of basic questions to which we have only a few suggestions rather than answers, largely because of important methodological shortcomings of much of the research which has been done in this area" (Tart, 1965a, p. 97).

Tart suggests that most of the relevant research has failed to consider adequately the demand characteristics of the experimental situation, has ignored idiosyncratic interpretations of instructions by experimental subjects, has naively assumed that the subject's response invariably reflected the experimenters' instructions directly, and lacks support by physiological measurement.[3]

A summary of four major criticisms leveled by Tart (1965a) at the studies he reviewed, is given in Table 4.3. Ninety per cent of the studies lacked EEG monitoring, 73 per cent inadequately described the trance level attained by the subjects, and 67 per cent did not clearly designate the relation-

---

3. In defense of hypnosis dream researchers, let us point out that Tart's charges can properly be leveled at the bulk of published reports in every area of hypnosis research.

TABLE 4.3   Methodological defects of dreams research using hypnosis

	No EEG Monitoring	Inadequate Data on Hypnotic Level of Subjects	Experimenter-Subject Relationship Unclear	Conclusions Based on Experimenters' Opinions
Number of studies	27	22	20	19
Per cent of studies	90	73	67	63

SOURCE: Data from Tart (1965a). Tart's own studies and four theoretical papers are not included.

ship between experimenter and subjects. There was "an almost total dependence on the experimenters' opinions for the assessment of results" in 63 per cent of the studies. The average study had three defects; no study suffered from fewer than two of the four.

SIMILARITY OF HYPNOTIC AND SLEEP DREAMS: SOME FACTS

The two types of dreams can be compared in four ways: circumstances of the occurrence, content, accompanying physiological state or reactions, and personal feeling-belief of the subject.

As Hilgard (1965b) points out, the circumstances within which the two kinds of dreams occur are evidently different. The hypnotic state is not an unconsciousness state. The time of the onset of hypnotic dreaming, and often the topic, is specified by the hypnotist, and the subject ordinarily is aware that he must report his dream.

Physiological aspects of the two kinds of dreams also differ largely, primarily because the trance lacks the electrophysiology of actual sleep. There are, however, interesting investigations (Schiff, Bunney, & Fredman, 1961; Brady & Rosner, 1966) that suggest that the rapid eye movements (REM) that accompany natural dreaming (and do not accompany waking fantasy) may also accompany the hypnotic dream. Domhoff (1964) believes that there is as yet insufficient evidence for a definitive conclusion, but the bulk of research bearing on physiological similarity must be regarded as negative.

The experimental literature is strikingly devoid of any large-scale comparison of the content of spontaneous and hypnotic dreams. More than half of the hypnotist-psychologists surveyed by Moss (1967) apparently believe that the contents are similar. Most of the handful of serious researchers in the dream area, on the other hand, would probably agree with Barber's (1962) contention that hypnotic dreams are ordinarily considerably shorter than sleep dreams, and "appear to be prosaic products without symbolizations or distortions." D. B. Klein (1930) once reported that the duration of hypnotic dreams was from 5 to 83 seconds with a mean of 36 seconds. Sleep dreams are now known to last from 3 to 90 minutes (Kleitman, 1963).

The hypnotic dreams of Tart's (1964) subjects never exceeded 4 minutes, while their sleep dreams ranged from 6 to 32 minutes with an average length of 14 minutes. The complexities of mental experiences lasting a few minutes, and those lasting a half-hour or more, are unlikely to be equivalent.

The early experiments with hypnotic induction of dreams usually assumed that the obtained responses literally reflected the stimulus suggestion —the report of a good hypnotic subject who is instructed to have a dream must be a dream. If the subject is asked whether he has been dreaming, he will undoubtedly respond affirmatively. Since the investigators ordinarily believed, without reservation, that they were studying a true dream analog, the demand aspect of the inquiry is very evident.

The hard-nosed, skeptical attitude and the sophisticated inquiry in Hilgard's laboratory at Stanford surely convey a different demand. Whether that demand inclines the subject to respond objectively or critically is impossible to determine, but the Stanford data indicate that for a majority of subjects, hypnotic dreams and spontaneous dreams are dissimilar experiences. Hilgard (1965b) reports that 9 of 39 subjects, only 23 per cent, considered that their hypnotic dreams were like a sleep dream. The remainder reported thinking, daydreaming, or watching a movie as responses to the suggestion to dream. Tart (1966a) found that only 15 per cent of 114 subjects felt that they were actually "in" a dream. The others reported ideational experiences similar to those of Hilgard's subjects. Thus it seems that only a small minority of those subjects who respond positively to the suggestion to dream really believe that they are dreaming.

The weight of the experimental evidence at this time, with and without due allowance for methodological deficiencies in relevant experiments, supports the view that hypnotically induced dreams and spontaneous sleep dreams are largely dissimilar and cannot be regarded as equivalents. This does not mean that the former is an area unfit for investigation. In essence, the intermediate positions taken by Hilgard, Moss, and others hold that the hypnotic dream is something more than a routine verbal response, and that it can yield meaningful experimental or clinical data even if it is not isomorphic with the sleep dream. The motor of the hypnotic dream is unclear. It may be primary process thinking[4] or an extension of the fantasy capacity for some other reason. Perhaps most people, like Nachmansohn's subjects (Rapaport, 1951), feel foolish responding to the instruction to dream in the waking state, but regard this as a very appropriate demand in the trance state, and hence perform more efficaciously.

It might be useful to clear the air of unnecessary semantic conflict. The expression, "hypnotically induced dream" implies the undemonstrated isomorphism. An expression like "hypnotically induced fantasy-dream" is more congruent with the currently available facts: a verbal production that

4. Wiseman (1962) suggests that the hypnotic dream may, in fact, be characterized by an increased amount of primary process material.

seems to be more than a daydream, but is definitely not a sleep dream. Future experimentation may be more fruitful if investigators do not need to feel that they must demonstrate that the hypnotic dream and the sleep dream are, or are not, isomorphisms.

Test Validation

Formal psychological assessment devices have sometimes been introduced to define dependent variables in hypnosis experiments. These investigations could be considered as tests of the construct validity of the instruments that were used, even though the investigator's intent had nothing whatever to do with establishing validity. In keeping with the approach of this chapter, the discussion in this section is limited to research in which it was the deliberate purpose of the investigator to examine the validity of a formal assessment device. The handful of appropriate studies constitute only a small minority of all those in which both hypnosis and formal instruments have been utilized. They illustrate three possible approaches to the problem of validity.

THE TRANCE AS A STATE OF HYPERINGENUOUSNESS

This approach is based on the conception that the hypnotized person is unable to dissemble. It is thus possible to determine whether an instrument like a verbal inventory, for example, is susceptible to such distorting phenomena as social desirability set, malingering, deliberate faking, or other dissimulation. A study of the California Test of Personality by Mellenbruch (1962) illustrates the procedure. He found considerable differences in subtest scores between the waking and trance states, concluding that in the former, "the individual tends to make a favorable case for himself."[5]

AGE REGRESSION

Most formal diagnostic instruments should reflect differences among adults, adolescents, and children. In submitting an instrument to such a validity check, the use of hypnotic age regression circumvents the problem of sampling differences. The same subjects can be tested at each age level. The technique is obviously restricted to those procedures that are applicable, without alteration, to both children and adults. It is illustrated by a study of Rorschach responses given by a single subject regressed to eight earlier ages (Bergmann, Graham, & Leavitt, 1947).

CONTRAST OF RESPONSES IN NORMAL AND
HYPNOTICALLY INDUCED STATES

The most common use of hypnosis as an approach to test validity entails a comparison of responses in the waking state and/or neutral hypnosis with

---

5. Mellenbruch's conclusion that the findings of his limited study "seriously undermines one's confidence in the fundamental validity of the personality inventory" is unjustifiably extreme.

those given in an hypnotically induced condition, usually an emotional state. The valid test ought to reflect the state differences.

Among those instruments that have been subjected to this approach are the Rorschach (Counts & Mensh, 1950; Lane, 1948; Levitt & Grosz, 1960; Pattie, 1954); the Hand Test (Hodge & Wagner, 1964; Wagner & Hodge, 1968); Taylor's Manifest Anxiety Scale and Barron's Ego-strength Scale (Grosz & Levitt, 1959); the Thematic Apperception Test (Levitt, Persky, & Brady, 1964); Zuckerman's Affect Adjective Check List and the IPAT Anxiety Scale (Levitt & Persky, 1962); the MMPI (Branca & Podolnick, 1961); and the polygraph (Germann, 1961; Weinstein, Abrams, & Gibbons, 1970).

Most of these investigations yielded positive results. Notable exceptions were the examinations of the lie detector. These clever experiments appear to indicate, with considerable clarity and definiteness, the relative ease with which several ordinary conditions of the subject can deceive the polygraph expert.

WHY HYPNOSIS IS SELDOM USED IN TEST VALIDATION

The use of hypnosis as a method of testing the validity of formal assessment devices is relatively rare. The primary reason would seem to be the fact that samples in hypnosis research are usually small and highly select. Few investigations of any kind in behavioral science research employ true random samples, but it is in the test construction area that the most attention is paid to the nature of the sample. Sophisticated test constructors must view with acute disfavor a sample of 20 hypnotic subjects which is the end product of a group of 50 intrepid or curious volunteers.

Furthermore, the belief in the hyperingenuous subject is a public misconception that has probably never been credited by hypnosis researchers, and possibly not by most experienced practitioners. Orne's (1961) conclusion that the hypnotic subject can deceive if sufficiently motivated to do so probably represents a consensus.

The perennial controversy over the validity of hypnotic age regression renders it a poor basis for inferences about test validity. In addition, there are not many formal instruments that cover a broad age range.

Reyher's (1962) claim that the contrast of normal and hypnotically induced states has been neglected by test constructors "more from the lack of criteria for determining relevance than from prejudice" is an unnecessary, and probably invalid, explanation. Interestingly enough, Reyher, in support of his position, cites a statement by Ainsworth (1954) that "hypnotic studies are open to the question of whether the hypnotically induced state is comparable enough to the 'genuine' state to provide validation evidence." Reyher implies that Ainsworth excluded hypnotic research from her review even though, in fact, she proceeded immediately to discuss six relevant investigations in a tone that clearly suggested she was not really questioning the genuineness of the hypnotically induced state.

The Study of Physiological Processes

Hypnosis has been used as a method in certain investigations of various physiological systems, primarily the cardiovascular, gastrointestinal, and sensory, but including also renal, respiratory, and endocrine systems. The general procedure is to use the trance to create an artifical state in the subject so that appropriate physiological measurements can be made.

Selecting studies is again a problem in this section. The most recent overview of psychophysiological studies involving hypnosis (Levitt & Brady, 1963) has a bibliography of more than 200 titles. The large majority are investigations of the hypnotic state, either to determine the effects of hypnosis on a physical system—for example, studying the effect of external sensory stimuli on gastric motility—or using physiological parameters to assess effects of an hypnotically induced internal feeling state. Fewer than 20 per cent qualify according to the criterion for inclusion in this chapter.

Hypnotic studies of physiology can be roughly divided into three categories: investigations of physical changes as response parameters of induced states, especially emotions, studies of physical states as etiological agents in physical and emotional pathology, and studies of physiological mechanisms of normal body system changes.

When hypnosis is used to study physiological change as an emotional response parameter, it is subject to the considerations and criticisms set forth in the section on induced states, though perhaps to a lesser degree. Physiological measures are more suitable than verbal and psychological measures for laboratory research because they are more objective and less subject to voluntary control.

Direct suggestion of specific emotional states and comparison of the physical response with baseline measures is the method most commonly employed in hypnotic studies of physiological response to emotional stimuli. Examples are investigations of metabolic and endocrine responses to suggested emotions (Black & Friedman, 1968; Levitt, Persky, & Brady, 1964; Whitehorn et al., 1930); gastric motility and secretory responses (Eichhorn & Tracktir, 1955a, 1955b; Ikemi et al., 1959); cardiovascular changes (Bennett & Scott, 1949); and respiratory responses (Dudley et al., 1964). Less common are studies of physical stress reactions using hypnotic recall of a previous actual stressful experience (Kline & Linder, 1969; Vandenbergh, Sussman, & Titus, 1966), and the paramnestic method (Eisenbud, 1937) as induction techniques. Tourney (1956) suggests that paramnestic methods may be more fruitfully applied to psychosomatic research than they have been in the past, provided that more careful experimental controls are utilized.

A large group of studies concerned with physical response to induced states can be classified as psychosomatic research. The major issue in this area is the controversy over whether psychosomatic symptoms are the result of organ vulnerability (that is, genetically determined causes), or whether they can be interpreted as expressions of underlying psychodynamic phenomena and thus be precipitated by emotions or attitudes.

Attempts have been made to define psychodynamic etiology of certain physiological symptoms by investigators who measured physiological responses to hypnotically suggested "attitudes" that were hypothetically analogous to those present in clinically observed psychosomatic disorders. Examples of these include studies of Raynaud's disease (Gottlieb, Gleser, & Gottschalk, 1967; Stern et al., 1961), in which skin temperature alternations in response to induced "attitudes" were measured, and studies of autoerythrocyte sensitization (Agle, Ratnoff, & Wasman, 1967), in which the effect of suggested emotions on production of purpuric lesions was observed. Such research has offered evidence for the significance of the interaction of emotional variables with other etiological agents in psychosomatic disorders, and demonstrates that induced states can have at least some catalyzing effects on psychosomatic symptoms. The complex nature of this kind of research problem, however, is illustrated in Erickson's (1943) account of his observations of coincidental occurence of psychosomatic phenomena—for example, auditory difficulties—where in fact visual perceptual alterations had been hypnotically suggested. He points out that physical phenomena other than that which are suggested may accidentally occur and thus confound experimental results.

Studies of physical states as etiological agents in physical and emotional pathology are few, and are directly concerned with perhaps the primary consideration in this area of research, which is whether analogs of naturally occurring physiological states can be satisfactorily reproduced under hypnosis. A group of studies essentially examining this question is represented by Scantlebury and Patterson (1940), who compared effects of suggested food stimuli on gastric motility to actual responses to these stimuli, Scantlebury, Friek, and Patterson (1942), who reported a similar comparison involving natural and hypnotic dreams, and Dudley et al. (1966, 1967), who demonstrated that physical and psychological concomitants of head pain could be partially suggested in the waking state. Although identical analogs of physical states have not been produced, similarities have been found which suggest that, with better control of variables, it may be eventually possible to produce hypnotic analogs.

Methods in studies of mechanisms and theories about normal body system changes include direct suggestion of a specific physical response, or suggestion to recall a previous physical response. Representative of this area of investigation are studies by Chase (1963) and Johner and Perlman (1968) in which nystagmus was decreased by direct suggestion under hypnosis, enabling the authors to more carefully distinguish the nature of nystagmoid movements. These led to hypotheses regarding the physiological mechanisms responsible for nystagmus and the relationship of observable behavior to brain functions.

An Overview

Hypnosis has been used as a research technique in the study of content areas other than the hypnotic trance itself: emotions, psychopathology, defense mechanisms, dreams, physiological processes, and test validation, for example. Most of the proposed research advantages of hypnosis, such as the induction of "pure" states, and enhanced control of the experimental treatment, have not yet been subjected to systematic experimental test. But there seems little doubt that the hypnotic trance is a satisfactory mechanism for creating reasonable facsimiles of at least some naturally occurring conditions.

The power of hypnosis as a method of inducing states also remains to be assessed systematically. Comparisons with other artificial techniques are lacking. The available evidence, largely in the form of contrasts of hypnotically induced behavior with simulator behavior, suggests that hypnosis is at least as powerful as other laboratory techniques.

The most frequent use of hypnosis in research is in the artificial induction of emotional and psychopathological states. Three approaches have been employed: direct suggestion, a previous experience indirectly suggested, and paramnesia followed by induced amnesia.

Direct suggestion has been used most often; the length and complexity of stimulus suggestions has varied greatly. Comparisons of the relative power of the three techniques have not yet been carried out. Logical analysis suggests that each has its potential advantages and disadvantages, and that the choice of a technique for inducing a state depends largely on the experimenter's specific aim.

The use of hypnosis to study dream behavior is highly controversial. A survey of findings to date indicates that the hypnotically induced and the natural sleep differ on four significant dimensions: circumstances, content, physiology, and subjective feeling. However, it is still likely that the hypnotic dream is something more than a rote verbal production, and that investigations of it may be fruitful. It is suggested that the controversial term, "hypnotically induced dream" should be replaced by "hypnotically induced fantasy-dream."

Hypnosis has potential uses in test construction and validation, but the difficulty in assembling large samples of susceptible subjects, and the high probability of sampling bias, militate against its use in this area. These drawbacks are less likely to affect findings in research on physiological processes, especially investigations of the possible role of psychological factors in physical symptoms. Yanovski (1962), for example, believes that in using hypnosis to study cardiac dysfunction, even single subjects may furnish meaningful data.

Leuba (1941) once suggested that the hypnotic trance offers impressive advantages to experimenters in all content areas. One wonders why possibilities of its use are not being explored more extensively. Experiments employing hypnosis as a method of study constitute no more than an infinitesimal fraction of the total research effort in the behavioral sciences. There are several possible reasons for this neglect. One is that hypnosis has not yet proven itself powerful enough as a method of creating state facsimiles to overbalance the time and effort it involves. A second possible reason is the unusually high probability of sampling bias. The most important reason may be its shaky status in the community of scientists, its still uncertain respectability. Until the mystical aura of the centuries has finally been dispelled, hypnosis will not be afforded a full, fair opportunity to demonstrate its value as a research method.

Theodore Xenophon Barber *is Director of Psychological Research at the Medfield Foundation and Medfield State Hospital, Harding, Massachusetts. He received his Ph.D. in social psychology from the American University in 1956. His doctoral dissertation pertained to the relationship between light sleep and hypnosis. After his degree he became a National Institute of Mental Health Post-Doctoral Research Fellow at the Laboratory of Social Relations at Harvard University. This fellowship was sponsored by Professors William Caudill and Clyde Kluckhohn and pertained to "Cross-Cultural Aspects of Trance Behavior." In 1969 he accepted a research position at the Medfield Foundation and Medfield State Hospital where he was free to carry out full-time research in the area of hypnosis. He is author of* Hypnosis: A Scientific Approach *and* LSD, Marihuana, Yoga, and Hypnosis.

Barber *critically analyzes the basic underlying assumptions of the traditional hypnotic state paradigm. In its stead, he offers an alternative paradigm for conceptualizing the phenomena. The traditional paradigm postulates that responsiveness to test suggestions is increased to the extent that the subject enters into or is placed in a special state ("hypnotic trance") that is fundamentally different from and qualitatively discontinuous from the waking state of consciousness. Barber's alternative paradigm views high responsiveness to suggestions for limb rigidity, anesthesia, hallucination, age regression, amnesia, and so on as due to the following: the subject has positive attitudes, motivations, and expectancies toward the test situation and, consequently, allows himself to think with and vividly imagine those things that are suggested, while letting go of extraneous or contrary thoughts.*

5

Suggested ("Hypnotic") Behavior: The Trance Paradigm Versus an Alternative Paradigm

THEODORE XENOPHON BARBER

It has been traditionally assumed that certain types of procedures, labeled as "trance inductions," give rise to a special state of consciousness (hypnotic trance) in some individuals. It has also been assumed that as the hypnotic trance becomes deeper or more profound, the subject becomes more responsive to suggestions for age regression, analgesia, hallucinations, deafness, amnesia, and so on. In this chapter, I will critically analyze these and other assumptions that underlie the traditional (trance) paradigm and I will present an alternative paradigm for conceptualizing the experiences and behaviors that have been historically subsumed under the term "hypnotism" or "hypnosis."

Paradigms in Science

In a cogent analysis of the history of science, Kuhn (1962) has shown that scientists working in an area of inquiry usually share common basic assumptions pertaining to the nature of the phenomena they are investigating. The shared assumptions, which are often more implicit than explicit, together with a related set of criteria for asking meaningful questions and for selecting research topics, are termed a "paradigm."

Work on this chapter (Medfield Foundation Report #103) was supported by research grants (MH-11521 and MH-19152) from the National Institute of Mental Health, U.S. Public Health Service.

Each paradigm may give rise to more than one theory that aims to explain the phenomena. Although theories deriving from any one paradigm differ in various aspects, they share the same basic assumptions, the same methodological criteria, and the same framework for asking meaningful questions. As Braginsky, Braginsky, and Ring (1969) have pointed out, "In academic psychology, for example, competing behavioristic theories of learning were for a long time able to flourish despite widespread agreement concerning how the phenomenon [of learning] should be approached—a consensus that was particularly likely to be evident when such theories were challenged by the radically different assumptions of cognitively oriented theories (p. 30)."

In the history of science, there are many important instances when the consensually-shared paradigm could not easily explain new research data. In these instances, a few scientists began to question the basic assumptions underlying the traditional paradigm, a new way of viewing the phenomena (an alternative paradigm) was slowly developed, and after a period of debate, misunderstandings, and acrimony, the alternative paradigm was accepted by new generations of investigators and slowly became dominant. In astronomy, for example, the geocentric view of the planetary system was replaced by the heliocentric view; in chemistry, the phlogiston conception of combustion was replaced by the oxygen conception; in physics, theories pertaining to the ether were replaced by conceptions that did not postulate an ether; and, in psychology, introspective analysis gave way to behaviorism.

As Chaves (1968) has pointed out, it appears that a paradigm shift may be occurring at the present time in the area of inquiry historically subsumed under the term "hypnosis." In the next section, I will briefly describe the underlying assumptions of the traditional (trance) paradigm that has dominated this area of inquiry for more than a hundred years. Following this, I will formulate some of the postulates of an alternative paradigm.

The Special State (Trance) Paradigm

During the past century, terms such as "hypnotic trance state" (or "trance," "hypnosis," "hypnotic state," and "hypnotized") have been widely used by both scientists and laymen and have become part of the everyday vocabulary of children and adults. Although the implications of these terms have been slowly changing over the years, they seem to refer to some kind of fundamental change in the state of the organism.

During the nineteenth century, terms such as "hypnotic trance" or "hypnosis" typically implied that the subject resembled the sleepwalker or somnambule, that is, resembled the person who arises from his bed at night, walks around while "half asleep," and responds in a dissociated, rather automatic way to a narrow range of stimuli. Some present-day investigators also think of the "hypnotic trance" subject as resembling a sleepwalker. As Hilgard (1969a) has pointed out, "Hypnosis is commonly considered to be a 'state' perhaps resembling the state in which the sleepwalker finds himself, hence the term 'somnambulist' as applied to the deeply hypnotized person (p. 71)." Other present-day investigators who utilize the terms "hypnotic trance" or "hypnosis" do not seem to mean that the subject resembles the sleepwalker. Although, as Bowers (1966) has noted, "Most [present-day] investigators interested in hypnosis believe that there is an hypnotic state which fundamentally differs from the waking state" (p. 42), they differ among themselves as to the exact meaning to be assigned to the terms.

Bowers (1966) views hypnosis as "an altered state within which suggestions have a peculiarly potent effect" (p. 50). However, Gill and Brenman (1959) use the term "hypnotic state" to refer to an "induced psychological regression, issuing, in the setting of a particular regressed relationship between two people, in a relatively stable state which includes a subsystem of the ego with various degrees of control of the ego apparatuses" (p. xxiii). Other investigators attach different connotations to the term. For instance, among the essential characteristics of the hypnotic state, Orne (1959) includes a tolerance for logical inconsistencies ("trance logic") and alterations in subjective experiences induced by suggestions. Evans (1968) views hypnosis as an altered subjective state of awareness in which dissociative mechanisms are operating, Meares (1963) sees the basic element in hypnosis as an atavistic regression to a primitive mode of mental functioning, and Shor (1962) views the hypnotic state as having three dimensions—hypnotic role-taking, trance, and archaic involvement.

Although the above and other theoretical formulations attribute somewhat different properties to the hypnotic state, they derive from a common set of basic assumptions (an underlying paradigm). Some of the underlying assumptions of the hypnosis or trance paradigm appear to include the following:

1. There exists a state of consciousness, a state of awareness, or a state of the organism that is fundamentally (qualitatively) different from other states of consciousness such as the waking state, the deep sleep state, and the state of unconsciousness. This distinct state is labeled "hypnosis," "hypnotic state," "hypnotic trance," or simply "trance."

2. The state of hypnotic trance may occasionally occur spontaneously, but it is usually induced by special types of procedures that are labeled "hypnotic inductions" or "trance inductions." Although trance induction procedures vary in content—for example, they usually include, but they need not include, fixation of the eyes, suggestions of relaxation, and suggestions of drowsiness and sleep—they all appear to have two essential features

in common: they suggest to the subject that he is entering a special state (hypnotic trance) and investigators who adhere to the traditional paradigm agree that the procedures are capable of producing hypnotic trance.

3. The hypnotic trance state is not a momentary condition that the subject enters for only a few seconds. On the contrary, when a person has been placed in a hypnotic trance, he remains in it for a period of time and he is typically brought out of it by a command from the hypnotist, such as "Wake up!"

4. Subjects who are in a hypnotic state are responsive, both overtly and subjectively, to test suggestions for rigidity of the muscles or limbs, age regression, analgesia and anesthesia, visual and auditory hallucination, deafness, blindness, color blindness, negative hallucination, dreaming on a specified topic, heightened performance (on physical or cognitive tasks), amnesia, and posthypnotic behavior.[1]

5. As Sutcliffe (1960) pointed out, some investigators who adhere to the trance paradigm believe the suggested phenomena are "genuine" or "real," whereas others are far more skeptical. For example, some investigators who accept the trance paradigm view hypnotic deafness as indistinguishable from actual deafness, and the hypnotic dream as indistinguishable from the nocturnal dream. However, other investigators who accept the trance paradigm view the hypnotic deaf subject as a person who is able to hear but thinks that he cannot, and they perceive the hypnotic dream as differing in essential respects from the night dream. Although investigators who adhere to the trance paradigm disagree on the "reality" of the suggested phenomena, the important point to emphasize is that they all view the phenomena as associated with hypnotic trance, and they consequently label the phenomena as "hypnotic phenomena," not simply as "suggested phenomena."

6. There are levels or depths of hypnotic trance; that is, hypnotic trance can vary from light, to medium, to deep, to very deep (somnambulism).

7. As the depth of hypnotic trance increases, the subject's ability to experience suggested phenomena vividly and intensely also increases. For example, as the subject becomes more deeply hypnotized, he is more able to have a vivid and intense experience of age regression, analgesia, hallucination, or amnesia.

In brief, the dominant (trance) paradigm sees the person who responds to test suggestions as being in a fundamentally different state from the person who is unresponsive to test suggestions. The construct "hypnotic state," "trance," or "hypnosis" is used to refer to this state, which is conceived to differ, not simply quantitatively, but in some basic, qualitative way, from normal waking states and from states of sleep.

1. Henceforth, in this chapter, the term "response" or "responsiveness to test suggestions" will be used as a shorthand term to refer to both overt and subjective responses to each of the types of suggestions mentioned in this paragraph.

An Alternative Paradigm:
The Member of the Audience Analogy

There is another way of viewing responsiveness to test suggestions[2] that does not involve special state constructs such as "hypnosis," "hypnotized," "hypnotic state," or "trance." This alternative paradigm does not see a qualitative difference in the "state" of the person who is and the one who is not responsive to test suggestions. Although the alternative paradigm has many historical roots (discussed by Sarbin, 1962), it derives primarily from my more recent theoretical endeavors and those of Sarbin (Barber, 1964a, 1967, 1969b, 1970a; Sarbin, 1950; Sarbin & Andersen, 1967; Sarbin & Coe, in press). An analogy to members of an audience watching a motion picture or a stage play may clarify the paradigm.

One member of an audience may be attending a performance with the purpose of having new experiences. His attitude is that it is interesting and worthwhile to feel sad, to feel happy, to empathize, and to have the other thoughts, feelings, and emotions the actors are attempting to communicate. He both desires and expects the actors to arouse in him new or interesting thoughts and emotions. Although he is aware that he is watching a contrived performance and that he is in an audience, he does not actively think about these matters. Since this member of the audience has "positive" attitudes, motivations, and expectancies toward the communications emanating from the stage, he lets himself imagine and think with the statements and actions of the actors; he laughs, weeps, empathizes and, more generally, thinks, feels, emotes, and experiences in line with the intentions of the actors.

Another member of the audience had an anxious and tiring day at the office, wanted to go to bed early in the evening, and came to the performance unwillingly, in order to avoid an argument with his wife. He is not interested in having the emotions and experiences the actors are attempting to communicate. He does not especially desire and does not expect to feel empathic, happy, sad, excited, or shocked. He is continually aware that he is in an audience and that he is observing a deliberately contrived performance. Given this set of attitudes, motivations, and expectancies, this member of the audience does not let himself imagine and think with the statements and actions of the actors; he does not laugh, weep, empathize or, more generally, think, feel, emote, and experience in line with the communications from the actors.

The implications of this analogy are:

1. The experimental subject who is highly responsive to test suggestions

---

2. As stated in footnote 1, in the remainder of this chapter the term "responsiveness" or "response to test suggestions" will refer to both overt and subjective responses to suggestions for limb rigidity, age regression, analgesia, hallucination, amnesia, postexperimental ("posthypnotic") behavior, and so on.

resembles the member of the audience who experiences the thoughts, feelings, and emotions that the actors are attempting to arouse. The very suggestible subject views his responding to test suggestions as interesting and worthwhile; he desires and expects to experience those things that are suggested. Given these underlying "positive" attitudes, motivations, and expectancies, he lets himself imagine and think with the things suggested and he experiences the suggested effects.

2. The experimental subject who is very unresponsive to test suggestions resembles the member of the audience who does *not* experience the thoughts, feelings, and emotions that the actors are attempting to arouse. The very nonsuggestible subject views his responding to test suggestions as not desirable; he neither wants nor expects to experience those things that are suggested. Given these underlying "negative" attitudes, motivations, and expectancies, he does not let himself imagine and think with the things suggested and he does not experience the suggested effects.

3. It is misleading and unparsimonious to label the member of an audience, who is thinking, feeling, and emoting in line with the communications of the actors, as being in a special state (hypnotic trance) that is fundamentally different from the waking state. In other words, it is misleading and unparsimonious to restrict our conceptions of normal conditions or waking conditions to such an extent that they exclude the member of the audience who is having various experiences as he listens to the communications from the stage. Furthermore, since the member of the audience, who is responding to the words of the actors, and the experimental subject, who is responding to the words (test suggestions) of the experimenter, do not differ in any important way in their attitudes, motivations, and expectancies toward the communications or in the way they think along with the communications, it is also misleading and unparsimonious to label the subject who is responding to test suggestions as being in a special state (hypnotic trance).

4. Although the member of the audience who is responding to the words of the actors and the experimental subject who is responding to the test suggestions of the experimenter have similar attitudes, motivations, and expectancies toward the communications and are similarly "thinking with" the communications, *they are being exposed to different types of communications.* The messages or communications from the actors are intended to elicit certain types of thoughts, feelings, and emotions—to empathize, to feel happy or sad, to laugh or to weep, to feel excited or shocked —whereas the messages or communications (test suggestions) from the experimenter are intended to elicit somewhat different types of thoughts, feelings, or emotions—to experience an arm as heavy, to experience oneself as a child, to forget preceding events, and so forth. From this viewpoint, the member of the audience and the subject who is responding to test suggestions are having different experiences, *not because they are in different "states" but because they are receiving different communications.*

The above analogy exemplifies some of the basic assumptions underlying the alternative paradigm. These assumptions include the following:

1. It is unnecessary to postulate a fundamental difference in the "state" of the person who is and the one who is not responsive to test suggestions.

2. Both the person who is and the one who is not responsive to test suggestions have attitudes, motivations, and expectancies toward the communications they are receiving.

3. The person who is very responsive to test suggestions has "positive" attitudes, motivations, and expectancies toward the communications he is receiving. That is, he views his responding to test suggestions as interesting or worthwhile and he wants to, tries to, and expects to experience the suggested effects. Given these "positive" attitudes, motivations, and expectancies, he lets himself think with and imagine those things that are suggested.

4. The person who is very unresponsive to test suggestions has "negative" attitudes, motivations, and expectancies toward the communications he is receiving. That is, he views his responding to test suggestions as not interesting or worthwhile and he neither tries to nor expects to experience the suggested effects. Given these "negative" attitudes, motivations, and expectancies, he does not let himself imagine or think with the suggestions; instead, he verbalizes to himself such statements as "This is silly" or "The suggestion won't work."

5. The three factors—attitudes, motivations, and expectancies—vary on a continuum (from negative, to neutral, to positive) and they converge and interact in complex ways to determine to what extent a subject will let himself think with and imagine those things that are suggested. The extent to which the subject thinks with and vividly imagines the suggested effects, in turn, determines his overt and subjective responses to test suggestions.

6. Concepts derived from abnormal psychology—such as "trance," "somnambulism," and "dissociation"—are misleading and do not explain the overt and subjective responses. Responsiveness to test suggestions is a normal psychological phenomenon that can be conceptualized in terms of constructs that are an integral part of normal psychology, especially of social psychology. Social psychology conceptualizes other social influence processes, such as persuasion and conformity, in terms of such mediating variables as attitudes, motivations, expectancies, and cognitive processes. In the same way, the mediating variables that are relevant to explaining responsiveness to test suggestions include attitudes, motivations, expectancies, and cognitive-imaginative processes.

7. The phenomena associated with test suggestions are considered to be within the range of normal human capabilities. However, whether or not the suggested phenomena are similar to or different from phenomena occurring in real-life situations that bear the same name, is viewed as an open question that needs to be answered empirically. For example, such questions as the following are open to empirical investigation: To what extent is suggested

analgesia similar to the analgesia produced by nerve section or by anesthetic drugs? What are the similarities and differences between suggested and naturally-occurring (nonsuggested) blindness, color blindness, deafness, hallucination, dreaming, and amnesia? The empirical evidence at present indicates that, although there are some similarities between the suggested and nonsuggested phenomena, they also differ in very important respects. For example, suggested color blindness has only superficial resemblances to actual color blindness, and suggested amnesia is much more labile or transient than actual amnesia. (Since these issues have been discussed in detail elsewhere—Barber, 1959b, 1961b, 1962a, 1962b, 1963, 1964b, 1964c, 1965b, 1969b, 1970a—they will be discussed only peripherally here.)

Which paradigm is more successful in explaining responsiveness to test suggestions for limb rigidity, age-regression, analgesia, hallucination, amnesia, etc.—the traditional one that postulates a special state that is fundamentally different from the waking state, or the alternative one that focuses on attitudes, motivations, expectancies, and thinking with and imagining those things that are suggested? I will next summarize experimental data, pertaining to responsiveness to test suggestions under control ("waking") conditions, which indicate that the alternative paradigm provides a more successful and more parsimonious explanation.

Response to Test Suggestions Without "Hypnosis"

A substantial number of subjects are highly responsive to test suggestions when no attempt is made to place them in a "hypnotic trance state." Let us look at a few examples.

HUMAN-PLANK FEAT

The stage hypnotist suggests to a selected subject that his body is becoming stiff and rigid. When the subject appears rigid, the stage hypnotist and an assistant place him between two chairs, one chair beneath the subject's head and the other beneath his ankles. The subject typically remains suspended between the two chairs for several minutes, as if he were a human plank. The traditional paradigm assumes that the subject is able to perform the human-plank feat because he is in a state—a hypnotic trance state—that is qualitatively different from ordinary states of consciousness. This notion is not supported by the empirical data.

Collins (1961) demonstrated conclusively that, when male and female control subjects are told directly (without any special preliminaries) to keep their bodies rigid, practically all perform the human-plank feat, that is, they remain suspended between two chairs for several minutes, one chair beneath the head and the other beneath the ankles. In fact, Collins demonstrated that control subjects are able to perform the feat just as easily as subjects who have been exposed to a trance induction procedure and who are ostensibly in "hypnotic trance." The control ("awake") subjects and also the experimental ("hypnotized") subjects stated, at the conclusion of Collins' experiment, that they were surprised at their own performance because they did not believe initially that they could so easily perform the human-plank feat.

At times, stage hypnotists ask a person to stand on the chest of the subject who is rigidly suspended between two chairs, one chair beneath his shoulders and the other beneath his calves. The traditional paradigm assumes that the suspended subject is able to support the weight of a man on his chest because he is in a special state of consciousness—a hypnotic trance state. The empirical evidence does not support this assumption. In my laboratory, six unselected male subjects were told under control conditions (without any special preliminaries) to make their body rigid and to keep it rigid. They were then suspended between two chairs, one chair beneath the shoulders and the other beneath the calves. Each subject was able to support the weight of a man on his chest. All subjects were surprised that they could so easily support the weight of a man and all disagreed vehemently with the statement that they were in a trance.

RESPONSE TO OTHER TEST SUGGESTIONS

Experimental studies that I have summarized elsewhere (Barber, 1965a) have demonstrated that a substantial proportion of individuals are responsive to various kinds of test suggestions when no attempt is made to place them in a "hypnotic trance." In these experiments, 62 unselected college students were assigned at random to a control condition (they were simply told that they were to receive a test of imagination). They were then assessed individually on objective and subjective responses to the eight standardized test suggestions of the Barber Suggestibility Scale: Arm Lowering (the subject's right arm is heavy and is moving down); Arm Levitation (the left arm is weightless and is moving up); Hand Lock (the clasped hands are welded together and cannot be taken apart); Thirst "Hallucination" (he is becoming extremely thirsty); Verbal Inhibition (his throat and jaw muscles are rigid and he cannot speak his name); Body Immobility (his body is heavy and he cannot stand up); "Posthypnotic-Like" Response (when he hears a click postexperimentally, he will cough automatically); and Selective Amnesia (when the experiment is over, he will not remember one specific test-suggestion).[3]

3. The subject receives a maximum Objective score of 8 points on the Barber Suggestibility Scale (one point for each of the eight test suggestions) if: the right arm moves down 4 or more inches; the left arm rises 4 or more inches; the subject tries to but fails to unclasp his hands; he shows swallowing, moistening of lips, or marked mouth movements and states postexperimentally that he became thirsty during this test; he tries but does not succeed in saying his name; he tries

(Continued on P. 124)

As Table 5.1, column 1, shows, about one-fourth of these control subjects, who were given the eight test suggestions immediately after they were
simply told that they were to receive a test of imagination, passed the Arm
Lowering, Arm Levitation, Verbal Inhibition, and Body Immobility items
both objectively (manifesting the suggested overt behavior) and subjectively
(testifying postexperimentally that they actually experienced the suggested
effect). In addition, nearly half of these control subjects passed the Thirst
"Hallucination" item and 40 per cent passed the Hand Lock item (that is,
they tried to unclasp their hands but had not succeeded after 15 seconds,
and they testified that they actually felt that their hands were stuck). Furthermore, about 13 per cent of these control subjects passed the "Posthypnotic-Like" Response and the Selective Amnesia items.

Although a surprisingly high proportion of subjects were responsive to the
test suggestions under the control condition, even more dramatic results
were obtained when another group of 62 subjects, randomly selected from
the same college population, were tested individually on the same test
suggestions after receiving task-motivational instructions for 45 seconds.
These task-motivational instructions, which aimed to produce favorable motivations, attitudes, and expectancies toward the test situation and to
heighten the subject's willingness to imagine and think about those things
that would be suggested, were worded as follows:

> In this experiment I'm going to test your ability to imagine and to visualize.
> How well you do on the tests which I will give you depends entirely upon
> your willingness to try to imagine and to visualize the things I will ask you
> to imagine. Everyone passed these tests when they tried. For example, we
> asked people to close their eyes and to imagine that they were at a movie
> theater and were watching a show. Most people were able to do this very
> well; they were able to imagine very vividly that they were at a movie and
> they felt as if they were actually looking at the picture. However, a few
> people thought that this was an awkward or silly thing to do and did not try
> to imagine and failed the test. Yet when these people later realized that it
> wasn't hard to imagine, they were able to visualize the movie picture and
> they felt as if the imagined movie was as vivid and as real as an actual movie.
> What I ask is your cooperation in helping this experiment by trying to imagine
> vividly what I describe to you. I want you to score as high as you can be-

---

but does not succeed in standing fully erect; he coughs or clears his throat when
the cue is presented postexperimentally; and he does not refer to the critical item
during the postexperimental interview but recalls at least four other items and
then recalls the critical item when told "Now you can remember."

In addition to the Objective scores, assigned as described above, the subject
also receives a maximum Subjective score of 8 points on the Barber Suggestibility
Scale (one point for each of the eight test suggestions) if he states, during the
standardized post experimental interview, that he actually experienced each of
the suggested effects and that he did not respond overtly to the test suggestion
simply to follow instructions or to please the experimenter.

TABLE 5.1   Percentage of subjects passing each test suggestion both objectively and subjectively

Test Suggestion	Per Cent of Subjects Passing		
	control	task-motivational instructions	trance induction procedure
1. Arm lowering	26b	61a	72a
2. Arm levitation	24b	56a	56a
3. Hand lock	40b	81a	69a
4. Thirst hallucination	48b	76a	74a
5. Verbal inhibition	27b	69a	64a
6. Body immobility	27b	66a	63a
7. Posthypnoticlike response	14b	42a	29ab
8. Selective amnesia	13b	39a	35a

SOURCE: Barber, 1965a.
NOTE: Percentages in the same row containing the same subscript letter do not differ from each other at the .05 level of confidence.

cause we're trying to measure the maximum ability of people to imagine. If you don't try to the best of your ability, this experiment will be worthless and I'll tend to feel silly. On the other hand, if you try to imagine to the best of your ability, you can easily imagine and do the interesting things I tell you and you will be helping this experiment and not wasting any time (Barber & Calverley, 1962, p. 366).

The subjects who received these task-motivational instructions showed a dramatically high level of objective and subjective responsiveness to the test suggestions (manifesting the suggested overt behaviors and testifying that they subjectively experienced the suggested effects). As Table 5.1, column 2, shows, from 56 per cent to 69 per cent of the subjects who received task-motivational instructions passed the Arm Lowering, Arm Levitation, Verbal Inhibition, and Body Immobility items, 76 per cent passed the Thirst "Hallucination" item, and 81 per cent the Hand Lock item. In addition, around 40 per cent of the subjects who received task-motivational instructions passed the Selective Amnesia and "Posthypnotic-Like" Response items.

As stated above, 62 subjects were tested individually under the control condition and 62 were tested under the task-motivational condition. In addition, 62 subjects, randomly chosen from the same population of college students, were assessed individually on response to the same test suggestions after they were exposed to a standardized 15-minute procedure of the type traditionally labeled as a "trance induction." This trance induction procedure, which is presented verbatim elsewhere (Barber, 1969b), included the following salient features: (a) Instructions were administered to produce favorable attitudes, motivations, and expectancies (for example, "Hypnosis is nothing fearful or mysterious. . . . Your cooperation, your interest, is what I ask for. . . . Nothing will be done that will in any way cause you the least embarrassment . . . you will be able to experience many interesting things."). (b) The subject was asked to fixate on a light blinking in synchrony with the sound of a metronome and was given suggestions of eye heaviness and eye closure (for example, "The strain in your eyes is getting greater and greater. . . . You would like to close your eyes and relax completely"). (c) Suggestions of relaxation, drowsiness, and sleep were administered repeatedly ("comfortable, relaxed, thinking of nothing, nothing but what I say . . . drowsy . . . deep sound comfortable sleep . . . deeper and deeper. . ."). (d) It was suggested to the subject that he was entering a unique state, a deep trance, in which he would be able to have interesting and unusual experiences

As table 5.1, column 3, shows, subjects exposed to the trance induction procedure were generally as responsive to the test suggestions as those subjects who had received the brief task-motivational instructions under waking conditions. Also, Table 5.1 shows that the subjects who received the trance induction procedure as well as those who received the task-motivational instructions were significantly more responsive to the test suggestions than the control group.

Table 5.2 shows the number of test suggestions that were passed by subjects in each of the three experimental groups. The reader will note that 13 per cent and 10 per cent of the subjects under the task-motivational instructions and trance induction conditions, respectively, and none of the controls, passed all eight of the test suggestions. Also, 16 per cent, 60 per cent, and 53 per cent of the subjects under the control, task-motivational instructions, and trance induction condition, respectively, were relatively highly responsive to test suggestions, passing at least five of the eight items.

The data presented above indicate the following:

TABLE 5.2 Number of test suggestions passed (both objectively and subjectively) by subjects in control, task-motivational instructions, and trance induction groups

Number of Test Suggestions Passed	Per Cent of Subjects Passing		
	control group	task-motivational group	trance induction group
8	0	13	10
7	3	16	16
6	11 } 16	15 } 60	16 } 53
5	2	16	11
4	11	16	15
3	6 } 38	8 } 27	13 } 36
2	21	3	8
1	16 } 45	10 } 13	6 } 11
0	29	3	5

SOURCE: Barber, 1965a.

1. When subjects are tested on response to test suggestions under a control condition (immediately after they are simply told that they are to be given a test of imagination), the majority respond to some test suggestions and a small proportion manifest a rather high level of response. Under the control condition, subjects typically passed two of the eight test suggestions and 16 per cent passed at least five of the eight.

2. Although most subjects respond to some test suggestions under a control condition, a markedly higher level of response is found when subjects are given task-motivational instructions, that is, instructions designed to produce positive motivations, attitudes, and expectancies toward the suggestive situation and a consequent willingness to think with and imagine those things that are suggested.

3. A trance induction procedure, which focuses on repeated suggestions of eye heaviness, relaxation, drowsiness, and sleep, also raises response to test suggestions above the control or base level.

4. Comparable high levels of response to test suggestions of arm heaviness, body immobility, inability to say one's name, selective amnesia, and so forth, are produced when task-motivational instructions are given alone (without a trance induction procedure) and when a trance induction procedure is given alone (without explicit task-motivational instructions).[4]

Why is enhanced responsiveness to test suggestions produced both by task-motivational instructions and also by a trance induction procedure? There are at least three possible interpretations:

1. From the traditional (special state) paradigm, one might hypothesize that both task-motivational instructions and a trance induction procedure

---

4. Additional experiments, summarized elsewhere (Barber, 1969b, pp. 60–70), also found comparable high levels of response to test suggestions (suggestions for analgesia, gustatory "hallucination," enhanced cognitive proficiency, dreaming on a specified topic, time distortion, color blindness, visual-auditory "hallucination," and amnesia) in subjects exposed to task-motivational instructions alone and in those exposed to a trance induction procedure. However, several considerations noted by Hilgard and Tart (1966) and by Edmonston and Robertson (1967) led to an additional experiment (Barber & Calverley, 1968), which indicated that task-motivational instructions given alone are slightly less effective in facilitating suggestibility than task-motivational instructions given together with a trance induction procedure. Barber and Calverley (1968) hypothesized that the slightly higher level of suggestibility that was found when the task-motivational instructions were combined with the trance induction procedure was due to the fact that under this condition the situation was defined to the subjects as "hypnosis" and, vice versa, the slightly lower level of suggestibility found with task-motivational instructions alone was due to the fact that under this condition the situation was defined as a "test of imagination." This hypothesis clearly merits testing, especially since earlier experiments (Barber & Calverley, 1964e, 1965) indicated that, with everything else constant, a higher level of responsiveness to test suggestions is produced when subjects are told they are participating in a "hypnosis" experiment rather than in an "imagination" experiment.

give rise to a hypnotic trance state. However, with few exceptions, subjects who have received task-motivational instructions appear awake, claim they are awake, and do not show a limp posture, passivity, a blank stare, or any other sign of trance. Are task-motivated subjects, who show no signs of being in a trance, actually in a trance? This question, which derives from the traditional paradigm, cannot be answered by any empirical method available at the present time.

2. Also, from the special state paradigm, one might hypothesize that (a) subjects who are highly responsive to test suggestions after they have received a trance induction procedure are in a hypnotic trance state whereas (b) those who are highly responsive after receiving task-motivational instructions are not in a hypnotic trance but are responsive for other reasons, for example, because they are highly motivated to respond. This interpretation also leads to an anomaly for the special state paradigm because it is now being said that the kind of high response to test suggestions that has been traditionally associated with hypnotic trance can also be produced as easily without hypnotic trance.

3. From the alternative paradigm, which does not postulate a special state, one could hypothesize that both task-motivational instructions and a trance induction procedure raise response to test suggestions above the level found under a control condition because they produce more positive attitudes, motivations, and expectancies toward the suggestive situation and a greater willingness to think with and to imagine those things that are suggested. This hypothesis can be empirically confirmed or disconfirmed by (a) assessing attitudes, motivations, expectancies, and willingness to think with the suggestions prior to and also after the administration of a control, a task-motivational, and a trance induction treatment to three random groups of subjects and (b) testing responsiveness to suggestions after the second assessment (of attitudes, motivations, etc.).

A PERSONAL REPORT ON RESPONDING TO TEST SUGGESTIONS

As stated above, some individuals manifest a high level of response to test suggestions when no attempt is made to hypnotize them. I also manifest a high level of response. Let me now give a personal, phenomenological report of the factors underlying my own responsiveness to test suggestions (Barber, 1970b).

An experimenter states that he would like to assess my responsiveness to suggestions and I agree to be tested. Since I believe that it is an interesting and worthwhile learning experience to respond to the kinds of test suggestions that I expect he will give me, I have a positive attitude toward the test situation and am motivated to experience those things that will be suggested. Furthermore, I expect that suggested effects, such as arm levitation, age regression, and amnesia can be experienced. Since I have positive attitudes, motivations, and expectancies, I will not evaluate, analyze, or think contrary to those things that are suggested; for example, I will not say to myself, "This suggestion is not worded correctly," "The suggestion will not be effective," or "This is just an experiment." On the contrary, I will let myself think with, imagine, and visualize those things that the experimenter will describe.

The experimenter asks me to extend my right arm and then suggests repeatedly that it is solid, rigid, like a piece of steel. If I had a reason not to respond to the suggestion, I could prevent myself from thinking of the arm as rigid. However, since there is no reason to resist, on the contrary, since I am motivated to experience the suggested effects, I let myself think with the suggestion—I verbalize to myself that the arm is rigid and I imagine it as a piece of steel. When the experimenter then states, "Try to bend the arm, you can't," I do not say to myself, "Of course I can bend it." Instead, I continue to think of the arm as rigid, I continue to picture it as a piece of steel, and when I make an attempt to bend it, I find that I cannot.

(Thinking back to the suggestion, after the experiment is over, I realize the following: (a) when I was imagining my arm as rigid, I involuntarily contracted the muscles in the arm, (b) the involuntary muscular contractions made the arm feel rigid, (c) the actual rigidity in the arm reinforced the thought that the arm was rigid and immovable, and (d) when told to try to bend the arm, I continued to think and imagine that the arm was a piece of steel and I continued to maintain the involuntary muscular contraction. Although these considerations are clear to me retrospectively, during the experiment I was picturing the arm as a piece of steel and I was not actively thinking about these underlying mechanisms.)

The experimenter next suggests repeatedly that my left hand is dull, numb, a piece of rubber, a lump of matter without feelings or sensations. I think with the suggestions and I picture the hand as a rubbery lump of matter that is separated from the rest of my body. The experimenter then places the hand in a pain-producing apparatus that brings a heavy weight to bear upon a finger. Although this heavy weight normally produces an aching pain in the finger, I do not think of the stimulation as pain. Instead I continue to think of the hand and finger as a rubbery lump of matter "out there" and I think of the sensations produced by the heavy weight *as sensations* that have their own unique and interesting properties. Specifically, I think of the sensations as a series of separate sensations—as a sensation of pressure, a cutting sensation, a numbness, a feeling of heat, a pulsating sensation. Although under other circumstances I would label these sensations as pain, I do not let myself think of the sensations in this way; instead, I think of them as a complex of varying sensations in a dull, rubbery hand and I state honestly that although I experience a variety of unique sensations I do not experience anxiety, distress, or pain.

The experimenter then suggests that I see a cat in the corner of the room. Since I have a positive attitude toward the suggestive situation and am motivated to experience the suggested effects, I inhibit the thought that there is no cat in the room. Instead, I let myself vividly visualize a black cat that I have often seen before and I think of it as being in the corner of the room. Since I continue to think of the cat as being "out there," and since I inhibit the thought that I am visualizing it in my mind's eye, I state that I see the cat in the corner of the room.

The experimenter next instructs me to close my eyes (presumably to remove visual distractions that might interfere with the forthcoming tasks), and then suggests that I am in Boston Symphony Hall and I hear the orchestra playing. I let myself vividly imagine that I am at the symphony and that the orchestra is playing Beethoven's Fifth Symphony. I inhibit the thought that I am really in an experimental situation, I focus on the idea that I am in Symphony Hall, and I "hear" the music, which becomes continually more vivid.

(Afterwards, thinking back to the suggestion for auditory hallucination, I realize that I was "making the music in my head." However, at the time I received the suggestion I was vividly imagining and thinking about Beethoven's symphony and I was not thinking about such matters as where the music was coming from. Although I could have stopped thinking with the suggestion, for instance, I could have said to myself that I was actually in an experimental situation, I had no reason to verbalize such contrary thoughts to myself and I continued to imagine vividly and to think of myself as being in Symphony Hall.)

The experimenter next suggests that time is going back, my body is becoming small, and I am a child of six years of age. I do not say to myself that I am an adult, that I cannot become a child, or that this suggestion won't work. On the contrary, since I have positive attitudes, motivations, and expectancies toward the suggestive situation, I think with the suggestion. I let myself imagine vividly that my body is small and tiny (and I begin to feel that I am actually tiny), I think of myself as a child, and I vividly imagine myself in the first grade classroom. I then let the imaginative situation "move" by itself; the first-grade teacher talks to the students, two boys in the back of the room throw spitballs when the teacher turns her back to the class, and later the bell rings for recess. Since I focused on the idea that I was a child, since I felt myself as small and tiny, since I could "see" the events occurring in the classroom, since I did not say to myself "I am really an adult," I testify afterwards that I actually felt that I was six years old and that I found this part of the experiment vivid and very interesting.

Later, the experimenter suggests that when the session is over I will not remember anything that occurred. Soon afterwards he states that the experiment is over and asks me what I remember. Since I have no reason to resist the suggestion for amnesia, I say to myself that I do not remember what occurred, I keep my thoughts on the present, I do not think back to the preceding events, and I state that I do not remember. The experimenter subsequently states, "Now you can remember." I now let myself think back to the preceding events and I verbalize them.

In summary, speaking personally and phenomenologically, I can experience arm rigidity, hand levitation, analgesia, visual and auditory hallucination, age regression, amnesia, and other suggested effects that have been traditionally thought to be associated with hypnotism. I do not need a "trance induction procedure" in order to experience these effects. Since I am ready at any time to adopt a positive attitude, motivation, and expectancy toward the suggestive situation, I am ready at any time to think with and to imagine or visualize those things that are suggested. On the other hand, if I had a reason not to respond to the test suggestions, I could adopt a quite different set of attitudes, motivations, and expectancies toward the situation, I could tell myself that I shall not respond, and I could easily prevent myself from thinking with and vividly imagining those things that are suggested.

Three additional points should be emphasized:

1. If the experimenter first suggests to me, as has happened on several occasions, that I am becoming relaxed, drowsy, sleepy, and am entering a hypnotic trance state, I can think with these suggestions and can feel relaxed, dowsy, sleepy, and passive. However, when the experimenter subsequently gives suggestions that involve effort, for example, suggestions of arm rigidity or analgesia, I no longer feel relaxed, sleepy, or passive and I may, in fact, feel very alert and aroused. The traditional "trance induction procedure" comprised of repetitive suggestions of relaxation, drowsiness, sleep, and hypnosis, appears to me to be just another set of suggestions that I can accept and it is not necessary or especially important in determining my responsiveness to test suggestions.

2. When I am experiencing suggested analgesia, age regression, amnesia, and so on, I do not feel that I am in a special state—a hypnotic state or a trance—that is discontinuous with or qualitatively different from my ordinary state of consciousness. In fact, when I am responding to test suggestions I do not feel that my "state" differs in any important way from the state I am in when I watch a motion picture or stage play. When I am in an audience, I let myself imagine and think with the communications from the stage and I empathize, laugh, feel sad, cry, and have the other emotions, feelings, and vicarious experiences that the actors are attempting to communicate. In essentially the same way, when I am in an experimental situation and am being assessed for response to test suggestions, I let myself think with and vividly imagine those things that are suggested and I have the experiences that the experimenter is attempting to communicate.

3. If I wish, I can give myself the same suggestions that are given by the experimenter. For instance, I can suggest to myself that time is going backwards, my body is becoming small and tiny, and I am a child of a certain age. I can then think about and vividly imagine a situation that occurred

when I was a child and I can inhibit contrary thoughts. Similarly, in a dental situation I can give myself suggestions that the sensations are interesting and not uncomfortable and by thinking of each of the varying sensations (drilling, pressure, pricking, heat, and so forth) as sensations per se, I can inhibit anxiety, distress, and pain. I have also found that the same technique—focusing on the sensations as sensations—is sufficient to block the pain and distress associated with various methods used in the laboratory to produce pain, for example, pain produced by immersing a limb in ice water and pain produced by using a tourniquet to cut off the blood supply to an arm. Although these experiences have been traditionally subsumed under the term "autohypnosis," I do not feel that I am in a special state (a hypnotic trance state) fundamentally different from my ordinary state of consciousness; on the contrary, when I am having these experiences I feel as normal and as awake as when I am watching a movie, a stage play, or a television show.

Data Ostensibly Supporting the
Traditional (Special State) Paradigm

At first glance, the traditional notion that a special state underlies high responsiveness to test suggestions appears to be supported by data such as the following:

1. Stage hypnotists appear to elicit unique or special behaviors from subjects who seem to be in a special state (hypnotic trance).

2. Experimenters have reported that a variety of amazing or special effects can be elicited from subjects who are ostensibly in a hypnotic trance.

3. High response to test suggestions is associated with observable trance-like characteristics.

4. Some highly responsive subjects testify that they experienced a special state of consciousness.

5. Some highly responsive subjects do not "come out of it" immediately —they seem to remain in a trance after the experiment is over.

6. Some highly responsive subjects spontaneously forget the events and spontaneous amnesia is a critical indicant of a special state.

7. Highly responsive subjects show a special type of logic—"trance logic"—which indicates that they are in a special state.

Let us look at each of these sets of data in turn.

STAGE HYPNOSIS

The traditional special state (hypnotic trance) paradigm seems to be supported by the very unusual or special behaviors elicited by stage hypnotists. At first glance, it appears that after the stage hypnotist has placed his subject in a hypnotic trance state, he can make him perform weird antics (such as dancing with an invisible partner or singing like Frank Sinatra) and can exert an amazing physiological control over the subject (such as stopping the circulation and pulse in the arm). A close look at stage hypnosis, however, does not support the special state paradigm. Let us look at the procedures and techniques used in stage hypnosis that my associate, William Meeker, and I learned when we received training in this area (Meeker & Barber, 1971).[5]

Although no two stage hypnotists use exactly the same methods, there are four major principles and four secondary principles that underlie stage hypnosis. Let us first look at the four major principles and then at the secondary ones.

Major Principle 1. Responsiveness to test suggestions under "waking" conditions is much higher than is commonly assumed. Stage hypnotists know that a substantial proportion of normal individuals are highly responsive to test suggestions when no attempt is made to hypnotize them. For example, the *Encyclopedia of Stage Hypnotism* states emphatically that "it is possible to produce very striking hypnotic effects in the waking state, entirely independent of the trance" (McGill, 1947, p. 28) and describes in detail how to use "waking" suggestions to produce an inability to separate the hands, an inability to close the mouth, a forgetting of one's name, getting drunk on a glass of water, and hallucination of a mouse. Arons (1961) has clearly described the use of "waking" suggestions in stage demonstrations and has emphasized that "this phase of the demonstration illustrates forcibly that the hypnotic 'trance' is not needed to perform a hypnotic demonstration" (p. 10). Most other writers on stage hypnosis also note that "hypnotic trance" is not necessary to elicit a high level of suggestibility from a substantial proportion of volunteer subjects (Lonk, 1947, p. 34, and Tracy, 1952, p. 152, for example).

Major Principle 2. Subjects who are highly responsive to test suggestions can be easily selected. Early in their training, stage hypnotists learn how to select subjects who are highly responsive to test suggestions. The technique used to select subjects is very simple: members of the audience or volunteers are given one or two test suggestions and only those subjects are used who are very responsive. For instance, the stage hypnotist may ask the entire audience or the volunteers to clasp their hands together tightly and then suggests repeatedly that the hands are stuck and cannot be taken apart, or the potential subjects are asked to close their eyes and then are given suggestions of inability to open the eyes. Only those subjects who pass these (or similar) test suggestions are used.

Major Principle 3. When the situation is defined to subjects as "hypnosis," it is clear that a high level of responsiveness to requests, suggestions,

---

5. I am indebted to William Meeker for permission to summarize our collaborative work in stage hypnosis.

and commands is desired and expected. The stage hypnotist invariably defines the situation as "hypnosis." Recent experiments (Barber & Calverley, 1964e, 1965) have demonstrated that simply telling subjects that the situation is "hypnosis" is sufficient by itself to raise response to test suggestions above the already rather high base level. Post experimental interviews with subjects participating in these recent experiments indicated that the reason why subjects are more responsive to test suggestions when they are told that they are participating in a "hypnosis" experiment rather than in some other kind of experiment are as follows: When subjects are told that they are in a "hypnosis" situation, they typically interpret this to mean that (a) they are in an unusual or special situation in which high response to suggestions, requests, and commands is both desired and expected and (b), if they actively resist or try not to carry out those things suggested, they will be considered as uncooperative or "poor" subjects, the hypnotist will be disappointed, and the purpose of the experiment will be nullified. Contrariwise, when subjects are told that the situation involves something other than "hypnosis," they are being told by implication that they are not necessarily expected to show a high level of response to test suggestions of the type traditionally associated with the word "hypnosis."

Since the introduction of this one word into an experimental situation heightens subjects' responsiveness to test suggestions, we can expect a high level of response in the stage situation that is emphatically defined as "hypnosis" and that includes a prestigious performer who has been widely advertised as a highly effective hypnotist.

Major Principle 4. The stage hypnotist capitalizes on the unique characteristics of the stage setting. The stage setting has several unusual features. First of all, it has unique expectancy characteristics. As the *Encyclopedia of Stage Hypnotism* points out, "the lights, the music, the curtains, the tenseness of being on the stage, and above all the expectancy centered on each subject by the audience—expectancy that he will be hypnotized, are factors working . . . powerfully in the performer's favor" (McGill, 1947, p. 248).

Secondly, the stage setting has unique "fun" characteristics. In addition, the stage setting has unique features that lead subjects to "help out the show." These aspects of the stage setting are discussed by Nelson (1965):

> To revolt or to rebel is to . . . stand out among the others as a "hold out". . . . The subject subconsciously gets the idea and *gets into the act.* It's fun—the ham in them exhibits itself and they are *actors* (acting the part of a hypnotized subject). They realize they have a perfect shield to hide behind if they engage in any odd or silly tactics (they are *hypnotized* which is the excuse), and begin competing among each other for the best performance—like a real *actor.* There are always one or two of the subjects out of a group that will out-do the others and give an outstanding performance. They sense the audience re-actions and applause, and love it and are impelled on in

their efforts like a hungry actor. Many times they will react in a slightly exaggerated manner, which the hypnotist must anticipate and capitalize on. Once the ball has started to roll, they all fall into the fun idea and play the role of an actor, the hypnotist merely being the *director* in the ensuing entertainment." (P. 30)

The *Encyclopedia of Stage Hypnotism* also emphasizes the "helping out the show" aspects of the stage situation: "Considerable numbers of subjects, especially in the extravert enterprise of performing on the stage, tend to simulate. . . . This simulation is not necessarily voluntary deception, for it is frequently born of an extreme desire to cooperate with the performer and help out the show" (McGill, 1947, p. 257).

In summary, to produce "amazing" performances, stage hypnotists rely *primarily* on the high level of "waking" suggestibility that is present in a substantial proportion of subjects, careful selection of the most responsive subjects, the further enhancement of suggestibility that is produced when the situation is labeled as "hypnosis," and the unique characteristics of the stage setting. These four factors are sufficient by themselves to produce most of the performances observed during stage hypnosis. However, well-trained stage hypnotists also have four additional techniques in their repertoire which they at times utilize. These techniques can be subsumed under four supplementary principles which will now be described.

Supplementary Principle 1. Stage hypnotists at times whisper private instructions to their subjects. The *Encyclopedia of Stage Hypnotism* instructs the stage hypnotist to make "gentle pass-like gestures in the air" while whispering to the subject, "We are going to have some good laughs on the audience and fool them . . . so when I tell you to do some funny things, do exactly as I secretly tell you. O. K? Swell!" (McGill, 1947, p. 236) The *Encyclopedia* also points out that any volunteer who is handled in this way will henceforth carry out the stage hypnotist's instructions and that, even when volunteers are first told to "help fool the audience," there soon arises a point where it is practically impossible to determine which responses on the part of the subject are deliberate and which are involuntary (McGill, 1947, pp. 237, 247).

The direct request to "help fool the audience" was more widely used by stage hypnotists in former years than it is at present. In modern performances, stage hypnotists tend to use a less blatant "whispering technique" to elicit the subject's cooperation. For instance, if the stage hypnotist wants a subject to dance with an invisible partner or to sing like Frank Sinatra, he may whisper privately to his most extroverted subject, "Give the audience a good act of dancing with an invisible partner (or singing like Frank Sinatra)." Also, the stage hypnotist may whisper to a subject, "Please close your eyes and let your body go limp." When he then makes passes over his subject, as the subject is complying with his request, the audience typically assumes that the stage hypnotist has very quickly and amazingly placed his subject in a hypnotic trance state. Along similar lines, the *Encyclopedia* points out that, when the subject is receiving suggestions of body sway, the hypnotist should whisper, "Let yourself go and don't resist. Let yourself come right back towards me." The *Encyclopedia* adds that *"These little intimate asides to the subject are most important*. The audience only hears the major portions of your comments that describe and explain the experiment, but the subject receives full benefit of your confidences that tend to make him feel very much obligated to properly perform his portion of the experiment" (McGill, 1947, p. 150).

Supplementary Principle 2. Stage hypnotists at times use the "failure to challenge" technique which misleads the audience to believe that subjects who may be unresponsive to test suggestions are actually responsive. When using the "failure to challenge" technique, the stage hypnotist (a) administers a suggestion to the subject, (b) does not determine whether the subject has accepted the suggestion, but (c) leads the audience to believe that the subject has accepted it. Schneck (1958) has carefully documented the use of this technique and has given examples such as the following: A famous stage hypnotist suggested to a subject that her right arm was insensitive. He then asked the subject to touch the right arm with her left hand in order to note the lack of sensation. Although the stage hypnotist did not ask the subject if the arm actually felt insensitive, "many in the audience accepted the implication that having gone through the motions, this girl actually did experience anesthesia" (p. 175). Similarly, the stage hypnotist suggests to a subject that his outstretched arm is rigid and immovable, but he does not challenge the subject to try to bend his arm. However, the stage hypnotist tells the audience that the subject cannot move his arm and the audience apparently accepts the hypnotist's statement. Also, stage hypnotists at times administer a trance induction procedure to some of their subjects and then assure their audience that the subjects are in a hypnotic trance, but they do not question the subjects about their experiences or assess their responsiveness to test suggestions.

Supplementary Principle 3. Stage hypnotists at times use pretrained subjects to insure the success of their show. Manuals of stage hypnosis assert that during the days of vaudeville, pretrained subjects were commonly used in stage performances and that the audience was not told that the subjects were trained ('Calostro,' 1949; Gibson, 1956; Lonk, 1947; Lustig, 1956; Nelson, 1965). This practice has markedly declined in recent years. Nowadays, some stage hypnotists use pretrained subjects to demonstrate some of the more difficult stunts, for instance, the one in which two or three men are supported on the subject's rigidly outstretched body, but the stage performer usually informs the audience that in order to demonstrate this difficult feat, he will use a trained subject.

Supplementary Principle 4. Stage hypnotists at times use tricks to elicit "amazing" performances. Manuals of stage hypnosis describe a series of "amazing" performances that can be easily elicited. These performances, which can be labeled "tricks," include, among many others, the human-plank feat, the anesthesia demonstration, stopping the blood flow, and production of "hypnotic trance" by pressure on the carotid baroreceptors. Let us look briefly at each of these tricks in turn.

As stated previously in this chapter, practically all normal individuals can easily remain suspended for several minutes between two chairs (one chair beneath the head and the other beneath the ankles). Also, practically any normal male subject can keep his body rigidly suspended between two chairs (one chair beneath his shoulders and the other beneath his calves) while, at the same time, he is supporting the weight of a man on his chest. However, since laymen are unacquainted with these facts, they assume that the subject who is performing these human-plank feats must be in a hypnotic trance state.

An anesthesia demonstration that is performed at times by stage hypnotists can also be labeled a trick. When the stunt is to be demonstrated, the subject is asked to extend one arm horizontally with the palm facing downward. The stage hypnotist then makes passes over the subject's hand, suggests that it is numb and insensitive, and then moves the flame of a cigarette lighter slowly under the outstretched palm. The subject typically shows no reaction to the flame and the audience assumes that hypnotic anesthesia has been demonstrated. However, when performing this stunt, stage hypnotists keep the flame about one inch from the subject's palm and do not hold it at one spot but, instead, move it slowly (Lonk, 1947, p. 35; Tracy, 1952, p. 133). If the reader tries it, he will find that he will not be bothered at all by the heat of the flame, provided that the flame is at a distance of about an inch from his palm and is moved slowly.

Stage hypnotists also at times place a lighted match directly upon the subject's palm and then move it slowly. If the reader tries it on himself, he will find that the fire from a match is not especially uncomfortable and no burning results, provided that the match is moved along the palm. The only possibility of burning occurs if the lighted match is brought toward the palm to slowly or is held at one spot.

Stage hypnotists, at times, also demonstrate the "stopping the blood flow" stunt, conducted as follows: the stage performer suggests that the blood is leaving the subject's arm and makes mysterious passes over it. The subject's arm appears white and lifeless. Next, the performer suggests that the blood is returning to the arm, and its natural coloring returns. During this test, a member of the audience (preferably a physician) is asked to test the subject's pulse, which often proves imperceptible (Lonk, 1947; Lustig, 1956; McGill, 1947). Although there are several methods for performing this trick, the one most commonly used is that, prior to the performance, a golf ball is placed in the armpit of a stooge and fastened there by an elastic. When the hypnotist suggests that the blood is leaving the arm, the stooge presses his arm against the golf ball, and the circulation and pulse are temporarily obliterated (Lonk, 1947, p. 58; Lustig, 1956, p. 15).

The carotid trick is also described in detail by most of the manuals of stage hypnosis (Nelson, 1965; McGill, 1947; Lonk, 1947, for example). When using this trick, the stage performer exerts pressure on the baroreceptors at the carotid sinus. This produces a vagus-induced bradycardia and vasodilation, which leads to sudden hypotension and fainting (Ganong, 1967, pp. 508–9). The manuals state that, when using this technique, the stage performer should make passes over the subject with his free hand in order to lead the audience to believe that he is placing the subject in a hypnotic trance state. However, the manuals also warn the stage hypnotist that continued pressure on the carotid is dangerous, the pressure should not be continued for much more than 15 seconds, and the technique should be used only on rare occasions, for example, when a smart-aleck subject dares the performer to hypnotize him.

In summary, the traditional (special state) viewpoint would conceptualize stage hypnosis along the following lines: the stage hypnotist places his subjects in a state (a hypnotic trance) fundamentally different from ordinary states of consciousness, and subjects on the stage behave in unusual ways because they are in the special state. These notions are misleading. The alternative viewpoint, which does not posit a special state, postulates that stage hypnotists induce their subjects to behave in apparently unusual ways primarily because of the following:

1. A substantial proportion of individuals show a rather high base-level response to test suggestions.

2. Only selected subjects, who show a high level of response to test suggestions, are used in the stage demonstration.

3. Since the situation is emphatically defined as "hypnosis," it is clear to all of the selected subjects that obedience to requests, commands, and suggestions is desired and expected.

4. Unique characteristics of the stage situation—the expectancy centered on each subject by the audience, together with the "fun" and "helping the show" atomosphere—are helpful in eliciting obedience.

Although these four features of the stage situation are sufficient to elicit most of the ostensibly amazing behaviors, stage hypnotists also at times use the following to enhance the dramatic nature of their show: the technique of private whispers, the failure to challenge technique, pretrained subjects to demonstrate the more difficult stunts, and one or more tricks that lead the audience to believe that extraordinary effects are being produced.

Although the stage performer is viewed, from the traditional (special state) paradigm, as a highly effective hypnotist who places his subjects in a hypnotic trance state, a more valid conception is that the stage performer is an actor playing the part of a hypnotist. As manuals of stage hypnosis point out: "The successful hypnotic entertainer is actually not interested whether or not the subjects are really hypnotized—his basic function is to *entertain*. He is interested in his ability to *con* his subjects into a pseudo performance that appears as hypnotism—to get laughs and to entertain his audience. . . . [The subjects] enjoy their part and react as they are *told* to do. Hypnotism, as done for entertainment, is as simple as all this" (Nelson, 1965, pp. 29–31).

"AMAZING" EFFECTS ELICITED IN EXPERIMENTAL SITUATIONS

The traditional (special state) viewpoint seems to be supported by experimental reports that amazing or special effects were produced when suggestions were given to highly responsive subjects. These effects include the production of blisters, the cure of warts, the production of analgesia sufficient for surgery, and the production of actual age regression, hallucinations, and deafness. Let us look at the data pertaining to each of these effects.

Production of blisters

It has been claimed that blisters appear in some subjects who have been exposed to a trance induction procedure, who are highly responsive to test suggestions, and who have been given suggestions that a blister will form at a specified place on the skin. This widely-publicized claim seems to lead to the conclusion that the subjects must be in a unique or special state when they manifest such a unique effect. However, a close look at the data indicates that the so-called "blister" phenomenon is far more complex than it first appears, and that there is no need to postulate a special state (hypnotic trance) in order to explain it:

1. During the past 100 years, many researchers suggested to their hypnotic trance subjects that a blister would form on the skin. With very few exceptions, no skin changes whatsoever were observed (Barber, 1969b, Ch. 9).

2. About 12 researchers reported that suggestions for blister formation gave rise to cutaneous alterations; some of these alterations were labeled "blisters." These reports should be viewed within a broader context by noting the following points, which have been delineated in a series or reviews (Barber, 1961b; Gorton, 1949; Pattie, 1941; Paul, 1963; Sarbin, 1956; Weitzenhoffer, 1953).

3. With very few exceptions, the positive findings were obtained between

1886 and 1927, prior to the advent of rigorous experimental controls in this area.

4. With very few exceptions, careful controls were not used to exclude the possibility that the subject may have deliberately injured his skin in attempting to comply with the suggestion for blister formation. Furthermore, one subject attempted to injure his skin by pricking it with a needle (Schrenck-Notzing, 1896), another vigorously rubbed snow on the area where the blister was supposed to form (Ullman, 1947), and another rubbed poison ivy leaves where the skin change was supposed to appear (Wolberg, 1948, p. 49).

5. With very few if any exceptions, the positive results were obtained with patients who were either suffering from various skin ailments (neurodermatitis, hysterical ecchymoses, wheals, or neurotic skin gangrene) or who were diagnosed as hysterics (hysterical blindness, hysterical aphonia, hystero epilepsy, or hysterical hemianesthesia).

6. With one or two exceptions, it is not clear from the studies reporting positive results whether the skin alterations were blisters, wheals, or dermographism. A study that carefully considered each of these possibilities (Borelli, 1953) showed conclusively that the skin change that was produced by suggestion was dermographism, not a blister. It should be emphasized that dermographism (wheal formation in response to a single moderately strong stroking of the skin) is more common than is usually supposed. For instance, in testing 84 young men, T. Lewis (1927) found a clear-cut swelling of the skin as a reaction to a single firm stroke in 25 per cent and in 5 per cent a full wheal developed. Furthermore, as Graham and Wolf (1950) have documented, some normal individuals show wheal formation at sites of mild pressure stimulation, such as around a collar, a belt, or a wristwatch strap. These data are important in understanding the positive results obtained in the studies mentioned above because in all but one of the successful studies tactual stimulation was used to localize the place where the blister was to form, and in many of these studies the stimulus object was a small piece of metal.

7. All of the studies in this area lack a control group; suggestions for blister formation were never given to subjects who were not exposed to a trance induction procedure. It was always assumed, without apparent justification, that a hypnotic trance state is necessary in order to produce blisters by suggestions.

Further studies are needed to determine whether suggestions for blister formation are effective in producing blisters in any present-day subjects under "hypnotic trance" conditions and also under "waking control" conditions. I will venture three hypnotheses: under both the hypnotic trance and the waking control conditions, fewer than 1 per cent of the subjects will show any skin alterations, the alterations will resemble dermographism or wheals rather than blisters, and the few subjects who show a cutaneous effect when given suggestions for blister formation will normally manifest marked dermographism when appropriately stimulated on the skin.

Removal of warts

Sinclair-Gieben and Chalmers (1959) and Ullman and Dudek (1960) reported that suggestions given to hypnotic trance subjects were effective in some instances in removing warts. However, although suggestions for wart removal appear to be effective at times when they are given under "hypnotic trance" conditions, they also appear to be effective at times when they are given under "waking control" conditions. A series of investigators (Bloch, 1927; Dudek, 1967; Sulzberger & Wolf, 1934; Vollmer, 1946) found that warts at times disappear when they are simply painted with an innocuous dye and the "awake" subjects are told that the placebo-dye is a powerful wart-curing drug. Furthermore, in those instances in which suggestions for wart disappearance were effective, there is evidence that the warts may have been of the labile type, that is, of the type that would have disappeared spontaneously within a rather short period of time if no suggestions had been given (Clarke, 1965; Memmesheimer & Eisenlohr, 1931; Stankler, 1967).

Analgesia

From time to time accounts are published of hypnotic trance subjects who underwent minor or major surgery without analgesic or anesthetic drugs. These accounts imply that a unique or special state, a hypnotic trance state, is necessary in order to undergo surgery without drugs. However, the available data do not support this implication:

1. Most "hypnotic trance" subjects who undergo minor or major surgery without drugs show signs of pain. Some subjects cry, others show a "hideous expression of suppressed agony" (Barber, 1970a, p. 228) and, in many instances, chemical analgesics or anesthetics have to be administered in order to complete the surgery (Anderson, 1957; Barber, 1970a, Ch. 5; Braid, 1847; Butler, 1954).

2. A few "hypnotic trance" subjects manifested very little or no pain when they underwent minor or major surgery without drugs. However, a few subjects who were not exposed to a trance induction procedure also manifested little or no pain when they underwent minor or major surgery without drugs (Chertok, 1959, pp. 3–4; Elliotson, 1843, pp. 15–17; Esdaile, 1850, pp. 214–15; Haim, 1908; Leriche, 1939, pp. 55–56; Lewis, 1942, p. 10; Mackenzie, 1909; Mitchell, 1907; Propping, 1909; Sampimon & Woodruff, 1946; Trent, 1946).

3. The pain involved in most surgical procedures is highly overestimated. Although the skin is sensitive, most of the muscles and organs of the body

are relatively insensitive to pain. More precisely, the skin is sensitive to a knife cut, but the skilled surgeon cuts through the skin smoothly and quickly and the underlying muscles and internal organs are relatively insensitive. Lewis (1942) has documented the fact that the muscles, the internal organs, and most other parts of the body (with the exception of the skin) are insensitive to incision (although they may be sensitive to other stimuli such as pulling or stretching). For instance, Lewis (1942) has noted the following:

> [The subcutaneous tissue] gives rise to little pain when injured by . . . incision. . . . [The pain in somatic muscles] is slight when elicited by . . . knife cut. . . . Compact bone may be bored without pain. . . . The articular surfaces [of joints] . . . are insensitive. . . . Puncture of a vein is nearly always painless. . . . The dura mater. . . . pia mater and the cortex are generally regarded as insensitive. . . . the lung and visceral pleura are insensitive . . . the surface of the heart is found to be insensitive . . . [surgeons] have often and painlessly removed pieces of the oesophageal wall of the conscious subject for histological examination. . . . It is common knowledge that the solid organs such as liver, spleen, and kidney, can be tightly gripped, cut, or even burnt without the subject's being conscious of it. . . . All parts of the wall of [the stomach] may be cut, burnt, stretched, or clamped without pain. . . cutting [the jejunum and ileum] . . . is accomplished painlessly . . . . The insensitiveness of [the colon] attracted early attention . . . cutting [the great omentum] is accomplished painlessly. . . . The body of the uterus can be cut . . . painlessly. (Pp. 2–8)

In brief, there are rare cases of individuals who were said to be in a "hypnotic trance state" and also individuals who were said to be "awake" who underwent minor or major surgery without drugs and without manifesting much pain. These cases seem much more dramatic than they actually are because it is assumed that all parts of the body are as sensitive to pain as the skin. The truth of the matter is that, although the skin is sensitive, most tissues and organs in the body are insensitive to the surgeon's scalpel. Furthermore, there is no reason to postulate a special state of consciousness in order to explain the ability to undergo noxious stimulation of the skin without manifesting distress or pain. The following points are relevant:

1. Pain is at times markedly reduced in awake subjects when placebos are administered with the implication (or the explicit statement) that they are pain-relieving drugs (Barber, 1959b; Beecher, 1959).

2. Instructions or suggestions intended to produce relaxation are at times effective with "hypnotic trance" subjects and also with "awake" subjects in reducing subjective and physiological responses to noxious stimuli (Barber & Calverley, 1969a; Jacobson, 1938, 1954; Hilgard et al., 1967).

3. Responsiveness to painful stimulation is reduced in some "hypnotic trance" subjects and also in some "awake" subjects by instructions or suggestions intended to alleviate anxiety and anticipation or fear of pain (Hill et al., 1952a, 1952b; Kornetsky, 1954; Shor, 1967).

4. Suggestions of anesthesia or analgesia are effective in reducing subjectively reported pain in a substantial proportion of subjects who have been randomly assigned to a trance induction treatment and in an equal proportion of subjects who have been randomly assigned to a control treatment (Barber & Calverley, 1969a; Spanos, Barber, & Lang, 1969).

5. Subjectively reported pain is reduced in awake subjects when they are distracted during exposure to noxious stimulation (Kanfer & Goldfoot, 1966). Furthermore, both subjectively reported pain and physiological responses to noxious stimulation can be reduced by instructing control subjects to try to think about and to imagine vividly a pleasant situation during the stimulation (Barber & Hahn, 1962). Also, pain is reduced to an equal degree in "waking control" subjects and in "hypnotic trance" subjects when both groups of subjects are distracted during the pain-producing stimulation by having them listen to and try to remember the details of an interesting story presented on a tape recording (Barber & Calverley, 1969a). These results are consistent with the conclusion reached many years ago by Liébeault (1885) that, if and when suggestions are effective in reducing pain in "hypnotic trance" subjects, the mediating processes can be conceptualized as focusing of attention on thoughts or ideas other than those concerning pain. These results are also consistent with the conclusion drawn by August (1961) from a large-scale investigation with 1,000 patients, that trance induction procedures and suggestions are effective in reducing pain during childbirth to the extent that they direct "attention away from pain responses toward pleasant ideas"(p. 62).

Age regression

Several studies pertaining to hypnotic age regression also seem to support the contention that subjects who are highly responsive to test suggestions are in a "special state." These studies, by Gidro-Frank and Bowersbuch (1948), Parrish, Lundy, and Leibowitz (1969), and True (1949), appeared to indicate that, when given suggestions to regress to infancy or childhood, "hypnotic trance" subjects show an amazing reinstatement of a physiological reflex which is characteristic of infancy, an amazing recall of events that occurred during childhood, and an amazing childlike performance on objective tests. A close look at these studies, however, fails to support the special state paradigm. Let us look at each of them in turn.

Gidro-Frank and Bowersbuch (1948) reported that when three selected "hypnotic trance" subjects were given suggestions to regress to four months of age, they showed a Babinski toe response, that is, stimulation of the sole of the foot produced dorsiflexion of the large toe and fanning of the other toes. Several neurology texts stated that the Babinski toe response is present in infants up to four months of age but is not present after six months of age. Consequently, it appeared that Gidro-Frank and Bowersbuch had demonstrated that suggestions to regress to early infancy, when given to "hypnotic trance" subjects, reinstate a long-dormant physiological reflex that is characteristic of early infancy. However, the neurology texts were mistaken. Researchers who have actually looked at infants have consistently observed that the typical response of the four-month-old infant to stimulation of the sole of the foot is *not* the Babinski response, but rather sudden withdrawal of the limb with variability in response of the toes. In fact, the Babinski toe response is very rarely if ever observed in early infancy (Burr, 1921; Mc-Graw, 1941; Wolff, 1930). Since the Babinski response is rarely if ever observed in infants, the question at issue is not how suggestions given under "hypnotic trance" revive an infantile reflex, but why these "hypnotic trance" subjects showed a Babinski toe response (not characteristic of early infancy) when they were given suggestions to regress to early infancy. There are at least two explanations of these weird results: the subjects may have realized what response the experimenters were looking for and may have voluntarily performed that response (Barber, 1962a; Sarbin, 1956); or, since the Babinski toe response is at times observed during profound relaxation, the subjects may have become very relaxed when they assumed the "sleeping posture of the infant" (Barber, 1970a, Ch. 6).

True (1949) reported that most adult subjects who were placed in hypnotic trance, and who were given suggestions to regress to ages 11, 7, and 4, recalled the exact day of the week on which their birthday and Christmas fell in the particular year involved. Six subsequent studies failed to confirm these results (Barber, 1961a; Best & Michaels, 1954; S. Fisher, 1962; Leonard, 1963; Mesel & Ledford, 1959; Reiff & Scheerer, 1959). However, in a series of attempts I made to validate True's results, one "hypnotic trance" subject, who received suggestions to regress to *each* of her previous birthdays, correctly named the day of the week on which *each* of her previous birthdays fell. After the hypnotic trance session, the subject testified that she was able to perform this remarkable feat simply because she knew that the days of the week go backward one day each year and two on leap years and, knowing the day of the week on which her birthday fell in a recent year, she could easily and quickly (within 20 seconds) figure out the day of the week it must have fallen in an earlier year (compare Sutcliffe, 1960; Yates, 1960). In brief, although True's study seemed to support the contention that the "hypnotic trance state" gives rise to nearly miraculous feats of memory, subsequent studies strongly suggest that "hypnotic trance" is irrelevant in performing this feat and that the relevant factor is prior knowledge of the fact that the days of the week go backward one day each year and two on leap years.

Parrish, Lundy, and Leibowitz (1969) reported that highly suggestible subjects, who were exposed to a trance induction procedure and given suggestions to regress to ages nine and five, were affected by two optical illusions (the Ponzo and Poggendorff illusions) in a similar manner as children who are actually nine and five years of age. Since there is no reason to believe that adults can figure out how children are affected by these complex illusions, the results presented by Parrish et al. could be interpreted as indicating that the highly suggestible subjects were in an unusual state (hypnotic trance) when they manifested such an unusual effect.

However, the results of the study could not be confirmed in two subsequent investigations. Ascher and Barber (1968) closely replicated the experimental procedures used by Parrish et al., that is, subjects who were highly responsive to test suggestions were exposed to a trance induction procedure and were given suggestions that they were nine and five years of age. Under the regressed condition, the subjects' performance on the Ponzo and Poggendorff illusions was virtually the same as their adult performance and not at all similar to the performance of children who are actually nine and five. Spanos and Barber (1969) also replicated the experimental procedures of Parrish, Lundy, and Leibowitz, but used only exceptionally suggestible subjects who had previously passed a large number of very difficult test suggestions. When placed in "hypnotic trance" and given suggestions to regress to ages nine and five, these exceptionally responsive subjects performed on the Ponzo and Poggendorff illusions in practically the same manner as their adult performance and their performance did not remotely resemble that of children of ages nine and five.

In brief, the traditional (special state) paradigm seemed to be supported by several studies that reported very amazing effects produced in "hypnotic trance" subjects by suggestions to regress to an earlier chronological age. However, a close look at the data fails to support the traditional paradigm. The notion of a special state is also not supported by the following considerations pertaining to suggested regression:

1. Practically all investigations in this area found that "hypnotic trance" subjects who were given suggestions to regress to a specified age performed at a level superior to the level actually found at the specified age; for example, when regressed to age six, "hypnotic trance" subjects typically performed at a nine-year-old level (Barber, 1969b, Ch. 11).

2. "Hypnotic trance" subjects who tend to act in a childlike way when given suggestions to regress to childhood also give an equally convincing portrayal of an older person or of a senile individual when given suggestions to progress to the age of 70, 80, or 90 (Kline, 1951; Rubenstein & Newman, 1954). Also, some "hypnotic trance" subjects who tend to give a childlike performance when regressed to childhood also give a convincing performance when regressed to prenatal life in the womb or to a time that preceded their present life (the "Bridey Murphy" phenomenon) (Bernstein, 1956; Kelsey, 1953).

3. When subjects who have been randomly assigned to an "awake" group or to a "trance" group are given suggestions to go back or to regress to an

earlier chronological age, the same proportion of subjects in both groups report that they imagined, felt, or believed that they had returned to the earlier age (Barber & Calverley, 1966a).

4. Although various theoretical formulations might possibly account for the foregoing data, one formulation that can parsimoniously explain the results is as follows: When it is suggested to "hypnotic trance" subjects or to "awake" subjects that they are in the past (or in the future), (a) some "hypnotic trance" subjects and also some "awake" subjects try to the best of their ability to think about continuously and to imagine vividly that they are in the past (or in the future), (b) some of the "hypnotic trance" subjects and also some of the "awake" subjects succeed in focusing imaginatively on the past (or future), and (c) when thinking about and vividly imagining themselves in an earlier time (or in a future time), some subjects in both groups feel as if they are in the past (or in the future) and trend to behave to a certain limited degree as if they are in the past (or future).

Hallucinations

Two studies (Brady & Levitt, 1966; Underwood, 1960) indicate that highly suggestible subjects, who were first exposed to a trance induction procedure and then given suggestions to hallucinate, behaved as if they actually perceived the suggested (hallucinated) object. These data were interpreted as lending support to the notion that the subjects must have been in a unique state (hypnotic trance) in order to manifest such unique behavior. However, a closer look at the data does not support the special state notion.

Brady and Levitt (1966) attempted to ascertain whether a suggested visual hallucination of an optokinetic drum (a revolving drum with alternate black and white vertical stripes) gives rise to involuntary nystagmoidlike eye movements that resemble those found when an individual actually perceives an optokinetic drum. When highly suggestible subjects were exposed to a trance induction procedure and given suggestions to hallucinate the optokinetic drum, a small percentage behaved as if they were actually perceiving the drum—manifesting nystagmoidlike eye movements. However, a subsequent study by Hahn and Barber (1966) showed that an equally small percentage of unselected subjects under a waking control condition manifested nystagmoidlike eye movements when they were simply instructed to imagine vividly the optokinetic drum. Also, Reich (1970) recently presented data indicating that some subjects are able to produce nystagmus "through conscious, voluntary effort while awake."

To ascertain whether suggested visual hallucinations produce objective consequences that resemble those produced by actual visual stimulation, Underwood (1960) used two optical illusions in which a series of lines distorts a geometric figure. The subjects were shown the geometric figures without the distorting lines and were given suggestions to hallucinate the lines. Underwood found that when given the suggestions to hallucinate the lines, a small percentage of selected "hypnotic trance" subjects reported a few effects that tended to resemble those actually produced by the optical illusions. However, Sarbin and Andersen (1963) found that an equally small percentage of unselected waking control subjects reported the same effects when they were simply instructed to imagine the lines vividly.

In brief, suggestions to hallucinate an object, given to subjects who are said to be in hypnotic trance, at times gives rise to some objective effects that tend to resemble those found when a person actually perceives the object. However, the same objective effects are produced when waking subjects are simply asked to imagine the object vividly.

Suggested deafness

Erickson (1938a, 1938b) concluded from experimental studies that a condition indistinguishable from actual deafness can be produced by suggestions, provided that the suggestions are given to highly responsive subjects who have been exposed to a trance induction procedure. Erickson's data seemed to support the traditional notion of a special state (hypnotic trance); that is, it appeared that in order to manifest such a special or unique effect (deafness produced by suggestions), the subjects must have been in a special state. Let us look at the data presented by Erickson.

Erickson (1938a) administered suggestions of total deafness to 30 subjects who were preselected as highly suggestible and who had been exposed to a trance induction procedure. Of the 30 subjects, 24 (80 per cent) did not show signs of deafness. However, Erickson judged the remaining six subjects to have become deaf as indicated by such signs as "failure to show any response to deliberately embarrassing remarks," "failure to raise voice when reading aloud while an irrelevant continuous extraneous noise becomes increasingly disturbing," and failure to react to unexpected sounds. Erickson concluded from these and similar data that "there was produced a condition not distinguishable from neurological deafness by any of the ordinarily competent tests employed" (p. 149).

Erickson's conclusion is not clearly supported by his data. For instance, failure to react to unexpected sounds does not demonstrate that the sounds were not heard. In a study carried out by Dynes (1932), three selected suggestible subjects, who were judged to be in hypnotic trance and who received suggestions of deafness, did not become noticeably startled when a pistol was fired unexpectedly; however, each subject testified postexperimentally that he had heard the pistol shot. Similarly, lack of response to a disturbing noise or to embarrassing remarks does not demonstrate that the subject is deaf, since these responses can be rather easily inhibited voluntarily.

In a supplementary study, Erickson (1938b) found that two of the "hypnotic trance" subjects who appeared to be deaf did not manifest a handwithdrawal response that had been conditioned to a sound. He interpreted this outcome as demonstrating that the subjects were "unconscious of the sound." The interpretation is not valid; many studies have demonstrated that subjects can voluntarily inhibit hand-withdrawal responses that have been conditioned to a sound (Hamel, 1919; Hilgard & Marquis, 1940, pp. 269–70).

In five more recent studies, the technique of delayed auditory feedback was used to evaluate suggested deafness produced under "hypnotic trance" (Barber & Calverley, 1964c; Kline, Guze, & Haggerty, 1954; Kramer & Tucker, 1967; Scheibe, Gray, & Keim, 1968; Sutcliffe, 1961). Each of the five experiments showed that "hypnotic trance" subjects who have received suggestions of deafness are affected by auditory stimuli in essentially the same way as any normal person who hears perfectly well; that is, when exposed to delayed auditory feedback, the "hypnotic deaf" subject and the person with normal hearing (but not the person who is actually deaf) typically stutters, mispronounces words, and speaks more loudly and more slowly. One of these studies (Barber & Calverley, 1964c) also showed that suggestions of deafness are at least as effective with "waking" control subjects as with "hypnotic trance" subjects in eliciting subjective reports of deafness; however, both the "waking" control subjects and the "hypnotic trance" subjects who accepted the suggestions of deafness responded to the delayed auditory feedback in the same way as individuals who hear normally.

Although both "hypnotic trance" subjects and "waking" control subjects who have received suggestions of deafness may be trying not to hear, they simply do not succeed in blocking out sounds. The fact that the subjects can hear is often obvious. After suggesting deafness to "hypnotic trance" subjects, the hypnotist may ask, "Can you hear me?" A few subjects reply, "No, I can't," thus admitting that they can hear. The other subjects, however, do not reply and appear to be deaf. How does the hypnotist remove the deafness? He typically states, "Now you can hear again," and since the subjects now respond normally it is obvious that they could hear all along.

OBSERVABLE TRANCELIKE CHARACTERISTICS

The special state paradigm also seems to be supported by the fact that a substantial proportion of subjects who are highly responsive to test suggestions actually appear to be in a trance. Numerous investigators (Erickson, Hershman, & Secter, 1961, pp. 55–58; Gill & Brenman, 1959, pp. 38–39; Pattie, 1956a, p. 21; Weitzenhoffer, 1957a, pp. 211–12) have pointed out that subjects who are highly responsive to test suggestions often show signs of trance such as a blank stare, a rigid facial expression, a lack of spontaneity, a limp posture, psychomotor retardation, disinclination to talk, lack of humor, and literal-mindedness. Although these observations, at first glance, seem to support the assumption that a special state (hypnotic trance) underlies high responsiveness to test suggestions, a closer look at the data fails to support the assumption:

1. When subjects who are highly responsive to test suggestions manifest trancelike characteristics, the characteristics have been explicitly or implicitly suggested. That is, the experimenter has suggested to the subject that he is becoming relaxed, drowsy, sleepy, and is entering a hypnotic trance state. These suggestions imply to subjects that they should become passive or lethargic, behave in a trancelike manner, move or respond slowly (show psychomotor retardation), and not look actively around the room (Barber & Calverley, 1969b).

2. Since the trancelike characteristics have been suggested, they can also be removed by suggestions. For instance, several years ago, I carried out the following informal study with eight suggestible subjects. The subjects were first exposed to a trance induction procedure, comprised of repeated suggestions of relaxation, drowsiness, sleep, and deep hypnosis. All subjects appeared to be in a hypnotic trance—manifesting a lack of spontaneity, psychomotor retardation, and passivity or lethargy—and also responded to test suggestions for arm heaviness, arm levitation, inability to unclasp hands, and thirst hallucination. Next, the subjects were told to become awake and alert, to stop acting as if they were in a hypnotic trance, but to continue to remain responsive to test suggestions. The subjects remained highly responsive to test suggestions for inability to say their name, body immobility, and selective amnesia, but they no longer showed signs of trance; in fact, they appeared to be just as awake as subjects who were not responsive to test suggestions.

3. Some subjects who have been exposed to a trance induction procedure manifest a high level of responsiveness to test suggestions but they do not show signs or characteristics of hypnotic trance (Erickson, 1962).

4. Some subjects who have been exposed to a trance induction procedure and who show signs of hypnotic trance are not responsive to test suggestions for analgesia, age regression, amnesia, and so on (Barber, 1957, 1963; Barber & Calverley, 1969b).

5. As pointed out previously in this chapter, some subjects who have not been exposed to a trance induction procedure manifest a high level of response to test suggestions without showing signs of hypnotic trance (Barber, 1969b; Klopp, 1961). Stated otherwise, when no attempt is made to induce a hypnotic trance, and especially when subjects are not asked to close their eyes, a substantial proportion of subjects experience such suggested effects as limb rigidity, analgesia, age regression, hallucination, amnesia and so on, without manifesting signs of hypnotic trance such as blank stare, rigid facial expression, and passivity.

In brief, trancelike characteristics on the part of the subject appear to be artifacts that the experimenter can put into the suggestive situation and can also take out of the situation, and they certaintly are not necessary (and may be extraneous) for high response to test suggestions.

SUBJECTS' TESTIMONY OF BEING IN HYPNOTIC TRANCE

At first glance, the traditional viewpoint seems to be supported by the fact that some subjects who are highly responsive to test suggestions testify that they are hypnotized or are in a hypnotic trance. A close look at subjects' testimony, however, fails to support the traditional notion that a state discontinuous with ordinary states of consciousness underlies high responsiveness to test suggestion for limb rigidity, analgesia, hallucination, and so on:

1. As stated previously in this chapter, some subjects manifest a high level or response to test suggestion when no attempt is made to hypnotize them. With few exceptions, these highly responsive subjects testify that they are *not* in a hypnotic trance. The remaining few testify that they must be hypnotized, even though they do not feel that they are hypnotized, because they actually experience those things that are suggested. These subjects are not using the term "hypnotized" to refer to a state that is basically different from ordinary states of consciousness; they are using the term "hypnotized" synonymously with the phrase "high responsiveness to suggestions."

2. A substantial proportion of subjects who are given suggestions to enter a hypnotic trance state and who are highly responsive to test suggestions state that they are not sure if they are hypnotized. The proportion of highly responsive subjects unable to state whether they are in a hypnotic trance varies from 25 per cent to 67 per cent depending on the wording of the questions submitted to them in order to elicit their statements (Barber, Dalal, & Calverley, 1968; Hilgard, 1965b, p. 12).

3. As implied in the preceding paragraph, subjects' testimony pertaining to whether they think they are in hypnotic trance depends, in part, on the wording and tone of the questions that are used to elicit their testimony (Barber, Dalal, & Calverley, 1968).

4. Subjects' testimony pertaining to whether they are in hypnotic trance depends, in part, on their preconceptions of what hypnotic trance is supposed to be. Subjects differing in preconceptions give different testimony even when they are equally responsive to test suggestions. For instance, one highly responsive subject believes hypnotic trance is a state of relaxation, whereas another highly responsive subject believes that a hypnotized person experiences spontaneous amnesia. When both of these highly responsive subjects become relaxed during the session and both fail to experience spontaneous amnesia, the former testifies that he was hypnotized or was in a hypnotic trance, whereas the latter testifies that he was not in a hypnotic trance.

5. Subjects' testimony pertaining to whether they are hypnotized is also dependent, in part, on subtle situational variables such as whether the exper-

imenter states or implies that he believes they are hypnotized (Barber, Dalal, & Calverley, 1968).

6. Subjects who state that they are in a hypnotic trance are not necessarily saying that they are in a state that is clearly different from ordinary states of consciousness. On the contrary, they often appear to be saying no more and no less than that they are ready and willing to respond to test suggestions. Gill and Brenman (1959) have documented this important point:

> First, we would induce hypnosis in someone previously established as a "good" subject; then we would ask him how he knew he was in hypnosis. He might reply that he felt relaxed. Now we would suggest that the relaxation would disappear *but he would remain in hypnosis*. Then we would ask again how he knew he was in hypnosis. He might say because his arm "feels numb"—so again, we would suggest the disappearance of this sensation. We continued in this way until finally we obtained the reply, "I know I am in hypnosis because I *know* I will do what you tell me." This was repeated with several subjects, with the same results. (P. 36)

The subject's final assertion—"I *know* I will do what you tell me"—does *not* support the traditional paradigm, which assumes that the subject who shows high response to test suggestions is in a state fundamentally different from the waking state. However, it is in line with and can be deduced from the alternative paradigm, which views the subject who is highly responsive to test suggestions as being as awake and as normal as the member of the audience who is ready and willing to have a wide variety of experiences as he listens to the communications from the stage.

DIFFICULTY OR DELAY IN "COMING OUT OF HYPNOTIC TRANCE"

At first glance, the special state (hypnotic trance) paradigm also seems to be supported by the following two sets of interrelated data. On rare occasions, subjects who are highly responsive to test suggestions do not open their eyes immediately when told to wake up—they seem to remain in a hypnotic trance. When the experimenter leaves the room without having told the subject to wake up, subjects who are said to be in a hypnotic trance remain sitting passively with eyes closed for a longer period of time than simulating subjects who have been asked to act as if they are in a hypnotic trance. Let us look at these two sets of data in turn.

Refusing to "wake up"

When told that the experiment is over, practically all subjects who have been exposed to a trance induction procedure open their eyes and converse normally (Kroger, 1970, p. 172). However, in very rare instances, subjects who have been exposed to a trance induction procedure do not open their eyes when told to wake up. They remain sitting passively with eyes closed and it appears, from the traditional special state viewpoint, that they are having difficulty making the transition from the hypnotic trance state to the waking state. The empirical evidence, however, does not support the special state viewpoint. Williams (1953) and Weitzenhoffer (1957a, pp. 226–29) have summarized data that cogently indicate that these few subjects (who do not open their eyes when told to wake up) have some special reason or motive for refusing to open their eyes; they either (a) have been given a suggestion to carry out postexperimentally that they do not want to carry out, (b) are deliberately resisting the hypnotist, (c) are testing the hypnotist's ability to control them, (d) are manifesting spite toward the hypnotist, or (e) are attempting to frighten the hypnotist by refusing to "wake up."

If a "hypnotic trance" subject does not open his eyes when told to wake up, Weitzenhoffer (1957a) recommends the following: "The simplest way of proceeding is to ask him why he does not wake up. Most subjects are quite willing to explain why. If the subject is uncooperative you may have to request an answer more forcefully. Usually the answer tells the hypnotist what to do." Weitzenhoffer adds that if the subject remains intractable, you "simply say to him, in a final tone, 'Very well then, if you will not wake up I will just have to leave you as you are.' You then ignore the subject entirely and go on to other things" (p. 228). Since the subject now cannot accomplish his purpose by remaining passive with his eyes closed, he soon opens his eyes.

Remaining in hypnotic trance when the experimenter leaves the room

Orne and Evans (1966) and Evans (1966a) contended that it is possible to test the hypothesis that a trance induction procedure leads to a qualitative change in the organism in highly suggestible subjects. They reasoned as follows: If the highly suggestible subject actually enters a special state (a hypnotic trance) when he is exposed to a trance induction procedure, and if the hypnotist leaves the room without telling the subject to awaken, then the subject should slowly bring himself out of the special state. An active effort would be required for the subject to initiate the volitional act of arousal and, consequently, the voluntary termination of the hypnotic trance would not be immediate—it would subsume a period of time.

Two experiments were conducted with the aim of testing this hypothesis (Orne & Evans, 1966; Evans, 1966a). Both experiments utilized two groups of pretested subjects. Subjects in one group were highly responsive to test suggestions (suggestible subjects) and those in the other group were very unresponsive (nonsuggestible subjects). Prior to the formal experiments, the nonsuggestible subjects were told, by a person other than the experimeter, to try to simulate hypnosis—that is, they were told to try to fool the experimenter by faking or acting as if they entered a hypnotic trance. The suggestible subjects were not told to simulate and thus were categorized as real hypnotic subjects. During the experimental sessions, both the suggestible (real) and the nonsuggestible (simulating) subjects received a trance induction procedure by means of a tape recording. The suggestible (real) subjects presumably entered a hypnotic trance state and the nonsuggestible (simulating) subjects presumably did not enter a hypnotic trance state even though they acted as if they had entered such a state. In the middle of the experimental session, a switch was purposively thrown in another room, thus stopping the tape recording with a marked slur. The experimenter then left the room, ostensibly to repair the fuse that had stopped the tape recording. Both the real subjects and the simulating subjects were then observed to determine how long they would remain sitting quietly with eyes closed.

In both the first and second experiments, the real hypnotic subjects, who were presumably in a hypnotic trance state, did not open their eyes immediately; they remained sitting quietly with eyes closed for quite some time after the experimenter had left the room. In the first experiment, the simulating subjects also remained sitting quietly with eyes closed; in fact, they did not open their eyes at all until the experimenter again entered the room about one-half hour later. In the second experiment, the simulators opened their eyes soon after the experimenter left the room. The inconsistent behavior of the simulators in the first and second experiment was due to the following: In the first experiment there was a conspicious one-way mirror in the room and the subjects knew that they were being observed. In the second experiment, the one-way mirror was completely blocked by a blackboard and the subjects believed that they were not being observed. (They were observed, however, through a peep hole that they were not aware of.) Since, in both experiments, the real hypnotic subjects, who were presumably in a hypnotic trance state, did not open their eyes for quite some time after the experimenter left the room, whereas the simulators opened their eyes when they believed they were not being observed but did not open their eyes when they believed they were being observed, Evans (1966a) concluded that the experiments had demonstrated that the highly suggestible (real) subjects were actually in a special state of consciousness (hypnotic trance).

Evans's (1966a) conclusion, of course, does not clearly follow from the data he presented. The experiments are open to another interpretation, namely, that the differences between the two groups were due to the fact that subjects in one of the groups (but not the other) had been instructed to try to fool the experimenter and to make him believe that they were hypnotized. When subjects are instructed to try to fool the experimenter into believing they are hypnotized, it can be expected that, after the experimenter leaves the room, they will act as if they are hypnotized if they believe they are being observed by the experimenter or by his surrogates, and they will not act as if they are hypnotized if they believe they are not being observed. The appropriate comparison is not between subjects who are asked to fool the experimenter and those who are not asked to fool the experimenter. The appropriate comparison is between a group of suggestible subjects who are exposed to a trance induction procedure and who are presumably in a hypnotic trance state, and a group of control subjects who are simply told to relax. It can be hypothesized, from the viewpoint that does not postulate a special state, that control subjects who are simply told to relax will remain sitting quietly with eyes closed as long as the subjects who are presumably in a hypnotic trance. This hypothesis has been tested experimentally by Dorcus, Brintnall, and Case (1941). Let us now look at their experiment.

The experimental group was comprised of 20 subjects who had previously demonstrated that they were highly responsive to test suggestions. After these subjects had been exposed to a trance induction procedure, an assistant came into the room and said to the experimenter, "You are wanted on the telephone about an appointment downtown." The experimenter replied to the assistant that he had forgotten an appointment and that he would be gone for the remainder of the day. Both the experimenter and the assistant then left the room hastily. The subject was then kept under observation through a peep hole in an adjacent room. Twenty-five subjects in a control group were asked to simply close their eyes and relax and then were told that, after a few minutes of relaxation, they would be given further instructions. During the period of relaxation, the same conversation about the appointment was carried out. After the experimenter left the room, the suggestible subjects, who had been exposed to the trance induction procedure and who were presumably in a hypnotic trance state, remained passive with eyes closed for a mean time of 28 minutes. The control group, which had been simply told to relax, remained passive with eyes closed for an insignificantly shorter average period of 23 minutes.[6] Postexperimental interviews showed that the behavior of both the "hypnotic trance" subjects and the "relaxation control" subjects was influenced by the same factors; that is, some subjects in both groups thought they should wait for the experimenter to return, others thought the experiment was over, and others had to leave because they had previous appointments. Clearly, this study does not support the contention that suggestible subjects who have been exposed to a trance induction procedure have entered a special state that is qualitatively different from the ordinary state of consciousness present when people relax.

The foregoing experiments by Orne and Evans (1966), Evans (1966a), and Dorcus, Brintnall, and Case (1941) indicate that subjects who are asked to simulate hypnosis may perform differently from "hypnotic trance" subjects and also from control subjects (who are not asked to simulate), and that control subjects may behave in the same way as "hypnotic trance"

---

6. It should be noted that in the Dorcus et al. experiment, both the "hypnotic trance" subjects and the "relaxation control" subjects remained passive with eyes closed about as long as the real hypnotic subjects in the Evans (1966) experiment.

subjects. These results suggest extreme caution in interpreting studies that compared simulating subjects with "real hypnotic subjects." The simulators are in a special situation—they are trying to fool the experimenter. Also, when given their original instructions, the simulators are told not to let themselves experience any of the suggested effects. Consequently, if a control group is not used, differences in performance between simulators and hypnotic subjects can be easily misinterpreted as indicating that the hypnotic subjects behaved unusually, when it was actually the simulators who behaved unusually. Other studies that found differences in the performance of simulating subjects and real hypnotic subjects, such as in the performance of posthypnotic behavior outside of the experimental setting (Orne, Sheehan, & Evans, 1968; Sheehan & Orne, 1968) and in the performance of "source amnesia" (Evans, 1968, p. 483), need to be redone with the addition of a control group that is not asked to simulate.

SPONTANEOUS AMNESIA

Individuals usually have spontaneous amnesia for the events that occurred when they were in a special state of consciousness. For instance, upon awakening, individuals usually forget the dreams and other events that occurred when they were in the special state of sleep. With these considerations in mind, the traditional (special state) paradigm seems to be supported by the fact that, after "awakening," some highly suggestible subjects state spontaneously that they have forgotten what occurred during "hypnotic trance." However, a close look at the data fails to support the special state paradigm:

1. A rather large number of subjects have been assessed on response to test suggestions for limb rigidity, analgesia, age regression, etc., without receiving either suggestions for relaxation, drowsiness, and sleep, or suggestions to forget what occurred. To the best of my knowledge, no subject has ever manifested spontaneous amnesia under these conditions. It thus appears that all subjects, including those highly responsive to test suggestions, remember the events perfectly well if they are not exposed to a trance induction procedure and are not told to forget (Barber & Calverley, 1966b). Stated otherwise, high responsiveness to test suggestions is not necessarily associated with spontaneous amnesia.

2. No subject has ever forgotten the events occurring during the time he was highly responsive to test suggestions (or, in the traditional terminology, was in a hypnotic trance) if told during the session that he was expected to remember the events (Barber, 1962b; Orne, 1966a; Watkins, 1966).

3. If not told explicitly to forget, almost all subjects, including those who have been exposed to repeated suggestions of relaxation, drowsiness, and sleep, remember the events perfectly well. In other words, if amnesia is not explicitly suggested, very few subjects who are highly responsive to test

suggestions (or who are judged from the traditional viewpoint to be in a hypnotic trance) manifest spontaneous amnesia (Barber & Calverley, 1966b; Hilgard, 1966).

4. When a trance induction procedure is administered but subjects are not told explicitly to forget what occurred, a very small number of subjects manifest apparent spontaneous amnesia. However, this apparent spontaneous amnesia can almost always be readily removed if the experimenter suggests or insists that the subject can remember. Furthermore, there are at least three reasons (specified in the following three paragraphs) why it is seriously questionable that the apparent amnesia in these rare cases is actually spontaneous (nonsuggested).

5. These rare subjects, who seem to manifest amnesia spontaneously, have received repeated suggestions of drowsiness and sleep. Since the subjects know that people usually forget the dreams and other events that occur during sleep, the direct suggestion to sleep may include the indirect suggestion to forget the events occurring during "sleep." In other words, the apparent amnesia in these instances may not be spontaneous but may be due to implicit suggestions for amnesia conveyed by the explicit suggestions to sleep.

6. In some of these infrequent cases of apparent spontaneous amnesia, the subjects received suggestions to sleep and suggestions for amnesia in a previous session, and may have generalized or extrapolated the suggestions to apply to the present session.

7. Subjects who manifest apparent spontaneous amnesia have received suggestions to enter a "hypnotic trance state." Since subjects generally believe that a hypnotic trance state is followed by spontaneous amnesia (Dorcus, Brintall, & Case, 1941; London, 1961), they may say that they have forgotten in order to be good subjects and to meet what they believe are the expectations of the hypnotist.

To recapitulate, several compelling considerations indicate that the rare occurrence of apparent spontaneous amnesia that follows a trance induction procedure may not be spontaneous but, instead, may have been either explicitly or implicitly suggested in the present session or in a previous one. Even if some of these instances of apparent amnesia were actually spontaneous (nonsuggested), they would not clearly support the notion that a special state underlies high responsiveness to test suggestions because when amnesia is not suggested, almost all subjects highly responsive to test suggestions and judged by traditional investigators to be in a hypnotic trance state assert after the session that they remember everything that occurred.

"TRANCE LOGIC"

Orne (1959) presented the following data from an informally conducted study: Subjects who were highly responsive to test suggestions and who were exposed to a trance induction procedure stated that (a) they could see a suggested (hallucinated) person in a chair and, at the same time, they could see the back of the chair through the (hallucinated) person, and (b) they could see the suggested (hallucinated) coexperimenter in the chair and, at the same time, they could see the (actual) coexperimenter in another part of the room (that is, they could "see" two images of the coexperimenter). Orne also stated that nonsuggestible subjects instructed to fool the experimenter into thinking that they were hypnotized (simulators) did not give these types of reports; for instance, although the simulators reported that they could see the suggested (hallucinated) coexperimenter in the chair, they refused to see the (actual) coexperimenter in another part of the room or they claimed that they could not recognize him. Orne (1959) concluded from these informal observations that the highly suggestible subjects who were exposed to a trance induction procedure and who were presumably in a hypnotic trance state manifested a special type of logic, "trance logic," defined as the "simultaneous perception and response to both hallucinations and reality without any apparent attempts to satisfy a need for logical consistency" (p. 295). Orne also concluded that trance logic was part of the essence of hypnosis.

At first glance, it appears that Orne's data support the special state paradigm; that is, since the highly suggestible subjects who had been exposed to a trance induction procedure manifested a special type of logic, they most likely were in a special state. However, since Orne derived his data from informal observations (not from a structured experiment), the "trance logic" contention can be viewed as suggesting a hypothesis that needs to be confirmed experimentally.

Johnson, Maher, and Barber (in press) carried out two experiments to test Orne's "trance logic" hypothesis. In the first experiment, 70 subjects were pretested on response to test suggestions. Following the pretest, 10 subjects, who had shown high response to test suggestions, were given additional "hypnotic training." They received practice in responding to a wide variety of difficult test suggestions. These 10 "trained" subjects were exposed to a trance induction procedure in the experimental session. The remaining 60 subjects were subdivided into high and low responders to test suggestions, and then equal numbers of high and low responders were randomly assigned to the following three groups with 20 subjects to each group: a group that was exposed to a trance induction procedure in the experimental session, a group of simulators who were first asked to fool the experimenter by acting as if they were hypnotized and then were exposed to a trance induction procedure, and a control group that was simply asked to imagine the various suggested effects.

All subjects were tested for "trance logic" according to the two criteria specified by Orne (1959). By the first criterion, trance logic is considered to be present if the subject states that he sees the suggested (hallucinated) person in the chair and, at the same time, sees the back of the chair through the

158 THEODORE XENOPHON BARBER

hallucinated person. By this criterion, trance logic occurred equally often among the control subjects, the trained hypnotic subjects, and the untrained hypnotic subjects. The second criterion for trance logic refers to the subjects seeing both the hallucinated coexperimenter sitting in the chair and also the actual coexperimenter in another part of the room. By this criterion trance logic was found to occur equally often among all groups (controls, simulators, trained hypnotic subjects, and untrained hypnotic subjects). Also, in each of the three groups, the high suggestible subjects did not differ from the low suggestible on either criterion of trance logic.

The second experiment included two groups of subjects. One group was selected from a large population as the most responsive to test suggestions. These very suggestible subjects were exposed to a trance induction procedure during the experimental session (real hypnotic subjects). The second group also included only very suggestible subjects; this group was first asked to simulate hypnosis and then was exposed to a trance induction procedure (simulators). Trance logic was assessed in both groups, using the criteria specified by Orne (1959). With respect to the first criterion, 60 per cent of the real hypnotic subjects and 50 per cent of the simulators exhibited trance logic. With respect to the second criterion, 60 per cent of the real hypnotic subjects and 67 per cent of the simulators exhibited trance logic.

In brief, the experiments by Johnson, Maher, and Barber (in press) demonstrated that trance logic is *not* unique to subjects who are highly responsive to test suggestions and who have received a trance induction procedure. Not only is "trance logic" not a characteristic of the presumed "hypnotic trance state," but it is also not found to a greater degree in "hypnotic trance" subjects than in simulating subjects, in "hypnotic trance" subjects than in control subjects, in highly suggestible subjects than in nonsuggestible subjects, or in subjects who are "trained in hypnosis" as opposed to those who are not trained. Johnson, Maher, & Barber concluded that "Since trance logic was not found to be a discriminating characteristic of hypnotic subjects, investigators who seek the essence of hypnosis must now search elsewhere—that is, if there is an 'essence.' "

The Search for a Physiological Index of the Presumed "Hypnotic Trance State"

Since the organism is a psychophysiological unity, special states of consciousness or special states of the organism are expected to have some physiological concomitants that distinguish them from nonspecial states. Investigators who adhere to the traditional paradigm have been trying for many years to find a physiological concomitant or index of the presumed special state that they call "hypnotic trance." Not only have they failed to find any special physiological changes associated with the presumed special state, but they have also consistently found that physiological functioning during the postulated special state varies in the same way as in nonspecial or ordinary states. The relevant data are as follows:

1. Electroencephalographic (EEG) criteria indicate that subjects who are highly responsive to test suggestions (and who are judged by traditionalists as being in a hypnotic trance) do not show any special patterns on the EEG that might distinguish them from subjects who are relatively unresponsive to test suggestions (Barber, 1961b; Chertok & Kramarz, 1959). Similarly, subjects said to be in a hypnotic trance do not show special changes on any other known physiological measure that might serve as an index of the presumed special state.

2. The EEG of the person who is responding to test suggestions varies continually with the instructions or suggestions he is given and with the activities he is asked to perform (Barber, 1961b; Chertok & Kramarz, 1959). Similarly, other physiological measures vary continually when subjects are responding to test suggestions. Subjects who are said to be in hypnotic trance show continually varying (high, medium, or low) skin conductance, basal metabolic rate, heart rate, blood pressure, respiration, peripheral blood flow, blood clotting time, oral temperature, and so forth (Barber, 1961b; Cogger & Edmonston, in press; Crasilneck & Hall, 1959; Levitt & Brady, 1963; Timney & Barber, 1969). There is no need to postulate a special state of consciousness to account for these continual variations in physiological functions that are found in subjects responding to test suggestions (or said to be in hypnotic trance). Physiological variables vary in hypnotic subjects in the same way as in normal individuals, that is, in accordance with whatever activity they are engaged in. Normal individuals tend to show a high level of skin conductance, basal metabolic rate, heart rate, blood pressure, and so forth, when they are active or aroused, and a low level when they are relaxed or passive. In the same way as any other normal individual, the subject who is highly responsive to test suggestions (and said to be in a hypnotic trance) shows a high level of skin conductance, basal metabolic rate, heart rate, and so forth, when he is given suggestions that lead to activity or arousal, and a lower level when he is given suggestions leading to quietude or relaxation. Similarly, if a normal individual is not anxious about a painful stimulus, he will tend to show a small change in skin conductance when he is exposed to the stimulus; and, if a normal individual is anxious about a painful stimulus, he will tend to show a larger change in skin conductance. In the same way, the subject who is responsive to suggestions intended to reduce his experience of pain will show a small rise in skin conductance when he is exposed to the noxious stimulus, and the subject who is unresponsive to the suggestions for reduced pain reactivity will show a larger rise in conductance (Barber & Hahn, 1962).

"Hypnotic Trance" as a Misnomer
for a Responsive Waking State

Some present-day investigators who use the traditional term "hypnotic trance" (or "hypnosis" or "hypnotic state") do *not* seem to mean that the subject is in a special state basically different from ordinary waking states. On the contrary, by the term "hypnotic trance" they seem to refer to a person who is as awake and as normal as you or I and who is as ready to respond to test suggestions as I am while I write these lines and as some readers are as they read these lines. (If, as I write these lines, an experimenter entered the room and wished to assess my response to test suggestions, I would have positive attitudes, motivations, and expectancies toward the test situation and I would be ready, willing, and able to respond to the test suggestions and to experience the suggested effects. Some readers of these lines would be just as ready as I am to respond to the test suggestions.) To illustrate these contentions, let us look at how the term "hypnotic trance" is used by Erickson (1967a), who has written extensively on this topic:

1. Erickson often judges subjects to be in a hypnotic trance when, from all indications, they are in a waking state. For instance, he writes: "In the well-trained subject, the [deep hypnotic trance] is that type of trance in which the subject is seemingly awake and functioning adequately, freely, and well in the total hypnotic situation, in a manner similar to that of a non-hypnotized person operating at the waking level" (1967a, p. 13).

2. Erickson notes that psychologists, psychiatrists, and experienced hypnotists often view his hypnotic trance subjects as being in the waking state. For instance, he offers the following illustrative example: "the author, as a teaching device for the audience, had a subject in a profound somnambulistic trance conduct a lecture and demonstration of hypnosis (unaided by the author) before a group of psychiatrists and psychologists. Although many in the audience had had experience with hypnosis, none detected that she was in a trance" (1967a, p. 14).

3. Erickson's subjects disagree with his judgment. For instance, in a study with 48 subjects presented by Secter (1960), Erickson judged how many subjects had entered light, medium, or deep hypnotic trance and how many did not enter trance. Each of the 48 subjects also rated himself as having attained one of the four levels. By chance, Erickson and the subjects should agree 25 per cent of the time. The actual percentage of agreement was 29 per cent, which did not significantly exceed chance expectations.

In brief, when Erickson states that a subject is in a hypnotic trance, the subject often appears to be normally awake and is often judged by other investigators as being awake. Furthermore, Erickson's subjects do not agree with his judgment that they are not in a hypnotic trance or are in a light, medium, or deep trance. It appears that when Erickson judges one of his subjects to be in a hypnotic trance, he does not mean that the subject is not awake or that the subject is in a trance in the traditional sense of the term. What then does the term "hypnotic trance" mean in Erickson's work? A close reading of his papers provides the following answer: Whenever Erickson states that a subject was in a hypnotic trance, he almost always states on the same page that the subject was highly responsive to test suggestions. In fact, it appears that quite often Erickson first observes that the subject is very responsive to test suggestions and then infers that, since he is responsive to test suggestions, he must be in a hypnotic trance. The term "hypnotic trance," as used by Erickson, appears to refer to high responsiveness to test suggestions.

When pushed to specify what he means by the term "hypnotic trance" (or "hypnosis" or "hypnotized"), Erickson states that he is referring to "a state of intensified attention and receptiveness and an increased responsiveness to an idea or to a set of ideas" (1958, p. 117) and to a person who "tends to want to understand or to receive or to respond to the stimuli which are given to him or which he can derive from his situation" (1962, p. 240). It appears that Erickson may be misusing the term to refer to the same thing I have been describing in this chapter, namely, to an awake subject who has positive attitudes, motivations, and expectancies toward the situation and is ready and willing to think with and to imagine those things that are suggested.

Attitudes, Motivations, and Expectancies

In this chapter, the variables that mediate response to test suggestions for limb rigidity, analgesia, age regression, hallucination, amnesia, and so forth, have been conceptualized in terms of attitudes, motivations, and expectancies that determine whether the subject thinks with and imagines those things that are suggested. This section will focus on the relevance of attitudes, motivations, and expectancies; the next section will focus on the process of thinking with and imagining those things that are suggested.

The reader will recall from the previous discussion, that the following kinds of attitudes, motivations, and expectancies are being referred to:

Attitude continuum

The subject views his responding to test suggestions as interesting or worthwhile and he views the suggested effects as falling in the category of things he should experience (positive attitude); or, at the other end of the continuum, he views his responding to test suggestions as not interesting or worthwhile and he views the suggested effects as falling in the category of things he should not experience (negative attitude). If the subject has been told that he is in a hypnosis situation, then the attitude continuum needs to be conceptualized somewhat differently; in this case, the subject views his being "hypnotized" as interesting or worthwhile and as falling within the category of things he should experience (positive attitude); or, at the other end of the continuum, he views his being "hypnotized" as not interesting or worthwhile and as falling within the category of things he should not experience (negative attitude).

Motivational continuum

The subject desires to and tries to experience those things that are suggested (positive motivation); or, at the other end of the continuum, the subject does not desire and does not try to experience those things that are suggessed (negative motivation). If the situation is defined to the subject as hypnosis, the subject desires to be "hypnotized" and tries to enter "hypnotic trance" (positive motivation); or, the subject does not want to be "hypnotized" and tries not to enter "hypnotic trance" (negative motivation).

Expectancy continuum

The subject believes that he can experience those things that are suggested (positive expectancy); or, at the other end of the continuum, the subject does not believe that he can experience those things that are suggested (negative expectancy). If the situation is defined to the subject as hypnosis, the subject believes that he can be "hypnotized" (positive expectancy); or, he does not believe that he can be "hypnotized" (negative expectancy).[7]

Two sets of studies have evaluated the effects of the variables specified above. In one set, the subjects were simply asked to rate their attitudes, motivations, or expectancies; in the other set an experimental attempt was made to manipulate these variables. Studies that utilized the subjects' self-ratings will be reviewed first. Next, experiments that tried to manipulate attitudes, motivations, or expectancies, and which obtained more dramatic results, will be reviewed.

SELF-RATINGS OF ATTITUDES, MOTIVATIONS, AND EXPECTANCIES

David Calverley and I (unpublished data) assessed motivations toward hypnosis in 55 subjects by a scale worded as follows: "In this experiment I want to be deeply . . . medium . . . lightly . . . or not hypnotized." The subjects were then individually exposed to the trance induction procedure and the test suggestions of the Stanford Hypnotic Susceptibility Scale (Form A). The subjects' self-rated motivations were significantly correlated ($r = .36$) with their responsiveness to the test suggestions.

In an investigation by Barber and Calverley (1966c), 13 female subjects participated individually in eight hypnotic sessions conducted on eight con-

7. Another type of expectancy also plays a role in determining response to test suggestions. This other type of expectancy, namely, an expectancy of what kinds of behaviors are appropriate in the situation, will be discussed later in this section.

secutive days. Attitudes and expectations toward the hypnotic situation were assessed at the beginning of each of the eight daily sessions. Attitudes were measured by a Likert-type questionnaire, which asked the subject whether she viewed hypnosis as (a) interesting . . . equally interesting and boring . . . boring, (b) satisfying . . . unsatisfying, (c) pleasant . . . unpleasant, etc. Expectations were assessed by a questionnaire that asked the subject whether she expected that she would be hypnotized and, if so, if she expected to be hypnotized to a deep, medium, or light level. Immediately following the daily assessment of subjects' attitudes and expectations, a standardized trance induction procedure and the Barber Suggestibility Scale were administered by a tape recording of the experimenter's voice. Responsiveness to the test suggestions of the Barber Suggestibility Scale decreased continually during the course of the eight days. Changes in the subject's attitudes and expectations were correlated with this reduction in responsiveness. For instance, the average correlation over the eight days between one of the attitude measures (perceiving hypnosis as interesting) and Objective scores on the Barber Suggestibility Scale was .55, and between preexperimental expectations and Objective scores was .41.

In another study (Barber & Calverley, 1969b), 110 subjects first completed a questionnaire that assessed their expectations concerning whether or not and to what degree they would be hypnotized. Next, half of the subjects were exposed to the standardized trance induction procedure and test suggestions that comprise the Stanford Hypnotic Susceptibility Scale. The other half of the subjects were told to close their eyes for 5 minutes and place themselves in hypnosis; after 5 minutes, they were assessed on response to the test suggestions of the Stanford Scale. Responsiveness to the test suggestions was significantly correlated with subjects' expectations in the group exposed to the trance induction procedure *(r = .33)* and also in the group told to place themselves in hypnosis *(r = .40)*.

Melei and Hilgard (1964) had previously obtained similar results. These investigators assessed subjects' attitudes to hypnosis and expectations of their own hypnotizability prior to the hypnotic session. The subjects were then exposed to the standardized trance induction procedure and test suggestions of the Stanford Hypnotic Susceptibility Scale. For the female subjects, significant positive correlations (around .30) were obtained between attitudes toward hypnosis and response to test suggestions. For the male subjects, the correlations were also in the positive direction but not significant. Also, for subjects participating in a hypnotic experiment for the first time, expectations of their own hypnotizability were positively correlated *(r = .16 to .29)* with scores on the test suggestions.

Anderson (1963) also obtained a significant correlation of .47 between responsiveness to test suggestions in a hypnotic situation and a preexperimental scale measuring attitudes toward hypnosis (such as, "There are things that would worry me about being hypnotized," and "I would feel uneasy or uncomfortable as a subject").

Dermen and London (1965) found that subjects' expectations of their own hypnotizability were correlated with responsiveness to test suggestions in a hypnotic situation *(r* = .28 to .49 for females and .33 to .35 for males). Similarly, other studies (London, Cooper, & Johnson, 1962; Rosenhan & Tomkins, 1964; Shor, Orne, & O'Connell, 1966) generally yielded small positive correlations (which were more often significant for females than for males) between suggestibility in a hypnotic situation and their preexperimental attitudes toward hypnosis and their preexperimental expectations of their own responsiveness.

EXPERIMENTAL MANIPULATION OF ATTITUDES, MOTIVATIONS, AND EXPECTANCIES

In the studies summarized above, subjects' self-ratings were used to assess either their attitudes, or their motivations, or their expectancies. Let us now look at a series of studies that experimentally manipulated these three variables in various combinations, and which showed that attitudes, motivations, and expectancies play very important roles in determining response to test suggestions.

Attempts to produce positive attitudes, motivations, and expectancies

Earlier in this chapter, a series of experiments were summarized in which subjects were given a set of instructions labeled as "task-motivational instructions." Although this label emphasizes the motivational elements in the instructions, a close look at the wording of the instructions indicates that they were aimed to produce not only positive motivation, but also positive attitudes and expectancies. For instance, the so-called task-motivational instructions included the following statements:

1. Statements intended to lead the subject to view his responding to suggestions as interesting or worthwhile (positive attitude): "I want you to score as high as you can because we're trying to measure the maximum ability of people to imagine. If you don't try to the best of your ability, this experiment will be worthless and I'll tend to feel silly. . . . If you try to imagine to the best of your ability . . . you will be helping this experiment and not wasting any time."

2. Statements intended to lead the subject to desire to and to try to experience those things that are suggested (positive motivation): "How well you do on the tests which I will give you depends entirely upon your willingness to try to imagine and to visualize those things I will ask you to imagine. . . . What I ask is your cooperation in helping this experiment by trying to imagine vividly what I describe to you."

3. Statements intended to lead the subject to believe that he can experience those things that are suggested (positive expectancy): "Everyone passed these tests when they tried. For example, we asked people to close their eyes and to imagine that they were at a movie theater and were watching a show. Most people were able to do this very well; they were able to

imagine very vividly that they were at a movie and they felt as if they were actually looking at the picture. However, a few people thought that this was an awkward or silly thing to do and did not try to imagine and failed the test. Yet when these people later realized that it wasn't hard to imagine, they were able to visualize the movie picture and they felt as if the imagined movie was as vivid and real as an actual movie . . . if you try to imagine to the best of your ability, you can easily imagine and do the interesting things I tell you."

As stated previously in this chapter, these so-called task-motivational instructions, which were intended to produce positive attitudes, motivations, and expectancies, raised both overt and subjective responses to test suggestions to about the same level found in a group exposed to a procedure traditionally labeled as a "trance-induction" and markedly above the base level found in a control group. More specifically, as Table 5.2 showed, 60 per cent of the subjects who received the task-motivational instructions showed a relatively high response to test suggestions (passing at least five of the eight items on the suggestibility scale) as compared to 53 per cent of the subjects in the trance-induction group and 16 per cent in the control group.

Attempts to produce negative attitudes and motivations

In an attempt to produce negative attitudes and motivations toward the test situation, Barber and Calverley (1964d) told one group of 16 subjects that they were to be tested for gullibility. Seventeen other subjects, randomly assigned to an imagination control group, were told that they were to be tested for ability to imagine. All subjects were then assessed individually on the Barber Suggestibility Scale, administered by a tape recording of the experimenter's voice. Seven subjects (41 per cent) in the imagination control group and only one subject (6 per cent) in the group told they were to be tested for gullibility manifested a relatively high level of suggestibility (Objective scores of 5 or above on the 8-point suggestibility scale). Presumably, the statement to the subjects that they were to be tested for gullibility produced negative attitudes toward the situation (they viewed their responding to test suggestions as not good or worthwhile) and negative motivations (they did not want to and did not try to experience those things that were suggested). If this conjecture is valid, then the experiment demonstrated that negative attitudes and motivations produce a marked reduction in responsiveness to test suggestions.[8]

---

8. Further experiments are needed in which subjects' attitudes, motivations, and expectancies are assessed after the experimental manipulation—after the subjects are told they are to be tested for gullibility, and prior to assessment of their responsiveness to test suggestions. This consideration applies to all of the experiments discussed in this section; that is, each experiment should not only be replicated but also extended by assessing to what extent the experimental manipulation actually produced positive or negative attitudes, motivations, and expectancies.

Barber and Calverley (1964b) subsequently conducted another experiment along similar lines. First, 24 student nurses were tested individually on objective and subjective responses to the Barber Suggestibility Scale, administered without any special instructions. In a second series of sessions, held one week later, the subjects were tested again individually after they were randomly assigned to one of the following three experimental groups with eight subjects to each group:

Group A (Task-Motivational Instructions) was retested on objective and subjective responses to the Barber Suggestibility Scale after receiving the task-motivational instructions presented verbatim earlier in this chapter. (As stated previously, these task-motivational instructions include statements intended to produce positive attitudes, motivations, and expectancies toward the test situation.)

Group B (Control) was retested on objective and subjective responses to the Barber Suggestibility Scale in the same way as all subjects had been tested in the first session (without special instructions).

Group C (Negative Instructions) was retested on the Barber Suggestibility Scale after an attempt was made to produce negative attitudes and motivations toward the test situation. To produce negative attitudes and motivations, these subjects were told the following by their supervisor (the Supervisor of Student Nurses):

> It's being rumored by doctors and administrators, and I don't know who else, that nursing students are too easily directed and easily led in their responses to suggestions. It's kind of shocking and discouraging to hear that the students are so easily directed and can't decide things for themselves. We've got a job to do—to impress the administrators and doctors around here with the fact that nursing students are not as gullible and as easily directed as they appear to have been showing during this research study. Well it sure is up to each of you as to how easily led people around here think student nurses are. (P. 459)

Table 5.3 shows that during the first session, in which all subjects were tested without any special instructions on the Barber Suggestibility Scale, Groups A, B, and C obtained very similar average scores on the scale. Table 5.3 also shows that in the second session, in which Groups A, B, and C received different sets of instructions, the scores of the three groups were markedly different. On the average, Group A (Task-Motivational Instructions) passed four of the eight test suggestions in the second session, Group B (Control) passed two, and Group C (Negative Instructions) passed none. With the exception of one subject, who obtained an Objective score of 1 on the Barber Suggestibility Scale, all subjects in Group C failed all test suggestions in the second session. The table shows that, depending on whether task-motivational instructions (Group A) or negative instructions (Group C) were administered, the percentage of subjects who obtained an objective

TABLE 5.3 Objective (and subjective) scores on Barber Suggestibility Scale with task-motivational, neutral, and negative instructions

	Group A			Group B			Group C	
Subject	Session 1 (neutral instructions)	Session 2 (task-motivational instructions)	Subject	Session 1 (neutral instructions)	Session 2 (neutral instructions)	Subject	Session 1 (neutral instructions)	Session 2 (negative instructions)
A	7.5 (8)	8.0 (8)	I	7.0 (7)	4.0 (4)	Q	7.0 (6)	0.0 (0)
B	7.5 (8)	8.0 (8)	J	6.0 (6)	4.0 (4)	R	6.0 (4)	1.0 (0)
C	5.0 (5)	3.5 (4)	K	3.0 (2)	2.0 (2)	S	5.0 (4)	0.0 (0)
D	3.5 (4)	2.5 (3)	L	3.0 (4)	1.0 (1)	T	5.0 (3)	0.0 (0)
E	2.5 (3)	2.0 (2)	M	2.5 (3)	2.5 (2)	U	3.0 (3)	0.0 (0)
F	1.0 (1)	2.5 (3)	N	2.0 (2)	1.5 (2)	V	2.0 (3)	0.0 (0)
G	1.0 (1)	5.0 (4)	O	1.5 (0)	2.0 (1)	W	1.5 (2)	0.0 (0)
H	1.0 (2)	2.5 (3)	P	1.0 (1)	0.0 (0)	X	1.5 (2)	0.0 (0)
Mean	3.6 (4)	4.2 (4.4)		3.2 (3.1)	2.1 (2)		3.9 (3.4)	0.1 (0)

SOURCE: Barber, 1964d.

NOTE: Subjective scores are in parentheses.

score and also a Subjective score of at least 1 on the suggestibility scale varied from 100 per cent (Group A) to 0 per cent (Group C).

In this experiment, an attempt was made to ascertain whether negative attitudes and motivations mediated the lack of suggestibility in Group C. To determine whether negative attitudes and motivations were actually among the mediating variables, the following procedure was utilized: The day after the experiment was completed, but before the collaboration of the Supervisor of Student Nurses with the experimenter was admitted to the subjects, the subjects were asked by the Supervisor to write out the answer to the following questions: "Did my statement to you yesterday about the experiment impress you in any way?" Answers to this question strongly indicated that the failure of subjects in Group C to be responsive to test suggestions in the second session was due to the statement made by the supervisor, which was effective in inducing negative attitudes and motivations toward the test situation. Typical replies by the subjects in Group C were as follows:

Subject S: "I was impressed by the manner in which you expressed your concern over the project and the possible effect the outcome will have on the nursing profession. I agreed that we should have a mind of our own and should use it and that nurses should be firm in their decisions."

Subject W: "The fact that many student nurses were suggestible irritated me somewhat. (I didn't like the idea that this particular group of people were suggestible.) I was resistant to the first test but even more to the second test because I did not want to be associated with this branding" (p. 462).

Attempts to vary expectancy

In three experimental studies (Barber & Calverley, 1964e; Klinger, 1970; Wilson, 1967), attempts were made to lead the subjects to expect that they could or could not experience those things that were to be suggested.

To produce positive expectancies, Barber and Calverley (1964e) told one random group of subjects that it would be easy to respond to the test suggestions that would be given. To produce negative expectancies, subjects in another random group were told that the test suggestions would be difficult to pass. Subjects given the instructions intended to produce a positive expectancy were significantly more responsive to the test suggestions of the Barber Suggestibility Scale than those given the negative expectancy instructions.

To produce positive expectancies in one random group of subjects and negative expectancies in another random group, Klinger (1970) proceeded as follows: Before being assessed on response to the Barber Suggestibility Scale, each subject observed another person (a stooge) responding to the test suggestions. The stooge had been secretely instructed to role play a very suggestible person half of the time and a very nonsuggestible person the

other half of the time. The subjects who observed another person responding without difficulty to the test suggestions presumably would conclude that
they themselves could respond without difficulty (positive expectancy), and
those who observed another person who was unresponsive would presumably conclude that they themselves would find it difficult to respond (negative
expectancy). Subjects who presumably had a positive expectancy (who had
observed the responsive person) obtained high scores on the Barber Suggestibility Scale (an average score of 6 on the 8-point scale). Subjects who
presumably had a negative expectancy (who had observed the unresponsive
person) obtained low scores on the suggestibility scale (average score of
2.6). The experimental treatment (whether the subject had observed the
suggestible or nonsuggestible person) accounted for a rather large percentage of the variance (40 per cent) in the subjects' scores on the suggestibility
scale.

To produce a positive expectancy that the suggested effects can be experienced, Wilson (1967) proceeded as follows: Subjects who were randomly
assigned to an experimental group were asked to imagine various suggested
effects while ingenious methods were used to help them experience the effects without their knowing that they were receiving such aid. For instance,
each subject was asked to imagine that the room was red while at tiny bulb
was lighted secretly that provided a faint red tinge to the room. Following
these procedures, each subject was assessed on the Barber Suggestibility
Scale. Other subjects, who were randomly assigned to a control group, were
tested individually on the suggestibility scale with no attempt made to produce an expectancy that the suggestions were easy to experience. Subjects in
the experimental group obtained an average score of 5 whereas those in the
control group obtained a significantly lower average score of 3 on the 8-
point suggestibility scale.

In brief, three experiments that employed different methods to induce an
expectancy that the suggested effects can be experienced converge on the
conclusion that expectancy plays an important role in determining responsiveness to test suggestions.

Expectancy of appropriate behavior

A study by Orne (1959) showed that performance in a hypnotic situation
is also affected by another type of expectancy, namely, an expectancy pertaining to what types of behaviors are appropriate in the situation. An experimental group was told in a class lecture that hypnotic subjects typically
manifest catalepsy of the dominant hand whereas a control group was not
told anything about catalepsy. Subsequently, subjects in both groups were
tested individually in a hypnotic session on response to various test suggestions and on response to a test for catalepsy. Since 55 per cent of the subjects in the experimental group and none in the control group showed

catalepsy of the dominant hand, it appears that subjects' expectations concerning what behaviors are appropriate in a hypnotic experiment play an important role in determining their performance.

In brief, a series of experimental studies converge on the conclusion that responsiveness to test suggestions for body immobility, hallucination, amnesia, posthypnotic behavior, and so forth, is determined in part by the subjects' attitudes, motivations, and expectancies.

Thinking with the Suggestions and Imagining the Suggested Effects

If a subject has negative attitudes, motivations, and expectancies toward the test situation (that is, if he views his responding to test suggestions as not worthwhile and does not want to, does not try, and does not believe that he can experience those things that are suggested) he (a) will not think with the suggestions (instead he will verbalize to himself such statements as "This is silly" or "The suggestion won't work"), (b) will not imagine those things that are described by the experimenter, and (c) will not perform the suggested behaviors or experience those things that are suggested.

On the other hand, if a subject has positive attitudes, motivations, and expectancies toward the test situation (that is, if he views his responding to test suggestions as interesting or worthwhile and desires to, tries to, and believes that he can experience those things that are suggested), he (a) will think with (subvocally verbalize to himself) the statements of the experimenter, (b) will imagine those things that are suggested, and (c) will perform the suggested behaviors and experience the suggested effects.[9]

How does thinking with the suggestions and imagining those things described lead to the overt behaviors and the subjective experiences that have been traditionally associated with the word "hypnosis"? An important paper by Arnold (1946) provided a preliminary answer to this question.

First, Arnold pointed out that words are symbols that stand for the situation or activity to which they refer. As we hear words or speak them to ourselves, the experience to which the words refer tends to be reinstated in a fragmentary way. When a situation is described verbally, we tend to visualize ourselves or feel ourselves in the situation and to reexperience our attitudes and reactions in the situation.

Secondly, Arnold pointed out that thinking about and vividly imagining a

9. To simplify the discussion, I am emphasizing only the extremes of a continuum, that is, I am focusing only on the extreme negative end or positive end of a continuum of attitudes, motivations, and expectancies toward the test situation. Of course, most subjects are not at the extreme ends of the continuum; most subjects have neither extremely negative nor extremely positive attitudes, motivations, and expectancies, and they show neither very high nor very low response to test suggestions.

suggested movement or activity tends to bring about that activity. Arnold referred to the experiments of E. Jacobson (1930, 1932), which showed that an imagined movement (for example, imagining bending an arm) results in electromyographic activity in the flexor muscles of the arm. If the muscles are relaxed when the subject begins to imagine, these slight muscle contractions occur only in the limb that is imagined as being moved and do not occur in other limbs. Schultz (1932), Hull (1933), Arnold (1946), Mordey (1960), and other investigators have shown that these tiny muscular contractions that are produced when the subject imagines a movement may at times increase up to the point where they result in observable movements. In these experiments, subjects were asked to imagine that they were falling backward or forward, that an arm was moving, or that a Chevreul pendulum (which they held by two fingers of one hand) was moving to the right or left. With very few exceptions, subjects who imagined the movement tended to move either slightly or markedly in the imagined direction. In general, subjects who reported that they imagined the most vividly showed the most marked movements in the imagined direction. It is important to emphasize here that "The experience of 'intention,' of 'willing,' is . . . absent from these imagined movements" (Arnold, 1946, p. 111).

Sarbin (1950) has pointed out that "Common experience verifies the same notion [concerning the effects of imagining]. In imagining a former embarrassing situation we can feel our ears reddening and our faces flushing; in imagining a former painful experience we may involuntarily withdraw from the direction of the imagined stimulus, or in imagining something extremely unpleasant or disgusting we may experience nausea" (p. 266). In line with these assertions are a series of experimental studies, which indicate that vividly imagining a sensation can produce physiological changes associated with the actual sensation. For example, Schultz (1926) found that relaxed subjects who imagined that a hand was exposed to heat tended to experience a sensation of warmth associated (in 15 of 18 subjects) with an objectively measurable rise in skin temperature (up to $2°$ C. above normal). Conversely, imagining the forehead to be cool was associated in some subjects (5 of 14) with a fall in the temperature of the forehead, presumably produced by contraction of the superficial blood vessels.

Along similar lines, Harano, Ogawa, and Naruse (1965) instructed subjects to repeat to themselves and to concentrate on the phrase, "My arms are warm." When repeating and focusing on these words, the subjects generally showed a change in the felt warmth of the arms, an increase in the surface temperature of the arms, and an increase in the blood volume of the arms. The same investigators found that there were no significant subjective or objective changes in the temperature of the arms when the subjects tried purposively to raise the temperature of the arms without vividly imagining that the arms were warm. As Richardson (1969) reminds us, the results presented by Harano, Ogawa, and Naruse are in line with the contention of

Coué (1922) that "To make good suggestions it is absolutely necessary to do it *without effort* . . . the use of the *will* . . . must be entirely put aside. One must have recourse exclusively to the imagination" (Richardson, 1969, p. 10).

Menzies (1941) and Hadfield (1920) also presented data indicating that some individuals show vasodilation and a rise in skin temperature when instructed to imagine or to think of a limb as warm, and show vasoconstriction and a drop in skin temperature when thinking about or vividly imagining a limb as cold. Although other studies, summarized by Luthe (1970, pp. 50–57), failed to replicate the indicated relationship, the positive results indicate that, in at least some subjects, vividly imagining heat (or cold) is associated with a measurable rise (or fall) in skin temperature.

In a series of studies (Barber, 1965a), summarized earlier in this chapter, control subjects were asked to imagine that the right arm was becoming heavy and then were given repeated suggestions that it was becoming heavy ("Imagine that your right arm is feeling heavier and heavier. . . . It's becoming heavier and heavier. . ."). Similarly, each control subject was asked to imagine that his left arm was becoming light, his clasped hands were stuck together, he was very thirsty, his throat was rigid and he could not say his name, and he was stuck in the chair and could not get up. As Table 5.1, column 1, shows, more than one-fourth of these control subjects who were asked to imagine the suggested effects passed each of the test-suggestions both objectively and subjectively, that is, they experienced arm heaviness, arm lightness, hand lock, thirst hallucination, verbal inhibition, and body immobility.[10]

Recent studies (Spanos, 1971; Spanos & Barber, in press) probed more intensively into the relationship between imagining or fantasying and responding to test suggestions. In the first study, Spanos worked with 24 female subjects, of whom approximately half were highly responsive to test suggestions. Before beginning the experimental session, Spanos told each subject individually:

> I am interested in what is going on in people's minds when they are hypnotized. I'm interested in what they are thinking, imagining, feeling, and saying to themselves during hypnosis. In this experiment I am going to hypnotize you and ask you to carry out some suggestions. After each suggestion, while you are still hypnotized, I'll ask you to tell me what was passing through your mind while you were carrying out the suggestion. In giving me your answer it's very important that you be honest and tell me everything that was

10. In the same experiments, the control subjects were also given suggestions for "posthypnoticlike" response and selective amnesia. However, they were not given instructions to imagine these suggested effects. Instead, they were simply told that they would carry out the postexperimental response and would forget one of the preceding test suggestions.

passing through your mind—everything that you were thinking, imagining, feeling and saying to yourself—even if you think it silly or unimportant (p. 88).

A trance induction procedure was then administered and the subject was given test suggestions (for arm levitation, limb rigidity, and selective amnesia, for example). Immediately after responding to the first test suggestion, and also immediately after responding to each of the subsequent test suggestions, the subject was asked to report what was passing through her mind during the time she was responding. In most instances, the subjects who experienced the suggested effects stated that, when they were responding to the suggestions, they were imagining in a specific way; namely, they were imagining a situation which, if it actually transpired, would result in the behavior that was suggested. Typical examples of this type of imagining, which Spanos labeled "goal-directed fantasy," were:

1. A subject who experienced suggested arm heaviness reported: "I imagined that there were all kinds of rocks tied to my arm. It felt heavy and I could feel it going down."

2. A subject who experienced suggested arm levitation reported: "I imagined that my arm was hollow, there was nothing in it, and somebody was putting air into it."

3. A subject who passed the suggestion to forget the number 4 (selective amnesia) stated that she first pictured the numbers in a row (1, 2, 3, 4, 5, and so on up to 10), and then she pictured taking the number 4 out and, finally, she pictured the numbers 1, 2, 3, 5, and so on up to 10 with a blank space where the number 4 was formerly.

In a second experiment (Spanos & Barber, in press), 40 female subjects who had not previously participated in a hypnotic experiment were randomly assigned to four experimental groups with 10 subjects to each group. All subjects were exposed to a trance induction procedure, were given a test suggestion for arm levitation (worded differently for each of the four experimental groups), and then were asked to report what was passing through their minds when they were responding to the test suggestions. The subjects' reports were scored for the presence or absence of goal-directed fantasy. (These judgments could be made easily and reliably by two independent raters who agreed in every instance; for example, it was clear that the following type of report should be scored as a goal-directed fantasy: "I imagined a balloon tied to my arm and the balloon was slowly rising.") The subjects who passed the test suggestion also completed a Likert-type scale that asked them to state whether they attributed the arm levitation to their own voluntary effort ("I only had the experience of causing it [the arm] to rise") or whether they considered it an involuntary occurrence ("I experienced it rising completely by itself"). In those subjects who showed arm levitation, goal-directed fantasy and the experience of volition were related as follows:

of those who reported a goal-directed fantasy, none stated that they experienced the arm rising as volitional; while of those who did not report a goal-directed fantasy, 60 per cent stated that they experienced the arm rising as volitional. In brief, if a subject carries out a goal-directed fantasy when given a suggestion—that is, if he imagines a situation which, if it actually transpired, would result in the suggested effect—he tends to feel that his response to the suggestion is involuntary (reporting, for example, "My arm rose by itself").

Let us now summarize the data presented in this section and in the preceding one:

1. Studies that used subjects' self-ratings to assess either their attitudes, or motivations, or expectancies toward the test situation generally found small but significant relations between each of these variables and response to test suggestions.

2. Studies that experimentally manipulated attitudes, motivations, and expectancies in various combinations found a marked enhancement of response to test suggestions when an attempt was made to induce positive attitudes, motivations, and expectancies toward the test situation, and a marked reduction in response when an attempt was made to induce negative attitudes, motivations, and expectancies.

3. An underlying assumption or axiom of the alternative paradigm is that when a subject has positive attitudes, motivations, and expectancies toward the test situation he thinks along with and imagines those things that are suggested.

4. A series of experimental studies indicates that thinking along with and vividly imagining those things that are suggested tends to produce both the overt response and the subjective experience that is suggested.

5. Two recent studies indicate that subjects experience suggested effects, such as arm levitation, as occurring nonvolitionally when they imagine a situation which, if it objectively transpired, would produce the suggested behavior, for example, they imagine a rising balloon tied to the arm, which is lifting the arm up.

Tangible Antecedent Variables

In this chapter, I have focused on the intervening variables (subjects' attitudes, motivations, expectancies, and cognitive processes) that mediate response to test suggestions. In other papers and books (Barber, 1969a, 1969b, 1970a) I have focused primarily on denotable antecedent variables that are functionally related to subjects' overt and subjective responses.

There appear to be at least three important antecedent variables that directly affect how subjects report their experiences:

1. The wording of the questions used to elicit the subjective reports (Barber, Dalal, & Calverley, 1968).

2. Whether or not honest subjective reports are demanded (K. S. Bowers, 1967; Spanos & Barber, 1968).

3. Whether the subjective reports are elicited by the experimenter or by another person (K. S. Bowers, 1967; Spanos & Barber, 1968).

Other tangible antecedent variables appear to affect subjects' overt and subjective responsiveness to test suggestions by first affecting their attitudes, motivations, and expectancies, and their willingness to think with and imagine the suggested effects. These antecedent variables include the following:

1. How the situation is defined to the subject (as a test of imagination, as a test of gullibility, as "hypnosis," etc.) (Barber, 1969b).

2. Whether preexperimental instructions that aim to alter the subjects' attitudes, motivations, and expectancies toward the test situation are administered.

3. Whether the test suggestions are worded in a permissive or authoritarian manner, for example, "Try to forget" versus "You will forget," or "Try to dream on a specified topic" versus "You will dream on the topic" (Barber, 1966b).

4. Whether the test suggestions are given in a firm or lackadaisical tone of voice (Barber & Calverley, 1964a).

5. Whether the subject has been repeatedly assessed on response to the same test suggestions in previous sessions (Barber & Calverley, 1966c).

6. Whether the subject volunteered to participate in the experiment or was coerced (Boucher & Hilgard, 1962).

7. Whether the subject's performance was observed by an audience (Coe, 1966).

8. Whether the subject was provided with a clear conception of the experience that was desired and was given verbal reinforcement for each appropriate response (Giles, 1962; Sachs & Anderson, 1967).

9. If the situation is defined as hypnosis, whether an attempt was made to remove the subjects' misconceptions and fears about hypnosis (Cronin, Spanos, & Barber, 1971; Macvaugh, 1969).

The effects of these nine antecedent variables can be more satisfactorily explained by the alternative paradigm than by the traditional (trance) paradigm. For instance, it is difficult to conceive how suggestions for amnesia worded in different ways have any relevance whatsoever to whether the subject enters, remains in, or goes deeper into a state (trance) that is fundamentally different from ordinary states of consciousness. However, it is not at all difficult to see how permissive suggestions for amnesia ("Try to forget") are more effective than authoritarian suggestions ("You will forget") in motivating the subject to put the previous occurrences "out of mind" (Barber & Calverley, 1966b). Similarly, it is difficult to conceive how the experimenter's tone of voice (firm or lackadaisical) in administering test suggestions for arm heaviness, inability to unclasp hands, and so forth, is

relevant to whether the subject enters, remains in, or goes deeper into a special state (trance). However, since subjects who received test suggestions in
a lackadaisical tone of voice tended to report that they thought the experimenter did not expect them to respond to the test suggestions, it is not difficult to conceive how the tone of voice used to administer test suggestions
might affect the subjects' attitudes, motivations, or expectancies toward the
test situation (Barber & Calverley, 1964a). The trance paradigm might be
able to explain why subjects exposed in repeated sessions to the same test
suggestions showed a continual reduction in responsiveness. However, the
alternative paradigm is more consistent with the empirical data, since subjects participating in these repeated sessions testified that they became bored
and lost interest, and this change in attitude was correlated with their reduced responsiveness (Barber & Calverley, 1966c). Similarly, the trance
paradigm might explain the effects of some of the other antecedent variables listed above; for example, it might explain why coerced subjects are less
responsive to test suggestions than volunteers (Boucher & Hilgard, 1962),
why subjects are less responsive when they believe they are being observed
by an audience (Coe, 1966), and why verbal reinforcement for each appropriate response enhances subsequent responses to test-suggestions (Giles,
1962; Sachs & Anderson, 1967). However, without belaboring the point
and going into further details, it should be clear that these antecedent variables can be more satisfactorily conceptualized as affecting subjects' attitudes, motivations, and expectancies toward the test situation and their willingness to think with and imagine the suggested effects.

The antecedent variables listed above are functionally related to the dependent variable we have labeled "response to test suggestions." A few of
the above-mentioned variables also overlap with other antecedent variables
to determine response on two additional dependent variables: whether and
to what degree subjects (a) manifest a trancelike appearance and (b) report that they were "hypnotized."

As implied previously in this chapter, whether subjects who are highly responsive to test suggestions appear to be in "hypnosis" (that is, manifest
trancelike characteristics such as a limp posture, passivity, a blank stare,
rigid facial expression, and so forth) is dependent primarily on two tangible
antecedent variables, namely, whether the situation was defined to the subjects as "hypnosis" and whether or not they were asked to close their eyes.
If the situation is not defined as "hypnosis," but in some other way—as a
"test of imagination," for example—and if the subjects are not asked to
close their eyes, very few if any subjects who are highly responsive to test
suggestions for limb rigidity, analgesia, age regression, amnesia, and so
forth, manifest a trancelike appearance. If the situation is defined to the subjects as "hypnosis" and they are told to close their eyes, then whether and to
what extent the subjects manifest a trancelike appearance is functionally related to such antecedent variables as (a) their preconceptions of what "hyp-

nosis" is supposed to involve, (b) their preexperimental attitudes toward whatever they conceive "hypnosis" to be, (c) their preexperimental expectations concerning their own performance, (d) the suggestions they receive (implicit suggestions to be passive, or repeated suggestions that they are becoming relaxed, drowsy, sleepy, and are entering hypnosis), and (e) whether the experimenter, at some point, speaks to them along the following lines: "Wake up, stop acting as if you are in a trance, and continue to respond to my suggestions" (Barber, 1969b; Barber & Calverley, 1969b).

Whether subjects who are highly responsive to test suggestions report that they were in "hypnosis" is also dependent primarily on two tangible antecedent variables, namely, whether the situation was defined to the subjects as "hypnosis" and whether they were told to close their eyes. If the situation is not defined to the subjects as "hypnosis" and they are not told to close their eyes, very few if any subjects who show a high level of response to test-suggestions state that they are in hypnosis. If the situation is defined as "hypnosis" and the subjects are told to close their eyes, the antecedent variables that determine whether the subjects will report that they were in "hypnosis" to some degree or were not "hypnotized" at all include (a) their preconceptions of what "hypnosis" is supposed to involve, (b) their preexperimental expectations of their own performance, (c) whether they received repeated suggestions that they were becoming relaxed, drowsy, sleepy, and were entering a hypnotic state, (d) whether they observed that they were or were not responsive to test suggestions, (e) whether the experimenter stated or implied that he believed they were or were not hypnotized, and (f) the wording and tone of the questions used to elicit their reports (Barber, 1969a; Barber & Calverley, 1969b; Barber, Dalal, & Calverley, 1968).[11]

---

11. As noted above, whether a subject who is highly responsive to test suggestions manifests trancelike characteristics and whether he reports that he was "hypnotized" is dependent, in part, on whether he was told repeatedly that he was becoming relaxed, drowsy, sleepy, and was entering a hypnotic state. Repeated suggestions of this type (relaxation, drowsiness, etc.) may also affect the subjects' performance on other variables, for example, they may reduce their strength and endurance (Barber & Calverley, 1964f) and they may change their responses to projective tests, such as the Rorschach or TAT, in the direction expected when a person is relaxed or sleepy. However, whether repeated suggestions that the subject is becoming relaxed, drowsy, sleepy, and is entering hypnosis influence the subjects' responsiveness to test suggestions of analgesia, hallucination, age regression, amnesia, etc. depends primarily on how they affect subjects' attitudes, motivations, and expectancies toward the test situation. I have noted (unpublished observations) that a substantial proportion of individuals, especially those who are relatively uneducated, are anxious or fearful with respect to whatever they think "hypnosis" is supposed to be. When these individuals receive repeated suggestions that they are becoming relaxed, drowsy, sleepy, and are entering hypnosis, they seem to have negative attitudes, motivations, and expectancies toward the test situation and they perform less well on test suggestions than they would have if they had not received such repeated suggestions. Most college students, however, are eager

Continued on p. 178

In brief, the dependent variables (response to test suggestions, trancelike appearance, and reports of having been hypnotized) are functionally related to the many denotable antecedent variables mentioned above and also to other tangible variables that have been discussed elsewhere (Dalal, 1966; McPeake, 1968; Nichols, 1968; Richman, 1965; Spanos, 1970; Spanos & Chaves, 1970). In fact, these behaviors and experiences appear to be as complexly determined as any behaviors and experiences that psychologists have ever attempted to study. Although the antecedent variables are many and complex, a substantial number of them can be viewed as converging on a set of mediating variables that we have called attitudes, motivations, and expectancies toward the test situation and thinking with and imagining the suggested effects. These mediating variables are part and parcel of normal psychology, especially of present-day social psychology. They mediate behavior and experiences in a wide variety of situations; for instance, they mediate the experiences of the member of the audience who is listening to an orator, or who is observing a motion picture, a stage play, or a television show. It is misleading to subsume these mediating variables, which are an integral part of normal psychology, under a construct ("trance," "hypnosis," or "hypnotic trance") that derives from the psychology of the abnormal, that has been historically loaded with surplus connotations (including the connotation that the person resembles the sleepwalker), and that is used to refer to a special state basically different from ordinary states of consciousness.

Résumé and Prospects

As Kuhn (1962) pointed out, a change in scientific paradigm is preceded by a period in which research yields data that do not fit into the prevailing paradigm. Recent research has produced data incongruous with the prevalent trance paradigm. Some of the anomalous data include:

1. Some individuals are very responsive, both overtly and subjectively, to test suggestions when they are tested under a base level (control) condition (without any special instructions). Also, when unselected subjects are simply exposed to brief instructions intended to produce positive attitudes, motivations, and expectancies toward the test situation ("task-motivational instructions"), they are about as responsive to test suggestions for body immobility, hallucination, age regression, analgesia, amnesia, etc. as unselected subjects who have been exposed to a procedure of the type traditionally

---

to experience whatever they think "hypnosis" is supposed to be. Consequently, when given repeated suggestions of relaxation, drowsiness, sleep, and entering hypnosis, they seem to have positive attitudes, motivations, and expectancies toward the test situation and they perform better on test suggestions than they would have if they had not received such repeated suggestions.

termed a "trance induction" and who are, presumably, in a hypnotic trance. The trance paradigm could not have predicted these results and it requires ad hoc assumptions in order to explain them. It has to assume, after the fact, that highly responsive control subjects or task-motivated subjects who have not been exposed to a trance-induction procedure, who do not appear to be in a trance, and who do not think they are in a trance are actually in a hypnotic trance.

2. The anomaly mentioned above appeared earlier in the work of hypnotic state theorists such as Erickson. To maintain the logic of the trance paradigm, Erickson was compelled to contend that some subjects are in a deep hypnotic trance even when they do not think they are in a trance, are judged by psychologists and psychiatrists as being in a normal waking state, and are even judged by Erickson himself as being "seemingly awake and functioning . . . in a manner similar to that of a nonhypnotized person operating at the waking level" (Erickson, 1967a, p. 13). Why was Erickson compelled to categorize subjects as being in a deep hypnotic trance even though the subjects appeared, to objective observers and to themselves, to be normally awake? Because Erickson was certain that the subjects would respond to his suggestions. This logic led to another serious anomaly for the trance paradigm: subjects were judged to be in a hypnotic trance because they would show high response to test suggestions and, turning around circularly, the high response to test-suggestions was explained as due to the presence of hypnotic trance (Barber, 1964a).

3. Since all investigators conceive of the human organism as a psychophysiological unity, special states of the organism are expected to have some physiological concomitants. For more than 50 years, investigators have been trying to find a physiological concomitant or index of the presumed special state labeled "hypnosis" or "trance." Not only have they failed to unearth any special physiological change associated with the presumed special state, but they have also consistently found that physiological functioning during the postulated special state varies in the same way as in nonspecial or ordinary states. Of course, many failures over many years to find a physiological index does not prove that such an index does not exist or will never be found. Nevertheless, consistent findings that physiological functions during the presumed special state vary in the same way as in nonspecial states are becoming more and more anomalous for the trance paradigm as time goes on.

A traditional paradigm is not overthrown simply because some of the relevant data are incongruous with it (Kuhn, 1962). In addition to pointing out data that are anomalous for the traditional formulation, an alternative paradigm must also be able to explain all of the relevant phenomena at least as well if not better than the traditional one. The underlying contention of this chapter has been that the alternative paradigm, which has had a rather brief period of development (Barber, 1961b, 1964a, 1967, 1969b, 1970a;

Barber & Calverley, 1962; Sarbin, 1950, 1956, 1962, 1964; Sarbin & Anderson, 1967; Sarbin & Coe, in press), can explain the relevant phenomena more satisfactorily than the trance paradigm which has had more than a hundred years of development. Specifically, this chapter has shown how the alternative paradigm explains not only the "amazing" phenomena of stage hypnosis, such as, the human-plank feat, stopping the pulse in the arm, and performance by the subject of weird antics such as dancing with an invisible partner, but also explains the following phenomena that can be elicited by suggestions in experimental or clinical situations: production of blisters, removal of warts, analgesia, age regression, age-progression, visual and auditory hallucinations, deafness, trancelike characteristics, difficulty or delay in coming out of trance, suggested and also spontaneous amnesia, and trance logic. These phenomena, which were explained in this chapter from the alternative paradigm, were not selected at random. On the contrary, they were selected as representing the strongholds of the trance paradigm—as representing the phenomena that had been universally accepted as explainable only by positing a special state of the organism.

Looking to the future, I will venture four predictions:

1. As more investigators adopt the alternative paradigm, the kinds of questions that are asked and the focus of research will change. Instead of asking what the most effective methods for inducing a deep hypnotic trance are or how the hypnotic state differs from the waking state, researchers will ask questions such as the following:

a. What kinds of instructions are most effective in eliciting positive attitudes, motivations, and expectancies toward the test situation?

b. Are all three factors—positive attitudes, positive motivations, positive expectancies—equally necessary for high response to test suggestions? How does a subject respond to test suggestions when he believes it is interesting and worthwhile to be responsive (positive attitude), when he tries to experience those things that are suggested (positive motivation), but when he does not believe that he can experience either a specific suggested effect, such as visual hallucination or amnesia, or all of those things that are suggested (negative expectancies)? A rather large number of additional questions can be formulated along similar lines. For instance, how does a subject respond to test suggestions when he believes he can experience the suggested effects (positive expectancy) but he has negative attitudes and motivations toward the test situation?

c. How can subjects be helped to imagine vividly those things that are suggested?

d. How can subjects be given practice in thinking with suggestions? Stated somewhat differently, how can they be given practice in covertly verbalizing the suggestions to themselves while, at the same time, inhibiting contrary thoughts such as "This suggestion won't work," or "It's impossible to experience this [suggested effect]"?

2. As the alternative paradigm becomes accepted by more researchers, the kind of response to test suggestions that has been traditionally subsumed under the term "hypnosis" will no longer be viewed as closely related to abnormal phenomena such as sleepwalking and fugue states (Gill & Brenman, 1959). Instead, the processes involved in responding to test suggestions will be analyzed in a similar manner as, and will be found partially to overlap with, such social psychological influence processes as conformity, attitude change, and persuasion (Barnlund, 1968; Bettinghaus, 1968; Hartley & Hartley, 1958, pp. 15–158; McGuire, 1969; Secord & Backman, 1964, pp. 93–231). The recent formulation by Sarbin and Coe (in press), which subsumes "hypnotic" behavior under the psychology of influence communication, will be viewed as a major turning point in this area. I will also venture to predict that, in the more distant future, a unified theory of social influence processes will be used to explain not only conformity, attitude change, and persuasion but also responses to test suggestions and other types of responses that were previously thought to be associated with a qualitatively distinct state (trance).

3. Conceptions of *normal human abilities* or "human potentialities" (Otto, 1966) will be markedly broadened when the subject who is responsive to communications (test suggestions) from an experimenter is seen to be as normal and as awake as the member of the audience who is responsive to communications from the actors. Investigators will no longer think in terms of rare individuals ("somnambulists") who possess unusual capacities, who differ in some basic way from other human beings, who are able to enter a special state ("deep somnambulistic trance"), and who are able to have experiences that other human beings find it very difficult if not impossible to have. On the contrary, investigators will think in terms of a wide range of normal human abilities that can be manifested when individuals adopt positive attitudes, motivations, and expectancies toward the test situation. These abilities, which will be viewed as within the normal human repertoire, will include: the ability to perform feats such as the human-plank feat; the ability to control or block pain (analgesia) by thinking of other things or by thinking of the sensations as sensations; the ability to imagine and to visualize vividly (hallucination and suggested dream); the ability to imagine or fantasy events that occurred at an earlier time (age regression) or that may occur in the future (age progression); and the ability to block or stop thinking about earlier events (amnesia).

4. As Chaves (1968) has pointed out, attempts have already been made to subsume the alternative paradigm under the traditional (trance) paradigm. I expect that further attempts will be made along these lines (Kuhn, 1962). That is, adherents of the traditional paradigm may contend that hypnotic trance (or hypnosis or hypnotic state) refers to (or is) positive attitudes, motivations, and expectancies and thinking with and imagining the suggested effects. To be consistent, adherents of the traditional para-

digm may also contend that all procedures, instructions, and experimental manipulations that aim to produce positive attitudes, motivations, etc—for example, task-motivational instructions (Barber & Calverley, 1962), or having the subject first observe another person who is highly responsive to test suggestions (Klinger, 1970)—are actually trance induction procedures. Also, to be consistent, they may contend that the member of the audience who is laughing, crying, empathizing, and so on, as he receives communications from the actors, is also in a hypnotic trance. These contentions will change the meaning of the term "hypnotic trance"; the term will no longer refer to a special state basically different from ordinary states of consciousness. Of course, such attempts to change the meaning of the central construct (trance) will be self-defeating for the traditional paradigm. Since the construct "hypnotic trance" (or "hypnosis" or "hypnotic state") has always referred to some kind of basic, qualitative change in the organism and has accreted many associated connotations (including connotations of somnambulism or sleepwalking), attempts to give it a new meaning and new connotations will lead to confusion rather than clarity and, sooner or later, the construct and its many associated assumptions will be viewed as a historical curiosity by students of human behavior.

Theodore R. Sarbin *received his Ph.D. from Ohio State University in 1941. From 1938 to 1941, he served on the staff of the University of Minnesota. For several years he was in private practice and engaged in part-time teaching. In 1949, he went to the University of California at Berkeley. He was made Professor of Psychology in 1957 and Professor of Criminology in 1966. In 1969, he moved to the University of California, Santa Cruz. He is presently Professor and Chairman of the Board of Studies in Psychology and also a member of the graduate faculty of the History of Consciousness Program. His interests include social and cognitive psychology, behavior disorders, and theoretical psychology. A definitive statement of his theoretical position on hypnosis is contained in* Hypnotism: The Social Psychology of Influence Communication *with W. C. Coe, in press.*

Robert W. Slagle *is an Assistant Professor of Psychology at Sonoma State College, California. He earned his Ph.D. in 1968 from the University of California, Berkeley, while working with an interdisciplinary brain research project. Expanding his neurobiological background to the immediacy of human experience, he accepted a postdoctoral research and training fellowship at the Psychology Clinic of the University of California, where he received intensive training in psychotherapy and drug counseling. In response to his growing concern regarding people and drugs he has served as a drug consultant in a variety of positions including an Oakland high school, an experimental drop-in center sponsored by the City of Berkeley, and in private practice as a licensed psychologist. His interests are now centered in humanistic psychology with an emphasis on integrating biological and psychological disciplines and bringing them to bear on issues of social growth and individual well-being.*

Sarbin and Slagle *survey the salient literature on physiological concomitants of hypnosis and find no evidence for a physiological process that could serve as an independent criterion of the postulated hypnotic state. They do, however, find strong evidence that symbolic stimuli and imaginings can produce impressive changes in physiological processes. They formulate their findings within a general theory of social role enactment, and conclude that the greater the intensity of organismic involvement in the enactment of the hypnotic role, the more extensive are the associated physiological concomitants.*

6

Hypnosis and Psychophysiological Outcomes

THEODORE R. SARBIN AND ROBERT W. SLAGLE

Hundreds of reports addressed to the problem of hypnotic influence on somatic processes have been published. The motivations behind these reports appear to fall into two general categories: to use hypnotic techniques in the clinical treatment of somatic and psychological disorders, and to identify an independent criterion for the hypnotic trance. These categories are not exclusive: Some writers have referred to clinical research reports as evidence for the independent existence of the hypnotic trance. Because clinical studies in general are characterized by the absence of appropriate controls, they can only be citied as "hypothesis-finding," rather than "hypothesis-testing" studies. On the other hand, studies addressed directly to the problem of identifying an independent criterion for the hypnotic trance are usually characterized by attempts to incorporate principles of experimental design, including controls.

Not every laboratory report makes explicit that the search for a physiological indicant is to demonstrate that hypnosis is a special state of mind or an altered state of consciousness. The hypotheses are stated in such a way, however, that the reader may safely conclude that the intent is to demonstrate that the altered physiological process is a function of a hypnotic trance brought about by the hypnotic induction.

The search for a physiological indicant of the hypnotic state cannot be appreciated without placing it in the more general context of the search for a criterion that is independent of the postulated mental state. No sophisticated analysis of hypnosis can avoid recognition of the tautology contained in classical explanations of hypnosis. The tautology can be expressed simply: behaviors ordinarily subsumed under hypnosis, such as catalepsies, rigidities, paramnesias, and posthypnotic feats, are the effects of the hypnotic trance; the presence of the hypnotic trance is noted by the catalepsies, rigidities, paramnesias, and posthypnotic feats. The circularity follows from the lack of an independent criterion.

The recognition of the circularity has put pressure on exponents of the trance concept deliberately to seek independent criteria. Two types of independent criteria have been sought: "Phenomenological" tests for an altered state of consciousness, and physiological indicators.

The problems inherent in employing phenomenological criteria are discussed in detail by Sarbin and Coe (1972) in the context of the docility of reports of imaginings to role demands, to the effects of organismic involvement on stimulus inputs, to the selectivity involved in making public one's imaginings, and to the conditions that influence the assigning of credibility to imaginings. Their conclusion is that phenomenological tests of the hypnotic trance have been ineffective for breaking out of the circularity. Such ineffectiveness of phenomenological tests makes crucial the search for somatic indicators if the trance concept is to remain scientifically viable.

Experiments designed to reveal physiological indicants of the hypnotic trance are of two sorts. The first monitors somatic responses that occur consequent to the hypnotic induction procedure. In the typical experiment, a measure such as heart rate, GSR, or body temperature is assessed before, during, and after the induction procedure. If subjects are used as their own controls, the same measurements are taken under conditions where other instructions (such as imagining) are employed. If the independent group design is used, readings may be taken before, during, and after the induction for the experimental sample. In the control sample, the hypnotic induction is omitted.

The second type of experiment focuses on physiological responses to suggestions made after the induction is completed. To study hypnotically-induced analgesia, for example, hypnotized subjects are given a painful stimulus; the experimenter, besides noting the subjects' verbal and expressive responses, records physiological responses, such as blood volume, that normally vary with the administration of traumatic stimuli. Experiments may be conducted with independent groups, where the subjects of the control sample are not hypnotized. Frequently, experiments are reported where the subject is his own control—hypnosis is employed at one sitting, other instructions are given at a second sitting.

After presenting a review of selected studies, we shall return to a critique of the experimental designs in studies of the physiological effects of hypnosis. Suffice it to say now that the type of experimental design selected is not without relevance to the interpretation given positive findings.

In attempting to discuss and account for physiological manifestations of hypnosis we must keep in mind not only the technical, methodological, and terminological considerations that are essential to any type of in vivo biological investigation, but also considerations concerning "hypnosis" as an independent variable. The controversial status of hypnosis both in theory and in practice should direct the investigator to scrutinize the assumptions and "givens" behind the choice of experimental designs employed in examining physiological aspects of hypnotic phenomena. Not only must we be sensitive to biological base rates but to behavioral base rates as well. We must also be sensitive to the social and cultural context in which we make our observations.

The use of the dramaturgical metaphor of "role" will permit a systematic way of defining and measuring the many contextual, historical, and imaginal accompaniments of hypnosis in the experimental situation. Some examples of the kinds of cautions that we should attend to are: What is the basis for the selection of subjects? Do the subjects in any given experiment have special characteristics such as high responsiveness to hypnotic instructions? Are they students, or patients, or otherwise representative of only a special population? Are they all men? or women? or of a particular age or socioeconomic status? If "hypnotic induction" is used, what other type of instructions are and should be administered to control groups? What indices of involvement in the hypnotic role are employed? In what way is the phenomenon termed "hypnosis" in any given experiment representative of the historical and natural observations on the presumed process under consideration as observed and reported outside the laboratory? Who are the experimenters and what subtle biases might they implicitly carry to the experimental situation? And, in general, what role demands are placed on the subjects?

With these questions as a backdrop, we now turn to a survey of the literature on physiological correlates of hypnosis with emphasis on exemplary experiments from recent publications. The review could be organized according to the type of physical measurement used; for example, bioelectrical recordings, measures of changes in pressure or volume as in the case of blood pressure or volume of tidal air, temperature, presence and concentration of chemical substances, and so forth. Or, we could group experiments according to the presumed physiological events, such as changes in muscle tone, skin resistance, heart rate, and so forth; or we could organize according to the intended effect of the induction—for example, to bring about relaxation, to call out particular emotional responses, or to cure an illness. Many different kinds of events in the body are measured by changes in electrical parameters, so the first approach has little heuristic value. We have chosen to organize our review according to the bodily organs or processes in which changes are alleged to occur as a result of hypnotic instructions.

Survey of the Experimental Literature

The literature on physiological correlates of hypnosis has been reviewed by several investigators: Barber (1961b), Crasilneck and Hall (1959), Gorton (1949), Levitt and Brady (1963), Sarbin (1956), and West (1960). For this reason, we shall not attempt a thorough survey, but rather point to selected investigations for purposes of illustrating experimental design and interpretation of findings.

RESPIRATORY FUNCTIONS

Barber (1965b) reviewed and criticized a number of reports on the hypnotic cure of asthma and other respiratory ailments. He pointed out that control groups are often omitted in these reports of improved respiratory function via hypnotic suggestion. The absence of a waking control group that receives suggestions for improvement without hypnosis makes it particularly unparsimonious to attribute the improvement to the specific antecedent condition, namely, the "hypnotic state."

In discussing hypnotic effects on breathing, Sarbin (1956) concluded that for subjects in "deep" hypnosis a decrease in breathing rate could be observed. However, the pneumographic record is easily affected by the type of suggestion given. For example, relaxation suggestions bring about decreased respiratory rates, while the introduction of emotional stimuli usually increases the rate.

In a study that gives particular attention to individual differences, Dudley et al. (1964) reported systematic respiratory alterations with pain and exercise and from hypnotically suggested emotions, pain, and exercise. Experiments were carried out on 10 hypnotically-naive medical students and a tuberculosis patient with previous hypnotic experience. These men were each interviewed to determine events in their past lives associated with strong emotion. Hypnosis consisted of "eye fixation on a light and the repeated suggestion of relaxation and drowsiness" (p. 47). Suggestions were then made involving the emotion-laden interview material, and the subjects were questioned about their feelings both during and after the hypnotic session. An independent investigator took continuous measurements of alveolar ventilation, and tidal air concentration of CO_2 and O_2. Blood pressure, pulse rate, and skin temperature were also monitered but not reported. By regarding each subject as his own control, the hypnotic condition had minimal effect on respiration except for a decrease in O_2 consumption. Behavioral observations and self-reports from these subjects corroborated that they felt as if they were undergoing (experiencing) the suggested emotions.

CARDIOVASCULAR FUNCTIONS

Heart rate

It is common to observe tachycardia during the initial period of the hypnotic induction procedure (Sarbin, 1956). This speeding up of the heartbeat can probably be attributed to the excitement and unfamiliarity of the situation. With Barber (1961b) we agree that three critical factors must be controlled in a satisfactory demonstration of hypnotic cardiac acceleration:

level of "arousal," respiratory rate, and the capacity of a subject voluntarily to increase his heart rate without an hypnotic induction. Barber concluded that no experiments to date have met these criteria. Recent experiments aimed at manipulating heart rate via hypnotic instructions seem to bear out this conclusion. For example, one means of asking about possible unique effects of hypnosis on cardiac function is to compare two groups of subjects who are performing the same behaviors, except that one group is told not to "slip into hypnosis" but to fake the requested performance.

Damaser, Shor, and Orne (1963) employed suggested emotional behavior to execute such an experiment. Seventeen undergraduate men and women were divided into two groups: "Real" hypnotic subjects who had had previous experience as hypnotic subjects, and "Simulators" who were not susceptible to hypnosis and who were asked to fool both the experimenter and the polygraph. The experimenter was not informed which subjects were Simulators. During the experiment all subjects were asked to try to *feel* the requested emotions of fear, calm, happiness, and depression. When the emotion was requested, the subject was given a description. For instance, for fear he was told, "You feel terribly frightened. You're horribly scared." Continuous recordings of heart rate, muscular activity in the forehead, and electrodermal potentials were measured. No significant differences between Reals and Simulators were observed in the physiological variables. Both groups showed significant and comparable physiological responses to the requested emotions and in the directions predicted. Fear and happiness were most active while calm and depression were least active.

In an experimental design much like that of Damaser, Shor, and Orne (1963), Hepps and Brady (1967) paid 25 undergraduate men who were either Real hypnotic or Simulator subjects to undergo a fear-arousing set of taped instructions. As with the Damaser et al. study, Real and Simulator subjects showed a significant cardiac acceleration and higher score on the Taylor Manifest Anxiety Scale with the fear stimulus, but differences between Reals and Simulators were not significant. In postsession interviews, the Reals reported that they felt fearful more often and to a greater intensity than did the Simulators. Hepps and Brady also report that Reals showed a significant positive correlation between heart rates during all aspects of the experiment, and hypnotic responsiveness as measured by standardized scales. It is appropriate to question this finding: Since the basis for selection of Reals was different from that of Simulators, this correlation may be the result of subject selection and experimental interaction, or of base rate phenomena in the population from which the subjects were chosen. The conclusion of Damaser et al. seems applicable to this type of research at this point in time: "the evidence does not support the view that either (1) effects in the hypnotic state are larger than in the waking state, or (2) effects in the Real group are more frequent than in the Simulating group" (p. 340).

Hemodynamics and vasomotor functions

Barber (1961b, 1965b) and Sarbin (1956) have reviewed numerous articles reporting local vasoconstriction and/or vasodilation with some hypnotized persons by appropriate verbal stimulation. Although these local effects can be demonstrated under hypnotic conditions, the absence of control studies makes it impossible to determine the effects of symbolic stimulation, role demands, and expectations without hypnosis. The extent to which the subjects could voluntarily control these processes without any special instructions at all is not usually assessed.

An example of a more recent report on hemodynamics during hypnosis is that of May and Edmonston (1966). They measured changes in peripheral blood volume in six male hypnotically-naive students and attempted to determine whether these men were less attentive to incidental startling stimuli when hypnotized. A six-man control group was matched on the Barber Suggestibility Scale and the Taylor Manifest Anxiety Scale. The procedure included no training sessions. During the first experimental session, all subjects were seated and blood volume was monitored with a photoelectric plethysmographic finger pickup. The experimental group listened to 19 minutes of taped induction that paraphrased the Stanford Hypnotic Susceptibility Scale (SHSS). Control subjects listened to three taped short stories for an equivalent time. In a counterbalanced fashion, all subjects received either "anxiety" producing instructions, or an unexpected blast from an automobile horn. May and Edmonston's groups did not differ significantly for changes in blood volume in terms of base rate, or responsiveness to the horn or to the fear producing stimuli. Within the experimental group, blood volume did not change significantly during induction; however, the control group showed a significant drop in finger blood volume relative to the experimental group during the 19 minutes of taped stories. In their discussion, these investigators point out that neither their hypothesis of differential plethysmographic changes nor differential inattentiveness to extraneous stimuli during hypnosis and nonhypnotic conditions was supported. Furthermore, the "anxiety" instructions were not rendered physiologically more effectual by virtue of the hypnotic induction.

The subjects of the May and Edmonston experiment were apparently in a "light" depth of hypnosis (the criterion was eye closure). Under these conditions, one would expect the "hypnotized" subjects to be responsive to the blast of an automobile horn. Differential thresholds to extraneous stimuli would probably not have been noticeable with such intense stimuli had they been present in the first place. Also, since subjects received tests of suggestibility *before* the experimental session, they might have expected hypnosis. Thus when the control group hears taped "stories" it is reasonable that they would interpret this to mean they are in a "control condition" and not become involved in their roles. The hypnotized subjects, however, would be expected to become more involved. Finally, the hypnotized subjects in fact responded at about the same level as control subjects to "anxiety" instructions. If hypnotized subjects are less attentive to extraneous stimuli, they would hear fewer of the anxiety instructions than would control subjects. Yet hypnotized subjects were hypothesized to be more suggestible. It follows that they would be more responsive to the smaller portion of "anxiety" stimuli that they do attend to. These opposing processes, lessened attention and enhanced responsivity, may cancel each other, making the hypnotic group comparable to controls on this measure.

Reports on hypnotic effects on anatomically proximal blood flow seem scarce; an example of this type of investigation is that of Maiolo, Porro, and Granone (1969). Five normal but deeply hypnotized subjects were compared with six normal, alert subjects in terms of cerebral blood flow, cerebrovascular resistances, and cerebral metabolic rate of oxygen consumption. No statistically significant differences between alert and hypnotized subjects were found on any of these measures, although standard deviations for the alert subjects were somewhat larger than for the hypnotized group. Maiolo and coworkers suggest that "anxiety" accounts for the greater variance among alert subjects. Hypnotic procedural details were not available in this brief report.

GENITOURINARY FUNCTIONS

As is revealed by the reviews of Dunbar (1954) and of Kroger and Freed (1943), the majority of reports on genitourinary functioning are in the form of anecdotes and clinical case histories. However, within this corpus of literature practically every type of urological, gynecological, and reproductive function can be ablated or produced through procedures that have been termed "hypnotic." Examples of hypnotic control of menstrual cramps, frigidity, impotence, and changes in menstrual periodicity and painless childbirth are commonly reported (Sarbin, 1956).

A recent experimental report involving hypnosis and the genitourinary system is a study of immersion diuresis (urine excretion) published by McCally and Barnard (1968). Water excretion by the kidney is regulated by vasopressin, an antidiuretic hormone (ADH) secreted by the posterior lobe of the pituitary gland. Secretion of this hormone is controlled by two known mechanisms, neural cells in the hypothalamus that are sensitive to osmotic pressure, and efferent impulses from receptors in the heart, primarily the atrial "volume" receptors, which respond to an increase in intrathoracic blood volume. When a person is immersed in water (at body temperature) up to his neck, there occurs an increase in urine flow with a concomitant change in its chemical properties. This phenomenon of immersion diuresis is presumably a result of inhibition of ADH from stimuli from the "volume" receptors of the heart.

McCally and Barnard have shown that immersion diuresis can be significantly modified through suggestion. They analyzed urine samples from seven unpaid volunteer men who had previous autohypnotic training. Experimental conditions were: rest, rest with hypnosis, rest with hypnosis plus suggestions of thirst, immersion, immersion with hypnosis, and immersion with hypnosis and thirst suggestions. These authors acknowledge that they had no measure of hypnotic depth nor suggestion-without-hypnosis condition. However, it is notable that suggestions of thirst versus no such suggestion in the immersion situation resulted in diuretic changes in the directions that might be expected: (a) urine output fell significantly $(p < .05)$, (b) urine osmolarity increased (not significant), (c) urine solute excretion decreased (not significant), (d) sodium excretion increased (not significant), (e) glomerular filtration decreased significantly $(p < .05)$, and (f) free water clearance decreased significantly. "The present study demonstrates that the hypnotic suggestion of thirst inhibits diuresis during immersion" (p. 294).

Like so many other studies, the independent variable is not fully specified. Those differences that met usual standards of statistical reliability could have been produced under "imagination" conditions. Because of the small number of subjects, mean differences could be a result of the responses of but one or two subjects.

GASTROINTESTINAL FUNCTIONS

That hunger contractions, stomach secretions, and a variety of other gastrointestinal functions can be modified by appropriate social-psychological stimulation is evidenced by both experimental and clinical reports (Eichhorn & Tracktir, 1955c; Ikemi et al., 1959; Kehoe & Ironside, 1964; Lewis & Sarbin, 1941; and others). Which of the myriad of variables incorporated into experimental hypnotic treatments are necessary and sufficient for the respective gastrointestinal events has not been ascertained. Hall et al. (1967) examined gastric motor and secretory function during suggested symptoms in healthy volunteers using a standard test meal under controlled conditions with and without hypnosis. Subjects (unspecified as to age or sex) were selected from university student volunteers on the basis of no history of gastrointestinal disorders, high hypnotizability, and diagnostic testing to exclude people with severe emotional problems. Measurements and feeding of a standard meal of dextrose in a phenol red solution was accomplished by nasogastric intubation. During the first and fifth of five sessions each subject heard tape-recorded Chopin nocturnes. The intervening three sessions consisted of a taped hypnotic induction plus suggestions of indigestion or constipation for experimental subjects. Control subjects received the hypnotic induction and then listened to Chopin nocturnes. After each session the subject completed a questionaire about his sensations, then his stomach was emptied, and he was dehypnotized and interviewed in a separate room.

Hypnosis alone resulted in the greatest residual stomach volume and least passage through the pyloric sphincter; this is as compared to music alone and to indigestion and constipation sessions. The rate of emptying of the stomach during the first hypnotic session was significantly lower than during hypnosis plus suggestions of indigestion, but was also significantly lower than during the fifth session of music and no hypnosis. Considering only data for the six out of eight subjects who reported sensations of indigestion or constipation does not change the results of this experiment.

ENDOCRINE FUNCTIONS AND METABOLISM

A number of metabolic processes have been reported susceptible to hypnotic manipulation. Respiratory exchange has been cited above. Sarbin (1956) and Barber (1961b) have reviewed a number of cases reporting hypnotic modification of blood glucose levels, basal metabolic rate, and calcium metabolism. Studies on metabolism and hypnotic stimulation have added to the methodological difficulties mentioned for other types of hypnotic research, since there is extreme liability of temperature, hormone titers, activity, or in general the level of "arousal" in the human body. And since many of these reports involved patients such as diabetics the data are even further confounded.

Few endocrine functions have been studied in relation to hypnosis other than via indirect manifestations through such processes as digestion, circulation, or respiratory alterations. Some work on adrenocortical steroids and hypnosis has been published. In a very simplified way we can think of a feedback loop between the anterior pituitary and the cortex of the adrenal glands. Apparently the pituitary release of ACTH can be affected directly by emotional stimulation, chemical stimuli, or limbic system trauma via the reticular activating system. Release of ACTH from the anterior pituitary into the blood stream stimulates the adrenal cortex to release cortisol (a glucocorticoid) back into the blood stream to affect central nervous system control of ACTH release. High circulation of cortisol inhibits ACTH secretion. The circulating levels of plasma cortisol are also dependent on diurnal cycles. Detectable levels of ACTH are quite low early in the morning and around six in the evening, and reach a peak in the early afternoon.

Sachar and others have reported in replicate a drop in plasma cortisol titers to significantly low levels 90 minutes after hypnotic induction (Sachar, Fishman, & Mason, 1964; Sachar, Cobb, & Shor, 1966). Four graduate students with no previous hypnotic experience were given hypnotic training over a six-week period during which diurnal cycles, medication, and time of reading hypnotic instructions and blood sampling were controlled. At two-week intervals a 90-minute "passive trance" was induced. One hour before and one hour after this session and immediately before and after this session blood samples were taken from each subject. The samples were frozen and later analyzed.

At the end of the six weeks, control blood samples were taken without hypnosis. The day before each of the three "passive trance" sessions the Stanford Hypnotic Susceptibility Scale (Form C) was administered to each subject. With the use of interviews each subject was rated on degree of "nonconscious involvement in the hypnotic role," degree of "trance," and degree of "archaic" relationship with the hypnotist. In 4 out of 12 posttrance assays, 17-HOCS (17-hydroxycorticosteroid includes primarily cortisol and its derivations) fell below a biologically significant cutoff level (2 micrograms/100cc of blood plasma). The 17-HOCS measures never reached this low level in 50 other blood samples (p < .0001). These low plasma cortisol levels did not appear to be correlated with scores of hypnotic susceptibility, nor degree of "trance," nor degree of nonconscious involvement, but did for the one applicable subject seem to be related to the degree of "archaic" transference to the hypnotist. For this subject the induction sessions were exhilirating; he felt that he was becoming dependent on the hypnotist and this pleased him; he had dreams involving the hypnotist and during sessions it seemed to him that the hypnotist was doing his thinking for him. Further nonhypnotic control sessions would have been useful. Sachar and coworkers refer to the "hypnotic state" a term that arises out of his operations inducing the "passive trance." The metatheory of the investigators is revealed in that the "state" occurs at finite times and can be monitored by plasma measures from samples taken before and after the "passive trance."

Reid and Curtsinger (1968) report hypnotic effects on several metabolic-related indices including oral temperature, respiration rate, blood pressure, and pulse rate. Their conclusion is that "neutral hypnosis" is generally accompanied by increased oral and skin temperature. Seventeen men and three women, between the ages of 15 and 60, volunteered to participate in an experiment in hypnosis; 10 of these people had been previously hypnotized. All subjects were seated in a nonhumid, draft-free room maintained at 25° C. Hypnotic inductions were not read or taped, but an attempt was made to make them invariant from subject to subject. In progressive steps the subjects were told to close their eyes, to relax their muscles, to visualize a pleasant scene, and to relax deeper and deeper while the hypnotist counted to 20. Pulse rate, respiration rate, systolic and diastolic blood pressure, and oral temperature were measured several times before and after the "trance." Temperatures were nearly identical pre- and posttrance, that is, 10 minutes before and after the entrance and exit ceremonies. During "trance" the oral temperature went up an average of 0.6° F.

In a second portion of the study, four experimental subjects received the same treatments and four controls were simply told to relax while seated as above. A rise in oral temperature comparable to the first group occurred for experimental subjects, but only a .1° F. rise occurred for controls. Pulse rate, respiration, and blood pressure dropped slightly during "trance," so the increase in oral temperature is not attributable to increases in heart rate or respiration. However, it should be noted that oral temperature is highly dependent upon how a person breathes, as well as upon the rate of respiration and what he is doing with his mouth. Independent measures of body temperature other than intraoral would be helpful to validate the findings of Reid and Curtsinger. Using infrared heat detection techniques, the distribution of temperature changes over the body surface might be monitored during hypnotic and control instructions to explore further relationships between biothermodynamics and social-psychological stimulation.

CUTANEOUS FUNCTIONS

Skin blisters and wheals

The cure, exacerbation of, and production of dermatitis has been attributed to hypnotic stimulation. Reviews of this type of research have been reported by Barber, 1961b; Pattie, 1941; Sarbin, 1956; Paul, 1963; and others. Paul (1963) reviews literature from 1886 to 1962 that has dealt with hypnotic blister production. Of 21 reported attempts to produce nonherpetic skin blisters through suggestion, Paul finds only 14 to be satisfactory in accounting for their methodology, procedures, and controls. Of these 14 reports only 3 appear substantially free of alternative explanations for the reported skin anomolies; and these 3 reports are all from the early literature (prior to 1926). The remaining 11 studies involved procedures wherein self-injury, mechanical stimulation, contact dermatitis and/or mechanical edema could account for blister formation. In some studies, hypnotic suggestion included touching a certain part of the skin of a subject and suggesting that a burn would result. Paul reviews evidence that for some persons mechanical stimulation alone can trigger dermatitis. In those studies where a metal object such as a coin was used to touch the skin, he reviews evidence that the metals involved are known to produce contact dermatitis in some individuals. In other studies, the subjects were found to have irritated the skin in question at some time after the hypnotic induction and before blisters were evident (self-injury).

A unique study of skin reactivity with hypnotic induction is that of Ikemi and Nakagawa (1962). They selected 13 subjects highly allergic to the poisonous leaf of the Japanese wax tree. These subjects were not sensitive to the nonpoisonous leaves of the chestnut tree. Five of these people were administered a hypnotic induction, blindfolded, and told they were being touched with the chestnut leaves. In fact their arms were touched with the poisonous wax leaf. Chestnut leaves were touched to the opposite arm, but now these people were told that they were being touched with the wax leaf. The eight remaining subjects were blindfolded, not given an hypnotic induction, but were given exactly the same treatment with the leaves and suggestions. All subjects showed slight to marked dermatitis (such as flushing, erythema, and papules) when touched with the nonallergenic chestnut leaf but told it was the wax leaf. Five of the hypnotic and seven of the waking control subjects showed no noticeable allergic responses to the poisonous leaves of the wax tree.

Dermal excretions

Little or no experimental literature is available on this subject. A recent case report describes the control of sweat glands of the axilla via hypnosis (Sacerdote, 1967b). An 18-year-old girl had tried various medicants to stop armpit sweating, which became uncontrolled when she was at a social gathering. Sacerdote hypnotized her and over several separate sessions suggestions were given that she could control her involuntary responses and feel gay and happy at future parties. The reported effect of these hypnotic sessions was to bring this patient's sweating back to a normal level of responsivity to excess heat.

Skin temperature

Some reports of vasoconstriction and dilation have been mentioned in the section on cardiovascular functions. A number of reports dealing with surface body temperature alone have also been published. Gottlieb, Gleser, and Gottschalk (1967) examined the effects of hypnotically suggested attitudes on several physiological measures, including blood pressure and skin temperature. The suggested attitudes were: "hives"—described as a feeling of being mistreated but having no desire to act; and "Raynaud's" (after Raynaud's Syndrome)—described as a feeling of being mistreated with a desire to strike the mistreater. Although this investigation employed a standard hypnotic induction for the 12 male high-school subjects, there was no waking control given comparable suggestions. Skin temperature rose significantly for subjects receiving the suggestions characterizing people with hives. A significant drop relative to "hives" temperature occurred with suggestions of Raynaud's attitude. However, over all subjects hypnotic induction produced a rise in skin temperature. (Regrettably, there was an increase in room temperature throughout the induction and testing.)

Interview material revealed that 46 out of 48 suggested attitude periods were accompanied by self-reports of the suggested attitudes. The "hives" attitude did not affect blood pressure, but Raynaud's attitude increased heart rate and systolic (but not diastolic) blood pressure. The data were statistically significant when the attitudes were directed toward the experimental assistant, but not when directed toward the hypnotist. It may be noted that "hypnosis" in this study was used as a vehicle to induce certain attitudes, rather than as the object of a physiological investigation.

Electrodermal changes

Ravitz (1950, 1951a, 1951b) and O'Connell and Orne (1962) found a reduction in spontaneous electrodermal activity during hypnosis as compared to a waking condition. Pessin, Plapp, and Stern (1968) randomly assigned 40 male psychology undergraduates to four groups of 10 each. All subjects were informed that the study concerned hypnosis, but the different groups were not told they would be hypnotized (or not) until just prior to the experimental session. Subjects reclined in a chair and were hypnotized by a standardized form of the SHSS such that words about hypnosis, sleep and drowsiness were removed. The experimental design is given in Table 6.1.

There were spontaneous fluctuations (SF) in the electrodermal response (EDOR) during all treatments. Mean hypnotic SF was 40.75 while for the nonhypnotic groups it was 63.80 *(p* > .025). The SF *between* tone trials were significantly lower for Group I than for Group III. There was no significant difference in rate of habituation of the EDOR between induction and rest groups. The Hypnosis Group I had consistently lower basal levels of skin resistance (BSR) during the rest period before tones than Group III, but this was not statistically significant. These authors comment that relaxation or sleep can result in a decrease in SF, but should be characterized by an increased level of BSR. Since the induction groups had lower BSR after induction, they say that "it seems unlikely that the effects of hypnotic induction in the present study are explainable in terms of heightened relaxation or sleep" (p. 204). Looking at this study critically, we might suggest that Groups I and III were first entertained, via the hypnotic induction, and then asked to perform a signal detection task. Groups II and IV, bored during the rest periods, were asked to perform a scanning task. Entertainment and excitement versus boredom and neutrality could no doubt be reflected in overall "arousal," a generalized somatic condition that would mediate the EDORs and BSRs and SF.

Tart (1963) found a high positive correlation between BSR and depth of hypnosis on a self-report depth scale. He selected "potentially good hypnotic subjects" by testing 345 undergraduate psychology students for arm levitation, interest in participating in the study, and lack of serious maladjustment as judged by MMPI profiles. Eleven men were chosen. These subjects were

TABLE 6.1 Experimental design of Pessin, Plapp, and Stern

Group	Initial Treatment	Final Treatment
I	15 min. Induction	Suggestions to count tone stimuli (intermittent)
II	15 min. of Rest	Suggestion to count tone stimuli (intermittent)
III	15 min. Induction	Suggestions to attend visually to a slide projection and ignore other stimuli while counting squares on the screen
IV	15 min. of Rest	Same as for Gr. III

given two hypnotic training sessions to "familiarize them with the hypnotic state." The procedure the subjects went through suggests that they might be aware of an expectation to be "good subjects" and to report a large magnitude of depth. Tart says there was a high correspondance between subjective depth reports and traditional criteria for depth such as amnesia—for example, 87 per cent of the subjects who reported a depth of 30 or more also reported amnesia. The BSRs were always measured just before or after events such as arm rotation. (If these are sequential items from the previous training sessions, a person might have learned the sequence and expect when the next event will occur; perhaps BSR measures sequential associations.) Tart mentions that a simulator control group with BSR measurements would be valuable. Another control group should just estimate degree of physical relaxation without hypnosis.

CENTRAL NERVOUS SYSTEM FUNCTIONS

Evoked potentials

Just as the spontaneous electrical activity of some mass population of neural elements can be measured by electrodes placed on a person's scalp (electroencephalogram), the sudden "jump" in the EEG tracing following a sudden loud clap of the hands or sudden flash of light into the eyes can also be measured. This sudden change in brain voltage that is driven by an external stimulus is referred to as an "evoked potential."

Evoked potentials are claimed to be affected by hypnotic suggestions by Hernández-Peón and Donoso (1959), and by Clynes, Kohn, and Lifshitz (1963). However, Beck, Dustman, and Beier (1966), Beck and Barolin (1965), and Halliday and Mason (1964) have failed to find a significant effect of hypnotic suggestions on evoked potentials. In the report by Beck, Dustman, and Beier (1966), visual evoked potentials were measured in 10 normal subjects selected for known hypnotic suggestibility, who were hypnotized and given suggestions that light flashes of a constant intensity were in fact brighter or dimmer than a referent flash. Two hypnotists were assigned subjects who were hypnotized for two or more sessions. "Before any suggestion of light intensity was initiated certain behavioral criteria of hypnosis were evaluated, such as suggested catalepsy and anesthesia" (p. 398). Seven subjects reached somnambulism as rated by the Davis and Husband scale (1931). All subjects were photically stimulated by a uniform hemispheric surround. One hundred low intensity flashes were presented to each reclining subject at 2 to 3 second intervals. Summated evoked responses were determined by a computer of average transients for each 100 flashes. During this photic stimulation, subjects received hypnotic suggestions of bright light or dim light. Summations of evoked responses were also made before hypnosis, after hypnosis, and randomly between suggestions of bright and dim light. Evoked responses were also measured for 10 control subjects who actually received just-noticeably brighter, dimmer, or intermediately intense photic stimulation.

Individual records of all 20 subjects plus composite records for experimental and control groups were analyzed for (a) time to peak delay of 7 wave components of the visual evoked response (VER), (b) peak to trough amplitude for each component, (c) total excursion of the recording pen as it traced out the 7 components. Results showed differences in these measures only for the subjects who actually received different intensities of photic stimulation. That is, total excursion and amplitude increased with increased stimulus intensity, but not with hypnotic suggestion of increased or decreased brightness.

The results of this experiment give no support to theories that posit an altered state of consciousness. The possibility remains that instrumentation and analysis were not sensitive enough to detect suggested dimness and brightness. Additional variables could have been assessed that might have offered some indirect support for such a posited altered state. For example, the experimenters could have assessed self-reported changes in brightness and correlated this assessment with changes in photic stimulation.

Spontaneous EEG activity

In earlier reports, the EEG record after hypnotic induction has been claimed by some researchers to be indistinguishable from waking patterns (Blake & Gerard, 1937; Chertok & Kramarz, 1959; Ford & Yeager, 1948; Loomis, Harvey, & Hobart, 1936; True & Stephenson, 1951; Weitzenhoffer, 1953. However, differences between sleep and hypnosis have become a controversial issue, since other workers have found the postinduction EEG to resemble "light sleep," (Barker & Burgwin, 1949; Darrow et al., 1950).

Dittborn and O'Connell (1967) reported an experiment that was designed to show relationships between hypnotizability and sleep as measured behaviorally, physiologically, and by the subject's report. Seventy-five paid undergraduate volunteers were administered the SHSS Forms A and C, and a preexperimental hypnotic induction wherein hypnotizability was assessed behaviorally. In addition, electroencephalograms were obtained to determine alpha content during a waking period. Of these subjects, 51 (mostly men) showed 40 per cent or more waking alpha prior to the experiment. These subjects were then seated in a reclining chair in a dark room and instructed to press a telegraph key each time they heard a stimulus buzzer. All of these subjects were given instructions that they would fall easily into natural sleep, *not* hypnosis, as they listened to the buzzer (which sounded about every 9 seconds). Thus behavioral sleep was defined by failure to press the key when the buzzer sounded, subjective sleep was determined if the subject reported after the experiment that he had "dozed off" or "fallen asleep," and physiological sleep was determined by traditional criteria for Stage 1 EEG sleep.

In terms of hypnotizability, 28 subjects rated 1-4 while the remaining subjects were rated as extremely hypnotizable. Seventeen subjects evidenced 1.5 minutes or more of EEG defined sleep (no mention is made of observations for other than Stage 1 sleep); 10 of these 17 responded to the buzzer while "asleep." Responding to the buzzer during EEG "sleep" was uncorrelated with hypnotizability. The subjects who showed no EEG sleep but did show behavioral sleep were highly hypnotizable subjects (a significant correlation, $p = .01$). Also, these subjects *reported* that they were asleep. Dittborn and O'Connell also found in this study that if subjects did not have the expectation that they were to "fall asleep" in their experimental situation, then they did not; however, if subjects were told that it is likely that people fall asleep in this situation, they do.

These findings offer little substance to the search for sleep correlates of hypnosis because of the multifaceted nature of the sleep variable. The various criteria of the "state of sleep" are poorly related.

In another type of study relating hypnotic susceptibility to phenomena of sleep, Evans et al. (1969) found a tendency of subjects to carry out a verbal suggestion administered during light sleep (EEG Stage 1 sleep). Procedurally, 19 male nurses slept two nights in the laboratory. After at least 120 seconds of Stage 1 sleep by EEG criteria, a suggestion such as "whenever I say the word 'itch,' your nose will feel itchy until you scratch it," was administered. During that same period of Stage 1 sleep, or during a later period, or on the second night of sleep, if the cue word "itch" was spoken, the subject would scratch his nose (latency was about 32 seconds). These subjects did not respond to the cue word when it was spoken in a word association test when the subjects were awake during the day. (It is not clear whether the experimenter ever gave the cue words alone without suggestions, or if subjects would respond to the cue word if awake but it was nighttime). Evans et al. report that responsive subjects at night had waking amnesia for the cue words as well as the behavior they performed in their sleep. Yet these investigators report that with no repetition of the suggestion, the cue word elicited the response sometimes five months later in a follow-up laboratory sleep session. Could this be a result of conditioning to the laboratory setting? Is the response the effect of the cue word alone?

These authors found a high correlation between frequency of responses to the cue words during light sleep and hypnotizability scores. This positive correlation reached significance for subjects who could respond to the cue word on the second night of sleep when suggestions were given only on the first night. Also the subjects who were able to remain asleep while responding to the cue word instructions slept more soundly and claimed that they were sound sleepers (multiple $R = .68$, $p = .01$). Also these more hypnotizable subjects sleep better in the laboratory than the insusceptible subjects, who were easily aroused by verbal stimulation during Stage 1 sleep. Finally, "frequency of sleep response did not correlate with score clusters (factor analysis) derived from the hypnosis scales measuring various aspects of motor suggestion. Instead, sleep response frequency was related to the clusters typically consisting of phenomena obtained with somnambulistic hypnosis: hallucinations and posthypnotic effects" (p. 475). In the light of the analysis by Coe and Sarbin (1971) of the unidimensionality of hypnotizability scales, the findings of Evans et al. fit the notion that some subjects are skillful in performing difficult cognitive acts. The basis of the skill appears to be in the use of "as if" or hypothetical constructions.

The ultimate explanation for this finding, if replicated, will depend upon the meaning given to Stage 1 sleep. If it is discontinuous from waking, then the strategy of research will return to a paradigm not unlike Braid's first theory (1843) that equated hypnosis and sleep.

London, Hart, and Leibovitz (1968) compared EEG alpha activity in subjects that varied in scores of hypnotic susceptibility. [They proceed from the assumption that there are "waking and hypnotic states of consciousness" (p. 71).] They state that many experiments show that people with high and those with low susceptibility to hypnosis also differ considerably in operant performance measures of strength, endurance, psychomotor coordination, and rote memory. London and McDevitt (1967) found that there are also differences in base-rate measures of autonomic nervous system functions.

Women volunteers, $N = 154$, of ages 16 to 61, participated in an experiment on "brain waves and hypnosis." One week before an individual measurement of EEG activity, these subjects were administered the Harvard Group Scale of Hypnotic Susceptibility. The EEG recording session was divided into 10 trials of 2 minutes duration. Subjects were told only to relax with eyes closed ("operant task"). This was followed by a single 2-minute EEG sample after instructions to perform a visual imagery task.

Mean alpha durations were compared for subject falling into four levels of hypnotic susceptibility (10th, 25th, 75th, and 90th percentiles). Between the operant and visual imagery task there were no significant differences in alpha duration. There were significant differences between the 10th and 25th and between the 75th and 90th percentile groups with an increase in alpha duration with increased hypnotic susceptibility scores.[1]

At first glance, this report suggests that hypnotizability is correlated with a fundamental somatic process. It should be made clear, however, that relaxation increases alpha. Perhaps the authors were monitoring the EEG correlates of the ability to accept the relaxation instructions that are implicit, if not explicit, in most inductions.

Katzenstein (1965) reports some electrobiological data on 100 patients at the German Academy of Science Research Institute, (Berlin-Buch, Ger-

---

1. If these highly susceptible people have such high alpha durations during waking periods, this ceiling effect might very well obliterate any expected differences in alpha duration when they are hypnotized.

many). He interprets the presence of alpha activity to indicate hypnotic effect. In some patients he found beta rhythms (signs of vigilance), which he interprets as an indication of the effectiveness of hypnotic influence. In many patients he found delta waves and sleep spindles after induction when the hypnotist had left the room. With a sensitive actograph he found a "remarkably uniform drop" in motor activity in all subjects. This observed immobility exceeded by far the decrease in motor activity that characterized normal sleep. He suggests this hypothesis: "subjects with strong internalized behavioral inhibitions would tend to react more fully to an initial hypnotic induction procedure than those with less strongly developed inhibitions" (p. 323).

We cannot make much of this report because of the lack of measures of hypnotic depth and statistical analyses.

OCULAR MOVEMENTS AND INTERNAL ALTERATIONS

Rapid eye movements

A considerable interest in eye movements has evolved over the past 15 years as a result of work in the early fifties by Aserinsky and Kleitman (1953) showing that concomitant with dreaming are bursts of conjugate rapid eye movements (REMs). One interpretation of this phenomenon is that the dreamer is scanning visual images. Another interpretation suggests that REMs are a nonspecific correlate of attentive activity. The reports that dreaming can occur without REMs and vice versa also raise the possibility that REMs cannot be accounted for by either of these interpretations.

In relation to hypnosis, Amadeo and Shagass (1963) have attempted to test two hypotheses. The more general hypothesis is that eye movements (an increase in intensity or frequency) are a nonspecific concomitant of attentive activity. The more specific hypothesis is stated as follows: "If it were found that eye movements increase in frequency with heightened attention and decrease in the hypnotic state, these findings would support the hypothesis that overall attentive activity is diminished during hypnosis" (p. 139). We should note that two assumptions are implicit in this hypothesis: the assumption that "the hypnotic state" is a given, and the assumption that in that "state" attention is narrowed or reduced in intensity.

Thirteen women and fifteen men, paid volunteers, were subjects in two separate experiments. In an attention experiment 10 subjects had their eye movements measured (EOG) while reclining with eyes closed on a couch. Subjects were instructed to relax while the EOG was recorded for 3 minutes. Next the EOG was recorded while subjects recalled as vividly as possible a scene from a recently viewed movie. Finally subjects were given a word association test with auditory stimuli and the EOG was recorded during the "ready" period, presumably a time of heightened attention. In a hypnosis experiment the remaining 20 subjects were exposed to three conditions in partially counterbalanced design: waking condition—EOG recorded with eyes open, closed, and closed with instructions to perform mental arithmetic (doubling a single digit spoken every 2 seconds); hypnosis condition—subjects were hypnotized by a variation of Kraines's "sleeping method," then the EOG was measured as in the first condition: eyes open, closed, with performance of mental arithmetic; voluntary prevention of eye movement condition—subjects were instructed to concentrate on keeping their eyes perfectly still while EOG was again recorded with eyes open, closed, and during mental arithmetic.

Mean REM/min. were counted for subjects in each condition. REM were defined by a predetermined cutoff amplitude and duration of movement of the recording needle. The results of the attention experiment showed a mean REM/min of 7.6 in the initial resting condition, 20.4 during imagining of the movie, and 17.7 during the "ready" phase of the word association test. The REM rate was significantly lower $(p < .01)$ in the resting phase than in the other two conditions. For the hypnosis experiment the hypnotized subjects and voluntary control subjects had a significantly lower REM rate than nonhypnotized subjects across all three subconditions: eyes open, closed, and during the arithmetic task. The voluntary control REM rate was higher than the hypnotic rate across these subconditions (not statistically significant). Support for the hypothesis of increased eye movements with attentive activity comes from the observation that there was a high REM rate during auditory attention comparable in magnitude to the rate during vivid imagery. These investigators conclude from the hypnosis experiment that "there is antagonism between the hypnotic state and attentive performance" (p. 142). This conclusion is based on the low REM rate for hypnotized subjects plus data that only about half of the subjects when hypnotized succeeded in performing the arithmetic task.

It is important to note that reduced attentive activity was attributed to the presumed "hypnotic state" rather than to different instructions. A "state" is not a necessary given for the interpretation of these data if role theory is employed. If subjects are instructed to behave as if they are sleepy ("sleeping method" of hypnotic induction), the role demands and expectations in that situation are simply contrary to performing mental arithmetic. The high REM rate for these subjects probably reflects the higher degree of arousal accompanying the demand to perform implicitly contradictory tasks, namely to behave as if they were sleepy and relaxed. Unfortunately Amadeo and Shagass cannot validate their "state" proposition by comparison of hypnotized subjects instructed to imagine vividly the movie scene with waking subjects given identical instructions.

The instructions given the voluntary control subjects to "concentrate on holding your eyeballs perfectly still" is logically an instruction for a high level of attention—attention to keeping the eyeballs fixed. Interpretation of these data becomes difficult since in this situation the experimenter is essentially telling the subject to voluntarily interfere with the dependent variable. An interesting comparison would be to record the EOG while the subject is instructed to concentrate on holding his hand or tonque perfectly still.

Another example of recent work on possible relations between hypnosis and bursts of rapid eyeball movements is a study by Brady and Rosner (1966), who compared ocular activity during hypnotically induced dreams with that during imagined dreaming.

Undergraduate paid volunteers (five men and six women) were assigned to the hypnotically-induced dream group (H) on the basis of their reporting dreaming during preexperimental hypnotic suggestions to "have a dream." The mean score of these subjects on the SHSS Form C was 8.2. Three men and two women were assigned to the imagined dream group (C) on the basis that they did not report hypnotically induced dreams. The mean score for this group on the SHSS was 5.6. All subjects were then given identical treatment except that group H was given a hypnotic induction, whereas group C was simply instructed to imagine dreaming (this group was never told that they would not be hypnotized). EEG and EOG were recorded from all subjects during an initial resting phase, after hypnotic induction for group H, during mental arithmetic, during suggested dreaming, during a postdreaming resting phase, and during postdreaming mental arithmetic.

Hypnotized subjects showed the expected increase in EEG alpha relative to preinduction alpha in the same subjects. (Did subjects have eyes closed at all times?) Within group H the range of ocular activity was significantly reduced from waking-resting to hypnotic-resting phases; rest, activity, and amplitude of eye movements did not differ significantly between these two phases. The hypnotic dreams significantly increased the range of eye movements. Mental arithmetic produced a larger range of eye movements after hypnosis than before. The marked differentiation between groups H and C was a significantly lower base rate of all measures of ocular activity for group C. For example, median ocular activity during "dreaming" for group C was 4.8, while for group H the median was 40.3. In fact, imagined dreams never raised any measure of ocular activity above the level for mental arithmetic in the same group (C).

Brady and Rosner conclude that their data supports that of Amadeo and Shagass (1963) that eye movements decrease during hypnotic trance, and that attentiveness is reduced during hypnotic trance as indicated by reduced EOG activity and increased alpha EEG activity.

In any comparison between groups H and C we do not know if differences in EOG activity during any experimental phase were consequences of hypnotic induction, or the preselection of subjects who did or did not manifest hypnotic dreaming. The fact that the initial EOG base rates were so different between groups C and H suggests that these groups differed importantly even before hypnosis. Also, group C not only was not hypnotized, but was given different dream instructions—group H was told to "have a dream," while group C was told to "imagine" having a dream. Therefore the effects of hypnosis per se must be evaluated from data within group H. As was the case with the Amadeo and Shagass experiment, there is no independent measure of hypnotic trance apart from the induction that brought it about. Nor is there a waking control group that is *identical* on preselection criteria. Therefore attributing changes in EEG or EOG to a "state" rather than to different instructions is unwarranted at this time.

Slow eye movements

Weitzenhoffer (1969) has reported observations of slow eye movements (SEMs) during deep hypnosis. In connection with another type of experimentation on hypnosis, he recorded eye movements in 15 subjects who were students, secretaries, and laboratory technicians. Subjects ranged from 0 to 12 on the Stanford Scale of Hypnotic Susceptibility, Form A. The low-scoring subjects were used as simulators, while high-scoring subjects served as hypnotic subjects. Following induction, eye movements were recorded while subjects carried out a variety of tasks including opening and closing their eyes, going into hypnosis with their eyes open, resuming the nonhypnotic state, and then reentering hypnosis at a signal.

Nonhypnotized persons, sitting quietly without specific instructions, produce saccadic eye movements that are irregular and of high amplitude. With eyes closed, the same persons show the same type of REM but of lower amplitude. Reduced REM and micro eye movements occur during induction of hypnosis, (suggested eye closure involved). Somewhat late in hypnosis, and only for the high-scoring subjects on the SSHS (scores combined = 22 or better, scales A, C) a slow eye movement appeared with a period of about 4 seconds and an amplitude of about one-third that during waking REMs. In contrast to REMs, the SEM is a slower and smoother movement. Thus SEMs were produced only by the most hypnotizable and presumably most deeply hypnotized subjects. SEMs were produced when outward judgments of depth were highest (LeCron type of depth estimations). These SEMs were the same as described for stage 1 sleep (light sleep); the subjective report was of lessened awareness but definitely not of sleep. The subjects had no idea what was being measured. In these deeply hypnotized subjects, instructions to open the eyes abolished the SEM, but it returned with eye closure. Subjects who had produced the SEM pattern were unable to reproduce it voluntarily without extensive coaching and practice. Weitzenhoffer states: "It can be said with reasonable confidence that the reported results could not have been the product of demand characteristics of the situation, even if this could be a factor under other conditions" (p. 225).

He cannot discount that the subjects might have fallen into light "natural" sleep since EEG and GSR measures were not taken; it is entirely possible that the somatic mechanisms activated in light sleep which are responsible for the accepted indices of Stage 1 sleep are also activated in hypnosis" (p.

226). The SEM subjects were in contact with and responsive to the hypnotist, however this may also be true of light sleep as was reported by Evans et al. Weitzenhoffer suggests the interesting notion that laboratory sleep studies never have studied "natural sleep," and that in fact there is reason to believe that instructions to the subjects are such as to suggest that they are in a hypnoidal if not an hypnotic state. Weitzenhoffer quotes a report where, physiologically speaking, a subject required to move his legs and arms rhythmically to loud music while viewing synchronized flashes of light produced episodes of *light sleep* alternating with episodes of wakefulness. The subject was unaware of the sleep episodes during this "monotonous" activity. Apparently the EEG record and eye movements of Stage 1 sleep also occur under LSD and with other circumstances. "The fact remains that individuals who, on the basis of well-known and accepted behavioral criteria, must be judged as having been hypnotized, and probably deeply so at the time, have been found conjointly to produce SEM" (p. 227).

According to Weitzenhoffer, light sleep and hypnosis can be the same at this level of physiological manifestation. He quotes Heiman and Spoerri (1953), who suggest that hypnosis can coexist with sleep as distinct but simultaneous states. This notion that two or more ordinarily exclusive "states" can occur simultaneously in the same individual is the basis for the following suggestion by Weitzenhoffer: "one might consider the possibility that subjects who exhibit hypnotic-like behavior in the absence of SEM are merely exhibiting a high degree of waking suggestibility, and those who also produce SEM are exhibiting much suggestibility in the presence of an altered state of awareness, otherwise to be identified as 'hypnosis' as distinct from 'suggestibility' " (p. 227).

Optokinetic nystagmus

During the turning of the head about a vertical axis, there occurs a deviation of the eyes in a direction opposite to the turning. This conjugate eye movement maintains the image of a fixed object on the retinas. After a certain degree of deviation, the eyes are quickly shifted back in the same direction the head is turning. These two movements of the eyes, when cyclically repeated, constitute nystagmus. It is the quick component of eye deviation that defines the direction of nystagmus.

If a person with normal vision gazes at a rotating drum that has alternating black and white vertical lines, he will show horizontal optokinetic nystagmus. A blind person will of course not show this response, but presumably an hysterically blind person or a person faking blindness *will* show the nystagmus. Backus (1962) tested a single subject under three conditions: waking with visual fixation on the rotating drum, deeply hypnotized with eye fixation on the drum, and deeply hypnotized with eyes fixed on the drum but with negative hallucinations suggested, such as that the drum was absent from the room. This subject showed horizontal nystagmus under the first two conditions, but no nystagmus under the third condition. Thus a deeply hypnotized subject was able to respond as if the drum were absent, as though he were truly blind, and in a manner that a faker could presumably not do.

Backus explicitly assumes that the subject was in a "trance" state. Neither the effects or specifics of the induction nor the subject's personal history can be evaluated since details are not reported. It is not clear whether in the third condition the subject continued to fixate on the drum after the negative hallucination instructions; if he discontinued one would of course expect a cessation of the nystagmus. Finally we must ask if the subject might not have shown the absence of nystagmus in a waking condition with fixation on the drum, but also with nonhypnotic instructions to imagine that the drum was absent.

In a controlled experiment Aschan, Finer, and Hagbarth (1962) studied hypnotic suggestion effects on "good hypnotic subjects" during rotary nystagmus. With four experimental treatments it was found that hypnotic suggestions of increased or decreased rotary sensation had the predicted effect of enhancing or diminishing the intensity of eye movements. Unfortunately they did not include a control for suggestions without hypnosis.

Pupillary diameter

Bartlett, Faw, and Liebert (1967) studied the effects of traditional hypnotic relaxation instructions versus alertness instructions on pupil size of a deeply hypnotized subject. A young adult woman who scored in the upper 20 per cent on the SHSS:C was pretested to determine that she could have the subjective experience of hypnosis with her eyes either open or closed. She was then deeply hypnotized (no measure) by the traditional induction procedures of the SHSS:C. A 16mm movie was taken of one of her eyes while she was given suggestions either of relaxation or of alertness and attention. It was found that her mean pupil diameter increased by about 2mm during alertness suggestions, yet after the experiment she reported being in a hypnotic state through both types of instructions. These investigators conclude that "various parameters of arousal apparently associated with hypnosis may be attributable to specifiable characteristics of the instructions used rather than to stable characteristics of the 'state' of hypnosis" (p. 189).

Subjects are known to behave in accordance with their interpretation of the experimental expectation. Did this subject know what the experiment was about? There is no base rate measure of pupil size. Therefore it remains as a possibility that her pupil spontaneously cycled through the diameter changes measured regardless of the type of instructions. Other questions are: Was the subject dark adapted? Were both eyes open? Which eye was measured? What was the variability in pupil diameter?

Ocular anatomy

Strosberg and Vics (1962) studied subepithelial physiological and anatomical changes in the eye of 10 patients who had all been "previously hypnotically conditioned." In a procedure that took only 12 minutes per patient the eye was microscopically examined with a slit lamp before, after, and in one case during hypnotic induction. By using natural landmarks such as a blood vessel on the surface of each individual eye examined, these workers measured the blood supply in the vascular anastomosis, the relucency of the arcades, changes in the curvature of the cornea, and the degree of engorgement of the vessels on the sclera. Unfortunately these investigators give no measure of degree of hypnosis; the hypnotic state is a given and the only statement about the induction procedure is that the patient was "hypnotized." Comparison of observations and measurements during and after hypnosis showed the following results: (a) deepening of color and increase in width of an arbitrarily chosen blood vessel on the sclera (no statistical analyses are reported), (b) the normally open meshwork at the junction of the cornea and sclera became a solid mass, (c) the distance from the corneal-scleral junction to the tops of the vascular arcades decreased (from 50 to 30 of the units marked on the microscopic objective), (d) decrease of blood supply in the anastomosing vessels near the corneal-scleral junction, and (e) a shift in the degree of axis of astygmatism in those patients with this corneal abnormality.

This study shares the faults of many reviewed above. The "hypnotic state" is presented as a given. No control subjects were employed. There was no examination of effects of other types of instructions or of instructions to perform tasks during the "hypnotic state." No statistical test are reported.

Design Problems

To better evaluate the research reports, some of the problems of experimental design should be noted here. The most commonly employed experimental design, subjects-as-own-controls, developed out of the clinical method. Often employing a single subject, the experimenter (or therapist) would first monitor certain physiological processes during the waking (resting) condition. After hypnosis was induced, he would utter either direct suggestions ("your heart is beating faster") or indirect suggestions ("you are about to be attacked by the grizzly bear just behind you"). Any change in monitored physiological responses was attributed to the power of the hypnotic trance. Such clinical reports have been rejected by modern behavioral scientists as support for psychosomatic theories, mainly because generalizations cannot be drawn from single-case studies.

The subjects-as-own-control design is a logical outgrowth of the single-case study. By increasing the number of subjects, and by using standardized experimental treatments, changes in physiological indicators can be traced to antecedent conditions, one of which is the hypnotic induction procedure. A tenuous assumption must be held to give empirical warrant to such a procedure, to wit, that the subject carries no information from one experimental condition to the other. To make the subject "blind" to the experimental hypotheses, the experimenter usually instructs the subject to be amnesic to the earlier treatments. The available evidence makes dependence on the assumption a risky business. For example, Barber (1962c) demonstrated that subjects who expect to be hypnotized during a later phase of an experiment perform differently from subjects who do not hold this expectation.

The independent groups design has been introduced to counter the problems inherent in the subjects-as-own-control design. Those who employ this design are in general interested in demonstrating that the effects attributed to the hypnotic trance can be more parsimoniously attributed to task-motivation, imagination, specialized instructions, and so on. In this design the experimenter employs two or more samples of subjects: to one sample is administered a standard hypnotic induction; the other sample receives nonhypnotic treatments, such as instructions to "imagine vividly." This design has not been widely used in experiments to assess changes in somatic processes. Where it has been employed, the results until now have failed to show any clear support for the existence of a physiological variable that could serve as an independent criterion of the hypnotic trance.

The independent groups design has been criticized as being insensitive to small, but significant, differences. In studies designed to tease out such small differences, Hilgard and Tart (1966) recommend repeated measures on the same subjects, under different conditions. In their study, they first assessed responsiveness to suggestion for three samples of subjects: one sample was tested in the waking condition, another in an imagination condition, and a third in a hypnotic condition. A second session assessed responsiveness of each of the samples to hypnotic induction. A small but significant increase in responsiveness was found for the two groups who had been tested previously under the waking and imagination conditions, but not for the sample that had been tested under the hypnotic condition. They drew the conclusion that a small effect in responsiveness can be attributed to hypnotic induction.

Experiments from Barber's laboratory (Barber & Glass, 1962; Barber & Calverley, 1963b) are not consistent with this finding. The imagination instructions in the Hilgard-Tart experiment are more like those of "unmotivated" subjects in Barber's laboratory. When proper task-motivation instructions are given, different responsiveness under the hypnotic conditions is more difficult to obtain.

The controversy over the relative merits of the own-controls design and the independent groups design has been carried on primarily within the study of hypnotic responsiveness as assessed through hypnotic susceptibility scales. Our search of the literature reveals no parallel controversies where physiological indicators serve as dependent variables.

Another experimental design focuses on base rates. Although widely-used in public health research, base rate design is seldom encountered in hypnosis research and almost never when physiological processes are being monitored. The purpose of the base rate design is to show that subjects are not preselected for characteristics that are relevant to the criterion variable.

An implicit assumption held by many researchers is that the somatic responses under scrutiny have a zero base rate. That is to say, responses such as marked changes in heart rate, skin conductance, and blood sugar levels are nonexistent under ordinary basal conditions in the general population. Therefore, the observation of atypical changes after a hypnotic induction procedure may be attributed to the hypnotic state. Rates of response greater than zero are presumed to result from the induction procedures, when in fact they may already exist in the experimental sample.[2]

When psychophysiological experiments are conducted with small numbers of subjects, it is imperative to have a base rate in order to assess the effects of the experimental treatments. Underwood (1960) reported the results of an experiment that appeared to support the claim that a visual illusion can be influenced by the hypnotic trance. His interpretations suggested the altered operation of perceptual-physiological processes. Sarbin and Andersen (1963) repeated the experiment using imagination instructions rather than the hypnotic induction. Underwood's conclusions were based on the performance of a half-dozen subjects (3 per cent of his total subjects). Sarbin and Andersen demonstrated the same "hallucinatory" phenomenon —without hypnosis—in 9 per cent of their subjects. Had Underwood conducted an assessment of the base rate for this particular task, he would not have concluded that the "hallucination" was specific to the hypnotic induction.

It is obvious why base rates are not usually obtained in psychophysiological research. The time and expense involved are enormous. Each subjects must be assessed individually. In order to establish reliable base rates for infrequent occurrences, hundreds of subjects would have to be assessed.

2. Some years ago, one of us (T.R.S.) was exploring the possibility of studying the effect of hypnosis on reflexes. An adult volunteer was administered a standard hypnotic induction procedure. Depth of hypnosis was assessed by the Friedlander-Sarbin scale. At the conclusion of the testing, the subject was told to relax even more and that his reflexes would be tested by a physician. Imagine the astonishment of the physician when he obtained an apparent infantile Babinski in an intact well-functioning adult. The inference was immediately constructed that the infantile Babinski was a form of regression brought about by the hypnotic induction. Later it was discovered that this patient could exhibit the anomolous reflex under nonhypnotic conditions. The assumption that such anomolies occur only as a result of neuropathology led to the unwarranted expectation of a zero base rate.

Theoretical Integrative Considerations

In reviewing the literature on the somatic effects of hypnosis, we paraphrase William James's comment about his review of the literature on emotion: It would be more rewarding to count and catalog the rocks of New Hampshire than to reread the literature on the somatic effects of hypnosis. Two conclusions can be drawn from our review. Conclusion 1 concerns the question, Are observed alterations in physiological processes specific to the hypnotic "trance"? The answer is an unqualified no. Conclusion 2 concerns the question, Can symbolic processes produce changes in biological processes? The answer is an unqualified Yes. That somatic processes can be influenced by symbolic stimuli is an observation that goes back at least to Aristotle. The reviews of Dunbar (1954) and the reports to be found in *Psychosomatic Medicine* make clear that the introduction of a large variety of stimulating conditions, including symbolic stimuli and imaginings, can influence life processes.

Our theoretical efforts must be redirected. Instead of persevering in the search for an elusive physiological indicator for the trance, we can try to understand the more general problem contained in Conclusion 2. In short, can we illuminate the proposition that physiological processes can be influenced by social psychological stimuli?

The concepts of role theory are helpful in formulating some propositions that help to account for the observations. As a point of departure, we begin with the suggestion that hypnotic performances can be regarded as role enactments, the subject taking the role of the hypnotized person within limits imposed by his expectations, skills, self-conceptions, and by the demands of the situation, including audience effects. Role enactment is the independent variable, and one of its components is organismic involvement in the role performance.[3]

The enactment of any role may be conceptualized in terms of more or less intensity, or rate of energy transformation. "Intensity" is the descriptive term applied to the molar observed event; it is tied to the increased functioning of the organism as a whole and can be monitored by various physiological assessment procedures. In fact, the change in intensity of the molar act depends in part on changes in the internal physiology. For example, the intense role of "quarterback making an end run" cannot be enacted unless the visceral and somatic organ systems are acting synergically.

The organismic-involvement dimension, of course, applies to any social role, be it shaman, professor, shortstop, or mother. It is a matter of everyday observation that roles are enacted with varying degrees of organismic involvement, although in most roles, of course, it is minimal—otherwise the

---

3. The paragraphs dealing with the concept of organismic involvement are freely adapted from Sarbin (1956).

physiological expenditures would be out of proportion to available reserves. One approach to the assessment of the organismic dimension, commonly used by clinically oriented investigators and reporters, is that of global observation of the role. The investigator observes the patterned activity of visible effector organs and then records his observations, using for examples such qualitative terms as agitated, surprised, anxious, heated, calm, matter-of-fact, apathetic. The investigator may further organize his perceptions into social concepts such as frenzied behavior, passive role, assertive conduct, "little-boy" role, etc. To such observations our knowledge of general physiology can be added and we can predict (and test the predictions) that certain physiological changes will be associated with certain degrees of organismic involvement in a particular role.

As an everyday example, take the husband of a primiparous woman who is in labor in a modern hospital. From a time-sample observation we would say that he is tense, anxious, pacing, restless, and so on. We could further organize these qualities on the basis of knowledge of the situation into the role concept of "expectant father." We could further place his conduct at a high level of organismic involvement and predict elevation in blood pressure, increase in temperature, cessation of gastric function, increased palmar sweating, and other characteristics that are part of the adaptive techniques of the organism to stress. Furthermore, we can predict reversals of the global behavior within a finite time interval following the announcement of the birth of the child and the reassurances of the physician that all is well. The shift in behavior will be organized around his everyday occupational role, one that is normally enacted with low-level involvement. Associated with the taking up of his everyday role are the reversals of the physiological changes mentioned before. The concept of organismic involvement in role enactment is, for the present, organized around such global conceptions. That such involvement can be monitored by appropriate psychophysiological and physiological techniques has been amply demonstrated.

For purposes of this exposition, we will illustrate eight levels of organismic involvement in role taking. Hypnotic subjects may perform with intensities that can be classified at any point on this organismic dimension, except perhaps at the extremes.

Level 0. This level can be characterized by latent roles peripheral to everyday actions; there is absence of involvement.

Level 1. This is everyday casual role enactment. There is little affect, little involvement of self in role. Performances are more or less automatic, routinized, effortless. The actions of the hypnotic subject cannot be classified at this level: to volunteer for an experiment in hypnosis or to seek hypnotic therapy denotes greater involvement in the social role than level 1.

Level 2. At this level, mechanical acting, we can observe the behavior of hypnotic subjects who score low on depth scales. Here the hypnotic subject, like the mechanical actor, performs stereotyped ritual movements in order to validate his occupancy of the social position. Again we see little affect and little effort, although more than in level 1. According to retrospective accounts of "mechanical" actors and of hypnotic subjects classified at this level, there is little involvement of self in role.

Level 3. Heated acting ("living the role") shows, of course, more effort, more activity on the part of the subject, such as grimacing, increased rate of respiration, and tension, and more side effects of such voluntarily initiated activity. In order to manifest rage, for instance, an actor may work himself up emotionally by violently shaking a ladder in the wings before appearing on the stage. Among the easily observed side effects are erythema, rapid pulse, increased sweating, and vocal effects. Here we can see much involvement of the self in the role. Many hypnotic subjects behave in ways that allow them to be classified at this level.

Level 4. This level is denoted by hypnotic behavior of the somnambulistic type. The classical behavior of the deeply hypnotized subject, the perceptual-motor effects, the compulsive posthypnotic behaviors, the amnesias, the hallucinations, all show much involvement of the self in the role. There is apparent effort, a striving to do what the experimenter requests. Here is illustrated most forcefully the operation of the "as if" mechanism, the influence of covertly taking the role in a relatively complete way, with reduction of possibilities for performing competing roles. The subject tries to perform as if he were blind, or deaf, or analgesic, or anosmic, or whatever the role instructions demand.

Level 5. The behaviors subsumed under the rubric histrionic neurosis or conversion reactions are used as a frame of reference on the organismic dimension. The histrionic patient responds as if he suffered some sensory or motoric affliction. The range of intensity overlaps the range of behaviors of the deeply hypnotized person, level 4. However, expression of affect associated with the maintenance of the "as if" behavior is the rule. The involvement of the self in the role of the invalid is immediately apparent when efforts are made to modify the behavior. At the same level of intensity are trance states of the Plains Indians (Benedict, 1934) and the couvade (Crawley, 1927), the custom where the husband lies-in during parturition.

Level 6. Only occasionally are hypnotic performances classified at level 6. Ecstatic states are usually associated with the suspension of voluntary action. They are seen in socially initiated situations such as religious conversions, mystical states, possession, and religious revivals. In addition to the greater involvement of the skeletal musculature, there is an increased involvement of the organs served by the autonomic nervous system. Here we see, in extremis, affect and effort. The nearly complete submergence of the self in the role is observed. Obviously, such performances cannot be prolonged over time without damage to the organism. As a general rule, automatic equilibratory controls terminate such intense behaviors through institutionalized rituals, fatigue or exhaustion, and/or autonomic regulation.

Level 7. This level is not applicable to the usual experiment in hypnosis. It is an extension of the previous range but is characterized by the failure of equilibratory mechanisms. Well-authenticated cases of voodoo death have been described by Cannon (1942) and others. The focus is on role taking as the initiatory phase of complex and irreversible physiological activity.

Conclusion

Within a naturalistic framework, which asserts that hypnosis is not necessarily a transcendental phenomenon but rather a specialized kind of social situation, our point of departure for theory building must depend upon objective observation of the events in question, interpreted against a background of available knowledge drawn from psychology and physiology.[4]

4. Because of space limitations, we have had to forego considering general theories of psychosomatics against which physiological changes in hypnosis may be evaluated. Theoretical accounts have been offered by Arnold (1959), Kraines (1969), Roberts (1960), Sarbin (1956) and others. The importance of the brain stem reticular system, diffuse projection systems, and "recruiting" response and "attentional" processes in general are clearly underscored in current theories. Arnold, Kraines, and Roberts each relate hypnosis to those same processes that underly attention and sleep. All three agree that the neural substrates for hypnosis fall between the classical sensory and motor systems. These neurophysiological hypotheses account for most of the "symptoms" of hypnosis. They are sufficiently general, however, to be a basis for many types of behavior other than hypnotic behavior. The definition of hypnosis in these accounts remains unspecified, taken for granted without rigorous attention to operational designations of the phenomena for which the neural substrates are hypothesized. Unlike such theories that focus on dependent variables, the views advanced in the theory proposed by Sarbin (1956) take into account the vagaries in the independent variable "hypnosis." Because no physiological variable has been discovered that is *specifically* tied to hypnosis, the most obvious place to begin a theory is at the juncture of the symbolic stimulus and the initial molar somatosensory response.

Leslie M. Cooper *is a Professor of Psychology at Brigham Young University. He received his Ph.D. from the University of Illinois in 1962. Upon obtaining his degree, he joined the staff at Brigham Young University. In 1964, he joined the Department of Psychology at Stanford University as an Assistant Professor. While there, he was associated with the Laboratory of Hypnosis Research for two years. In 1966, he returned to teaching and research at Brigham Young University. He has been a consultant to the Utah State Training School, the Alpine House (halfway house) Project, and the Utah State Prison. He is a diplomate in experimental hypnosis and licensed as a psychologist in the state of Utah. His research interests include hypnosis, learning, and imagery.*

Cooper *presents a comprehensive review of current knowledge about hypnotic amnesia as derived from experimental studies. The chapter begins with a definition of hypnotic amnesia and describes the standardized assessment procedures used to measure it in the laboratory. Different types of hypnotic amnesia are described, methodological problems and research evidence are reviewed, and the variables that influence hypnotic amnesia are discussed along with the issues of authenticity and underlying mechanisms. Cooper argues that hypnotic amnesia needs to be redefined in order to eliminate mere verbal inhibition, and to integrate the role of normal forgetting. He also stresses that better ways should be found to incorporate clinical sources of evidence into laboratory settings.*

7

Hypnotic Amnesia

LESLIE M. COOPER

As one of the phenomena that prominently characterize hypnosis, amnesia has long figured in the lore and anecdotes relating to hypnosis. References to its occurrence and effects are found in some of the earliest literature on hypnosis. Experimental investigations of amnesia began in the early twentieth century. Much of the early experimental work lacked an objective, standardized measure of susceptibility to hypnosis. It is little wonder that there was difficulty in uncovering the parameters of hypnotic amnesia, or any other hypnotic phenomena for that matter, when there was not much objective agreement as to how to measure hypnosis. In 1959, the first of a series of susceptibility scales was published, which overcame this problem. The scales, discussed later in this chapter, possess the psychometric properties of high reliability, internal consistency, and validity, making it possible to measure susceptibility to hypnosis in a controlled manner. They yield results that can be meaningfully compared from study to study. The development of these scales made it possible to study rigorously various hypnotic phenomena, including amnesia.

The previously unpublished studies by the author reported in this chapter were supported by a University Research Fellowship from Brigham Young University; by Research Grant MH-3859, National Institute of Health, U.S. Public Health Service; Contract AF 49 (638)-1436, U.S. Air Force Office of Research to Dr. Ernest R. Hilgard, Principal Investigator, Laboratory of Hypnosis Research, Stanford University; and by Grants MH-08598 and MH-12853, National Institute of Health, U.S. Public Health Service to Dr. Perry London, Principal Investigator, University of Southern California. I wish to express my appreciation to Drs. Hilgard and London for their assistance and support in carrying out the research, and to Dr. Robert J. Howell and Mr. John D. Richards for their comments and suggestions in the preparation of this chapter.

This chapter attempts to review current knowledge about hypnotic amnesia and to present the experimental evidence supporting these conclusions. The survey of the literature should be considered representative, rather than exhaustive. An attempt has been made, however, to comprehensively cover the areas associated with hypnotic amnesia. Experimental evidence for, and procedures used to study, hypnotic amnesia are surveyed, rather than clinical case studies. The organization of the chapter is topical rather than chronological. The first section discusses the definition of amnesia and the means devised to measure it. A typical procedure used to assess amnesia is presented in detail, so that the reader will understand the nature of the instructions commonly used, the task of the subject, and the manner of assigning a score to the response.

"Hypnotic amnesia" is an inclusive term used to label any of a number of different types of amnesia occurring as a result of a hypnotic procedure. The second section of this chapter defines and discusses a number of different types of amnesia, such as posthypnotic recall amnesia and source amnesia. It briefly describes representative studies investigating each type, including the evidence for their occurrence as well as their relationship to one another.

A third section discusses the variables that have been found to give rise to and affect the nature of hypnotic amnesia. This section discusses the independent variables when considering amnesia as a dependent variable. The role of demand characteristics as conveyed through the instructions of the experimenter and the expectations of both the hypnotist and the subject, the role of normal forgetting, and the role of hypnotic susceptibility are discussed. A consideration of the authenticity of hypnotic amnesia is also discussed in this section.

Finally, various mechanisms that have been proposed to theoretically explain amnesia are discussed. The concepts of functional ablation, repression, regression, and dissociation are presented. Some of the supporting evidence for each of these explanatory positions is given.

Definition

"Amnesia" means a loss of memory, due usually to brain injury, shock, fatigue, repression, or illness. Webster also gives a second definition: "a gap in one's memory." "Hypnotic amnesia," then, is a forgetting that is associated with a hypnotic experience, rather than brain injury, fatigue, or illness.

The Marquis de Puységur is given credit for "discovering" hypnotic amnesia in 1784. It is said that he mesmerized a shepherd boy, who immediately fell into a deep trance and began sleepwalking. When the boy awakened from the trance, he had no recollection of what had occurred during the trance. It was believed that sleepwalkers could not remember what they had done while "somnambulistic"; the term "somnambulist" was applied to deeply hypnotized persons because they were thought to be amnestic for what was done while hypnotized. While it is generally agreed today that the hypnotized individual is not asleep, the term remained to describe the deeply hypnotized person.

Amnesia is present when a subject fails to recall either the material or events that have been associated with a hypnotic experience or whatever the hypnotist has specifically suggested to forget, and when this material can be recovered at some later time either through appropriate suggestions or a reinduction of hypnosis. Thus, while hypnotic amnesia is distinct from simple forgetting, the two phenomena cannot be told apart as long as the amnesia remains. The recovery of the material, however, serves to distinguish hypnotic amnesia from forgetting. But as we shall see, all too often little more than lip service has been paid to the importance of demonstrating the recoverability of the material. (It is just assumed that the material would have been recovered if appropriate procedures had been utilized.) Unfortunately, this has sometimes encouraged the use of language (if not constructs) to define and explain hypnotic amnesia not different from that used to define and explain forgetting.

Empirically, a concept is ultimately defined in terms of the operations used to measure it. A typical example of such operations for recall amnesia is found in the procedures used in the Standard Hypnotic Susceptibility Scale, Forms A and B (Weitzenhoffer & Hilgard, 1959). Recall amnesia is suggested toward the end of the hypnotic session by telling the subject "you will probably have the impression that you have slept because you will have difficulty in remembering all the things I have told you and all the things that you did or felt. In fact, you will find it to be so much of an effort to recall any of these things that you will have no wish to do so. It will be much easier simply to forget everything until I tell you that you can remember. You will remember nothing of what has happened until I say to you: 'Now you can remember everything!' You will not remember *anything* until then" (pp. 23-24). After the subject is awakened from hypnosis, he is asked to tell in his own words everything that has happened since he began looking at the target. After having an opportunity of responding, and having come to a block, he is then asked, "Anything else?"; after stopping again he is told, *"Now you can remember everything*—anything else now?" and he is given the opportunity to add to those events that he experienced under hypnosis but could not remember prior to the recovery signal.

The number of items reported prior to the recovery signal is recorded, and the subject is scored as passing amnesia if the number reported is three or fewer. The number of items reported after the recovery signal is obtained; however, this information has not often been used as part of the scoring definition of amnesia.

These procedures give credit to any item that is not reported. Literally, this does not require that the subject has forgotten the material (in either a chemical, physiological, or psychological sense). All that is required is that the subject not report it. The failure to report may be a result of having temporarily forgotten the item, of having permanently forgotten it (a test of recoverability permits the evaluation of this alternative), or it may be a result of an unwillingness or an inability to report the item for various reasons. For example, when asked to describe the experience of posthypnotic amnesia, some subjects have remarked: "I feel that if I thought hard enough I could remember, but I just can't get down to business," and "I haven't any inclination to go back over it," or "I do remember but I can't say, I can't think of the word . . ." (White, 1941, p. 491). Wells (1940) noted that this could occur as a result of an inhibition of voluntary recall and suggested that it be called "pseudo-amnesia." It might also simply be a form of verbal inhibition. There is a lack of agreement as to whether responses of this nature should be considered true amnesia.

Hull (1933) suggested that inasmuch as the amnesia could be reversed, that is, the material recovered, the underlying mechanism was not at the level of registration or retention, but rather at the level of reproduction. Can verbal inhibition be construed as a problem of reproduction? Hilgard (1966) proposed that hypnotic amnesia may be explained, in part, as a form of inhibition of motor speech, although he recognized the problems in such a formulation. Many studies have purposely used measures other than direct recall to assess the presence of amnesia to control for verbal inhibition (Barber & Calverley, 1966b; Bitterman & Marcuse, 1945; Imm, 1965; Patten, 1932; Scott, 1930; Strickler, 1929; Thorne, 1969; Williamsen, Johnson, & Eriksen, 1965). Orne (1966a) has suggested that verbal inhibition should be differentiated from subjectively real amnesia.

Whatever may be ultimately meant by amnesia, so long as the operations currently utilized in most susceptibility scales are used to assess it, all of the response types discussed here are classified as amnesia.

Kind of Amnesia

Observation has suggested that there are various forms and/or kinds of hypnotic amnesia. They can be distinguished from one another by the tasks presented, the absence or use of specific suggestions and their nature, and the time at which the testing of amnesia is carried out.

Thorn (1960), Evans (1966b), and Hilgard (1965a, 1965b, 1966) have suggested and discussed classification schemes differentiating the various types of hypnotic amnesia. Two major forms of hypnotic amnesia are spontaneous amnesia, which occurs without any explicit suggestion for its occurrence, and suggested amnesia, which comes about following a specific suggestion by the hypnotist that the amnesia will occur. This clear-cut distinction cannot always be made in the practical situation, since what appears to be spontaneous amnesia may be indirectly suggested through the expectations of the hypnotist or through subtle cues and consequently be, in fact, suggested amnesia. However, this difficulty is not so great as to void the usefulness of the distinction.

Hilgard (1965b) lists and discusses the following types or kinds of amnesia: (a) posthypnotic (recall) amnesia, an amnesia for the events within the hypnotic session; (b) posthypnotic source amnesia, a *retention* of material learned within the hypnotic state, but a forgetting of the fact that it was learned under hypnosis; (c) posthypnotic amnesia for material learned within the hypnotic conditions; (d) posthypnotic partial amnesia, an amnesia for only some of the events or materials learned within the hypnotic session; and (e) amnesia within the trance for earlier within-trance events while the subject remains hypnotized. While other types of amnesia have been proposed, such as symbolic amnesia (Strickler, 1929), sensory amnesia, and amnesia of integration (Wright, 1966), little systematic work has been done to further our understanding of them.

POSTHYPNOTIC RECALL AMNESIA

Spontaneous posthypnotic amnesia for the events occurring within hypnosis has been considered by many as intrinsic to, and characteristic of, deep hypnosis. Since Puységur discovered it, posthypnotic amnesia has functioned as one of the distinguishing signs of hypnosis. Virtually all scales that have attempted to assess hypnotic susceptibility or hypnotic depth have included some type of amnesia item.

Braid maintained that his patients were not truly hypnotized unless spontaneously and completely amnesic. Charcot and his associates used amnesia to distinguish somnambulism from catalepsy and lethargy as qualitatively different hypnotic states. Richet used amnesia as an index for two of his three degrees of hypnotic depth. Liébeault and Bernheim both utilized spontaneous amnesia as a characteristic of the deeper stages of their scales. All of the nineteenth-century scales heavily weighted spontaneous posthypnotic amnesia as a criterion of deep hypnosis (Hilgard et al., 1961).

Even the more recent susceptibility scales have incorporated an item involving some form of amnesia, usually suggested amnesia. The Davis and Husband scale (1931), the scale proposed by Barry, MacKinnon, and Murray (1931), the scale of Friedlander and Sarbin (1938), and the scales developed by Eysenck and Furneaux (1945), LeCron and Bordeaux (1947), and Watkins (1949), all used some type of amnesia item as an index of susceptibility or depth. This is also true of the still more recent widely used susceptibility scales such as the Stanford Hypnotic Susceptibility Scale, Forms A and B (SHSS:A and B) (Weitzenhoffer & Hilgard, 1959) and Form C, (SHSS:C) (Weitzenhoffer & Hilgard, 1962) and its variations; the Harvard Group Scale of Hypnotic Susceptibility (HGSHS) (Shor & Orne, 1962), and the Children's Hypnotic Susceptibility Scale (CHSS) (London, 1963). Posthypnotic selective partial amnesia (amnesia for one item) is employed in the Barber Suggestibility Scale (Barber, 1965a and 1969b).

Very few present-day investigators claim that spontaneous amnesia is the only defining phenomenon of hypnosis. In the more recent scales, neither spontaneous nor suggested amnesia is treated as the sole defining characteristic of the hypnotic state. Rather, amnesia is treated as just one of many phenomena comprising the operational definition of hypnosis, with which it is less than perfectly correlated. For example, the suggested amnesia items of the SHSS correlate from .23 to .62 with the other items of the scale, the average correlation being .42; and its correlation with the total scale minus the amnesia item is .69. The better controlled research on amnesia defines susceptibility as the total score with the amnesia item deleted (for example, Hilgard & Cooper, 1965).

In attempting to assess the actual frequency of occurrence of amnesia, it must be remembered that the frequency with which amnesia occurs depends on the criterion by which it is measured. It has been pointed out that most of the recent scales of susceptibility consider posthypnotic amnesia to be manifest if some specified number of the events that occurred in the hypnotic session are not recalled after the subject has been awakened. For example, as already mentioned, a subject is credited with having passed the amnesia item on the SHSS if three or fewer items are recalled. Unfortunately, there has been a wide discrepancy from study to study in the arbitrary selection of the number of items that must be forgotten to pass amnesia, making comparisons difficult. Very seldom, if ever, is the recoverability of the memory incorporated as a necessary part of the criterion.

Furneaux (1946) reported that 17 per cent of the subjects spontaneously failed to recall more than one-third of the 17 items in the scale devised by Eysenck and Furneaux (1945). He concluded that spontaneous amnesia for the events within hypnosis is a result of hypnosis and not an artifact suggested by the operator. Evans and Thorn (1966) tested for spontaneous amnesia in three different samples and found that 20 per cent, 16 per cent, and 26 per cent of the subjects in the three samples forgot at least two-thirds of the 17 items presented. They further concluded that normal forgetting could account for much of the failure to remember, since 24 per cent of a waking control group also failed to remember at least two-thirds of the items. They also suggested that some of the forgetting may be due to the demand characteristics of the situation.

A greater proportion of the subjects pass the amnesia item when it has been suggested. Friedlander and Sarbin (1938) found that 24 per cent of their subjects remembered three or fewer items of their seven-point scale when it was suggested that they would not remember. Weitzenhoffer and Hilgard (1959) found that 32 per cent of the students comprising the standardization sample of the SHSS passed suggested amnesia.

Although few studies have tested for both spontaneous and suggested posthypnotic amnesia, Hilgard and Cooper (1965) did obtain comparative figures of the prevalance of both forms of posthypnotic amnesia. Ninety-one introductory psychology students were divided into two groups. A standard induction procedure was used, and suggestibility items that served to measure susceptibility and to test for amnesia were presented. For one group, spontaneous amnesia was tested on the first day, and suggested amnesia on the second day. The order was reversed for the second group. Evidence for amnesia was determined by the subject failing to remember more than 5 of the 10 items possible. Seven per cent showed spontaneous amnesia on one of the two days, while 35 per cent (a significantly larger proportion, $p = .001$) showed suggested amnesia. It was further found that the highly susceptible hypnotic subjects showed no more spontaneous posthypnotic amnesia than did the other subjects. There was some effect of suggested posthypnotic amnesia for all levels of susceptibility, but it became very pronounced only with susceptibility scores of 6 and above.

These findings do not disprove the occurrence of spontaneous posthypnotic amnesia, but suggest that it is less frequent than has been previously supposed, and less frequent than suggested amnesia. They also suggest that when a high frequency of spontaneous posthypnotic amnesia is reported, it may be a result of the experimenter giving subtle and unintentional cues or suggestions that it occur.

POSTHYPNOTIC SOURCE AMNESIA

Posthypnotic source amnesia, first discussed by Thorn (1960), occurs when something is learned under hypnosis and the result of the learning is carried into the waking state, but the fact that it was learned under hypnosis is forgotten. The phenomenon is typical of memories related to knowledge obtained in childhood. We all know when the Declaration of Independence was signed, who gave the Gettysburg Address, where the Pilgrims landed, but we seldom have any specific idea where or how we obtained the information. The concept basis to source amnesia had been subtly imbedded in the memory literature for some time, relating to the difference between what subjects could retain and what they said they could remember (Strickler, 1929; Hull, 1933). Banister and Zangwill (1941) used an experimental procedure similar to that used to investigate source amnesia, but described their investigation as one of paramnesia.

In studies investigating posthypnotic source amnesia, hypnotized subjects are taught answers to questions not generally known, such as "What is the mean diameter of the earth?" "What is the population of Singapore?" (Cooper, 1966a). Later, after being awakened, subjects are tested to see if they remember the information and its source. They are credited with posthypnotic source amnesia if they can give the correct answers to the questions but cannot state the circumstances under which the information has been learned.

Evans and Thorn (1966) reported that 13 per cent, 11 per cent, and 7 per cent of three samples met the criterion of spontaneous source amnesia on at least four out of six items. Only one subject (2 per cent) in a waking control group met this criterion.

In a test for both suggested and spontaneous source amnesia (Cooper, 1966a), 93 students from an introductory psychology course were randomly assigned to one of two groups. The standard induction of the SHSS:C was utilized, and modified items from the SHSS:C as well as source amnesia items were presented. For one group, source amnesia was suggested on one day and not suggested on the second. This order was reversed for the second group. In order to be considered as passing source amnesia, subjects were required to know the correct answers to all three source amnesia items, but to fail to state the source of the information. Two per cent showed spontaneous source amnesia, and 9 per cent, a significantly larger proportion (p = .05), showed suggested source amnesia. Using the less rigid scoring criterion of requiring the subjects to fail to remember the origin of only one of the questions, the frequency of spontaneous source amnesia increased to 9 per cent, and of suggested source amnesia to 14 per cent. It was further found that there was little effect of source amnesia below a susceptibility score of 4, and that both spontaneous and suggested source amnesia increased as hypnotic susceptibility increased. Spontaneous source amnesia correlated .57 (p = .001) with susceptibility and suggested source amnesia, .34 (p = .05) with susceptibility.

Thus, spontaneous source amnesia has been demonstrated to occur, but again it occurs less frequently than when it is suggested, and careful consideration should be given to the possibility of giving subtle cues for its occurrence when testing spontaneous source amnesia.

Evans and Thorn (1966) have argued that the distinction between recall amnesia and source amnesia arises from different underlying mechanisms, and thus that they should be considered as independent phenomena. When submitted to factor analysis (Evans, 1966b; Thorn, 1960), recall amnesia was found to load on a factor relating to compulsively executed posthypnotic actions. They found that only 4 out of the total of 243 subjects developed both types of amnesia. However, Cooper (1966a) found that the correlation between spontaneous and suggested source amnesia (.53) was only slightly higher than the correlation between the two forms of source amnesia and recall amnesia (.48 for spontaneous and .49 for suggested), suggesting that subjects who are more amnesic for the events within hypnosis are more likely to yield both spontaneous and suggested source amnesia. Gheorghiu (1969) has more recently claimed that all subjects manifesting recall amnesia can subsequently be led to manifest source amnesia.

Some investigators have maintained that recall amnesia is related to posthypnotic responses in that subjects not manifesting amnesia also tend not to carry out other posthypnotic suggestions (Hilgard, 1965b). Barber (1962b) and Sheehan and Orne (1968) have shown that amnesia is not a necessary or sufficient condition for posthypnotic behavior to occur, but the latter authors report that amnesic and nonamnesic subjects do respond differently to posthypnotic suggestions.

AMNESIA FOR LEARNED MATERIAL

Strickler (1929) was one of the first to investigate this type of amnesia. He tested for savings of nonsense material that had been learned under hypnosis and for which amnesia was suggested. He compared the results with a group who had not previously been submitted to the hypnotic condition and found that the hypnotized group took just as many trials. A series of studies (Graham & Patten, 1968; Huse, 1930; M. Mitchell, 1932; Nagge, 1935; Orne, 1966a; Takahashi, 1958) utilized this type of amnesia to investigate the hypothesis that there should be less retroactive inhibition if hypnotic amnesia for the interpolated material was suggested. Although there is some inconsistency in the results, the general findings do not support the hypothesis. More will be said about this in a discussion of functional ablation as an underlying mechanism of hypnotic amnesia.

Patten (1932) and Wells (1940) showed that the extent of this type of amnesia is a function of the susceptibility of the subjects, the explicitness of the suggestions for amnesia, and the apparent relevance of the procedures utilized to assess the amnesia. A more recent study is that of Williamsen, Johnson, and Eriksen (1965).

In order to understand the controls used in this study and others to be reported later, it is necessary to explain a simulation group as utilized in hypnotic research. A simulator is a subject who has not been hypnotized, but has been instructed to fool a hypnotist (who is blind to the true hypnotic or waking state of the subjects) into thinking that the simulator is responding appropriately, that is, is truly hypnotized. Simulators are not given any special training about how a hypnotized person should or does act so that their behavior is a result of the instructions, expectations, and demand characteristics of the experiment. It is necessary to have determined that the simulators are unhypnotizable and thus will not enter hypnosis. Previous studies have shown that simulators cannot be detected from experimental (hypnotized) subjects when these conditions are met, but their behavior serves as a control for the effects of instructions and expectations.

In the study by Williamsen, Johnson, and Eriksen (1965), a list of six words was read to the subjects in three different groups, and the subjects were asked to repeat them. The words were presented under hypnosis to an experimental group, to whom suggestions for amnesia were also given; subjects in a simulation group were asked to pretend they were hypnotized, then given the words and the instructions for amnesia; the words were presented to a control group with instructions to forget them. All subjects were subsequently asked to recall as many of the words as they could. Amnesia impaired recall for the experimental group, and they reported more than the simulating group but fewer than the control group. The same trends were found for the recognition test. However, amnesia did not reduce the availability of the words for the experimental group as associative responses. A signal to remove the amnesia was given to the hypnotized and simulating subjects, and they were again asked to give as many of the words as they could remember. While not all of the words were recovered (approximately 82 per cent), a significantly larger number of words were recalled than under the amnesia condition. The study was replicated by Barber and Calverley (1966b) with additional control groups added, and they concluded that the differences were attributable to instructional and motivational differences rather than to the effects of the hypnotic condition. Thorne (1969) used recall amnesia to investigate the effects of different instructions.

There are a number of methodological problems associated with the experimental investigation of this type of amnesia. One has to do with the control of the learning task and the opportunity for rehearsal. If it cannot be demonstrated that the subjects in all groups have learned equally well, differences in amnesia may be due to differences in learning rather than or in addition to the hypnotic suggestions. The confounding of these two factors will not permit an unequivocal interpretation. While a separate experiment was run by Williamsen, Johnson, and Eriksen (1965) to evaluate this influence, such a control is all too often lacking. The finding that subjects may learn less well when hypnotized by the more usual procedures makes this possibility more critical. Liebert, Rubin, and Hilgard (1965) have suggested that the failure to find superior hypnotic performance in learning studies may be due to the passive, lethargic, induction procedures utilized, and if an alert trance were utilized different results might occur.

When subjects are used as their own control by administering different conditions to them at different times, but similar measures are utilized to assess amnesia, then the opportunity for rehearsal may have a relevant effect. Day-to-day effects have been found when both Forms A and B of the SHSS have been utilized. Although susceptibility generally increases (even though slightly) from the first to the second day, it has been found that there is a slight decrease in the number of items forgotten. Since memory is restored before concluding the first day's session, it appears that this helps to facilitate recall on the second day. The two sets of recall scores correlated .67, and when the effect of regression toward the mean was eliminated, the rehearsal or practice effect was found to increase the recall score from .5 to 1.5 items (Hilgard, 1965b). It was found that a change from a waking suggestion to a hypnosis condition can lead to a decrease in the amount of amnesia, which could lead one to the paradoxical conclusion that there is less amnesia under hypnosis than there is as a result of a waking suggestion. The results are more probably due to the interaction of the amnesic effect and the practice effect.

Very few studies attempt to distinguish between normal forgetting and amnesia. Analyzing the amount recovered upon a signal or the reinduction of hypnosis to break the amnesia would serve as a control, but this is seldom incorporated, or if incorporated, analyzed. Thorn (1960) has shown that amnesia is uncorrelated with the ability to retain, posthypnotically, nonsense syllables learned during hypnosis. In studies using a learning task (especially when it involves recognition), care must be taken not to confound source amnesia with recall amnesia, in addition to not confounding amnesia with normal forgetting (see, for example, Thorne, 1969).

PARTIAL POSTHYPNOTIC AMNESIA

A few studies have systematically investigated the effects of suggesting that some, but not all, of what has transpired within hypnosis will be forgotten —certainly a common procedure in hypnotherapy. The client is frequently told that he may or may not remember everything that has happened or been discussed, permitting the client to decide what to remember and what to forget. Clemes (1964) used this kind of amnesia to test the hypothesis that amnesia is related to repression. If so, then under a suggestion for partial amnesia, it would be hypnothesized that the subject would be amnesic for the more anxiety-provoking material. He determined by means of a word association test the words that were neutral for a subject as opposed to those that produced a longer reaction time (critical words). He then had subjects memorize under hypnosis a list composed half of neutral and half of critical words, after which he suggested partial amnesia. Using an adequate control to insure that all words were memorized equally, he found that subjects did forget a larger number of the critical words.

Variables Affecting Hypnotic Amnesia

The studies reviewed thus far make clear that hypnotic amnesia is a multidimentional rather than a unitary process, manifesting itself in many different ways. It is also multiply determined. Most investigators would agree that many factors give rise to the measured phenomena called hypnotic amnesia. Such factors as normal forgetting, verbal inhibition, and instructions have already been referred to in this chapter. While it is of interest to speculate about the most important processes or factors producing it, probably no one explanation will be found to account for it ultimately; there will more likely be many explanations that account for a proportion of the variance found in a given condition. We will now briefly consider some of the variables recognized as being of some importance.

HYPNOTIC SUSCEPTIBILITY

Many investigators interested in hypnotic phenomena believe that some of the variance will be found to be attributable to a hypnotic state, which differs in some fundamental ways from the waking state (Barber and Sarbin are exceptions). As an independent variable, this concept has been variously called "hypnotic induction," "hypnotic trance," "hypnotic state," "hypnotic susceptibility," and so forth. If the standardized susceptibility scales are measuring this variable or factors related to it, we should find hypnotic amnesia related to susceptibility. A large number of studies have shown that amnesia is positively correlated with susceptibility (Barber & Calverley, 1966b; Boyers & Morgan, 1969; Cooper, 1966; Evans & Thorn, 1966; Hilgard & Cooper, 1965; Imm, 1965; Orne, 1966a; Wells, 1940).

Field, Evans, and Orne (1965) have further shown that the occurrence of amnesia is perhaps more a function of the level of hypnosis at the time of the suggestion for amnesia than it is of the susceptibility score, a stable overall index of hypnosis. Tape-recorded modifications of the HGSHS, one with the items in an increasing order of difficulty, and the other with a decreasing order of difficulty, were presented to two groups. Although the mean susceptibility score for the two groups did not differ, the group having the easier items last—which increased the probability of the subjects' responding —showed significantly more posthypnotic amnesia.

Orne (1966a) has reported that amnesia can be facilitated by tying it to a hypnotic suggestion that the subject is known to be able to carry out.

DEMAND CHARACTERISTICS

Orne (1959, 1962b) has pointed out that the experimental subject, in psychological research, is a thinking being who is attempting to understand the procedures and to evaluate the hypothesis being tested when actively participating in an experiment. He has shown that the expectations and perceptions of the subjects may subtly alter the results of a psychological experiment. For example, subjects who had been told that catalepsy of the nondominant arm was an invariant characteristic of hypnosis displayed catalepsy of the nondominant arm when later hypnotized, while control subjects, who had not been given this information, did not. He proposed several control and quasicontrol procedures to assist in evaluating the role of "demand characteristics" in hypnotic research. The postexperimental inquiry, the "nonexperiment," and the use of simulating subjects are three quasicontrols. Such controls have been utilized in research investigating hypnotic amnesia by Williamsen, Johnson, and Eriksen (1965), Barber and Calverley (1966b), and Bowers (1966). The possible role of demand characteristics in producing spontaneous recall and source amnesia has already been pointed out. Frequently, the demand characteristics come about as a result of instructions and/or expectations.

Instructions

Many different suggestions and instructions are used to elicit amnesia. We have already discussed different types of amnesia, most of which are produced through different suggestions and/or instructions. It may be that subjects formulate an implicit "contract" with the hypnotist in regard to amnesia in terms of what is expected of them on the basis of the instructions given. This may concern what is to happen, with whom it is to happen, how long it should persist, and so forth. Even within a specific type of amnesia, differing suggestions may produce different results.

The following implicit instructions, which are given simultaneously, can be detected in the suggestions for amnesia in the SHSS:A: (a) You will have difficulty in remembering, (b) You will have no desire to try to recall (implying perhaps that the subject could recall if he tried?), (c) It will be easier to forget everything, and (d) You will remember nothing (pp. 23–4). It is hardly surprising, therefore, to find subjects reporting different subjective impressions about their experience of amnesia. Some report it is like trying to think of a name that does not come; others say it is like "knowing" the material but not being able, or not desiring, to put it into words; others emphasize the lack of desire to expend the energy necessary to recall (Hilgard, 1965b; White, 1941). Barber and Calverley (1966b) and Thorne (1969) have proposed that authoritative suggestions for amnesia, such as, "You will not remember," may produce different results from more permissive suggestions such as, "Try to forget."

Orne (1966a) reported that when, without the removal of amnesia, the subjects were interviewed by a different experimenter about the material for which they were amnesic, some subjects related everything, and frequently indicated that they knew the material at the time they were originally questioned by the hypnotist, but felt compelled to inhibit it verbally; others indicated that they did not have recall of some of the material originally, but that it gradually came to them as they were being interviewed; still others remained amnesic.

Damaser (1964) found that when the subjects were questioned one week later, again by a different experimenter, some subjects reported that spontaneous recall occurred during the week, perhaps being triggered by some event in their daily lives. But again, others continued to maintain the amnesia.

Boyers and Morgan (1969) attempted to evaluate the influence of the instructions and expectations by presenting to subjects a series of invitations to break amnesia. For one group of subjects, the invitations were made by a confederate secretary in the office, and for another group, by the experimenter. The invitations consisted of the standard request to report everything that had happened, a request to try *very* hard to remember, the changing of rooms to dissociate the subject from the hypnotic situation, a financial bribe, and, when the invitations were presented by the confederate, she gave the release signal usually given by the experimenter. The experiment was replicated twice.

Of seven subjects recalling fewer than three items in their first hypnotic experience, the invitations to break the amnesia elicited a mean of five additional items for three subjects, two of them in the confederate group and one in the experimenter group. The average number of additional items elicited by the invitations for all subjects was approximately two out of the nine possible. A second replication made use of eight subjects who had previously scored 10 or above on SHSS:A and reported complete recall amnesia. Only one subject showed any effects of the invitations. This subject was in the experimenter group, and four additional items were elicited by the bribe of paying one dollar for each new item recalled. The authors concluded that the inability to recall was more than merely role playing, and that the amnesic response from a highly hypnotizable subject can generally be accepted as valid.

Expectations

If the expectation of a subject can influence the results of an experiment, then it is of some value to determine the expectations of prospective subjects about amnesia as it is related to hypnosis. Studies have shown that amnesia is one of the phenomena associated with hypnosis and is an expected result of an hypnotic experience for college students, at least, and perhaps the general public. London (1961) conducted a survey of 645 students in introductory psychology courses at the University of Illinois, in which he asked a number of questions about hypnosis aimed at assessing the direction of popular prejudices rather than the accuracy of people's knowledge. Seventy-four per cent of the students agreed with the statement, "People usually forget what happened during the trance as soon as they wake up from it." Ninety-three per cent of the sample felt that the general public would agree with this statement as well. Fifty-two per cent of the respondents agreed with the statement, "After they come out of a trance, people will ordinarily remember what has happened unless the hypnotist suggested that they forget," and 42 per cent felt that the public would agree. London concluded that "a large minority of the respondents obviously feel that spontaneous amnesia is intrinsic to the experience of hypnosis and a large majority feel that some form of amnesia is to be expected as a result of hypnosis" (p. 157).

In a more recent survey (Cooper, 1969) the same trends were found. Students in introductory psychology courses at Brigham Young University were asked a series of questions to determine their expectations and beliefs regarding hypnosis. Of those surveyed, 498 students had never been hypnotized previously. Of these, 57 per cent agreed that if they were to be hypnotized, they would not be aware of what was going on at the time it occurred. Fifty-nine per cent felt that if they were to be hypnotized, they would not remember what had happened after they woke up. Sixty-seven per cent felt that if they were to be hypnotized, they would remember what had happened unless the hypnotist suggested that they forget. While a minority felt that some form of amnesia would occur, a larger proportion thought that it would appear if suggested, rather than spontaneously.

The college students used in most hypnosis laboratories today are probably more sophisticated about hypnosis than were the naive subjects used in much of the early work in hypnosis. This may account for the failure to find a universal expectation that spontaneous amnesia would occur; nonetheless, even in 1969, a small majority of the college students did associate amnesia with hypnosis.

This finding presents somewhat of a paradox when compared with the incidence of amnesia. Despite the fact that amnesia is associated with hypnosis for approximately 57 to 74 per cent of college samples, it is spontaneously manifested by only 20 per cent (the maximum percentage found by Evans and Thorn, (1966). Young and Cooper (1970) did a pilot study investigating the number of items forgotten in response to the amnesia suggestion of the SHSS:A as a function of whether the subject had previously indicated an expectation for amnesia. With 10 subjects in each group (one group with the expectation and the other without), no significant difference was found in the number of items forgotten. A more extensive elaboration of this study is currently underway in my laboratory. We did find a mean difference of 1.70 items in the number of items forgotten between a group that had been told as part of a lecture on hypnosis that amnesia was a predominant characteristic of hypnosis and a group that had been told it was not (Cooper and Young, 1971). The difference was significant at the .01 level. If subjects were responding only in accordance with their expectations or the demand characteristics, or in a manner to please the hypnotist, there would be a larger number of college students showing spontaneous amnesia. While these influences may account to some extent for the amnesia in certain individuals, they do not solely account for its occurrence or lack of occurrence.

Many of the common induction techniques make use of reference to sleep. Sleep, when directly suggested to the subject, may act as an indirect suggestion to forget, since many people believe that we do not remember what occurs when asleep. [It should be noted that some interesting, contemporary findings give partial support to this idea (Evans et al., 1966, 1969).] Dittborn and Aristeguieta (1962) found that they were able to vary amnesia by changing the references to sleep in the instructions to a highly hypnotizable subject. The use of a single subject precludes drawing any definite conclusion, but the study does suggest the way in which expectations may alter results, and suggests a replication with appropriate modifications to assess the effect more adequately.

Just knowing that they are involved in a hypnosis experiment may be sufficient to motivate subjects to enhance their hypnotic performance. Although not specifically studies of amnesia, the following findings have implications for research on amnesia. When subjects were tested in the order of waking condition followed by hypnosis, there were no differences in the performance. However, when hypnosis preceded the waking condition, waking performances were significantly less successful than the hypnotic performance (Evans & Orne, 1965). If a subject knew before a waking test that he would subsequently be retested during hypnosis, his waking perform-ance fell below his hypnotized performance (Zamansky, Scharf, & Bright-hill, 1964).

An interesting and unexpected finding in regard to expectation was re-ported by Evans (1968) in a study concerning source amnesia. Ten of 37 deeply hypnotized subjects selected from the highest 5 per cent of the distri-bution of hypnotic susceptibility showed source amnesia, whereas all simula-tors not only acted as though they forgot where they learned the material (source amnesia), but also acted as though they forgot the material (recall amnesia). This suggested that the expectation for the source amnesia in-structions was that posthypnotic recall amnesia should occur. Consequently, the occurrence of source amnesia may be interpreted as contrary to the re-sults anticipated from a compliance with expectations.

ROLE OF NORMAL FORGETTING

The similarities between amnesia and simple forgetting have already been referred to. As early as 1933, Hull, in his book *Hypnosis and Suggestibility*, raised the question of how much of the reported amnesia was caused by a process of forgetting, a question that has since been raised by others (Evans, 1968; Hilgard, 1966). In an attempt to gain empirical data relevant

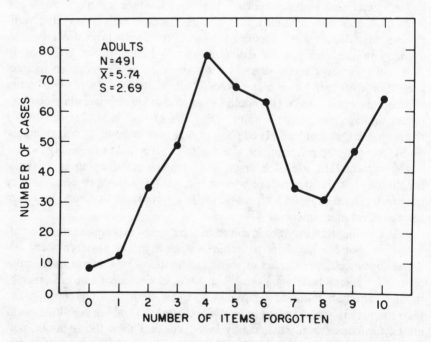

FIGURE 7.1. *Distribution of Posthypnotic Amnesia in College students.*

to this issue, I began a series of studies in 1966 focusing on normal forgetting in posthypnotic amnesia (Cooper, 1966b).

When the number of items forgotten by 491 college students of both sexes, ranging in age from 17 to 22 years, in response to the SHSS:A were analyzed on a pass-fail basis (a pass score requiring the subject to forget seven or more items presented during the course of the hypnotic testing), 177 or 36 per cent passed the item. This percentage is quite consistent with that reported elsewhere (Hilgard et al., 1961; Hilgard, 1965b).

The number of items forgotten may also serve as the index of amnesia, and an examination of the distribution of actual number of items forgotten is instructive. Figure 7.1 shows the distribution for the 491 college students. It is obvious that amnesia when so measured forms a continuum, some subjects forgetting everything, some forgetting a few items, and others forgetting almost none of the items. More subjects forget all the items than forget only one or two of them, which has led Hilgard (1966) to suggest that this may be so because having remembered one or two items, the subject is led to remember more through some associative process that breaks the amnesia. It should be noted that the distribution is bimodal. This bimodality has been found for other similar samples, and is also found for the amnesia item of subsequent administrations of other forms of susceptibility scales. While bimodality may be artifactually produced by certain scaling procedures, such as the bimodality found in the distribution of susceptibility scores (see Hilgard et al., 1961; Hilgard, 1965b), it may also occur when the phenomenon being studied is caused by separate and unrelated variables.

Evans (1966b) and Hilgard (1966) have both conjectured that the bimodality of the distribution of items forgotten as a result of suggested amnesia may be explained by the lower mode being a result of forgetting, while the upper mode may be the result of truly amnesic subjects. Thus, the bimodality of Figure 7.1 may be conceptualized as the result of combining two separate curves, one with a mode at 4 representing a curve of the forgetting of a series of tasks when there were no instructions to try to remember them, and the other representing an amnesic curve. Figure 7.2 shows the distribution of amnesic forgetting with two normal distributions superimposed. These fitted curves were obtained by using both a standard procedure and a reduction method (D. Lewis, 1960). The curve to the left was based on a N of 306. The mean is equal to 4.06 and the standard deviation equal to 1.67. A chi square of 6.97 yielded a *p* value of .70, suggesting that it was a reasonably good fit. The other normal curve has a mean of 9.00 and a standard deviation of 2.30, and was fitted by assuming the second mode at 10 of the original distribution represented an undistributed maximum.

It is difficult to obtain a direct empirical index of the role of "normal" forgetting in amnesia; however, an attempt can be made to infer some estimate from indirect evidence. An estimate of the amount of forgetting that *can* occur with such items would provide some base for comparison. Evans

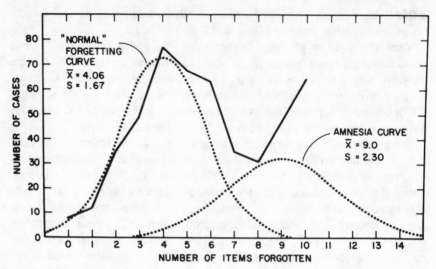

FIGURE 7.2. *Distribution of posthypnotic amnesia in college students with hypothesized theoretical forgetting and amnesia curves superimposed.*

and Thorn (1966) reported the amount of forgetting of 17 items comprising a battery of standard hypnosis items by a waking control group that had received no induction procedures. On the average, the subjects forgot approximately 40 per cent of the items. If consideration is given to the fact that 17 items were administered rather than 10, the estimated mean that would have been obtained had there been 10 items would not be too unlike the mean of 4.06 for the derived normal forgetting curve.

In order to make the comparisons more similar, Cooper and Moore (1967) administered directions requesting compliance with the motor items used in the SHSS but without any hypnotic induction, or any reference to hypnosis, or to such words as "relax," "drowsy," or "sleepy." These instructions were given in a group setting to 96 college students ranging in age from 17 to 22 years. As soon as the items were administered, the subjects were asked to write down everything they could remember of what had occurred since beginning the activities; they were allowed 10 minutes to do so. The instructions indicated that the responses need not be listed in order, nor need the language utilized by the experimenter be used; the subjects were allowed to express themselves in their own words.

Figure 7.3 shows the resulting relative frequency distribution indicating the percentage of the total number of subjects forgetting each of the number of items under this condition superimposed upon the fitted theoretical "normal" forgetting curve. The mean for the empirical distribution is 3.60 and the standard deviation is 1.74. When it is remembered that the mean and standard deviation of the theoretically derived curve were 4.06 and 1.67 respectively, it is apparent that the two curves are highly similar. The two

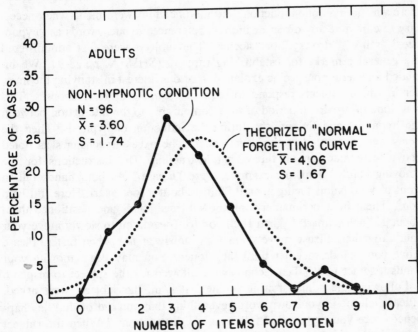

FIGURE 7.3. *Percentage distribution of number of items forgotten by college students in non-hypnotic condition with hypothesized theoretical forgetting curve superimposed.*

standard deviations are not significantly different from each other $(X^2 = 103; p = .25)$. Although the two means are just significantly different $(p = .05)$, it must be remembered that the procedures for fitting the theoretical distribution allowed a relatively large amount of leeway. Under these conditions, the similarity for the two distributions is rather remarkable.

It must be noted that, in a strict sense, this condition cannot be considered a control for the hypnotic condition. There were at least two important differences between the two conditions; first the amnesia results were obtained by an individual administration of the SHSS while the normal forgetting measures were obtained in a group setting; and second, the time allowed to respond in the normal forgetting conditions was longer than that usually found in testing for amnesia. In the latter, after the second block by the subject, the hypnotist not very subtly discourages further attempts to remember under amnesia by giving the cue to remember, thus terminating the amnesia. Both of these differences preclude exact comparisons between these conditions.

In an attempt to overcome these limitations, Cooper and Harrison (1969) individually administered to 49 students from an introductory psychology class directions that requested compliance to the motor items of the SHSS. The exact wording and procedures of the scale were utilized, except there was no hypnotic induction, and modifications were made when necessary to eliminate any direct or indirect references to such words as "hypnotize," "relax," "drowsy," or "sleepy." The subjects were first administered the general remarks for establishing rapport (SHSS:A, pp. 8-9). We included a general nonspecific explanation of our interest in studying the manner in which subjects respond to requests to make motor responses. This was done to provide a period of time comparable to the interaction between the hypnotist and the subject during the induction of hypnosis. Then the items were presented in the usual order. The necessary changes as noted above were made in all the verbal instruction. The instructions for the "moving hands" item, for example, were "Please hold both hands out in front of you, palms facing inward, hands about a foot apart. Here, I'll help you." Then the experimenter took the subjects' hands and positioned them about 12 inches apart. "When I tell you to, I want you to slowly move your hands together. Please move them very slowly at first, then faster. Please move your hands together until they touch. You may begin moving your hands together now." Ten seconds were allowed for the subject to respond.

Following the administration of the last item, the subjects were asked, "Please tell me in your own words everything that you did or that has happened since you first started following my instructions." When the subject reached a block, the experimenter asked, "Anything else?" Thus, the procedures in this experiment were made to duplicate as closely as possible those in the hypnotic condition. It was found that every subject forgot at least one item. The mean number of items forgotten was 3.22 and the standard deviation was 1.23. There were no significant differences between the means ($p > .10$) nor the variances ($F = 1.98$, $p > .05$) of the group administered and individually administered "normal" forgetting conditions. These results make it clear that normal forgetting may be accounting for some of the posthypnotic amnesia that is found.

Additional indirect evidence involving the interaction of age with normal forgetting and its role in amnesia may be found by examining the analogous findings for children. The responses relating to amnesia of 286 children ranging in age from 6 to 15 years to the CHSS were analyzed, and 222 or 78 per cent passed the item. This is comparable with the percentages reported elsewhere (Cooper & London, 1966; London & Cooper, 1969; Moore & Lauer, 1963). A comparison with the 36 per cent of the adults that passed the item suggests that hypnotic amnesia is more likely to be found in children than in adults. Because the first 12 items of the CHSS are very similar to those of the SHSS and the test of amnesia applies to 10 of these items as it does on the SHSS, the two distributions of the actual number of items forgotten can be meaningfully compared.

Figure 7.4 shows this distribution for the 286 children. Unlike the distribution for the adults, there is only one mode and, apparently, only one curve is represented. As indicated by the per cent passing the item, children

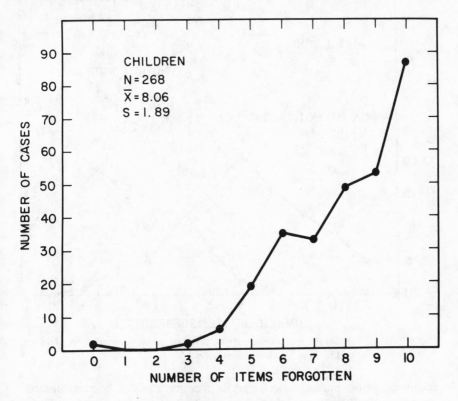

FIGURE 7.4. *Distribution of posthypnotic amnesia in children.*

forget more items than do older college students; the mean number of items forgotten by the children was 8.06 (SD = 1.89) as compared to the mean of 5.74 for the adults. This difference is significant at the .01 level.

It might be concluded that the memory task for children is simply more difficult than it is for young adults, and that this distribution for children represents a "normal" forgetting curve with an undistributed maximum. However, the children were significantly more hypnotically susceptible (p = .001) than the college students, with a mean susceptibility score of 7.41 (SD = 2.91), based on the first 11 items scored on a pass-fail basis, as compared with 5.39 (SD = 3.00), for the adults. This susceptibility score did not include the amnesia item, so the curve may represent the effect of hypnotic suggestions for amnesia. Another alternative is that both of these effects were operating simultaneously.

In addition to the adult sample, Cooper and Moore (1967) also administered the instructions that deleted references to hypnosis requesting compliance to the motor tasks utilized in the CHSS to 157 children varying in age from 9 to 15 years. Again, these instructions were administered in group

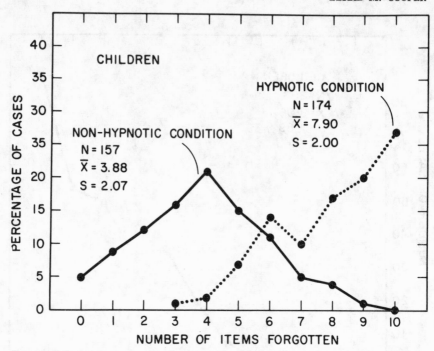

FIGURE 7.5.   *Percentage distribution of number of items forgotten by children in both hypnotic and non-hypnotic condition.*

sessions, and the limitations referred to previously should be remembered. The mean number of items forgotten was 3.88 and the standard deviation was 2.07. However, because age was significantly correlated with the number of items forgotten in this condition (as will be discussed later), all children below the age of 9 in the hypnotic condition were eliminated for purposes of analysis, and meaningful comparisons must be made with this restricted sample, whose mean was 7.90 and standard deviation was 2.00.

Figure 7.5 shows these two distributions. No theoretically-fitted distributions have been presented for those analogous to the adult distributions, because the distribution of items forgotten in the amnesia condition was not bimodal. In Figure 7.5, however, if we assume that the accumulation of scores at 10 for the hypnotic condition is an undistributed maximum, then a rough fit to this distribution would be a normal curve with a mean at 7.30 and a standard deviation of 1.15. It is obvious that such a curve is a poor fit to the obtained curve under the nonhypnotic condition, and is displaced toward the higher end of the scale.

As has been pointed out, the time to respond in the nonhypnotic condition was longer than that usually found in the hypnotic condition. The time allowed for reminiscence may be more important for children than for adults, which would account for the larger mean number of items forgotten in the hypnotic condition by the children. On the other hand, the differences between the mean number of items forgotten under the two conditions might also be due to the greater susceptibility of the children, so that the suggestions for amnesia were more effective for all children.

It was hypothesized that the number of items forgotten in the nonhypnotic condition would tend to be an inverse function of age up to some asymptote; that is, to some point, the older the subject, the fewer the items that would be forgotten. For the adults, there were no significant differences between the mean number of items forgotten at the different ages for the "normal" forgetting condition $(F = .48; df = 4, 73; p = .20)$, and, as would be expected, the correlation between age and number of items forgotten was not significantly different from zero. Likewise, there was no correlation between age and number of items forgotten under the amnesia condition. This suggests that the two regression lines were virtually horizontal at the means of 3.60 for the normal forgetting condition and 5.74 for the suggested amnesia condition. At every age there were some items forgotten in the "normal" forgetting condition, and at every age the number forgotten in this condition was less than those forgotten in the hypnotic condition.

There was a decreasing number of items forgotten with increased age by the children in the nonhypnotic condition. A square root transformation was made on the raw scores to produce greater homogeneity of variance, and an analysis of variance was performed. The overall test was significant at the .001 level of significance $(F = 181.17; df = 5, 141)$. The overall mean number of items forgotten was 3.88 (SD = 2.07). The combined results from both the children's and the adult's data suggest that the asymptote of forgetting was reached at about 15 or 16 years of age.

While the trend is not so pronounced, there was a negative correlation between age and the number of items forgotten as a result of suggested amnesia of $-.28$ $(p = .01)$. Again, at every age tested, there were some items forgotten in the "normal" forgetting condition, but at every age there were fewer items forgotten under this condition than under the hypnotic amnesia condition.

While the important differences between the two conditions should again be remembered, these data suggest that "normal" forgetting does play a role in hypnotic amnesia. Furthermore, these data suggest that this influence is more important in younger children, and decreases with age. Other variables, such as, susceptibility, may become of greater influence with increased age. This conjecture is supported by the correlation between number of items forgotten in the hypnotic condition and susceptibility for different age spans. For the 6 to 8 year olds the correlation was $-.06$ $(p = .20)$, for the 9 to 11 year olds it was .37 $(p = .001)$, and for the 12 to 15 year olds it was .46 $(p = .001)$, while for the adult sample it was .52 $(p = .001)$. There is then some indirect evidence for the role of "normal" forgetting in hypnotic amnesia from the data discussed thus far.

Although a technically precise definition of amnesia must incorporate the recoverability of the material through some appropriate procedures, very little serious attention has been given to this requirement, as has been previously suggested. Such a test is not usually incorporated into the passing criterion of amnesia in the currently used susceptibility scales, nor discussed in the majority of the studies investigating amnesia. It is usually assumed that the material would be recovered if the appropriate procedures were utilized. The research discussed here, however, suggests that at least some of the items are truly forgotten, and may not be recoverable. If the material is not recovered, this should at least suggest the possibility that the amnesia was simply a matter of natural forgetting and not a result of the suggestion to forget temporarily, since part of that suggestion was that the material would be remembered at the signal, "Now you can remember everything." It could be claimed that if nothing is recovered, the subjects have in fact not complied with the suggestions.

In an attempt to obtain some evidence concerning this hypothesis, the number of items recovered after the signal to remember had been given was analyzed for each group. The results are presented in Table 7.1. Both distributions were markedly positively skewed with the larger frequencies recovering the fewer number of items. Of the 491 adults, 201 or 41 per cent, and of the 286 children, 131 or 46 per cent, recovered none of the material. This is a relatively large proportion of each sample. None of the adults recovered more than nine items, and only 12 recovered more than seven items. Not only were there many who did not recover any of the items, but

TABLE 7.1   Number of items recovered in the adult and children sample

Number of Items Recovered	Frequency	
	adult sample	children sample
10	0	1
9	5	0
8	7	2
7	17	0
6	25	6
5	45	13
4	31	20
3	51	35
2	52	38
1	57	40
0	201	131
Number	491	286
Mean	2.10	1.50
Median	1.28	.80
Standard Deviation	2.37	1.83

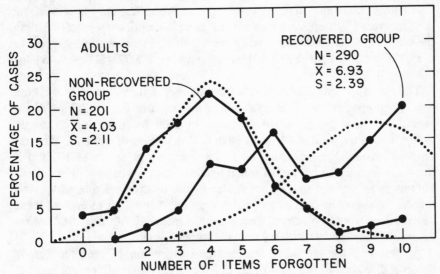

FIGURE 7.6. *Percentage distribution of the number of items forgotten by college students under hypnotic condition for both recovered and non-recovered groups.*

generally speaking, surprisingly few items were recovered. These findings point out the fallacy of assuming that the amnesic material would be recovered if appropriate procedures were utilized, and call into serious question such statements as, "With few if any exceptions, hypnotic and nonhypnotic subjects who claim they have forgotten, verbalize the 'forgotten' events when the hypnotist or experimenter simply states, 'Now you can remember'" (Barber, 1969b, p. 212), and emphasize the importance of testing for the recoverability and incorporating it into an operational definition of amnesia.

In the light of these findings, it was decided to divide each sample into two groups on the basis of a conservative definition of amount recovered. One group consisted of those subjects who recovered at least one item or more, and the other group consisted of those who recovered nothing.

Figure 7.6 shows the number of items forgotten by these two subgroups for the adult samples, superimposed upon the theoretically-derived distributions. The mean number of items forgotten by the "nonrecovered" group was 4.03, the standard deviation was 2.11, and the distribution is very similar to the theoretically fitted "normal" forgetting curve. The mean number of items forgotten by the "recovered" group was 6.93 and the standard deviation was 2.39. While this distribution is far from a perfect fit to the theoretical "amnesia" curve, there are suggestive similarities, and it must be remembered that the subjects comprising this group had not recovered everything, but some recovered no more than one item. The mean number of items forgotten by the "recovered" group was significantly larger *(p =*

.001) than that of the "nonrecovered" group. Also, the subjects comprising the "recovered" group were significantly more susceptible *(p* = .001) than the subjects of the "nonrecovered" group, with mean susceptibility scores of 6.55 (SD = 2.80) for the former as compared with 3.73 (SD = 2.45) for the latter.

The corresponding distributions of the number of items forgotten by these two subgroups for the children's sample as shown in Figure 7.7 yielded a mean of 7.61 and a standard deviation of 2.09 for the "nonrecovered" group, and a mean of 8.44 and a standard deviation of 1.60 for the "recovered" group. Each distribution had a piling up of scores at 10, and if these are assumed to be undistributed maxima, then we can use these distributions in an attempt to gain some idea of the relative position of the two theoretical curves analogous to those for adults. A rough fit to each of these distributions would be normal curves with a mean of 7.00 for the "nonrecovered" group, and at 9.00 for the "recovered" group.

As was true for the adult sample, the distribution of the "recovered" group is displaced to the right of that of the "nonrecovered" group, and the mean of the former was significantly larger *(p* = .001) than that of the latter. In comparison with the adult sample, both of the child groups forgot a larger number of items than the corresponding adult group, but the separa-

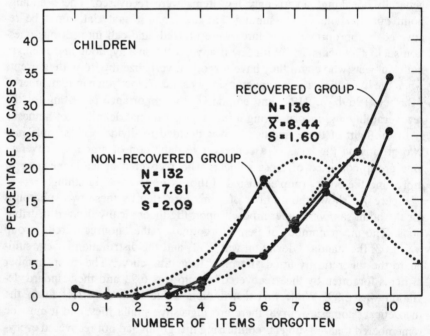

FIGURE 7.7. *Percentage distribution of the number of items forgotten by children under hypnotic condition for both recovered and non-recovered groups.*

tion between the groups of children was not as pronounced as that for the adults. The "recovered" group was significantly more susceptible *(p =* .001) with a mean of 8.24 (SD = 2.60) than the "nonrecovered" group, whose mean susceptibility score was 6.43 (SD = 2.94). While there was no significant difference between the mean ages of the two subgroups in the adult sample, there was in the children's sample. The "nonrecovered" group was significantly younger than the "recovered" group. The mean age of the former was 10.04 (SD = 3.53), while for the latter it was 11.87 (SD = 3.04; *p* = .001). Since age is negatively correlated with the number of items forgotten through normal forgetting, this would work against the finding that the mean number of items forgotten for the "recovered" group was larger than that for the "nonrecovered" group, because the "recovered" group should have remembered more if only "normal" forgetting effects were operating. When the number of items forgotten in both groups for each sample was analyzed as a function of age, it was found that there were more items forgotten by the "recovered" group than by the "nonrecovered" group at every age.

Perhaps the number of items recovered per se is not of crucial importance. Those who forget more may well recover more, and therefore it might be of greater significance for an individual who forgot only three items to recover all three of them. In order to evaluate this possibility, a per cent recovered score was computed for each person by dividing the number of items recovered by the number forgotten. If this rationale were true, a high correlation between the number forgotten and the per cent recovered would be expected. Such correlations, however, were not found. For the college group, per cent recovered correlated .49 with the number of items forgotten and .89 with the number recovered. When the correlation between the number of items forgotten and the number of items recovered was partialed out, per cent recovered correlated −.48 with number forgotten and .89 with number recovered. For the children, the per cent recovered correlated .20 with the number of items forgotten and .97 with the number recovered. When the correlation between the number forgotten and the number recovered was partialed out, per cent recovered correlated −.48 with the number forgotten and .98 with number recovered. These results do not support this rationale and suggest that a consideration of the number of items recovered is sufficient for our present purposes.

In order to complete our understanding of the association between the number of items forgotten, the number of items recovered and their relationship to amnesia, the correlations between the number of items forgotten and the number of items recovered was examined. This correlation was .72 (*p* = .001) for the adult sample, but only .32 (*p* = .001) for the children's sample. Of greater importance is the fact that the correlation between these two variables tends to increase with age. For the 6 to 8 year olds the correlation was .26 *(p = .05)*, for the 9 to 11 year olds it was .56 *(p = .001)*, for the 12 to 15 year olds it was .51 *(p = .001)*, and, as has been indicated, .72 for the adult sample.

These results suggest that age is an important moderating variable in posthypnotic amnesia. In the younger individual, both the number of items forgotten and the number of items recovered are less a function of susceptibility, and because the two are not highly correlated, the number of items forgotten is more a function of forgetting. For those who do recover something, the number of items forgotten is a function of susceptibility. For the older individual, the number of items forgotten and the number of items recovered are more highly correlated, and both are a function of susceptibility; the number of items forgotten is less a function of forgetting per se.

These results emphasize the importance of giving serious consideration to testing the recoverability of the material forgotten when attempting to demonstrate hypnotic amnesia. If the conservative operational definition of recoverability adopted for the purpose of analysis in this research had been incorporated into the original criterion of amnesia, while none of those who failed to recover would pass the item, 21 or 4 per cent of the adult sample, and 87 or 30 per cent of the children sample who passed the item would fail it.

Authenticity of hypnotic amnesia

The emphasis on the role of demand characteristics, instructions, expectations, and normal forgetting in hypnotic amnesia as compared to that devoted to hypnotic susceptibility should not be interpreted as implying that the former are more important or more powerful in producing the phenomenon. It should be interpreted rather as an attempt to stress the importance of controlling for these independent variables so that we may better evaluate the true role of the hypnotic state.

As is true of other phenomena, clinical experience and clinical reports seem to uphold without any doubt the existence of hypnotic amnesia (see, for example, Erickson & Brickner, 1943). Experimental evidence does not conclusively support the existence of the phenomenon, however.

Barber (1969b; and Barber & Calverley, 1962, 1966b) has challenged the concept of the hypnotic state and its use in explaining hypnotic phenomena. He has suggested that "performance of behaviors traditionally associated with the word 'hypnosis' may be more parsimoniously conceptualized under the more general psychological concept of task motivation," and further that the "the concepts of 'trance' and 'hypnosis' may be no longer useful" (Barber & Calverley, 1962, p. 388). As this challenge applied to all hypnotic phenomena, the authenticity of hypnotic amnesia is questioned.

The basis for this challenge to the genuineness of hypnotic phenomena is twofold. First, it is claimed that all the behavioral responses characteristic of the hypnotic state can be obtained, and with the same intensity, by procedures that are not hypnotic in nature; and second, that because the responses are the same, the basic mechanism giving rise to the responses must also be the same. Both of these claims will be discussed with specific references to hypnotic amnesia.

The first claim implies that the kind and degree of hypnotic amnesia that can be obtained through hypnotic procedures can also be obtained through nonhypnotic ones. While the conclusions drawn must be tempered by the problems regarding the definition and measurement of hypnotic amnesia discussed previously, there is evidence helpful in evaluating this claim.

Most of the investigators interested in hypnotic behavior do not claim that the behaviors obtained through hypnotic procedures are unique to hypnosis, nor that they cannot be obtained through any other means. The amnesia associated with fugues or produced through chemical means (see, for example, Osborn et al., 1967) is a forgetting of material that is frequently recoverable, but not brought about through the use of hypnotic procedures. This does not make the amnesia brought about through hypnosis any less real. Nonhypnotized subjects and simulators may manifest amnesia as a result of certain instructions. Analogously, however, this does not make the amnesia of hypnotic subjects any less an amnesia. A relevant and important question is whether the hypnotic procedure can enhance the manifestation of the behavior over what it is through a nonhypnotic procedure. While Barber (1969b) makes such statements as "very few if any 'deeply hypnotized' subjects forget the hypnotic events when amnesia is not directly or implicitly suggested" (p. 206), it seems to me somewhat too convenient to dismiss the following evidence by attributing the amnesia to implicit suggestions.

Hilgard and Tart (1966) administered the SHSS:C (which included an amnesia item) under a waking-suggestion condition, a vivid-imagery condition, and a hypnotic condition, and found that total scores for the hypnotic condition were significantly greater than for the other two conditions. Evans (1966b) administered a battery of hypnotic phenomena including recall and source amnesia to both a hypnotic group and a waking group. Both of the amnesia items discriminated between the waking and the hypnotic conditions. While we have noted that the occurrence of spontaneous recall amnesia occurs less frequently than may have been originally thought, nonetheless its occurrence has been demonstrated, and Evans and Thorn (1966) have shown that it occurs more frequently as a result of a hypnotic experience than in a waking state. The same can be said of spontaneous source amnesia (Evans & Thorn, 1966).

In regard to suggested amnesia, the conclusions are somewhat more equivocal. What appears to be, and is described as, amnesia can and does occur as a result of suggestions without involving hypnotic procedures (Barber & Calverley, 1966b; Evans & Thorn, 1966; Thorne, 1969; Williamsen, Johnson, & Eriksen, 1965). It is difficult, however, to determine that in fact it does occur under this condition with the same frequency and intensity as obtained by a hypnotic procedure because controls for learning, practice effects, and normal forgetting are seldom incorporated.

Even if we ultimately find that the frequency of its occurrence without any hypnotic procedure is similar to its frequency as a result of hypnotic suggestions, it does not logically follow that the same antecedent variables are giving rise to the phenomenon under the two conditions. The amnesia produced by drugs is not necessarily equivalent to the amnesia produced hypnotically, nor are both necessarily the result of the same mechanisms.

Nonhypnotic simulators may show the same amnesia that hypnotized subjects show, but for quite different reasons. The former may do so primarily because of the operation of demand characteristics and instructions. That is, they are subtly informed what hypnotic behavior should be like and that they are expected to behave in a hypnoticlike fashion. On the other hand, the hypnotic subjects are often told just to let happen whatever they find is happening without any attempt to hinder or help it along. The observable behaviors may be the same, but it does not necessarily follow that the bases for the behaviors are the same.

Edwards (1965) gave suggestions for the slowing of reaction time to two groups, a hypnotized group and a control group. Instructions for amnesia for the suggestions were subsequently given to both groups. While no significant differences between the groups were found in reaction time, striking differences were found in response to a post experimental inquiry concerning the subjective quality of the experience. The hypnotized subjects "manifested perplexity—a puzzling difficulty" in recalling the original suggestion. The control subjects remembered the original suggestion and manifested no perplexity. Edwards emphasized that "it is difficult not to conclude that the original hypnosis has produced an impairment of mental functioning which is a phenomenon *sui generis,* and which cannot be adequately accounted for as a reflection of social control or role-playing" (p. 322).

Bowers (1966) gave instructions to subjects in both a hypnotic condition and a simulating condition to begin all sentences to an apparent experimental task of making up sentences with "he" and "they." Suggestions were also given that the subjects would be unaware of and amnesic for this suggestion. There were no significant differences between the two groups in the tendency to use the "correct" pronouns in two test situations. In a postexperimental inquiry, however, significant differences were found between the two groups in regard to their verbalizing using the "correct" pronouns and their justifications for using them.

Even though Thorne (1969) did not find significant differences in amount of amnesia as a function of susceptibility, in interpreting the findings he was led to conjecture that the same results may have been brought about through different subjective experiences.

Barber too has recognized that different basic processes may be producing the same results in the different groups. In explaining the fact that nonhypnotized subjects, in a replication of the study of Williamsen, Johnson, and Eriksen (1965), showed more amnesia, and more of them than of hypnotized subjects claimed they had actually forgotten the words, Barber stated: "The suggestions . . . may be congruent with the type of instructions or suggestions that are expected in an awake situation but not in a hypnotic situation. Subjects may expect that if forgetting is to occur in an awake situation it is necessary for them to strive to 'control their memory' whereas in a hypnotic situation amnesia should occur effortlessly, not by willful striving" (1969b, p. 209).

Because amnesia can be produced by mechanisms other than hypnosis we should not, therefore, deny the subjective reality of the hypnotic amnesia. Orne (1959, 1962b, 1965b) has warned that hypnosis cannot be understood in terms of observable, overt behavior only, and that we must bring the subjective experiences into the domain of the laboratory if we are ultimately to understand hypnosis. Even though Barber, Abdulhusein, and Calverley (1968) have protested using subjective reports as indices of actual experiences or of the hypnotic state, further studies should continue to do so. A precedent for so doing with appropriate cautions has been established in the investigations of the role of awareness in learning (see Dulany, 1961, and Eriksen, 1962).

Underlying Mechanisms

The demonstration of hypnotic phenomena can be dramatic and impressive. Demonstration of occurrence is, however, only the beginning of scientific interest. The questions, How commonplace is it? What are the parameters which give rise to the results? immediately follow. Subsequently, the question, What are the underlying mechanisms? must be raised and answered. Unfortunately, even with the amount of research that has been done on hypnotic amnesia, relatively little research has been devoted to elaborating its underlying mechanisms systematically. A brief discussion of some proposed underlying mechanisms follows.

FUNCTIONAL ABLATION

An early explanation of amnesia was that of a functional isolation, removal, or obliteration of the neural representation of specific experiences or events so that they could no longer influence behavior. This was not thought to preclude the recovery of the material, as an opposite effect, reinstatement, was also proposed. By testing for the influence of the amnesia on responses other than direct recall, an attempt was made to evaluate how complete the amnesia was. When the amnesia was measured by relearning (Strickler, 1929), practice effects (Life, 1929; Patten, 1932), conditioned reflex responses (Scott, 1930), autonomic responses to single words (Bitterman & Marcuse, 1945), associative responses (Barber & Calverley, 1966b; Thorne,

1969; Williamsen, Johnson, & Eriksen, 1965), and memory for colored patterns (Goldstein & Sipprelle, 1970), the amnesia was found to be far from complete. As early as 1929, Strickler concluded that "the posthypnotic amnesias which appear to be complete are by no means so" (p. 116).

Other investigators have studied the effects of amnesia on retroactive inhibition. When subjects learn a list of words or nonsense syllables, later learn another list, and are subsequently asked to recall the first list, the material of the second list interferes with or retroactively inhibits the recalling of the first list. The functional ablation hypothesis suggests that if amnesia is produced for the second list, there should be less retroactive inhibition. Some investigators have claimed to have found this effect (Messerschmidt, 1927; M. Mitchell, 1932; Nagge, 1935; Stevenson, Stoyva, & Beach, 1962; Sturrock, 1966). Many of these studies have suffered from small sample sizes (in some cases only two subjects were used), differing instructions, and the failure to suggest amnesia, assuming that it would spontaneously occur because the subject was hypnotized. In well-designed and carefully controlled replications of these studies, both Orne (1966a) and Graham and Patton (1968) found no support for the hypothesis that retroactive inhibition is decreased when the interpolated material is subjected to hypnotic amnesia. All of these studies indicate that the functional ablation hypothesis is not tenable as such, and although the subjects are unable to recall verbally material for which amnesia has been suggested, when tested by methods other than direct verbal recall, effects of exposure to the material were found.

Such a conclusion need not be interpreted as challenging the authenticity of hypnotic amnesia. An alternate explanation is that amnesia may be a form of posthypnotic suggestion, which is discussed below.

By comparison, Stern et al. (1963) found that the adaptation of the electrodermal orientation response to a sound stimulus occurred more slowly for a hypnotized group given suggestions for amnesia than for other control groups. However, they suggested that amnesia was not a passive but rather a very active process; that it was not an obliteration of memory traces but rather an alteration of perception or a disturbance in the expression of the amnesic material. They concluded that the study demonstrated "not only at a verbal level but also at a physiological level that amnesia is a 'real' phenomenon" (p. 400). Analogous findings have been reported by Plapp and Edmonston (1965).

SPECIFICITY OF HYPNOTIC SUGGESTION

Amnesia, like any other posthypnotic behavior, has been traditionally viewed as being outside of the subject's volitional control and carried out automatically (Erickson & Erickson, 1941; Weitzenhoffer, 1957b). This view has been challenged by Fisher (1954, 1955), who has suggested that posthypnotic behavior occurs only in the specific context where the subject perceived that the hypnotist expects that it should occur. It has since been shown that posthypnotic behavior occurs in those situations in which the subject expects that it is to occur. Although similar to Fisher's statement, this latter finding is different in some important ways. The expectations of the subject are a function of the instructions and the demand characteristics. It may be that the instructions for amnesia, as understood and interpreted by the subject, are very specific in their action, so suggestions that the subject may be amnesic are effective only in those situations and under those conditions where it is apparent to him that memory is being evaluated. If requests for direct recall are seen as tests of memory, but association tests, or tests for practice effects are not, then we might expect to see the effects of amnesia in the former but not in the latter.

Hull (1933) noted that the effectiveness of suggestions for amnesia diminished as the way in which it was measured varied from specific learned content to more remote results of practice. He stated:

[The subjects] uniformly deny any recollection of trance events, i.e., as tested by general symbolic recall, amnesia is 100 per cent. By detailed specific recall this amount of amnesia is reduced for nonsense material probably to about 97 per cent. By the relearning method amnesia falls to approximately 50 per cent. Manual habits learned in the stylus maze show by the relearning method an amnesia of about 50 per cent. With specific training in arithmetical addition and general training in memorizing nonsense material the amount of posthypnotic amnesia is reduced to zero. (1933, p. 155)

An analogous, though somewhat different, result has been found in regard to memory for events while asleep. When suggestions such as "Whenever you hear the word 'itch' your nose will itch until you scratch it," were given while subjects were in stage 1 sleep, some subjects responded by scratching their noses when the cue word "itch" was spoken, although they remained asleep. Even though they responded when tested as long as six months later, they were amnesic for the suggestions and their responses when awake (Cobb et al., 1965; Evans et al., 1966). Subsequent research has shown that a presleep set that learning can occur during sleep leads to a waking recall of material presented during sleep (Cooper & Hoskovec, 1966; Evans & Orchard, 1969). Just as the manipulation of the set may break the amnesia for the events occurring while asleep, so the manipulation of the analogous set may break the amnesia for events occurring while hypnotized.

Orne, Sheehan, and Evans (1968) and Sheehan and Orne (1968) have effectively shown that posthypnotic behavior is not *entirely* dependent upon the context in which the suggestion is tested as implied in Fisher's position, but may occur outside the experimental setting. Orne (1966a) has reviewed a number of findings that lend support to this explanation of hypnotic amnesia.

REPRESSION

The similarities between posthypnotic amnesia and clinical repression have long attracted attention. The recoverability of the amnesic material, the suggestions of an active rather than a passive process, and the finding that there is differential amnesia as a function of the affective content of the material are characteristics common to the two phenomena. Brenman (1947) tested in the waking state the preference for completed and incompleted tasks that occurred within hypnosis and for which amnesia had been suggested. In general, preference was for the completed tasks. Hilgard and Hommel (1961), taking advantage of the fact that even though suggested, posthypnotic amnesia is often incomplete, studied the types of items that were forgotten. They found that subjects tended to forget relatively more frequently those items that they failed (that is, did not respond to as a hypnotized person), than those they passed. They accounted for these results by suggesting that the failure to respond as a hypnotized subject was disappointing and led to repression. They recognized, however, that an alternative explanation might account for the findings equally well; namely, that successful hypnotic performance may have been very dramatic and was remembered by the subjects because of its being so accentuated. The study by Clemes (1964), previously described, lent partial support to their first explanation. He found that subjects were more amnesic for critical than for neutral words, supporting the repression hypothesis.

A subsequent study by O'Connell (1966) supported an enhancement explanation. He also analyzed the nature of the items recalled and, like Brenman, found an overall tendency for passed items to be recalled more frequently than failed items. Further analysis showed, however, that this was more pronounced for those subjects relatively unhypnotizable than for those highly hypnotizable. He interpreted this to suggest that it was the rather unusual or unexpected nature of the passing of the items for those subjects who passed relatively few items that enhanced the passing and increased the probability of its being remembered. Had the explanation been one of repression, the subjects who passed the larger number of items, that is, the more susceptible subjects, would have been expected to show the effect to a greater degree.

Bobbitt (1958), Imm (1965), and Levitt et al. (1961) have also investigated the relationship between amnesia and repression. While there are similarities, it does not appear that hypnotic amnesia can be entirely explained by the mechanism of repression.

DISSOCIATIVE PROCESS

Hypnosis has been conceived by some as an altered state due to a dissociative process. This implies a capacity for various processes to occur simultaneously, but to be relatively independent of each other. In the case of amnesia, functionally (structurally?) distinct modes of thought may operate in such a way that the material in one cannot be readily translated into the other. While little research has directly investigated this explanation, there is much clinical evidence and tangentially related experimental evidence that supports it.

Kihlstrom and Evans (1971) have recently suggested that the suggestions for posthypnotic amnesia may result in disruptions in cognitive processing and the distortion of cognitive materials. This led them to hypothesize that subjects manifesting partial hypnotic amnesia would retrieve events in a more random manner than the "organized and sequential remembering of the insusceptible subjects" (p. 775). They found significant differences $(p =$ .001) in both the organization of recall and the sequence of recall for the items comprising SHSS:C supporting their hypothesis.

The amnesias that occur in multiple personalities; the amnesias associated with hypnoticlike states reported to occur in a large number of primitive societies; Orne's (1959) discussion of trance logic; the work of Gill and Brenman (1959), which conceptualizes hypnosis as a regression in the service of the ego; the work of Schachtel (1947) and Reiff and Scheerer (1959) dealing with the styles and modes of thought; the contribution of Eriksen (1958) on awareness and its manifestation through different response modalities; the amnesia for events occurring during sleep, which have been previously described (Cobb et al., 1965; Evans et al., 1966, 1969); and clinical observations (Orne, 1966a)—all bear on this issue. There is a need for more direct testing of hypotheses generated from this formulation.

With our present limited state of understanding and sophistication about hypnosis in general, it would be premature to accept any one explanation of amnesia as comprehensive.

Summary

In summary, it should be noted that hypnotic amnesia is not a simple phenomenon. Like any other psychological concept, as we employ more sophisticated methodologies to analyze it, we find it to be more and more complex in terms of its manifestations and the variables that give rise to it. The present survey reviewed a relatively large number of studies. Although amnesia has attracted the interest and attention of both clinicians and laboratory investigators for a long time, many questions still need to be answered. Sequentially planned programs of a series of investigations of hypnotic amnesia are needed. The payoff will be many times greater than for the one-time shotgun type of study that has all too often characterized the research in this area.

Our attention in this chapter has been directed specifically toward amnesia; yet it is only one of a number of hypnotic phenomena that are interrelated. As our understanding of these other phenomena as well as of the underlying nature of hypnosis itself increases, there will be relevant implications for the nature of amnesia. For example, findings of a physiological nature about hypnotic susceptibility may generate hypotheses about amnesia.

This survey has been directed primarily toward the experimental evidence for and procedures used to study hypnotic amnesia rather than toward clinical case studies. Reference has been made from time to time regarding the differences that occur in amnesia in the clinical setting as compared with the experimental setting. The effects are often startlingly dramatic and conclusive in the former, but less so in the latter. Important differences distinguish the two settings; they should be kept in mind. The relationship that exists between the hypnotist and the client or subject, the motivation for participating in the experience, or the personally relevant, ego-involving nature of the material for which amnesia is suggested, and the expectations of the client or subject differ radically for the two settings. It should not be too surprising that different observations have been made in the clinical as opposed to the experimental setting. What needs yet to be done is to systematize and carefully record the important factors in the clinical situation, and then study their influence in a clinical laboratory setting, that is, a laboratory setting in which the clinical factors are maximally operative.

I am not convinced that the phenomenon of hypnotic amnesia can be entirely explained on the basis of demand characteristics, instructions, expectations, desires to please the experimenter, or role playing. Over and above all of these variables, there is a responsiveness to hypnotic suggestions that is part of a unique subjective state, and which supports the authenticity and genuineness of hypnotic amnesia. The crucial problem is to establish procedures and controls that will allow us to evaluate the hypnotic state influences so that we can, in turn, assess and understand their authenticity. It has been suggested that this may involve defining hypnotic amnesia more carefully, so that the definition eliminates verbal inhibition as part of amnesia. This may require changes in the operational definitions used to measure amnesia so that the recoverability is an integral part of the definition. It will require the systematic incorporation of procedures to evaluate the role of normal forgetting. The presence of such confounding variables makes the task more difficult and increases the need for caution in drawing conclusions from any particular study, but their presence does not destroy the concept itself.

Kenneth S. Bowers *received his Ph.D. from the University of Illinois in 1964. Since then he has been at Ontario's University of Waterloo, where he pursues his research interest in hypnosis. He served for two years as Director of Clinical Training at University of Waterloo, and for four years served as a consultant to the Ontario Training School for Girls. In the latter capacity, Dr. Bowers became interested in the subtleties of behavior change as understood by attribution theory, which he has recently combined with his interest in hypnosis. In 1970–71, he spent a sabbatical year at Stanford's hypnosis lab, where he completed experiments concerned with an attributional analysis of operant conditioning. With his wife Patricia, Dr. Bowers has investigated the relationship of hypnosis and creativity; their contribution to this book reflects his interest in this area.*

Patricia Greig Bowers *is an Assistant Professor of Psychology at the University of Waterloo, Ontario. She received her Ph.D. from the University of Illinois in 1965. Since then she has done some clinical work, chiefly psychotherapy, as a psychologist at the Kitchener-Waterloo Hospital, and later as a consultant to Grandview School, a training school for girls in Galt, Ontario. Her teaching interests have been primarily in the field of personality. Cognitively-oriented theories of personality development are her special concern.*

Bowers and Bowers *are interested in the systematic study of subjective experience in hypnosis. For them subjective reports are primary data. They argue that the behavioristic tradition at best tends to place secondary interest on the heart of the matter—the striking changes in subjective experience. The phenomenological emphasis brings to light similarities between hypnosis, other altered states, and the creative process. Creativity is viewed as involving regression in the service of the ego (adaptive regression). This involves constructive integration of primary and secondary process thinking and employment of fantasy in the service of realistic ends. A careful review of empirical studies is made in the light of this theoretical viewpoint.*

8

Hypnosis and Creativity: A Theoretical and Empirical Rapprochement

KENNETH S. BOWERS AND
PATRICIA GREIG BOWERS

Hypnosis: The Behavioral Approach

While hypnosis has both experiential and behavioral characteristics, the latter have been the traditional target of experimental investigation. This behavioristic bias in the study of hypnosis has more or less identified hypersuggestibility as *the* defining feature of hypnosis (Hull, 1933; Weitzenhoffer, 1953). Behavioral responses to suggestions have thus been of unique importance in determining subjects' hypnotic susceptibility. Very often, however, nonhypnotized subjects who are either task motivated or simulating hypnosis behave much like hypnotized subjects (Barber, 1969b; Orne, 1959). The frequent failures to differentiate hypnotic behavior from simulated hypnosis or task-motivated behavior can suggest, however unintentionally, that there is no important difference between waking and hypnotized subjects. That is, the behavioral strategy in hypnosis often minimizes or even ignores quite striking differences in the subjective experience of hypnotized and control subjects. Unfortunately, the epistemological assumptions of behavioristic psychology do not easily accomodate to a distinction between objective reality and the subjective experience of it. Thus, from a strict behavioristic point of view, if the outward manifestations of hypnosis

This paper was assisted by Grant No. 217 of the Ontario Mental Health Foundation. The authors wish to thank Don Meichenbaum, Gary Griffin, Paul Lerner, and Ken Keeling for their helpful comments on this paper.

can be simulated or otherwise engendered, the very reality of hypnotic phenomena is cast into doubt.

Behavioristic skepticism about the nature of hypnosis is compounded when the notion of trance is invoked to explain various hypnotic phenomena. It is not yet at all clear that there are any behavioral or physiological concomitants that uniquely identify its presence; consequently, trance simply does not exist within the purview of a behavioristic psychology, and is in no position to explain anything (Barber, 1969b).

More recently, some investigators have abandoned a strict behaviorist orientation and have taken seriously the behavior and especially the testimony of hypnotized subjects as corresponding to profound alterations in their experience of themselves and the world. The use of subjective reports as primary data is not new in psychology. The whole tradition of psychophysics, for example, is an attempt to plot subjective experience as a function of stimulus input. But subjective reports of hypnotic experience have been less honored. And in a way skepticism regarding the subjective reports of hypnotic subjects is understandable. For instance, it does seem incredible that analgesic suggestions—mere talk—can render an ordinarily painful stimulus more or less unhurtful. So incredible does it seem, that reports of "no pain" by a hypnotized subject can themselves be dismissed as mere talk, more calculated to satisfy the hypnotist (Barber, 1963; Kroger, 1957) than correspondent to subjects' real experience. In psychophysics, the relationship between stimulus input and response output describes a predictable and continuous function that is acceptably mathematical and scientific. However, for the skeptical among us, the disjunction between rather innocuous hypnotic suggestions and subjects' reports of their rather dramatic effects is so great as to render the latter generally unbelievable, and *therefore* of little scientific value. In response to skepticism of this kind several recent experiments have demonstrated, beyond reasonable doubt, the credibility of subjects' testimony regarding hypnotic pain analgesia (Hilgard, 1969c; Lenox, 1970; McGlashen, Evans, & Orne, 1969) and other hypnotic phenomena (Bowers, 1966; Bowers & Gilmore, 1969).

Hypnosis: The Experiential Approach

The cautious acceptance of subjective reports of private experience as primary data allows an experiential orientation to the study of hypnotic phenomena. The experience of hypnosis can thus be studied in its own right, as it relates to hypnotic suggestibility, to other altered states, and to spontaneous, trancelike experiences. Several studies show that hypnotic experiences are characterized by important alterations in consciousness. As and Ostvold (1968) rated female subjects on the basis of their responses to a 27-item scale covering a variety of subjective experiences during hypnosis. Three factors accounted for half of the variance of these ratings. Factor I represented the "experience of trance," Factor II, the "experience of ego control," and Factor III, the "desire for regression." The following correlations between factor scores and depth of hypnosis as assessed by a standardized susceptibility scale were found: Factor I: r = .69; Factor II: r = −.41; Factor III: r = .07.

Field and Palmer (1969), using an empirically derived inventory that assessed subjects' experience during hypnosis (Field, 1965), factor-analyzed the intercorrelations of all items from both the experience inventory and the Stanford Hypnotic Susceptibility Scale (SHSS; Weitzenhoffer & Hilgard, 1959). Thus, the emerging factors are not pure experience factors as were those of Ås and Ostvold, but rather composites of experience and suggestibility. A general factor of hypnotic depth emerged, with challenge SHSS items, together with inventory items reflecting experiences of absorption, unawareness, compulsion, and unusualness loading on it most highly. This factor accounted for 16 per cent of the factor variance. Of six rotated factors found, two dealt with alterations of consciousness. One of these two factors described "the dimension from awareness to unawareness of the environment and the experimental situation," while the other factor was "a dimension from waking to dazed drowsiness" (Field & Palmer, 1969, p. 59). The total hypnotic inventory score correlated .51 with the SHSS.

Tart (1970b) correlated several indices of experiences during hypnosis with each other and with the behavioral score of the more demanding SHSS, Form C (SHSS:C; Weitzenhoffer & Hilgard, 1962). He reports that the mean of a subject's estimates of how deeply hypnotized he is correlates .74 with the SHSS:C behavioral score. The same subjective estimate or "state report" correlates .77 with SHSS:C "experiential score." This latter score reflects the "intensity and degree of involuntariness of each major suggestion" of the previously administered SHSS:C. The state report correlates .66 with Field's Inventory (above). In an interesting attempt to separate "state report" from the effects of following suggestions, the *initial* state report, requested after induction but before any experience of reactions to specific suggestions, was correlated with several variables. The results of this analysis were correlations between initial state report and the SHSS:C behavioral score of .56, between this report and SHSS:C experiential score of .69, and between this report and Field's Inventory of .69.

Hypnotized subjects can evidently articulate their experiences reliably. Such experiences are distinct from hypersuggestibility, but predict it to a moderately high degree (.56). Subjects' estimates of hypnotic depth prior to any response to specific suggestions predict the subjective intensity of subsequent hypnotic responses to an even greater extent (.69).

Trancelike Experiences and Hypnosis

The above studies have found evidence for important hypnotic experiences that are conceptually distinct from suggestibility per se. These trancelike, unrealistic experiences imply in large part an absence of the usual awareness of the environment and one's place in it. Accordingly, Shor has written several papers directly concerned with the loss of a "generalized reality orientation" (GRO) as one basic aspect of hypnosis (Shor, 1959, 1962). Shor recently described the GRO and its temporary abeyance in this way:

> In all our waking life we carry around in the background of our awareness a kind of frame of reference or orientation to generalized reality which serves as a context or arena within which we interpret all of our ongoing conscious experiences. Under certain conditions—of which hypnosis is just one—this wide frame of reference or orientation to generalized reality can fade into the very distant background of our minds so that ongoing experiences are isolated from their usual context. When that happens the distinction between imagination and reality no longer exists for us. (1970, p. 91)

As this passage suggests, the loss of GRO is by no means confined to hypnosis. Witch doctors, mystics, as well as the ordinary man in the street report occasional loss of awareness of their environmental frame of reference. For example, in the same paper from which the above quotation was taken, Shor described what he calls the "book reading fantasy" to illustrate how a loss in GRO can be a rather ordinary event for some people.

> When these people read a story, particularly an adventureful novel, they are able to enter the story in imagination so completely that it seems equivalent to living the experience itself. During the time of this fantasy the reader is completely oblivious to the true reality about him. The fantasy world is an encapsulated unit, and it seems totally real. There is nothing else beyond it. (P. 92)

A fading of GRO results not only from complete absorption in a complex story; as Deikman (1963) has shown, simply concentrating on a simple object like a blue vase can also have potent effects on one's perception of reality. Deikman's four subjects experienced rather unusual perceptual distortions during their 12 brief (usually 15-minute) meditation periods. The terms "more vivid" and "luminous" were often used to describe the vase. The shape of the vase appeared unstable; there were reports of a loss of the third dimension and a diffusion or loss of the vase's boundaries. One subject said in her fourth meditation session: "The outlines of the vase . . . seem almost literally to dissolve entirely . . . and for it to be a kind of fluid blue." This subject often felt herself merging with the blue. Another subject, when looking at a landscape immediately after one meditation session, reported that the "view didn't organize itself in any way. . . . There were no planes. . . . Everything was working at the same intensity" (Deikman, 1963, p. 208*).[1] The next day this subject, viewing the same scene after his

---

1. Throughout this paper, asterisks identify page numbers for the papers as they appear in Tart (Ed.), 1969. This convention facilitates access to otherwise widely scattered papers.

meditation, described very few objects but talked of pleasure, luminescence, and beautiful movements.

Other valued states have been described in which lack of awareness of any differentiation between the self and the surround is associated with emotions of joy or ecstasy. Subjective events of this kind have been termed "peak experiences" or "mystical experiences." An extreme loss of GRO is also experienced by the yoga, who after much practice can become oblivious not only to his reality context, but also to any thought or emotion arising from within. Other characteristics common to various altered states of consciousness are discussed by Ludwig (1966).

Physiological evidence that supports the assumption of similarities among altered states is accumulating. Alpha EEG activity is characteristic of yoga (Anand, Chhina, & Singh, 1961), Zen meditation (Kasamatsu & Hirai, 1966), and of the period just before sleep (Foulkes & Vogel, 1965; Vogel, Foulkes, & Trosman, 1966). It is true that subjects under hypnosis usually show no particular predominance of alpha waves; EEG activity during hypnosis is of the normal waking variety (Weitzenhoffer, 1953). However, London (1969; London et al., 1969) has found that in comparisons of resting, nonhypnotized baseline measures, high susceptible women have significantly longer alpha duration than low susceptible women. Similarly, beginners in yoga who have well-marked alpha activity in resting records, "showed greater aptitude and zeal for maintaining the practice of yoga" (Anand, Chhina, & Singh, 1961, pp. 505-506*).

Kamiya (1969) has trained people to increase or suppress alpha activity. To maintain a high alpha state, subjects "stop being *critical* about anything, including the experiment" (p. 514*). They report that this state of uncritical relaxation is very pleasant. Kamiya notes that those subjects who are better able to learn the control of alpha are characterized by having practiced some form of meditation in the past. Brown's (1970) subjects successfully learned to increase alpha EEG duration with eyes open using the feedback of a light that was on only when alpha activity was present. They answered a short general questionnaire after each of four practice sessions regarding their experiences in the session. Subjects "who lost awareness of all environmental factors except the light, or who felt 'dissolved into the environment' tended to have higher levels of alpha abundance" (p. 449). Consonant with the above findings may be Reyher's (1964) physiological theory of hypnosis, which suggests certain similarities between hypnosis, sleep, personality disturbance, and primary process on the basis of the greater influence of lower levels of cortical integration.

In sum, the GRO may be reduced in many ways: via hypnosis, various training techniques, or spontaneously. Altered states can also be induced by drugs (Huxley, 1963), by fatigue (Morris & Singer, 1966), and also by sensory deprivation, about which we will have more to say later.

Although losses in GRO are not as uncommon as one might suppose, people do differ a great deal in the frequency and/or completeness with which they experience such losses. Indeed, the frequency and/or intensity of waking subjects' spontaneous trancelike experiences has been the only index that consistently correlates with hypnotic susceptibility. The so-called experience inventories, which tap such spontaneous, waking experiences, should not be confused with the scales of hypnotic experience mentioned earlier. The Personal Experience Questionnaire (PEQ; Shor, 1960) was the first experience inventory that was employed in an attempt to relate spontaneous losses in GRO with hypnotic susceptibility. Forty-five items empirically selected from the original questionnaire correlated .46 with susceptibility when cross-validated (Shor, Orne, & O'Connell, 1962).

As, O'Hara, & Munger (1962) constructed a similar but theoretically derived experience inventory, which incorporated some of Shor's items. A factor analysis of 24 items representative of the 60-item inventory found two main factors, "role absorption," and "experience and tolerance of unusual experiences, the latter factor also representing some regressive elements." Examples of the first factor are having one's fanciful elaborations of an incident seem as real as the actual incident, and being so caught up in music and dancing as to become enraptured and lose the sense of self. An example of the second factor is having completed some task during the night with no memory in the morning of having done so. Total scores on the inventory correlated .36 and .31 with a standardized measure of hypnotic susceptibility for two samples of female subjects, and .47 with a sample of male subjects (As, 1962). Those items highly related to susceptibility in one sample were not consistently related to it in other samples. However, hypnotizability seems related to the type of item representing essentially the same psychological dimension as the inventory factors of role absorption and experience and tolerance of unusual experience (As, 1963).

There appear to be complex sex differences as well as similarities in the relationship between unusual, trancelike experiences and hypnotizability. While for both males and females unusual experiences are related to hypnosis, females have more such experiences, and take them more for granted. Females seem to relinquish ego control in favor of experiences of a nonrational, slightly mystical kind, while males are inclined toward more emotional, especially aggressive outlets (As, 1962). This is the first time that sex differences in correlates of susceptibility have been emphasized, and, as we will later show, such differences may be quite important in our understanding of hypnotic phenomena.

It is reasonable to suppose that spontaneous trancelike experiences are related to altered states other than hypnosis. And indeed, McGlothlin, Cohen, and McGlothlin (1968) have found that scores on an experience inventory (As, O'Hara, & Munger, 1962) also correlate with the intensity of reactions to LSD.

Suggestibility and GRO

When GRO is weakened a person tends to become involved with a surrogate reality either suggested by an external agent (person or book) and/or inspired by primary process dominated fantasy. Thus, subjects give more primary process on the Rorschach when they are hypnotized than they do in the waking state (Fromm, Oberlander, & Gruenewald, 1969). The suggestibility enhancing effect of hypnosis is ordinarily assumed, though as previously noted, there is recent documentation for the fact that subjective reports of trance depth correlate with behavioral measures of responses to suggestions (see also Hilgard & Tart, 1966; Tart & Hilgard, 1966; Tart, 1970b). While the content of the hypnotized person's ideation may conform to suggestion, the rules of thought are nevertheless heavily infiltrated by primary process. Such a condition is exemplified by trance logic (Orne, 1959), in which logical contradictions are tolerated easily by the hypnotized subject but not by the simulator.

Heightened suggestibility concomitant with a fading of GRO, while characteristic of hypnosis, is found under other conditions as well. That there should also be heightened suggestibility during sensory deprivation was hypothesized by Gill and Brenman (1959) and found recently by Sanders & Reyher (1969). They found that 4 to 6 hours of sensory deprivation leads to enhanced hypnotic susceptibility as measured by responsiveness to SHSS suggestions, which enhancement lasts at least a week. Wickramasekera (1969) reports greater hypnotic susceptibility in women after half an hour of sensory restriction. There is even some evidence that subjects highly susceptible to hypnosis will respond to simple motor suggestions while maintaining stage 1 EEG sleep; low susceptible subjects do not, however, respond in this way (Cobb et al., 1965). The most dramatic examples of hypersuggestibility occur in "brainwashing." Gill and Brenman (1959) have noted important similarities between brainwashing procedures and those used in sensory deprivation and in hypnosis.

GRO and Fantasy

Although a loss in GRO is one condition for enhanced suggestibility, it is also, as previously noted, a condition in which subjects are more receptive and responsive to internal sources of stimulation. In so-called hypnagogic states before sleep, "regressive content in mentation appears only with, or after, some loss of contact with the external world" (Vogel, Foulkes, & Trosman, 1966, p. 87*). The invasion of "reality" by fantasy under conditions of reduced GRO is especially clear in a recent autokinetic experiment by Mayman and Voth (1969). Persons who were less oriented to the memory of the (darkened) room tended to interpret the pinpoint of light less in terms of realistic considerations than in terms of their own fantasies. One subject, for example, saw the light as "the headlights of an automobile which is driving along a distant mountain road." Moreover, there seemed to be a dynamic, fostering relationship between the amount of autokinesis, the loss of GRO, and fantasy. Thus, the more subjects were aware of their surroundings, the less autokinetic movement they perceived $(r = -.51)$, and "the more autokinetic movement seen, the more elaborate, vivid, and compelling was the phantasy evoked in the autokinetic situation" (Mayman & Voth, 1969, p. 638). A later study was more ambiguous regarding the relationship between the amount of autokinesis and fantasy (Bush, Hatcher, & Mayman, 1969).

The tendency for some subjects in Mayman and Voth's (1969) study to fantasize in a 10-minute autokinetic procedure is somewhat reminiscent of reports by subjects serving in sensory deprivation tasks. Zuckerman (1964), in a review of the perceptual isolation literature, lists several studies in which from 30 per cent to 80 per cent of subjects in sensory deprivation reported a drifting of thought with fantasies and daydreams. From 79 per cent to 90 per cent of subjects in various samples had difficulty in directed thinking. Across all studies, approximately 43 per cent of subjects reported unstructured visual sensations and 19 per cent had structured visual sensations. The more complete the isolation conditions (and therefore, presumably, the more the loss in GRO) the more subjects reported highly intimate fantasies (Zuckerman, 1964, p. 273). Other similar effects are cited as well. A later report indicates that feelings of being cut off from reality, together with increases in primary process thinking, are unique to sensory deprivation and are not produced simply by confinement or social isolation (Zuckerman et al., 1968). Thus, the loss of GRO as induced specifically by sensory deprivation procedures increases primary process dominated fantasy.

Most persons find sensory deprivation somewhat stressful. There are, however, substantial differences in the ability of people to cope with the discomforts of sensory deprivation. Surprisingly, the correlates of adaptability to sensory isolation have been difficult to determine. However, Cambareri (1959) found that suggestible subjects were more adaptive to deprivation conditions than unsuggestible subjects, despite the fact that suggestible subjects experience more regressive phenomena than unsuggestible subjects.

Wright and Zubek (1969) were quite successful in predicting subjects' endurance under conditions of sensory deprivation. For predictive purposes, these authors employed an index of control derived from the Holt system of scoring the Rorschach (Holt & Havel, 1960). The 31 men in the experiment were rank ordered on this index and a median split was performed on the resulting distribution. Fourteen out of 15 subjects who were high on the index of control lasted the entire week in sensory isolation, whereas 12 of 16 subjects low on this score failed to do so ($\chi^2 = 12.17$, p

< .01). The authors concluded that "the effectiveness of subjects' control and defense mechanisms was positively related to success or failure in isolation" (Wright & Zubek, 1969, p. 616).

Since the Holt system of Rorschach scoring has been successfully employed in other investigations of interest to us, a description of this scoring system is in order. Basically, its purpose is to evaluate the manifestations of primary process in a Rorschach protocol, and the effectiveness with which these primitive modes of thinking are controlled and integrated into a realistic and socially acceptable form.

There are two basic measures derived in this system of scoring: a compound measure of primary process, called defense demand, and a compound measure of defense effectiveness. The primary process score is based on the number of responses with aggressive and libidinal content, together with various nonlogical or bizarre formal characteristics in the protocol. Defense demand rates "the intensity and primitiveness of the drive content and the extent to which the formal aspects of the response deviate from logical, orderly, realistic thinking" (Blatt, Allison, & Feirstein, 1969, p. 275). Defense effectiveness "is an assessment of the degree to which drive-laden, nonlogical thinking is integrated into a more realistic and understandable response" (Blatt, Allison, & Feirstein, 1969, p. 276). The product of the above two measures yields the Adaptive Regression score. Wright and Zubek's (1969) Index of Control was evidently derived from the ratio of defense effectiveness to the defense demand.

Turning now to other studies using the Holt method of scoring Rorschach, Feirstein (1967) found that Holt's (1963) measure of adaptive regression was correlated with subjects' ability to tolerate unrealistic experiences as derived from a battery of tests. It must be emphasized here that the measure used to assess subjects' tolerance for unusual experiences differed from the so-called experience inventories mentioned earlier. Feirstein evaluated subjects on the phi phenomenon, a set of reversible figures, performance utilizing aneisikonic lenses, and a series of pictures involving stimulus incongruity. From the four tests, he derived nine measures, on which the subjects' average score correlated .49 with the Holt adaptive regression score *(p < .01)*. Thus, tolerance for unrealistic experiences seems to be related to subjects' ability to integrate primary process material into a realistic and acceptable form. This finding is corroborated by an investigation using the Holt system showing that divinity students who had more intense conversion experiences (that is, unusual or unrealistic experiences) also had more "adaptively controlled regressive thinking" than students who had less intense conversion experiences, or none at all (Allison, 1967). Maupin (1965) compared the adaptive regression scores from the Rorschach of 28 male college students who subsequently were rated high, medium, and low in their response to a series of Zen meditation exercises. The relationship *(tau = .49)* was significant at *p < .001*.

Finally, in a frequently cited study by Pine and Holt (1960), a defense effectiveness Rorschach score correlated with a composite creativity score .80 for men *(n* = 13) and .52 for women *(n* = 14). Surprisingly, the adaptive regression score, though correlating with creativity in men *(r* = .90), was not correlated with creativity in women *(r* = .28).

A summary of the above findings is in order. Subjects' effectiveness in controlling primary process and integrating it into a realistic form is related to endurance in sensory isolation, the tolerance for unusual and unrealistic subjective experience, response to Zen meditation exercises, and creativity.

In this section, we have reviewed evidence indicating that the loss of GRO is accompanied by the escalating influence of primary process mentation. We have also seen how the ability to tolerate and control such mentation is evidently a disposition of some importance in determining a person's experiences. It is now appropriate to extend these findings, as well as ones mentioned earlier, into a more thorough examination of creative functioning.

Comments on Creativity

The creativity literature is not particularly cohesive. Definitional and criterial problems persist, and the need for theory-guided research is apparent. Our views of creativity have been guided mostly by theoretical considerations of a more or less ego analytic variety; Kris's (1952) and Schachtel's (1959) ideas regarding creativity have been particularly influential in the following account. A broader view of theories and research in creativity may be gained by referring to several valuable reviews, such as those by Dellas and Gaier (1970), Guilford (1967), and Barron (1965). Other reviews of creativity have been written by Golann (1963), Stein (1968), and Tryk (1968). Although technically not a review, we would also like to recommend the work by Wallach and Kogan (1965), which is a good treatment of some of the measurement problems that beleager the creativity area.

Having made these preliminary remarks, we will now present a view of creativity that relates to some of the concepts introduced above.

A Working Concept of Creative Functioning

Creativity involves the process of seeing things in a new way, of generating new forms that transform one's perception of the world (Jackson & Messick, 1965). At the peak of its realization, the creative vision of one man can literally reshape the world, as the inventive genius of Copernicus, Newton, Darwin, Freud, and Einstein have amply demonstrated. Their insights revealed a world subtler, more differentiated, and more challenging than imagined by their predecessors.

But human endeavor does not have to reach such exalted heights before it earns the right to be called creative. Consider children: According to Piaget (Flavell, 1963) a child becomes more differentiated as he successively accomodates his schema in order to assimilate the world in ways that were literally unimaginable at an earlier stage in his development. For the infant, the dawning recognition that he and the world are twain can hardly be less creative or dramatic in his life than the historical realization that man does not occupy the center of the universe. Perhaps it is a child's need to accomodate continually to the world, to apprehend and appreciate it in ever changing ways that is the basis of creativity in children.

As he grows older, however, the child's experience becomes conventionalized (Schachtel, 1959). He tends to depend upon words to tell him how things are, and he reduces his experiences to fit the stereotyped dimensions of language. Thus, however liberating language can be, it is also very limiting, subtly forcing us to exclude from consideration and even from consciousness those aspects of our subjectivity that evade easy articulation. Language may adapt us to the world that is, but it is the enemy of the as yet unimagined. Even for the poet, "the greatest problem . . . is the temptation of language" (Schachtel, 1959, p. 295).

It is our interior life that saves us from utter stereotypy. A momentary feeling of disgust, or awe, an intuitive hunch, a fantasy, all of these subarticulate experiences, if seized upon and elaborated, can create a new form, a new insight into reality. It matters little whether the product of such a transformation be a poem, an architectural landmark, or simply creative conversation. The point is, a new and satisfying reality has emerged. Moreover, the new insight, the new form, however familiar it may be to others, is nevertheless new and vital to the creator.

Maintaining one's perceptual vitality in the midst of conventionalizing forces seems to require a capacity for "partial, temporary, controlled lowering of the level of psychic functioning to promote adaptation"—Schafer's (1958, p. 122) definition of adaptive regression.[2] There are two aspects of

2. This definition is employed because it is more inclusive than many similar ones, which emphasize the role of primary process and drive discharge in the creative act. Schachtel (1959) is one influential theorist who specifically states that "regression to primary process thought is not typical of the creative process. . . . What distinguishes the creative process from regression to primary process thought is that the freedom of the approach is due not to drive discharge function but to the openness in the encounter with the object of creative labor" (p. 244–55). He further suggests that "the unseeingness which in all of us. . . stands in the way of a more creative vision is due more often to the encroachment of an already labelled world upon our spontaneous sensory and intellectual capacities than to the repression of a libidinal impulse" (p. 243). However, Schachtel does emphasize the role of "relatively undirected, freely wandering play of perception, thought and phantasy" (p. 245) in the creative process and seems therefore, to acknowledge the importance of the *formal* as opposed to

Continued on p. 266

this concept that we would like to stress. First, adaptive regression, also called regression in the service of the ego (Kris, 1952), implies a capacity and tolerance for unrealistic and unregulated thinking and experience. We have already reviewed evidence indicating that such experiences are more characteristic of some people than of others. Moreover, we have seen how such experiences are caused or at least accompanied by an abeyance in generalized reality orientation.

The second important aspect of adaptive regression is that the unregulated thinking and experience implied by regression is organized in terms of realistic considerations, that is, is adaptive. We will later consider *how* such an adaptation of unrealistic thinking to realistic purposes might ordinarily take place. For now, however, it seems reasonable to consider evidence which suggests *that* creative functioning involves (a) unrealistic thinking which is (b) adaptively integrated into an acceptably realistic form.

Creativity: Some Empirical Findings

The ability to experience in both a primitive and a mature mode, and to integrate the two effectively, has been studied empirically in several ways. We have already mentioned the scoring system for the Rorschach devised by Holt (1960) to assess primary process and its controlled expression. We have seen that Holt's measures of the extent to which primary process is effectively integrated in fact correlated highly with tests of creativity (Pine & Holt, 1960).

Another more traditional index of a person's ability to coordinate fantasy and reality is the number of M (human movement) responses given in a Rorschach protocol. Since the blots obviously do not move, whatever movement a person sees represents a projection of his own inner fantasy life (Lerner, 1967). If the movement is "well seen," that is, if it respects the formal characteristics of the blot, then the projected movement represents a creative embellishment of an inanimate form; one's inner life has enriched and enlivened the blot, making it at once more interesting and satisfying. Rorschach (1949) originally spoke of M responses as an index of the person's "capacity for inner creation." Schachtel (1950) basically agrees, and further argues that "M responses refer to the capacity for *creative experience,* not to the capacity for *creative production*" (p. 94, italics in original). He further argues that the capacity for creative experience is a necessary but not sufficient condition for creative production. This is probably true of

---

drive discharge characteristics of primary process in creative functioning. A compromise formulation might propose that when one looks freely at an idea or an object, the "primary process" brings to mind both conventionally unacceptable drive related associations as well as unconventional, nondrive related thoughts. Both kinds of associations are probably hindered by the too-complete acceptance of cultural labels.

other indices of adaptive regression as well. What follows, then, is a brief review of some of the relevant studies on inkblot perception that have assessed the use of M, and of primitive and mature responses in general as a means of investigating creativity.

Myden (1959) compared Rorschach protocols of 20 renowned subjects in stage, visual, and literary arts with 20 subjects successful in various nonartistic fields. The Piotrowski (1950) scoring system was used. Myden found that the artists gave significantly more M and primary process responses. Dudek (1968a) compared persons giving five or more M responses on the Rorschach to those giving two or less. She found that the high M producers found it much easier to express themselves creatively on the TAT, Figure Drawings and Mosaics. Within the high M group, there was a significant correlation between M production and creative expression, while this was not true within the low M group. Creativity was not related to the number of responses in this study. In another study, Dudek (1968b) compared 41 successful artists (writers, painters, and sculptors) with 19 unsuccessful artist and 22 high-M nonartists. The subjects were matched for education and socioeconomic status, but not age. Using Piotrowski's (1950) system of scoring the Rorschach, she found that the successful artists were far more productive of primary process than the other two groups, but that the groups did not differ on M.

Griffin (1958), using the Levy Movement Blots, found that 20 college women designated creative by their teachers and fellow students did not differ on M from 20 women designated as noncreative. Barron used 27 inkblots scaled for M-evocative power to ascertain a subject's M threshold. (M threshold is low when M is seen on a card of low M-evocative power). Subjects were 100 military officers taking part in a three day living-in assessment. M threshold was uncorrelated with measures of intelligence, originality, and associational fluency. Rather it was related to staff assessments that seem to indicate a preference for "intrapsychic living as opposed to interest in action, practical affairs, and 'the world outside' " (Barron, 1955, p. 38).

Hersch (1962) studied three groups of male subjects: 20 eminent artists, 20 noncreative normal men of mixed occupations, and 20 hospitalized schizophrenics. They were selected on the basis of similar age, intellectual level, and Rorschach response productivity. Six categories of the Genetic Scoring System (Phillips, Kaden, & Waldman, 1959) were used. Movement, Integrative, and Form Dominant responses were considered "mature" while Form Subordinate, Physiognomic, and Primitive Thought Responses were considered "primitive." The major hypothesis of this study was that "creative individuals have a greater availability of both mature and primitive operations than non-creative normals" (Hersch, 1962, p. 195–96). In corroboration of this thesis, the artists gave more Movement and Form Dominant responses than normals, as well as more responses in each category of primitive responses. They exceeded schizophrenics in each category of mature responses, and did not differ from them in two categories of primitive responses. In the third category, Physiognomic Responses, the artists had higher scores.

Two studies not utilizing inkblot assessment of primary process and its control should be mentioned in the light of Hersch's hypothesis and results. Gamble and Kellner (1968) predicted that, in a comparison of low and high creative subjects, the latter could more effectively utilize both primitive and mature modes of thinking. They utilized the Remote Associate Test (Mednick & Mednick, 1967) as a measure of creativity and the Stroop Color-Word Test (Stroop, 1935) as a measure of subjects' ability to coordinate both levels of thinking. The more creative subjects in fact performed significantly better on the Stroop test. In an earlier comparison of subjects who did well and poorly on the Stroop test, the former subjects saw significantly more movement on the Rorschach than the latter (Holt, 1960).

Barron reported another very interesting finding, which substantiates the coexistence of more primitive and mature thinking in creative individuals. He found that the MMPI profiles of high (peer nominated) creative architects and writers revealed that they "are almost as superior to the general population in ego strength as they are deviant on such pathological dispositions such as Schizophrenia, Depression, Hysteria, and Psychopathic Deviation" (Barron, 1965, p. 64; see also Barron, 1969, p. 110–11).

Stein and Meer (1954) studied the degree to which 18 research chemists rated by superiors and colleagues as high and low creative gave well-integrated responses to Rorschach cards presented at four exposure levels: .01 seconds, .1 seconds, 3 seconds, and full exposure. They used a weighting system developed on a previous sample, such that well-integrated responses to cards empirically determined as the most difficult to integrate at the shortest exposure received highest weights, while autistic responses and rejects at full exposure received the greatest penalties. A biserial correlation between the weighted form level score and the rating on the creativity variable was $+.88$ $(p < .01)$. High creatives achieved higher scores than low creatives at all four exposure levels. Only the first response to each card was used, but high creative subjects gave more total responses than low creative subjects, because the latter rejected cards at every level of exposure. When the number of rejects was held constant, the groups did not differ in the number of well-integrated responses.

Gray (1969) administered the Holtzman Inkblot Test (Holtzman et al., 1961) and six Guilford tests of divergent thinking to 100 college men. Using Holt's primary process scoring system, a correlation of .23 $(p < .05)$, was obtained between primary process and creativity scores. The number of words a subject used on the HIT correlated .24 $(p < .05)$ with the number of responses to the creativity battery. With either or both "productivity" scores partialled out, the correlation between primary process and creativity was insignificant. Gray concludes that primary process and creativity are not related. However, fluency is often considered a concomitant of creative production. Certainly the number of words describing a percept may be related to the richness and subtlety of the percept.

There are other studies that emphasize the role of primary process thinking and its realistic integration (see, for example, the review by Dellas and Gaier, 1970). The above studies are among the better known, and represent the general trend of findings. While the empirical results are not entirely consistent, the weight of evidence favors the view that the creative process involves the coexistence of more and less realistic modes of perception and their integration.

The Creative Process

The above findings do not, however, yield any useful insights into just how the integration of primary and secondary thinking takes place. Hilgard (1962) proposes that such integrations can be conceived as either fusions or mixtures of primary and secondary process thinking. In fusions, both types of thinking are homogenized in varying proportions in any given response. The mixture scheme suggests that a vacillation between primary and secondary thinking takes place, with each kind of mentation remaining more or less distinct and intact. Although Hilgard (1962) lists several of the more prominent ego analytic proponents as favoring the fusion view of integration, we are impressed with how often oscillation from one kind of thinking to another is implied in describing the process of adaptive regression. For example, in discussing creativity, Kris says:

> The capacity of gaining easy access to id material without being overwhelmed by it, of retaining control over the primary process, and perhaps specifically, *the capability of making rapid or at least appropriately rapid shifts in levels of psychic function* suggest psychological characteristics of a definite but complex kind. (Kris, 1952, p. 25; italics added)

In Bellak's (1958) words, creativity involves "a brief *oscillating reduction* [italics added] of *certain adaptive* functions of the ego in the service of (i.e., for the facilitation of) other, specifically the 'synthetic' ego functions" (p. 367).

Schachtel is somewhat less explicit about the shifting or oscillating aspect of mentation during creative functioning, but nevertheless strongly implies it:

> Both the period of immersion in the ever renewed encounters [with an object] and the period of articulating and connecting the experiences won in the free play of the varied approaches are essential for the growth and expansion of the person's relation to the world through creative experience. (Schachtel, 1959, p. 242)

The following remarkable passage by the artist Max Ernst describes the psychological origins of his painting *"Natural History,"* and exemplifies how thought can swing back and forth from realistic to primitive and imaginative modes of functioning during the actual course of an act of creation.

It all started on August 10, 1925, by my recalling an incident of my childhood when the sight of an imitation mahogany panel opposite my bed had induced one of those dreams between sleeping and waking. And happening to be at a seaside inn in wet weather I was struck by the way the floor, its grain accentuated by many scrubbings, obsessed my nervously excited gaze. So I decided to explore the symbolism of the obsession, and to encourage my powers of meditation and hallucination I took a series of drawings from the floorboards by dropping pieces of paper on them at random and then rubbing the paper with blacklead. As I looked carefully at the drawings that I got in this way—some dark, others smudgily dim—I was surprised by the sudden heightening of my visionary powers, and by the dreamlike succession of contradictory images that came one on top of another with the persistence and rapidity peculiar to memories of love.

Now my curiosity was roused and excited, and I began an impartial exploration, making use of every kind of material that happened to come into my field of vision: leaves and their veins, frayed edges of sacking, brush strokes in a "modern" painting, cotton unwound from a cotton-reel, etc., etc. Then I saw human heads, many different beasts, a battle ending in a kiss *(the wind's sweetheart)*, rocks, *sea and rain, earthtremors*, the *sphinx in its stable*, the *small tables round about the earth, Caesar's shoulderblade, false positions*, a *shawl covered with flowers of hoar frost, pampas*.

The *cuts of a whip, trikles of lava, fields of honour, inundations and seismic plants, scarecrows*, the *edge of the chestnut wood*.

Flashes of lightning before one's fourteenth year, vaccinated bread, conjugal diamonds, the *cuckoo (origin of the pendulum)*, the *meal of death*, the *wheel of light*.

A solar coinage system.

The *habits of leaves*, the *fascinating cyprus tree*.

Eve, the only one remaining to us.

I put the first fruits of the *frottage* process together, from *sea and rain* to *Eve, the only one remaining to us*, and called it *Natural History*. (Ghiselin, 1952, pp. 64–65)

Note that this passage also nicely illustrates how fantasies catalyzed by some mundane feature of the environment (floorboards) can be seminally important to the creative act. Note also that the fantasy does not simply serve to remove the observer from the environment in the tradition of Walter Mitty; quite to the contrary, it casts the artist more fully into it. But the world now becomes identified with the limited focus of the artist's attention. And that limited portion of reality becomes more engaging and involving as it is perceived, not in its staid, familiar surround, but in a novel context of fantasies, feelings, and associations that enrich and enliven it. Schachtel

(1959) has referred to this kind of "oneness" with the object as allocentric perception, which "transcends, in some respect, that part of the labelled, traditional, cultural world with which the perceiver is familiar" (p. 178).

We are in effect arguing that the juxtaposition of focused attention and fantasy and an oscillating relationship between them may well be an important condition of adaptive regression, and hence of creativity. There are limiting conditions on this proposal; for example, the richness of fantasy that a person has certainly constrains the creative use of that fantasy. We shall have to forgo consideration of this limiting condition and concentrate on two others—the limitation created by the relative amount of fantasy a person has, and the problems inherent in retrieving fantasy.

Basically, the problem is this: Our inner life is elusive, and often such fleeting thoughts and images as we have are consigned to an oblivion from which they cannot be easily retrieved. For example, at one time or another, everyone has had the experience of remembering that a dream occurred, without remembering specifically what the dream was about.

There is another illustration of the evanescent quality of waking fantasy which is, for our purposes, both more instructive and less frequently noted. Nearly everyone reading this article has had the experience of perusing a paragraph or page of a book, and then suddenly realizing that nothing of it has registered. There is little to do but reread the entire passage. If however one stops long enough to consider what was happening during the attentional lacuna, a second surprise often awaits the introspective reader—it is often difficult to recall the thoughts and fantasies that one was having in lieu of reading. On those occasions when one manages to capture the gist of the interpolated reverie, it is usually clear that the fantasy itself escaped attention initially, and what one has now grasped is a reverberating memory of it.

In conversations with various people about this phenomenon, several other aspects of the interpolated reading reverie have emerged. People have noted (or at least agreed) that when trying to recapture the content of an association or fantasy, they tend to remain perfectly still; "suspended" is a word that captures the flavor of this bodily and mental condition. This strategy of postural quiescence is quite reminiscent of Rorschach's injunction to remain motionless after awakening, the better to remember a dream. Another quality of the interpolated reading reverie that is sometimes noted is that its content often seems worth retrieving; there is a sort of prescience that the lost thought is pertinent to the topic at hand, perhaps catalyzed by some fragment of the commentary, and potentially enriching and extending the written word. Under these circumstances, it is often helpful to read the particular page or paragraph again with an associative and uncritical set, in the hopes that one's mind will of its own accord go back to where it came from.

Perhaps this example makes clear that there are several distinct qualities or phases of mental activity that characterize the reading reverie: attention begins to wander from the discourse and the reader becomes lost in thought; then rather abruptly he may find himself back in the real world, but often at some risk of losing the thought. Subsequently he begins actively scanning for the fading traces of the reverie. The oscillating process of first attending to the world, in this case the printed page, being transported thence into an oblivion of reverie, then suddenly "coming to" and internally scanning the reverberating memories of the reverie should have measurable concomitants. If there be such, they should arouse the interest of those who study creative functioning, for it is this very oscillation from directed to undirected thinking that is presumably a condition for adaptive regression. Since we have proposed that fantasy, so unwilled and evanescent, is the level of cognitive functioning to which people "regress" when attention wanes, let us look at some of the work on waking fantasy. The work out of Jerome Singer's (1966) laboratory is perhaps the best place to start.

Eye Movements and Fantasy

Antrobus, Antrobus, & Singer (1964) report that subjects actively attempting to suppress a conscious wish or fantasy showed significant increases in eye movement over the rate exemplified during the passive "indulgence" of such a wish or fantasy. The study was later replicated (Singer & Antrobus, 1965). Again the authors found that the frequency of eye movement during the imagine-suppress condition was higher than during the imagine condition $(p < .001)$, whether or not the eyes were covered with a Ganzfeld.

From the evidence so far presented, one might infer that eye movement during the imagine-suppress condition reflects subjects' attempts to escape the fantasy in the mind's eye by actively processing visual information. It seems that this interpretation is too specific, however, for eye movements were also quite high under conditions where subjects were told to "make their thoughts race as fast as possible" (Antrobus, Antrobus, & Singer, 1964, p. 246). Thus, the authors suggested that rate of eye movement is less linked to visual input than to the rate of change of cognitive content.

Somewhat similar conclusions were reached by Amadeo and Shagass (1963). They found that subjects displayed more eye movement during a task of auditory vigilance than they did during a resting base level. Since subjects' eyes were closed during the vigilance task, they could not have been seeking actual visual cues, and it was deemed unlikely that subjects' eyes were following imagined visual cues. Consequently, the authors suggest that a higher rate of eye movement is a nonspecific concomitant of attentive activity. This interpretation is particularly reasonable in light of the results of a second portion of the same experiment. Utilizing different subjects and procedures, the authors consistently found the highest rate of eye movement under conditions where a subject was instructed to perform arithmetic manipulations in his head. Inasmuch as this relative superiority was obtained under both eyes-open and eyes-closed conditions, the eye movements again seem to be less a concomitant of looking at things than of being mentally active and attentive.

Incidentally, in the same experiment, the authors also found that the state of hypnosis led, under eyes-closed conditions, to a much lower rate of eye movement than could be achieved even under waking instructions "to do your utmost to keep your eyeballs from moving" (Amadeo & Shagass, 1963, p. 140). Evidently active attention paid, even in keeping one's eyeballs fixed, is accompanied by more eye movement than is the uncritical passiveness of the hypnotic state. Thus, when subjects are in an essentially passive and uncritical state of mind, such as during daydreaming or hypnosis, eye movements are minimal. But when subjects' thinking is actively directed toward and/or attentive to *either* exterior *or* interior events, eye movements are significantly higher. It seems that the relative rate of eye movements may in fact reflect the two different kinds of thinking: undirected, fantasy-dominated thought on one hand, and directed, regulated thinking on the other.

There do seem to be occasions, however, when a passive, uncritical orientation toward the visual field, instead of toward fantasy, is accompanied by a somewhat unusual pattern of eye movement. An excellent paper by Silverman (1968), describes eye movements characteristic of persons under LSD, and of (nonparanoid) schizophrenics. When these persons are oriented toward the visual field, their eye movements often reflect an intense preoccupation with a narrow range of reality. Such subjects show attenuated scanning movements, which implies a narrowing of attention, but the rate of saccadic eye movements is also somewhat increased, suggesting the intensity of concern for that narrow range of reality. Whether such a pattern of environmentally-oriented eye movement is characteristic of a normal, undrugged person in an altered state is unclear. However, it would not be surprising if, for example, the subjects in Deikman's study of experimental meditation showed a similar eye pattern while gazing at a blue vase (Deikman, 1963). These subjects reported various perceptual anomalies regarding the vase that are quite characteristic of the experiences accompanying the unusual eye movement pattern described above. The combination of low scanning, high saccadic movement is ordinarily accompanied by overestimation of object size and brightness, exactly the kind of phenomena reported by Deikman's subjects.

We might mention here that such an orientation toward a narrow range of reality, as described by Silverman and Deikman, is perhaps misleadingly described as "attention," at least in the active, scrutinizing sense of that word. Deikman, for example, specifically enjoined his subjects not to analyze the vase or think about it, but simply "to see the vase as it exists in itself . . . [to] perceive it as directly, as completely, as intensely as possible" (p. 202*). Thus, the subjects' attention, such as it was, seems more passive and uncritical than active and directed.

To summarize, evidence suggests that eye movement is usually reduced under conditions of uncritical, undirected thinking characteristic of hypnosis and fantasy. However, under certain conditions of uncritical preoccupation with a narrow visual field, eye movements, at least of the saccadic variety, may be intensified, though scanning movements seem to be much reduced. In any event, active thinking and attention, whether directed to exterior or interior events, is ordinarily accompanied by a higher rate of eye movement, and seems to suppress fantasy, (Antrobus, Antrobus, & Singer, 1964; Singer & Antrobus, 1965).

An interesting question is: What happens when one actively pays attention to fantasy? If there is anything to the hypothesis that fantasy is suppressed by attention in general, it is at least arguable that attention directed specifically at a fantasy may tend to make it less vivid. Experientially, it often seems as if attention is a solvent in which fantasies tend to dissolve; when we try to pay attention to our fantasies we seem to find only their residue. This is not to say that undirected thoughts and fantasies can not themselves be a noticeable and salient facet of experience, even to the point of being peremptory and terrifying (G. S. Klein, 1967). It is interesting, however, that this latter condition occurs precisely under circumstances when a person finds it difficult to pay attention to something, to direct and control his thinking. For example, in an article previously cited, Zuckerman (1964) noted that difficulty in directed, secondary process thinking is the most frequent, and for the subjects, most unexpected effect of sensory deprivation. It is this inability to attend that seems to be the conditon for another frequent symptom of isolation, namely the upsurge in primary process fantasies and daydreams. Thus, attention serves us not only by processing information; it may also serve to inhibit and control our fantasy life. A somewhat similar point is made by Silverman, who thoroughly reviewed various mechanisms involved in the production of altered states of consciousness. He concludes his article by saying that "the overall pattern of attentional response and psychological state relationships . . . indicates clear-cut associations between 'styles' of paying attention and the experience of 'reality'" (1968, p. 1215).

We have been stressing the relationship of eye movement to attention and fantasy, but it is possible that eye movements are a specific instance of how body motility in general adversely affects fantasy. Lerner (1967) has recently reminded us of Rorschach's original proposal that body movement and kinesthetic fantasy are inversely related, and Schachtel (1959) has noted that "bodily movement is the basic and simplest form of all activity endangering memory" (p. 281). In this context, "memory" is less for space-time events than for the elusive fantasies that permeate one's being, as in hypnagogic reveries (see also Reiff & Scheerer, 1959). Consistent with this hypothesis is a finding of Rossi, Fuhrman, and Solomon (1967), who found that during sensory deprivation, body motility and degree of reality orientation in imagery are directly related. Lerner cites several other studies which also suggest that immobility during isolation is the major contributor to increases in movement (kinesthetic) responses on the Rorschach, and that "the facilitating role of immobility in kinesthetic fantasy is a general one which holds true both in and out of dreams" (Lerner, 1967, p. 93).

A corroborating observation of a somewhat different kind is that sleep-deprived subjects rarely move their heads to check an illusion (Morris & Singer, 1966). Presumably, head and eye movements are often a means of gaining alternate prospects, the better to coordinate and test reality. Absence of such movements seems to suggest an unwillingness or inability to engage actively in reality testing, one result of which is visitation by the various illusions and unrealistic experiences that characterize sleep-deprived subjects, and altered states of consciousness in general.

We have been suggesting that eye and body movements, or rather their lack, may represent externally the "regression phase" of adaptive regression. We will need to follow this evidence with another kind that may better represent the "adaptive phase" of adaptive regression. Before doing so, however, we should like to extend the above findings to a consideration of hypnosis as an altered state, the better to indicate the psychological relationship of hypnosis and creativity.

Hypnosis and the Outside In

Perhaps the reader will recall again how subjects gazing at the blue vase in Deikman's (1963) meditation procedure experienced it as becoming boundaryless and super blue. To achieve these effects it was crucial for subjects to concentrate on the vase, but not in an analytic, scrutinizing way. That is, subjects were to remain passive with respect to their perception of the blue vase, just as we are ordinarily passively oriented with respect to our fantasy life. The significance of this last remark is that it is precisely under conditions of such attentional passivity that it can be difficult to discriminate the degree to which one's experience is determined by objects in the world on one hand, or by fantasy on the other. There is a sort of merging of inside and outside, a breakdown in the usual self-object boundary (Gravitz & Forbes, 1963). Indeed one of the scary things that occasionally happens under such altered states is a sudden burst of anxiety at the depersonalization implicit in this boundaryless condition.

This merging of inside and outside is rather reminiscent of Piaget's descriptions of infant perception. For the infant, the action performed on the object is identical to the object; the nipple *is* the sucking behavior performed on it—there is no separation between the activity of perceiving and the object perceived. Similarly, when a person's eye movements and body motility are drastically reduced, so are his perspectives of reality. The blue vase, for example, becomes less and less coordinated in space and time by multiple, analytic perceptual acts performed on it; consequently, it becomes more and more identified with and identical to the particular and limited perceptual act by which it is apprehended. It becomes, so to speak, a part of the person, rather than a separate and distinct object. As one of Deikman's subjects commented, "at one point it felt . . . as though the vase were in my head rather than out there: I knew it was out there but it seemed as though it were almost a part of me. I think that I almost felt at that moment as though, you know, the image is really in me, it's not out there" (1963, p. 206*).

It has been simpler to introduce the general idea of subject-object merging by recourse to a visual illustration. However, it seems reasonable that such phenomena also take place via the auditory modality as well, though there is no evidence that the admirable ability to move one's ears is in any way a functional analogue of eye movement. If there is nevertheless an analogous "regression" with respect to auditory stimulation, the dramatic effect of hypnotic suggestions may simply derive from the fact that a profoundly hypnotized subject has in effect ceased actively directing his own thinking and behavior, and experiences suggested phenomena in the same passive way that he experiences his fantasies, that is, as fantasy equivalents. Thus when such a person behaves in accordance with suggestion, it is less by reason of being realistically responsive to the demand characteristics of the situation (Orne, 1959) than by reason of experiencing the suggested state of affairs in the more or less uncontrolled and peremptory way that subjects in sensory isolation experience their fantasies. Indeed, some hypnotized subjects also experience nonsuggested phenomena, which may represent the unexpectedly potent effect of their own fantasies in the relative abeyance of their directed thinking.

The fantasies and/or suggested state of affairs thus perceived and experienced by a profoundly hypnotized subject constitute a kind of surrogate reality. Whether or not this reality surrogate is accepted as veridical seems to depend on factors other than its vividness or clarity (Neisser, 1967, p. 150). As Kolers has noted, "there is nothing in an experience that testifies to its correspondence with 'reality,' nothing in a perception that guarantees its truth. Judgments of reality and truth must come from other sources than the experience or the perception" (1964, p. 99).

Reality testing of this kind is not totally foreign, even to the deeply hypnotized subject. For example, Orne (1962c) notes that a deeply hypnotized person will not bump into a chair he is negatively hallucinating. An even more impressive instance of reality testing occurred when a deeply hypnotized subject discriminated a real and hallucinated person by seeing which image would raise its hand in response to a mental directive to do so (Orne, 1962c).

Gill and Brenman (1959), in their otherwise fine book, rendered a somewhat tortuous explanation of how a hypnotized subject maintained a certain residual contact with reality. They invoked several arcane concepts including an ego subsystem that regressed during hypnosis, leaving the ego proper free to navigate reality. This theoretical venture has been criticized by another writer of ego psychological persuasion (van der Walde, 1965). We submit that a conception of hypnosis emphasizing the fantasy-equivalent status of the suggested state of affairs finesses many of these theoretical pitfalls. The problem of responding to reality residues while hypnotized should be no more difficult than responding to fantasy residues while in a normal alert state. To put it another way, "reality" may be as peremptory to the hypnotized person as fantasy can be to the person who is not. Thus, a hypnotized subject is not apt to behave in accordance with suggestions that involve clear and present danger (although compare Orne & Evans, 1965). The extent to which reality invades fantasy in this way undoubtedly varies as a function of persons and circumstances.

Two more points should be quickly mentioned here. First, it seems clear, as we have pointed out early in the paper, that people differ in the ability to give up their generalized reality orientation and to tolerate the unusual experiences attendant upon this loss. Moreover, this ability to tolerate unusual experiences correlates about as highly with hypnotic susceptibility as any other measure. Since the unusual experiences are in part fantasy derived, or concomitant with the subject-object merging described above, it should not be surprising that people who can passively experience vivid fantasies with some satisfaction should ordinarily be willing to passively experience hypnotic suggestions.

Second, we began the section on adaptive regression by an illustration—the interpolated reading reverie. We mentioned then how evanescent one's passively experienced fantasies are, and how difficult it can sometimes be to retrieve them. It can be no accident that amnesia for one's hypnotic experiences is a frequently cited (but by no means universal) sequel of a hypnotic experience. No doubt, forgetting of both fantasies and hypnotically-suggested experiences is most apt to occur when the subject is unwilling or unable to quickly scan the internal residue of the experience. Having fantasy is one thing; having access to it is another. The same can be said for hypnotic experiences. We shall now turn to some possible manifestations of the fantasy retrieval process.

Fantasy Retrieval

We have been arguing that eye movements accompany directed thinking and that the relative lack of eye movements suggests the presence of undirected waking fantasy. Furthermore, we have suggested that adaptive regression may in certain circumstances be represented by an oscillating pattern of eye motility and quiescence. Whether creative subjects tend to have more interspersed episodes of ocular quiescence and motility than less creative subjects is a hypothesis that needs to be tested.

The simple oscillation of directed and undirected thinking, though perhaps a condition of adaptive regression, is clearly not a sufficient condition. For one thing, it seems quite likely that many people rarely connect their "real" and fantasy life. That is, each level of thinking can exist in relative isolation from the other, making it difficult to employ one's fantasy life in the service of realistic aims. In terms of the reading reverie example introduced earlier, it is quite possible that many people seldom attempt to retrieve their interpolated fantasies, or rather their fantasy residues, through an act of directed internal scanning.

Eye movement seems to reflect only the presence of attention, but does not differentially reflect whether attention is directed to interior or exterior events. Consequently, even though eye movement measures may be of value in representing the presence and absence of fantasy, they would probably be of less value in informing us whether the fantasizer was attempting to retrieve fantasies by directed, internal scanning. Fortunately, there is a measure that helps to identify whether and when attention is directed to external or internal events. The measure is cardiac variability; unlike the eye movement research, some evidence exists that directly relates heart rate variability and creative functioning. Again, let us begin with a finding from Singer's lab.

In the Singer and Antrobus (1965) study previously cited, the authors also employed heart rate in an attempt to assess subjects' arousal during various stages of the experiment. Using the imagine condition for a baseline they found that "Heart Rate under the suppress condition increased with eyes covered [with a Ganzfeld] and decreased when eyes were uncovered" (p. 73). These findings were quite contrary to the authors' expectancies that suppressing fantasy would, under all conditions, be more arousing than simply imagining it, and should therefore be uniformly accompanied by higher heart rate.

Although these cardiac findings did not make much sense from the point of view of arousal theory, they are quite consistent with Lacey's notion that heart rate reflects cognitive aspects of subjects' functioning. Basically, Lacey (1959, 1967) suggests that a person's orientation toward or attention to external sources of stimulation is accompanied by heart rate deceleration, and that conversely, tasks requiring "the internal manipulation of symbols and the retrieval of stored information" (Lacey et al., 1963, p. 170), is accompanied by heart rate acceleration. Therefore, in the Singer and Antrobus (1965) study, when subjects' eyes are not covered by a Ganzfeld, a reasonable strategy of fantasy suppression is to become attentive to environmental cues, a state of affairs that would be accompanied by heart rate decrease, which was in fact observed. The fact that heart rate did not decrease during the eyes-covered condition also makes sense because there was, in effect, no environment to take in, and some other strategy of image suppression was required. For example, a reasonable image-suppress strategy under the eyes-covered condition might be to direct one's thoughts to solving some mental arithmetic, a cognitive activity that yields concomitant heart rate increases over a resting baseline (compare Lacey et al., 1963).

The fact that heart rate probably reflects the shifts of attention from external to internal events makes it a potentially revealing way to assess the oscillation of attention from an external focus of concern toward the internal events they trigger, a process that we have argued is one aspect of creativity.

A recent study (Bowers & Keeling, 1971) examines this possibility. Bowers and Keeling reason that the oscillation of attention from reality to fantasy residues proposed as a basis of creative functioning should have a pattern of cardiac acceleration and deceleration. Specifically, more highly creative subjects should show more variability in their heart rate than less creative subjects, who presumably are more constant in their concern for the outer reality and less attentive to their interior fantasies. Heart rate in the study was continuously monitored for 20 males instructed to respond creatively to 10 Holtzman blots (Holtzman et al., 1961) selected for their low movement "pull." A measure of heart rate variability derived from this task correlated .49 with subjects' average creativity score derived from the Remote Associates Test (Mednick & Mednick, 1967) and the Revised Art Scale (Welsh & Barron, 1963). Thus, more creative persons tended to show higher cardiac variability. These results are consistent with those of an earlier study by Blatt (1961). Utilizing a complex cognitive task, Blatt found that efficient problem solvers generated significantly more variable heart rate than inefficient problem solvers. They also showed that efficient problem solvers showed significant differences in cardiac variability from problem solving to nonproblem solving (such as resting) phases of the experiment, whereas this was not true for the inefficient problem solvers. Since efficient problem solving is one kind of creative functioning (Guilford, 1967, p. 435), the results of this study are germane to our hypothesis that attention shifts from exterior to interior events are integral to the creative process.

Blatt himself did not interpret the results of his study in the way we have. He employed cardiac variability as a measure of arousal, and assumed that efficient problem solvers would be more aroused than inefficient ones. However, a recent finding by Bowers (1971a) suggests that cardiac variability is diminished under conditions of heightened alertness or arousal. The cardiac variability in Blatt's study may thus be better understood as exemplifying attentional shifts rather than arousal.

The combination of cardiac and eye movement measures in studies of creative functioning might prove most instructive as a test of the adaptive regression hypothesis. The presumed cycle of attention directed outward (analysis), fantasy, attention directed inward (fantasy retrieval) should have distinctive eye movement and cardiac patterns that accompany it. During the analytic phase, eye movement should be relatively high, and heart rate decelerated. During the fantasy phase, heart rate should be near its resting base, and eye movement should be attenuated. During fantasy retrieval, eye movement should again be high, but heart rate should now be accelerated.

This pattern would be particularly discernible if the creative "cycle" were of relatively short duration. If the oscillation from directed to undirected thinking were fairly long, however, it may be less easy to detect. Various time-correlated changes in physiological functioning would tend to obscure the pattern of such longer cycles.

While we are qualifying our position, we should admit to another "idealization" in our interpretation of creative functioning. The reading reverie illustration and much of the subsequent discourse has suggested that directed attention and undirected fantasy are more or less exclusive and alternating states of mind. There is, however, evidence that subjects may process reality and fantasy simultaneously (Antrobus, Singer, & Greenberg, 1966; Neisser, 1967). Singer (1966) in fact seems to argue that fantasy is a continuously ongoing backdrop to everything we do, only becoming salient as attention to external sources of stimulation abates.

Neisser suggests that information processed preattentively (which processing he thinks is analogous to the primary process) may come to our attention when it is particularly relevant to us, for example, to our name printed or spoken in an "ignored" part of our perceptual field, (Neisser, 1967, 1969). Just how an ongoing fantasy crosses the threshold of relevance is a problem of some considerable interest for the psychology of creativity (Rugg, 1963). It seems likely that the process is not substantially different from recognizing the relevance of incidental cues in the environment (Mendelsohn & Griswold, 1964).

Returning briefly to Blatt's (1961) study on the cardiac concomitants of creative functioning, we should note that the complex cognitive task employed in that study has been employed in several other studies as well. Blatt, Allison, and Feirstein (1969) found that the cognitive efficiency with which 50 male subjects approached the task, correlated $-.46$ with the defense effectiveness score (derived from Holt's system of scoring Rorschach), and $-.40$ with the adaptive regression score.[3] Effective, modulated control over primary process as measured on the Rorschach is thus correlated with both creative functioning (Pine & Holt, 1960) and cognitive efficiency, and the latter measure is associated with a characteristic pattern of high cardiac variability.

---

3. Cognitive efficiency is assessed by the number of unnecessary questions that subjects pose; the fewer questions posed, the more cognitively efficient a person is. Consequently, the relationship between cognitive efficiency (that is, questions posed) and defense effectiveness is negative.

In another study (Blatt & Stein, 1959), 35 research chemists were run on the complex problem solving task used in the study previously citied (Blatt, 1961). Cognitive efficiency correlated .50 *(p < .01)* with the Aesthetic value of the Allport-Vernon-Lindsey Study of Values (1951). Seventeen of these subjects had been previously split into high and low creative groups on the basis of supervisor ratings, and comparisons within only these 17 subjects were computed. There was a tendency for the creative chemists to be more cognitively efficient *(p < .10)* than uncreative chemists. On other measures, which themselves were significantly related to cognitive efficiency, the superiority of creative chemists was more clear-cut. For example, the creative chemists asked a larger proportion of questions in the earlier phases of problem solving *(p < .05)*, and they more clearly shifted from an analytic to a synthetic phase of problem solving *(p < .05)*.

The Blatt and Stein (1959) study indicates that, even within a highly homogeneous sample, a challenging task of cognitive efficiency can discriminate subgroups of more and less creative individuals. As several reviewers have noted (Dellas & Gaier, 1970, Stein, 1968), very few of the standard psychometric tests of creativity are successful in discriminating criterion groups of creative and uncreative persons. It is interesting that a (nonpsychometric) measure of cognitive efficiency, which was at least partially successful in differentiating high and low creative subjects, is also related to the success with which primary process thinking is integrated into a more realistic and acceptable form (Blatt, Allison, & Feirstein, 1969). This process of integrating unregulated into more regulated thinking is implicit in the notion of cognitive shifting proposed as a basis for creative functioning.

We shall now consider several studies that take the notion of cognitive shifting in creativity quite seriously. As we shall see in the first study, the operations for measuring cognitive shifts are also quite successful in differentiating criterion groups of presumably creative and uncreative persons.

Creativity and Cognitive Shifting

In a paper entitled "Creativity and Adaptive Regression," Cynthia Wild (1965) emphasized cognitive shifting "as particularly applicable to the concept of regression in the service of the ego, for it involves both a capacity to engage in unregulated thinking and an ability to return adaptively to more regulated thought, implying some degree of control of regression" (p. 162). This general theme is by now becoming very familiar. What was novel in her paper was the way she operationalized the concept of cognitive shifting. She provided subjects with a word association test and an object sorting task given under natural (that is, spontaneous) conditions, and then under two different instructional conditions. Under one set of instructions, subjects were asked to perform on the task like a highly conventional, cautious person "who prefers an orderly, structured universe and values good common sense." The other set of instructions asked subjects to perform like an "unregulated" character given to "novel thoughts and . . . acute perceptions that may startle other people" (p. 163). The instructional conditions were of course counterbalanced. The extent of a subject's movement from conventional to original associations and sorts constituted his shift score.

Three different groups of subjects were used in the experiment: 26 teachers, 26 schizophrenics, and 30 art students. The art students were hypothesized to be more creative. Some warrant for this assumption derived from the finding that under spontaneous (that is, uninstructed) conditions, artists were significantly more unconventional in their thinking than the other two groups. Moreover, these differences paralleled Wild's anecodotal reports of the art students' greater enthusiasm for and involvement in the tasks.

The findings on the cognitive shift measures were consistent. In practically all comparisons the art students showed greater cognitive shifts than either schizophrenics or teachers. Internal analysis demonstrated that these differences derived primarily from subjects' performance during the unregulated condition, since whatever group differences existed during the regulated conditions were relatively small or nonexistent. Note also that there were very few differences between teachers and schizophrenics of any kind, whether under spontaneous or instructed conditions.

A subsidiary analysis was based on teachers' ratings of the art students' creativity. Though interrater reliability was somewhat problematic, the results are consistent with the expectancy that the art students judged most creative had higher shift scores than the students judged least creative. Other analyses performed on the data are in accord with the major findings. It seems clear that the ability to shift cognitively from more to less regulated thinking is characteristic of the creative person.

While word associations and object sorts may not appear on the face of it to "creative" activities, the above study suggests that since these measures differentiate criterion groups of more and less creative people, they in fact tap this important psychological domain. A theoretical stance regarding creativity prompted the use of these measures, and it is through such theory-based research, rather than "blind" empiricism, that the investigation of creativity will progress.

The extent to which the tasks utilized by Wild do have an interesting conceptual basis is demonstrated in a study similar to hers, conducted by Fitzgerald (1966). He used the same word association and object sorting tasks as Wild, and generally followed her procedures. However, the groups he employed were composed of extreme scorers on an Experience Inquiry he devised specifically for the experiment. The inventory is in the genre of those mentioned early in this paper, and in fact borrowed many items from a similar scale devised by Ås, O'Hara, and Munger (1962).

The rationale for Fitzgerald's study derived largely from Schachtel's (1959) concept of "openness to experience," and Fitzgerald's Experience Inquiry presumably assesses the person's tolerance for the unrealistic and unconventional experiences implied in Schachtel's concept. Moreover, Fitzgerald argues that a tolerance for such experiences characterizes the person who has a flair for the original, and "the ability to shift from more to less regulated thinking with facility" (p. 656). This hypothesis was in fact supported. Subjects scoring high and low on the Experience Inquiry differed significantly on both the word association and the object sorting tasks, and these differences emerged under spontaneous (that is, uninstructed) conditions, and on the shift scores. In all comparisons, subjects scoring high on the Experience Inquiry were superior to low-scoring subjects. Again, internal analysis showed that the significant differences in shift scores derived primarily from subjects' performance under the unregulated and not from the regulated condition.

The results of Fitzgerald's (1966) study were partially replicated by Feirstein (1967), who obtained cognitive shift scores only on the word association task, and who assessed tolerance for unrealistic experiences by a battery of four tests (instead of by a questionnaire). The correlation between this battery and the cognitive shift score was .62 *(p* < .01).

Hypnosis and Creativity

This chapter has reviewed evidence that unrealistic or fantastic experiences: (a) are concomitants of various altered states of consciousness, including hypnosis, (b) occur spontaneously to a greater extent in subjects who are high as opposed to low in hypnotic susceptibility, (c) may occasionally occur in the context of a creative act, but in any event, (d) are often experienced by creative subjects who, as a group, seem more adept than their less creative counterparts at shifting cognitively from a "higher" to a "lower" level of psychic functioning.

We have suggested that creativity involves regression to passively experienced fantasy and than progression to integration of the fantasy with reality. Both Krippner (1969) and Silverman (1968) have noted certain similarities between altered state processes and the inspirational stage of creativity. While Hilgard (1968) discounts the likelihood of finding direct relationships between hypnosis and creativity, such evidence and arguments as we have marshalled lead us to predict that creativity and altered states like hypnosis should be related to a moderate degree. The regressive aspect is similar in both, but only creativity implies any constructive use of the regressive experience. In the hypnotic state there is increased primary process, but control of it as shown in adaptive regression scores may not increase (Fromm, Orberlander, & Gruenewald, 1969; 1970; and Chapter 16 of this book). And at least for men, creativity is more related to adaptive regression scores than to primary process itself (Pine & Holt, 1960).

A relationship between hypnosis and creativity does seem probable, but the precise nature of this link is far from clear. Does a trancelike experience often precede a creative insight or is the route more indirect? If there is a direct connection between trancelike experience and creativity, being hypnotized, taking certain drugs, and so forth should significantly increase many persons' creative performance. A study using mescaline, but unfortunately employing no control group, suggested that 27 subjects actively engaged in seeking solutions to practical professional problems did increase their creativity (Harman et al., 1966). The authors state: "Tentative findings based on tests of creativity, on subjective reports and self ratings, and on the utility of problem solutions suggested that, if given according to this carefully structured regimen, psychedelic agents seem to faciliate creative problem solving, particularly in the illumination phase" (p. 461*).

The first study in our own series of investigations was concerned with the impact of the state of hypnosis on creativity (P. Bowers, 1967). At that time, we conceptualized "defensiveness" as a process that kept some people from primitive and unconventional experience, and therefore from the possibility of using this experience creatively. If, as reported in the literature, hypnosis could lower the barriers to regressive experience, the result should be looser, freer combinations of ideas and better performance on divergent thinking tasks. Accordingly, the instruction in a waking state to be "free" in one's thinking would be less apt to affect the defensive barrier typically preventing this freedom than such instructions given under hypnosis. The subjects chosen were college women who were all susceptible to hypnosis, having scored 7 or above on the Harvard Group Scale of Hypnotic Susceptibility (HGSHS; Shor & Orne, 1962). They were seen by the second author in small groups of two to five persons. There were two sets of instructions, one merely giving subjects a cognitive set to be creative and flexible on the tasks, and the other giving strong encouragement to let their thoughts run freely without any constraints as to what others might think, and so on. The latter was termed the Defense Reducing instruction.

After waking "Cognitive Set" premeasures, subjects were either hypnotized or encouraged to relax in a waking state by closing their eyes and listening to music. Half of the waking and half the hypnotized subjects again received the Cognitive Set instruction; the other half of each group received the Defense Reducing instruction. They then completed post measures of four divergent thinking tasks (Guilford, 1959): Alternate Uses, Consequences, Plot Titles, Simile Insertions, and of one test of clerical performance (Minnesota Clerical Test; Andrew, Paterson, & Longstaff, 1933). The latter was given to assess purely motivational effects of the instructions. No effect was found on the latter measure, nor were there differences due to type of instruction. A significant difference $(p < .01)$ between hypnotic and waking conditions was found on the eight scores from the divergent thinking battery when an overall F was computed by the Multiple Discriminant Function Analysis. By far the major component of this difference between groups was attributable to performance on the Consequences Test. More remote—but appropriate—consequences were given as possible effects of improbable events by hypnotized subjects than by waking subjects. Only on this score were differences between hypnotic and waking groups found in covariance analysis *(p* < .001). Hypnotized subjects did not give significantly more unscorable or inappropriate responses than did waking subjects.

The results of this experiment were consistent with the hypothesis that hypnosis could reduce defensiveness and facilitate creative expression. However, perhaps the results had nothing to do with the actual "state" of hypnosis, but rather resulted from potent sanctions of the hypnotic situation. A hypnotized subject could simply tell himself he was "not responsible" for his unconventional ideas; a similar sanction might obtain for subjects told to simulate hypnosis. This latter possibility was investigated in a second study (Bowers, 1968).

Subjects susceptible to hypnosis (HGSHS of 8 or more) were seen individually and given defense-reducing instructions under two conditions: hypnosis and hypnosis simulation. The Consequences Test was the measure of creativity. No differences on either Remote or Obvious Consequence scores were found. The mean scores for both hypnotic and simulator subjects were similar to those of hypnotic subjects in the first study. The subjects of the two experiments were drawn from a different population, however, and so the question of whether subjects in Bowers's (1968) study would have differed from a waking relaxed group was unanswered. Accordingly, the third study in this series (Bowers & van der Meulen, 1970) compared waking subjects with hypnotized and simulator subjects on a variety of creativity measures, including movement perception to Holtzman Inkblots, Guilford's Consequences Test, and a word association test. Virtually no treatment effects emerged. So it seems at this point unlikely that there is anything unique about hypnosis per se that directly enhances creativity test performance. Actually, this state of affairs seems eminently reasonable. It seems unlikely that people who are good at such tasks literally go off into a trancelike condition to dredge up, say, the correct associate to a Remote Associates Test (Mednick & Mednick, 1967) item. It is nevertheless possible that persons who are more *able* to experience such trancelike states are better on such tasks than persons less able to do so.

Previous experiences of an unrealistic kind, with the fantasies and fluid associations that accompany them, may enrich a person's cognitive resources. Theorists such as J. McV. Hunt (1965) and Butler and Rice (1963) suggest that there is a basis in such enriched cognitive structures for creativity *motivation,* the importance of which Maddi (1965) and even Guilford (1967) have stressed. Persons with complex cognitive structures enjoy and seek novelty and complexity, and are able to provide, by their own imaginative and reflective processes, the very novelty and complexity they require. He who has a "need for novelty" (Maddi, 1965) might find the experience of altered states most useful. The person who has not only tolerated but also integrated a number of unrealistic, trancelike experiences might have many more unusual responses in his repertoire. He might be so used to experiences in which conventional labels are not applicable that he no longer depends upon them. He has learned a habit of creativity on the basis of his past, well-integrated, unusual experiences. Barron notes that "originality is almost habitual with individuals who produce a really singular idea. What this implies is that a highly organized mode of responding to experience is a precondition for consistent creativity" (1969, p. 19). Indeed, the creative person may have developed techniques that, when applied, result in "creative" responses.[4] In essence, his previous experience of trance with concomitant enriched fantasy associations to objects may have given him more ability to act in a creative way without the necessity of an altered state at the moment of creation.

Such reasoning leads to certain predictions: People who have spontaneous regressive experiences should be more interested in the novel and complex. They should be less dependent on conventional labels to identify their experience. When adequate adaptation to such regressive experiences has occurred, waking state responses and associations should be more flexible and original, more creative.

The catalog of personality attributes that seem to go along with people designated "creative" either by judgments or test criteria are consonant with these hypotheses. Creative people are nonconforming, tolerant of ambiguity, adventurous. They like reflective thinking. They are not meticulous or disciplined (Guilford, 1967). The Revised Art Scale (Welsh & Barron, 1963) is the most successful test predictor of creativity (Gough, 1964; Dellas & Gaier, 1970), and it is simply a scale of preference for visual complexity. Renner (1970) trained subjects to understand the complexity of art works. Compared to appropriate controls, this training led to both significantly higher scores on the Revised Art Scale *and* greater originality on the Consequences test.

We have previously shown that susceptibility to hypnosis is correlated with a person's ability to let go of a reality orientation and experience more primitively. Consequently, susceptibility should also be related to creativity, since such regressive experiences should contribute to the cognitive complexity and therefore to the creativity of those able to integrate such experience.

Accordingly, in the study cited earlier (Bowers & van der Meulen, 1970), high and low susceptible subjects were compared to investigate whether the former would do better on a battery of creativity tests than the

---

4. Guilford stresses the recall of stored information in creativity. Shifting to more primitive, freer thinking, dispersed attention, and so forth may enable a wider search of our memory. He suggests that creative people may have learned how to achieve the goal of original responses by using broader search techniques.

latter. The results unambiguously supported the hypothesis. On eight out of nine creativity subtests, the high susceptibles scored significantly higher than the low susceptibles. Subsidiary analysis revealed that irrespective of susceptibility level, women were consistently more creative than men.

Separate studies have indicated that hypnotic susceptibility was related both to creativity test performance (Bowers & van der Meulen, 1970) and to various experience inventories (Shor, Orne, & O'Connell, 1962; As, 1963; Lee-Teng, 1965). Since a tolerance for unusual experiences also appeared related to measures of adaptive regression (Fitzgerald, 1966), which in turn have been found to correlate with creativity (Wild, 1965), Bowers (1969) investigated the interrelationships of hypnotic susceptibility, creativity, and tolerance for unusual trancelike experience. On all 39 subjects unselected for susceptibility, he found virtually no relationships of any kind! However, when the data was analyzed separately for the 27 men and the 12 women, some rather dramatic sex differences emerged. The gist of the findings quite consistently indicated that for males, the intercorrelations were zero or even negative, but for females the various correlations between susceptibility, creativity, and Shor's Personal Experience Questionnaire (Shor, Orne, & O'Connell, 1962) were .40 and higher.

Because of these unexpected results, another investigation was conducted (Bowers, 1971b). A rectangular distribution of susceptibility was employed, with 3 men and 3 women at each of the 12 points along the susceptibility continuum as measured by the HGSHS. The 36 men and 36 women in this study were assessed on five separate measures of creativity: the Consequences Test, movement responses to the Holtzman Inkblot Test (Holtzman et al., 1961), a word association test (adapted from Gardner et al., 1959), the Revised Art Scale (Welsh & Barron, 1963), and the Remote Associates Test (Mednick & Mednick, 1962). From this battery of creativity tests eight measures were derived, and a subject's average Z score on these measures constituted his composite creativity score. In addition to the creativity tests, each subject also received the WAIS vocabulary subtest and Shor's PEQ. The results showed quite clear sex differences. For women, the correlation between susceptibility and the creativity composite was .41; for men it was −.08. For women, the correlation between susceptibility and the intensity of trancelike experiences was .39; for men the same correlation was .09. For women, the correlation between creativity and PEQ intensity was .33; for men it was .16. All the relationships for women are significant at $p < .05$. Intelligence accounted for none of these correlations.

More interesting than the sex differences across the entire range of susceptibility, however, was the patterning of relationships within low (1-4), medium (5-8), and high (9-12) levels of susceptibility. For men, the three correlations between susceptibility, creativity, and PEQ intensity were virtually zero within each level of susceptibility. For women, however, the correlations varied from zero or negative to quite positive as a function of susceptibility level. For example, within low susceptible women, the correlation between PEQ intensity and overall creativity was −.47; for high susceptible women the analogous correlation was .63 *(p < .05)*. The correlation in high susceptible women between creativity and susceptibility was somewhat lower *(r = .48)*.

The moderating effect of susceptibility and sex on the correlates of susceptibility was further confirmed in a supplementary analysis employing the SHSS:C scale. Only 31 women and 27 men in this study took the SHSS:C, and women scored significantly higher on it than men *(p < .05)*. The relationship between creativity and susceptibility across the entire range of SHSS:C was *not* significant for *either* men *or* women. However, a similar correlation performed on the 21 women scoring at or above the median of 7 on the SHSS:C was .55 *(p < .01)*; for the 11 men scoring above the median, *(r = −.11)*.

The results of this last study are a fairly convincing demonstration that both sex and susceptibility serve as moderator variables in the correlates of susceptibility. The moderating role of sex has also been explicitly recounted in an article by Rosenhan (1969), who found that men and women of high and low anxiety had differing patterns of susceptibility correlates. Other kinds of evidence, though less explicitly pointing to the moderating role of sex in susceptibility, nevertheless emphasize differences in men and women in their tolerance for unusual trancelike experiences. Several such findings might briefly be mentioned. In Bowers' (1971b) study, women scored higher on PEQ intensity than did men, which confirms earlier similar results (Shor, 1960; Gravitz & Kramer, 1967; Ås, 1962). And although sex differences in hypnotic susceptibility have not been widely acknowledged, the evidence of Bowers' (1971) study shows significant superiority of women over men on the SHSS:C. This difference emerged even though sexes were initially matched on the HGSHS, a much less challenging scale of susceptibility. Similar superiority of women over men on susceptibility was also reported by Shor, Orne, and O'Connell (1966).

Palmer & Field (1968) have underlined that "both hypnotizability and imaging ability seem to relate to a tolerance for unrealistic experiences," and that their findings "indicate consistently stronger relationships between imagery and hypnotizability for females than for males" (p. 459). That is, the tolerance for unrealistic experiences seems to have played a greater role for females than for males in determining the correlates of susceptibility, a result thoroughly confirmed in Bowers' (1971b) study. The fact that autokinesis and fantasy adumbration of the effect are more correlated in women than in men (Mayman & Voth, 1969) also suggests that tolerance for unrealistic experiences is more generative of interesting relationships in women than in men.

In Bowers' (1971) study, not only sex but susceptibility itself served as a moderator variable in the correlates of susceptibility, and there are some clues in the hypnosis literature that serve as harbingers of these findings as well. For example, there is the suggestion of bimodality in the distribution of susceptibility (Hilgard, 1965b, pp. 221–28), and various factor analytic studies in the field (Hilgard, 1965b, p. 270–82) consistently yield factors such as "dissociation" that do not seem differentially represented in low susceptible subjects. Both these observations are consistent with a view that the correlates of susceptibility should vary as a function of the dominant factors represented within various levels of susceptibility. The results of Bowers's recent findings, together with evidence antedating his, suggest that the notorious absence of susceptibility correlates (Hilgard, 1965b) may derive from the moderating function of both sex and susceptibility in these relationships. Future measurement-oriented studies of hypnotic susceptibility should be cognizant of these moderating effects, perhaps by employing enough subjects of both sexes ranged *within* levels of susceptibility, the better to examine effects there, as well as across the entire range of susceptibility.

While the reasons for the sex differences in the correlates of creativity are unclear, the reader will perhaps indulge us a few more lines for a speculative hypothesis. Perhaps creative imagination can be inspired primarily by impulses and drives or by external reality. If men and women differ in the source of their inspiration, and only one of these is related to hypnotic susceptibility, we might account for the observed sex differences.

There is evidence that men and women are differently affected by impulses and environment. We have already mentioned Ås's (1962) findings of sex differences in the type of spontaneous, trancelike experiences that relate to hypnotizability. He found that hypnotizable women are willing to relinquish ego control for experiences of a nonrational, slightly mystical kind, while hypnotizable men prefer to relax ego controls to indulge in emotional experiences. His men and women subjects differed not so much on total scores on his Experience Inventory, but in the relative predominance of certain types of experiences. Women experienced more changes in mental states due to social influences, or reading, and had more illogical experiences. Men exceeded women in experiences characterized by impulsivity, such as enjoying wild parties or wanting to hit someone who made them angry. Other evidence suggests that boys are more impulsive and aggressive and girls more passive (Maccoby, 1966). Helson (1968) suggests that women in general have a lower level of resistance to incoming stimuli than men, and that creative women can focus and direct this awareness. Pine and Holt (1960) hypothesized that women were able to change their set toward giving either controlled or freer imaginative responses to tests, depending upon the type of test, while men maintained their set to give controlled imaginative responses regardless of the type of test.

These studies suggest that women are indeed less responsive to impulses and more to environmental factors. To take our argument one step further, Josephine Hilgard (1970) reports that the type of imagination a subject has may predict his hypnotizability. She says that "the distinction between stimulus-incited and autistic, or impulse-incited, imagnation appears to be an important one in relation to hypnotic susceptibility, with such evidence as we have pointing to greater hypnotizability on the part of those capable of stimulus incitation" (1970, p. 103).

We propose then, that women may be more apt to show stimulus-incited rather than impulse-incited imagination. If men receive higher creativity scores more on the basis of impulse-incited responses and women more on the basis of stimulus-incited responses, one would expect the obtained correlation of creativity and hypnosis in women but not in men. It seems likely that creativity tests rely somewhat more on stimulus-incited imagination, and this could account for the higher scores of women on such tests than men.

Summary and Conclusion

In this paper, we have reviewed evidence that hypnosis and related states involve a loss in generalized reality orientation, and a concomitant rise in fantasy or suggestibility. The role of fantasy in creative functioning has also been noted, with particular emphasis on fantasy retrieval as a crucial antecedent of its creative use. Moreover, we have argued that the occurrence of fantasy and its retrieval may be well represented in patterns of ocular and cardiac activity, a possibility that may redound to the benefit of research on adaptive regression as an important concept in creativity.

Our own interpretation of creativity and hypnosis has been influenced by, and is largely compatible with, the ego psychological concepts of regression in the service of the ego (Kris, 1952), and of the relative autonomy of the ego from both drives and environment (Rapaport, 1958). Because hypnosis per se constitutes a kind of regression phenomenon, it seems reasonable to expect that hypnotic techniques might simply facilitate creative performance. Although this hypothesis at first seemed supported, failure to replicate the initial findings suggest that the rapprochement between hypnosis and creativity must be more complex. The personality characteristics that allow one person to be more susceptible to hypnosis than another might coincide to some extent with those characteristics that make him more creative. Perhaps the ease with which one can deconventionalize experience and accept the unrealistic and fantastic contributes both to susceptibility and creativity. Our evidence to date suggests that something like this is the case: creativity, hypnotic susceptibility, and spontaneous trancelike experiences are interrelated in women but not in men. Some speculations about these sex differences with respect to creativity were considered. It should be noted, however, that even in men fairly consistent correlations seem to be reported between hypnotic susceptibility and spontaneous trancelike experiences.

We have argued that hypnotic phenomena are usefully conceived as fantasy equivalents, and that both fantasy per se and the hypnotically suggested state of affairs are a kind of reality surrogate. While both creativity and hypnosis involve the construction of a new reality, the creative act is generally enduring and, in some sense, worthwhile; the reality suggested under hypnosis is more apt to be transient, if not trivial.

A strong argument can be made that the constructive processes in fantasy and hypnosis are not basically different from perceptual processes in general. Neisser (1967) in his book, *Cognitive psychology,* emphasizes that *"the mechanisms of visual imagination are continuous with those of visual perception*—a fact which strongly implies that all perceiving is a constructive process" (p. 96; italics in original). The differences that do exist in the realities constructed out of perception and imagination inhere in the extent to which environmental input determines the constructive process. In perception, "the constructive act is closely controlled by present or recent stimulus information" (Neisser, 1967, p. 305), whereas this is much less the case for fantasy, and hypnotically suggested fantasy equivalents. The governing relation of reality input on the constructive process is perhaps helpful in understanding how hypnosis and creativity are *not* alike. Conventional reality is relatively unimportant for the daydreamer and the hypnotized person. The importance of conventional reality is guaranteed to the creative person, however, for it constitutes his worthy adversary—it is the "stuff" that creative imagination transforms.

Peter W. Sheehan *is Senior Lecturer in Psychology at the University of New England, Australia. He received his Ph.D. from the University of Sydney in 1965 working on imagery and some of its correlates under the direction of J. P. Sutcliffe, who initially fired his enthusiasm for hypnosis. After obtaining his doctorate, Dr. Sheehan accepted a two-year appointment as Research Associate at the Unit for Experimental Psychiatry and Instructor in the Department of Psychiatry at the University of Pennsylvania. From there he went to the City College of the City University of New York, where he was Assistant Professor in Psychology. He returned to Australia in 1968. He is Australian Co-ordinator for* The International Society For Mental Imagery Techniques *and is currently editing a book on the function and nature of imagery. His research interests lie mostly within the fields of experimental cognition, hypnosis, and the logic of artifact.*

Sheehan *presents a comprehensive review of theoretical and experimental evidence on the role of mental imagery, imagination, fantasy, and primary process thinking in hypnotic performance. He argues that Sarbin's "as if" formulation best conceptualizes the important role of imagery and fantasy in hypnosis. Among the issues scrutinized are the enrichment of imagery in hypnosis, the relationship between hypnotizability and enduring aptitudes for vivid imagery; imaginative involvements and tolerance for fantasy experiences; and the relationship between hypnotic hallucinations and perceptual processes.*

9

Hypnosis and the Manifestations of "Imagination"

PETER W. SHEEHAN

Introduction

THE PROBLEM

Many workers in the field of hypnosis have held tenaciously to the view that there are personality correlates of hypnosis and that the hypnotizable person manifests aptitudes or abilities for trance that lie waiting to be discovered within the realms of his personality. Researchers into hypnosis used to be quite definite in their assertions about the personality correlates of hypnotizability. Currently, however, summaries of empirical findings on the correlates of trance are much less positive in outlook; much conflicting evidence has accumulated. Deckert and West (1963) concluded, after a comprehensive survey of the literature, that the correlation of any personality trait by any means of measurement with hypnotizability awaits consistent confirmation across laboratories and that the search for specific traits has not at all clarified the concept of hypnotizability.

Mischel (1968) has shown convincingly how rare it is for consistencies to occur across studies in the field of personality assessment. The ambiguity of research findings is not due entirely to the problem of measuring the various dimensions of traits; other factors are also responsible. Barber (1969b) has stated that equivocal findings in the area may be due to the lack of comparability in drawing subject samples, and the use of different scales to measure suggestibility, as well as the crudeness of available techniques for assessing personality attributes. Subjects may also vary their response to suggestions according to their task motivation, or the nature of the particular relationships they have with their *E*s. It may be that even some of the positive correlations that have appeared in the literature are due to the impurity of the criteria of hypnotizability, selective personal appeals of different hypnotists, or other situation-specific factors (Shor, Orne, & O'Connell, 1966).

Differences among individuals in hypnotizability, although related to differences in attitudes toward and relationship with the hypnotist, must reflect the aptitudes or enduring characteristics of the personality of the *S*s themselves. It can be argued that a *S*'s personality will strongly determine the ways in which he can relate to the hypnotist however skillful the hypnotist is in engendering attitudes such as "basic trust" and "confidence." The importance of the *S*'s personality is not diminished by the fact that some *S*s with similar characteristics may respond differently to hypnotic induction by different hypnotists. To do so would be to deny that people relate quite differently to different people. A person's behavior is influenced both by the interaction among personalities, and by his own particular abilities and capacities.

The importance of subject characteristics is stated succinctly by Sarbin (1950), who after reviewing the effects of various kinds of induction techniques concluded that "since the induction procedure per se cannot account for the differential responsiveness of subjects, this leaves the subject as a person as the more fruitful focus of study" (p. 257). This statement avoids commitment to the host of determining variables other than induction that have been isolated by Barber and his associates (Barber, 1969b), but it does draw attention to one significant feature of the hypnotic setting: the presence of individual differences in susceptibility to trance. Not all *S*s exhibit "hypnotic" behavior (Hilgard et al., 1961; Hilgard, 1965b), and it is clear that explanation for this individual variation in hypnotic response must often be sought in other factors than the process of induction. One place we may look is to the subject characteristics that differentiate hypnotizable from nonhypnotizable people.

Not only are *S*s differentially susceptible to hypnosis, but wide individual differences also exist in their capacities to engage in fantasy, daydreaming, and mental imagery of a sensorily vivid kind (Betts, 1909; Foulkes, 1966; Lindauer, 1969; Schonbar, 1961; Singer, 1966). There are, for example, important patterns of individual differences in frequency of daydreaming (Singer, 1966) in normal adults and children, and the reinforcement or motivation for the continuous cognitive processing of daydreams has been shown to be very powerful. Antrobus, Singer, and Greenberg (1966) found that *S*s are able to engage in a high degree of spontaneous fantasy even when they are under heavy pressure to attend to a signal presentation task. The authors judged it as remarkable that "*S* can receive signals at the rate of 1/sec., accurately judge whether each signal is the same or different from the pitch of the preceding signal, indicate his judgment on a hand switch while storing the signal for comparison with the next, and at the same time imagine sailing with his friends during his forthcoming holiday" (p. 406). Grossberg and Wilson (1968) found that self-produced stimulation arising from instructions to imagine fear scenes produced more tension or arousal in a *S* than did the externally presented stimulation of *E* reading the scene to him. These and other studies attest to the significant and measurable effects of *S*'s engagement in fantasy activity. In view of the wide individual differences present in both imaginal activity and susceptibility to trance as judged by response to standard tests of hypnosis, it is conceivable that the various manifestations of imagination and hypnotizability bear a strong, positive relation to each other. This hypothesis is the specific concern of this chapter.

DEFINITION OF TERMS

A sizeable barrier to ordering studies in the area of fantasy, imagery, and hypnotizability is the semantic confusion resulting from authors using different terms to explain what appear to be essentially similar processes, and also their using the same term to cover apparently different processes. Moss (1967) reports that a majority of "hypnotic dreams" reported in the literature seem to consist of brief products that are often difficult to discriminate from verbal associations to the suggested dream topic. In a comprehensive analysis of over 400 "hypnotic dreams" reported by a sample of 16 students, Quay (1952) found that many of the dreams could be classified simply as verbal associations. Use of words like "dream" to *S*s in an experiment often carries with it semantically ambiguous demands. Only detailed questioning of *S*s can decide whether *S* is reporting fantasy, imagery, or merely nonimaginal thoughts. The problem of classifying the nature of *S*'s cognition is considerably aggravated by the fact that an experimenter can give cues to the *S* about the expected response that the *S* may respond to in a way that leads the *E* to classify *S*'s behavior mistakenly. Barber (1964c), for example, has drawn attention to the possibility that when an experimental *S* is told explicitly to see objects and to hear sounds that are physically absent, the *S* is actually being instructed to classify or categorize what are really imaginal events as perceptual ones. Sarbin (1967) is making the same point when he states "when we reflect that the behavior labeled hallucination is an imagining that is publicly reported, the question must be rephrased as follows: What are the antecedent and concurrent conditions that lead a person publicly to report his imaginings in such a way as to lead a psychologist, psychiatrist or other professional to designate the described imagining as an hallucination?" (p. 363).

The concept of hallucination has proved particularly obstinate to tidy classification. McKellar (1957), Barber (1964c), and Sarbin (1967) talk of hallucinations as involving mental imagery. Sidis (1904a, 1904b), Erickson and Erickson (1938), Arnold (1959), and others, however, talk of hallucination as involving actual perception of the hallucinated object. The problem of classification appears to lie with the relative importance of the ideational and delusory components of hallucination. As Binet and Féré (1886) pointed out, in every image presented to the mind there is always the germ of a hallucination that needs development. Binet and Féré maintained that it was in the hypnotic state that such development is most clearly seen to occur. It is only necessary to name a given object to the susceptible subject, that is, to simply say "here is a bird," in order that the image suggested by the E's words should become a hallucination. Schneck (1954a) has shown, however, that subtle changes in E's instruction may determine E's classification of S's behavior as imaginal or hallucinatory. Schneck reports the case of a patient in therapy who reported imagining sounds in hypnosis and actually "hearing" them. The nature of S's report was quite dependent on the wording of the E's inquiry.

It appears that the processes of imagination play an important part in hypnotic hallucinations and that the hypnotic setting affects, either artifactually or otherwise, the judgment of S as to the reality of his imaginings. As Barber (1964c) has indicated, suggestions to hallucinate include two components: explicit suggestions, which influence imaginative processes, and implicit instructions, which affect verbal reports. When such implicit suggestions are operative S may classify his imaginings as actual perceptions. This account of hallucinations is consistent with Sarbin's contention that hallucinations occur only in persons who are particularly skillful in imagining the presence of stimulus-objects that are physically absent (Sarbin, 1964). The importance of imagery to hypnotic hallucination makes it particularly fruitful to explore the nature of the imaging capacities of hypnotizable Ss.

As imagery and hypnotic hallucination appear related, so also are fantasy and imagery; yet distinctions in process may be raised. Ullman (1959) identifies one of the primary formal aspects of dream consciousness as the employment of concrete means of presentation predominantly in the form of visual imagery. Fantasy is traditionally regarded as a form of creative imagination "where the images and trains of imagery are directed and controlled by the whim or pleasure of the moment" (Drever, 1952; p. 209–10). "Fantasy," however, is a term that not so much denotes the faculty of imagery as it signifies the imaginary world and its contents, "the imaginings or fantasies into which the poet or the neurotic so willingly withdraws" (Laplanche & Pontalis, 1968). It suggests a constructive organization of past experience which, although dependent on the revival of imagery, is especially subject to the vicissitudes of the motivational and emotional state of the organism.

In summary, then, the terms "image," "hallucination," and "fantasy" may be defined as follows: With imagery there is no object present to the senses as in perception; it is somewhat introspective in fashion to speak of "seeing," "picturing," or "visualizing" something. This difference is true also for recalling and hallucinating, but these processes differ from "imaging." The objects of recall lack the "thing-quality" alleged for the imaged objects, and objects of hallucination, though they may be ideationally based, are accompanied by S's conviction of their external locus. Fantasy may be distinguished from imagery in that it appears to be more of a reproductive synthesis, largely motivational in origin, of a totality of past experiences. As used in the literature, the term "imagine" is a more general one, which may denote more than one of these processes. A person who is imagining may be engaging in either "fantasy" or "imagery" activities.

Any definitions must to some extent be inadequate in that they cannot do justice to the richness and variety of psychological experience. As Holt (1964) and Horowitz (1967) have pointed out, a multitude of processes can be subsumed under the term "visual imagery" alone, and classification is made especially difficult by the subtle variations in S's experience as to the reality of his imaginings. In this respect, even the auditory hallucinations of schizophrenic patients differ greatly from each other (Brady & Levitt, 1966); one may talk about a continuum from ill-defined "thoughts" originating from within the body to voices that appear to be external to, and independent of, the self. The special difficulty of isolating the delusional and ideational components of cognitive events can be seen clearly in Sidis's (1906) observation of the hallucinations of a deeply hypnotizable S. For this S the delusional component broke down and S described his experience of E's suggested hallucinations as "fixed ideas" and "mental pictures." After a posthypnotic suggestion to see a snake, S claimed he saw one but wrote "I see a snake. I see it in my mind" (p. 255). Here, the ideational and delusional aspects of the hypnotic hallucination interchanged confusedly.

Some agreement on terms is necessary, however, to attempt an accurate evaluation of the evidence available on the relationship between imagery and fantasy to hypnotizability. For example, studies that report mainly on verbal associations (e.g., Erle, 1958) are less relevant than others. Even an arbitrary classification draws attention to the fact that different terms as used by hypnotists (e.g., "imagine," "image," "see," and "make-believe") may carry special connotations to Ss that are quite specific and that may implicitly direct the nature of Ss' responses.

With this classification in mind we move now to a consideration of the evidence. First, we will consider the theoretical grounds that lead one to hypothesize a relationship between hypnotizability, fantasy, and imagery. Subsequent sections will review the "empirical" data (both clinical and experimental) that bear on this relationship, and present a framework within which the relationship can be conceptualized.

Review of Evidence: Theoretical

HYPNOSIS AS AN "ALTERED STATE OF CONSCIOUSNESS"

Experientially speaking, hypnosis is easily recognizable as a change in consciousness and the emergence of imagery in altered states of consciousness is well acknowledged (Freedman & Marks, 1965; Horowitz, Adams, & Rutkin, 1968; Ludwig, 1966; Moss, 1967). Similarly occurring changes are those that are associated with prolonged stimulus deprivation (see, for example, Gibson, 1953), extreme boredom (Heron, 1957), hypnagogic and hypnopompic states (Ludwig, 1966) and other related phenomena.

In the most general sense the altered state of consciousness may be defined as a "mental state induced by various physiological, psychological, or pharmacological maneuvres or agents, which can be recognized subjectively by the individual himself . . . as representing a sufficient deviation in subjective experience or psychological functioning from certain general norms for that individual during alert waking consciousness" (Ludwig, 1966, p. 9–10). The description of hypnosis as a loss of Generalized Reality-Orientation (Shor, 1959) has gone furthest to highlighting the features of hypnosis that relate to this more general class of phenomena.

The concept of Generalized Reality-Orientation refers to the background of awareness, the frame of reference that denotes the context within which one interprets all ongoing conscious experiences. Shor argues that under hypnosis this orientation to reality fades into the background so that ongoing experiences become relatively isolated from their usual frame of reference. The structure of the Generalized Reality-Orientation permits what in Freudian terminology is called secondary process thinking. Viewed in this way the ability temporarily to give up reality orientation corresponds to a regression to primary-process functioning. The phenomena that pertain to the concept of "primary process" share with hypnosis the feature that they occur in isolation from ordinary reality. It has long been assumed that hypnosis reduces alertness and such a reduction may facilitate the flow of free associations, thus bringing the hypnotized person into contact with prelogical ideational processes. In a similar fashion, vigilance is reduced through sleep. This reduction is known to be associated at some stages of the sleep cycle with unusually expressive mentation illustrative of primary process functioning (Bertini, Lewis, & Witkin, 1964; Fiss, Ellman, & Klein, 1968).

With the loss of the Generalized Reality-Orientation, the distinction between reality and imagination fades and primary process modes of thought such as imagery and fantasy are allowed to flow more easily into awareness. Conceptually speaking, the consequences of viewing hypnosis as a loss of this reality orientation are twofold. First, it can be argued with Shor (1959) that if primary process material flows more easily into consciousness, then the new orientation that is created (namely, in this instance, "trance") should show some of the qualities of the dream state itself. This implies that hypnosis involves a greater preoccupation with internal sensations or mental processes than does the waking state. Vivid imagery, hallucinations, and other dreamlike phenomena may be expected to be generated as an integral part of the altered state. Many so-called "state" theorists refer to primary process thinking that is activated in trance (Gill & Brenman, 1959; Janet,

1925; Kubie, 1961). Gill and Brenman, for example, talk of the emergence of fluid, archaic forms of thought that employ visual images and symbols as material in trance. Kubie (1961) argues that there can be little doubt that under hypnosis changes occur in S's capacity to reproduce vivid images of experiences that are more remote in time and space.

Very few studies have been carried out to test the assumption that there is an actual enrichment of imagery experience in hypnosis. Those studies that have been conducted, however, generally have been supportive. Rossi, Sturrock, and Solomon (1963) instructed Ss to experience images under normal, hypnotic, and placebo conditions. The Ss' responses to a questionnaire given under the experimental treatments showed that imagery was more vivid in hypnosis than under the nonhypnotic conditions. Stross and Shevrin (1962) found, using tachistoscopic presentation of a rebus stimulus, that imagery occurred more often in hypnosis and dreaming than in the waking state. Naruse and Obonai (1953) found, using a sensory conditioning procedure, that hypnosis appeared to facilitate imagery. Deeper levels of trance as reported by Ss were associated with clearer imagery.

In what is perhaps the most pertinent series of experiments on this issue, Stross and Shevrin (1967) found that hypnosis facilitated dream recall. In one study dreams were recalled by 44 Ss first in the waking state and then in hypnosis. No Ss recalled their dreams in the waking state itself and not in hypnosis afterwards, whereas 28 Ss recalled their dreams exclusively in hypnosis. In a second study the order of state was counterbalanced. The waking state following hypnosis was significantly associated with more dream recall than the waking state preceding hypnosis. The better recall of dreams in hypnosis suggested that "cognitive processes in hypnosis may resemble dream thinking more closely than the predominant mode of thinking that governs the waking state" (p. 69). In further support of the enhancement hypothesis, Fromm, Oberlander, and Gruenewald (1969) found that over all Ss tested, primary process responses on the Rorschach were appreciably greater in trance than in the waking condition. Amount of the effect was related in part to the level of adjustment of Ss, the order of conditions (hypnosis-waking, or waking-hypnosis), and the sex of Ss.

The experimental literature on the issue of enhancement is not entirely in confirmation, however. A study by Poe (1967) found no difference between hypnotic imagined practice on motor and cognitive tasks and waking imagined practice for good hypnotic Ss. This may be because Poe's study dealt less with the primary process features of imagery than did the previously reported studies. A series of experiments by Stross and Shevrin (1968) has also produced somewhat contradictory evidence for the hypothesis. In these studies Ss described their images of stimuli, that were presented subliminally, either in the hypnotic or in the waking state. Data indicated that hypnosis enhanced secondary rather than primary process mentation. Hypnotic induction in combination with freely evoked images gave rise consistently to conceptual subliminal effects, which were indexed by the number of rational associates appearing in the Ss' image descriptions of the experimental stimuli. Hypnosis failed to be distinguished from the waking state on the basis of differences in primary process thinking as assessed by the more irrationally-oriented rebus technique. As the authors acknowledged, however, results against the enhancement hypothesis were not definitive. Some of the words that appeared as conceptual associates may have been more drive-determined than the Es could detect within the formal laboratory setting. Generally speaking, the hypothesis that imagery ability is enhanced under hypnosis has not been tested sufficiently fully. It awaits systematic exploration.

The second consequence of regarding hypnosis as a loss or fading of the usual reality-orientation can be stated more simply. This position implies merely that imaginal capacities of the S must be relevant to the trance experience. Here, a correlation is posited between hypnotizability and aptitude for imagination. The occurrence of primary process mentation in trance, combined with the assumption that not everyone is susceptible to hypnosis, suggests that certain cognitive abilities must exist for S in order that he may function as a good hypnotic S. The implications of such a correlation are complex and require elaboration.

IMAGINATION AND "CREDULOUS" VERSUS "SKEPTICAL" ACCOUNTS OF HYPNOSIS

The correlation of hypnotizability with imaginative capacities does not necessarily commit one to belief in a "special state" view of hypnosis. The several implications of the correlation for the nature of hypnosis are best considered in terms of the distinction made by Sutcliffe (1960) between "credulous" and "skeptical" accounts of hypnotic phenomena. The skeptical view states that S agrees verbally with the hypnotist's suggestions and acts as if the suggested state of affairs were so. The credulous viewpoint stresses the reality of hypnotic phenomena where the reaction of the hypnotic S is identical in form with the sensory experience produced by a parallel objective reality. The skeptical viewpoint does not state that the hypnotic S is simulating. Most theorists agree that the hypnotic subject plays his role in some way differently from the waking simulator (Orne, 1959; Sutcliffe, 1958; Young, 1940).

Obviously, imagery or fantasy activation is not the solution to the problem of defining hypnosis. The complexity of hypnotic phenomena excludes this conclusion outright. The ability of the hypnotic S to image well may be accounted for in several ways. Imagery, for instance, could be the result of dissociation through trance induction giving rise to primary process thinking, or simply a manifestation of an ability that S happens to bring to the trance setting.

One cannot image without some capacity to do so, and no theory of hypnosis is discounted by this capacity being evident in the waking state. As imaging is manifested in both the waking and trance states, it is evident that the hypnotizable person has a cognitive ability suitable for the eliciting of various hypnotic phenomena, but either a credulous or skeptical viewpoint may be tenable. If the capacity to image is evidenced in the hypnotic state, but not in the waking state, then there has been a change in personality functioning that supports the credulous view of hypnosis. It is difficult, however, to test the hypothesis that imaging is evidenced only in the trance state. Before this assertion is accepted, conditions for evocation of imagery must be equated for both the trance and the waking states, except with regard to that which truly distinguishes one state from the other. Aside from the problem of knowing what this criterion for distinguishing the two sets of events is, the motivation and expectations of *S*s must be similar for the same *S* in both the waking and trance conditions, since imagery and fantasy may be aroused voluntarily.

A hypnotized person performs convincingly in hypnosis, and this fact raises issues such as Sarbin's "organismic involvement," or Sutcliffe's "delusion." The hypnotized person accepts suggestions to a degree where self and role appear to be de-differentiated (Sarbin, 1954), or the *S* deluded as to the real state of affairs (Arnold, 1959; Sutcliffe, 1958). Such characteristics of behavior may be necessary to define the nature of hypnosis, but the association of imagery with these features of hypnotic performance does not necessarily support either the credulous or the skeptical viewpoint. It is difficult to analyze the nature of an association. Imagery, for example, may be the result of delusion or simply a manifestation of it.

The correlation, then, of imagery ability with hypnotizability is consistent with but not a test of a variety of theories of hypnosis. The presence of a positive relationship may support either a credulous or a skeptical view. The association does imply that *S*s have certain abilities that make it likely that they will be hypnotizable. This includes consideration of a *S*'s aptitude for trance as distinct from his attitudes towards hypnosis itself or the person who is doing the hypnotizing.

THE HYPNOTIC SETTING

The nature of the hypnotic setting itself provides further theoretical support for positing a relationship between imaginal capacities and hypnotizability. In sharp contrast to the notion that hypnosis leads to an increase in primary process functioning, one may view the hypnotic context as a setting that carries with it strong inherent demand characteristics for engagement by the *S* in imaginal activities. A person may engage in fantasy or call up mental images easily at will (Betts, 1909). The intentional development of *S*s' capacities for daydreaming (Singer, 1966) highlights the voluntary nature of *S*s' imaginal processes. The voluntary nature of imagery and fantasy allows *S* to respond appropriately to the hypnotist's implicit direction to him to lay aside his usual reality orientation. When *S*s' responses to standard induction procedures are analyzed, it is difficult to decide just how much of the quality of

*S*s' mentation is due to their perception of cues to respond in a make-believe fashion, and how much the quality of cognition is uniquely distinctive of their experience of an "altered state of consciousness." A hypnotist typically suggests to *S* that things are other than they are and so implicitly requests that *S* accept his fantasy play and respond appropriately in like manner. Because of the example set by the hypnotist the *S* may indulge his predilection for fantasy (Sutcliffe, Perry, & Sheehan, 1970). The hypnotist characteristically, it seems, instructs *S* to place aside reality testing and allow more "primary" mentation to occur. No study has been done to separate the suggested features of primary process thinking in hypnosis from those features that might be expected to occur (on theoretical grounds) because of the presence of a change in consciousness. It is largely due to the traditional emphasis of hypnotic testing on phenomena such as hallucinations ("response to objects that do not really exist") that ability to indulge in make-believe or fantasy appears to be so important a dimension of hypnotic behavior.

On theoretical grounds, hypnosis defined in terms of a loss of Generalized Reality-Orientation is a particular instance of an altered state of consciousness and as such might be expected to highlight ideational aspects of the stream of consciousness such as imagery and fantasy. If one accepts the connotations of "altered state" at more than the experiential level, it can be argued that primary process functioning will be augmented in trance as compared to the normal waking state. Laying aside the question of whether such augmentation is supported on empirical grounds, the mere occurrence of primary process mentation in trance implies that there is a positive correlation between *S*'s aptitude for hypnosis and his proneness to ideational activity. This correlation is consistent with either a credulous or skeptical approach to hypnosis. Any attempt to analyze the role of imaginal processes in hypnosis must, however, take some account of the nature of the hypnotic setting, which carries strong cues for *S* to respond in a make-believe fashion as directed implicitly by the hypnotist. The fact that *S* may respond as suggested and manifest appropriate fantasy responses does not diminish the importance of the particular cognitive abilities that *S* brings to the trance situation.

Any theoretical proposition must ultimately be dependent for its justification on empirical tests. The following section reviews the empirical evidence available. Both clinical and experimental data that are relevant to the hypothesis of a positive association between susceptibility to trance and ability to engage in ideational activity are considered.

Review of Empirical Evidence: Clinical

The relevance of imagery and fantasy to hypnosis is seen most readily in the clinical observations hypnotists make on the *S*s they test. Sarbin (1950) writes that "clinically, [he] has never found an adult with eidetic, or vivid imagery who was not a good hypnotic subject" (p. 268). Wolberg (1948) notes that in trance imagery seems to play a special role, and Orne (1951) talks of age regression in hypnosis as being actively hallucinated and vividly imagined. The ability of the hypnotic subject to imagine well is noted also by Binet and Féré (1886), Lundholm (1932), and Hilgard (1965b). Hilgard (1965b), for example, reports that the more hypnotizable *S*s give the most "dreamlike" hypnotic dreams and dream more frequently than less hypnotizable *S*s when a dream is suggested in hypnosis.

The role of imaginal activity in hypnosis is stressed by therapists using a variety of hypnotic techniques (Kanzer, 1945; Krojanker, 1962; Schneck, 1953; van den Berg, 1962; Wolberg, 1945). Krojanker (1962) employed a hypnodramatic reenactment technique in which the *S*'s dreams were used specifically in the treatment process. His technique together with those used by others draw their validity from the psychiatrist's assumption that pictorial representations can be enlivened with affect in a way that conceptual representations can not, and therapeutic gain may derive from them. According to this view, hypnosis is helpful in that it facilitates the occurrence of fantasy involvement. Other studies have used imagery to deepen the trance state. Wiseman and Reyher (1962), for example, explicitly utilized the sleep-dream cycle to facilitate a deepening of hypnosis.

Inadvertently, hypnosis may be induced by *S*s receiving imagination instructions (Hilgard, 1965b; Tart, 1966a). Subjects given such instruction, and no hypnotic induction, sometimes report being hypnotized and show signs of trance such as psychomotor retardation and waxy flexibility. Hilgard and Tart (1966a) have found within the experimental setting that the degree to which some *S*s felt themselves hypnotized was highly predictive of the dreamlike character of the fantasy they produced regardless of whether they had received a formal induction procedure. Evidence from the experimental studies of Barber and his associates (Barber, 1969b; Barber & Calverley, 1962; Barber & Glass, 1962) relates to Hilgard and Tart's data. These studies have demonstrated consistently a high rate of response by *S*s to the Barber Suggestibility Scale under imagination instructions. In a study by Barber and Calverley (1968), 12 per cent of *S*s showed a high level of suggestibility, and 36 per cent showed moderately high suggestibility under instructions where *S*s were asked simply to try to imagine those things that would be described to them. Barber interprets these instructions as "non-hypnotic" and uses them to establish what he terms "base-control rates of response." Hilgard and Tart prefer to consider at least some of these instances of high suggestibility response under imagination instructions as possible examples of hypnotic involvement. Leaving details of this controversy aside, the data reported in the literature do suggest that in some instances the behavioral consequences of instruction to imagine bear a striking enough similarity to hypnotic outcomes that some prefer to label them as the effects of trance.

Shor (1970) has reported in detail an analysis of book reading fantasy that illustrates the separate dimensions of hypnosis as he has conceptualized them elsewhere (Shor, 1959, 1962). The occurrence of fantasy in circumstances very different from the traditional hypnotic setting illustrates that the underlying processes of hypnosis bear some clinical similarity to imaginative activities. Some people read a story so completely that they enter imaginatively into the story to a degree almost equivalent to reliving the experience. During the time of the fantasy the person becomes totally oblivious to the reality around him. Shor draws the parallel between the level of involvement in the fantasy and the loss of Generalized Reality-Orientation, which is a dimension of hypnotic depth. The reader actively creates the fantasy for himself, thus instituting a nonconscious level of deep involvement typical of the hypnotized *S*. Josephine Hilgard (in E. R. Hilgard, 1965b; J. R. Hilgard, 1970) has related book reading fantasy to hypnotic susceptibility. In a series of interviews she found that people who became absorbed in tales of romance and adventure tended to be highly hypnotizable.

Although there is much evidence from anecdotal reports on experimental *S*s, therapeutic case studies, and interview data indicating that fantasy and imaginative involvement are associated with hypnosis, the clinical method is especially ill-equipped to interpret the nature of the association. The richness of mentation typically reported under hypnosis may be elicited from patients who are not hypnotized and do not report the experience of trance. Instructions to visualize a scene evoke elaborate dream imagery from psychoanalytic patients even when no "hypnosis" is employed. As Barber (1962d) points out, carefully controlled experiments are lacking to exclude the possibility that primary process functioning of the kind typically reported in the literature can be elicited without the use of hypnosis. The experimental method is needed to clarify whether the association between imagery and hypnosis is purely an incidental one.

Review of Empirical Evidence: Experimental

INDIRECT MEASURES

Jenness (1944) found evidence to support the hypothesis that persons whose imagery is generally vivid would be more readily hypnotized than those whose imagery is poor. Working with Jorgensen (Jenness & Jorgensen, 1941), he found that the imagery of somnambulists tended to be more vivid than that of nonsomnambulists where somnambulism referred to *S*s who walked or performed other coordinated acts while asleep. Later Jenness (1965) reported a relationship between somnambulism, vividness of imagery, and hypnotic ability. In his study *S*s rated the vividness of their imagery in response to phrases read aloud by *E*. Forty-one sleepwalkers averaged higher in visual imagery and hypnotic susceptibility (as measured by standardized hypnotic scales) than 84 Ss who denied walking or talking during sleep.

A similar indirect approach to the study of imagery and hypnotizability was made by Arnold (1946), who used the postural sway technique and asked Ss to imagine falling forward. Comparisons were made between the amount of sway and the reported vividness of imagery. She found a correlation between amount of body sway and vividness report, and concluded there was a relationship between vividness of imagery and hypnotic depth. This relationship has been confirmed most recently by Richardson (1969), who found that vivid uncontrolled imagery was more obviously related to greater body sway than weak, less vivid imagery. McBain (1954) chose the "memory for designs" test from the 1937 revised version of the Stanford Binet, a paper cutting test, and the "progressive finger tracing" test as tests of imagery to further investigate Arnold's hypothesis. Using the body sway technique and administering standard imaging instructions, he found that Ss with higher imagery scores were more susceptible to hypnosis when the finger tracing test was used.

Arnold's and McBain's studies are open to objection. Arnold specified no operation or procedure for selecting those Ss who could imagine well, and inferred a correlation of imagery with hypnotic depth using the body sway test as her measure. Insufficient recognition was given to the fact that the body sway test is not a direct measure of hypnotizability. Arnold's instructions to Ss may also have had implicit effects. She used the word "imagine" rather than the word "image," and Ss may have simply "thought hard" about swaying. A S asked to imagine something does not necessarily have to evoke imagery in order that his attention be focused on an object. As used in many studies in hypnotic literature, instructions to imagine may have slightly different effects for some Ss from instructions to image; I can imagine, for example, that a man is not standing next to me far more easily than I can image his absence. In McBain's study, tests were used that were intended to index objectively the imagery aroused. More accurate performance was taken to indicate more vivid imagery. Accuracy of test performance, however, is not always a sure criterion of type or quality of imagery used. McBain's tests were tests of intelligence rather than tests of mental imagery, and accuracy of reproduction may indicate any of a variety of mental processes.

Suggestibility as measured by other than the body sway test has shown some relationship to imagery capacity. Camberari (1958) divided his sample into suggestible and nonsuggestible groups on the basis of a battery of many different tests. Suggestibility was positively correlated with a greater number of reports of visual imagery in an isolation situation. Roberts (1965) tested Ss in a similar situation. Using as his measure of fantasy the degree of hallucinatory activity in perceptual deprivation, he found no relationship between Ss' willingness to enter fantasy and performance on the SHSS, Forms A and C.

QUESTIONNAIRE STUDIES

Studies have met some degree of success in establishing predictors of hypnotic susceptibility through the tapping of personal subjective experiences (As, 1963; London, Cooper, & Johnson, 1962; Shor, Orne, & O'Connell, 1962). Subjects' self-reports of hypnotic experiences have been shown by Freedman and Marks (1965) to be related to some forms of imagery aroused in the experimental setting. Segal (1968) also found that in a sensory deprivation situation Ss who indicated a high tolerance for unrealistic experiences aroused more vivid imagery than Ss with a low tolerance for such experiences. The Freedman and Marks study and Segal's study both suggest that S's capacity for fantasy and imagery (as evaluated independently of questionnaire assessment) are related to those aspects of subjective experience that denote susceptibility to hypnosis.

In the aftermath of the mass of conflicting data on the personality correlates of hypnosis the literature has not sufficiently recognized that good hypnotic Ss quite consistently have shown that some forms of imaginative activities have played a significant part in their everyday waking experiences. The consistency of data runs counter to the general failure by studies in this area to replicate their findings. In an investigation reported by Barber (1960), 61 items from the Guilford-Zimmerman Temperament Survey, the Webster-Sanford-Freedman version of the F scale, and a specially constructed questionnaire were found to discriminate suggestible from nonsuggestible Ss. A questionnaire containing these items was given to four groups in a series of two studies (Barber & Glass, 1962). Analysis of results showed that the four items differentiated suggestible from nonsuggestible Ss in all groups. A fifth sample was given the questionnaire in further test of replicability of findings. The highly suggestible and nonsuggestible Ss in the new sample answered each of the four items in the predicted direction. Examination of the content of these items showed that three of the four items were concerned with fantasy activity. One item dealt with book reading fantasy *(p < .001)*, the second with daydreaming *(p < .02)*, and the third with vivid imaginary playmates *(p < .001)*. The fact that over five groups these items discriminated Ss consistently (even when groups were tested by two different Es) and that the items were characterized particularly by ability to engage in imaginative activity, suggests that the relation between hypnotizability and the various manifestations of imagination has considerable support. This support is limited only by the fact that replication was specific to college students and items did not differentiate those Ss who were moderately susceptible from the other Ss in the sample.

Using the Stanford Hypnotic Susceptibility Scale, Sarbin (1964) in another laboratory confirmed the trend of Barber's data. Sarbin reports the construction of a questionnaire of 117 items which was administered to 93 Ss as part of an ongoing study of student attitudes. Twenty-three items discriminated between Ss high and low on role enactment. A logical clustering of these items revealed that one of the five major dimensions being tapped by them was concerned with fantasy and other forms of "as if" behavior.

Recently a substantial amount of data has been brought to light on the relation between hypnotizability and one particular questionnaire measure of vividness of imagery. A test (Betts QMI), as devised by Sheehan (1967a) from Betts's Questionnaire Upon Mental Imagery (Betts, 1909), was administered to a sample of 95 Ss after Ss were tested hypnotically on the SHSS:C and a scale specially constructed for the study (Sutcliffe, Perry, & Sheehan, 1970). The Betts QMI correlated significantly with both hypnotic scales for the total sample and for males, but not females. Close analysis of the results indicated that the relationship departed significantly from linearity. Vivid imagers were both susceptible and insusceptible to hypnosis, but Ss with very poor imagery tended to be insusceptible. Vividness of imagery, then, predicted insusceptibility to hypnosis better than susceptibility. In experimental confirmation of clinical data reviewed above, diagnostic subgroups of susceptible and insusceptible Ss, as rated by independent Es after hypnotic testing, were clearly differentiated with respect to the vividness of their imagery. Susceptible Ss imaged more vividly than insusceptible Ss. Shor, Orne, & O'Connell (1966), using a variation of the Betts QMI, also found for a sample of 25 volunteer Ss a significant correlation (r = .56) between vividness of imagery and plateau hypnotizability as measured by clinical diagnostic ratings. Sutcliffe (1958), using Betts's original questionnaire and Gordon's test for "control of imagery," found that highly susceptible Ss exhibited more vivid imagery than did Ss who were insusceptible to hypnosis. In an attempted replication of the imagery study by Sutcliffe, Perry, & Sheehan, J. R. Hilgard (1970) found over all Ss a small but significant correlation (p < .01) between the Stanford hypnotic scale and the Betts QMI, but the sex differences were reversed. The relationship was significant for the female sample only. Her data replicated the nonlinearity of relationship noted in the earlier study. The correlation was determined largely by those completely lacking in imagery.

Only one study using the Betts QMI as a measure of imagery has reported negative findings. In an unpublished investigation reported in a Hawthorne House Research Memorandum, Morgan and Lam (1969) found no relationship between the Betts QMI and SHSS:C scores for particular subgroups of susceptible Ss and for the total sample of 322 student Ss. In Morgan and Lam's study, however, Ss were not particularly well selected for extremes in hypnotic ability. Sutcliffe, Perry, and Sheehan discriminated susceptible from insusceptible Ss not only on SHSS:C scores but also on the basis of clinical ratings agreed upon independently by separate hypnotists. In view of the positive trend of findings on the Betts QMI to date, it is difficult to account fully for Morgan and Lam's failure to replicate using the same instrument.

THE PROBLEM OF SEX DIFFERENCES

Research into the association between imaginal activity and hypnotizability has shown considerable inconsistency of data on sex differences. Sutcliffe, Perry, & Sheehan (1970) found a relationship for males, and J. R. Hilgard (1970) found an association for females, yet the two studies used very similar measures of hypnotizability and vividness of imagery. Palmer and Field (1968) measured visual imagery under sensory restriction and under rhythmic photic stimulation to test the hypothesis that Ss with good visual imagery would be more susceptible to hypnosis. Their results showed a consistently stronger relationship between imagery and hypnotizability for females than for males.

The fact that Palmer and Field's study and Hilgard's study were conducted on American student volunteers and Sutcliffe, Perry, and Sheehan's study was carried out on Australian volunteer samples suggests that the pattern of sex differences among the studies may, to a degree, be culturally based. A very recent study on American Ss by Rhoades and Edmonston (1969), however, suggests otherwise. These authors used Cattell's IPAT questionnaire and scores based on second-order factors of Cattell's 16PF scale to relate a number of different aspects of personality functioning to susceptibility as measured by the Harvard Group Scale of Hypnosis. Tests were given to two samples: 32 male undergraduate students and a second sample of 14 male executives and 10 female housewives or students. Only the data for the second sample indicated a positive relationship between imaginative activity (as measured by Cattell's Factor M) and responsiveness to hypnotic suggestions. This relationship was highly significant for males but absent for females. Rhoades and Edmonston made a special point of reporting that their second sample of males was highly homogeneous with respect to socioeconomic level (all were executives and were with the same company). Their results suggest that the pattern of sex differences across studies may, in part, reflect socioeconomic variation among Ss tested, rather than cultural or sex differences. It appears significant that the female sample in Rhoades and Edmonston's study that showed no relationship was much more heterogeneous (housewives and students) than the usual sample of student Ss in terms of Ss' occupational and socioeconomic status. If American female student samples are more homogeneous in socioeconomic background than American male samples, the difference in sample structure may account for the higher incidence of positive relationships found for female as compared to male Ss.

The above hypothesis to explain sex differences can only be proposed tentatively because other factors also appear to be relevant. Special care should be taken, for example, to equate male and female Ss for imagination ability. Michael (1967) has reported evidence that male and female Ss differ in imaging ability. Using American student samples, he found a factor of visual imagery to account for the performance of female but not male Ss. A battery of tests was given to groups of students differing in educational grade level. The visual imagery factor did not appear in the male population even when it was dissected as to grade level. Another variable to be considered in analyzing the issue of sex differences is that of "imagination control." It appears that male and female Ss may handle their imaginative capacities differently. Antrobus, Singer, & Greenberg (1966) found that male Ss controlled and excluded their fantasy tendencies when threatened with financial loss for failures in signal detection. Fromm, Oberlander, & Gruenewald (1969) have presented evidence to suggest that male rather than female Ss increase primary process mentation in trance as compared to the waking state.

THE ISSUE OF CONJOINT ATTRIBUTES

Studies reviewed above generally have attempted to correlate hypnotic test scores with single dimensions of cognitive function. Evidence from these experiments has been both positive and negative in support of an association between imaginative ability and susceptibility to hypnosis. Results, though, have been more positive than negative, and have shown an unusual degree of consistency over subject samples. Close analysis of the data from these studies indicates that investigation of conjoint attributes of cognitive functioning may bear an even closer relationship to hypnotizability.

The curvilinear nature of the relationship between imaginative activity and susceptibility to hypnosis (J. R. Hilgard, 1970; Sutcliffe, Perry, & Sheehan, 1970) suggests that accurate prediction of susceptibility to trance may depend on knowledge of more than one capacity of the S. The experimental literature is in some support of this contention.

M. J. Roberts (1965) found no relationship between hypnotizability and willingness to enter fantasy as assessed by degree of hallucinatory activity in perceptual deprivation. This measure of fantasy, however, used in a multiple correlation with other measures (for example, test for tolerance for unrealistic experiences) predicted susceptibility much better than the fantasy measure did alone. In another investigation, Perry (1965) extensively investigated proneness to fantasy as indicated by Ss' morning recall of their nocturnal dreaming and found no significant relationship between hypnotizability (measured both clinically and by standardized scales) and either incidence of dreaming or dream distortion. This finding should be considered in light of the fact that spontaneous morning recall of dreams is subject to extraneous influences that are minimized (though not completely) when dream reports are collected at the time dreaming occurs. Although the data for fantasy proneness as measured by "dream distortion" only tended to be in the same direction as predicted by the study, this measure taken conjointly with vividness of imagery was related obviously to hypnotizability (Sutcliffe, Perry, & Sheehan, 1970). Those Ss with moderate degrees of one or both characteristics had high or medium susceptibility to trance and the absence of both characteristics was associated with insusceptibility to hypnosis. Consideration of both fantasy proneness and vividness of imagery led to more accurate prediction of high susceptibility than the imagery variable did alone.

Coe and Sarbin (1966) have also demonstrated the predictive value of the multivariable approach. Employing measures of congruence between self and role, role expectation, and role-taking aptitude they found that any group of Ss that scored more highly on more role theory variables than another group scored significantly higher on the hypnotic test. Multiple correlation analyses using the Personal Experience Questionnaire, which bears a positive relationship to experimentally produced imagery, have also been successful (London, Cooper, & Johnson, 1962; Shor, Orne, & O'Connell, 1966). Indeed, in the light of the trend of data it seems feasible that the failure of many studies to consider conjoint cognitive attributes is partially responsible for the lack of their success in predicting hypnotic susceptibility with more than only a moderate degree of accuracy.

Quite another view to that which has just been proposed has been put forward by E. R. Hilgard (1964) and J. R. Hilgard (in E. R. Hilgard, 1965b), who have argued that the low correlations found generally with personality measures and other tests arise because Ss enter hypnosis with wide individual differences in experience and background. The Hilgards raise the possibility that a single favorable predictor leads to high susceptibility in the absence of other favorable predictors. This point of view conceives of there being "multiple paths" into hypnosis, any one of which leads to a high score. Personality tests yield low correlations with hypnosis, for example, because scores on many predictive items do not equal the effect of single more influential items. Hence, reliance should be placed on single, strong predictors.

In support of this view, E. R. Hilgard (1964) considered separate, significant correlations between the SHSS and measures of adventuresomeness and childhood fantasy. Fantasy and adventure can be said to represent alternative routes into hypnosis. Results showed that for low (but not high) fantasy Ss the correlation of adventuresomeness and hypnotizability was significant, and that for low (but not high) adventuresome Ss the correlation of fantasy with susceptibility was significant. It was concluded that for those Ss whose path into hypnosis was by way of fantasy, interest in adventure was indifferent; for those whose path into hypnosis was by way of adventure, interest in fantasy was irrelevant.

The above findings somewhat contradict the data reported by Sutcliffe, Perry, & Sheehan (1970), which suggested that at least in some instances multiple predictors of hypnotizability are more effective in discriminating susceptible Ss than single predictors. The hypothesis of "multiple paths" into hypnosis has not as yet been tested fully. Reported correlations have been very small (of the order .23 to .34) and need replication; also, research has been at a preliminary stage. Data, however, draw much needed attention to the fact that joint analysis of relevant predictors of susceptibility may help us to understand the full ramifications of the term "susceptibility to hypnosis."

SUMMARY OF DATA

A review of the literature indicates that hypnotic data and data arising from Ss utilizing their cognitive capacities for fantasy and imagery are not always in one-to-one correspondence. As has been recognized elsewhere (Barber, 1969b; Barber & Glass, 1962), the relationship between sets of data of this kind may be multidetermined by a host of variables. Situational factors, the characteristics of the *E,* the interaction of these factors with the personality of the *S,* and an interaction between *S*'s characteristics and the nature of the experimental situation all may affect *S*'s behavior. Review of the evidence raises seven factors that can be singled out more than others as pertaining particularly to the interpretation of experimental findings in this area. These factors are: differences in form and quality of Ss imaginative activities; the homogeneity of samples tested with respect to factors such as socioeconomic status and control of imagination; the nature of the technique of investigation: correlation method or analysis of diagnostic subgroups; the essential weaknesses of subjective studies; the adequacy of imagination measures adopted; the cues given *S* as to the most appropriate response; and the efficacy of single versus multiple predictors of trance susceptibility. Consideration of one or more of these factors may nullify the presence of positive findings in the area or explain the absence of confirmatory data.

Differences in imaginative activity. Both imagery and fantasy may vary in form and content. Any relationship with hypnotizability may likewise vary with such differences in mentation. Richardson (1969) found, for example, a more positive relationship between suggestibility and imaginative activity for uncontrolled as opposed to controlled imagery. In further confirmation of the importance of individual differences in mentation, E. R. Hilgard (1964) reports the impression that stimulus-bound fantasy leads more readily to hypnosis than impulse-driven fantasy. This hypothesis was confirmed by Josephine Hilgard (1970) in a comprehensive interview analysis of the fantasy proneness of 289 Ss. Studies to date have also indicated a more apparent relationship for imagery as distinct from fantasy. To the extent that imagery and fantasy are different cognitive functions, hypnosis may be more related to the former than to the latter. Binet and Féré (1886) suggested that vividness of imagery was the basis of hypnotic hallucination. They argued their position on the basis of the perceptual clarity of imagery rather than on the inventiveness or fluidity of imaginative capacity that seems to denote fantasy more clearly. Their conclusion seems important. Studies conducted independently of the hypnotic context have shown that under certain conditions vivid imagery may reinstitute the original clarity of perceptual experience (Sheehan, 1966a, 1966b, 1967c). Vividness of imagery might be a more suitable aptitude for some aspects of trance behavior than fantasy, because it enables the hypnotic S to experience events specifically suggested by the hypnotist in a way that is close to the literalness of perception. With the special aid of imagery, hypnotic events may be experienced with a degree of vividness approaching that of sensory experience. It is well to recognize, however, that the term "imagery" may itself denote a variety of processes. That mental imagery is not a unidimensional phenomenon is well illustrated by the work of Palmer and Field (1968). In their study, correlations between different tests of imagery and susceptibility were so uneven as to challenge seriously the concept of a single, unitary process underlying all visual imagery productions.

Homogeneity of subject samples. Discrepancies among findings in studies employing different subject samples suggest that heterogeneity of sampling may be responsible for at least some variation in results. Evidence may be interpreted more clearly in the future if studies list, as far as possible, the age, sex, socioeconomic status, and imaginative abilities of the Ss being tested. Careful note should be made also of any Ss who attempt to control their fantasy; the data of Antrobus, Singer, and Greenberg indicate that such control may be sex-specific. Whenever paper-and-pencil questionnaire measures of personality attributes are used, sex differences may be expected to result (Hilgard, 1965b). It is useful to note in this context that the Betts QMI, the measure of imagery that has most consistently yielded a relationship to hypnotizability, was especially constructed to minimize sex differences in Ss' imaging responses to its items; it is also reliable (Sheehan, 1967a, 1967b).

Technique of investigation. The majority of studies in the field have employed the correlational method for analyzing the association between hypnotizability and imaginative capacity. This technique, of necessity, includes for analysis those Ss who have only a moderate degree of hypnotic aptitude. These Ss are neither characterized by a special aptitude for trance nor by a particular inability to experience hypnosis. Studies that have found a relationship for very susceptible Ss as distinct from moderately susceptible Ss (such as Barber & Glass, 1962; Sutcliffe, 1958; Sutcliffe, Perry, & Sheehan, 1970) indicate the value of considering results for diagnostic subgroups of the hypnotic population. The method of correlation is insensitive to those attributes that appear to characterize very susceptible Ss. In addition, studies that have employed the correlational technique have invariably assumed that the relationship they are investigating is a linear one. Recent data suggest that the hypothesis of linearity is untenable and that curvilinear methods of analyses are the more appropriate ones to adopt.

Weaknesses of subjective studies. Studies in this area are especially open to the problem of quantifying subjective experience. The criticism that can be made of such experiments is that imagery, fantasy, and hypnosis all denote essentially private phenomena directly observable only to the experiencing subject. Consequently, *S*s may have differing experiences with objects imaged or fantasied, and these differences contribute to unreliability of data. The meaning of points on appropriate rating scales for the measurement of imaginative abilities may also vary widely from one person to another. In the light of such difficulties, experiments that report on the relationship between imagination and hypnosis must cite all available evidence on the reliability of the measures adopted. Special consideration must be given to the problems of translating both imaginative and hypnotic experiences from subjective into objective terms.

Adequacy of measures. The adequacy of measures is obviously related to the problem of the weaknesses of subjective studies. Particular attention should be paid, though, to whether the measure selected by *E* is examining the form of imagery he really intends to study. Lindauer (1969) has drawn attention to the fact that inconsistencies in the literature on the effectiveness of imagery may be due to the use of materials that do not fully or effectively maximize the occurrence of imagery. He argues that one essential attribute of imagery, namely its reference to sensory modalities, has been especially neglected in the selection of measures of imagery. Inattention to sensory characteristics has produced materials that are uneven in their capacity to arouse imagery. In addition, care should be taken that techniques of measuring imagery are relatively free of obvious trance-inducing qualities. Palmer and Field (1968) found a relationship between hypnotizability and directed imagery in both a Ganzfeld and photic stimulation setting for female *S*s. Results suggested that the imagery test was actually trance inducing, since the Ganzfeld-directed imagery was correlated with photic-directed imagery more than photic-directed was correlated with photic-free imagery. Directed imagery in this situation was defined as imagery that *E* specifically requested from the *S*.

Implicit cues as to appropriate response. It is well known that the demand characteristics (Orne, 1959) in the experimental situation may determine the nature of *S*'s response. Cues may derive from the tests of imagination themselves, the experimental procedures, the nature of instructions, or from the *E* personally. In a nonhypnotic study Davis (1932), for example, designed tests meant to be associated with a particular form of imagery.

Much of the reasoning behind Davis's work was based on the assumption that visual work requires visual imagery and auditory work requires auditory imagery. The objection that can be raised specifically here is that a person could recall an object being a sounding object without any image of the sound at all. The implicit suggestion of auditory imagery in the nature of the test could lead S to report an auditory "image" when only nonimaginal recall was present.

The nature of E's instruction is important also. The early work of Schneck (1954a) attests to the influence on S's responses of subtle changes in the wording of E's hypnotic suggestions. The wording in one instance yielded evidence of "hallucination" and in another evidence of "imagery." Barber and Calverley (1968) have shown that hypnotic instructions may yield behavioral differences over other sets of instruction due to the subtle definition of the hypnotic situation as one in which unusual manifestations (such as hallucinations) are expected to occur. The E's demand for honesty is known also to affect the nature of hallucinatory behavior (K. S. Bowers, 1967). Indeed, it is very difficult to assess to what extent fantasy and imagery responses are determined by the demand characteristics of the hypnotic situation. This is particularly so because the hypnotist characteristically directs the S to engage in imaginative activity. Fantasy involvement is clearly an expected feature of S's hypnotic response.

The efficacy of multiple predictors. Finally, one should consider the accuracy of prediction of susceptibility afforded by conjoint cognitive and personality attributes. Since (theoretically at least) one may distinguish between imagery, fantasy, and hallucination, different functions may be served differently by the various manifestations of S's ability to engage in imaginative activities. On a priori grounds it seems reasonable to argue that a person proficient in the various manifestations of imagination will be more susceptible than a person who manifests one aspect singularly. This prejudges, however, the thorough exploration that yet needs to be carried out to investigate whether there are multiple paths to hypnosis.

Imagination, Hypnosis, and the As If Formulation

The positive nature of a considerable body of evidence and, in particular, the consistency with which some studies have yielded similar results in different settings suggest that the functioning of imaginative activities in trance should be analyzed more closely. The question may be raised as to the most appropriate framework within which to conceptualize the function of imaginal processes within the hypnotic setting.

Fantasy play may be initiated and directed by the hypnotist in a relationship between subject and hypnotist much akin to a form of *folie à deux* (Sutcliffe, Perry, & Sheehan, 1970). In this sense imaginative activity may be free in form and relatively unconstrained by physical reality. At the same time, however, the hypnotic situation puts considerable pressure on *S* to experience some hypnotic events in quite a literal fashion—as if these events were actual, in fact. The fact that imaginal events have been shown to reinstate the clarity of the perceptual experience serves to emphasize this function.

Consider suggestions to hallucinate and make-believe as a small child. In both these suggestions, as distinct from, say, suggestions for a hypnotic dream, the "demand characteristics" of the situation serve to emphasize that considerable accuracy is required on the part of the hypnotic *S*. Here, the hypnotist typically uses standards of reality against which he evaluates the performance of *S*. In hypnotic age regression, the hypnotic *S* must perform in a way at least consistent with true or real experiences of an eight-year-old child if he is at all going to satisfy the hypnotist about the genuineness of his performance. His recall of a classroom, for instance, must be roughly equivalent to that of a small child. In hypnotic hallucination the constraints for accuracy may even be more obvious. The hypnotic *S* must report literally on his experience as if what the hypnotist suggests to be present is actually so. Only the specificity of the original suggestion determines to what extent *S* may embellish his report.

It is in the above sense that Sarbin (1954) has applied the as if dimension to the conceptualization of drama, hypnosis, imagination, and role taking. The learning of role taking, for example, is associated with *S*'s ability to treat an object or event as if it were something else, and the skill a *S* shows in undertaking his play is defined as the degree of his success in use of "as if" behavior. Sarbin's use of the as if dimension to define imaginative behavior can be extended more fully to draw out some of the logical implications of this position.

When *S* images or fantasies an object he has seen recently, and reports on his experience, he can be said to be acting in testimony, as if previously experienced situations were now current. This is directly analogous to *S*'s response to the hypnotist's suggestions of hallucination and regression, which were analyzed above. A hypnotic *S* who says he has a mental picture of a garden is not contemplating a resemblance of the garden in any substantive sense, but, as Ryle (1955) would say, he resembles a spectator of the garden in that he behaves in report at least as if he were perceiving it. It is from such pretending behavior that one infers the process of imagining.

Consider the proposition "the imager acts as if previously experienced situations were now current." The words "as if" logically demand a comparison of two terms. The way a person who is imagining acts is equated with the way he acts when he has the perceptions on which his imagery depends. The first implication that follows from the as if formulation is that the imager must act exactly as he did when he actually had these perceptions. The words "as if," however, are conditional; they imply that the condition is unreal or impossible. Imagining is distinct from perceiving but not to be identified with it. It is not the impossible case itself that is assumed to be real, but the manner of regarding the case in question is equated with the consequences that follow from it, and are necessarily bound up with it.

The notion of the imager acting as if he were perceiving (as in a hypnotic hallucination) logically denies an identity of process between imaging and perceiving, while asserting that there may be a close correspondence between imaging behavior and perceptual behavior. Just how close this correspondence is will depend on the constraints for accuracy that are suggested by the hypnotist. If the imager is acting as if something were the case, the good or vivid imager must be a convincing enough pretender that another observer may fail to detect pretense. If one acts "as if" poorly, the likelihood of confusion is increased. The as if formulation applied to imagining in hypnosis suggests that the good imager acts as if the "hallucinated" object perceived were present, and if he acts as if convincingly, then behavior toward the imaged object will be as it is (usually) suggested by the hypnotist —akin to that of perception.

This view of imaginative activity and its relevance to hypnosis conflicts with some current assertions in the literature. Structural similarity of imaging and perceiving, implying an identity of process, has been proposed by many. Oswald (1962) holds to the view that the neurophysiological response present when an object is actually perceived by means of one's sense organs is similar to that present when a hallucination or image is experienced. Richardson (1969) also acknowledges that it may prove to be the case that quasiperceptual experiences labeled by us as "images" involve the reactivation of the neurophysiological processes of the central nervous system that are aroused during original perceptions. Along similar lines of argument Erickson (1958) maintains that hypnotic hallucinations are identical to actual perceptions. It is not altogether surprising that research over a long period has aimed to demonstrate that the hypnotist's suggestions about events that do not actually take place lead to consequences identical to those occurring when those events are perceived in fact (for example, Brady & Levitt, 1966; Rosenthal & Mele, 1952; Underwood, 1960).

The special relevance of the "as if" dimension to the association between imaginative activities and hypnosis can be examined in part by analyzing the evidence available to support the position implied by the as if formulation that there is no identity of process between imagination, hypnotic hallucination, and perception.

The first experimental study to add weight to the hypothesis that imaging "revived" perceptual processes was that of Perky (1910), whose findings have been replicated more recently by Segal and Nathan (1964). Data showed that under suitable experimental conditions a supraliminal visual perception may be mistaken for and incorporated into an image of imagination without any suspicion from the observer that an external stimulus is present. Perky interpreted her results as evidence for similarity between the processes of imagination and perception. All her results imply, however, is that an individual can be led to mistake an actual percept for an image. A distinction between processes cannot be made on the basis of introspective evidence alone.

Two conditions must be satisfied before it is legitimate to infer that there is a basic process similarity between imaging or hallucinating and perception. The behavioral product of imaging that is being investigated must be typically only a result of perceptual stimulation, and the *S*'s imaging response must be genuine. If *S* is asked to image the color red for 2 minutes and is then shown a blank card, he will see a green afterimage if the mechanisms of perceiving are akin in structure to those of imaging. Before process identity can be inferred, however, the *E* must be sure that the *S* has actually experienced a genuine negative afterimage. If the experimental design allows one to conclude alternatively that the *S* may be giving his imaging response because it is expected of him, the design cannot be said to indicate unequivocally that imaging involves a similar mechanism to perceiving. No study has satisfied these two requirements for positing similarity of process between imaging and perceiving.

The most striking evidence in support of structural similarity comes from a recent series of experiments by Brooks (1967, 1968). Brooks devised a number of techniques that set imagery and perception into direct competition with each other for the same organizing processes. In one study (Brooks, 1967) *S*s were presented with a series of messages that described spatial relations. Some of these were just spoken, and others spoken but accompanied by a simultaneous exposure of a typewritten copy of the message. After each message *S*s were asked to repeat it verbatim. It was hypothesized that reading the message would lead to less accurate repetition than listening to the message, since listening alone would not conflict with the use of the visual system for visualization of the spatial relations. Results showed that listening to the messages produced less interference with visualization than did reading the messages. Findings suggested that the mechanisms of imagery and those of perception are similar. Results were interpreted to indicate that the reading-visualization conflict resulted from the internal representation of spatial material using mechanisms specialized for *visual* perception. Brooks, however, acknowledged that this interpretation, although persuasive, was tentative. The most important thing about the visualization might not have been its sensory modality, but rather that it was organized quite differently from the verbal message itself. Also, *S*s in the experiment ascribed to visualization a whole range of mental events. Only two *S*s reported what might be judged as a "clear image."

Research on whether hypnotic hallucinations result in an activation of perceptual processes is also inconclusive. Evidence on this issue has shown that *S*s report afterimages to hallucinated colors (Barber, 1959a; Hibler,

1940; Sutcliffe, 1960), but that they may do so because they perceive the demand characteristics present in the situation. Brady and Levitt (1966) have offered data in support of the "reality" of hypnotic hallucinations. They found that hypnotized Ss who reported vivid hallucinations of a visual situation that ordinarily elicited optokinetic nystagmus showed nystagmus under the hallucinating condition. None of the Ss who demonstrated visual hallucinations by this criterion were able to fake the response in the waking state, nor could an independent set of control Ss. It is not surprising, however, that hypnotic Ss did not duplicate their hypnotic behavior and show nystagmus in the waking state. This group was subject to strong demand characteristics for behavioral change. Susceptible Ss could have perceived these cues and been led to expect that nystagmus was no longer required in the waking state, after they had demonstrated it previously in trance.

In summary of the evidence to date, no study supports unequivocally the hypothesis that hypnotic hallucinations or imagined events reinstitute the process of perception. Data are not in conflict with the logical implications of the as if formulation of the role of imagination in hypnosis.

Imaginal events are best conceptualized as serving an "as if" function. Under the direction, implicit or explicit, of the hypnotist, they enable S in a special way to react to suggestions as if they were literally true. The wording of the hypnotist's suggestion and the type of imaginative activity (fantasy or imagery) set limits on just how literal S is in conforming to the hypnotist's suggestions. Suggestions vary considerably in their constraints on S. In a suggestion to dream, S may fantasy freely in response to the hypnotist's instruction. In a suggestion to hallucinate a mutual friend, S is required to act as if a particular person were physically present, but instructions may still implicitly give him the freedom to describe the friend in one of a number of different ways. Under instruction to hallucinate a moving drum, S is required to duplicate even more closely perceptual-type responses; at least, it is the explicit intent of the hypnotist that he do so.

It may well be that the hypnotist's instruction also determines the relative exercise of imagery and fantasy. Insofar as these processes are distinct, imagery serves to reinstitute perceptual experience in a more literal way than fantasy when close correspondence of behavior with perception is requested by the hypnotist. Where imagery is invoked the apparent concrete nature of "something imaged" emphasizes the thing-quality of specific objects as suggested by the hypnotist. Fantasy, however, seems particularly suited to the hypnotic S where suggestions are for make-believe involvement that is relatively unconstrained by the explicit demands of the hypnotist for S to conform to reality. Both processes have in common that they are skills required by S to allow him to behave as if what the hypnotist is saying were true.

As proposed in this way, the as if formulation stresses the function of imaginative activities in hypnosis. It does not lead one necessarily to adopt a role taking account of hypnosis. Hypnotic events are extremely complex and require careful analysis. Role theory may be insufficient to explain them. If the hypnotic *S,* for example, exercises his imaginative capacities and acts as if his imaginings were real, he may do so in such a way that he not only reports his imaginings as true but he himself subjectively experiences them as such. This state of affairs can be explained in a number of different ways. It may result from "nonhypnotic" conditions of the trance setting developing naturally the germ of a belief in reality that is contained in every image; or *S* may have become so involved in the role that he is playing that self and role become de-differentiated; further, a special state of hypnosis may have been induced by the hypnotist which, as its essential characteristic, creates for *S* the delusion that what the hypnotist says is true.

As argued earlier in this chapter, the association between imaginative capacity and hypnotizability may be formulated so that it is consistent with a variety of theories of hypnosis. To the extent that any distinction can justifiably be drawn between role taking and state theories of hypnosis, studies exist that both support and conflict with either approach. Empirical data on the nature of hypnosis aside, the "as if" formulation appears to conceptualize most adequately the important function of imagery and fantasy within the hypnotic setting.

III

Lines of Individual Research

William E. Edmonston, Jr. *is an Associate Professor of Psychology at Colgate University. After receiving his Ph.D. from the University of Kentucky in 1960, he became an Instructor of Medical Psychology and Director of the Psychology Clinic in the Department of Psychiatry of the Washington University School of Medicine (St. Louis). In 1964, he terminated the clinical phase of his career and moved to Colgate, where he could devote a greater portion of his time and energy to teaching. During the academic year 1970–71 he was a Senior Fellow in the Department of Physiology and Biophysics, University of Washington School of Medicine (Seattle). Since 1961, when he received the Bernard E. Gorton Award (First) for meritorious scientific writing in hypnosis for his study on hypnotic age regression, the major portion of his research time has been devoted to hypnosis. His present research interests are the experimental and physiological parameters of hypnosis, the central nervous system physiology of altered states of consciousness and aesthetics. He has been Editor of the* American Journal of Clinical Hypnosis *since 1968.*

Edmonston *presents an experimental analysis of Pavlov's cortical inhibition theory of hypnosis. This theory predicts that as hypnosis deepens there is increasing interference with the voluntary but not with the involuntary components of conditioned responses, due to a progressive spread of cortical inhibition.*

Edmonston points out that previous experimental work on this prediction has been sparse and inconclusive. In a series of painstaking and logically converging studies he unravels the complexities, methodological flaws, and inaccurate interpretations inherent in the research that has centered on the Pavlov predictions. In Edmonston's own studies hypnosis is induced in a simple and neutral way, avoiding complicated instructions that might confuse the observation of primary relationships.

10

The Effects of Neutral Hypnosis on Conditioned Responses

WILLIAM E. EDMONSTON, JR.

> Thus the sight, or even the recalled *idea* of grateful food, causes an
> uncommon flow of spittle into the mouth of a hungry person; and the
> seeing of a lemon cut produces the same effect in many people.
> R. WHYTT, 1763

In the main, hypnotic studies have been concerned with the effects of complex hypnotic phenomena (such as amnesia and age regression) on conditioned responses or the effects of hypnotic induction on complex motor and verbal learning. Few investigations have been conducted on the more basic issue of the effects of neutral hypnosis; that is, the presentation of hypnotic induction instructions without further motivational instructions, on relatively simple conditioned responses.

Conditioned responses and their relationships to hypnosis have been of primary concern to the Russian investigators. Pavlov (1927), in his early work on two dogs (Bek and John), concluded that hypnosis, brought about by prolonged, monotonous environmental stimulation, creates in the cells of the cortex a state of irradiated inhibition. (For a detailed explication of Pavlov's theory see Edmonston, 1967.) In order to account for the loss of motor function during hypnosis in conjunction with the retention of the conditioned alimentary reflex, Pavlov concluded that hypnosis is the inhibitor of

Portions of the work described here were supported by Colgate University Research Council and completed while the author was a Sloan Foundation Fellow. The author is particularly indebted to the following individuals for their assistance in the experiments: Christopher D. Rhoades, John F. Kihlstrom, Mrs. Patricia A. Trumbull, Martin W. Ham, Anthony P. Conti, and Barrett J. Katz.

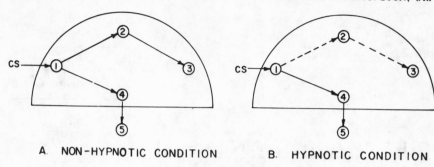

A. NON-HYPNOTIC CONDITION   B. HYPNOTIC CONDITION

1. VISUAL AUDITORY ANALYZERS
2. MOTOR ANALYZER
3. MOTOR RESPONSE CENTER
4. ALIMENTARY ANALYZER
5. ALIMENTARY RESPONSE CENTER

FIGURE 10.1.   *Schematic presentation of Pavlov's theory of the effects of hypnosis on the cerebral cortex.*

motor activity through the inhibition of the cortical motor analyzer. However, the other analyzers retain their excitation during hypnosis, and the salivation portion of the total conditioned response in the classic bell-food paradigm continues through hypnosis.

According to Pavlov, not only are the motor (voluntary) components lost during hypnosis, they are lost in a progressive fashion. Those motor behaviors most active just prior to hypnosis are inhibited first, while those furthest removed in time from induction are the last affected. For example, as hypnosis occurs in the dog, the first motor responses to be inhibited are the masticatory and lingual, the last are the postural. Very clearly, Pavlov felt that hypnosis affected cortical rather than subcortical anatomy, for his observations indicated that motor (cortical) functions subsided while alimentary (subcortical) did not. Figure 10.1 presents a schematic drawing of this idea. In Figure 10.1a, the nonhypnotic condition, the conditioned stimulus (CS) activates a focal point in the cortex, which in turn activates the motor and alimentary analyzers, which then lead to motor and alimentary responses. During hypnosis, however, the motor analyzer and responses are inhibited (the degree depending on the depth of hypnosis), while the alimentary analyzer and responses continue in a state of usual excitation (Figure 10.1b).

Pavlov, then, was quite clear with respect to the portion of the central nervous system involved in hypnosis—the cortex: "We are dealing with a complete inhibition confined exclusively to the cortex, without a concurrent descent of the inhibition into the centres regulating equilibrium and maintenance of posture." He also states: "Thus in this form of sleep [hypnosis] the plane of demarcation between the inhibited regions of the brain and the regions which are free from inhibition seems to pass just beneath the cerebral cortex" (Pavlov, 1927, p. 266). However, while initially separating the alimentary from the motor analyzer, placing the former in the subcortex and the latter in the cortex itself, Pavlov did leave some confusion as to the type of conditioned response that might be affected by hypnosis. This confusion seemed to be resolved by a consideration of hypnotic depth: "all the cases of dissociation of the secretory and motor reactions can be attributed to a different localization of inhibition at the onset of the hypnotic state and in the course of its development" (p. 365). This then was a statement of the progressive irradiation of inhibition over the cortex with increasing hypnotic depth.

In addition, what Pavlov seemed to be implying was that as the hypnotic state developed we might see interference (inhibition) not only with the degree of a given conditioned response, but with different kinds of responses as well. The former point seems to have been well established by Korotkin and Suslova (1951, 1953, 1955a, 1955b, 1955c, 1959, 1960, 1962), who demonstrated a progressive difficulty in the formation of conditioned eyelid responses as the depth of hypnosis increased to a point where they could not be formed at all. Platanov (1959) as well has offered evidence to the effect that hypnosis interferes with the establishment of new conditioned responses and the elicitation of old. In line with Pavlov's notions of motor (voluntary) inhibition under conditions of hypnosis, Platonov's review reported changes in motor chronaxie, which seemed to indicate a similarity between suggested (hypnosis) and natural sleep.

There is not complete unanimity among the Russian investigators. Pavlov and Povorinskii (1953), for example, indicate that motor responses are more rapidly formed in hypnosis, while Livshits (1959) has offered data that seem to be at variance with the general notion of a diminution in conditioned response elicitation during hypnosis. Livshits (1959) conditioned differential vascular dilation and contraction to a buzzer and a bell prior to hypnosis, and then demonstrated that "conditioned reflexes elaborated in the waking state were preserved in the state of hypnosis" (Livshits, 1959, p. 752). Even though Livshits based his conclusion on a single subject (out of the 43 with whom he initiated the study), it is clear from the forgoing discussion of Pavlov's position that the retention of this conditioned response would be expected since it was an involuntary, nonmotor response. Only through a deepening of the hypnotic state would we expect, from Pavlov's viewpoint, any interference (inhibition) with this type of conditioned response.

In addition to the study reported by Livshits, a few non-Russian works have reported no interference with conditioned responses during hypnosis (McCranie & Crasilneck, 1955; H. D. Scott, 1930). However, McCranie and Crasilneck (1955) did find that a voluntary conditioned response (hand withdrawal) disappeared following the addition of age regression instructions to the hypnotic induction, whereas a less voluntary response (eyelid) was uninfluenced. LeCron (1952) earlier had also reported the loss of a conditioned hand withdrawal response during age regression. Although with respect to neutral hypnosis these works did not support the cortical inhibition view, when age regression instructions were added they fit Pavlov's original formulation with respect to inhibited motor responsivity.

Moravek (1968) also showed the inhibition of motor activity under suggested hypnoanesthesia. All 25 subjects who were tapping with their fingers showed motor inhibition during hypnotic anesthesia but not during a nonhypnotic period. In addition, 4 of the subjects were trained to two similar acoustical stimuli, which evoked the motor response. The effect of one of these stimuli was inhibited in the anesthetic hand, but not in the other hand. This inhibition carried over into the nonhypnotic period; the stimulus had lost its ability to elicit the response.

What becomes most clear from this brief survey of the scanty experimental data is that there is "no clear-cut conclusion as to the fate of a previously established conditioned response following the induction of hypnosis" (Plapp & Edmonston, 1965, pp. 378–79). What was needed at that time (1965) was a series of studies systematically investigating the effects of hypnotic induction (neutral hypnosis) on a variety of conditioned responses, some involving voluntary motor behavior and others involving involuntary nonmotor behavior.

The model chosen for the studies in this series under my direction consisted of five basic phases: conditioning, experimental instructions, first extinction period, termination of experimental instructions, and finally, second extinction period. The second study in the series (Plapp, 1967), involving eyelid conditioning, consisted of a slightly different format, although it adhered basically to the general model of the other works. As will be described, conditioning procedures varied with the particular response involved. Experimental instructions in each of the studies consisted of hypnotic induction for one group; instructions to relax, but not to be hypnotized for another group; and other instructional sets as dictated by the variety of control groups employed in each study. Both extinction periods consisted of the presentation of the conditioned stimulus (CS) without reinforcement for a specified number of trials. Instructions countermanding the particular experimental instructions were interposed between the two extinction periods.

Finger Withdrawal Conditioning

According to Pavlov's view, the formation of conditioned responses (CRs) during hypnosis is inhibited. Scott (1930), however, not only found that a finger withdrawal CR could be elaborated more easily in hypnosis than in nonhypnosis, but that the extinction of the response demonstrated continuity from trance to nontrance. The first study in our series (Plapp & Edmonston, 1965) used a slightly different model and, as seen below, produced markedly different results.

Method

Of 30 original volunteer students, 12 served as subjects for this study. Fourteen of the original group did not condition—a problem of no little consequence, as we shall see progressively through this series—and 4 discontinued participation. A conditioned finger withdrawal response was established to a 2000 Hz tone (CS) by pairing the tone with a noxious electric shock (UCS). A conditioning trial consisted of a .5 second CS, a .5 second interval, and a .5 second UCS; intertrial intervals ranged randomly between 20 and 40 seconds. One of every five conditioning trials was designated a test trial (CS presented alone), and the criterion of conditioning was the elicitation of four CRs (finger withdrawal) out of five consecutive test trials.

Once conditioned, the *S*s were equally and randomly divided into two groups, one receiving the eye closure section of the Stanford Hypnotic Susceptibility Scale (SHSS), Form A (Weitzenhoffer & Hilgard, 1959) as a hypnotic induction, and the other instructed to remain comfortable with their eyes closed (Plapp & Edmonston, 1965, p. 380). The experimental group was tested for hypnosis with the hand lowering, arm rigidity, and eye catalepsy portions of the SHSS; the control group was instructed to perform these tasks voluntarily. Following these procedures, 12 extinction trials (CS alone) were presented to each *S* in each group. At this point the hypnosis was terminated for the experimental group, the control group was told to open their eyes, and the second series of 12 extinction trials was presented to all *S*s.

Results

The results of these procedures were quite striking, as can be seen in Figure 10.2. Except for one CR given by one experimental *S* on trial 3, no experimental *S* gave any CRs during the first extinction period. The control group, which was not hypnotized, continued to yield CRs. During the second extinction period, following the termination of the hypnotic condition in the experimental *S*s, we note that the two groups are showing similar patterns of slow extinction.

Discussion

These data are precisely what Pavlov would have predicted: the motor (voluntary) components of conditioned responses are lost during hypnosis. However, it was precisely the voluntary aspects of the finger withdrawal response that posed a problem. Initially, we were willing to attribute the dramatic change in the CR from nonhypnotic to hypnotic condition to the spe-

TABLE 10.1 Summary of experimental design

Group I	Test for hypnotic suscepti-bility	Hypnosis	Conditioning	Presentation of control verbal material I and control verbal II	Extinction I	Hypnosis termination	Extinction II
Group II	"	Presenta-tion of control verbal material I	Conditioning	Presentation of control verbal II and hypnosis	Extinction I	Hypnosis termination	Extinction II
Group III	"	Hypnosis	Conditioning	Presentation of control verbal material I and hypnosis termination	Extinction I	Presentation of control verbal material II	Extinction II

SOURCE: Plapp, 1967, p. 26.

cific hypnotic induction instructions received by the experimental group. However, we were somewhat concerned that the experimental *Ss*, through their personal perception of what should or should not happen during hypnosis, had withheld their response during the first extinction period. Thus, the very behavior that Pavlov held as prima facia evidence for hypnosis is confounded by the fact that the finger withdrawal response has the potential of being manipulated by the subject—without special training.

Quite obviously, one way of assuring that such was not the case was to remove the subject's ability to maintain any control over the response, either before or after conditioning, by the choice of the response to be conditioned. Thus, by choosing a series of progressively less voluntary responses it was possible to eliminate one confounding aspect of this first study, although we may have eliminated the crux of Pavlov's theory in the process. At the very least, we felt that there was further need to investigate hypnosis per se as a separate experimental procedure from hypnotic suggestions such as amnesia, age regression and so forth.

Eyelid Conditioning

As indicated in the general introduction above, the effects of hypnosis on conditioned eyelid responses have been reported in the literature (Korotkin & Suslova, 1951, 1953, 1955a, 1955b, 1955c, 1959, 1960, 1962; McCrainie & Crasilneck, 1955). Korotkin and Suslova (1951) reported that as the "somnabulistic phase" of hypnosis is reached there is increasing difficulty in achieving a conditioned eyelid response. In those *Ss* where the response could be achieved, acquisition was greatly retarded. These same findings were replicated in the 1959 and 1960 studies of these same authors. With respect to McCrainie and Crasilneck (1955), both a hand withdrawal and an eyelid response were conditioned in two groups of six *Ss* each. Contrary to the findings of Korotkin and Suslova, the induction of hypnosis did not affect either response. It was only after hypnotic age regression was introduced that the hand withdrawal response disappeared. The eyelid response, on the other hand, was not affected.

Up until 1967 these investigations were the only studies offering some direct measure of the effects of neutral hypnosis on a conditioned eyelid response; yet the findings of Korotkin and Suslova are at variance with those of McCranie and Crasilneck. Reviewing these and related portions of the literature, Plapp (1967) concluded that "although motor conditioned responses established in the waking state and tested for in the hypnotic state appeared during extinction to be inhibited in those hypnotized Ss by either neutral hypnosis, hypnosis plus age regression, or hypnosis plus stimulus-lessening or stimulus-absent instructions, controls have not been adequate to determine whether this effect is due simply to the hypnosis treatment, to specific instructions during hypnosis, or to pre-existing differences between

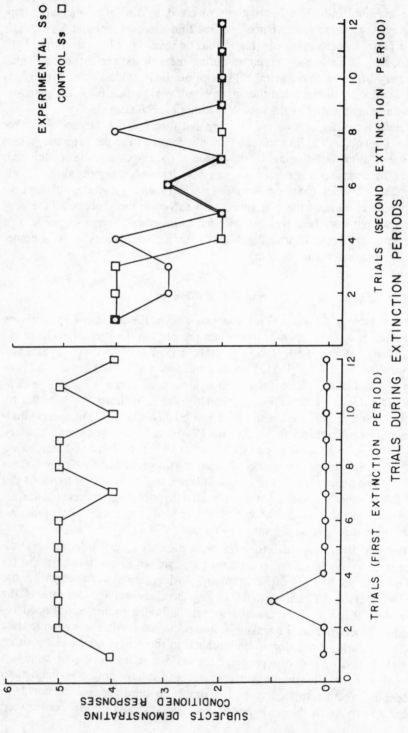

FIGURE 10.2. The number of subjects giving CRs on each extinction trial (From Plapp & Edmonston, 1965, p. 380).

experimental and control Ss" (Plapp, 1967, p. 10). With these difficulties in mind, Plapp (1967) undertook to investigate the effects of neutral hypnosis on both the acquisition and extinction of a conditioned eyelid response. In addition, he obtained reaction time, electrodermal, and plethysmographic orienting response measures in the course of his data collection.

Method

Table 10.1 summarizes the experimental design employed by Plapp (1967). Plapp's Group II follows the model set forth in the finger withdrawal study above and followed in the subsequent studies to be reported. Therefore it is this group on which we will focus our main attention. The inclusion of the other two groups stems from Plapp's interest in not only the effects of hypnosis on an already established CR, but on the acquisition of a CR as well. All of Plapp's subjects were pretested through a tape-recorded presentation of the Harvard Group Scale of Hypnotic Susceptibility (Shor & Orne, 1962). Hypnotic induction instructions were an adaptation of the Stanford Scale of Hypnotic Susceptibility (Weitzenhoffer & Hilgard, 1959), and the other verbal materials were taken from a book on the topic of social mobility.

Plapp used 35 acquisition trials that were defined as the presentation of a signal light (10 seconds), followed by a tone (450 msec.) whose termination coincided with a 60 msec. air puff directed at the right eye of the *S*. The signal light continued for 2 more seconds after this sequence, during which the *S* was to push a reaction time key. Each extinction period involved 10 trials in which all the stimuli with the exception of the air puff were presented.

Results

Figure 10.3 depicts the per cent of conditioned eyeblinks occurring during acquisition and the two extinction periods for Plapp's three groups; Groups I and III received the acquisition trial during hypnosis, and Group II received them prior to hypnotic induction. Hypnosis was induced in Group II prior to the first extinction period and terminated prior to the second extinction period. For all groups there was a decided reduction in the frequency of Ss yielding a CR on the first extinction trial as related to the last acquisition trial, but this was not unexpected due to the intervention of another experimental procedure—instructions.

Plapp notes that during the first extinction period: "following the induction of hypnosis in what was originally the nonhypnosis group (Group II), the number of conditioned eyeblinks falls to a low level for almost all Ss, with this reduction in CRs being greater than for Ss hypnotized prior to acquisition (Groups I and III)" (1967, p. 54). This finding is elaborated in further discussion of the data: "Only Group II Ss, hypnotized prior to the first extinction period, gave a significantly reduced number of eyeblink CRs

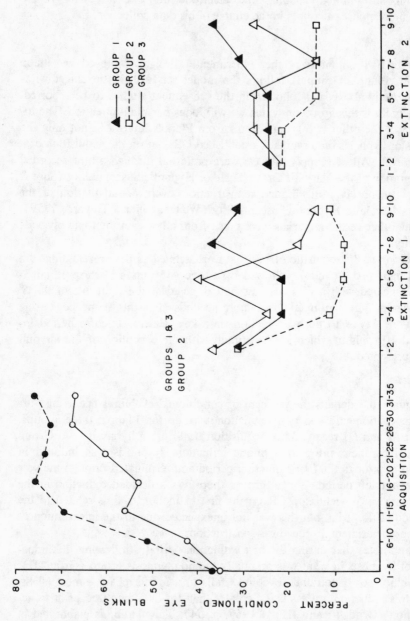

FIGURE 10.3. *Per cent conditioned eyeblinks over blocks of acquisition and extinction trials (From Plapp, 1967, p. 39).*

on the first extinction as compared with that of the last acquisition trial. Further, examination of Figure 10.3 suggests that extinction was more rapid for this group. The number of CRs given by Group II Ss decreases more rapidly and remains at a lower level during the first extinction period" (p. 71). However, the analysis of the second extinction period failed to detect a conclusive reversal effect for Group II, as had occurred in the finger withdrawal study. Finally, one other measure taken during this experiment is also of significance to us in our interpretation of Pavlov's views of hypnosis. Plapp found that the reaction time measure (a more voluntary motor response) significantly increases for Group II following the induction of hypnosis.

Discussion

The eyelid findings are in direct contradiction to those of McCranie and Crasilneck (1955), who did not find a decrement in either finger withdrawal or eyelid conditioning upon the induction of hypnosis. Both the eyelid and the reaction time responses tend to support and elaborate further the findings of Korotkin and Suslova and the theoretical position of Pavlov. Both of the responses, which contain clear elements of potential voluntary control, were influenced by the induction of hypnosis. However, the nature of the eyelid response does raise some doubt as to the accuracy of Pavlov's cortical-subcortical demarcation of hypnotic influence. Marquis and Hilgard (1936) pointed out that the response is not dependent upon cortical areas for its maintenance. Ablation of the occipital lobes did not disturb a conditioned lid response, thus indicating a subcortical locus of action. Although eyelid responses may contain voluntary control potential, they also contain *both* cortical and subcortical elements, the former being less prominent as conditioning is established.

In spite of a general overall failure of hypnosis to influence physiological measures, Plapp did find a significant negative correlation between the number of spontaneous electrodermal fluctuations (SF) and hypnotic susceptibility. Highly susceptible subjects tended to give few SF, while less susceptible subjects tended to yield more. From this finding Plapp concluded that "the effects of hypnosis may go beyond the primarily voluntary kind of response to also depress responses which are not directly under voluntary control and are not obviously subject to S-expectations regarding hypnotic effects" (1967, p. 67). Such a suggestion also runs counter to Pavlov's theory, but will be taken up in the studies to follow.

Electrodermal Conditioning

EXPERIMENT 1

The next logical step in our series of studies was to investigate the effects of neutral hypnosis on a less voluntary CR—the electrodermal response

(EDR). Prior to the report of this study (Edmonston, 1968), no investigation of the effects of neutral hypnosis on EDR conditioning had been reported. A number of investigators had reported data concerning the alteration of electrodermal responses during hypnosis (Barber & Coules, 1959; Davis & Kantor, 1935; Edmonston & Pessin, 1966; Estabrooks, 1930; Fehr & Stern, 1967; Levine, 1930; O'Connell & Orne, 1962; and Pessin, Plapp, & Stern, 1968), but none yielded data regarding the conditioning of this response.

Method

The basic methodology outlined in the introduction was used: conditioning, experimental instructions, first extinction period, termination of experimental instructions, and finally, a second extinction period. In the initial portion of this study 45 individuals served as Ss. They were equally divided into three groups, the first two of which were equated for Harvard Group Susceptibility Scale Scores (Shor & Orne, 1962) and the third of which contained Ss of far less susceptibility. The groups were equated also for mean Maudsley neuroticism and extroversion scores, and age (see Table 10.2). Following 20 habituation trials to a 7 second, 500 Hz tone, each of the Ss received 20 conditioning trials, which paired the same tone with a .5 second electric pulse. Following the administration of the experimental instructions, 10 extinction trials (tone alone) were presented. The instructions were then countermanded and 10 more extinction trials were offered. The first experimental groups (group 1) received as experimental instructions a tape-recorded hypnotic induction procedure based on the eye closure portion of the Stanford Hypnotic Susceptibility Scale, Form B (Weitzenhoffer & Hilgard, 1959). The second experimental group (group 2) was told: "Let yourself become very deeply relaxed but do not allow yourself to enter hypnosis; allow yourself to become deeply relaxed but do not become hypnotized" five times during a 17-minute time control period. The final, control group (group 3) sat in the experimental room for 17 minutes without instructions.

Some time later a fourth group was run in the same experimental procedures; the results were not reported with the original data (Edmonston,

TABLE 10.2   Means and Standard Deviations of Subjects' Ages, Harvard Group Scale Scores, and Maudsley Neuroticism and Extroversion Scores

| | Group 1 | | Group 2 | | Group 3 | | Group 4 | |
	M	SD	M	SD	M	SD	M	SD
Age	27.13	8.11	30.93	8.45	29.13	7.27	18.83	2.76
Harvard	6.07	3.43	5.93	2.55	2.93	1.12	5.27	1.92
Neuroticism	25.93	13.04	25.13	13.07	19.60	9.02	—	—
Extroversion	32.33	8.58	34.40	8.29	30.33	8.23	—	—

SOURCE: Edmonston, 1968, p. 19.

1968), but will be reported here. During the running of the first three groups, concern developed with the notion of how the *S*s would perform if in fact they knew what the experimenters wanted of them. That is, what if a group of subjects was told that neutral hypnosis abolishes a conditioned electrodermal response? Thus, almost a year after the original data collection, a fourth group was added to the study. An instruction sheet was presented to the *S*s informing them of our desires and expectations for the results of the study. Basically, the question was, Can a subject role play to the extent of abolishing a conditioned nonvoluntary response? This group was equated with the others on Harvard scores and received the same hypnotic induction at the same time in the methodological sequence as the first experimental group.

Results

Records were kept of the following measures with respect to the electrodermal response on all *S*s during all of the periods: electrodermal orienting responses (OR), electrodermal conditioned responses (CR), electrodermal spontaneous fluctuations (SF). Figure 10.4 shows the results of the ORs. All four groups performed in the same manner during the habituation period to the CS—the tone. For the conditioning period, however, a rather striking difference appears among the groups. Groups 1, 2, and 3 of the original study show no significant differences with respect to ORs during the conditioning period. We see, of course, an increase of these responses over the last block of trials of habituation and then a diminution of these responses over the blocks of conditioning trials. Group 4 is the curiosity here, in that it shows a decided difference from the other three groups. Since at this point in the study, the only difference between group 4 and the other groups was that group 4 knew what was expected, it is rather striking to see this significant diminution in the OR. Either a subject selection bias had occurred or the *S*s were able, in some manner or form, to reduce the ORs to the tone during conditioning. The two extinction periods show no differences among groups on the ORs. Group 4 is consistently lower than the other groups, but this can be attributed to the reduced number of ORs during the conditioning. Thus, it would seem, as Plapp (1967) concluded earlier, that the induction of neutral hypnosis, as opposed to relaxation, does not affect the electrodermal OR, whether the *S*s are knowledgeable or not with respect to the expected outcome.

Figure 10.5 shows the electrodermal CRs during the conditioning and two extinction periods. A conditioned response was a drop in *S* resistance of 300 ohms or more, between 3.5 and 8.5 seconds following the onset of the tone stimulation. There are two things to notice about the conditioning aspect of Figure 10.5. The first is that both group 1 and group 4 (group 4 is the knowledgeable group) showed a rather clear habituation pattern during the conditioning; group 1 from the first block to the last block of trials, and

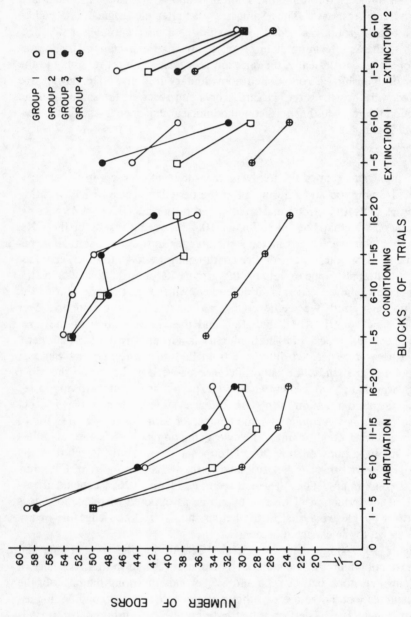

FIGURE 10.4. Total number of EDORs for each group over blocks of trials during habituation, conditioning, first, and second extinction periods (From Edmonston, 1968, p. 19).

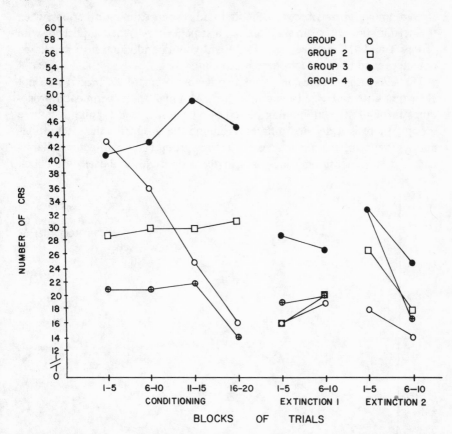

FIGURE 10.5. *Total number of CRs for each group over blocks of trials during conditioning, first, and second extinction periods (From Edmonston, 1968, p. 21).*

group 4 from the third block to the last block of trials. This finding in group 4 may not be unusual because those Ss, after all, knew the results anticipated. In fact, they had shown a decided difference in the number of orienting responses produced during this period. The real puzzle is group 1, because these subjects did not know the purpose of the study. Perhaps, as has been suggested, the idea was inadvertently conveyed to the Ss in this group that they were to demonstrate fewer and fewer conditioned responses as the experiment progressed. Even if this were essentially true, it offers no explanation as to how the Ss might have done this. That they did seem to habituate during conditioning in a manner unlike the two major control groups is evident.

A covariance analysis between the last block of conditioning trials and the first block of first extinction trials demonstrated no significant differences among groups. In addition, no significant differences were demonstrated among groups between the first and second extinction periods when the termination of neutral hypnotic instructions was accomplished with groups 1 and 4. Thus, we concluded that hypnotic induction instructions do not affect conditioned electrodermal responses.

However, this conclusion seemed somehow premature, since it was not clear that CRs had ever been established. Although the experimental procedures through the conditioning period had been identical for the first three groups, there is a decided difference among the groups in their conditionability. It appears that the main experimental group (group 1) actually habituated, despite continuing increases in the amplitude of the electric shock

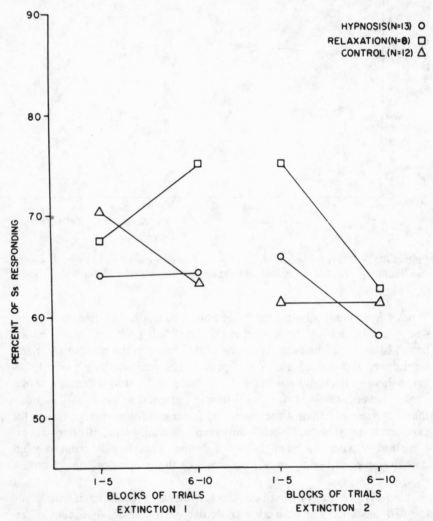

FIGURE 10.6.   *Per cent of subjects meeting conditioning criterion who yielded CRs during the first and second extinction periods.*

for all Ss in order to avoid this very phenomenon. In fact, there was some question as to whether any conditioning at all occurred over this period of 20 trials in the groups. Notation of this failure of conditioning leads to the second phase of this investigation, described below.

EXPERIMENT 1A

Although the covariance analyses above indicated that neutral hypnosis had no effect on the level of electrodermal conditioned responding, more substantial evidence was needed as to the degree of conditioning obtained before stable conclusions could be drawn. While the groups as units did not demonstrate consistent conditioning, certain individuals within each group did meet a reasonable criterion of conditioning.

Method

The data for those Ss who yielded at least four conditioned electrodermal responses (as defined above) out of five consecutive conditioning trials were selected for further analysis. In group 1, 10 Ss conditioned; in group 2, 8; in group 3, 12; and in group 4, 3. The conditioned members of groups 1 and 4 were combined into one hypnosis group and compared with the other two groups during the two extinction periods.

Results

Figure 10.6 presents the percentage of Ss yielding an electrodermal CR during the first and second extinction periods. Recall that the experimental instructions (hypnosis for groups 1 and 4, and relaxation for group 2) were introduced before the beginning of the first extinction period and terminated prior to the start of the second.

These data are commensurate with those from the total groups. Neutral hypnosis did not affect an electrodermal CR in any different manner than either no instructions or instructions to relax. In fact, the group that demonstrated the most variability was the relaxation group (group 2), although, with the exception of the first trial of the first extinction period, these three groups did not differ.

Discussion

Whether one looks at the data for all the group members (experiment 1) or just for those Ss who conditioned, the conclusion is the same—neutral hypnosis does not influence conditioned electrodermal responses. At this point the series of studies seemed to be supporting Pavlov's original contention that hypnosis inhibits the motor analyzer, leaving the other analyzers (alimentary, in his case) relatively uninhibited, so that CRs or portions of CRs not involving the voluntary musculature would continue in essentially the same form as we might expect in the unhypnotized person. Yet, we were not fully satisfied with our electrodermal data and continued our investigations in the following form.

EXPERIMENT 2

Method

In the context of a study of the effects of neutral hypnosis on conditioned heart rate, electrodermal measures were also recorded. Again we used undergraduate and graduate students and their wives as Ss. While we used the same basic methodology as before, the stimulus condition was considerably different. Instead of the simple tone and shock pairing used before, the stimuli sequence was as follows during the conditioning period: (a) a 500 Hz tone (6 second duration), (b) a flash of light (1/1500 sec.) 6 feet and to the left oblique, from the eyes, (c) the illumination of a 200 watt bare incandescent light bulb in the same position as the flash (6 seconds), and (d) a blast of a 12 volt auto horn located behind and beneath the subject's chair (6 seconds). The subject was seated in a comfortable, reclined chair with EDR electrodes attached to his right index and ring fingers and EKG electrodes attached to his right and left wrists.

Our original intention was to utilize the tone as a CS and the flash and light as the UCS for a conditioned electrodermal response. The light was also to serve as a CS for heart rate conditioning, with the auto horn as the UCS. However, the startle effect of a flash of light is not nearly as long-lived as an electric pulse, and consequently all of our Ss habituated to the flash-light within several trials. On the other hand, the auto horn, being a meaningful stimulus in our society, maintained its startle effect throughout 20 conditioning trials for several subjects, who developed electrodermal CRs to the light-horn pairing in the sequence.

On the basis of the previous studies it was apparent to us that the most meaningful control group for hypnotic studies was the relaxed, but not hypnotized group. Consequently, the 20 Ss of this study were equally divided, on the basis of Harvard Group Scale Susceptibility Scores (Shor & Orne, 1962), into two groups, one receiving the same hypnotic induction instructions and the other receiving the same relaxation instructions as described in the first electrodermal study. Instructions were introduced before the first extinction period (after conditioning) and terminated prior to the second extinction period. Again, both extinction periods were 10 trials long, a trial being the presentation of the tone and flash-light stimuli alone.

Results

The groups showed little evidence of conditioning. However, using the same criterion as before (four CRs out of five consecutive trials), three hypnosis and two relaxation Ss were selected for further evaluation. The data from the two extinction periods yielded the same conclusion as before: Neutral hypnosis has little or no affect on conditioned electrodermal responses. Five CRs were elicited from one hypnotized S during the first extinction period, and one during the second. One other hypnotized *S* gave one CR on the second trial of the second extinction period, and the other *S* in this group gave no CRs during either extinction period. Likewise, one relaxed *S* yielded two CRs during the first and one during the second extinction period, while the other gave only two CRs, both during the second extinction period.

EXPERIMENT 3

Dissatisfied with the post hoc approach outlined in experiments 1a and 2, we undertook a final brief study of the effects of hypnosis on the electrodermal response. Instead of groups of *S*s our efforts were concentrated on four deep trance *S*s with whom we had worked during the summer of 1969 (three faculty wives and one student wife). Each of the *S*s participated in at least 10 hours of trance phenomena including hypnotic amnesia, age regression, and hallucinatory behavior. With each we had established a signal for rapid induction, so that they were able to reach "depths" of between 90 and 100 on a subjectively reported depth scale of 0 to 100.

Method

Electrodermal conditioning was attempted in the same manner as in experiment 1, using a 500 Hz tone as the CS and a randomly increasing electric pulse delivered to the right arm as the UCS. The criterion of conditioning was the elicitation of a CR in four out of five consecutive trials.

Results

Although upwards of 60 trials were given to some of the *S*s, only one developed a stable conditioned electrodermal response.

This particular subject conditioned within 38 conditioning trials, yielding her cluster of criterion CRs on trials 34, 35, 36, and 38. An individually induced deep hypnotic trance was obtained, with the subject reporting a "depth" of 95. (She had previously engaged in clinicially authentic age regression, hallucinations, and amnesia at "depths" of 92.) Her performance during the extinction periods that followed is most instructive. During the first 10 presentations of the tone alone—in hypnosis—she yielded four CRs, on trials 1, 2, 3, and 4. During the second 10 presentations of the tone alone —after the termination of hypnosis—no CRs were elicited. What we see then is an unremarkable extinction record; the induction of hypnosis had no effect on the usual processes that we might expect under normal (nonhypnotic) conditions.

Discussion

Thus, it seems that our post hoc procedures employed in experiments 1a and 2 were justified, and did not lead to spurious conclusions. In this brief study of one *S*, we assured ourselves of a conditioned response and of a degree of hypnotic trance that should have influenced the CR, if it were in fact to be influenced. At this point our evidence appears to yield the interpretation that as the S loses voluntary control over the response conditioned, the effects of neutral hypnosis are minimized, whether or not the physiological loci are cortical, subcortical, or both.

Heart Rate Conditioning

One of the major difficulties with studies of conditioned heart rate (HR) is the designation of the response. The literature is far from clear on whether its nature is accelerative or decelerative. Comparison across studies is an added difficulty because of the noncomparability of stimuli, intra- and intertrial intervals, and number of conditioning trials. Some investigators have reported acceleration as the conditioned HR response (Zeaman, Deane, & Wegner, 1954; Zeaman & Wegner, 1958), while others found deceleration to be the form of the response (DeLeon, 1964; Notterman, Schoenfeld, & Bersh, 1952a, 1952b; Zeaman & Wegner, 1954). Both auditory (Notterman, Schoenfeld, & Bersh, 1952a, 1952b; Zeaman & Wegner, 1954) and visual (DeLeon, 1964) stimuli have been used as CS, and both electric shocks (Notterman, Schoenfeld, & Bersh, 1952a, 1952b; Zeaman, Deane, & Wegner, 1954; Zeaman & Wegner, 1954, 1958) and loud noises (DeLeon, 1964) have served as UCS. The number of conditioning trials also appears to influence the interpretation of the response; that is, a small number of trials (11) appears to lead to an accelerative form of the CR, while a longer series of trials (20) produces, at first, an acceleration, then a deceleration (Dawson, 1953). Even this finding does not appear to be stable, because one factor that seems crucial is the precise time in the conditioning sequence when the response is measured. Needless to say, the state of human HR conditioning is itself in a state of unsteady flux. In fact, even to attempt to use such an unknown response to measure the effects of another as yet unknown (hypnosis) may have been premature.

Few studies of the effects of hypnosis on heart rate per se have appeared in the literature, and here too the results seem to be in conflict. Jenness and Wible (1937), Tsinkin (1930a, 1930b), Whitehorn et al. (1932), and Wible and Jenness (1936) reported a deceleration upon induction, while True and Stephenson (1951) reported an acceleration. Crasilneck and Hall (1959), after a review of this literature, concluded: "In summary, heart rate normally declines in neutral hypnosis, but may increase as the result of specific psychodynamics or induction techniques" (1959, pp. 19–20). They felt that the decelerative findings were due to the general relaxation inherent in most induction procedures. No investigations of the effects of hypnosis on conditioned HR have appeared in the literature, and only one study of the effects of neutral hypnosis on a conditioned plethysmographic response has been reported (Livshits, 1959), with negative results on one *S*. May and Edmonston (1966) have also reported that plethysmographic responses to startle stimuli are unaffected by hypnotic induction.

Two studies of the effects of neutral hypnosis on conditioned HR have been conducted in our laboratories.

EXPERIMENT 1

Method

Twenty-four male undergraduates, matched into four groups on the basis of performance on the SHSS, Form A (Weitzenhoffer & Hilgard, 1959) served as *S*s for the first study. In one group (1), conditioning occurred during hypnosis, extinction after hypnosis termination; in another (2), both conditioning and extinction were carried out without hypnosis, while in a third group (3) both the conditioning and extinction trials were during hypnosis. The final group (4) was conditioned prior to hypnosis and received extinction trials after induction. Induction procedures were tape recordings of the eye-closure instructions of the SHSS; time control instructions consisted of two taped short stories of an equivalent time period.

A 10 watt 120 volt white light bulb served as the CS, with the same auto horn described in the electrodermal experiment 2 as the UCS. Both stimuli durations were 6 seconds, their consecutive presentations constituting one conditioning trial. Ten habituation trials (light alone) preceded 20 conditioning trials (both stimuli), after which 10 extinction trials (light alone) were presented. Appropriate instructions were interjected into this sequence in accord with the group to which the particular *S* was assigned. The habituation trials were presented to ascertain their necessity in future studies; habituation for the light stimulus was found to be unnecessary, because HR shows no natural response—either increase or decrease—to this form of visual stimulation.

Results

All four groups demonstrated a statistically significant increase in HR between the last five trials (6–10) of habituation and the first five of conditioning, but there were no differences among groups on the first five trials of the extinction period. This finding was noted despite the fact that there had been a change in experimental conditionings prior to the onset of extinction for groups 1 and 4. Thus, it appeared from these results that a conditioned increase in HR was unaffected by either the induction of hypnosis or by trance termination, when the conditioning occurred during hypnosis. Neutral hypnosis did not appreciably affect a conditioned HR. However, this finding remains in some doubt because of the nature of the conditioned HR obtained in this and the follow-up study.

Discussion

As it turned out, about all that could be ascertained from this investigation was that, given the stimuli used and their specific time relationships, a conditioned HR is accelerative in form, but only for a very short duration of trials. The conditioned HR of this and the following study seemed to reach a maximum during the second (this exerpiment) or third (the following experiment) block of conditioning trials (6–10 or 11–15). What seems to this author to be most outstanding about HR is not its conditionability but its adaptability in the form of rapid habituation to novel stimuli.

EXPERIMENT 2

The second HR conditioning study was begun as the first was being completed. The procedures have been previously described in experiment 2 of the electrodermal conditioning series. Instead of the four groups used by Conti (1968), 20 Ss were divided into two groups: a hypnosis group and a relaxation control group. The Ss, composed of graduate students and student wives, were divided such that the two groups were comparable with respect to Harvard Group Scale Susceptibility Scores (Shor & Orne, 1962).

Twenty conditioning and two periods of 10 extinction trials each were given to all Ss. The same hypnotic induction and relaxation instructions as used in the EDR experiment 1 were introduced prior to the first extinction period and countermanded before the second. Measurement consisted of tabulating the HR in beats per 6 second periods (pre-CS; CS, light; UCS, horn) summed across Ss in blocks of five trials each. In addition, the number of beats during the 6-second periods directly preceding and following the stimuli sequence were similarly tabulated and grouped. Since the light served as the CS, the main evaluation was of potential shifts in HR during this period in both the conditioning and extinction trials.

Results

We discovered that no matter whether we compared beats per unit time or a ratio of the number of beats during the light period to those in either or both of the preceding 6-second periods, no statistically discernible conditioned HR was evident in the groups as units. In fact, in the groups as groups no appreciable change in HR was noted even during the UCS (horn) period. Without the elaboration of a CR, the groups as units could not be used to evaluate the effects of neutral hypnosis. Once again we reverted to looking to the data of those few subjects (two hypnosis Ss and two relaxation Ss) in whom a conditioned response of reasonable magnitude had been developed.

Even the evaluation of these few data posed some presentation problems (see Shearn, 1961). When using a change of rate as a response, the measure tabulated must be a ratio of some sort, most preferably between the rates of an ongoing rate period and a rate period that has potentially changed. In our case an increase (Conti, 1968) HR should occur across trials during the CS (light) period. This increase should be absolute and yet relative to the pre-CS 6-second period. However, in addition, we should also observe a decrease in HR across trials during the UCS (horn) period as conditioning occurs. A presentation of data for this investigation must then include the data from all three periods (pre-CS, CS, and UCS) in a manner such that the progressive increase HR during CS and decrease HR during the other two periods is clearly evident.

Figure 10.7 presents the average beats per 6 seconds averaged across blocks of five trials each during the pre-CS, CS, and UCS periods for two of the Ss from the relaxation control group. Looking first at the conditioning trials, we see that the HR during the pre-CS period remains fairly constant, with the exception of the increase (3 beats/min.) during the second block of trials (6–10). The HR also increases during these same five trials during the horn presentation (1/25 beats/min.), but then decreases (3 beats/min.) as the trials continue. On the other hand, during CS period, these Ss yielded an increase HR that maximized during conditioning trials 11–15 (5.7 beats/min.) and leveled off at 3 beats/min. by trial 20. Five sets of instructions to relax but not to become hypnotized were presented during the next 17 minutes, followed by 10 extinction trials. Following the instructions, an average drop in HR of 5 beats/min. was noted. As can be seen in Figure 10.7, this new level of HR did not change during the first five extinction trials for any of the measurement periods. In fact, for both the UCS and the CS a continued drop (2 beats/min.) occurs as the first extinction period progresses.

Instructions to become more alert followed. During the second set of extinction trials there appears an initial increase in HR during the CS period (2 beats/min.), followed by a decrease of 4 beats/min. as the extinction continues. The initial increase can be attributed to spontaneous recovery. Both the pre-CS and UCS periods show a progressive increase HR across these last 10 extinction trials.

Turning now to the data for the two Ss from the hypnotic group (Figure 10.8), we see similar rate patterns during the conditioning trials, except that the habituation during the pre-CS and UCS periods is more marked than for the Ss in the control group. During the pre-CS period the HR drops 3 beats/min. from the beginning to the end of the conditioning with a maximum drop of 7 beats/min. between the second and third blocks of conditioning trials. With respect to the UCS period during conditioning there is a progressive habituation across trials amounting finally to 8 beats/min. However, during the CS period no such habituation is evident. Between the beginning of the conditioning and the third block of trials (11–15) the HR increases 2.3 beats/min. and then falls approximately to its initial level.

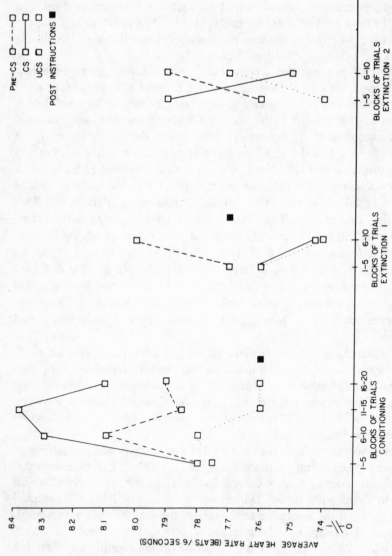

FIGURE 10.7. Average heart rate (beats/6-second periods) measures in two relaxation subjects during the pre-CS, CS, and UCS periods throughout the conditioning and first and second extinction periods.

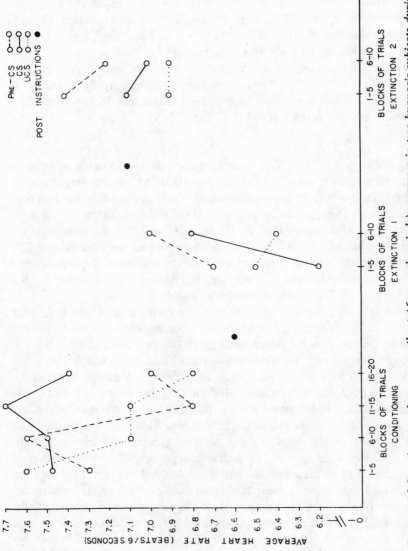

FIGURE 10.8. *Average heart rate (beats/6-second periods) measures in two hypnosis subjects during the pre-CS, CS, and UCS periods throughout the conditioning and first and second extinction periods.*

Hypnotic induction instructions (electrodermal conditioning experiment 1) were introduced prior to the first extinction period, following which there was a decrease of 8 beats/min. (as compared to 5 beats/min. for the control *S*s) prior to the beginning of the first extinction trial. During the CS period of the first five extinction trials there was a further decrease of 4 beats/min. (as compared to no decrease for the control *S*s). The pre-CS and UCS periods showed no appreciable change during this block of extinction trials. As this extinction period progresses, both the pre-CS and the CS periods yield increasing HRs, the UCS showing a slight opposite trend.

With the termination of the hypnotic instructions the HR reverts to a level 5 beats/min. above that immediately following hypnotic induction. The second extinction series of trials yielded unremarkable data in all three measurement time periods (pre-CS, CS, and UCS).

Discussion

As with the Conti (1968) investigation, HR conditioning appears to reach its maximum effect within the first 10 to 15 conditioning trials. In both studies it was clear that although some degree of conditioning had been achieved with some *S*s, the introduction of the different instructions did not take optimal advantage of the CR. Because of that fact it was difficult to say precisely what effect the hypnotic instructions had on conditioned HR. However, in this second study we were able to introduce the instructional sets while the conditioned HR was still in effect, at least for four *S*s. But here again the interpretation of results is difficult.

What appears to be a dramatic elimination of the conditioned HR in the two hypnotized *S*s as compared to the two control *S*s may be attributable to a subtle difference in the instructions given the two groups. Relaxation *S*s were told to relax only five times during the 17 minutes in which the hypnotized *S*s received continual instructions for trance development. Both groups showed an appreciably decreased HR following instructions (5 beats/min. for the relaxed; 8 beats/min. for the hypnotized), so that it may be that the intermittent nature of the relaxation instructions forestalled what would also have been a dramatic decreased HR for that group, had their instructions been continuous throughout the instruction period. The interpretation of what appears to be the elimination of a conditioned nonvoluntary response by neutral hypnosis must await further studies in which relaxation instructions are as continuous in presentation as hypnotic induction instructions.

The weight of evidence to this point would indicate that the elimination of the conditioned HR in two *S*s was an artifact of instructional differences between groups, and this interpretation seems most likely. However, if the finding is not an instructional artifact then we have what may be an inconsistency in our series of studies, which must be resolved on some other basis. Either way, further study of HR is indicated.

Conclusion

Pavlov's theory poses two mutually interrelated problems; that of the locus of hypnotic inhibition, and that of the *S*'s voluntary control over the responses influenced by hypnosis. To state that hypnosis involves the irradiation of cortical inhibition is an oversimplification. While it seems obvious that some cortical functions are involved in the perception of the various conditioned and unconditioned stimuli of these studies, the separation between cortical and subcortical involvement in conditioning is not a simple matter. We have already pointed out that eyelid conditioning, although involving certain cortical areas, is not dependent upon these areas for the maintenance of the CR (Marquis & Hilgard, 1936). The fact that decortication does not appreciably impair classical Pavlovian learning alone indicates the involvement of subcortical areas (Campbell, 1965).

Several investigators of hypnosis (Akstein, 1965; Arnold, 1959; and Roberts, 1960) have suggested blockages either in the reticular activating system itself or between this system and cortical functioning. The effects of such a blockage on conditioned responses would seem to be response dependent, for our data and those of other investigators indicate the inhibition of some CRs, but not others. Either the inhibitory effects of hypnosis are much more widespread than Pavlov originally supposed or there is another factor operative in the investigations. Initially, the apparent differential influence of hypnosis would lead us to consider the voluntary aspects of responses as the third prime factor (the other two being cortical and subcortical). However, we suspect that it is not the "willful" control wielded by the *S*, but the general inhibition of the entire organism inherent in hypnosis, yet seldom isolated through experimental design.

All of the CRs used in our studies and those of other investigators have both cortical and subcortical components. To erect a cortical inhibition theory of hypnosis on the basis of the action of CRs during hypnosis is to confound both the process (hypnosis) and the measure (CRs).

For example, the works of Korotkin and Suslova (1951, 1953, 1955a, 1955b, 1955c, 1959, 1960, 1962), taken in conjunction with the demonstrated relationship between conditionability and hypnotizability (Das, 1958a, 1958b), would indicate that these two functions may be mutually interfering, and therefore involve similar or the same neurophysiological mechanisms and analyzers regardless of their cortical or subcortical locale. It may just be that the incompatibility of *simultaneous* hypnosis and conditioning is attributable to the fact that both utilize the same mechanisms. Perhaps hypnosis subjects make double use of the same physiological mechanisms, adding to the facilitation of any responses (hypnosis being one) involving these areas when the responses are separately but not simultaneously elicited. In that case separate measures of conditionability and hypnotizability would be positively related, while simultaneous hypnosis and conditioning would be mutually interfering.

However, the studies reported here have demonstrated that the situation is not one of simply overloading the neurophysiology. The introduction of hypnotic induction instructions between the conditioning and the extinction of a response leads to the elimination or drastic reduction of responses that contain voluntary, motor components (finger withdrawal, eyelid) but not of responses whose voluntary components are minimal (electrodermal, HR— the latter clearly needing further study). The trend of these investigations leads us to believe that hypnotic induction influences solely the voluntary motor systems of the organism, regardless of cortical or subcortical considerations. It is through the general relaxation inherent in hypnosis that the induction exercises its influence. Therefore, the one crucial factor that must be accounted for in evaluations of the influence of neutral hypnosis is the concomitant relaxation state. Both nonhypnotic relaxation and hypnosis involve the relaxation of the voluntary motor systems. To hypnotize a S and then point to a motor response that has been adversely affected as proof that hypnosis affects the motor system, without also showing that relaxation without hypnosis does not similarly affect the same system, is to confound the interpretation of the data. This has been the basic fault with Pavlov's, other Russian, our own finger withdrawal, and Plapp's eyeblink studies.

ELECTRODERMAL SPONTANEOUS FLUCTUATIONS

In the series of electrodermal conditioning studies, the importance of determining the influence of relaxation per se on the response measured became fully apparent. The state of the organism during hypnosis was clarified by the electrodermal SF data from experiments 1 and 2. Earlier, Fehr and Stern (1967) had suggested that the hypnotic S is more vigilant and less responsive to extraneous internal and external stimuli. This conclusion was based on a reduced number of SFs during hypnosis. The more basic factor, to which our data seem to point, is the state of relaxation of the S, which allows him to exclude the influence of other stimuli including CS, so long as they pertain to voluntary functions.

In Figure 10.9 we see the electrodermal SFs during the five periods of the study (habituation, conditioning, instruction period, first extinction, and second extinction) for the four groups of experiment 1.

The differences between group 3 and groups 1 and 4 may, of course, be attributable to some susceptibility factors, since the no instruction group (group 3) had significantly lower Harvard Scale scores than the other three groups. We might speculate on the possibility of a hypnotic susceptibility referent here, in that by SF standards this group was considerably more activated than the other two groups. It is conceivable that those individuals who are more susceptible to hypnosis are generally less physiologically active,

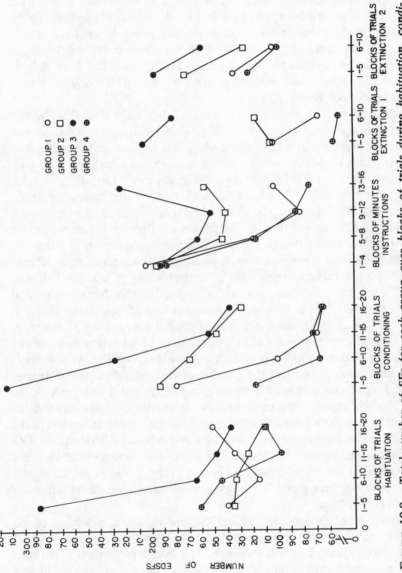

FIGURE 10.9. *Total number of SFs for each group over blocks of trials during habituation, conditioning, first, and second extinction periods; also included are 4-minute blocks of time during instructional period (From Edmonston, 1968, p. 20).*

and do not maintain the same level of physiological arousal as individuals who are less susceptible (see also Plapp, 1967).

With the exception of the first block of habituation trials, the four curves do not differ significantly from one another. At least by the end of the habituation period we could consider all four groups to be equated with respect to SF production. We see again in the first block of trials of conditioning the separation of the groups with group 3, the uninstructed, less hypnotizable group, yielding significantly more SFs than the other groups. Interesting to note here is the fact that the fourth group, which was added later, follows both the same relative and absolute patterns of group 1, the original experimental hypnotized group.

At the beginning of the instruction period, it was quite clear that the four groups were equated with respect to SF production. By the second block of minutes we begin to see a separation, which has become quite profound by the third block of minutes and continues through the fourth block of minutes. The separation that became apparent in minutes 9 through 12 reaches significance in minutes 13 through 16, with group 1 demonstrating significantly fewer SFs than group 3. Thus, our experimental Ss demonstrated a reduction of SFs beyond that for the uninstructed group 3, but not for the relaxed control group, that is, group 2. What we see clearly is that our two hypnotized groups, 1 and 4, demonstrate a progressive reduction in SF production over a relaxed group and a noninstructed group. As indicated above, the hypnotic groups did not differ significantly from the relaxed group (group 2), which falls intermediate between groups 3 and 1 and 4.

The split of group 3, the noninstructed control group, from groups 1, 2, and 4 became even more evident in the first block of extinction trials following the instruction period. Covariance analysis between the last five trials of the instruction period and the first five of this extinction period demonstrated a significant difference between groups 1, 2, and 4 and group 3, the latter showing significantly more SFs. A covariance analysis between the first and second five of the first extinction trials gave some indication of the relationship between hypnotic instructions and relaxation instructions. Covariance analysis between the first and the last five of the first extinction trials also showed us a curious difference, in that group 1 had produced significantly fewer SFs than group 3. However, there was no significant difference between groups 2 and 3.

Initially, we might have interpreted this finding as an indication of the durability of hypnotic relaxation, in that both the hypnotic and the relaxed groups were virtually identical during the first five extinction trials, but then split apart—the former maintaining its degree of relaxation depicted by low SF production, group 2 becoming rearoused during extinction. However, we must keep in mind that the relaxed group received instructions to relax only five times during the 17-minute instruction period, so that the difference in the effectiveness of instructions could be attributable merely to the amount of verbalization the respective groups received in the instruction period. Finally, looking at the first five trials of the second extinction period, following arousal instructions to groups 1 and 4, we see that all four groups produced the same amount (statistically) of SFs. However, groups 1, 2, and 4 showed a significant increase in SF production from the last five trials of the first extinction period to the first five trials of the second extinction period.

Figure 10.10 shows the data of the electrodermal conditioning experiment 2. It is quite evident that during the habituation and conditioning periods, these two groups produced similar SF patterns of habituation. During the instruction period, when one group was receiving hypnotic induction and the other relaxation instructions, we also see similar patterns. (The lack of a data point for the last 4 minutes of the instruction period for the relaxed group was due to experimenter error, but we suspect that the projected SF would continue to approximate very closely those of the hypnotized group.) Finally, in the two extinction periods we also note no difference between the two groups.

In Figure 10.11 we have combined the SF data for experiments 1 and 2 so that the hypnosis group is a combination of the three hypnosis groups, the relaxation data is from the combination of the two relaxation groups, and the no-instruction data is from group 3 of experiment 1. While it is quite clear that in the habituation and conditioning periods the no-instruction group produced more spontaneous fluctuations than the other two groups (which, as indicated before, may be related to some hypnotic susceptibility factor), it is the instruction and extinction periods that are of the most interest to us.

Once again with these combined data we found no difference in SF production during the first 4 minutes of the instruction period and then a progressive separation of the curves representing the three groups, with the relaxation group falling intermediate between no-instruction and the hypnotic instruction group. Once again we found significant differences between the hypnotized and the no-instruction group, but not between the hypnotized and the relaxation group. However, following the instruction period, in the first extinction period we see quite obviously significant differences between the relaxation and hypnosis groups and the no-instruction group. There were significant increases in SF production for the hypnotized group following arousal instructions (in the second extinction period), but not for the relaxed and no-instruction groups. Both the hypnotized and the relaxed groups remained considerably less productive of SFs than the no-instruction group during this period.

FINAL REMARKS

As we pointed out in the introduction to this chapter, Pavlov considered hypnosis to be the inhibitor of voluntary motor activity. Such inhibition was considered to be progressive in a fashion suggestive of a generalization gra-

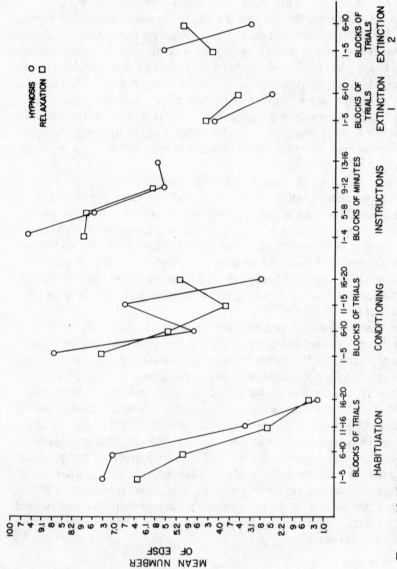

FIGURE 10.10. *Mean number of SFs for each group over blocks of trials during habituation, conditioning, first, and second extinction periods; also included are 4-minute blocks of time during instructional period.*

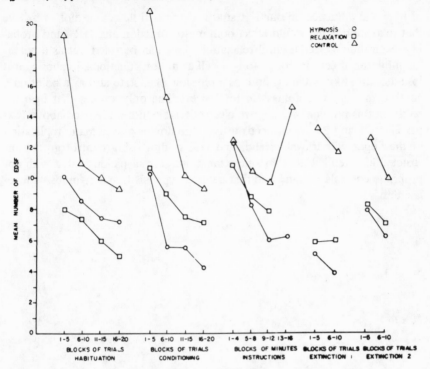

FIGURE 10.11. *Mean number of SFs for combined groups (Figures 10.9 and 10.10).*

dient over more to less involved functions. Our overall data tend to support this viewpoint and yet raise the doubt that hypnosis is unique in its inhibitory capacity. In fact, a major stumbling block to understanding the nature of hypnotic phenomena may be the propensity of investigators to consider hypnosis (or trance) as a state, separate from other states of the organism. Although the experimental evidence to this effect is weak (see Edmonston, 1967), such an assumption can lead to a reasonable experimental tactic. The only question is, At what point do we agree that the evidence has reached such a critical mass as to obviate the assumption? At what point do we agree that the data is sufficiently clear to warrant the abandonment of the assumption of a state of hypnosis?

What is clear from our data is that voluntary motor functions are inhibited by hypnotic induction, just as Pavlov stated they would be, and nonvoluntary functions appear not to be. However, the extensive conclusions and theory drawn by Pavlov and elaborated by his followers do not necessarily follow, because of the lack of appropriate experimental controls. The data themselves cannot be accurately interpreted unless controls that isolate nonhypnotic relaxation have been applied.

As seen in our data the introduction of nonhypnotic relaxation alone could account for the results obtained. Nonhypnotic relaxation could also account for the finding, inconsistent with the voluntary-involuntary division of hypnotic influence, in our HR study. There is little reason not to believe that relaxation alone would affect both motor function and HR (and probably respiration as well). Until relaxation alone can be ruled out as a potential inhibitor of certain nonmotor, as well as motor, functions, hypnosis must lose its claim to uniqueness both as a physiological state and as a point on a continuum from wakefulness to total sleep. The only studies that bear directly on this problem are the two electrodermal studies reported above (experiments 1 and 2). What needs to be done now is a systematic replication of the finger withdrawal, eyelid, and HR studies using control groups instructed in extended nonhypnotic relaxation. Our suspicion is that with appropriate controls we may find that neutral hypnosis is synonymous with relaxation.

Gerald S. Blum *is Chairman and a Professor of the Department of Psychology at the University of California, Santa Barbara. After receiving his Ph.D. in psychology from Stanford University in 1948, he joined the University of Michigan faculty, where he remained until moving to the University of California in 1968. During that time he also served as a consultant in clinical psychology to the Veterans Administration (1949–59), devoted some time to research in Italy as a Fulbright Scholar (1954–55), spent a year as fellow at the Center for Advanced Studies in the Behavioral Sciences (1959–60), and also was the recipient of a Social Science Research Council Faculty Research award (1961–62), a Ford Foundation behavioral science grant (1956–61), and several National Institute of Mental Health research grants covering the period from 1953 to the present. His research interests have focused on the experimental investigation of psychoanalytic theory and the development of a conceptual model of the mind by means of hypnotic research techniques. Publications in-*clude The Blacky Pictures, Psychoanalytic Theories of Personality, A Model of the Mind, *and* Psychodynamics: The Science of Unconscious Mental Forces.

Blum *describes the line of research he and his students have been following for more than a decade. Blum's research is an attempt to develop models of mental processes patterned after those of cybernetic circuitry. Cognitive arousal is viewed as analogous to an electronic gain control that serves to amplify the signal regardless of the informational content. Affective arousal is conceptualized as ranging from free-floating pleasure to free-floating anxiety.*

Blum has developed hypnotic training techniques to teach subjects how to gain precise and systematic control over their levels of cognitive and affective arousal. He calls these hypnotic training techniques "programming."

11

Hypnotic Programming Techniques in Psychological Experiments

For me, hypnosis is a research tool par excellence for peering into black boxes and deciding how to diagram their contents. The particular black boxes I find intriguing contain functions of the human mind that are involved in processing stimulus inputs for eventual response. Central topics for research therefore include such items as the role of amplification level, or cognitive arousal, in mental functions; factors affecting the reverberation of thoughts; the influence of various types of affective arousal; and the like. Together these and other functions comprise a conceptual model of the mind that we have been evolving through laboratory experiments over the past decade and a half. For an account of the origins of the model, see Blum, 1961.

Very early in the efforts of our research group it became apparent that such an undertaking requires an exceptional degree of control over experimental variables, not possible with conventional psychological techniques. In 1957 we decided to enlist the aid of hypnosis in programming our subjects' minds, and a whole new dimension of research immediately opened before us. As a research strategy, we choose to work intensively with small numbers of highly trained hypnotic subjects, usually undergraduate students, who are paid to participate in many different investigations throughout the course of a year or more. On the basis of a brief screening interview, anyone with past or present cardiac illness or a severe nervous disorder is excluded.

Revision and extension of a paper presented in a symposium entitled "Hypnosis as a Research Tool" at the 1968 annual meeting of the Society for Clinical and Experimental Hypnosis, Chicago, Illinois. Research studies referred to in this chapter were supported by NIMH Grants 0847-01 through -04, and 16970-01.

If the prospective S is a minor, his parents are asked to indicate in writing their willingness for him to take part in experiments involving hypnosis. Next the Stanford Hypnotic Susceptibility Scales are administered, usually with the purpose of eliminating low scorers. Those selected for training are then given a personal history questionnaire to fill out.

Each S typically is scheduled for two sessions a week, each lasting about two hours, throughout the academic year. At the outset S is told that he will be given feedback concerning the research after he has completed all the experiments. He is asked to respect the confidential nature of the tasks, just as his own responses are kept in confidence by members of the research staff. A sharp distinction is continually preserved between the "outside world" and the laboratory, so that crossing the threshold signifies the transition from one realm to the other. This psychological separation further cuts down the possibility for laboratory responses to occur outside. Very likely it also contributes to the effectiveness of training inside the laboratory by minimizing interference from everyday preoccupations. Upon termination S is given a lengthy debriefing in both hypnotic and waking states. The procedures and experiments are explained in detail and all suggestions are carefully removed and tested for their disappearance. Stress is also laid on the inadvisability of indulging in self-hypnosis or attempting to hypnotize others.

The various hypnotic programming techniques utilized to pursue our conceptual variables experimentally will be illustrated in the course of an overview of several major research topics chosen for laboratory study in recent years.

Cognitive Arousal

Some years back our conceptual model led us to differentiate two aspects of arousal, "cognitive" and "organismic." Before describing research that has grown out of this distinction, a brief account will be given of the hypnotic training in which S learns to control his level of cognitive arousal in varying degrees.

Under hypnosis (H), lying on a couch with eyes closed, S is told that we can conceive of the human mind as always operating at a particular level of amplification or "mental arousal" ranging anywhere between a peak of alertness and concentration, where mental contents are especially vivid and clear, and a low point approaching stupor, where thoughts are very fuzzy and unclear. The analogy is drawn to the gain control on a TV set, which affects reception regardless of the channel tuned to at the moment. Just as that gain control can be turned up or down, so also can the amplification level of S's mind be brought under systematic control with the aid of H. Only the contents of the mind are to be affected by this manipulation, *not* the muscles or senses (thereby excluding the organismic component of arousal). Then S is told to view his mental amplification as if under the control of a dial, the midpoint of which corresponds roughly to his normal waking level of mental arousal.

E next instructs *S* that his dial is now gradually being turned up and up until it reaches the very top, and as this happens his thoughts are becoming more and more clear and distinct. (Clarity is singled out for emphasis by *E* during the arousal induction for two reasons: Change in clarity was the one dimension common to the subjective experiences of a group of *S*s when we began exploring the manipulation of cognitive arousal without specific instruction as to its effects, and some experimental tests designed to isolate various dimensions, including clarity, magnitude of imagery, and speed of thought, revealed that alterations in clarity alone duplicated the effects of cognitive arousal induced as an unspecified whole.) *S* nods when he thinks he is at the peak of arousal and *E* asks him to make a mental note of what his mind is like at that point and also to describe it aloud. *E* then exhorts *S* to turn his amplification dial up even more until *S* is certain he can go no higher. This peak level of cognitive arousal is labeled "plus double A" (+ AA) for *S*. The imaginary dial is returned to the midpoint, labeled "zero" (0), and *S* notes and reports mental contents at that level. Next he is instructed to move up the scale halfway between 0 and + AA, a level designated as "plus A" (+ A). Repeated practice is then given at each of the three levels, typically by asking *S* to visualize and describe the same scene, such as the contents of the experimental room, under 0, + A, and + AA.

If *E* deems the reports appropriate and sufficiently discriminable in terms of their clarity and vividness, and *S* can easily move from one level to another, the next phase of training is begun. Now the amplification dial is turned downward from 0 until it reaches the lowest point at which contact with *E* still remains *(S* is carefully instructed that he must never go so deeply into a stupor as not to be able to hear *E*'s voice). This low point, also duly noted and described, is labeled "minus double A" (− AA). *E* then proceeds to have *S* fill in the fifth degree of cognitive arousal halfway between 0 and − AA, which is called "minus A" (− A). Repeated practice is given first at the lower levels, and then the whole range is eventually brought into play, both with standard thoughts suggested by *E* and freely varying contents supplied spontaneously by *S*. A typical account of imagery under − AA is: "There's no shape to the room, I'm just in something, lying on something, everything's gray and fuzzy, no images or anything"; in contrast to + AA where minute details of the room are visualized and the mental image is described as "very clear, very perfect, delineated exactly, with vivid colors." If at any time *E* discovers that affects, such as pleasure or anxiety, occur concomitantly with the changes in cognitive arousal, he immediately severs the connection via hypnotic instruction and proceeds to check on the efficacy of the instruction. A problem that often needs additional work at this stage is the speed with which *S* can reach the desired level of arousal. Speed is timed by having *S* say "Now" when he thinks he is at the correct level. For our experimental purposes it is essential for S to learn to respond appropriately within a few seconds of E saying a cue.

The next step involves practice with S's eyes open, still under H. Now the arousal cues are acting upon externally based percepts as well as upon thoughts and internally based percepts. After this series is mastered, he goes through similar routines while sitting up under H with eyes open. Successful execution is followed by instructions to the effect that S will be able to do equally well with the cues in the waking state, at which time he is to be amnesic for the hypnotic training. He will not pay any attention to the fact that cues are given to him by E, but he will respond in the desired manner whenever a cue is presented in the laboratory (not outside). The response is to remain in effect at a constant level until E gives a signal to terminate. Nothing about the procedure will seem at all strange to him in the waking state. S is brought out of H and the cues are presented to him posthypnotically in either oral or written form until E is satisfied with the apparent level and timing of their execution. For most of our highly susceptible Ss, the procedures described thus far consume no more than one or two sessions. S's training is then ready to be put to a somewhat more rigorous series of experimental tests.

Two tasks currently routinely employed by us to check on the cognitive arousal training are hexagram salience and the Stroop Color-Word Test.[1] The salience technique consists of the oral presentation of a string of six consonants at the rate of one per second to which S merely listens, followed by an interval in which S engages in a filler activity such as counting beats of the metronome, and then a 6-second report period when S says aloud whatever consonant spontaneously pops into mind at each beat. Salience of stimulus consonants at the time of report is measured by a scoring system based primarily upon their reappearance in the report series, with some weight also given to correspondence in position. The cognitive arousal cues, if working properly, should produce an ordered set of salience scores ranging from low to high as arousal increases. This ordering should occur both when the cues are placed in effect during the hexagram presentation or during the filler activity immediately following, but not when the cue onset and offset precede the presentation at the start of a trial. The latter serves as a check on possible simulation by S. Likewise the cues should yield an ordered set of speeds when the color-word interference chart of the Stroop is read under each of the five levels of cognitive arousal. On the other hand, the simple chart containing only patches of color should be minimally susceptible to facilitation under heightened arousal beyond S's normal waking control performance, which is easily carried out in a highly motivated state.

1. The application of our cognitive arousal cues to the Stroop task was first undertaken by Paul Bakan at the Stanford Laboratory of Hypnosis Research. Our subsequent investigations are reported in Blum and Graef (1971).

The lower arousal cues though, $-A$ and $-AA$, can be expected to interfere even with execution of this simple task.

One of our first series of studies involving cognitive arousal cues was conducted in 1964–65 with a male S who had already participated in the research program for a couple of years. His data (Blum, Geiwitz, & Stewart, 1967) were used to clarify the effects of various sources of amplification control upon cognitive processing. Figure 11.1 portrays amplification routes in our conceptual model of the mind. It can be seen that sensory input, in addition to activating specific cognitive, affective, or motoric networks, also constitutes a major source of control over amplification in the system. The amount of nonspecific sensory input regulates boosting capacity (level of gain control) of the three amplifiers that process signals from their respective networks. The quantity of nonspecific input itself depends, at any given time, upon both external stimulation from the environment and sensory feedback of muscular and glandular responses of the effectors. In addition to this nonspecific amplification control route, there is another double line from cognitive networks to the gain control of the cognitive amplifier, suggesting that cognitive arousal can also be regulated directly by cognitive messages.

We operationalized the feedback of affective output by programming S to experience three degrees of anxiety and also three degrees of pleasure in response to cues. (The topic of affective arousal will be dealt with in a later section.) Motoric feedback was manipulated by five degrees of muscle movement ranging from complete relaxation to extremely active twitching and contracting of muscles. External sensory input was regulated by feeding in various intensities of white noise through earphones. The remaining source, cognitive control of amplification, was tapped by the low and high cognitive arousal cues.

Besides these independent variables, we needed a sort of "tracer" that could be sent repeatedly through the cognitive subsystem under the various arousal conditions so as to reveal the amounts of amplification actually available for processing. Here we utilized as the dependent variable a visual discrimination task. On a given trial S looked into a tachistoscope and was asked to identify one of seven stimuli flashed briefly. The stimuli were one-inch-square photographs of an X on a white background; they differed only in darkness of the lines. Each X stimulus was identified by a different letter of the alphabet. Unbeknown to S, the latency of his response in making a judgment was also recorded exactly by a timer. By means of the prior hypnotic training it was possible to induce each one of the several kinds of arousal in pure form, in a specified amount, and to control both the onset and offset of the particular arousal reaction. Analysis of their effects upon identification of the Xs enabled us to make significant comparisons among the reactions.

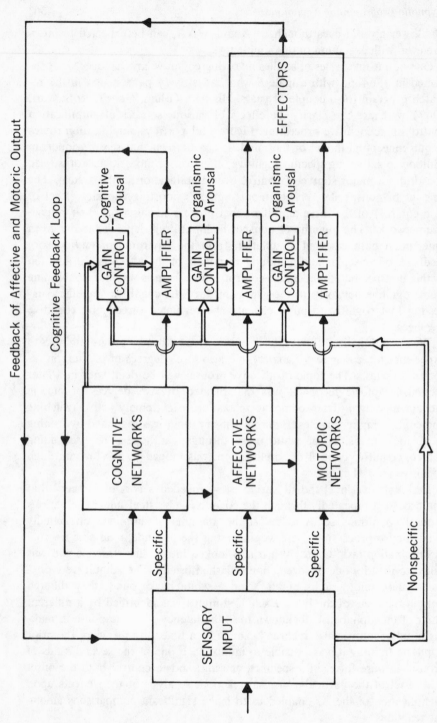

FIGURE 11.1. *A model of the mind (Form T): Signal routes (Single lines) and amplification control routes (double lines). (From Blum, Geiwitz, & Hauenstein, 1967).*

Figure 11.2 presents the order of median latencies for the 19 independent variables that were paired randomly with the X stimuli in 15 two-hour sessions of 90 trials each. The four cognitive arousal cues employed in the study clearly demonstrate the expected order of faster to slower responses as cognitive arousal varies from + AA down to − AA.

Hypnotic techniques also permitted further explorations not possible using conventional methods. For example, we were interested in discovering whether the cues were having their observed effects in the early perceptual registration or "perceiving" phase as opposed to the later "judgment" phase of a trial where *S* has to compare the perceived X with the file of Xs in his memory. The procedure, somewhat similar to that employed in the first experiment but involving selected cues and a smaller N, was identical in form for both the perceiving and the judging parts. The subject began by responding to a cue. When the X flashed, he closed his eyes and "fixed the image" of what he had just seen. In other words, he took a sort of mental photograph, without making any decision as to which X it was. Indeed, due

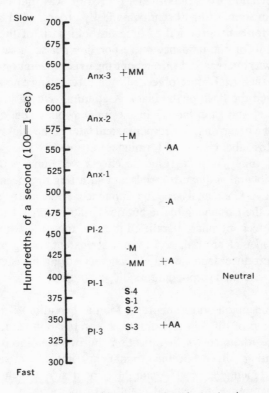

FIGURE 11.2. *Order of median latencies for cue conditions (From Blum, Geiwitz, & Stewart, 1967).*

to prior hypnotic instruction, his mental file of Xs was not consciously available to him during the process. When he had fixed the image clearly in his mind, he was to say "now" (producing a measurable latency by means of the voice relay), put the image aside for later recall, and open his eyes. A new cue was then inserted. After 9 seconds this cue was removed and the subject closed his eyes. Six seconds later he heard a distinct click through the earphones, which was a signal to "bring back" the previously fixed image along with his now available file of Xs and to judge which X it was (latency again recorded).

In the perceiving phase, cues were randomly assigned to the first phase of this two-part procedure, the image fixing. After viewing the stimulus under the influence of one of these conditions, the image was brought back by S and judged under the neutral condition. In the judging phase of each trial, image fixing was done under the neutral condition, whereas judging was affected by one of the eight cues. Thus the influence of each condition on perceiving and judging, separately, was assessed by response latency.

Another deviation from the original procedure was that the effect of the cue (other than sounds) had been hypnotically programmed to last through the response, for a fixed period of time, in both parts of the sequence. In order to control for cue influence on responding per se, a set of simple response trials was interspersed throughout the experimental ones. In the perceiving phase such trials were preceded by a card saying "no image," and S merely observed the flash of the blank X stimulus, closed his eyes without fixing an image, and said "now." In the judging phase the advance signal card contained a prearranged X response, and later at the click S just repeated the prescribed X label instead of forming a judgment.

In the data analysis, pure response effects were first partialled out by pairing experimental and control trials and adjusting the mean experimental latencies by covariance analysis. Cue differences achieved overall statistical significance in the *perceiving* phase but not in the judging. The directions of effect in the perceiving phase paralleled those of the earlier study: high anxiety, lowered mental arousal, and to a lesser extent strong muscle activity continued to produce decremental effects; very strong pleasure (Pl–3) and +AA both accelerated responding, as did the loud sound levels to a smaller degree.

Another kind of question important for the evolution of our model involves the action of different conditions in combination rather than singly. Here we chose for intensive investigation the two conditions that had exerted a facilitating influence in the original experiment, very strong pleasure and heightened mental arousal. Again the same design was employed except that S was programmed to respond simultaneously to the two cues shown together in the adapting field of the tachistoscope before the X flash. There were six combinations in all, Pl–3 and no pleasure being paired with +AA, +A, and 0 levels of cognitive arousal. Forty-two randomized trials were run for each of these combinations. The mean response latencies clearly indicate the *additive* nature of the interaction. The shortest latencies occur for the Pl-3 and +AA combination, the longest for the neutral pairing, and the intermediate in ordered progression for the remaining combinations.

A different line of investigation by Geiwitz (1966) applied the cognitive arousal cues and other hypnotic programming techniques in a comprehensive experimental approach to the phenomenon of boredom. Four male *S*s served in each of four experiments: (1) a "natural series" in which various levels of boredom were induced by varying durations of a simple repetitive task (making check marks on a piece of paper), and self-ratings were employed to assess levels of arousal, constraint, unpleasantness, and repetitiveness; (2) a "partly synthetic" series in which the synthesis of boredom was attempted by inducing various levels of arousal, constraint, unpleasantness, and repetitiveness by means of posthypnotic cues and the degree of ensuing boredom was indicated by *S*'s verbal report; (3) a "wholly synthetic" series identical to the preceding except that *S* was instructed additionally to keep the three other variables constant at a neutral level while the fourth was being manipulated; and (4) a "factorial" series in which, with arousal held neutral, constraint, unpleasantness, and repetitiveness were manipulated conjointly in a 2 x 2 x 2 factorial design.

Geiwitz found reported boredom to be associated with low arousal, increased feelings of unpleasantness, constraint, and repetitiveness. Boredom can be produced or synthesized by lowering arousal or by increasing one of the other three factors. Each variable tends to redintegrate a complex of all four which, in turn, results in a report of intense boredom. Each alone, however, with the others held constant, can produce boredom, a conclusion unequivocal for lowered arousal and constraint, but less certain for unpleasantness and repetitiveness.

In discussing the role of low cognitive arousal, he states:

> Several experimental findings deserve further research attention. For example, the association of boredom with low arousal, as we mentioned in the introduction, is by no means generally accepted. Subjective repetitiveness as the most equivocal factor is surely not in line with common interpretations of boredom. The major role of constraint, a factor typically ignored in scientific discourse, suggests that its absence is a serious oversight.
>
> In regard to arousal, we might suggest that theoretical disagreement is at least partly a semantic illusion. In this study, we defined and used the construct with major emphasis on its cognitive aspects. Let us then say that low *cognitive* arousal has been shown to be influential in boredom. Berlyne, the major theorist holding a high arousal position, may well agree with these results; the cause of high arousal in his system is inhibited cortical activity— low cognitive arousal? In other words, we may be discussing two distinguishable forms of arousal, one cortical or cognitive and the other more peripheral, sensorimotor, or organismic. All might agree that cortical arousal is low in boredom; the dispute would center on the second level. (Geiwitz, 1966. p. 599)

A recent illustration of our research use of the cognitive arousal cues lies in the domain of psychodynamics, a special concern of the conceptual model [see Blum (1967) for an overview of our earlier work in this area]. A fertile field for the pursuit of psychodynamic phenomena is of course dreamlike imagery. We chose to explore the influence of cognitive arousal level upon such imagery through hypnotic programming of three Ss, two males and one female, all of whom had previously been trained to experience the five degrees of mental amplification and had been given practice under H in having "dreamlike visual images, which can sometimes be quite bizarre." The Ss also were very familiar with the Blacky Pictures (Blum, 1950), having told stories about Blacky in the waking state, filled out the Defense Preference Inquiry, and narrated, under H, personal experiences of their own suggested by each of the pictures.

The aim of the study, conducted entirely under H, was to obtain dream-like protocols under conditions that minimize distortions in reporting and maximize interpretability. Accordingly, S was instructed to have his imagery grow directly or indirectly out of all three Blacky pictures shown to him at the start of a trial. Looking in a tachistoscope, S saw each of three pictures clearly for 0.5 sec. with an interval of 0.5 sec. between them. For the next 20 sec. he experienced his imagery with eyes closed until E said "Stop." At that point S's prior programming dictated that he give a detailed account of his just completed dream and to indicate its completion by saying "that's all," whereupon he proceeded spontaneously to give his own explanation of how each of the three pictures exposed on that trial played a part in the images. S's statements were recorded and transcribed for later analysis. At the end of each trial, S was told to rest, which meant that he sat back in his chair and made himself amnesic for the entire trial before going on to the next one.[2] This procedure minimizes distortion in reporting because S narrates his dream immediately after experiencing it and does not have to undergo a disruptive change of state, as from sleep to waking in REM research, between dream and report. Reporting under H also seems to promote an exceptional degree of candor, exemplified by the following from the female S: "There was an image of a penis right in front of me, in front of my face, and it started growing and it grew until it was about 20 times as big as I was and then crushed me on the ground." Interpretability of the imagery is aided by E's knowledge of the antecedent conditions, namely themes associated with the three Blacky pictures, plus S's own associations given immediately afterward.

The independent variable in the study was degree of cognitive arousal. Before each trial, E said "Ready," a signal for S to look into the machine, and then spoke one of the five cues ranging from −AA to +AA. Three sec-

---

2. The automatic invocation of amnesia between trials of an experiment is believed to facilitate the independence of those trials, at least to the extent that conscious rumination is precluded.

onds were allowed to elapse while *S* reached the appropriate level and then the picture presentation began. The cognitive arousal cue remained in effect by instruction through the 20 sec. of dreamlike imagery (until *E* said "Stop"), at which time *S* automatically returned to the normal level (0) for his report. The N for each *S* was 45 trials, 9 at each of the five cognitive arousal levels, carried out over three sessions of 15 randomized trials per session. Nine of the Blacky pictures in all were used, with various combinations of three presented randomly.

For the data analysis a team of three judges worked out a scoring guide that included cognitive alterations such as condensation, symbolism, lack of logic or morality, omnipotent wish-fulfilling fantasy, paranoid flavor, obsessive-compulsive quality, and depersonalization; stylistic variables such as productivity, activity of the scene, centrality of *S* and others in the dream, and presence of animals; and *S*'s mode of coping with aggression, sex, and rejection. Once the categories were agreed upon, the judges independently scored each protocol blindly, that is, without knowledge of the cue condition, and any disagreements were discussed and resolved consensually.

Those trends that emerged from this exploratory approach showed the lowest level of arousal, $-$AA, to be more associated with magical elements, paranoid flavor, and sex anxiety, and less with active imagery. The following $-$AA protocols exemplify these findings:

Male S: magical solution

I saw this big knife, great big knife that was coming at me and felt like I should do something to it to destroy it or something like that. It was out to get me. It started to melt and gradually became harmless, just kind of turned into a big round molten lump. I had a feeling that I was alone. I looked about and there was no one there—a totally blank, blank void in which I was sitting. I could see no one. That's all.

Other male S: paranoid flavor

I was giving a speech to a group of people out on the streets and I was talking about civil rights but nobody was listening. They were jabbering with one another. So I sat there talking and this one person was watching off to the corner of my eye. It was a little kid, about seven and he kept staring. And so I finished the speech and I was thrown off the stand. They just threw me out in the street and then they just all climbed up and looked and they all started laughing. And they all started talking and I was the one that was listening this time until finally they started dispersing. And so I got up and started walking down the street. Then I fell into like a manhole. And that was the end. That's all.

Female S: sex anxiety

There was the image of two dogs, a male and a female, and the boy was chasing the girl around in a circle and then the dogs changed into frogs. They were still hopping around with the boy chasing the girl in a circle and then they changed into turtles and it was like in slow motion. They were going very slowly, still chasing though. And then the girl all of a sudden pulled into her shell and stopped. And the boy caught up with her and climbed on top of her shell and sat there for a couple of minutes, kind of clawing at her shell or something and fell off and landed on his back. That's all.

In retrospect it seems likely that the general instruction to experience "dreamlike, often bizarre" visual imagery may have largely overshadowed the possible effects of cognitive arousal changes, since primary process elements abounded in all conditions. Nonetheless the form of hypnotic programming utilized in this study does seem to us promising for further work in the psychodynamic realm.

Cognitive Reverberation

A very different application of hypnosis as a research tool arose when we sought to explore experimentally that portion of the conceptual model relating to the "cognitive feedback loop" (see Figure 11.1). Each amplified signal is presumed to set up an autonomous feedback loop that sustains network activity until the loop gradually dies down, a process we refer to simply as "reverberation."

The construct of reverberation has its neuropsychological counterpart in the theories of Gerard, Hebb, Eccles, and others. Similar notions of perseverative activity have arisen in studies of information processing. Broadbent talks of "recirculation" through a short-term memory storage and Posner discusses a "central rehearsal," not necessarily overt or conscious. Most of the thought and research concerning reverberation has centered on its possible function. Typically the autonomous reactivation process is seen as strengthening the emergent structural trace—the consolidation hypothesis —or as retarding the natural decay of a cognitive network. Research on the consolidation hypothesis generally involves experimental interruption of the presumably active trace by means of electroconvulsive shock or chemicals. Such interruptions show the predicted effect, that is, memory decrement as an inverse function of time after stimulus presentation, up to a point. But interpretation of the data is not unequivocal. Alternative interpretations often include competition or interference, and lowered arousal. One of the major obstacles to a choice among these explanations has been a lack of knowledge regarding the precise effects on the organism of both electroconvulsive shock and chemicals. Discussion of the decay-retarding hypothesis is found most clearly in the area of human memory research. The interpretive problems here include the fact that many experiments attempt to prevent rehearsal in order to study the course of decay. The use of interpolated material for this purpose builds in the possibility for alternative explanation in terms of retroactive interference. [See Blum, Geiwitz, and Hauenstein (1967) for a more extended discussion of the above.]

Thus, a potential model-builder must conclude that the nature of reverberation and its function are poorly understood. Major questions remain: Is it possible to obtain clear-cut behavioral evidence with human subjects for the existence of autonomous reverberation? If so, how long does such activity last? To what kinds of influence is it responsive? This is how our empirical search began. We decided to attack the problem with our previously described "salience technique," which merely exposes S to stimuli without any learning set and, for reporting, only requires that he say those items that pop into mind spontaneously. It is assumed that strong networks will dominate mental activity if given the opportunity. This salience technique offers a purer measure of cognitive network strength than is provided by conventional methods such as recall, where the complex of learning, memory, and performance factors renders inference about an intervening process like reverberation especially hazardous.

In place of electroconvulsive shock or chemical interrupters, which are unsuited to normal human Ss, we substituted a brief excursion into the state of hypnosis. Some of our earlier work had indicated that the act of going into very deep H for a few seconds tends to impair conscious retrieval of immediately prior material from the waking state—an ideal probe which is easily applied with a trained S, can be manipulated precisely in time, and runs no risk of neurological damage.

In the first series of experiments (Blum, Geiwitz, & Hauenstein, 1967), S, a female graduate student in social work, was trained to enter deep hypnosis immediately upon receiving a tap on the left arm and to return to the waking state 5 seconds later in response to another prescribed signal. At the tap her eyes would close, her head would drop suddenly to one side, and she would report that her mind went blank. She described the hypnotic pause as disruptive of any ongoing train of thought—somehow she had to "start all over again" after the pause. Approximately three experimental sessions per week were then conducted throughout a summer. Each session typically consisted of three half-hour blocks of trials with 10-minute rest periods between blocks. All trials involved oral presentation, at the one-per-second rate, of a set of six consonants taken from a pool of 432 hexagrams, and S was instructed at the outset not to try to form associations to the consonants.

In the first study S counted beats during a standard 20-second interval between E's presentation and her own report. On the beat after she reached 15 she began reporting consonants. Experimental and control manipulations consisted of taps on the left or right arm during the interval. A tap on the left arm, as mentioned earlier, signified that she should automatically stop counting and enter H immediately. E then allowed five beats to elapse. On the sixth, S said a number that served a double purpose: It signaled S to be-

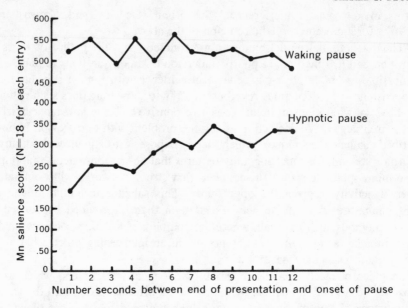

FIGURE 11.3. *Hypnotic interruptions of reverberation (From Blum, Geiwitz, & Hauenstein, 1967).*

come wide awake again and also told her where to resume counting aloud to 15. The control tap on the right arm merely signified that S was to remain awake with eyes closed during the subsequent 5-second pause—a period occupied by stray thoughts, usually concerning events of the day. Taps were delivered in random order by a ruler at prescribed beats ranging from 1 to 12 seconds after the end of the hexagram presentation. S could not anticipate their arrival because she sat with her back to E. The experiment required six sessions, with a total N of 18 trials for every waking or hypnotic pause at each one of the 12 seconds. The results in Figure 11.3 show the mean salience score for the H pause to be below that of the W pause at every point along the time dimension. This finding, under circumstances where S never thought about consonants during the 20-second interval, supports the notion of an ongoing process of reverberation vulnerable to disruption.

These data permit the inference that the hexagram network remains active during the 20-second interval; otherwise the H pause could not have had a disruptive effect upon network salience. But the basis for its continued activity is not certain, beyond the fact that conscious awareness need not be involved. In addition to autonomous reverberation, there is the possibility that S, knowing the relationship between her reported letters and those previously spoken by E to be under some kind of investigation, might be exercising an "unconscious intention" to retain the stimuli. Ideally one would like to replicate the findings in a situation where S does not realize she is performing in an experiment. Obviously the systematic execution of such a plan is not feasible, but we were able to insert a couple of nonintentional trials in the context of some later experiments. Nevertheless there was some statistical evidence in this first study that argued against intentionality. It turned out that the H pause not only disrupted reverberation of the stimulus hexagram but also reduced the likelihood of an intrusion from consonants given in the report on the preceding trial. Here the material was obviously not intended, by either S or E, to be carried over.

Another question concerns the duration of reverberatory activity. In the next study the 5-second hypnotic and waking pauses were inserted near the end of trials lasting 30 seconds, 1, 2, and 3 minutes. Instead of counting beats of the metronome, which is understandably tedious over long periods, S was shown colored travel slides as a filler activity. At every duration the same result obtained as before—mean salience scores for the H pause were significantly lower than for the W pause.

It was in this setting that we added one of the nonintentional trials referred to earlier. E presented a hexagram (KXTGWM) and then "by mistake" projected a blank on the screen instead of a slide. Acting flustered, he exclaimed "Oh nuts, skip it!" and told S that he would have to run quickly through a series of slides to reach the spot in the tray where a fresh start could be made. After 30 seconds of slide-changing E instructed S to say six consonants in time with the metronome. Incredulous, she asked "Now?" and proceeded to report KXTGMP. Thus five letters from the stimulus set reappeared when S obviously had no intention of retaining them.

Subsequent trials extending the length of the filler activity showed the same disruptive effect of the 5-second H pause even after 30 minutes. At this juncture a 2-hour nonintentional trial was introduced. E explained to S that he was expecting an important phone call and would have to terminate the session the moment it came. Presumably hearing a faint ring about 20 seconds after a stimulus set was spoken, he switched off the slide projector and went outside to answer the phone. S then departed for her job in another building where she typed letters. Two hours later E surprised her with a phone call and, holding the metronome against the receiver, asked for the report of six consonants. Three of the stimulus consonants recurred. Similar trials, discontinued shortly after S was given the hexagrams but with no further attempt to surprise her, were conducted with 3-, 4-, and 5-hour intervals. At 4 hours the H pause still yielded a lower score than the W pause, and only after 5 hours did the report drop to chance expectancy with the W pause.

The next question dealt with the influence of competition upon the reverberation process. This was explored by filling a 20-second interval with either a full 20-second H pause; a 20-second W pause; counting beats up to 20; or looking at a slide accompanied by E's narration of a relevant anecdote. As always, the H pause, in which S's mind remained essentially blank for 20 seconds, resulted in the lowest salience scores. The W pause, least demanding of S's attention with its leisurely stray thoughts such as buying furniture for her new apartment, yielded the highest scores. Counting and listening to the narration, both of which were described by S as more involving than the W pause, produced intermediate scores.

The H pause had proven its practical worth as an experimental probe, but the basis of its disruptive action was not apparent. Another series of investigations sought to clarify the nature of the effect. One possibility lay in the discontinuity of shifting between waking and hypnotic states. So an experiment was carried out with S under hypnosis throughout the whole trial. In this case the H pause did not involve a shift, whereas the W pause did. According to the discontinuity hypothesis, salience scores should be lower for the W than the H pause. Instead the same result as before was obtained; mean salience for the H pause was still significantly lower.

Another alternative invoked the concept of amplification level. The skill of quickly reaching a deep stage of hypnosis entails a sudden drop in cognitive arousal, reflected in the "blank mind" phenomenon. If the level of amplification in the system is turned down, then the reverberating signal along with any other ongoing signals should be affected according to our model.

Having the previously described experimental techniques at our disposal for manipulating degrees of cognitive arousal posthypnotically, we carried out the following study, again employing a 20-second counting interval and the standard waking context for presentation and report. The conditions included the usual 5-second H and W pause trials intermingled with 5-second pauses varying in the five degrees of cognitive arousal, and also a posthypnotic blank mind cued by E saying "Blank." Mean salience scores formed a perfect progression for the five degrees of arousal from − AA on up to + AA. Thus there seems no reason to doubt that the process of reverberation is sensitive to brief changes in amplification. It is important to note that 5 seconds of relatively content-free amplification raised beyond the normal level (from 0 to + A to + AA) resulted in higher scores, indicating that the strength of reverberation can be influenced in both directions. Moreover the comparability of scores among the H, − AA, and Blank conditions suggests that lowered amplification is the key to understanding the H effect. S also reported the three to be subjectively similar except that she is awake during − AA and Blank.

Next, a control experiment was carried out to check on the possibility of report bias, that is, S reasoning consciously or unconsciously that, since five degrees of arousal are involved, her responses should obligingly yield differential, ordered results. Here each cognitive arousal cue was given 10 seconds in advance of the hexagram and terminated 5 seconds before the presentation. Theoretically we should expect no effect on salience, but the opportunity for report bias still exists. The results showed that − AA in advance of the stimulus did not lower salience in comparison with 0, and

+ AA did not raise it. A further check on simulation was performed by tapping the best class of fakers we knew, psychologists, familiar with the salience design and even the scoring system. They tried to produce ordered responses for five different conditions announced to them just before the report period. Their efforts met with only very limited success.

We next undertook to replicate and extend the results with two male undergraduates (Blum, Hauenstein, & Graef, 1968). One *S* was given the same procedure as had been used in the initial experiment with the female *S*. The mean salience score for the H pause was again below that of the W pause at every point along the time dimension, consistent with the notion of an ongoing process of reverberation vulnerable to disruption.

The second *S* was used to replicate the finding that degree of cognitive arousal, or amplification level, directly affects the course of reverberation. Instead of the H and W pauses, he was given posthypnotic cues that triggered 5-second pauses of extremely high (+ AA), or normal (0), or extremely low (− AA) cognitive arousal. The data supported the original observation that lowered amplification in the system cuts down the normal strength of reverberation, whereas heightened amplification yields greater salience than normal. Of 36 possible comparisons among + AA, 0, and − AA, there was only one reversal and two ties, all other entries bearing the predicted relationship.

To confirm the influence of competition upon the reverberation process, both *S*s were asked to count metronome beats aloud (rather than silently) as the filler activity, based on the assumption that the aloud condition, with its sensory feedback of vocalization would constitute somewhat stronger competition. The salience scores did indeed reflect this seemingly slight difference in procedure. In trials testing the duration of reverberatory activity, one of the male *S*s also turned out to be a fairly long reverberator; the other showed clear evidence for reverberation after a 20-second interval, but by 50 seconds the H pause no longer had its characteristically disruptive effect.

The data obtained in all these studies with the three *S*s led us to formulate the following principles of cognitive reverberation for the conceptual model:

1. Reverberation consists of autonomous reactivation of a network by the signal transmitted from that network at the time of its original activation.
2. Reverberation takes place independently of conscious awareness.
3. The reverberating signal is strongest at the time of network activation and gradually decreases until it dissipates.
4. Barring disruption, a single series of reverberations from a transient network apparently can last for hours in some individuals.
5. Reverberation acts to retard, in proportion to its own intensity, the intrinsic rate of decay in network strength.
6. The course of reverberation is a direct function of current amplification level in the system.

7. For a given level of amplification, strength of the reverberating signal is an inverse function of the strength of competing signals in process.

Armed with these principles, we were eager to begin our advance up the ladder of stimulus complexity. First we escalated by presenting two hexagrams on a trial instead of one, guided by the notion that it should be possible to control experimentally the relative salience of the two by varying S's cognitive arousal immediately after the presentation of each stimulus. All three Ss participated in this experiment, the results of which are given in Table 11.1. The left-hand side of the table shows the results for hexagram I and the right-hand side for hexagram II. The first member of the listed cognitive arousal pairings was in effect after hexagram I and the second member came after II. The rank orders for individual Ss pertain to salience scores across the nine pairings. For example, we see from the left-hand side that putting $+AA$ after I and $-AA$ after II on a trial yielded the highest hexagram I salience rank for RM and EE, and the second highest for FS. The sum of ranks for all Ss conveys at a glance how well the manipulations bore fruit. The salience of hexagram I was maximized by strengthening it and simultaneously weakening II; minimized by weakening it and simultaneously strengthening II. The converse effects appear for hexagram II in the right-hand side, which is not surprising in view of the interdependence of the two hexagrams in a trial. The placing of $+AA$ after hexagram II, provided I is kept at $-AA$ or 0, maximized the salience of II; the combination of $+AA$ and $-AA$ minimized II. The high rank-order correlations between Ss, listed at the bottom of the table, attest to the strong consistency of findings across individuals.

TABLE 11.1 Salience Ranks for Various Cognitive Arousal Combinations Following Presentations of Two Hexagrams in a Trial

Cognitive Arousal Combinations		Hexagram I Ranks			Cognitive Arousal Combinations		Hexagram II Ranks		
	Σ Ranks	RM	FS	EE		Σ Ranks	RM	FS	EE
$+AA$ $-AA$	4	1	2	1	$-AA$ $+AA$	4.5	1.5	1	2
$+AA$ O	5	2	1	2	O $+AA$	4.5	1.5	2	1
O $-AA$	11.5	4	4.5	3	$-AA$ O	11.5	4	3.5	4
$-AA$ $-AA$	12	3	3	6	O O	12	3	3.5	5
O O	16.5	5	7	4.5	$+AA$ $+AA$	13	5	5	3
$-AA$ O	17.5	7	6	4.5	$-AA$ $-AA$	21	9	6.5	6
$+AA$ $+AA$	20.5	9	4.5	7	O $-AA$	21	7	6.5	7.5
O $+AA$	23	7	8	8	$+AA$ O	21.5	6	8	7.5
$-AA$ $+AA$	25	7	9	9	$+AA$ $-AA$	26	8	9	9
	Rho					*Rho*			
RM vs EE	.79				RM vs EE	.82			
RM vs FS	.73				RM vs FS	.90			
EE vs FS	.77				EE vs FS	.92			

SOURCE: Blum, Hauenstein, & Graef, 1968, p. 175.

In the next stage, we utilized meaningful content instead of hexagrams. The same two male *S*s took part in two related experiments that dealt with the effects of interference and cognitive arousal upon the processing of organized thought (Blum, Graef, & Hauenstein, 1968). Our aim was to present stimuli under conditions that would initiate thought organization. Then, while the still loosely connected thoughts were in the process of reverberating, we wanted to introduce experimental changes in level of interference and cognitive arousal. The effects of these manipulations were to be observed in *S*'s subsequent verbal output.

For stimuli we chose scrambled presentation of words from familiar phrases. On a given trial *S* was asked to read aloud, while in a state of lowered arousal, each of three words exposed on a card. After a 2-second pause another card with three more words was given him to read. The six words, if unscrambled across the two cards, comprised two familiar three-word phrases. Here are some sample pairings: roses are red—familiarity breeds contempt; french fried potatoes—power of suggestion; divide and conquer —on your mark. By prior hypnotic instruction *S* reverted to the normal level of arousal immediately after the second card was removed. A few seconds later he executed the salience task of saying any words at all that popped into mind over a 12-second period. The degree of organization in his verbal output was assessed by an objective scoring system for the unscrambling of the two phrases.

For the interference experiment, the manipulation consisted of *S*'s posthypnotic auditory hallucination of numbers while reporting words. There were three conditions: (1) after removal of the second card of words, *E* said three digits (for example, 2, 7, 4) in time with the metronome in a *loud* voice, which by prior hypnotic instruction meant that *S* was immediately to begin "hearing" those numbers loudly at successive beats over and over until told to stop; or (2) *E* said three digits in a *soft* voice, signifying soft background hallucination of the numbers; or (3) *E* said "No numbers," which meant that there would be no hallucination on that trial. The clearcut role of interference in disrupting reverberation and breaking down thought was demonstrated, the mean organization scores for both *S*s being ordered according to presence and degree of interference provided by the posthypnotic number hallucination activity.

For the cognitive arousal experiment, one of the five posthypnotic arousal cues was substituted for the numbers instruction and S performed the task under its influence. The unequivocal results are given in Figure 11.4. For both *S*s there was a progressive decrease in organization as arousal dropped from very high to very low. It is important to note that raising the level above normal again produced greater organization.

The foregoing series of investigations into the concept of cognitive reverberation illustrates the heuristic interplay of conceptual model and hypnotic research methodology. The model pointed systematically and insistently to

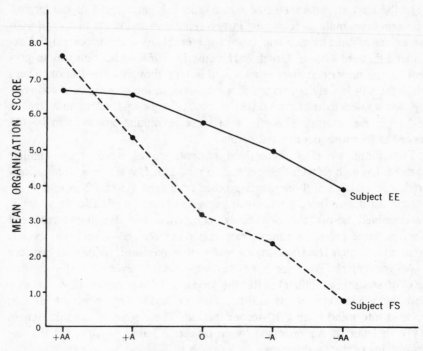

FIGURE 11.4. *Effects of cognitive arousal upon thought organization (From Blum, Hauenstein, and Graef, 1968).*

questions requiring empirical answers at a molecular level not often encountered in behavioral research. Hypnotic techniques permitted an unprecedented degree of rigor and control, which make possible such a molecular approach. At the same time the various cautions necessary in work with hypnosis, such as the operation of demand characteristics, intentionality, and simulation, were shown to be amenable to empirical check.

Affective Arousal

Currently we program our Ss hypnotically to respond to a set of 11 posthypnotic affective cues ranging from a peak of free-floating pleasure ($+5$) down to a neutral point (0) and up to a peak of free-floating anxiety (-5). A verbatim description of our anxiety procedures, at a time when Ss were programmed to experience only three degrees of intensity, is available elsewhere (Blum, 1967), so the present account will emphasize the pleasure training carried out with a male S who participated in a series of experiments during 1969-70.

Under H, while reclining on the couch, he was asked to recount a very pleasurable experience from his past. The episode he chose was a rock climbing venture in Yosemite (literally a peak experience!) where he led a group successfully. Next, in the course of reliving the episode he described his feelings as follows:

> Looking around where I was, a feeling of exultation, enjoyment, even a little superiority comes upon me. . . looking out over the valley, it's very beautiful, a very pleasant feeling, very enjoyable. . . so good to be here, so exciting, people congratulating me.

He was told to make a good mental note of the feeling of pleasure and instructed to dissociate the feeling from the actual experience in which it took place. During the practice of this detached free-floating pleasure, he felt "very happy and excited, like nothing else really matters, I would like it to last." Next he was exhorted to experience the pleasure ever more strongly until he felt it could go no higher, at which point he made another mental note. Asked to compare that feeling with real-life experiences of pleasure, S replied: "It's indescribable, so much better than anything bounded by earth, in real life. I'm just so happy and joyous, it's hard to believe such a wonderful thing could happen." The label $+5$ was attached to this peak of pleasure so that whenever S is presented with that cue *in the laboratory only,* either awake or under H, he responds appropriately. Next the intermediate degrees of pleasure ($+1$ up to $+4$) were trained in similar fashion and S was given practice in skipping around quickly from one level to another.

Prior to being brought out of H, S was informed that, as always, he would be amnesic for the training and respond to the posthypnotic cue presentations without conscious awareness or feelings of strangeness and curiosity. The scale from 0 to $+5$ was then practiced first with S lying awake on the couch and subsequently after he had moved to a chair. Typical waking comments about his feelings in $+5$ were "I'm *really* happy, don't know what about, just feel real good all over. . .exulted and high, an elevated thing. . .a feeling of pleasure is just pervading me."

Into each life some rain must fall, however, and the following session saw the induction of the other half of the affective scale, degrees of anxiety ranging from the weak -1 on up to the extreme of -5. This was accomplished by having S relive under H a personal experience narrated earlier in response to the picture of Blacky chewing on Mama's collar:

> I came home from school one day in the fourth grade. No one was home. My mother wasn't there for the first time. I got kind of worried and upset. I wondered if something bad happened. I was scared. . . my first time home alone.

During hypnotic reliving S described himself as "very worried, scary. . .I feel a little shaky like I'm breathing harder than usual . . . my mouth is dry. . .feels like my heart is beating faster."

The anxiety feeling was then dissociated by instruction from the originating episode and brought to a peak, labeled −5. At that level he described subjective experiences as follows: "Frightening, a feeling of impending doom . . . I don't know what I'm afraid of but it seems very real . . . I can't control it . . . my heart is beating faster, I'm breathing harder, I feel shaky with tingling sensations in my body, and my mouth is dry . . . anxiety is pervading my whole body and mind." The rest of the procedure paralleled the pleasure training, except that the GSR was used additionally to monitor S's physiological reactions.

Near the end of the session, back under H where amnesia is not in effect, E asked S what he thought about the anxiety training he had just undergone. His reply is illuminating:

> It was very interesting. Initially I thought it would be aversive but I understand it now. The anxiety itself is aversive but I understand why it would be important for the experiments. The anxiety is very real when it happens.

Asked if he were willing to tolerate that much anxiety in the course of future experiments, S replied in the affirmative. Care is always taken to keep S's anxiety reactions to the necessary experimental minimum. He receives considerable praise under H for having executed the cues properly. This friendly and sympathetic treatment by all members of the research team, combined with the displacement of the onus of anxiety onto the "experiments," probably help to cushion the impact. Whenever possible, pleasure cues are also interspersed to maintain some rough affective balance.

Evidence for the validity of S's cued anxiety reactions comes from several sources: his own subjective reports, observation by Es of facial expressions, body movements, and so forth, and recorded changes in galvanic skin resistance. In addition to these introspective, observational, and physiological indices, by now we have accumulated a large amount of data demonstrating that the anxiety cues interfere in degree with a variety of experimental tasks.

The validity of the cued pleasure responses cannot be inferred as easily by observation, nor does any particular physiological concomitant seem to be characteristic across Ss. "Face" validity (smiling, grinning, eyes lighting up) is often present in the case of expressive individuals, but more reliance must be placed on verbal report than with anxiety. Other independent checks are sometimes possible, however. In an unpublished study[3] with a female S, the monetary equivalents for each of the five degrees of pleasure were ascertained systematically under H. Money, duration, and degree of pleasure were manipulated so that two variables were held constant and S gave judgments regarding the third. Judgments of money rose in linear fashion as level and duration of pleasure increased. Each pleasure cue increased in average value 58¢ more than the preceding one, and every additional second of time in the pleasure condition increased subjective worth by 23¢. For

3. The experiment was carried out in my laboratory by Muriel Fabrikant.

example, *S*, not very well off financially, was willing to pay $2.00 in order to experience 6 seconds of +5 pleasure!

Now that the affective arousal training has been presented in some detail, we can turn to experiments that employ the hypnotically programmed degrees of anxiety and pleasure. Other affects have also been trained in our *S*s, such as degrees of anger for use in an investigation of factors in the appreciation of hostile humor (Hauenstein, 1970), and a scale of interest-boredom applied to studies of time estimation (Graef, 1969), but we shall restrict our illustrations to anxiety and pleasure.

Anxiety and pleasure were included among the independent variables in the series of visual discrimination experiments (Xs flashed tachistoscopically) summarized in the section "Cognitive Arousal." It has already been mentioned that the facilitating influence of very strong pleasure combined additively with degrees of cognitive arousal. From Figure 11.2 we see that the three degrees of anxiety exerted progressively greater decremental effects upon *S*'s response latency, a result similar to previous findings with the anxiety cues applied to other tasks (Blum, 1967). A follow-up study was able to localize the pleasure and anxiety effects primarily in the perceiving rather than the judgmental or responding phases of processing.

A subsequent investigation in that same series sought to break anxiety down into its cognitive and organismic components, a distinction between the vague feeling that "something bad is going to happen" and the physiological concomitants of anxiety. For this purpose *S* was trained to respond with the anxiety "thought only" or the "bodily sensations only" or both thought and bodily sensations intact as before. GSR recordings were used to validate this cognitive versus organismic distinction. From 42 trials in each of the 9 anxiety conditions (three degrees each of cognitive only, organismic only, and combined cognitive and organismic), interspersed with neutral and pleasure trials over four sessions, it was clear that the decremental effect of the intact anxiety cues upon response latency in identifying Xs was duplicated by the cognitive component acting alone, but not by the organismic alone.

This important finding about the molecular operation of anxiety was replicated and extended in a recent series of experiments with another male *S* (Blum and Wohl, 1971). The task was virtually the same as the salience one employed in the last cognitive reverberation experiment described in the preceding section: *S* read aloud 6 words in scrambled order from two familiar 3-word phrases and then reported whatever words popped into mind during a 15-sec. period. An objective scoring system reflected the amount of organization in *S*'s report. Eight independent variables were included in the design: cognitive only, organismic only, and intact whole reactions of peak anxiety (−5) and pleasure (+5); the neutral nonaffective level (0); and a condition of heightened muscular tension (10). On a given trial one of the 8 cues was presented visually to *S* during a 5 sec. reverberation period immediately after the stimulus presentations and turned off before his report. A total of 144 randomized trials over three sessions permitted an N of 18 in each condition. Concomitant GSR recordings independently confirmed the absence of organismic response to the cognitive anxiety, cognitive pleasure, and neutral cues. The results showed the thought organization score to be affected significantly more adversely by the cognitive component of anxiety than by the other 7 cues.

Having thus replicated with another S in a different task our earlier finding that the cognitive component is crucial in determining the action of anxiety, we then applied our hypnotic methodology in an attempt to discover the mode by which the cognitive component accomplishes its deleterious consequences. In terms of our conceptual model, two possibilities offer themselves: because of its cognitive strength, the anxiety thought competes successfully with other mental contents for access to the cognitive amplifier and thereby impedes the reverberation of phrase networks; or, as a consequence of early affective learning, the anxiety thought acquires the capacity to lower the gain on the cognitive amplifier by transmitting an attenuation signal, which automatically inhibits the strength of any and all contents being processed at the time. Of course, it is also possible that the cognitive component of anxiety could operate both by competition and attenuation.

To test this knotty distinction between competition and attenuation, we decided to introduce a facilitation in the cognitive strength of the phrase networks. If the anxiety component is acting solely through competition, the increment in thought organization scores resulting from the extra facilitation should be just as great for the anxiety condition as the increment in scores for the neutral and pleasure conditions, where there is no question of attenuation being involved. On the other hand, an automatic pervasive attenuation action resulting from anxiety should, as part of its indiscriminate effect, weaken the extra facilitation as well. The extra facilitation consisted of the presence of one of three patches of color along with the cue card on half of the trials during the 5 sec. reverberation period. Before a given set of three trials, each color had been associated with a pair of unscrambled phrases in a learning task. When S glimpsed the color after reading the scrambled words during a trial, it provided extra facilitation to the appropriate phrase networks as they reverberated prior to the report period. The other half of the trials were without color facilitation, the same as the previous experiment. Three sessions of randomized trials yielded an N of 24 in each of the color and no color conditions for the anxiety, pleasure, and neutral thought cues. Comparison of color minus no color organization scores across the three cue conditions unequivocally favored the competition alternative. The introduction of color added at least as much to the -5 no color scores as it did to the $+5$ and 0 scores. Of course, this result must be confirmed with other Ss, but at least we now have a methodology to provide direct empirical answers to a difficult question that in the past has been able to be attacked only at a very inferential level.

A separate control experiment to check on the possible operation of demand characteristics produced negative results. The cues were inserted only at the beginning of a trial prior to the stimulus presentation, a time when they should have no consequences for reverberation. No differences were noted among the anxiety, pleasure, and neutral conditions, in contrast to the dramatic effects obtained earlier.

Efforts to expand our knowledge of the influence of anxiety upon mental processing have also involved psychodynamic contents (see Blum, 1967). For example, an earlier investigation (Hedegard, 1968) witnessed a molecular analysis of the formation of defense mechanisms through the utilization of the anxiety cues in conjunction with an adaptation of the Blacky Pictures Defense Preference Inquiry (DPI). As level of anxiety rose, S's defensive choice proved to be increasingly distorted. More recently, in an unpublished study, we have contrasted the effects of defended versus undefended anxiety upon imagery and free association. Each of two Ss, a male and a female, were instructed hypnotically to identify completely with Blacky, so that Blacky's feelings would be his as well. Before each experimental trial, S, under H, was shown one of four Blacky pictures and given a brief description of Blacky's state of mind, which would characterize S's own state of mind whenever the picture was shown for a 1-sec. duration later in the waking state. The description either conveyed strong, undefended anxiety at the −5 level for a given picture, or a defense mechanism (selected from S's own earlier defense choices on the DPI), which reduced the anxiety to the mild −1 level.

Every experimental trial required a series of imagery and free association responses, each of which was preceded by a 1-sec. exposure of the critical picture to trigger the appropriate level of defended or undefended anxiety. Another manipulation involved cutting off cognitive reverberation by plunging S into the lowest arousal level, just prior to his associations. Data for both Ss yielded predictable results: shorter response latencies were found in the case of defended anxiety, disrupting reverberation produced longer latencies than when it was not cut off, affect ratings were more negative in undefended compared to defended anxiety, and also more negative when reverberation from exposure of the critical picture was not disrupted. These ratings were collected by means of another hypnotic innovation. S was trained, at a given signal, to enter a brief "dissociated" state during which he rated his just-experienced affect on the scale from +5 to −5 and then became amnesic for the rating as he returned from that altered state of awareness. The hypnotic programming procedures thus not only lead S to respond appropriately to cues but also enable him to rate his spontaneous subjective experiences along very familiar scales such as anxiety-pleasure and cognitive arousal.

Summary

In this chapter three broad objectives have been sought: to convey the flavor of our hypnotic programming procedures, to point out methodological advances possible with the experimental use of hypnosis, and to illustrate some of the seemingly elusive research problems that become amenable to study. Along with the accounts of how Ss are trained to experience degrees of cognitive arousal, pleasure, and anxiety, it has been shown that the necessary safeguards and independent checks for such work with hypnosis can be accomplished. Examples are the application of the cognitive arousal cues to hexagram salience and the Stroop Color-Word Test, the GSR as a reflection of degrees of organismic anxiety, and monetary equivalents for the levels of pleasure.

The potential number of methodological advances is virtually without limit. By means of posthypnotic cues, experimental variables can be shaped in pure form, such as free-floating anxiety, and manipulated systematically in degree. Their onset and offset can be brought about and timed with some degree of precision. Related variables commonly lumped under general rubrics such as arousal or boredom can be distinguished operationally and their effects studied in isolation or even in specifiable combinations. The conduct of experiments in the waking state, with S amnesic for the previous hypnotic training and not self-conscious about his programmed behavior, minimizes the opportunity for data to be confounded by spontaneous conscious deliberations on the part of S. Also, the conduct of postexperimental inquiries back under H, where amnesia no longer applies, typically provides a wealth of otherwise unattainable information about S's waking performance. Another experimental advantage of amnesia is its aid in keeping a series of trials independent, in the sense of eliminating conscious carryover from one trial to the next. Ss become highly sophisticated introspectors of their own mental states under hypnosis, and these judgments can themselves be utilized as data under circumstances where cognitive or affective arousal is free to vary, as noted above. We also saw the use of hypnosis itself as an experimental probe, substituting for electroconvulsive shock or chemicals in the studies on cognitive reverberation. The more one uses hypnotic methodology in research, the stronger the feeling grows that the surface of the potential has barely been scratched.

Finally, the range of research problems capable of attack is greatly broadened. Hopefully this point was driven home by such illustrations as the experimental separation of arousal effects along the perceiving-judging-responding sequence in the visual discrimination task; the breakdown of anxiety into its cognitive and organismic components to isolate the locus of decremental action and even to pin down empirically the competition versus attenuation explanations of such action; and the various extensions into the complex psychodynamic realm of primary process thinking, defense mechanisms, and the like, which expose *S*'s "natural" dynamic themes to laboratory scrutiny.

Josephine R. Hilgard *is clinical professor of psychiatry and research associate in the Department of Psychology at Stanford University. She received her Ph.D. in child psychology with Dr. Arnold Gesell at Yale in 1933, and her M.D. from Stanford in 1940. She completed her residency and psychoanalytic training under a Rockefeller Foundation grant in Chicago and Washington. Prior to her appointment at Stanford, she served as director of the Child Guidance Clinic of the San Francisco Children's Hospital. She has been involved in the work of the Laboratory of Hypnosis research at Stanford since 1957 and is the author of* Personality and Hypnosis: A Study of Imaginative Involvement, *based on her research there.*

Josephine R. Hilgard *demonstrates that hypnotizability is largely a matter of keeping alive the imaginative involvements of childhood. If these involvements fall into disuse or are replaced by too much vigilant concern with reality, hypnotic ability declines. Evidence from the Laboratory of Hypnosis Research at Stanford University is summarized, particularly her own extensive prehypnosis interview research. She illustrates how capacity for imaginative and adventurous involvements originating early in life are kept alive and functioning through continuous use in non-competitive physical activities, fantasies, and reading.*

12

Evidence for a Developmental-Interactive Theory of Hypnotic Susceptibility

JOSEPHINE R. HILGARD

A complete theory of hypnosis would doubtless have much to say about the relationship of the hypnotic state to known processes going on within the brain and nervous system, the various parameters influencing hypnotic performances, the subordinate processes of induction and trance deepening; however, such a complete theory is not available, at least not in a form to gain wide acceptance. The theoretical problem with which I am concerned is a far more limited one: To understand why one person tends to be much more hypnotizable than another. The empirical facts are clear. In whatever way hypnosis is defined—according to parameters affecting behavior (Barber & Calverley, 1963a), as some kind of established state (E. R. Hilgard, 1969a), as role enactments (Sarbin & Andersen, 1967), or as partial sleep (Pavlov, 1923; Platonov, 1959)—it is universally agreed that wide differences exist in responsiveness to suggestions given by the hypnotist.

Method of Investigation

The Laboratory of Hypnosis Research of the Department of Psychology at Stanford has been engaged for over a decade in the study of individual differences in hypnotizability. Early products of these investigations were the Stanford Hypnotic Susceptibility Scales (Weitzenhoffer & Hilgard, 1959,

This paper was presented at the American Psychological Association meetings, September, 1969. It summarizes some of the results presented in the author's book, *Personality and hypnosis: A study of imaginative involvement*, Chicago: University of Chicago Press, 1970. The research on which the findings are based was supported by grants from the National Institute of Mental Health (Grant MH-3859) the Wheeler Foundation, and the Air Force Office of Scientific Research.

1962). My role has been to direct and participate in an extensive interviewing program, in which, *in advance of hypnosis,* personality features that might potentially be related to hypnosis were assessed. In a number of interviews *following* hypnotic susceptibility testing we received the kind of feedback essential to improve our interpretation. The quantitative material here presented comes from the interviews prior to hypnosis; this protects against the tendency of rationalizing post facto connections between earlier and later behavior.

Findings

By way of introduction to the quantitative material, here are some of the conclusions reached regarding the development of hypnotic ability. While these conclusions often came after the data were collected, those reported were verified through replication. By presenting the conclusions first it may be easier to see the relevance of the data.

The first conclusion concerns the high susceptibility of young children to hypnosis. The trends with reference to age are shown in Figure 12.1.

This figure was constructed from unpublished data of our laboratory. We tested the hypnotic susceptibility of 277 children and 173 of their parents. Socioeconomic and educational status were relatively well controlled. The study is cross-sectional; the numbers tested at each age are shown on the figure. The main age trends are: a high level of hypnotic susceptibility between the ages of 6 and 15, a rather pronounced drop between 16 and 20, and a tendency for a gradual falling off thereafter through later middle age.

Because the ability to produce hypnoticlike behavior is so widespread in early childhood, our first conjecture was that some features of growing up —increased responsibility, heightened reality orientation, or increased competitiveness and achievement motivation—tend to reduce the earlier level of hypnotizability. For those who defy this trend and remain highly hypnotizable, it may well be that something in the later years sustains the kinds of experiences that are more nearly universal in childhood. As will be seen, we have evidence that those who, for one reason or another, kept alive the imaginative involvements of childhood, were the ones who retained their hypnotizability. It is possible, of course, that there were experiences that enhanced hypnotizability as well, but much of what we found can be explained on the basis of *retained* childhood susceptibility. If childhood imaginative involvements fall into disuse, or are replaced by a vigilant concern with reality, hypnotic ability will fail. This is the essence of the developmental theory to be presented here.

The other aspect of this theory—the interactive aspect—is concerned with how the words of the hypnotist capitalize on an imaginative background to produce the hypnotic state, and how they lead to the hypnotic reactions that Shor (1959, 1962) has well characterized as nonconscious role

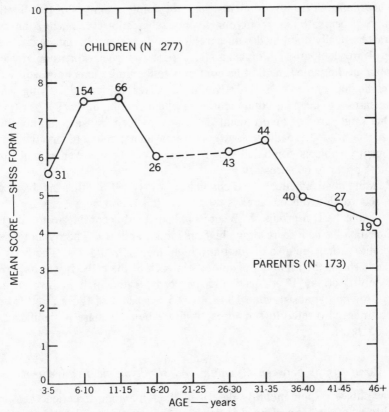

FIGURE 12.1. *Decline of hypnotizability with age. The data are from an unpublished study under way in the Stanford Laboratory and appear here through the courtesy of Arlene H. Morgan. A few parents between ages 21 and 25 were tested, but are omitted from the figure, which at all points except the last is based on upwards of 25 cases (from Hilgard, J., 1970).*

involvement and loss of reality orientation. In other words, hypnotic ability alone is not enough to explain why it is so easy for some individuals to become hypnotized; the conditions also must be right. Therefore our theory can best be described as a developmental-interactive one.

THE ROLE OF INVOLVEMENTS

The theory is that the *capacity* for imaginative and adventurous involvement, originating early in life, has been kept alive and functional through continuous use. Among the college students, the involvements that were found to be related to hypnosis included reading, drama, creativity, childhood imagination, religion, sensory stimulation, and adventurousness. The sum of these involvements correlated .35 with hypnosis, significant at the .001 level.

These imaginative involvements were not simply examples of free-floating primary-process thinking; in our hypnotizable subjects imagination was characteristically combined with careful cognitive control. Imagination and control are compatible. For example, a poet can give expression to deep emotion at the same time that he conforms to the limitations imposed by the meter he has chosen. Or the adventurous diver enjoys skin diving while being careful to keep his equipment in excellent condition.

One single area of involvement that has remained in use continuously is all that is needed: reading alone, or drama alone, religion, or adventure. Frequently subjects combined two or more areas of involvement, but this did not appear to be necessary.

Reading involvement showed characteristics typical of other involvements also; accordingly, this one area is used as an illustration.

In Table 12.1, a group of 82 subjects is divided according to the degree of their involvement in reading: high, medium, and low. The hypnotic susceptibility scores are also divided into high, medium, and low. The body of the table shows the numbers of subjects in each of the cells. It was apparent that only 2 of the 13 subjects (15 per cent) rated high in involvement scored low in hypnosis; while 18 of 40 (45 per cent) of those rated low in involvement also rated low in susceptibility. The chi square is significant at the .05 level.

Comparisons between Hypnotic and Nonhypnotic Involvements

A few subjects spontaneously described their hypnotic experiences as related to what they experienced in reading. Julie, who was highly hypnotizable, observed that "hypnosis was like reading a book. . . .When I get really involved in reading, I'm not aware of what is going on around me. I concentrate on the people in the book or the movie and react the way they react. The intense concentration is the same in a book or a movie or in imagination as it is in hypnosis. Reading a book can hypnotize you." Having affirmed the relationship, she went on to make clearer how she felt: "After each book, I'm completely washed out. After hypnosis it was the same. I

TABLE 12.1 Susceptibility to hypnosis as related to rated involvement in reading

Rated Involvement in Reading	Susceptibility to Hypnosis (Scores on SHSS:C)			
	low (0–3)	medium (4–7)	high (8–12)	Total
High involvement (6–7)	2	6	5	13
Medium involvement (4–5)	8	8	13	29
Low involvement (1–3)	18	16	6	40
Total	28	30	24	82[a]

SOURCE: J. Hilgard, 1970.
a. One case not ascertained.
Chi Square = 9.61, 4 df, p = .05

was completely washed out and couldn't keep my eyes open. I lacked the ability to communicate." This state of mind had lasted for a half hour.

The kinds of reading most conducive to the fantasy of participating in mental and physical activities, with appropriate emotion, include novels, mysteries, adventure stories, biography, and science fiction.

Sarah described her reading experiences in a way not too different from a description of hypnosis:

> I read two to three pages slowly, then I pick up speed (if the author is good) and am not aware of turning pages or of things around me. When I'm read-ing Faulkner, everything fades except what he's saying. . . . I start living with a book—I'm more identified with Faulkner in the emotion and ex-pression and totalness. I come out to meet him. It's as though nothing else is important. The room has faded—you separate from everything else. It's just the book.

Thus, in reading, Sarah tends to hold in abeyance all critical comment until afterwards; she also does this in hypnosis. Afterwards she reconstructs and criticizes. When asked how she made the leap from the more rational fantasies triggered by books to the occasionally irrational "magic" of hypno-sis, she denied that there was really much difference:

> Hypnosis is a different form of reality testing. You explore the possibilities inherent in something that doesn't really exist. You know what cold is by comparing it with hot. In hypnosis you are comparing an accepted irrational nonreality as real. Nothing's really wrong because some part of you is always aware that it's hypnosis though you don't verbalize it at all, not even to yourself. It's like dreaming when you know you're dreaming. When you first are hypnotized you lose your feet, you lose your hands, though you know they're there. Even though I'm doing just what the experimenter asks me to, that's secondary; my own recollection and activity are more important.

A valuable parallel arose in connection with a somewhat extreme demon-stration in which analgesia was produced through the posthypnotic sugges-tion that Sarah would awake from hypnosis to find that she had no hands, but that this would not bother her. When her "absent" (invisible) hands were then given quite a strong electric shock, she reported that she felt noth-ing, although there had been no specific analgesia suggestions. This experi-ence later reminded her of a book in which a hand had been lost:

> Dr. H. told me that I didn't have any hands. He had a little shocking ma-chine that kept floating around in the air. I was very interested in the fact that I didn't have any hands and I really felt I didn't. He told me it would be funny and I thought it amusing to see Dr. H. poking around in the air. My silly looking long sleeves with only circles at the end where the hands would be. Only those ridiculous ruffles were there.

When asked why she was not troubled, she replied:

Somewhere else I absolutely know I have hands. I know they're not cut off. I'm exploring the sensation of not having them. There's no anxiety. He said they would appear gradually at the count of five. He asked me how they came back and I didn't know. I had quit doing what I was doing that was keeping me from seeing them. But whatever it was I was doing was inside me, and I couldn't observe what I quit doing when my hands were again there. It's as though they were there all the time but I hadn't noticed them. They didn't suddenly appear as though they had come from nowhere, and they didn't appear gradually as though there were a film being developed.

The difficulty of describing just what had happened was extreme. The analgesia was doubtless genuine, for under hypnosis Sarah can tolerate keeping her hand in circulating ice water for several minutes remaining fully relaxed without feeling the pain, although insusceptible subjects find this quite impossible.

When asked if there were any bridge between this kind of an experience and what she felt in reading, she gave the following account:

In reading a novel, some misfortune happens. In one book I read, a hand was cut off—Howard Pease's book about a young man, Jewish-American, a talented musician, captured by Nazis, sent to a concentration camp; he has an arm injury which results in a hand amputation. The most powerful part was the last two to three chapters where he comes back to his friends. In one scene, he sits in front of the piano, plays crashing chords with his one hand, expresses his feelings of tragedy. Then he finds himself through composing music. The reader identifies with this young hero, goes with him through the experience of losing his hand. You *feel* how it is for him to lose a hand. You're able to feel with him and sympathize with him—even though you know you have both hands and aren't likely to lose a hand. I could feel the physical pain—I felt horrified—it made a great difference to me, yet I know I am still whole.

Although Sarah felt that she had shown to her own satisfaction that her reactions in reading and in hypnosis were essentially alike, there still seemed to be some lack of clarity. The interviewer urged her to talk further. Sarah added:

You can take an attitude, establish a new viewpoint. You can feel something that isn't there (like hallucinated heat) or you can lose something that is there (like your hand). You visualize what the author says—that's taking something on. You may visualize something gone, too, as when Dr. H. told me my hands were gone. It's not really losing anything; it's taking on an outlook. With the novelist it's not so personal; he leaves it up to you; among several characters you chose which one to identify with. With the hypnotist it is personal, it has to be you.

Involvements Not Related to Hypnosis

The question may well be asked whether the involvement theory is merely an alternate form of the role-enactment theory, because when subjects identify with a character in a book they are obviously adopting a role. As a matter of fact, many of our involved readers did *not* identify with the characters in books, although they empathized with the feelings expressed. These empathetic subjects, who did not take any specific role, were just as hypnotizable as those who became in their imaginations the characters they read about.

Even more striking evidence against an undiscriminating use of role theory came from cases in which strong role enactments were *not* associated with hypnosis unless other characteristics of imaginative involvement were also present. Two groups of subjects illustrated this position very well: athletes and scientists.

HYPNOTIZABILITY OF ATHLETES

Athletes tend to be highly motivated and to become deeply involved in their sports. However, it became necessary to make unanticipated discriminations if we were to predict which athletes would be hypnotizable. The main issue revolved around the degree of competitiveness. Competitive athletes in the team sports such as baseball, football, and basketball proved to be less hypnotizable than athletes who preferred individual skill sports such as boating, skiing, swimming, and riding. Of course this dichotomy is not absolute: There are ski competitions in the Olympics, there are teams of swimmers, and there are boat races. Nonetheless, it is possible to divide sports roughly into two major categories—those at the highly-competitive team-sport end of the continuum, and those at the less-competitive individual-skill sport end.

The relationship of type of sport to hypnotizability is shown in Table 12.2. Of the seven highly hypnotizable athletes, only one was in the highly competitive group; while of the 41 athletes with low hypnotizability, 28 of 41 (or 68 per cent) fell into the highly competitive group. The results were statistically significant, yielding a *p* of .001 by Fisher's exact probability test.

One of the athletes, Perry, received a low score of 3 on the SHSS. His only high involvement rated in advance of hypnosis was in athletics at the 7 level. He had played football for 10 years, and in the interview preceding hypnosis had said that the appeal was its aggressive nature and his need for

TABLE 12.2 Type of sport as related to hypnotic susceptibility

Hypnotic Susceptibility (Scores on SHSS: C)	Type of Sport		
	highly competitive; team sports	less competitive; individual skill	total
High (9–12)	1	6	7
Medium (5–8)	10	11	21
Low (0–4)	28	13	41
Total	39	30	69

SOURCE: J. Hilgard, 1970.
Fisher's exact probability *p* < .001.

power. He said he would become absorbed in his desire to win, to hit someone, and to crush him.

In contrasting his absorption while playing football with his absorption
during hypnosis, Perry said:

> The emphasis in athletics is to win and develop strength within the self; you
> have to strive constantly. In hypnosis you are taking emphasis off the self,
> and putting yourself in someone else's hands. You're relaxing instead of
> striving; when relaxing, my thoughts are wandering and I have no con-
> centration of attention then.

Perry's description of the total absorption and concentration on the game
that is demanded of the athlete continued:

> You train yourself to be conscious of movements of every other player; it
> becomes automatic, it's not conscious thought. Nothing else is in your mind
> than the game and your environment; at no time do you let down, you're
> always watching the other players. Your mind is directed toward one goal
> and that's the goal of winning. You're aware of your body and where it is
> in space. You develop reflexes so you know exactly where your hand is in
> space while you watch the ball, whether you're playing baseball, basketball,
> or football.

On the other hand, Chester, who enjoys swimming, provided an unusually
clear picture of the hypnotizable individual-skill sports enthusiast. His score
of 9 on the SHSS:C put him in the high group within our sample. Although
he had been on swimming teams, his own evaluation of the experience was
clearly on the side of enjoyment of the experience rather than enjoyment of
the victory. He said firmly:

> The competition is not as important as the enjoyment. . . . I love to get
> into the water and pretend I'm a seal. I can move like one in that wavy mo-
> tion. It's a fluid, effortless, almost frictionless feeling. . . . I like being
> underwater more than being on top. I look around and swim. . . . Every-
> thing underwater has a different appearance, though I guess it is more the
> feeling of suspended weightlessness, a feeling of easy, free movement.

HYPNOTIZABILITY OF SCIENCE STUDENTS

Another illustration of high concentration without the kind of involvement
associated with hypnosis was provided by the subjects interested in the natural sciences and engineering. When the students were classified according to
their majors in college, a difference in hypnotizability showed up (see Table
12.3). The humanities majors were nearly two-to-one in the more hypnotizable group, the social science majors were evenly divided, and the natural
science majors were three-to-one in the less hypnotizable group.

What these findings suggest is that there is a positive relationship between
hypnotizability and imaginative involvements of the kinds found in the
home in early childhood *if these involvements persist into college*. When, in

TABLE 12.3 College major as related to hypnotic susceptibility

Hypnotic Susceptibility (SHSS: C)	humanities	social sciences	Major biological sciences, physical sciences, engineering	total
More hypnotizable (Score 7–12)	9	21	10	40
Less hypnotizable (Score 0–6)	5	21	32	58
Total	14	42	42	98

SOURCE: J. Hilgard, 1970.
Chi Square, 9.53, df 2, $p < .01$.

the process of growing up, these imaginative involvements are replaced by high achievement strivings and vigilance as in the competitive team athlete, or by firm reality orientation and objectivity as in the natural scientist, hypnotizability tends to fade. One must not, however, overstate the magnitude of these tendencies, for there are scientists who keep their imaginations alive (by reading science fiction, for example), and occasionally there are highly hypnotizable competitive team athletes.

The Role of Childhood Punishment

Because of our interpretation that contagion between parent and child was one of the important facilitators of the persistent imaginative involvements and hence of hypnotizability, it was natural to infer that the relation between child and parent would be that of basic trust, as described by Erikson (1963). This would be a plausible background for the later trust in the hypnotist. Even though the hypnotist would be asking one to do and experience wholly new things, he could be trusted to do nothing disagreeable or harmful. This line of reasoning left us unprepared for one of the clearest findings to emerge from the study supporting a developmental point of view: A positive correlation between severity of punishment in childhood and hypnotizability. Table 12.4 shows the relationship.

TABLE 12.4 Severity of punishment as related to hypnotic susceptibility

Severity of Punishment	Low Hypnotizability SHSS: C score (0–5)	High Hypnotizability SHSS: C score (6–12)	total
High: ratings of 5, 6, 7	22	41	63
Medium: rating of 4	36	30	66
Low: ratings of 1, 2, 3	37	21	58
Total	95	92	187

SOURCE: J. Hilgard, 1970.
Chi Square, 9.53, df 2. p. 01.

Of those most severely punished, 41 of 63 subjects, or about two-thirds, fell in the upper half of hypnotic susceptibility scores. Of those least severely punished, only 21 of 58, or about one-third, had high hypnotic susceptibility scores. Those moderately punished fell between. The chi square was significant at the .01 level.

This is a developmental contribution because these punishments occurred early in childhood and were reported when the student was in the university. These may be interpreted as *successful* outcomes of punishment inasmuch as the recipients were doing satisfactory work in a highly competitive university.

We naturally wished to explore more deeply to find the rationale for this unexpected relationship between punishment and hypnosis. It soon appeared that the severity of punishment had very little to do with mother warmth. Those students who reported severity of punishment rated their mothers as very warm as often as those who rated their punishment low. Thus it was necessary to avoid the stereotype that the severely punished children grew up with cold and forbidding parents.

What then accounted for the correlation between severity of punishment and degree of hypnotizability? Two main factors suggested themselves, and both may in fact operate. The first has to do with training to accept commands immediately and without question. If during childhood this highly conforming response led to better relations with parents, it could become deeply ingrained as a mode of response to authority figures. If the hypnotist stands in loco parentis, he would then receive the same prompt response to his requests that the parent did. The second factor is quite different, although our interview material also bore it out. There was a tendency to avoid the pain and frustration of punishment through an imaginative evasion, which in itself may be a kind of hypnotic dissociation. One subject put it this way:

> My father would yell at me for long periods of time, even though he never touched me. I was frightened by him, I learned to become detached. I had to learn to escape. If I got angry, that would increase the yelling. I had to withdraw from my own anger. I learned to detach myself as though floating—a feeling of not feeling my body at all. If I had felt my body, I would have felt angry.

The subject, as a university student, was highly hypnotizable. He had no doubt that he had learned to dissociate in these childhood experiences of avoiding his father's verbal attacks.

Summary

Two developmental strands have been shown to provide a background for hypnotizability of young adults. The first was maintenance into young adulthood of the imaginative involvements prevalent in childhood; the second is an aftereffect of rather severe punishment in early childhood. This was less well understood. When either or both of these strands are present, the young adult is a good candidate for hypnosis. The hypnotic experience itself is an interactive one, in which the stage is set for the hypnotist to capitalize on the readiness that the developmental experiences have produced.

Martin T. Orne *is Director of the Unit for Experimental Psychiatry at the Institute of the Pennsylvania Hospital and Professor of Psychiatry at the University of Pennsylvania. He received his M.D. from Tufts University Medical School in 1955, and his M.A. and Ph.D. from Harvard University Graduate School in 1951 and 1958. After an internship at Michael Reese Hospital in 1956, he completed his residency at Massachusetts Mental Health Center in 1960. He became Senior Research Psychiatrist at Massachusetts Mental Health Center and Associate in Psychiatry at Harvard Medical School. From 1958 until 1964 he was Director of the Studies in Hypnosis project. In 1964 the research laboratory moved to the Institute of the Pennsylvania Hospital. The research group has continued as the Unit for Experimental Psychiatry with studies concerning the nature of hypnosis remaining one of its principal interests. Current areas of research also include sleep, psychophysiology, bio-feedback mechanisms, and the generic problem of objectifying alterations in subjective experience. Since each of these substantive areas of inquiry involves human subjects in experimental contexts, some work has inevitably been concerned with the basic problem of experimental methods in psychology and psychiatry, especially the social psychology of the psychological experiment.*

Orne *reported in 1959 on a special comparison group for the study of hypnosis, which involved the use of Ss instructed to simulate hypnosis. Simulators are selected from among unhypnotizable individuals and are not given any special training. Their behavior reflects therefore their own expectations about hypnosis and the information about what is expected of them that is provided by the hypnotist and the experimental situation. The procedure was developed in rough analogy to the double-blind placebo technique design as used in psychopharmacology. It has proved to have several important uses in hypnotic research, but the implications have been widely misunderstood and misinterpreted. This chapter seeks to clarify the issues. Orne shows that it is possible to simulate hypnosis, but he does not imply that hypnosis is simulation. Quite the contrary, his technique has helped shed light on important, unique characteristics of hypnosis.*

13

On the Simulating Subject as a Quasi-Control Group in Hypnosis Research: What, Why, and How

MARTIN T. ORNE

When a *S* capable of entering deep hypnosis agrees to do so, it is possible for him, within what appears to be a few moments, to alter dramatically his appearance, behavioral style, and responsivity to the hypnotist. The remarkable range of alterations in experience and memory that can now be induced has long puzzled and fascinated laymen and professionals alike. It is not surprising that such a dramatic phenomenon has resulted in innumerable claims about its potential benefit or harm, the way in which it may change or improve mental functioning, and how it might cause one individual to obtain a greater degree of control over another.

The process by which hypnosis is induced is remarkably innocuous when one considers the apparently dramatic changes that occur. Furthermore, entering hypnosis may take place almost instantaneously. As a result, the observer is fascinated by the implausibility of these events and, in trying to explain them, either assumes some basic alteration in neurophysiological function or is inclined to dismiss what he has seen as not real, play-acting, or faking.

The preparation of this chapter, as well as the substantive research conducted at the Unit for Experimental Psychiatry, was supported in part by grant #MH 03369 and by grant #MH 19156-01 from the National Institute of Mental Health, Public Health Service. The author wishes to express his appreciation to Harvey D. Cohen, Mary R. Cook, Frederick J. Evans, Charles Graham, A. Gordon Hammer, Ulric Neisser, Donald N. O'Connell, Emily Carota Orne, David A. Paskewitz, Arthur Shapiro, and Mae C. Weglarski for their helpful comments during the preparation of this manuscript.

From the time when hypnotic phenomena were first described, attempts have been made to explain away these occurrences as not being real. Inevitably, in attempting to account for hypnosis, there has been a great deal of concern about the extent to which the *S* honestly reports his experiences or the extent to which he may be dissimulating or deceiving the observers.

Traditionally then, questions were raised about the extent to which the *S*'s actions reflect what he is experiencing and whether the *S*'s reports about his experiences are honest and genuine. The most satisfying proof about the reality of hypnosis, therefore, was to demonstrate abilities of the hypnotized individual that were present only in that state. If it could be demonstrated that the hypnotized *S* can do things that the waking individual cannot, there is little need to worry about the reality of the phenomenon. It certainly is more satisfying to have hard evidence of this kind than to depend upon the *S*'s verbal description of what has occurred.

When it was first reported (Orne, 1959) that individuals are able to simulate hypnosis sufficiently well to deceive trained hypnotists, the observation aroused considerable skepticism, and its implications were widely misunderstood. It is the purpose of this paper to clarify some of these issues and to review the strategy of research that led to development of this technique.

Some Comments on the Nature of Hypnosis

It is recognized that there is no generally accepted definition of hypnosis, though considerable consensus exists at a descriptive level and observers readily agree that they have witnessed hypnosis after they have watched a highly responsive *S* responding to hypnotic suggestions. Although a large number of induction procedures have been described, it must be admitted that neither the necessary nor the sufficient conditions for hypnosis have yet been delineated. Thus, some *S*s under some circumstances will enter hypnosis without any formal induction procedures, while others fail to enter hypnosis despite extensive induction procedures designed to elicit such response. For these reasons it seems futile at the present state of knowledge to define hypnosis by the antecedent conditions. It seems more appropriate to stay closer to a descriptive level where consensus exists.

The presence of hypnosis can be identified by the way in which a *S* responds to suggestions. Heuristically, then, hypnosis is considered to be that state or condition in which suggestions (or cues) from the hypnotist will elicit hypnotic phenomena. Hypnotic phenomena can operationally be distinguished from nonhypnotic responses only when suggestions are given that require the *S* to distort his perception or memory. Accordingly, the hypnotized individual can be identified only by his ability to respond to suitable suggestions by appropriately altering any or all modalties of perception and memory (Orne, 1959). It follows, therefore, that if a *S* is told by a hypnotist, "Remove your left shoe," and he carries out the requested behavior, it would not be possible to conclude that the individual is hypnotized; since no distortion of perception is required, the behavior could be carried out by the unhypnotized individual. However, if the hypnotist suggests that the *S* see someone who is not physically present, hear music in a quiet room, or have gustatory experiences in the absence of food, and the *S* behaves as if he has these experiences, reports having these experiences and, as far as it is possible to ascertain, actually believes he has these experiences, one may say he is hypnotized; indeed, these are experiences which the nonhypnotized individual cannot simply choose to have.

Of particular importance for the diagnosis of hypnosis are suggestions that (1) distort the *S*'s perception so as to make him feel unable to carry out an action such as bending his arm, opening his eyes, and so forth (challenge suggestions), (2) induce hallucinatory experiences, (3) alter memory (such as suggested amnesias), and (4) elicit posthypnotic behaviors.

Individuals differ widely in the extent to which suggestions are able to elicit hypnotic phenomena from them. The concept of hypnotic depth generally is used to designate the range of phenomena that can be experienced, though, unfortunately, the same term is also used to describe the subjective conviction associated with the suggested alteration of perception or memory and the degree to which the *S* feels himself profoundly affected.

A great many questions may be asked about hypnosis, such as those that deal with individual differences, the dynamics and nature of the induction process, correlates of hypnotizability, and so on. However, the main thrust of our research program has focused on questions concerning the nature of hypnosis: In other words, research focused on trying to clarify the consequences of being in that state where suggestions are able to distort the perceptions and memories of an individual. If it is suggested to a *S* that he is six years old and he begins to act in a childlike manner and appears to believe that he is six, what consequences does this have for his actual mental functioning? How will his thought processes be altered? What will this do to his ability to recall past events, and so forth? If a *S* is told he has superhuman strength and accepts the suggestion, how does this alter his actual performance? If anesthesia is induced and he is exposed to painful stimuli, how does this alter his behavioral response; how does it affect his physiological responses, and so forth?

To the extent that the investigator is concerned about the effects of hypnosis on the psychological and physiological responsivity of the individual, it seems essential to be certain that the *S* is hypnotized. Consensus is easily obtained only with highly responsive *S*s, whereas with less responsive *S*s neither the observer, the hypnotist, nor the *S* himself is necessarily certain as to the extent of hypnosis or even whether hypnosis is present. The most appropriate strategy would therefore be to use only the most responsive *S*s. By selecting the extreme group of individuals who are deeply hypnotizable, it is possible to make highly reliable diagnoses and achieve general consensus that the hypnotic phenomenon is unequivocally present. The research approach to be discussed here, then, is based upon the assumption that in order to approach a poorly defined phenomenon one must be absolutely certain that it is really present in the situation. From this point of view, parametric questions dealing with the generalizability of the findings become important only after the general nature of the phenomenon has been delineated.

Problems in Hypnosis Research

Though it is generally agreed that hypnosis is that state where suggestions can elicit hypnotic phenomena from the *S*, the associated behaviors have been subject to continuing controversy. In historical perspective this is particularly striking. Thus, the behavior exhibited by Mesmer's patients at his *baquets* was characterized by hysterical seizures which he termed "crises." While these behaviors seemed to be an invariant accompaniment of his sessions, they certainly are not seen today. On the other hand, the fixed entranced expression often associated with hypnosis was shown by Bernheim (1889) not to be a necessary accompaniment of the phenomenon. Rapport, once believed to be an essential characteristic of hypnosis, was shown by P. C. Young (1927) not to be essential. At the present time, Erickson[1] insists that catalepsy is an inevitable accompaniment of hypnosis, a finding not substantiated by a number of other clinicians.

In the older literature particularly, many claims are made about hypnosis which, to the modern reader, appear naive. The "physical effects" of mesmeric passes, the transference of cataleptic states from one side of the body to another by means of magnets, and Charcot's (1886) observation that a hypnotized *S* could be brought from sleep to somnambulism by rubbing the top of his head are examples. It is worth noting that the investigators involved were often outstanding scientists whose incisive observations in other areas have stood the test of time. One could hardly consider Charcot—a pioneer in recognizing the distinction between neurological and psychiatric illness, who first described such classic signs as glove anesthesia—an untrained observer; nor is such a label appropriate for Binet, Braid, or Moll.

In order to understand the range of reports about hypnosis and the peculiar diversity of findings, it is necessary to take into account the deeply hypnotized individual's remarkable responsivity not only to explicit suggestions but also to very minute cues, often outside the observer's awareness. These cues are analogous to those discovered in the case of the famous Clever Hans (the horse who was apparently able to do arithmetic computations), a puzzle that was finally solved by Pfungst (1911) when he noticed that the animal responded as long as his trainer looked expectantly at his right fore-

1. Personal communication.

foot and stopped when the trainer raised his head. Many scientists, unable to explain the phenomenon, came to accept the extremely implausible hypothesis that the horse, Clever Hans, was actually doing arithmetic. If such a relatively simple set of cues could prove so deceptive, it should not be surprising that the elucidation of behavior characteristic of the hypnotized *S* has proven to be such a difficult and complex problem.

Not only does the deeply hypnotized *S* respond to implicit communication (which in and of itself is enough to create special problems of investigation), but there is a further complicating factor: The *S*'s own beliefs and expectations about appropriate behavior of hypnotized individuals also help to determine how he will behave when he is actually hypnotized. Thus it was possible to demonstrate that *S*s who were led to believe unilateral catalepsy of the dominant hand is a hallmark of deep hypnosis tend to display this item of behavior when they are subsequently hypnotized (Orne, 1959).

The search for behavioral characteristics of deep hypnosis that are "intrinsic" is, therefore, exceedingly difficult. An investigator might easily validate any plausible—or not so plausible—beliefs about what constitutes "typical" behavior of the hypnotized individual. The cues as to what is expected may be unwittingly communicated before or during the hypnotic procedure, either by the hypnotist or by someone else, for example, a previous *S*, a story, a movie, a stage show, etc. Further, the nature of these cues may be quite obscure, both to the hypnotist, to the *S*, and even to the trained observer.

Recognizing these problems, it seemed essential to develop special techniques that would make it possible to recognize which aspects of a *S*'s response, if any, were due to hypnosis, as opposed to those that were the result of a combination of the *S*'s prior knowledge and expectations in conjunction with cues provided by the situation.

The Need to Evaluate or Hold Constant
the Problems that Required Clarification

The generally accepted approach to hypnotic research, characterized particularly well by the work of Hull (1933), compared the effect of instructions or suggestions given to a deeply hypnotized individual with the identical instructions given either to a nonhypnotized independent control group or to the same individuals in the waking state.[2] Upon study of the results of dif-

---

2. The technical advantages of using *S*s as their own control are considerable in that inter-individual variability is eliminated, and it is therefore possible to obtain significant results with small samples (and also the hypnotizability variable is held constant); on the other hand, the effects of repeated measurements on performance can be highly complex and, especially in hypnotic research, these may seriously distort the picture. For a discussion of these issues, see Sutcliffe (1958) and Zamansky, Scharf, and Brightbill (1964).

ferent instructions it becomes clear, however, that while it is possible to hold the precise wording constant, it is extremely difficult if not impossible for an investigator to speak in the same fashion to a hypnotized as to a waking S—even when the investigator himself is convinced he has done so. Inevitably the instructions are more meaningful to the S and are given with more conviction and emphasis to an individual in whom the E had just induced hypnosis. [An empirical demonstration of these differences was carried out by Troffer and Tart (1964).]

It would appear that many of the differences observed between hypnotized and nonhypnotized individuals could be accounted for by the differential treatment of Ss in hypnosis as opposed to the waking state. The lyrics may be the same but the melody is vastly different! Moreover, even when one is aware of this problem, it is extremely difficult to treat Ss in the same way when they are hypnotized as when they are awake. This problem becomes especially poignant to the observer of the hypnotic interaction when he recalls how a hypnotist changes his voice to speak convincingly to the age-regressed S as a child, and how difficult it is for most Es, even in a role playing situation, to speak to the adult in front of them as if they were playing with a winsome waif making mud pies on the street outside their laboratory.

The importance of subtle interactional differences in the treatment of individuals has long been recognized in psychopharmacology. Thus, it eventually became clear that even the placebo control is not sufficient, since the physician characteristically (and appropriately) is more concerned with the patients on a new and presumably powerful drug than with those who are receiving an inert substance where "side effects" must be a matter of chance. Complaints of the former variety are carefully followed up, while those of the latter are quickly dismissed, though the etiology of complaints or "effects" in both instances may often, in fact, be identical. For reasons such as these, double- and triple-blind studies have been recognized as essential in order to demonstrate a therapeutic drug effect, particularly in the case of psychotropic agents where subjective experiences are involved. The problem here, analogous to studies of hypnosis, is the need to develop a control procedure for the behavior of the physician-experimenter and, particularly, the need to control for his natural inclination to delve into and follow up certain kinds of subjective experiences in one patient group but not in another.

The Need to Evaluate Subjects' Knowledge and Expectations

The classic experimental model, being based on the one used in physics, assumes that the S enters an experiment as a tabula rasa; that is, that the human S exposed to various treatment conditions has no relevant prior information, knowledge, or expectations. Further, the S in the classic psychological experiment is expected to respond only to those stimuli that are explicitly defined as relevant and important by the investigator. Certainly such is not the state of affairs.[3] On the contrary, Ss enter into any experimental situation—including those that employ hypnosis—with a great deal of prior information as well as very specific, though not necessarily correct, expectations about what is to occur. By the same token, they do not respond merely to the explicit suggestions; rather, these are interpreted, as are all other communications, in the context of a S's understanding of what is intended.[4]

Until relatively recently, little explicit attention had been paid to the S's interpretation of the situation. A striking exception was Asch's (1952) brilliant reinterpretation of the Lorge (1936) experiment on prestige suggestion. In this study the investigators had shown that Ss based their agreement with short statements not on their substantive content but rather on the individual to whom the statements were ascribed. Lorge argued that Ss' acceptance or refusal of substantive statements was based not on their content but on prestige suggestion, that is, the attitude toward the man to whom the statement had been credited. In repeating this study, Asch asked not only for the degree of acceptance but also for an elaboration of the meaning of the statements. In this way it became clear that a short sentence such as ". . . a little rebellion, now and then, is a good thing . . ." has in fact an entirely different substantive meaning if it is attributed to Lenin than it does if attributed to Jefferson. In other words, the ascription of a brief and ambiguous statement to a specific author about whose views the S is relatively well informed actually provides special contextual meaning to the statement. Agreement or disagreement is a function not of prestige suggestion but of altered meaning due to the additional information provided by the knowledge of who made the statement.

Asch's analysis is a penetrating one which can be used as a model for understanding much experimental work. Inquiry procedures (Orne, 1959) help clarify how the S perceived the total situation and how he interpreted explicit experimental demands. Unfortunately the interpretation of inquiry information involves considerable subjective judgment, a difficulty which can be only partially remedied by the use of judges. Further, there always remains doubt about how the S's perception may have translated itself into behavior on the experimental tasks. Another problem with post-experimental procedures is the difficulty of determining the extent to which the S's response represents hindsights gained from reflection about his own performance, which need not have affected his behavior during the actual experimental situation.

3. For a more extended discussion of these issues see Orne (1962b, 1969, 1970).
4. It has often been claimed (see Erickson, 1952) that the deeply hypnotized S is more literal in his interpretation of suggestions than the waking individual. Unfortunately, rigorous evidence for this very interesting observation is not yet available. The possibility that the observations are the result of subtle cues by the hypnotist of the kind described earlier cannot be dismissed.

A modification of the post-experimental inquiry procedure, which has been referred to as the "pre-experimental inquiry" or the "nonexperiment" (Orne, 1962b), partially deals with this problem; a similar technique was independently suggested by Riecken (1962). In such a nonexperiment, the procedure of the experiment is explained to the S, but he is never allowed to actually respond to the independent variables in order to eliminate cues stemming from his own behavior. He may then be asked to complete any post-experimental tests and be given a post-experimental inquiry. (For a description of this approach and a discussion of its limits see Orne, 1969.)

While a variety of inquiry techniques have proved useful in hypnosis research, none of these procedures can adequately deal with the nexus of problems stemming from (1) subtle cues that may communicate what the hypnotist desires, and other effects of differential treatment of the hypnotized and waking individual; (2) the effects stemming from the S's prior knowledge and expectations in interaction with the information provided by the particular study, as well as the E-bias factor discussed above. Consequently a procedure was needed that would permit the investigator to estimate the possible effects of these factors in a particular experiment. Specifically, a special control group was necessary, with which to compare the performances of deeply hypnotized Ss.

The Motivation of a Comparison Group

One of the characteristics of the hypnotized individual is a high motivation to play the role of a hypnotized person and carry out the requests of the hypnotist (White, 1941). The S's wish to please the hypnotist is an aspect of hypnosis that has also been commented on extensively by therapists describing its use in treatment (e.g., Brenman & Gill, 1947). Thus, it seemed essential to have an *unhypnotized* comparison group that would be highly motivated to please the hypnotist and to behave in a manner they believed characteristic of hypnotized Ss.

The Simulating Technique

In order to satisfy the requirements discussed above, the technique of asking Ss to simulate hypnosis as a comparison group was developed (Orne, 1959). The procedure was initially conceptualized as providing a group of individuals who would share the role playing aspects of hypnosis and the high level of motivation to behave like hypnotized Ss[5] but would not share

5. At the time, it was assumed that a high level of motivation to please the hypnotist uniquely characterized the hypnotic relationship. Since then it has become clear that a good subject-experimenter and certainly therapist-patient relationship may provide at least as high a level of motivation to please, and therefore I no longer assume a necessary motivational difference between the hypnotized and the unhypnotized S (see Orne, 1970).

the experiences of real hypnosis. That is, they would not be able to experience as subjectively real the suggestions of the hypnotist. However, they would have as a basis for their simulation behavior the usual prior knowledge and expectations as well as all of the information provided by the experimental procedure and those subtle cues from the hypnotist that communicate his implicit wishes.

Until recently the literature was in general agreement about the impossibility of simulating hypnosis in a way that would deceive the experienced hypnotist. When, nonetheless, we asked Ss to simulate hypnosis, it became clear why there was such agreement on this point (Orne, 1959). Ss found the task difficult and distasteful. Typically they gave a very transparent performance, tending to interrupt it by asking for reassurance with questions such as, "Am I doing all right?" or "Is this what you want?" When urged to resume the role, they would do so, frequently looking to the E for encouragement, smiling embarrassedly, and in many clearly discernible ways communicating their discomfort. From discussion of these experiences with the Ss it emerged that they felt foolish in carrying out a task that was manifestly impossible. They had been asked to simulate hypnosis but were aware that the request had emanated from the hypnotist who, of course, knew that they were simulating, so there was no conceivable way in which they could successfully comply with the request without appearing ridiculous.

It is necessary to make a small but absolutely vital change in the procedure: two Es must be involved so that the hypnotist-experimenter can remain absolutely blind as to which Ss are in deep hypnosis and which Ss are simulating. Ss are instructed by one investigator as follows:

> Today your task will be to work with Dr. X and to convince him that you are an excellent hypnotic subject and become deeply hypnotized. Dr. X will not know that you are pretending, though he will be aware that some individuals may be faking. If he becomes aware of the fact that you are not really hypnotized and are only pretending, he will immediately stop the experiment. So long as he goes on, you know that you are successful in your task.[6] I cannot tell you anything about what he will be doing with you today nor can I tell you anything about how a hypnotized individual might act in this situation. You will just have to use your judgment and do the best you can. This is a difficult task but we have found that intelligent subjects have been able to carry it out successfully. Good luck!

If one assumes that situations can be set up whereby an individual can simulate hypnosis and not be detected at greater than chance rate by the hypnotist-experimenter, then it becomes crucial to allow only those individuals to be part of the simulator comparison group who indeed cannot, with

---

6. The latter part of the instructions was added because we observed that some individuals would suddenly stop in the middle of an experiment because they mistakenly thought they must have revealed the fact that they were simulating. These instructions obviated this difficulty, and also served to reinforce the Ss.

repeated tries, enter any depth of hypnosis at all. The simulator comparison group is not useful to evaluate those responses which could be a function of cues in the situation rather than hypnosis if there is any possibility that some members of this comparison group have the ability to enter hypnosis.

Since it is essential that the Ss who are in the simulating group should not be hypnotized, we selected those individuals who had previously tried to enter hypnosis and had been unable to respond to any significant degree in a clinical diagnostic situation (Orne & O'Connell, 1967). It was important, however, in this context not to include those Ss who appeared negativistic or seemed, for purposes of their own, to have a need to demonstrate their inability to enter hypnosis. It is not uncommon to find individuals who view the situation as some form of power struggle and misuse the situation as a means of demonstrating to themselves that they are not easily influenced by others. As a rule they consider it a matter of pride to have a "logical mind," are not subject to suggestion, have an "indomitable will," and so forth. Such Ss can generally be identified during the induction process: They will sometimes sway forward when instructed to sway backwards; if told that they will be unable to bend their arm, they bend it even before they are asked to test the suggestion; or, if they wait, such Ss often display an overeagerness to demonstrate that they have not in fact responded. In addition to this characteristic mode of responding to the suggestions themselves, these individuals, while superficially extremely cooperative, sabotage the induction in a variety of ways and betray their underlying attitude by being manifestly pleased by their inability to experience suggestions. Such individuals not infrequently turn out to be capable of entering deep hypnosis if the induction procedure takes care to circumvent their defensive maneuvers. (For example, see Erickson, 1952.)

The reason that such a negativistic individual must not be used is that the simulating situation provides a setting where this type of S may respond to the challenge, again negativistically, but this time by becoming hypnotized! On the other hand, those individuals who are able to experience extremely limited effects of hypnosis, despite apparently genuine attempts to respond, almost never experience any hypnotic phenomena when asked to simulate. We intentionally avoided working with highly hypnotizable Ss under simulating conditions since we found it impossible to determine with certainty whether these individuals were or were not hypnotized in the simulating situation. The possibility that a highly hypnotizable S, instructed to simulate, might enter hypnosis and yet maintain that he was simulating was difficult to exclude.[7]

---

7. Austin et al. (1963) as well as Bowers (1966) have carried out studies utilizing highly hypnotizable and simulating controls. They have stressed the importance of selecting Ss from the same hypnotic population, and wished to demonstrate that the procedure was feasible. Personal communication with several of the

In the 1959 paper that first described the simulating technique, the statement was made that Ss instructed to simulate were drawn from the same population as those who were actually hypnotized (Orne, 1959, p. 287). By this it was meant that Ss shared the same general information about hypnosis and were drawn from the same population insofar as their expectations, beliefs, and knowledge about hypnosis were concerned. Unfortunately, in the original printing the statement that the simulating Ss were unhypnotizable was inadvertently omitted, and it should be emphasized that in terms of the hypnotizability variable, simulating and real Ss (as I have used the terms) are decidedly *not* drawn from the same population. For the reasons outlined, it is not possible to have Ss matched for hypnotizability in the simulating design without introducing serious doubts about the actual status of the simulation no-hypnosis comparison group. The possible effect of as yet undiscovered personality differences[8] between simulating and real Ss has, of course, important methodological consequences that must be taken into account in interpreting research findings, and places important limitations on some—but not all—applications of this technique. These issues will be discussed later. Our intent here is to clarify the essential characteristics of the real-simulator design. The nine points discussed below take up those characteristics of the design that have been misunderstood most frequently in the literature.

1. It should be emphasized that one crucial aspect of using simulators is that the hypnotist who is working with the S must truly be blind as to the latter's actual status. Thus, when the prospective simulator is told that the hypnotist-experimenter with whom he will work does not know which Ss are simulating, this must in fact be an accurate statement and, equally important, before the hypnotist-experimenter can be unblinded, the experiment must be *entirely* over, all Ss having completed *all* relevant sessions. If this is not the case, the E often second-guesses, "I had two reals, one simulator; the next one must be a simulator." In our experience it has not been possible for the investigator to treat a S whom he knows to be a simulator the same way as he would a S whom he believes to be hypnotized, even when he subjectively feels that he has been consistent in his approach. Subtle, but nonetheless real, differences exist, which will tend in turn to affect the S's performance (Troffer & Tart, 1964).

2. Such a situation is radically different from that obtained when individuals are asked to role play hypnosis or simulate with the knowledge of the E, or any variation of these. To emphasize this difference for studies with

authors suggested that these investigators encountered the very problems described above, that is, the problems upon which we based the decision to use only unhypnotizable simulators.

8. Numerous studies of personality correlates of hypnotizability (see Hilgard, 1965b) have as yet not been successful in isolating personality attributes unique to deeply hypnotizable Ss.

many different kinds of control groups, O'Connell, Shor, and Orne (1970) proposed the term *"crypto*simulator" to distinguish this control group— where the hypnotist *is blind* as to which Ss are simulating—from role playing Ss on the one hand, and from so-called "simulating" Ss where the investigator *is aware* of (not blind to) their true status, on the other. Neither of these groups can serve the purposes for which the cryptosimulator procedure was designed.

3. While the concept of the simulating design is a single-blind adaptation of the double-blind placebo technique in psychopharmacology, there are important and very significant differences between them. Whereas with the placebo both the E and the S are blind as to the presence or absence of the active pharmacological agent, only the hypnotist and not the S is blind in the simulating design. Further, while the simulator unavoidably knows that he is in a special simulating group, the real S does not know of the simulator's existence.[9] Neither real nor simulating Ss are deceived at all. There must be no deception about the blindness of the hypnotist-experimenter involved in dealing with the simulating S. It is crucial that the S correctly perceive that he has a chance of fooling the hypnotist-experimenter, or there is no "percentage" in his trying and he is apt simply to give up.

4. While it is crucial for the simulating Ss to have had several opportunities during which they have tried to enter hypnosis, preferably with different hypnotists using varying techniques, *no* special training may be given to this group. The very point of having simulating Ss to help evaluate the nature of the cues in the experimental situation is to determine how these would be interpreted by Ss who do not share the hypnotic experience but otherwise have access to the same amount of background information. It is, of course, particularly important that the instructions to simulators in no way communicate how a deeply hypnotized S would actually perform, either on the experimental procedures being tested or on any other aspect of hypnotic behavior. While simulators as well as real Ss may have seen hypnosis at some time in the past, neither group should include individuals who have special knowledge or experience.

5. Ss should be given simulating instructions at a time immediately preceding the experimental session. This will assure that they understand what is required of them and will tend to facilitate a high level of motivation. While in certain studies it may be more efficient to set up Ss two or three weeks in advance, they then do not tend to have a clear enough picture in

9. While it is motivating and important (to bring meaning to the task) for simulators to know of the existence of a real hypnotic group, when real Ss are confronted with the idea of a simulating group, of necessity the group is understood by them to cast doubt on their own performances. This inevitable conclusion does not allow them the necessary trust in the laboratory that is essential to their concentrating for full hypnotic depth. It is therefore not good practice that the simulating group be discussed with them, as it can distinctly hinder their cooperation.

their minds at the time of the experimental run as to their exact instructions. Perhaps even more important, the spontaneity and enthusiasm of participating in an exciting study in a very important control group is sometimes lost. With time, self-doubt about one's ability to successfully simulate looms large, and the *S* may become unduly concerned with possible failure. Instead of focusing on fooling the *E,* the *S* may become troubled about looking foolish himself. The model is designed to overcome this problem by assuring the *S* that the *E* is blind, thereby making it possible for him to succeed and making it worth his while to try his best to do so.

It is possible, however, to have the *S* simulate over a period of several sessions extending over a matter of weeks, provided that the "setup" takes place immediately prior to the first session. In this instance the *S* successfully completes the first session before he has an opportunity to become concerned. As a result, he will be less likely to fear failure—the experiment would have been terminated had he been unsuccessful—and he has also had actual experience in the role of simulation, making it very unlikely that he will forget the task. Further, in the pre-experimental setup interview it is very important for the *S* to be told precisely when his task as simulator will be completed, and also for the end point to be clearly marked by a final interview with the investigator who originally instructed him to simulate.

6. It is necessary to make clear to the *S*s that their simulation is a crucial part of the experimental situation, that it is their task as *S*s to fool the *E*. It is helpful in this regard that the *E* who is to be fooled be seen as competent and senior. Yet the *S*s ought not to see their role only as making a fool of the investigator, but rather as a vital control procedure contributing to the scientific process, success being difficult but possible.

Under these circumstances we have not encountered any difficulty with *S*s being concerned about deceiving the investigator. The only situation where we have observed such problems was when the *E* to be fooled was a relatively young and somewhat insecure graduate student with whom some *S*s tended to identify. Under these specific circumstances some *S*s felt uncomfortable since they perceived the situation as though the *E* were being tested. It is important in setting up *S*s to simulate not to reassure them about the legitimacy of faking hypnosis. To tell *S*s beforehand not to feel guilty about it clearly conveys that you feel they or others have indeed or should in fact feel guilty about faking. This problem is most effectively dealt with by clearly communicating that they are an essential control group, the existence of which is known to the investigator, but that which individuals are part of the control group is clearly not known by the *E*.

7. We have found it essential for the investigator who sets up the *S* to simulate to arrange, at that time, for a post-experimental interview with the *S* at the completion of the experiment. This provides a necessary audience for the *S* who is simulating, someone with whom he can eventually share his success, someone who will provide him with the feedback about the experi-

ment, and with whom he can discuss how he actually felt. Since the information the S provides at the very end has always been viewed as of crucial importance by our laboratory, arrangements for a final interview were routinely made whenever the simulator model was used. In retrospect, it seems very likely that an arrangement of this kind played a significant role in facilitating the simulator's performance.

8. A simulator rarely behaves so transparently that the blind E can recognize with certainty he is faking. If he should do so, the data from such a S must, of course, be excluded from the analysis.[10] However, we do not feel it appropriate to terminate the experiment at that point and embarrass the S; instead, in these rare cases the E's certainty is marked by his immediately shortening the normal experimental procedure, but not in such a way as to make it obvious to the S. We feel that every effort should be made to have any S participating in an experimental study perceive his performance as a success experience; his data are real and he has thereby contributed to science even if in a way that is uncongenial to E's aims. To bluntly inform a S that he has been unsuccessful in carrying out an experimental requirement is at best unkind and frequently quite traumatic for the S. It costs but little more time and effort to make certain that the S leaves the study with a good feeling. For ethical reasons alone, therefore, it is felt inappropriate for the blind E to ever stop an experiment and inform the S that he is faking. In addition, however, it seems likely that such behavior would make the task of subsequent simulating Ss more difficult, to the extent that it could conceivably become campus scuttlebutt that Ss who fail at simulating hypnosis are rudely dismissed.

It should be noted that even with great care it is possible—and we have seen two or three such instances—for a S instructed to simulate not to understand the instructions. In one instance, the S erroneously assumed that the simulating instructions were intended to facilitate hypnotizing him. In another, the S simply did not believe that the blind E actually would be blind. Under such circumstances, an experimental session is kept as short as possible, the blind E carrying out whatever experimental task might seem reasonable to the S without making him aware of his inappropriate behavior. The post-experimental interview is then used to explore the S's actual perception, again without making him feel that he has failed in his task as a S.

10. In our experience this is sufficiently unusual that there has never been more than one S in any given study who was identified with certainty by the blind E. This includes the kind of S who fails to understand instructions referred to below. Though such Ss would not tend to affect the group data to any significant degree, it is against the logic of the design to include them—except as a footnote. Unless the unhypnotized S instructed to simulate is able to perform the task required of him, he will not be treated equivalently by the blind E, thereby violating the assumption of the model.

9. We have found it useful to ask the blind *E* to specify whether a given *S* is hypnotized or simulating at the end of each run, although no feedback is provided. At the conclusion of the experiment it is then possible to determine whether the *E*'s perceptions of the *S*'s status affected the *S*'s behavior, especially when, as is frequently the case, his judgments prove to be random.

It is, of course, desirable to have the blind *E* know as little as possible about the design. He should certainly not know how many real and how many simulating *S*s he will see. When technically possible, it would be most desirable for the blind *E* not to know about the existence of the simulating *S*s (under such circumstances, of course, no judgments would be obtained). For various methodological reasons it may also be helpful to have only simulating *S*s or only real *S*s, which facilitates the evaluation of *E* expectancy effects in particular situations.

An Example of Simulating Instructions

Assuming that a *S* has shown himself unable to enter hypnosis in several sessions with different *E*s and has agreed to participate in another experiment, the simulating instructions would be given along the following line:

We much appreciate your participation in several of our sessions in the past. Today I would like you to take part in a very interesting experiment that is quite different from any in which you have participated to date. . . . You have attempted to go into hypnosis several times and found it quite difficult to respond. Though I understand you have been able to experience a certain lightness in your arm and felt quite drowsy at times, it was not possible to experience much else. . . . In this particular study there is a special group of subjects to which you will belong, all of whom were not able to enter hypnosis despite their honest efforts to do so. As you know, people vary in their ability to respond; some individuals find it very easy while some individuals find it quite difficult. This doesn't seem to be related to any other personality characteristics. In this instance your task will be to simulate being a very good hypnotic subject. You will be working with Dr. _____ who is a very experienced and competent hypnotist and will be carrying out an important piece of research. Your task will be to behave as though you were one of those subjects who is able to enter deep hypnosis with ease. There will be only two kinds of subjects in this experiment: those who are excellent subjects and can enter deep hypnosis, and several individuals like yourself who are unable to do so but will be trying to simulate hypnosis.

Dr. _____ does know that some subjects will be trying to simulate but has no idea who these subjects will be. Your task is to convince him that you are in fact an excellent hypnotic subject. Now this is a difficult task and you may well do something where you think you have given yourself away. Don't worry about this possibility, because if Dr. _____ recognizes the fact that you are simulating he will stop the experiment immediately. Therefore, as long as he continues with you, you know you have been successful in faking hypnosis. I point this out to you because in the past we have found some subjects would suddenly stop, thinking they had goofed and given themselves away, when, in fact, their behavior had been quite appropriate and the investigator had no idea that they were simulating. Keep in mind, then, that as long as the experimenter continues with you, you are doing all right; if he catches on he will stop the study immediately.

We realize that you have no experience in how to do this. You were chosen simply because you were not able to enter hypnosis and we know you have had no experience in this kind of task. However, we also know from previous studies—we have run a great many studies using this procedure—that intelligent subjects are able to do this. It is difficult but it is possible. . . . I can't tell you how to behave or what to do; you have to use whatever you know about hypnosis, whatever cues you get from Dr. _____, and whatever you learn from the situation to figure out how a deeply hypnotized subject would behave, and your task is then to use this information in your simulation of hypnosis. Keep in mind that you will be simulating the behavior of an excellent, highly hypnotizable individual and that your task is to maintain that you are going into hypnosis, to perform during hypnosis, and, when you are awakened, to respond as if you had been in hypnosis. In other words, this includes simulating not only while you are being hypnotized but afterwards as well. When Dr. _____ asks you about your experiences you should answer the way a deeply hypnotized subject would answer if he had actually been in trance. If Dr. _____ asks you how you did the last time, keep in mind that you are a good hypnotic subject and you would have gone into deep hypnosis on your previous efforts. You would have had several previous experiences with hypnosis just as you actually have, except that you would have entered deep hypnosis. All subjects will have had at least five such sessions with the laboratory.

At no time, once you leave this room, may you reveal to anyone that you are simulating. They will not know that you are simulating. Though it is known that some subjects will be simulating, no one knows who they are except for me. When you are completely finished with the experiment, the investigator will ask you to return to the waiting room, which you will do, and I will meet you there. I will eventually discuss your experiences with you back in this office. Until you are back here with me at the very end of the experiment, you are to reveal to no one that you are not actually hypnotized: this means the experimenter or anyone else who asks you about your experiences other than me when we are back in this room.

*S*s might ask questions such as:

"Could I ask you something about how to do it?"
    Answer: "Certainly."
"Let's say I am told to make a physical movement. How fast does a good subject react?"
    Answer: "I can't tell you that. I can only tell you to do what you think you should do."

"If I am told that I feel no pain, how will I be able to prevent myself from responding?"

Answer: "I really can't tell you how to simulate or what to do. It is a difficult task but we have found that other intelligent subjects have been able to do it successfully. Good luck! I will see you back here at the end of the experiment."

Early Experiences with Simulating Subjects

As soon as we began to experiment with the cryptosimulators, it became apparent that this situation produced a remarkable performance in simulating individuals. Initially I had hoped to develop a method to evaluate the effects of nonhypnotized Ss' perceptions of what was expected of them on the experimental tasks under investigation. However, as a clinician who had worked extensively with hypnosis, I never doubted that it would be easy for me personally to recognize Ss who were, in fact, simulating. It came as a complete surprise and was a considerable blow to my fantasies of omniscience to find that Ss tested over a one-session period were indeed able to deceive me. It turned out to be impossible to distinguish between simulating and hypnotized Ss with a high degree of certainty or, at any rate, greater than chance.

Many of the procedures that I had casually accepted as useful tests to determine the Ss' depth of response, and had assumed to be proof positive of the reality of the hypnotic response, failed to distinguish between the groups. Not only were simulators able to perform the many feats of strength —such as remaining suspended between two chairs—without hypnosis, but they also showed themselves capable of tolerating painful stimuli without flinching (Shor, 1964b) and were able to apparently recall material that ought to have been beyond their ken (O'Connell, Shor, & Orne, 1970). Simple behavioral tasks did not effectively discriminate between them, nor did a variety of procedures that tried to evaluate the individual's trust in the investigator (whether, for example, when told there was a chair behind him, he would sit down without actually testing its presence).

A very striking personal experience with this technique occurred when I tried to establish some simple differentiating criteria. Thus I set up Ss for my colleagues and carefully noted down a myriad of clear, definable differences between the behavior of simulating and deeply hypnotized individuals. Indeed it was hard for me to fathom how my colleagues were so inexperienced and unsophisticated as to fail to recognize a dozen or so fatal mistakes that simulators made in pretending to be hypnotized. It was all the more shocking, therefore, when I again took the role of blind E to realize that I too was quite incapable of successfully distinguishing the two groups. My experience as a clinician did not, in fact, allow a reliable differentiation. Perhaps this experience, more than any other, imbued me with an abiding awareness of capabilities for self-deception, and it has taught me not to place undue significance on impressions not rigorously tested.[11]

The Real-Simulator Technique Used to Evaluate the Capabilities of the Nonhypnotized Subject

A great many claims have been put forward about the effects of hypnosis to uniquely augment the *S*'s performance on a wide variety of tasks. Hull spoke of this class of questions as the problem of transcendence of normal volitional capacity (Hull, 1933).

Traditionally this category of questions has been answered by comparing the *S*'s performance in the waking state with his own performance in hypnosis. While the importance of controlling order effects had been recognized and dealt with by Hull, such controls do not deal with the effects of either differential treatment by the *E* of *S*s in the waking state and hypnosis, or the more complex effects where the *S* alters his response in the waking state in order to thereby maximize his apparent capacities in hypnosis. Hull already recognized this problem when he discussed the work of Sears (1932) on pain and noted the surprising finding that *S*s, instructed to flinch as little as possible when jabbed with a needle, actually flinched more than when they had received no special instruction. He suggested that they might have increased their flinching in order to give the appearance of greater relative control when tested in hypnosis. It is perhaps relevant that a special device was attached to the face to measure grimacing which, in and of itself, would be likely to communicate the *E*'s interest in such behavior. The *S*s' recognition that flinching was of concern to the investigator would have been emphasized further by the specific instructions which called attention to the behavior and were thereby likely to potentiate this kind of an effect. In an entirely different context, Zamansky, Scharf, and Brightbill (1964) have documented a similar effect more recently.

If the *S* is used as his own control and his performance during hypnosis exceeds the one he gives in the waking state, the difference may be due to an augmented performance in hypnosis or a diminished performance in the waking state (Evans & Orne, 1965). The latter, in turn, could be a function of the *S*'s wish to make his hypnotic performance seem better or merely a response to differential degrees of emphasis that the hypnotist uses with his instructions in the waking state and in hypnosis. In any case, however, it is difficult to demonstrate augmentation of *S*s' capacities with such a procedure.

11. Several distinguished colleagues, well known for their clinical skills, insisted that simulating *S*s could easily be distinguished from hypnotized individuals by experienced clinicians. In each instance, when they actually tried to do so with experimental *S*s who were set up for them according to the procedures outlined, they found themselves unable to make accurate and reliable differentiation on the basis of their clinical judgment during a single session.

Alternatively, if instead of using the *S* as his own control independent control groups are employed, new problems are introduced. Sample size must inevitably be increased considerably due to the introduction of interindividual variability. Most important, serious possibilities of dfferential treatment between experimental and control groups remain.

The real-simulating model is particularly well adapted to explore issues of this kind and permits the investigator to evaluate the likelihood of an alternative mechanism accounting for the behaviors observed during hypnosis. For example, it has often been asserted that if a deeply hypnotized *S* is given the suggestion to experience fear, guilt, anxiety, or depression, the appropriate state will almost instantaneously be produced in the *S*. In a straightforward psychophysiological study, Damaser, Shor, and Orne (1963) were able to show that striking changes in heart rate and GSR are induced in hypnotized individuals by such suggestions. However, in this study simulating *S*s were also used, and it was noted that equally large physiological alterations were seen in the comparison group. This demonstration suggested that physiological alterations, which otherwise might be viewed as proof of the unique capability of hypnosis to induce a suggested state, are not adequate evidence of this uniqueness. In this experiment the simulating control group served to demonstrate the capabilities of nonhypnotized individuals to alter some physiological functions—apparently mediated by way of imaging—in the total absence of the subjective experience of hypnosis.

Another example of this kind was a very detailed replication (O'Connell, Shor, & Orne, 1970) of the work of Reiff and Scheerer (1959) on hypnotic age regression. In their work, Reiff and Scheerer used the series of tasks that had been developed by Piaget in order to explore the cognitive development of children. In addition, they utilized the Word Association test and some behavioral measures which, they argued, were such that *S*s would have no way of knowing how to respond appropriately. They showed in an empirical study that age-regressed *S*s behave very differently from control *S*s instructed to role play the respective ages.

Reiff and Scheerer's original study had a number of methodological problems and, because of the significance of the findings, a careful replication and extension of the study was undertaken (O'Connell, Shor, & Orne, 1970). Of concern here is the inclusion of a new comparison group. This group served to provide a rigorous test for the assertion that *S*s *would not know* how to respond correctly. The study closely replicated the Reiff and Scheerer findings with deeply hypnotized *S*s; that is, our group of highly selected, exceedingly hypnotizable and highly trained *S*s behaved very much as did *S*s in the Reiff and Scheerer study. However, the simulating group, which was selected from unhypnotizable individuals and did not share any of the subjective experiences of age regression, yielded behavior which in all respects could not be differentiated from that of the deeply hypnotized group. Neither the objective tests nor the observational data of these individuals revealed any meaningful differences. Incidentally, both groups—the hypnotized and the simulating—behaved entirely differently from actual children when compared with such a group on a number of parameters.

For purposes of this discussion, the utility of a simulating comparison group should be clear. Here was a group of individuals who did not have the opportunity to experience age regression but were otherwise treated in exactly the same manner and given precisely the same cues and information by the hypnotist. The hypnotist was unable to treat these Ss differently because he did not know which were which. The fact that these individuals, without hypnosis, were able to produce the behavior of the hypnotized individuals conclusively demonstrates that, given the identical treatment, unhypnotized Ss can figure out the kind of responses that appear appropriate on the experimental tasks. It should be clear that it is *only* this assertion that is being tested by the inclusion of the comparison group of simulating Ss.

The conclusions that can be drawn from the behavior of simulating Ss need to be carefully considered. Certainly these studies do not suggest there are no differences between simulating and age-regressed Ss. The only permissible conclusion is that the particular technique that has been employed to "prove" that Ss could not have known enough without hypnosis to respond appropriately was inadequate to this task. The simulating procedure used in this fashion sheds light *only* on the adequacy of the experimental procedure. It says nothing about what mechanisms were actually involved. Thus, real and simulating Ss certainly may produce the same behavior mediated by different mental processes. In any case, our failure to observe any behavioral differences does not challenge the reality of the hypnotized individual's subjective experiences.

Thus, simulating Ss should not be considered a control group in the classical sense; that is, a group of Ss who are the same in all respects as the experimental Ss except that they are not exposed to the experimental treatment. They differ from the hypnotized group not only in their initial hypnotizability, but also in that they are functioning under entirely different instructions with presumably differing motivations and mental sets. The simulating Ss are best considered as a comparison group that helps to discover the kind of conclusions that a highly motivated S might draw from the procedure and from the behavior of the hypnotist interpreted in the light of the background information available to all Ss. The simulating group allows an estimate of the *capabilities* of unhypnotized Ss and obviates the need to speculate about what Ss could or could not do, or know, or figure out if they chose to do so. A finding of no difference indicates that the particular procedure was of a kind which, if the S had chosen to do so, could have been mimicked by an unhypnotized individual. It could therefore not be considered as proof of hypnotic potentiation.

In essence, the simulators are used to clarify the behavior of more typical nonhypnotized control groups. They help establish whether Ss could have figured out from the cues in the experimental situation what constituted the expected behavior without having been exposed to the subjective experiences of hypnosis. An example is Sheehan's (1969) replication of Reyher's (1961a, 1967) work. Reyher had carried out a number of studies using hypnosis to induce an artificial complex and testing the consequences of this procedure by administering projective techniques. He argued that the changes that were induced were of such a nature that Ss could not have anticipated the kind of changes that ought to occur and therefore the projective test data proved the reality of the unconscious complex that had been induced by hypnosis. To demonstrate that Ss would be unable to figure out the appropriate behavior on his tests, Reyher asked Ss to role play being hypnotized and exposed them to the same procedure. These individuals did not show the kind of changes observed in hypnotized individuals. In one experiment he even asked Ss to "simulate hypnosis"—in contrast to our procedure, the hypnotist was not blind, however—and, under these circumstances, these "simulating" Ss still did not respond to the projective tests in the same manner as the hypnotized individuals.

In a careful replication, Sheehan (1969) used the Luria technique to induce an artificial complex in the precise manner as reported by Reyher. His hypnotized Ss behaved in the same manner as those in the Reyher studies; however, in this instance, the simulating Ss were run blind as was specified by the model, and, under these circumstances, simulators responded to the projective tests in a manner indistinguishable from that of the hypnotized individuals. It is worth noting that the E in this study, which was run in our laboratory, initially was convinced that differences would emerge, but in accordance with the model he was not aware which Ss were and which Ss were not simulating. The striking differences between the behavior of the simulating Ss in Sheehan's study and those obtained by Reyher with Ss run by nonblind investigators illustrate the importance of the blind aspect of the simulator design.

Sheehan's findings do not, of course, invalidate Reyher's previous work. It is entirely plausible that changes observed in the projective techniques reflected genuine alterations in the subjective experience of hypnotized individuals. The important conclusion that must be drawn from Sheehan's findings, however, is that the procedure of using projective techniques is not sufficient to provide a criterion measure that could not volitionally be distorted by the S. The data from the simulators shed light only on what Ss *could* have done; it in no way proves what they did do. As long as we have no reason to distrust the projective test data of the hypnotized Ss, it should not trouble us unduly that these data can be reproduced by simulators exposed to the identical cues. It merely forces us to be cautious about making claims of having devised a foolproof test that demonstrates the reality of hypnotically induced complexes. [For a discussion of these issues, see Sheehan's (1971) rebuttal to Reyher's (1969b) comments.]

It should be clear then that whenever an investigator wishes to make assertions about what *S*s could not conceivably do without hypnosis because they would not have the ability or knowledge to do so, it behooves the investigator to test his belief, using the blind real-simulator design. This test is, of course, a very hard one, and it will readily throw into relief flaws in the procedure. As long as the procedure fails to distinguish between real and simulating *S*s, no meaningful statement can be made about an effect being uniquely due to hypnosis and demonstrating an ability not normally within the range of the waking individual's skills. Such a claim can be made only if the investigator hits upon a procedure that indeed does separate the two groups. However, even when he is able to accomplish this, it will still be necessary to determine whether these differences are due to an effect of hypnosis, a characteristic of hypnotizable individuals, or a function of *S*'s having been given simulating instructions. These questions cannot be answered within the real-simulating model and require different experimental approaches.

Are Simulating Subjects Hypnotized?

The publication of our experience with simulating *S*s, especially the failure to discriminate these individuals from the deeply hypnotized persons, led to a number of inappropriate conclusions. Two groups of colleagues holding diametrically opposed views of hypnosis concluded from our failure to find many differences between simulating and deeply hypnotized *S*s that these groups were the same. Many clinicians, particularly those whom Sutcliffe (1960) would have classified as belonging to the "credulous" group, promptly asserted that the fatal flaw was that *S*s, pretending to be hypnotized, were not really pretending but were, in fact, hypnotized. This being the case, it should surprise no one that differences could not be demonstrated. A similar position was adopted by some colleagues who took what Sutcliffe (1960) would call the "skeptical" position. These colleagues asserted that the failure to find differences between simulating and hypnotized *S*s was because there were no differences, since hypnosis actually was the same as simulation.

For a variety of reasons, however, it seems extremely unlikely that simulating *S*s are hypnotized. As has already been pointed out, great care is taken to select individuals who have found it impossible to enter hypnosis despite honest efforts to do so. While there are instances of an individual previously unable to enter hypnosis later successfully entering deep trance, they are extremely rare. After a single attempt at hypnosis, particularly if it is a standardized procedure, it is sometimes possible to increase a *S*'s response by working through his concerns and anxieties, using a more individualized approach (see Hilgard, 1964). Such a response is far less likely if the S has had several hypnotic sessions and the opportunity to discuss any concerns or anxieties with the hypnotist without any success. Indeed, with a number of sessions we have found it exceedingly difficult to increase the hypnotizability of individuals after the response has stabilized (see Cobb & Shor, 1964; Shor, Orne, & O'Connell, 1966). Since we select as simulators only those Ss who are unable to enter hypnosis over several sessions with different hypnotists, it is extremely unlikely that these individuals then enter hypnosis in the actual experiment itself.

It is again necessary to emphasize that simulators are not selected for their ability to simulate. Their sole qualifications are that they have volunteered and have been unable to enter hypnosis in several efforts beyond the level we have designated as 2– on the clinical scale (Orne & O'Connell, 1967). It is extremely infrequent to find a S who is unable to follow simulating instructions provided the situation that has been described earlier is set up—certainly no more than 1 individual in 20. These essentially unselected individuals are the ones who perform so well in the situation. If one were to assume that simulators are hypnotized, it would also be necessary to assume that we have effectively solved the problems of inducing hypnosis in all Ss with only a few moments of instruction.

Elsewhere (Orne, 1966b) I have emphasized that the hallmark of the hypnotic phenomenon is not the willingness of the S to do what he is requested to—this is characteristic of both clinical and experimental situations —nor that the S's behavior appears trancelike to the observer. Rather it is the nature and quality of the concomitant subjective events. Consider the case of a posthypnotic suggestion: If a S is told that he will run his hands over his hair when the E removes his glasses after he is awake and, in response to this cue, carries out the behavior, the event seems interesting and perhaps striking. The reason is not simply because the S did as he was told. Thus, it would not be considered noteworthy that a S runs his hand over his hair if he were instructed, "Please run your hand over your hair when I later remove my glasses," and he complies. However, when the S appears to carry out the action without apparently being aware of his behavior—or when he rationalizes his action and seems convinced that it is motivated by extraneous circumstances, or if he describes a peculiar compulsion or strange impulse as the basis for his action—one tends then to characterize the event as somehow different from what occurs in an individual's usual state of awareness. To a large extent one may infer from a S's behavior whether he experiences the situation as merely responding to a request or whether it is experienced differently.

To take another example, when a S is told his hand is so heavy that he cannot lift it and that he should try to do so, his behavior—that is, whether he does or does not lift his hand—will correlate fairly well with the presence or absence of heaviness of an experiential inability to lift his hand. To the extent that the behavior accurately reflects these experiences it is a useful criterion of hypnosis; however, the correlation is by no means perfect and, when the S's behavior fails to reflect alterations in his experience, it ceases to be a meaningful criterion of hypnosis. The S's response to hypnosis can never be evaluated adequately without a detailed exploration of the S's experience. It should be obvious, however, that simulating instructions are designed to create a lack of correlation between behavior and experience.

The need to examine the S's experience becomes particularly clear when working with the real-simulator design. Here the S's subjective response to the suggestions becomes the major criterion to determine the presence or absence of hypnosis. It is essential that this inquiry be carried out under circumstances designed to elicit an honest report. This is best done by the E who originally gave the simulating instructions. The inquiry should not be carried out in the presence of the hypnotist who had previously been blind since Ss may feel self-conscious about having deceived the E and could, for this and similar reasons, distort their account of the experience. It is essential, of course, that the investigator who carries out the inquiry communicate his genuine wish to know how the S felt in the situation. In any interview some biasing of the S's response is inevitable, and, since in this instance it is important not to overlook Ss who might have entered hypnosis, the E may communicate that quite often Ss experience a number of the hypnotic suggestions even though they had initially begun by simulating. In other words, the inquiry should be carried out in a way that would maximize the probability of the S's reporting subjective alterations even if he experienced none, in order to make certain not to overlook evidence of a hypnotic response. Under these circumstances, every so often a S will report experiences along lines such as, "When I was asked to straighten my arm and told that I couldn't bend it, the strangest thing happened to me. I actually found that the arm wouldn't bend. This was really weird. It scared me so much that I almost stopped simulating." A S reporting this had, of course, stopped simulating, at least as far as arm rigidity was concerned.

Even though the exploration of the S's experience is carried out in the most encouraging circumstances, it is exceedingly rare for Ss to report evidence of any subjective response to suggestions. Having even one such S in a study is unusual, but if this occurs, his data must be excluded from consideration. Incidentally, it should be noted that even these individuals do not experience the more difficult items. Thus, we have never seen *any* of our unhypnotizable Ss instructed to simulate who then reported experiencing a hallucinated person as though he were real or who felt that the amnesia suggestion had an effect on his recall.

In sum it would not be parsimonious to assume that Ss who are asked to simulate then become hypnotized, because (1) the inability to enter hypnosis despite repeated efforts to do so is a remarkably stable trait and (2) simulating Ss do not share the experiences of the hypnotized individual.

Are Hypnotized Subjects Simulating?

The purpose of developing the simulator design was to help differentiate artifactual components or epiphenomena from those aspects of hypnosis that are truly intrinsic. This work has been interpreted by some as raising questions about the existence of the phenomenon. The demonstration that simulators are able to produce behavior that even highly trained hypnotists were unable to distinguish from that produced by deeply hypnotized individuals resonates with the recurrent wish to explain away any apparently nonrational components in man's existence. When the simulator design is used, it soon becomes clear that many behavioral items that have been taken as self-evident proof of hypnosis—even by otherwise skeptical observers—are well within the repertoire of the nonhypnotized individuals. (These include such dramatic "proof" of hypnosis as the ability to remain suspended between two chairs, supported only at the heels and the head and supporting yet another person on one's midriff while in this position. Other behaviors such as a glazed look, passivity, talking in a monotone, the absence of a sense of humor, psychomotor retardation, and so forth, were once assumed to be uniquely characteristic of hypnosis. Similarly included is the ability to withstand without flinching being pinched or having a needle pass through one's arm.)

Though it is true that simulating *S*s are able to deceive experienced hypnotists, it is entirely incorrect to assume that spontaneous simulation can be used to account for the phenomenon of hypnosis. Spontaneous simulation under normal circumstances is rare, provided, of course, that the hypnotist does not create a situation where the *S* would make considerable secondary gains by simulating. Certainly it is unwise to tell *S*s that they will be permitted to participate in an exciting and well-paid research program if they are able to enter deep hypnosis. The problem of spontaneous simulation is somewhat similar to that of patients who willfully lie to their therapist. This occurs; however, it is rare under normal conditions because the therapist goes to considerable pains to create circumstances where no advantage can accrue to his patient from lying. (The difficulties encountered in treating patients where it is to their advantage to lie are well known and are attested to by the remarkably poor results with pension neuroses.)

For the most part, therapists evaluate the circumstances under which they are being consulted and recognize that in one or two sessions they would be unable to distinguish between a patient who is intentionally lying about a given difficulty and one who actually experiences the difficulties he describes. Indeed, it may be difficult to do so even with prolonged observation. Fortunately this realization does not cause the therapist to be unduly concerned about simulation unless it is clear that some benefit can be derived from such behavior. It seems strange that one should consider the hypnotized *S*'s reports of his experiences any differently.

It is currently fashionable to denigrate reports of subjective experience as evidence; however, it should be kept in mind that many "respectable" behavioral indices are subject to the same biases and distortions as verbal reports. On the other hand, it is essential to evaluate the circumstances under which subjective reports are obtained. During a properly conducted posthypnotic inquiry (which strives to elicit what the S actually experienced rather than attempting to lead him to obtain testimony to support one's point of view or, for that matter, to have the S fill out a questionnaire), the reports that are obtained are remarkably consistent with those obtained by other Es who are not the hypnotist, or in other contexts. At times we have gone to considerable lengths to obtain reports: for example, a research assistant may drive a S back home after an experiment and engage him in a casual conversation about his experiences; similarly we have explored the kind of reports that Ss give to roommates or spouses; and, at other times, we have provided an opportunity for Ss to talk informally in the waiting room while monitoring their conversation. It is striking that reports obtained under these widely differing circumstances agree on the major aspects of the S's experience during hypnosis.[12]

In talking with a S after an experiment, the unbiased listener cannot help but be impressed by the individual's uneven response to different suggested events. Why should a S describe a vivid visual hallucination and yet be unable to hear the buzzing of a fly with his eyes closed? Why should another S describe a startling inability to bend his elbow while indicating that an arm failed to get heavy when it had been suggested? The inconsistency of Ss' responses to different items, the lack of association between overall response and other indices of compliance, and the absence of any obvious motivation to spontaneously simulate make it extremely unparsimonious to assume that these individuals are reporting anything other than compelling and vivid subjective events. For these reasons, I would be convinced that deep hypnosis is an entirely different phenomenon from what we observe with simulating individuals even if we were unable to find a single clear-cut behavioral difference between these two groups. It is unfortunate that some colleagues misinterpreted my statements to suggest any other opinion. Though we will discuss some interesting examples where differences have emerged between

12. Barber and his associates (Barber, Dalal, & Calverley, 1968) have recently "discovered" that responses about the S's experience can be biased by the manner in which questions are asked. The fact that inappropriate wording of questions distorts Ss' responses is well known in the area of public opinion (e.g., Cantril, 1940; Maccoby & Maccoby, 1954) and ought not to be taken as evidence that the manner in which questions are phrased determines the experience that the S is reporting. Quite to the contrary, both the clinical techniques of interviewing as well as the techniques of social psychologists are designed to closely approximate how Ss actually feel about issues and experiences. To discover the wording of questions as antecedent variables determining responses is to confuse an artifact with substantive data.

simulating and hypnotized individuals, these data merely provided objective evidence of differences that clinically appear self-evident.

Differences Between Real and Simulating Subjects

The observation that even highly trained hypnotists are unable to distinguish deeply hypnotized *S*s from simulating *S*s seemed to introduce a more critical evaluation of those behaviors that many of us had assumed uniquely due to hypnosis. The fact that these behaviors can be mimicked cannot, of course, be taken as evidence that they are therefore not intrinsic to hypnosis. To take an analogy, if a *S* is asked to simulate sleep, the fact that he will lie down, close his eyes, and breathe in a regular rhythm in no way implies that these behaviors are not associated with true sleep. It merely means that this knowledge is shared by both *S* and *E* and cannot serve as the basis for reliably distinguishing between sleep and the simulation of sleep. Indeed, asking *S*s to simulate sleep will only serve to tell the investigator something about the preconceptions that all of us have about how the sleeping *S* behaves.

The reason why the simulating procedure seemed so important was that the behavioral characteristics of hypnosis are by no means as clear-cut as those of sleeping. Not only is hypnosis as described by Mesmer behaviorally different from the phenomenon observed today, but it is possible to demonstrate that when *S*s believe a behavioral item to be typical of hypnosis, they will manifest this item when they subsequently enter hypnosis. It is for these reasons that a detailed knowledge of the *S*'s expectations assumes such critical importance in hypnotic research. Thus, in the event that a simulating *S* can mimic the behavior of the hypnotized individual, it is still not possible to determine the extent to which the behavior is truly intrinsic to hypnosis and the extent to which it is a function of expectations of the subject population about hypnosis and therefore possibly an epiphenomenon. As we have repeatedly pointed out, in trying to successfully mimic the behavior of hypnotized individuals, simulating *S*s will utilize whatever knowledge is available to them from past experience as well as through cues provided by the experiment and subtle shaping procedures employed by the hypnotist, often without his own awareness. Successful imitation of hypnotized *S*s by the simulator in no way demonstrates a lack of genuineness of hypnosis. It does, however, show that the particular behavioral items cannot be employed to prove the genuineness of hypnosis. The best that one can say under these circumstances is that the behavior of hypnotized *S*s is such that nonhypnotized individuals placed in the same situation would know enough about what is expected to perform the same way.

The reason why it is so difficult for even experienced hypnotists to distinguish between hypnotized and simulating individuals is that the range of behavior observed in hypnotized *S*s is far greater than is generally recognized. However, some differences have gradually emerged. When such differences are observed, what conclusions can be drawn? First, it is likely that the simulating Ss simply do not know how the hypnotized individual would behave. Regarding the particular item of the investigation, the finding is counterexpectational. Further, the behavior of the hypnotized individual is not, in this instance, a function of the cues provided by the experiment or the behavior of the hypnotist. On the other hand, it would be premature, and at times incorrect, to assume that differences are due to the presence of hypnosis in the hypnotized group.

The simulating group is subjected to a treatment procedure different from hypnosis, but in many ways equally potent; namely, the instruction to simulate. Therefore differences between these two groups are as likely to be due to the presence of simulation in the simulating group as to the presence of hypnosis in the hypnotized group. For example, in early observations with simulators I observed that these Ss had a tendency to avoid committing themselves in an ambiguous situation, preferring to answer "I don't know" when such a response was plausible. This tendency, while reasonably consistent, was interpreted as analogous to the Rorschach findings with malingerers who typically gave few and vague responses (Orne, 1969). Differences between real and simulating Ss such as these are not particularly relevant or interesting since they are a function of the simulation treatment condition rather than the presence of hypnosis. While I have little doubt that, with sufficient effort, there are a number of ways that could be found that would trick simulators, findings of this kind would, perhaps, reassure those individuals who worry about the genuineness of hypnosis, but would fail to bring us to a closer understanding of the mechanisms of hypnosis.

Even if we are careful to avoid focusing on those behavioral items that might result from the simulation instructions, great care still is required before concluding that the behavior of a hypnotized S is due to the presence of hypnosis. It should be remembered that the real-simulator model compares highly hypnotizable Ss with unhypnotizable simulators, and, within the model, it is extremely difficult to discriminate between those aspects of behavior due to the presence of hypnosis as opposed to those due to differential hypnotizability of the S. This is an issue which, when relevant, must be resolved by a special study addressing itself to that question. However, it is, of course, unnecessary to worry about the problem when clear differences between simulating and hypnotized Ss are observed.

Clinical Observations Concerning Differences
Between Real and Simulating Subjects

Though it was not possible to reliably distinguish hypnotized from simulating Ss, some behaviors were observed only in deeply hypnotized individuals. This class of responses is characterized by a peculiar mixture of the suggested experience with components of accurate perception of the real world, and always characterized by a remarkable incongruity that does not appear to unduly trouble the *S*. An example would be a *S* who was told to hallucinate an individual sitting in a chair and describes his experience, "You know, it is the strangest thing. I see _____ sitting there and smiling in the chair. He's there and yet I can see the outline of the chair through him." Or another *S*, when asked to touch a hallucinated person, will describe a peculiar rubbery feeling, saying that somehow there is a tremendous amount of give as if he were able to feel through the person. Another type of incongruity reported earlier is equally characteristic of deep hypnosis (Orne, 1951). A *S*, regressed to age six, is instructed to write, "I am conducting an experiment which will assess my psychological capacities." Though printing in a childlike manner, he spells without any errors. Another *S* who spoke only German at age six and who was age regressed to that time answered when asked whether he can understand English, "Nein." When this question was rephrased to him 10 times in English, he indicated each time in German that he was unable to comprehend English, explaining in childlike German such details as that his parents speak English in order that he not understand. While professing his inability to comprehend English, he continued responding appropriately in German to the hypnotist's complex English questions. Incongruities of this kind (which simulators would readily recognize as inappropriate when they occur spontaneously) occur only with the deeply hypnotized individual—assuming of course that the simulator has not had access to these papers.

Since spontaneous evidence of the tolerance of incongruity, which I have called "trance logic" (Orne, 1959), is often not available, I have utilized a procedure to elicit this response. The technique was suggested by Milton Erickson[13] and consists of asking the *S* to hallucinate an individual (who is actually present)—say Dr. X—in a chair across the room. Once the *S* is clearly hallucinating, and interacting with the hallucination, the *S* is asked to indicate Dr. X. He will, of course, point to the hallucination. The investigator then points to Dr. X who is actually in the room—ideally somewhat outside of the *S*'s range of vision while he is looking at the hallucination—and inquires, "Who is this?" Simulating *S*s will tend to respond by saying, "I don't know," "Mr. Y," or "There is no one there." The hypnotized *S* will typically do a "double take," looking back and forth between the hallucination and the actual person, and then in a somewhat startled but not unduly disturbed manner will indicate that there are two Dr. Xs. In some instances, if the *S* is then asked to explain, it is not unusual to be told in a somewhat blandly quizzical fashion, "Mirrors perhaps," "He must have a twin brother," or something similar. If the situation is pushed still further,

13. Personal communication, 1949.

the S may be told that one of the Dr. Xs is a hallucination and the other is the real person and, when asked to indicate which is which, the S may experience varying degrees of difficulty.

Occasionally, especially if the S is not very deeply hypnotized, merely calling the S's attention to the real person will be sufficient to eliminate the hallucination. In other instances, being told that one is a hallucination may bring similar results. Again, Ss may describe fascinating and idiosyncratic differences between the hallucination and the actual person. Most illustrative and interesting, however, is the very occasional S who is usually both highly intelligent and experienced in hypnosis, who will look at both the hallucination and the real person and finally identify the real person. When asked the process by which this decision was reached, he will say that he thought Dr. X should carry out an action, perhaps raise his right hand, and one did and the other did not; he therefore decided that the one that raised his hand must be the hallucination. The possibility for such a highly sophisticated, logical process to co-exist with actually hallucinating is, in my view, uniquely characteristic of the hypnotic phenomenon.

The response of the simulating S under these circumstances is a function of his awareness that the same person cannot be in two places at once and, characteristically, when asked to explain why he behaved as he did, will indicate that having been told to hallucinate Dr. X in one place he assumed that he ought not to recognize him when the E pointed to him and said, "Who is this?" It goes without saying that simulating Ss who are given appropriate information can successfully mimic the behavior of hypnotized individuals. This may be accomplished either by informing simulating Ss in advance or by communicating what is expected in other subtle ways. The important issue, however, is that uninstructed simulators, working with a blind E who is careful not to communicate his desires, will spontaneously behave differently from most deeply hypnotized individuals able to hallucinate adequately, demonstrating thereby that the tolerance of incongruity in deeply hypnotized Ss cannot be explained as a function of their prior knowledge of, or expectations about, hypnotic behavior.

If the hypnotist clearly communicates to the S that he expects him to see Dr. X in two places, then, of course, both simulating and hypnotized Ss will yield this response, making it impossible to conclude anything about hypnosis with that particular procedure. The logic of the technique demands that extreme care be taken not to communicate expectations to the S; and the behavior of the simulating S is an indication of how effective the hypnotist is in avoiding such communication. Therefore, meaningful conclusions can be drawn only when E is able to set up the situation so that the simulating S does not know what constitutes the "right" response, and therefore denies the existence of Dr. X. Our experience under these circumstances is that only the S hypnotized deeply enough to experience a compelling hallucination will report that he sees Dr. X in two places.

The extent to which the kind of responses described above are actually characteristic of hypnosis or the extent to which they are characteristic of highly hypnotizable individuals is by no means established. Unfortunately the techniques presently available to evaluate trance logic are not very satisfying. In the occasional *S* who spontaneously reports such phenomena there is no difficulty; however, the absence of such spontaneous material is more the rule than the exception. Even though the double hallucination is useful, it is a difficult technique that must be used with great care lest it be communicated to the *S* what is desired, thereby inevitably ensuring that the response of the simulator will be the same as that of the real *S*s. In any case, it can be used only once and therefore does not lend itself to a comparison within the same *S* between hypnotized and waking conditions. Hopefully, better techniques to evaluate this parameter of mental function will be developed in the future. At this time, however, the question of whether this is a characteristic of hypnosis or hypnotizability remains both unanswered and technically difficult to resolve.

A study by Evans and Thorn (1966) provides a different but striking example of counterexpectational findings. They observed that two kinds of amnesia occur with hypnosis. The first is a tendency of hypnotized individuals to forget the actual events that transpired while hypnotized. This kind of amnesia the investigators refer to as "recall amnesia" and is well known. A different kind of amnesia is of equal interest. Thus, *S*s may continue to recall the associative content they have learned while hypnotized, but forget the source of this information. As a result, these individuals can honestly say that they do not remember what transpired while they were hypnotized, though careful testing reveals that information they had been given is available to them. This phenomenon is called "source amnesia." It is closely analogous to what is observed with patients who develop amnesia. Thus, while unable to recall their own names or identity, they hardly ever lose command of language, social skills, or even extensive professional knowledge.

To study source amnesia the following procedure was used: *S*s were taught a number of obscure facts during hypnosis, such as that amethysts, when heated, turn yellow. They then were wakened with suggestions of amnesia and somewhat later given tests of general knowledge, which included the obscure facts they had been taught. Interestingly, many good hypnotic *S*s, while unable to recall the events that transpired during hypnosis, nonetheless found themselves able to answer these questions correctly. When asked about where they learned this information, they were unable to correctly specify the *source* of their knowledge.

While source amnesia cannot be demonstrated with all *S*s, it is frequently found in deeply hypnotized individuals. On the other hand, simulating *S*s do not show this phenomenon, assuming, incorrectly, that the effect of amnesia suggestion should necessarily be the inability to recall the *content* of the events that occurred while hypnotized (Evans, 1971).

This behavior of simulating Ss does not help to elucidate the fascinating phenomenon of source amnesia. It does serve as an example of another failure to act as do hypnotized individuals, and indicates the difficulty of accounting for source amnesia in terms of Ss' expectations, or subtle cues provided by the hypnotist.

Methodological Developments Beyond the Real-Simulator Design

It has already been commented upon that the simulator group is not a true control group; rather, it is a different treatment group that under some circumstances is a necessary comparison group. An ingenious modification by London and Fuhrer (1961) achieves many of the advantages inherent in the real-simulator design without introducing the special problems inherent in simulation instructions. This technique takes advantage of the relatively high test-retest reliability of hypnosis. In brief, from an unselected population, a group of highly hypnotizable and essentially unhypnotizable Ss are selected. Both groups are told that they did well and are subsequently seen by another hypnotist who uses an induction procedure that would not reveal differences in hypnotizability, such as a progressive relaxation technique starting with eyes closed. The hypnotist remains blind by carefully avoiding any procedures that might reveal the S's degree of hypnotic responsivity as he gives the hypnotic suggestion to be tested. This interesting technique retains the advantage of being blind as far as the hypnotist is concerned as long as it is used with appropriate tasks, without introducing the problem of a simulation set.

To be fully effective in equating the mental set between the highly hypnotizable and the unhypnotizable group, the London-Fuhrer design requires an additional modification. Thus, it is essential to somehow convince the unhypnotizable group that they can, in fact, respond to hypnotic suggestions. Only if this is done successfully are the assumptions of the technique fully met. Also, the London-Fuhrer design as usually employed still has the problem of differentiating between the effect of hypnotism as opposed to the effects of differing hypnotizability. This can be accomplished most easily by within-group comparisons rather than by between-group comparisons and, in some instances, will necessitate an entirely different experimental procedure. [For an example of how the London-Fuhrer design can be adapted to complex experimental problems and how most of these problems can be circumvented, see McGlashan, Evans, and Orne (1969).]

Following the implications of the London-Fuhrer design further, one may wish to use a straightforward correlational approach in order to ask questions about the effects of hypnosis. Here hypnosis is assessed quantitatively and the assumption is made that an effect due to hypnosis will be more pronounced in individuals who are more hypnotizable. Whatever hypnosis is, there will be more of it in people who show more effects of hypnotism.

Given some questions, such an approach is the only appropriate one and the use of simulators, for example, quite superfluous [see, for example, Nace and Orne (1970)].

Types of Situations in Which the Simulator
Method Is Appropriate and Valuable

There are essentially three kinds of questions where the evaluation of the nonhypnotized *S*'s capabilities is best undertaken using the simulator design. These fall into three main categories:

1. *Where a claim is made the hypnotized individual is able to transcend his normal volitional capacities.* A typical example is the statement made after watching a *S* maintaining a cataleptic arm for a long period, "No unhypnotized individual could do this," or the claim that hypnosis facilitates recall of previously learned material not otherwise available to consciousness, leading to a level of recall that cannot otherwise be achieved. Whenever the assertion is made that hypnosis enables a *S* to do something not possible for an unhypnotized individual, the simulating comparison group puts the claim to its most rigorous test.

2. *Whenever hypnosis appears to result in an unusual willingness of the S to carry out behaviors that are requested of him,* it is necessary to evaluate how an unhypnotized individual would behave in such a situation. The question of whether a hypnotized individual could be compelled to carry out antisocial or self-destructive action is a well-known example of this issue. Similarly, whenever hypnosis seems to legitimize behavior that would appear inappropriate without hypnosis, simulators become useful. For example, much of what occurs in age regression is striking because, without any self-consciousness, adult *S*s carry out behavior that—from the observer's point of view—ought to make them feel ridiculous and foolish, such as playing in a sandbox and making mud pies. This is somewhat analogous to the behavior seen in some demonstrations of stage hypnosis where *S*s may be required to bark like a dog, crow like a rooster, or sing like Sinatra—all behavior that *S*s carry out with great aplomb and no apparent self-consciousness. The simulating situation provides an alternate kind of legitimization to evaluate the extent to which the *role* of being hypnotized rather than the *experience* of being hypnotized can account for the behavior.

3. Whenever an *experimental deception* is involved the simulator model provides an appropriate test of the manipulation's effectiveness. It asks in a very rigorous way the extent to which *S*s might have figured out what is actually going on.

While conceptually it is possible to separate these three kinds of problems where simulating *S*s may be useful, it must be noted that in many phenomena more than one aspect is involved. Age regression, for example, to the extent that one tests for augmented recall, may be conceptualized as a transcendence-of-normal-abilities question. However, to the extent that one wishes to evaluate the ease with which the S plays like a child or even perhaps wets his pants, it becomes a test of the S's willingness to engage in unusual behaviors. Simulating Ss may shed light in different ways on both aspects of such experimental problems.

The use of simulating Ss as a means of evaluating the transcendence of normal volitional capacities through hypnosis has been commented upon earlier. Suffice it to say that this is the only situation where a simulator's being able to carry out the identical behavior of the hypnotized individual provides conclusive negative evidence.

The second and third situations where simulators are useful will be discussed below.

A Detailed Example of How Simulators May Be Used to Evaluate Whether Hypnosis Leads to an Unusual Willingness to Carry Out Strange Behaviors

An experiment often cited as evidence to prove that deeply hypnotized Ss may be compelled to carry out antisocial or self-destructive actions is a study originally performed by Rowland (1939). He showed that deeply hypnotized Ss could be compelled to attempt to pick up a poisonous snake with their bare hands; to remove, with their bare fingers, a penny from a beaker of fuming nitric acid where it was obviously in the process of dissolving; and finally to throw this acid at a research assistant. Ss not only carried out these highly dangerous and antisocial behaviors but, when asked later in the waking state whether they would be willing to perform these actions, indicated with horror that they would not. Other waking Ss, asked whether they would be willing to perform these behaviors, also emphatically denied that they would do so. With relatively minor variations, the study was replicated by P. C. Young (1952) some years later with essentially similar findings.

These dramatic observations need to be contrasted with the contradictory findings of Erickson (1939b) who found that Ss could not be compelled even to tear up some pieces of paper that presumably were important documents, and it seemed as though striking discrepancies of this kind might well be due to the kind of variable that was originally described by Estabrooks (1943) as "operator attitude." [For an analysis of these issues, see Orne (1962a).]

A crucial factor in understanding the Rowland and Young findings seems to be the manner in which waking Ss would interpret the situation if they were actually exposed to it. To test the question of how truly dangerous, noxious, or antisocial waking Ss would perceive the situation to be, Orne and Evans (1965) replicated the entire study yet a third time, adding the simulator comparison group and subsequently several other nonhypnotized control groups.

The findings were striking and clear-cut: Using exactly the same procedure employed by Young and the analogous tasks, five out of six hypnotized Ss were compelled to carry out all of the requested behaviors. This replicated observations previously reported by Rowland and Young. But, when the simulating Ss were actually placed in the same experimental situation, all six of them also performed the identical actions!

The conclusions that were drawn from the behavior of the simulating Ss said nothing about the mental processes that were involved in bringing about the behavior of the hypnotized individuals. However, the situation now is such that we do not know whether the hypnotized Ss were or were not being "compelled to carry out self-destructive or antisocial actions." The only appropriate conclusion was that the experimental procedure previously employed to test this hypothesis was not adequate to do so. Regardless of the care with which the situation was contrived and the trouble taken to conceal the elaborate safety precautions from the S, the situation was perceived as sufficiently safe by the simulating Ss for them to carry out the requested behaviors. It should be emphasized that these Ss were quite unable to specify how they or the research assistant would be protected from harm. Nonetheless, they readily verbalized the conviction that the investigator would prevent anyone from being hurt. In this regard, they showed a clear recognition of the investigator's realities, pointing out that he could not afford to have anyone hurt in the course of his experiments.

It should be noted that when Ss were asked whether they would carry out these behaviors—as opposed to being instructed to do so—they said they would refuse. Nor were we able to persuade any of our faculty colleagues to perform any of these actions, an observation we interpret as due to the differences in role relationship. The simulating procedure, however, demonstrated to us that Rowland and Young's assumptions about what a nonhypnotized S would do in the actual situation were incorrect. Ss simply did not accept as plausible that either they or anyone else would be hurt.

Once we had the experience of seeing how nonhypnotized simulators behaved, it became possible for us to present instructions with sufficient conviction that even Ss picked at random from the corridor and co-opted to participate in the study complied with the requests. We noted that, depending upon the emphasis in the instructions, different degrees of compliance could be obtained and, with appropriate emphasis, the behaviors obtained from real and simulating Ss could also be elicited from the nonhypnotized individuals on first contact. The role of the simulating comparison group in this study seems particularly interesting. Thus, once the experiment was completed, the demonstration that the situation was perceived as safe by the Ss, and was therefore not a useful indicator of behavioral control exerted by hypnosis, no longer required reference to the simulating group but was un-equivocally demonstrated by the behavior of nonhypnotized Ss who were strangers asked to participate in the study.

In this study then, simulating Ss served the purpose of initially evaluating what Ss will do (rather than what Ss can do, as in the transcendence experiments). Their behavior helped clarify how an individual in the experiment actually perceives the situation, obviating the need for speculative polemics about what Ss will or will not do. The inference drawn from the behavior of the simulating Ss is concerned with assessing the adequacy of the procedure for answering the experimental question, rather than with answering the experimental question itself. In this sense it is a true quasi-control (Orne, 1969).

The Use of the Real-Simulator Model to Evaluate the Adequacy of a Laboratory Deception

Many important and meaningful problems are difficult to explore in the laboratory. There are a large number of questions where the S's behavior would be materially altered if he knew the precise variables under investigation, and one technique that has been widely used is to deliberately deceive the S in an experiment. Recently, ethical issues have been raised about laboratory deceptions.[14] While a detailed discussion of these would be beyond the scope of this paper, deception also raises serious methodological issues. When deception is used in an experiment, the reason is that it is felt to be necessary in order to create the required experimental context. It follows, therefore, that it makes a considerable difference whether the S believes the deception or is able to see through it. This crucial question has received almost no systematic attention. The procedure of merely asking S at the end

---

14. Most of the discussions focusing on the ethical dilemma of lying to a S appear to me naive and, at times, to border on the hypocritical. Ss expect not to be informed of the precise problem under study and anticipate that it may be necessary to deceive them for the sake of the experiment. In our experience the fact of deception has never been a source of difficulty to the S; on the other hand, it is vital that the E take responsibility for the consequences of his actions and make certain that no S leaves the laboratory with more problems than when he entered. Informing the S honestly about his homosexual conflict or of his inability to perform up to the level of the average college student or of similar findings without placing these observations in context is considerably more traumatic and, in my view, unethical, than the use of deception in a context where appropriate debriefiing is assured. The self-righteous position taken in the matter of laboratory deception is all too often associated with a lack of concern about how the S really feels and a lack of recognition that a S may be seriously traumatized even by being excluded from an experiment because he does not perform adequately on a given test or even by being informed that he cannot be hypnotized. The issue of protecting the welfare and safety of human Ss demands continual monitoring and close attention, and the E cannot shirk this responsibility by asserting that he has merely told the truth or that he was doing only a "learning" experiment.

of an experiment whether he had caught on to the deception is usually inadequate since the needs of both *S* and *E* tend to mitigate against learning *S*'s true perceptions and lead to what I have termed a "pact of ignorance." [For a discussion of these issues, see Orne (1959, 1962b, 1969).] It is vital, therefore, in many experimental situations that involve deception to determine whether *S*s saw through the experimental manipulation. To answer this question the simulating comparison group can be extremely useful.

An Experimental Example

Some years ago Fisher (1954), in a now classic paper, studied the nature of posthypnotic behavior. In an ingenious experiment Fisher suggested to deeply hypnotized *S*s that, on awakening, each time they heard the word "psychology" they would scratch their right ear. After waking the *S*s, he tested the suggestion by using the word and was able to elicit the suggested behavior. At this point one of his associates came into the room and by innuendo the experiment was terminated. The associate, Dr. Fisher, and the *S* entered into an informal conversation about current topics of the day. In the course of this informal conversation the word "psychology" came up spontaneously. Of the 12 *S*s, only 3 responded during this time. After some minutes of conversation the associate left and Fisher, by turning back to his *S*, implied resumption of the experiment, and conspicuously used the word "psychology" in a sentence. Under these circumstances all of his *S*s resumed responding by scratching their right ear. When asked about their behavior during the preceding period, several of the *S*s erroneously insisted that they had continued to respond, while others gave very transparent rationalizations. From these data Fisher concluded that the posthypnotic response is a function of the *S*'s understanding of what is desired at the time of responding, and would be carried out only as long as it was believed that the experiment was currently in progress.

An alternative plausible interpretation of Fisher's findings is, we felt, that *S*s perceived the *original* suggestion to be that they ought to respond by scratching their right ear whenever they heard the word "psychology" as long as the experiment continued—since, in the context where the suggestion was given, there would be no plausible reason for the hypnotist to mean for them to continue to respond indefinitely. If *S*s perceived the suggestion in this manner, one would expect them to stop responding when they believed the experiment to be over and Fisher's finding would not necessarily have any implications for the persistence of a posthypnotic suggestion outside of an experimental situation. It seemed to us that the study did not really test whether a *S* who is given a clear-cut, time-limited posthypnotic suggestion would carry it out even under circumstances that he perceived to be outside of the experiment where the hypnotist would not be likely to know or even care whether the suggestion had been complied with. This question has considerable theoretical importance and is closely related to the issue of whether the posthypnotic response is a function of the suggestion given to a deeply hypnotized S or whether it is an attempt to please the hypnotist, depending on the ongoing relationship.

In a carefully designed experiment Orne, Sheehan, and Evans (1968) required Ss to come to the laboratory on two successive days and to take a number of personality tests, some while hypnotized. The Ss were informed in advance that they would be required to come on two successive days. The first day, in addition to taking the tests which were, in fact, part of another experiment, Ss were also given the suggestion in deep hypnosis that for the next 48 hours each time they heard the word "experiment" they would run their right hand through their hair. It should be noted that this suggestion was legitimized by the fact that the Ss realized they would see the hypnotist on the following day. However, the suggestion was clear-cut and explicit in demanding a response each time S heard the word "experiment"; and by limiting it to 48 hours the expectation that the response persist for this period of time was clearly communicated.

The next day, when S came to the laboratory the E was informed by the receptionist of his arrival, and on meeting him in the waiting room and walking down the hall to the experimental room, the E would carefully say, "I appreciate your coming back to the 'experiment.' " This test, however, was not the crucial measure of the posthypnotic response.

The Ss taking part in our research are paid for their participation, and it is customary for them to return to the main office at the completion of a study where, after signing a receipt, they are reimbursed for their time. Each S, on the completion of the first day's tests, returned to the secretary who asked him to sign the usual form, asking whether it would be all right to pay him "now for today's 'experiment' and for the next part of the study tomorrow." The S's response under these circumstances, in a different room totally outside the experimental context, constituted the first criterion test. On returning the subsequent day, the S was met by the receptionist who asked whether he was participating in the physiological or the psychological "experiment"—two studies that were in progress at the same time. The S's response to the receptionist constituted the second test.

The results showed that, using a highly selected group of Ss who were capable of entering deep hypnosis, Ss responded in the waiting room and the main office much as they had in the presence of the hypnotist. Thus, in some instances, since the word "experiment" was used quite casually, Ss did not always seem to hear the cue; on the other hand, the fact that the context was different, that the E was not present, and that the test was carried out in a way that appeared totally unrelated to the study, did not seem to interfere with the response. Not surprisingly, those Ss who responded most consistently were those individuals who also were most deeply hypnotized.

Though the experiment as outlined above seems to deal with the experimental question, it fails to test the crucial issue of whether the test by the secretary was actually perceived to be outside of the experimental situation by the *S*. It might easily have happened that the way in which the study was carried out permitted *S*s to suspect that the secretary was really recording their behavior for the benefit of the hypnotist. Such a situation could readily arise if the hypnotist casually or implicitly added a comment that the *S* would respond not only with him but no matter who used the word "experiment," and so forth. Alternatively, the secretary might have unduly emphasized the word "experiment" in her speech, thereby marking the situation as a test. Under such circumstances the findings would not have permitted valid inference to be drawn about the extent to which posthypnotic responses generalize from one context to another. Obviously we would much rather have tested the posthypnotic suggestion totally away from the laboratory but, even if we had tested it in a classroom or dormitory, we would still need to ask whether the *S* might not have suspected what we were doing. So simulating *S*s were included in the study solely for the purpose of evaluating whether the test situation was recognized as related to the experiment. Their behavior served to tell us how likely it was that a *S* could catch on to the fact that the secretary was really a subtle but nonetheless crucial part of the experimental testing procedure.

In other studies we have noticed that *S*s asked to simulate hypnosis tend to be unusually suspicious. It is not surprising that the *S* asked to deceive someone else be alert lest he himself be deceived. Therefore we can expect the behavior of the simulating *S*s in such a situation to be exquisitely responsive to cues that would be missed by *S*s not sensitized by the simulating instructions. Used in this way the simulating comparison group intentionally "stacks the cards" against the hypothesis, thereby providing a particularly rigorous test for the adequacy of a given deception.

Running both groups of *S*s randomly mixed and without knowing to which group any given individual belonged, we observed that of 17 deeply hypnotized *S*s, 6 responded on both days, whereas of 13 simulating *S*s not a single *S* responded on both days. These differences are particularly striking since in the presence of the hypnotist the simulating *S*s tended to respond even more than the hypnotized *S*s.

It should be emphasized that the simulating comparison group was used in the Orne, Sheehan, and Evans study exclusively for the purpose of evaluating whether it is at all likely for even suspicious *S*s to see through the use of the secretary as a stimulus for and observer of posthypnotic behavior. The fact that simulating *S*s did not perceive the secretary in this way is taken as reasonable evidence for assuming that it is ecologically valid to accept the hypnotic *S*s' interaction with the secretary as representative of extra-experimental behavior. From the point of view of this particular experiment the simulating group served *no other purpose,* but they did thereby allow us to generalize about the hypnotized Ss' posthypnotic responses in settings outside the experiment.

In the context of this paper, however, the differences between real and simulating Ss in this study are of some interest. Not only do they demonstrate a behavioral difference between hypnotized and simulating Ss at an acceptable significance level, but they also show that the effect of a posthypnotic suggestion on hypnotized Ss persists even in situations where the hypnotist is apparently unable to know about the S's response. The effects of simulation instructions do not extend in this study to a situation where the S believes that his responses are no longer monitored. [For a more extensive discussion of studies on posthypnotic behavior, see Orne (1969).]

A Final Example

Another experiment that utilized the simulating control group as a means to evaluate the effectiveness of a deception serves perhaps best to illustrate the limitations on the conclusions that can be drawn from this comparison group. Orne and Evans (1966) carried out a study to investigate the question with which patients may betray their negative feelings as they are about to be hypnotized: "What happens if you drop dead while I am hypnotized?"

It is generally accepted that Ss will lapse into sleep and then spontaneously awaken after some time if the hypnotist should disappear; however, little hard evidence is available. Indeed, it is extremely difficult to tell what would happen if the hypnotist were to disappear once deep hypnosis has been induced. The only empirical study in the literature is by Dorcus, Brintnall, and Case (1941). In this experiment, after a S was deeply hypnotized there was a knock at the door and the secretary asked E to come quickly because of an emergency downtown. The E immediately left without any comment to S. Consequently, the hypnotized S remained alone in the room, and his behavior was observed surreptitiously. The group of Ss treated in this fashion was compared with others who were merely asked to relax in the same kind of situation. Unfortunately this study sheds no light on the question because in both instances the experiment was sufficiently transparent that Ss must have realized the deep interest of the investigator in how long they remained immobile or in trance.

To answer the question of what would happen if the hypnotist really disappeared, the situation must be contrived in a manner to seem plausible and truly accidental. This is also important in order to avoid doing violence to the implicit agreement between S and E that the latter is responsible for the welfare of the former during the course of an experiment. What would happen in a situation where the hypnotist truly disappears has, of course, considerable theoretical importance for an understanding of hypnosis. Thus, if one conceptualizes the phenomenon as a simple interpersonal transaction where the S behaves in certain ways only to please the hypnotist and comply with his demands, the disappearance of the hypnotist should lead to an immediate termination of the hypnotic condition. Conversely, if hypnosis leads to an altered state of the individual, the disappearance of the hypnotist should not automatically terminate trance but rather it should take a finite period of time for the *S* to somehow pull himself out of this state, either by awakening or perhaps by going to sleep.[15]

A situation was finally created that fitted the experimental requirements by requiring *S*s who had been previously trained to enter hypnosis readily to participate in a study requiring two sessions. It was explained to them that, in order to standardize the procedure, all instructions, including the induction and termination of hypnosis, would be carried out by tape recording.

The *E*'s task was essentially that of a technician—applying electrodes, turning on the tape recorder, presenting the experimental material, and so forth. He did not say anything throughout the study since every item of instruction was given by means of the tape recorder. Each *S* came for two such experimental sessions. During the second session, while the *S* was deeply hypnotized and tapping his foot in rhythm with hallucinated music, the tape recorder came to a grinding halt, the light went out, and the *E* tried in vain to reactivate the machine by flicking the switch. He then muttered under his breath, "The damn fuse," and dashed from the room.

The *S*'s behavior was observed by means of a one-way screen throughout the experiment in order to determine what would happen once the *E* had left the room. Would hypnosis be terminated immediately once the *S* was alone, as some theories would predict; or would it take a period of time for the *S* to pull himself out of hypnosis, as one would expect if the condition were some special altered state?

Despite the "cuteness" of the deception procedure of the simulated power failure, there was no certainty whether the *S* would accept it as such. For this reason a simulator comparison group was also included.

The findings were clear-cut: five of the six deeply hypnotized *S*s did not arouse immediately when the hypnotist left. They required varying periods of time to apparently pull themselves out of the state. When they did, they appeared somewhat disoriented and confused. However, five out of the six simulating *S*s also continued to appear hypnotized—but, in contrast, continued thus for the whole half-hour period until the technician returned, presumably having fixed the fuse. During the subsequent post-experimental inquiry it became clear that the simulators caught on to the fact that the

---

15. It should be noted that a role theory of hypnosis that conceives of the hypnotized *S* as playing a role at a nonconscious level leads to an identical prediction as the "state" theory. If one assumes that effects of a role persist in situations where the hypnotist does not know or would not care about what the *S* does, or that the continuation of a role is to a considerable degree independent of the actual or implied presence of the hypnotist, there is no discernible operational distinction between a role or a state view.

power failure was contrived and that they behaved as they thought a hypnotized *S* would if there were a true power failure. The simulating *S*s quite cogently pointed out that having been instructed to fool the *E* put them on their guard lest they themselves be fooled. In contrast, only one of the hypnotized *S*s reported suspecting that the power failure was contrived.

We observed statistically significant differences between the real hypnotized group and the simulating comparison group. What conclusions about the nature of the hypnotic phenomenon can be drawn from this difference? *In our opinion, no valid conclusion is justified.*

Once again the purpose of the simulating group was not to provide a comparison group for the actual subject population; rather it was a special treatment group included exclusively to test the adequacy of the experimental procedure. Specifically it was used here to determine whether the power failure in the experiment was sufficiently plausible to be accepted as genuine even by suspicious *S*s. The combined behaviors and reports of the simulating group clearly indicate that our efforts were inadequate in this regard. Five out of six simulating *S*s correctly perceived the power failure as a contrived part of the experiment. This leads to the unpleasant conclusion that the experimental procedure was inadequate to test the hypothesis. While according to inquiries—and in line with the experimental behavior—the hypnotized *S*s for the most part accepted the power failure as genuine, there were a sufficient number of cues in the situation to permit suspicious *S*s to see through the procedure. Therefore, the possibility that the hypnotized *S*s recognized the true state of affairs at some level cannot be discounted and the experiment cannot be interpreted at face value.

Having found the deception manipulation wanting, we re-examined in detail the cues that might allow the *S* to become aware that the power failure was a planned part of the experiment. The kind of nitty-gritty details that most investigators fail to publish and which, even if the investigators included them, most editors would delete for the sake of brevity, are crucial in this regard. For example, in the study just described, to facilitate observation after the "power failure" the overhead lights remained on and only the bright desk lamp went out as the tape recorder stopped; an obvious one-way mirror had always been in the room to which we had hoped (in vain) the *S* would have adapted; and a small polygraph continued to run in the experimental room after the "power failure." We now redesigned the study with considerable attention to such details. The one-way screen was eliminated and replaced by another less well known and carefully hidden means of observation. When the power failure occurred, all lights in the room were extinguished. Just enough light was filtered into the room through the window curtains from daylight—or from a strategically placed parking light outside at night—to make observation possible. Furthermore, physiological recordings were apparently made by means of a large Ampex instrumentation tape recorder and a small polygraph. Both of these machines stopped, along with the lights and the tape recorder, at the power failure. (Actually, the wires from the S were run through to another room at some distance in order to permit continuous recording of relevant data.) When the E left the room the hall lights were out. Every effort was made by scrupulous attention to such details to make the power failure plausible.

With these revised conditions, simulating and hypnotized Ss were run in another experiment by a blind E. Here four of six simulating Ss stopped simulating the moment the technician left the room, indulging in exploratory and other private behavior clearly indicating that they felt themselves to be unobserved. On the other hand, the hypnotized group behaved much as they had in the earlier experiment, pulling themselves out of this state only after a considerable period of time had elapsed. These behaviors were in line with the data provided during an inquiry, indicating that both real and simulating Ss now accepted the power failure as genuine.

Significant differences were again obtained but, in contrast to the findings of the first study, those from the second study allow meaningful inference. The behavior of the simulating Ss clearly indicates that the power failure was accepted as geunine. and therefore it is plausible to accept the behavior of the hypnotized individuals as validly indicating how they respond to the "disappearance" of the hypnotist.

It will be clear that the purpose served by the simulating Ss in this experiment was exclusively to determine whether or not there were sufficient cues in the experimental situation to allow a S to surmise that the power failure was staged rather than spontaneous. This issue is crucial, however, if one intends to extend inferences to a situation that is actually extra-experimental and perceived as such by the S. Though it entailed a great deal of trouble to test the adequacy of the experimental manipulation, without the simulating comparison group we would have had no empirical test of the procedure's adequacy. It is impossible without such a technique to evaluate the kind of cues presented to the S in an experimental situation. Yet it is the presence of such cues upon which the legitimacy of inference depends. In experiments requiring any form of deception, the simulators' performance puts into behavioral terms information usually gleaned only in in-depth interviews—and then often it is only one S, as in our first study, who will "break down" or break the pact of ignorance and be willing to tell that the whole experiment he has just taken part in has the kind of flaw that negates his own data and E's time.

In this experiment, as in the posthypnotic study previously reported, the differences between Ss who are pretending to be hypnotized and those actually hypnotized were not of much moment except to test the adequacy of the deception. The differences that emerge in both studies do, however, serve to support the assertions of both hypnotized and simulating Ss about the nature of their experiences and do argue for the existence of very different psychic mechanisms that may under certain circumstances result in similar behavior. The situation of the disappearing hypnotist undoubtedly is only one of a number of situations that could be contrived to demonstrate that behavioral differences do occur. In this instance, the behavior of Ss in the first unsuccessful deception experiment served to indicate that Ss' expectations or preconceptions are that the deeply hypnotized individuals ought to continue in the state of hypnosis if the hypnotist somehow were to disappear. The simulating Ss' behavior in the second experiment shows that insofar as they believe in the genuineness of the power failure they will stop pretending as soon as they believe that they are not longer under observation. The actual behavior of hypnotized individuals in both studies was, on the whole, unchanged: In both cases they gradually roused from hypnosis, taking several minutes to achieve full awareness of their surroundings.

Summary and Conclusions

This discussion has tried to clarify some of the misconceptions that have arisen concerning the use of the real-simulator design. What initially appears to be a simple control group is, in fact, an example of a category of techniques —"quasi-controls"—which serve special delineated purposes in experimental research. The observation that even highly trained hypnotists cannot reliably distinguish Ss pretending to be hypnotized from deeply hypnotized individuals without special procedures in no way challenges the genuineness of hypnosis or the subjective reality of the hypnotized individual's experiences. It does, however, force a careful reevaluation of a great many claims made for hypnosis, and challenges common beliefs in the infallibility of good clinical judgment.

The ease with which simulating Ss duplicate a wide range of behaviors once held to be uniquely associated with hypnosis cannot be explained by assuming that Ss pretending to be hypnotized are actually hypnotized. These Ss are purposely selected for their inability to enter hypnosis despite repeated efforts to do so, and extensive research has shown that the likelihood of such Ss entering deep hypnosis at some future time is very small. Furthermore, deeply hypnotized Ss report entirely different experiences in hypnosis from those reported by individuals pretending to be hypnotized. These reports tend to be stable whether they are given to an E formally, a research assistant informally, or are part of private conversations with other Ss, friends, or spouses.

Finally, while in our view such behavioral data are unnecessary to establish the difference between simulators and hypnotized individuals, a number of situations are described where clear behavioral differences do emerge.

The simulating comparison group serves a restricted purpose in hypnosis research. Many properly designed studies do not require such a group and, in some instances, it would merely serve to confuse the issues. However, three circumstances are described where such a group is essential:

1. Whenever the claim is made that a given phenomenon is produced because the *S* is hypnotized, where the *S*'s performance is taken as proof because unhypnotized *S*s are believed to be incapable of producing it. This includes all studies where a claim of transcending the waking *S*'s normal volitional capability is made. Simulating *S*s are required to provide a test of the motivated waking *S*s' capabilities given identical treatment by the hypnotist.

2. Whenever an individual in hypnosis performs an action that the investigator wishes to assert he would have refused if he were not hypnotized. In other words, when one wishes to demonstrate that hypnosis has led to a greater willingness to carry out a behavior required of the *S,* it becomes important to evaluate how unhypnotized *S*s would behave in the identical situation if the role were legitimized in some other fashion. In this context particularly, the inherent quality of the real-simulator model to prevent differential treatment of the comparison group by keeping the hypnotist blind is useful. Equally important is the effective manner in which the simulation instructions legitimize otherwise unacceptable behavior.

3. Whenever an experiment involves deception and the effectiveness of the deception is crucial to the interpretation of the conclusions. The inclusion of a simulating comparison group is needed to evaluate the adequacy of the deception procedure.

It should be emphasized that in each instance the simulating comparison group is included to allow the investigator to evaluate the capabilities of highly motivated, unhypnotized *S*s and the extent to which direct comparison between the behavior of this group and the hypnotized group is appropriate depends upon the nature of the hypothesis being tested.

The real-simulator model is difficult to use in practice. It demands not only several *E*s working together, but great care to meet the assumptions of the experimental model. In many instances alternative designs can be used to good advantage. Some experimental problems, however, demand the inclusion of such a comparison group. The complexities of this technique and its use may well serve to slow the flow of research. While a temporary inconvenience, such an eventuality may not be undesirable. In the long run it may be far better to have fewer studies that subject the phenomenon of hypnosis to a rigorous test while doing justice to its unique attributes than many studies that fail, under critical examination, to yield alternative explanations or, worse yet, fail to study the phenomenon at all.

Chárles T. Tart *is an Associate Professor of Psychology at the University of California's Davis campus. He received his Ph.D. from the University of North Carolina in 1963, and then had two years of postdoctoral training in hypnosis at Ernest R. Hilgard's laboratory at Stanford University. His research interests in hypnosis, sleep, and psychophysiology were supplemented by work on paranormal phenomena during a year as a Lecturer at the University of Virginia Medical School. Further contact with the burgeoning human potentials movement upon his return to California broadened his research interests to states of human consciousness in general, including drug-induced states and mystical experiences. He is now working on a comprehensive theory of states of consiousness and extensions of scientific methodology to allow objective investigation of many phenomena of states of consciousness usually considered unresearchable. He has written* On Being Stoned: A Psychological Study of Marijuana Intoxication, *and has edited* Altered States of Consciousness: A Book of Readings.

Tart *provides a comprehensive review of the five scales that have evolved to date to measure depth of hypnosis in terms of the subject's own experiential appraisals of how deeply hypnotized he feels himself to be. He discusses the differences among the five scales and their relationships to other methods for measuring depth; and presents a case study on one excellent hypnotic subject to illustrate his method and its potentialities.*

Tart conceptualizes his methods of measurement as extending beyond hypnosis to altered states of consciousness in general; and argues that experiential ratings should be adopted as the primary method for measuring depth in preference to conventional behavioral methods. He makes a strong case for the view that experiential ratings reach into areas of important hypnotic phenomena that are unavailable through behavioral approaches and argues that extensive research with the experiential approach is indicated.

14

Measuring the Depth of an Altered State of Consciousness, with Particular Reference to Self-Report Scales of Hypnotic Depth

CHARLES T. TART

Introduction

This chapter will propose a theoretical basis for measuring the depth of any state of consciousness (SoC) with particular emphasis on hypnosis, review the literature on previous attempts at self-report scaling of hypnotic depth, present data on two self-report scales of hypnotic depth used extensively in my laboratory, and conclude with some general comments on the practical uses of self-report scales.

As many SoCs exhibit quantitative or qualitative variation, either in terms of a subject's behavior or reports of his experiences, we commonly talk about the "depth" of a given SoC. This chapter will consider the problem of the depth of SoCs, with main reference to the hypnotic state, in terms of a theoretical model under development which is applicable to all altered SoCs. It will also systematically review the literature on self-report scales of hypnotic depth, one technique of measuring depth. Some new data will also be presented on the phenomenology of extremely deep hypnotic states in relation to a self-report technique for measuring hypnotic depth.

Theoretically, one may conceive of a subject's total state of being at a given time (behavior, experience, and physiology) as resulting from the interaction of a number of subsystems. These subsystems may be conceptual-

445

ized as behavioral, experiential, or physiological in nature, depending on their heuristic value. Such subsystems might be identity, memory, cognitive processing, limbic system interactions, and so forth. Each subsystem may exhibit one or several qualitatively different modes of action, and there may be *quantitative* variation within a given mode of action for a given subsystem. If we further postulate that the subsystems that make up the total organism interact with each other, and that this interaction may determine either the qualitative mode or the quantitative level of action within a mode for each subsystem, we are then led to the conclusion that there are a finite number of ways in which the total organism can be stably organized in terms of the interactive interrelationships between subsystems. These modes of organization or configuration each constitute a unique SoC, a gestalt of subsystems stabilized by feedback interaction between the subsystems.

For example, subsystems are organized in one fashion in the ordinary waking state but in a different fashion in a deep hypnotic state in the same subject. Note that the distinction between SoCs is thus based not on the *content* of SoC, the particular things a person experiences or the particular way he behaves, but on the altered configuration of interaction of the hypothesized subsystems, which results in a new organizational gestalt. For example, a person who has taken a large dose of LSD and a person who has been deeply hypnotized may both report that a given time they had no awareness of existing as a separate self; that is, the content of the experience seems identical, but we suspect that the manner in which this particular content came about in each state was not the same, that there was a different configuration of interacting subsystems, which happened to lead to the same content in a particular instance. Normally, different interacting configurations of subsystems will frequently lead to different contents, but this is not a defining criterion for SoCs.

The dimension of "depth" for a given SoC is a hypothetical construct that is useful to the investigator in ordering and conceptualizing changes seen in that SoC. In terms of the above model, changes in the depth of an SoC result from quantitative changes in the operation of some subsystems within the particular configuration of subsystems that comprises that SoC. Previous investigators have also used the term "depth" to cover what seem to be *qualitative* changes in the subsystem configuration, but as such changes may radically alter the overall configuration, a point is reached in which it is perhaps better to talk of a new SoC rather than a change in the depth of the original SoC. How large the qualitative change must be to initiate a new SoC is a point that cannot be decided theoretically. To illustrate, it is common in hypnosis for subjects to report that as they "went deeper," their perception of the environment around them became dimmer and dimmer, and that it finally faded out completely. This is a quantitative change that we would ordinarily associate with an alteration in hypnotic depth. If the same hypnotized subject spontaneously reported that he had suddenly found himself standing in a cavern near the sea, without there having been any suggestions to this effect, it is not clear from *content* alone whether this represents a further quantitative change in the operation of the subsystem that produced the fading of the environment, or whether a new subsystem had come into operation, or whether the mode of operation of a subsystem had qualitatively changed. Data presented later in this chapter will illustrate a case where deep hypnosis may have changed into another SoC.

Assuming now the existence of a depth dimension and some way to measure it, Figure 14.1 illustrates a few of the possible relations of the intensity or quality of observable effects to depth. Such effects may be considered a result of quantitative or qualitative changes in subsystem operation. The effects may be particular behaviors, reported experiences, or physiological indices. Intensity or quality of each effect is plotted on its own appropriate scale. Effect A is of the type present in ordinary consciousness at a low level, but which begins to increase with increasing depth part way along the depth dimension, and then levels off at some maximum intensity even though depth continues to increase. Effect B does not manifest at all until a threshold depth is reached, then increases with increasing depth, temporarily stabilizes at a maximum value, and then decreases and finally ceases to manifest with further increases in depth. Effect C suddenly manifests at full intensity when a certain depth is reached and suddenly disappears at a greater depth. Effect D manifests mildly at the lowest depth level and increases steadily in intensity all through the depth dimension; this sort of relationship to depth is commonly (but probably erroneously) assumed to be typical of altered SoCs and particularly of hypnosis. Effect E manifests strongly in normal consciousness, is unaffected by increasing depth up to a certain point, then is decreased in intensity or quality with increasing depth and finally levels off at zero. It may stay at zero with increasing depth or may, as in this particular example, suddenly return at a greater depth level, perhaps with an increased intensity. Many other possible relationships between the intensity of effects and depth may be presumed to exist other than those diagramed here.

In drawing Figure 14.1 it was assumed that we had some independent measure of depth. This assumption need no longer be made. If the important effects of a given SoC are measured with respect to each other as different effects take on different values, we may formally define the depth dimension of a given SoC as the obtained graphical plot of empirically obtained relationships of the above sort. Insofar as the plotted relationships are only of observed effects, "depth" is a purely descriptive concept, which may be useful in summarizing our observations but which actually adds no information not present in the first place. Insofar as the effects are considered as manifestations of alterations in the postulated subsystems, "depth" is a hypothetical construct and its value may be assessed on criteria of comprehensiveness, understanding, and testable predictions. In practice, any combina-

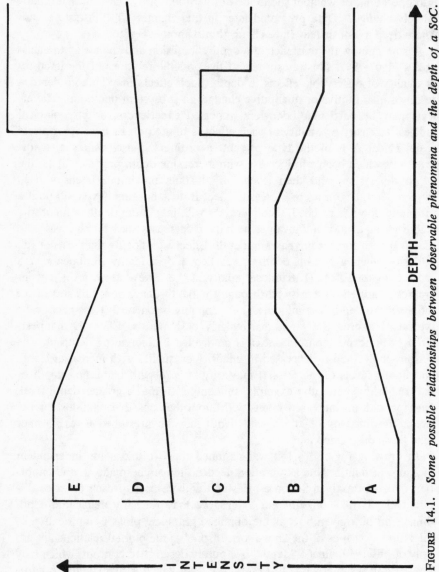

FIGURE 14.1. *Some possible relationships between observable phenomena and the depth of a SoC.*

tion of effects for a given SoC whose curves cover what we believe to be the entire depth continuum may be used as a minimal working index of the depth continuum, although effects of type D, those increasing linearly with depth, are most convenient.

The practical strategy for investigating the depth continuum for a given SoC would be to start with some important effect of that state that one could vary easily, say, for example, by suggestion in hypnosis. One would vary this effect through various values and at each value measure other effects, either experiential, physiological, or behavioral. Using the values of the deliberately altered variable for an axis, one would plot the other effects against them. If an effect that did indeed vary linearly with one's hypothetical concept of depth had been picked, then plots of the type shown in Figure 14.1 would be obtained; if the deliberately manipulated variable was of some other type, rather complex and confusing plots would be obtained, and one would repeat the investigation with other effects being deliberately manipulated. Statistical manipulations could be used to optimize the plot.

A number of cautions in applying this model of depth are necessary. First, some SoCs might consist entirely of type C effects, where the SoC is present and all effects are maximal, or is not present and all effects are zero, with nothing in between. Thus there really would be no "depth" for this particular SoC.

Second, some effects for a given SoC are "spontaneous," that is, they always appear without any special procedures needed to elicit them; others, however, are what might be called "potential" effects. Potential effects can be manifested in a given SoC but only if certain subject and situational variables take on the correct values. Insofar as the values of these variables are such as to routinely elicit the effect, but the variables are not recognized, we have a constant misinterpretation of the effect—we consider it spontaneous when in point of fact it is potential and must be produced in a certain manner. Insofar as the variables are nonconscious expectations of the experimenter we have the problem of demand characteristics and experimenter bias.

Third, the above model applies to a stable SoC. Because most subjects have little or no experience in functioning in altered SoCs, their early experiences with such SoCs will consist not only of the characteristic effects of such states per se but of many effects due to adaptation to the state and attempts to cope with the novelty of it. These transitional effects are worthy of study in themselves, but should not be confused with the stable and characteristic effects of the SoC. Gill and Brennan (1961) have reported on such effects occurring in the induction phases of hypnosis when patients were new to being hypnotized. Unfortunately, most of our knowledge of the effects of various SoCs stems from studies using unadapted subjects, producing an inextricable blend of adaptation-coping effects and effects of SoCs per se.

Fourth, several types of alterations in the configuration of subsystems might result in phenotypically identically observable phenomena, so too great an emphasis on single phenomena may be misleading. In the example mentioned earlier of an alteration of a subject's identity in an LSD state and in hypnosis, loss of personal identity might result in the first state because the subject feels identified with the cosmos as a whole, while in a hypnotic state it might result from no attention being mobilized for examining the characteristics that normally make up personal identity. In the case of LSD we have a profound alteration in the identity subsystem, while in case of hypnosis the primary change is in the attention subsystem. Only wide-range approaches to SoCs can adequately deal with them.

Fifth, some SoCs, particularly hypnosis, are highly "flexible," that is, out of a large number of observable effects potentially associated with that SoC only a small number will be seen at any time, and the particular subsets seen may be influenced by the experimenter, the experimental situation, and the subject's own predilections. In order to communicate with the subject about what he is experiencing and to ask him to scale the intensity of his experiences, we must hit upon a common vocabulary. In the course of communicating this vocabulary, however, the words may implicitly suggest what effects are desired, and so one can create an expected set of effects and possibly an expected set of interrelationships among these effects, which nevertheless represents only a small aspect of that SoC. It is important not to confuse this particular subset with the state of consciousness per se. Many of the differences of experimental results that come from different experimenters' laboratories may result from this. The language (and paralinguistic aspects of communication) with which we communicate with the subject sets up expectations and demands that may influence the subject's experiences per se, as well as influencing the way in which he reports them to us.

Sixth, there may be certain portions of the depth continuum of a given SoC that impair subjects' ability to adequately report their experiences or to carry out overt behavior, so these portions of the depth continuum will be hard to map. Subjects may or may not be able to report on these adequately in retrospect.

As a final note on practical difficulties, let us consider drug-induced SoCs, particularly those resulting from psychedelic drugs. Here it would seem that we have an independent measure of depth, namely the dose of the drug. It is clear, however, that there are tremendous differences between subjects and within the same subject from session to session with the same drug and dosage. The particular dosage of the drug will interact with the interpersonal situation, the experimenter-subject relationship, and the (changing) characteristics of the subject to produce different effects at different times; these are all "potential effects" in the model mentioned above, and worth studying, but they illustrate how crude dosage may be as a measure of depth.

The Depth of Hypnosis

Let us now consider the problem of the depth of hypnosis. Hypnotic "susceptibility" and hypnotic "depth" have frequently been confused in the literature. Hypnotic susceptibility refers to the degree of responsiveness to hypnotic suggestion administered under standardized conditions (Hilgard, 1965b), and in comparing subjects on the degree of hypnotic susceptibility we are comparing their *overall responsiveness to the assessment procedure.* Hypnotic depth on the other hand, refers to the *momentary* state of the subject along a hypothesized dimension. In the light of the above model, the hypnotic state would refer to the interacting, stable configuration of subsystems that comprise the hypnotic state, and hypnotic "depth" to each subsystem possessing a certain quantitatively variable level of operation within this configuration; that is, the *state* of hypnosis does not exist until the subsystems have taken up a certain, nonordinary configuration.[1] Once this configuration is taken up, quantitative variations of the sort illustrated in Figure 14.1 occur within the subsystems. While it is generally believed that a subject's hypnotic responsiveness, the measure of his "susceptibility," will vary directly with depth, it is possible for depth to vary quite rapidly in some subjects. Thus a standard assessment procedure, such as the Stanford Hypnotic Susceptibility Scales (Weitzenhoffer & Hilgard, 1962) may be confounded by changes in depth occurring through the lengthy assessment procedure for an individual subject. More importantly, in studies using the presence or absence of the hypnotic state of an independent variable, variations in depth in a given subject throughout the course of the experiment, as well as such variations across subjects, could seriously confound results, even to the point of increasing variance sufficiently to wash out genuine effects (see Tart and Hilgard, 1966, for an illustration of this).

It is clear from the above discussion that mapping the depth continuum for hypnosis or any other SoC is a laborious process, involving a great deal of trial and error to find what sort of dimensions make the best conceptual and theoretical sense. A possible starting point for mapping the depth continuum, which seems to offer a number of advantages, is found if we note that many subjects will spontaneously report on fluctuations in the depth of their hypnotic state when talking to an experimenter after a session. Ignoring for the moment the question of how subjects carry out this measurement process, it is conceivable that the subject himself may be an excellent direct observer of important aspects of the hypnotic depth continuum. Because of this observation, a number of procedures have been developed for teaching

1. The problem of where "waking suggestibility" leaves off and the hypnotic state begins will not be dealt with in this paper, as it belongs properly to a discussion of the nature of induction of altered SoCs.

the subject to scale and report the depth of his hypnotic state when requested during hypnosis.

In light of the above theoretical discussion, most of the empirical studies of self-report measurement of hypnotic depth leave much to be desired. In measuring the depth of any SoC, the problem of the degree of identity of that SoC across subjects is very important. Many subjects may be said to be "hypnotized" or "intoxicated with marijuana" or the like in conventional usage, but given the present sloppiness of specification of SoCs, each of the many subjects may have relatively unique components making up the gestalt configuration of his SoC. If these components are unique enough, we are seriously misled in giving the same name to the SoC across subjects. In the studies of self-report measurement of hypnotic depth to be reviewed in the next sections, the investigators (implicitly) assumed that the uniformity of the hypnotic SoC across subjects was high enough to ignore individual differences. Empirical investigation may eventually reveal this assumption to be very misleading. A later section of this chapter will present data illustrating an approach that is methodologically more conservative, investigating the depth continuum in an individual subject with the Extended North Carolina Scale. In this approach, the overall phenomenology of the SoC across subjects and the similarity of the individually obtained depth continua must show a satisfactory degree of commonality before the results can be combined into a "general" picture of that SoC.

Five Self-Report Scales of Hypnotic Depth

This section will consider the LeCron Scale, the North Carolina Scale, the Brief Stanford Scale, the Harvard Discreet Scale, and the Harvard Continuous Scale. The Long Stanford Scale will be considered in a separate section as it has been studied more extensively than the other scales. The Extended North Carolina Scale will also be discussed in a separate section.

LeCron (1953) reported that he was able to measure hypnotic depth as frequently as he desired, and with little effort, by simply instructing his subjects that they would be able to scale their hypnotic depth on a 100-point scale. He defined this scale to them somewhat vaguely (the values are shown in Table 14.1), but told them that their "subconscious minds" always knew how deeply hypnotized they were, and that whenever he asked them what their depth was a number would flash into consciousness from their subconscious minds and they would report it immediately. Although he reported few details of his studies, LeCron stated that these self-reports of hypnotic depth correlated extremely well with his clinical estimates of his subjects' depth, and could, for most purposes, replace other measures of depth, such as particular hypnotic phenomena.

LeCron's report led a number of other investigators to develop various methods for self-report of hypnotic depth (or hypnotic "state" in some stud-

TABLE 14.1 Characteristics of self-report scales of depth

Scale Name	Defined Values		Type of Answer	References
LeCron	0	= awake	Instant	Hatfield, 1961
	1–20	= light		LeCron, 1953
	20–40	= medium		
	40–60	= deep		
	60–80	= plenary		
	80+	= stuporous		
North Carolina	0	= waking	Instant	Tart, 1962, 1963, 1967
	1–12	= relaxed, detached, ideomotor movements		
	20	= analgesia		
	25	= dreams		
	30	= amnesia, mental quiet, very high suggestibility		
	40	= all effects completely real		
	50+	= mind sluggish		
Brief Stanford	0	= wide awake	Instant	Hilgard & Tart, 1966
	1	= borderline		Tart, 1966a
	2	= light		Tart & Hilgard, 1966
	3	= medium		
	4	= deep		
Long Stanford	0	= wide awake	Instant	Larsen, 1965
	1	= borderline		Tart, 1966b
	2	= light	Instant and	Present chapter
	5	= deep	Deliberate	
	10	= very deep, very high suggestibility		
Harvard Discrete	1	= awake	Deliberate	O'Connell, 1964
	10	= as deep as possible		
Harvard Continuous	1–10	= awake to deep as possible	Deliberate, Continuous	Field, 1966 Orne & Evans, 1966

SOURCE: Tart, 1970b.

ies). Names have been given to these scales according to where the work was done, and their main characteristics are summarized in Table 14.1. All these scales require the subject to report the depth of his hypnotic state when questioned about it, except the Hypnotic Depth Indicator (HDI), which requires the subject to adjust a dial or move his hands continuously along a ruled scale as his hypnotic depth increases or decreases.[2]

Since these five scales differ along many important dimensions, it is difficult to compare them. The first such dimension is the concept of hypnotic depth held by the experimenter, and the degree to which this was communicated to subjects explicitly (the formal instructions) and implicitly (demand characteristics). The second is the degree of definition of the scale. At one extreme (the HDI and Discrete Scales) only awake and deep are defined, while at the other (the North Carolina Scale, Tart, 1962) particular hypnotic phenomena that subjects can expect to experience at various scale points are mentioned in the instructions. The third is the amount of previous experience with hypnosis subjects may have had before being required to use the scale: If they have not had such experience, they are measuring on the basis both of hypnotic effects and of transitional effects of adapting to a novel situation. Fourth, the scales differ in whether subjects are asked to make conscious, deliberate estimates of their hypnotic depth or whether they are told that the answers will come automatically, instantly, in response to the experimenters query. The fifth dimension is the number of state reports obtained during the hypnotic session, varying from a low of one (the Discrete Scale) to obtaining a state report following every particular hypnotic phenomenon suggested (the North Carolina Scale) to continuous self-monitoring of subjective depth (HDI).

In attempting to assess the validity of self-report scales of hypnotic depth, all published studies to date have compared self-report measures for their subjects against some behavioral measure of hypnotic *susceptibility,* usually some version of the standardized Stanford Scales (SHSS) (Weitzenhoffer & Hilgard, 1959, 1962), or against particular hypnotic phenomena traditionally believed to require a certain minimum depth before they can be experienced well. The procedure of almost all experimental studies of hypnosis apparently assumes that depth stays constant after induction. If, however,

2. This scale was first used by Field in an unpublished report (1963), and required the subject to move a dial along a linear sliding scale. It was modified by Evans so that the subject could move the dial continuously, when appropriate, around a 12-inch diameter "clockface" with his eyes closed. Except for two early studies by Field (1965, 1966), a later, slightly modified version has been used in all studies (Evans, 1970; Evans & Orne, 1965; Field, Evans, & Orne, 1965; Orne & Evans, 1966), and is called in these reports the Hypnotic Depth Indicator (HDI). The Discrete scale, discussed below, is defined in the same fashion, but is usually presented to the subject only once after each termination of hypnosis. It asks the subject to rate the deepest level achieved (Evans & Orne, 1965).

depth does fluctuate rapidly for at least some subjects, then obtaining only a few self-reports of depth might well result in atypical values. Consequently, correlations of self-reported depth with overall susceptibility could not reach very high figures.

This consideration is particularly important in evaluating the published reports. Two studies, one of the original LeCron Scale (Hatfield, 1961) and one of the HDI (O'Connell, 1964), obtained only two reports and one report per subject, respectively, during the hypnotic state. Such designs are extremely susceptible to atypical reports from the subject. Both studies reported *statistically* significant correlations between the self-report measure and the susceptibility measure (.32 for Hatfield, .55 for O'Connell), but neither of these was high enough to uphold LeCron's original contention that self-report measures could replace ordinary measures of depth or be practically useful.

The North Carolina (Tart, 1962, 1963, 1967), Brief Stanford (Hilgard & Tart, 1966; Tart, 1966a; Tart & Hilgrad, 1966), and Long Stanford Scales (Larsen, 1965; Tart, 1966b) were designed to come much closer to LeCron's original technique—to require frequent reports and instructions to subjects that the reports would just flash into their minds instantly, rather than being something they had to deliberately estimate. With these scales, state reports were obtained immediately following the induction procedure and following every hypnotic test item.

One study with the North Carolina Scale (Tart, 1963) allows statistical comparison of a shortened version of the scale (only the first 30 points defined, rather than 50) and hypnotic phenomena: self-reports by subjects obtained just before item administration correctly predicted hypnotic dreaming 100 per cent of the time and posthypnotic amnesia 82 per cent of the time. Variations in self-reported depth on this scale also showed high parallelism with basal skin resistance during the hypnotic state (Tart, 1963), but there is some possibility of this parallelism being artifactual as, in most cases, the hypnotic state was not deliberately lightened to see if skin resistance would then fall, although this happened spontaneously in some cases.

There have been three studies with the Brief Stanford Scale. In the most extensive one (Hilgard & Tart, 1966), subjects were tested in a variety of conditions, all of which included administration of the SHSS:C. A total of 220 subjects were tested during the various hypnotic conditions. The depth reports on this 0–4 scale were obtained between all suggestibility test items, as well as immediately after the induction. Correlations from the various conditions between the SHSS:C score and the *mean* self-report score were .67, .68, .65, .75, and, quite surprisingly, in one group, − .01. Thus, the scale was generally quite significantly related to hypnotic behavior. Many of these subjects were also hypnotized on two different days, and the correlation between their mean self-reported depth from day 1 to day 2 ranged from .81 to .99 over the various groups, indicating that the self-report measurement of hypnotic depth has the same degree of reliability for this scale as does SHSS:C. Further, the *initial* state report, obtained just after the end of induction, was found to be highly predictive of subsequent hypnotic behavior. If the subject reported 0, indicating he felt not hypnotized at all, it was extremely rare for him to pass more than one or two of the easier suggestibility test items (mean score of 1.3 on the SHSS:C versus a mean score of 5.7 for those who reported a state of 2 or more, "definitely hypnotized").

The Brief Stanford Scale has also been found to correlate between .40 and .47 in various groups with the type of hypnotic dream the subject has when the type of dream is also scaled in terms of the profundity of the experience (Tart, 1966a). This finding has been confirmed by Honorton[3] and by Parker.[4]

The Long Stanford Scale

This study, reported in detail elsewhere (Tart, 1970b) is the most extensive study of self-report measurement of hypnotic depth to date. Thirty-five undergraduate male subjects who had experienced the Harvard Group Scale of Hypnotic Susceptibility (HGSHS) (Shor & Orne, 1962) and volunteered for further hypnotic experiments were tested individually. The subjects were randomly divided into two groups, such that while all subjects received otherwise identical instructions for measuring their hypnotic depth, 20 of them were told that such reports would come to mind instantly with no conscious activity on their part, while 15 were told to make deliberate, conscious estimates. The experimenter was blind as to which set of instructions the subject received. A tape-recorded version of the Stanford Hypnotic Susceptibility Scale, Form C (SHSS:C) (Weitzenhoffer & Hilgard, 1962) was then administered and self-reports of depth were obtained following the induction procedure and following every suggestibility test item. At the end of the SHSS:C testing a detailed inquiry about the nature of the subjects' hypnotic experiences was carried out. This leads to a score for each subject called C-experiential, and is described elsewhere (Tart, in preparation). It emphasizes the intensity of the subject's experience in response to the suggested hypnotic phenomena, rather than his overt behavior. Subjects also filled out the Field's inventory (Field, 1965) with respect to their hypnotic experience.

The exact instructions for self-report measurement of hypnotic depth for the instant and deliberate conditions were as follows (the first paragraph of the instructions being identical for each group):

> During your experience of hypnosis, I will be interested in knowing just how hypnotized you are. You will be able to tell me this by calling out a

3. C. Honorton, personal communication, 1968.
4. A. Parker, personal communication, 1969.

number from zero to ten, depending on how hypnotized you feel yourself to be. *Zero* will mean that you are awake and alert, as you normally are. *One* will mean a kind of borderline state, between sleeping and waking. *Two* will mean that you are lightly hypnotized. If you call out the number *five,* it will mean that you feel quite strongly and deeply hypnotized. If you feel really very hypnotized, you would call out an *eight* or *nine. Ten* will mean that you are very deeply hypnotized and you can do just about anything I suggest to you. Naturally, hypnosis can increase and decrease in depth from time to time, and that is the kind of thing I'll be interested in finding out from you.

The instructions for the Instant condition then went on:

Let me explain *how* you will report your state of hypnosis. When I ask "State?" you are to tell me the *first* number that pops into your mind, and this will represent your state at that time. We've found that this first impression is more accurate than if you stop to think about just what the number should be. This may seem a little hard at first, but it will get easy as you go along. Just call out the first number that pops into your mind when I ask, "State?" Remember the number zero means your normal waking state, five means quite strongly hypnotized, and ten means you are deep enough to experience just about anything I suggest. Just say the first number from zero to ten that comes into your mind when I ask, "State?" Let's try it now. State? [All subjects called out a zero at this time.] At various times during your experience I'll ask for your state, and you'll call out the first number that pops into your mind.

The instruction for the Deliberate condition read:

Let me explain *how* you'll report your state of hypnosis. When I ask "State?" I want you to estimate how deeply hypnotized you feel at that moment and call out this number to me. We've found that college subjects can give rather accurate estimates if they give it a few seconds' thought each time. This may seem a little hard at first, but it will get easy as you go along. Just call out your best estimate whenever I ask, "State?"

Remember, the number zero means your normal waking state, five means quite strongly hypnotized, and ten means you are deep enough to experience just about anything I suggest. Just call out your estimate between zero and ten whenever I ask, "State?" Let's try it now. State? (All subjects called out a zero at this time.) At various times during your experience I'll ask for your state, and you'll call out your estimate. You may take a maximum of 15 seconds to make your estimate.

The subjects in both groups, then, were told that hypnosis varies in depth, that they can accurately measure it and report it to the experimenter when asked, and that the deeper they feel, the more hypnotic phenomena they can expect to experience.

USE OF THE LONG STANFORD STATE SCALE

State reports (13 per subject), ranged from 0 to 8, but most of them (67 per cent were 1, 2, or 3, indicating borderline to moderately hypnotized.

One of the rationales for investigating state reports is the hypothesis that the depth of hypnosis may vary fairly rapidly with time. Time is here conveniently represented by the sequence of state reports obtained following each test item. For the subjects as a whole, graphs of mean state reports over time are essentially linear for both Instant and Deliberate conditions. In a group of unselected subjects, however, there will always be many who are not hypnotized, or who are only very lightly hypnotized, and such subjects would serve as a stabilizing influence on such a graph.

In Figure 14.2, state report for successive items has been plotted with subjects divided into high, medium, and low susceptibles on the basis of their SHSS:C behavioral score (high subjects scoring 7 or more; medium subjects scoring 4, 5, or 6; and low subjects scoring 3 or less). Instant and Deliberate conditions are combined. The low susceptible subjects show a mean state report for the whole session of 1.2 (range: 0–4.5 per subject); medium subjects, 2.5 (range: 1.7–4.6 per subject); and high subjects, 5.0 (range: 2.6–6.6 per subject). The differences between means of low and high subjects are significant $(t = 5.3, df = 25, p < .005,$ 1-tailed), as are the differences between medium subjects and high subjects $(t = 3.9, df = 13, p < .005,$ 1-tailed). The differences are only suggestive, however, between low subjects and medium subjects $(t = 1.65, df = 26, p < .10,$ 1-tailed). Considering mean state reports over the course of the suggestibility testing, the curve for the low susceptibles is essentially flat, while there is a suggestion of a rise for medium susceptibles and high susceptibles. Variability of the curves increases with items 6 (the dream), 7B (age regression), and 9B (sniff of ammonia without suggested anosmia). Statistical assessment of differences between the curves is not appropriate because of the con-

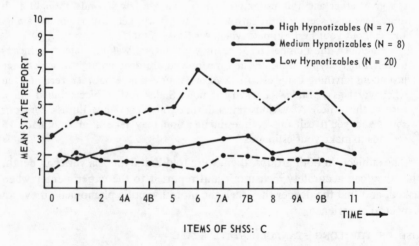

FIGURE 14.2. *Variation in mean state report over the course of testing for Ss of high, medium, and low hypnotic susceptibility (from Tart, 1970b).*

founding effects of: (a) time per se, (b) unequal increases in item difficulty over time, and (c) variations in item wording such that some items contain suggestions that might serve to deepen the hypnotic state, while others have suggestions that might lighten it.[5] This source of confusion, inherent in the use of SHSS:C, is regrettable, and the important possibility that suggestibility *testing* serves as a deepening or lightening procedure should be carefully noted for future investigations.

This analysis is sensitive only to long-term variability in state reports. Short-term variability, from one state report to the next, is also important. Considering all state reports from all subjects, most (50 per cent) of the time there was no change from one report to the next, and 35 per cent of the time the change was only 1 point. These figures can be misleading in the impression of stability they create, however, for, if state is important, a single state change of large magnitude might drastically affect the outcome of an experiment. If one examines the largest *absolute* (that is, without regard to sign) change from one state report to the next for each subject, one finds only 9 per cent showed 0 as their largest change, 34 per cent showed 1, 43 per cent showed 2, 11 per cent showed 3, and 3 per cent showed a change of 4 points. As subjects only used 8 points of the defined scale, changes of 2 points or more seem of considerable magnitude, and such changes were shown at least once by 57 per cent of subjects.

Another way of examining variability in the use of state reports is to consider the number of times each subject showed a change from one state report to the next, regardless of the size of such change. Figure 14.3 shows the frequency of such changes. It was common for subjects to have as many as eight or nine changes in state report during the session.

Thus, as originally hypothesized, subjects' reports of the depth of their hypnotic state do vary significantly in the course of a hypnotic session when examined over short time intervals, but are fairly stable when subjects' ratings are averaged together over the entire session.

At the end of the hypnotic session, all subjects were asked what criteria they had used in making their state reports or, if they reported their responses had been automatic, what sorts of perceived changes in their experience seemed to go along with changes in state report. One subject could report nothing; some subjects reported two or more criteria. Descriptive categories for grouping answers, staying as close to subjects' descriptions as possible, were evolved. The 34 subjects who reported their criteria mentioned 56 criteria among them. Because of the small number of cases that result if these categories are subdivided according to condition, and because of the statistical difficulties caused by varying numbers of criteria per subject, the following description is only suggestive.

---

5. Because there are several reports per subject in the graphed material, statistical comparison would not be legitimate.

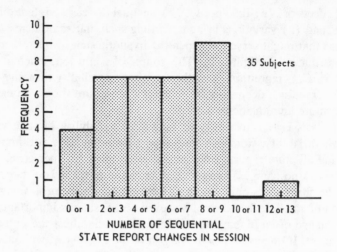

FIGURE 14.3. *Frequency of changes of sequential state reports (from Tart, 1970b).*

The following sorts of criteria, all positively correlated with increasing state report, were mentioned in at least 10 per cent of subjects' reports: (a) intensity of reaction to previous suggestibility test item, 21 per cent; (b) feelings of drowsiness, 20 per cent; (c) fading of the environment, 14 per cent; (d) changes in body image or perceived body position, 12 per cent; (e) relaxation, 11 per cent; and (f) feelings of compulsiveness of responses, 11 per cent. If categories (d) and (e) are combined with several other infrequent categories under the general category of bodily changes, 32 per cent of the reports are accounted for.

The subjects were also asked how well they felt their state reports correlated with the depth of their hypnotic state. They were given fixed response categories of Very Well, Fairly Well, or Poorly. Almost all subjects (97 per cent) reported they thought their reports correlated fairly well to very well.[6]

RELATION OF LONG STANFORD SCALE REPORTS TO BEHAVIORAL
INDICES OF HYPNOSIS

The relation of state report to a behavioral index of hypnotic responsiveness was ascertained by correlating each subject's mean state report with his total SHSS:C behavioral score. Figure 14.4 shows scatter plots for these two

6. I had attempted to run another group of subjects from advanced, rather than introductory, psychology courses in this study. Only two subjects made appointments for testing, so the results were discarded. It is interesting to note, however, that one subject in this group described clearly varying experiential correlates of his state reports, but stated that he had little confidence in their accurately reflecting hypnotic depth because he knew a lot about psychology and knew that subjective reports were of no value!

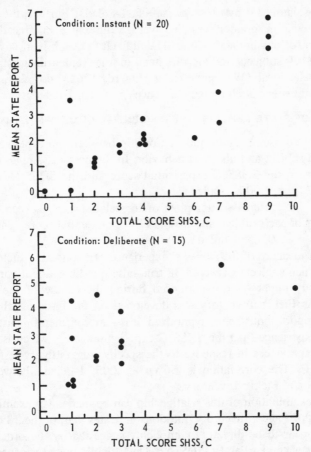

FIGURE 14.4. *Relationship between mean state reports and SHSS: C-behavioral scores for Instant and Deliberate conditions (from Tart, 1970b).*

measures for the Instant and Deliberate conditions separately. For the combined conditions, $r = .74$ $(p < .0005$, 1-tailed).

Because total scores on SHSS:C and mean state report are long-term measures, correlations between them are not an ideal way of assessing a relationship that may vary rapidly with time. A more sensitive measure is to compare the state report obtained just before each suggestibility test item was administered with whether or not that item was passed or failed by the standard SHSS:C behavioral scoring criteria. Item by item, the mean state report across all subjects was always greater for subsequently passed than for subsequently failed items; differences ranged from a low value of 1.12 to a high value of 2.76. Practically all differences for any given item[7] were

7. A test could not be carried out for item 2, as there was only one subject failing this item.

statistically significant by *t* test *(p < .005*, 1-tailed). Further, the more difficult an item, the greater was the average difference in preceding mean state report for passing and failing. The difficulty of each item, given by the percentage of subjects failing the item in the standardization data for SHSS:C behavioral (Weitzenhoffer & Hilgard, 1962), correlates .53 with the size of the mean state report difference *(p < .10*, 1-tailed).

RELATION OF STATE REPORTS TO EXPERIENTIAL QUALITIES OF HYPNOSIS

There is, of course, a significant relationship between the experience of the hypnotized subject and his overt behavior. In the present sample, the correlation between the SHSS:C experiential score and the SHSS:C behavioral score is .77 *(p < .0005*, 1-tailed).

Figure 14.5 presents scatter plots of the relationship between the mean state report of each subject and his SHSS:C experiential score. The correlation is .76 *(p < .0005*, 1-tailed).

Another measure of the subjects' experience of hypnosis is Field's Inventory, on which subjects answered 38 true-false questions about various phenomena they might have experienced during the course of the hypnosis session.[8] As Field's Inventory was developed on the basis of what people generally report about being hypnotized, it is a more general measure of the hypnotic experience than the SHSS:C experiential score, which is based on subjects' experiences in response to the specific suggestibility test items of the SHSS:C. The correlation is .66 *(p < .005*, 1-tailed) between mean state report and Field's Inventory.

A finer examination of this relationship can be made. My examination of the content of Field's Inventory questions indicates that, of the 38 questions, only 10 appear to be directly or implicitly suggested by the procedures of SHSS:C or of the earlier HGSHS:A.[9] Thus Field's Inventory score can be broken into a nonspecific score as well as a total score. Mean state report correlates .63 (*p < .005*, 1-tailed) with the nonspecific scores derived from the Inventory.

EFFECTS OF EXPERIENCE ON LONG STANFORD SCALE REPORTS

In the above analyses, subjects gained a fair amount of hypnotic experience in the course of making their state reports. In addition to the initial HGSHS:A, they had the induction of the SHSS:C and experience gained from the various SHSS:C items as the test proceeded. It is of interest to see how well state reports related to other aspects of hypnotizability with less

8. Subjects were obtained from three different psychology classes at various times: the third time subjects were run, the experimenter neglected to administer Field's Inventory, so the N for those analyses using Field's Inventory is 15 in the Instant condition and 10 in the Deliberate condition.
9. These 10 items are numbers 4, 6, 9, 10, 14, 16, 24, 29, 30, and 34.

hypnotic experience. This can be done by using only the first state report given by each subject, that is, the one immediately following the hypnotic induction section of SHSS:C, thus eliminating the experience of reactions to the suggestibility test items. Table 14.2 presents the correlation coefficients of initial state report with SHSS:C behavioral, SHSS:C experiential, and Field's Inventory across conditions. Although the correlations are generally reduced compared to those based on the full scale procedure, they are all statistically significant.

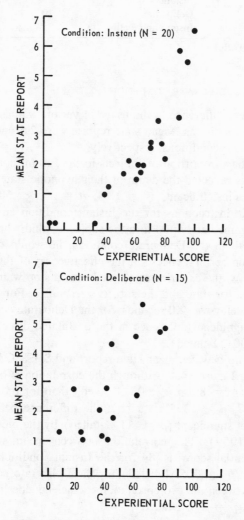

FIGURE 14.5. *Relationship between mean state reports and SHSS: C-experiential scores for Instant and Deliberate conditions (from Tart, 1970b).*

TABLE 14.2   Relation of initial state report to various measures

Measure	Condition	N	r	p < [a]
SHSS:C behavioral	Instant	20	.61	.005
	Deliberate	15	.58	.02
	Instant and Deliberate	35	.56	.0005
SHSS:C experiential	Instant	20	.79	.005
	Deliberate	15	.63	.01
	Instant and Deliberate	35	.69	.0005
Field's Inventory	Instant	15	.72	.005
	Deliberate	10	.69	.005
	Instant and Deliberate	25	.69	.0005

SOURCE: Tart, 1970b.
a. One-tailed values.

INSTANT VERSUS DELIBERATE CONDITIONS

There was no clear difference in the usage of various values of the state reports in the two conditions. Mean state reports were 2.5 and 2.6 in the Instant and Deliberate conditions, respectively.

A slightly higher proportion of subjects in the Instant condition reported their state reports reflected the depth of their hypnotic state Very Well, but the difference was insignificant ($\chi^2 = 1.84$, $df = 2$, $p < .50$, 1-tailed).

The state-scale instructions for the Instant condition emphasized that a number would immediately pop into the subject's mind when he was asked "State?" and that, in the Deliberate condition, he would *consciously estimate* the best number. To check on the effectiveness of the instructions in the two conditions, the experimenter timed with a stop watch the delay between the request for state and the subject's responses. For the Instant condition the mean delay was 2.0 seconds, for the Deliberate condition, 4.2 seconds, a highly significant difference in the postulated direction ($t = 4.07$, $df = 33$, $p < .001$, 1-tailed).

The relationship between mean state report and SHSS:C behavioral score was presented in Figure 14.4. Although the correlation is better for the Instant condition ($r = .85$, $p < .005$, 1-tailed) than for the Deliberate condition ($r = .67$, $p < .005$, 1-tailed), the difference between these two coefficients is not significant *(p = .11,* 1-tailed) by the method of Johnson and Jackson (1959). The correlation between mean state report and SHSS:C experiential scores is .84 for the Instant condition *(p < .005,* 1-tailed) and .75 *(p < .005,* 1-tailed) for the Deliberate condition. Again, the difference between the two correlation coefficients does not reach statistical significance *(p = .36,* 1-tailed).

The same pattern of correlation coefficients being higher, but not significantly so, for the Instant condition appears when comparing mean state report and Field's Inventory scores. The correlation for Instant condition is .69 *(p < .005,* 1-tailed) and for the Deliberate condition is .64 *(p < .02,*

1-tailed). The correlation between the Field's nonspecific scores with mean state report is .66 in the Instant condition *(p* < .005, 1-tailed) and .62 *(p* < .02, 1-tailed) in the Deliberate condition. Initial state reports, already presented in Table 14.2, also show this pattern.

In short, correlations with other measures of hypnotic performance are always higher for state reports from the Instant condition, but not significantly so.

The Extended North Carolina Scale

The Extended North Carolina Scale has been used in a large number of experiments in my laboratory, primarily where experienced hypnotic subjects are used repeatedly in various experiments. It is similar to the North Carolina Scale with the addition that subjects are told that there is really no "top" to the scale—that is, it is possible for them to go considerably deeper into hypnosis than the defined points. The exact instructions for the scale are:

We are interested in the ways in which the intensity or depth of your hypnotic state may vary from time to time. It has been our experience that we can get quite accurate reports of hypnotic depth or intensity by teaching you a way of scaling it and getting your first impressions whenever we ask you about your hypnotic state.

Basically, whenever I ask, "State?" a number will flash into your mind, and I want you to call it out to me right away. This number will represent the depth of your hypnotic state at the time. This number will flash into your mind and you'll call it out automatically, without any effort on your part. You won't have to think about what this number *should* be, or try to reason it out; you'll just call out the first number that comes to mind whenever I ask, "State?" If, of course, you then think the number is very inaccurate for some reason, I'd like you to tell me so, but people rarely feel the number is not accurate, even though they are sometimes surprised by it.

Getting these depth numbers is very important, because every person is somewhat unique in his reactions while hypnotized. Some people react at different speeds than others; some react to a particular hypnotic experience by going deeper into hypnosis, others sometimes find the depth of their hypnotic state decreased by the same experience. Thus by getting these state reports from you every so often I can tell whether to go a little faster or slower, where to put emphasis in the suggestions I use to guide you, etc. These depth reports are not always what I expect, but it's more important for me to know where you really are than just assume you're there because I've been talking that way!

Now here is the numerical scale you are to use. I'll give you various highlights that identify different degrees of hypnosis on the scale, but you can report any point on the scale when asked for your state.

Zero is your normal, waking state.

From *1* to *12* is a state in which you feel relaxed and detached, more so as the numbers increase toward *12;* in this range you can experience such hypnotic phenomena as your arm rising up or feeling heavy or moved by a force.

When you reach a depth of *20* or greater you feel very definitely hypnotized, and you can experience great changes in your feeling of your body, such as your hand getting numb if I suggested it.

By the time you reach a depth of *25* or greater you can have strong inner experiences such as dreams or dreamlike experiences.

At a depth of *30* or greater you can temporarily forget everything that happened in the hypnosis if I suggest it. Many other experiences are possible at this depth and greater, such as regressing into the past and reliving some experience, experiencing tastes and smells I might suggest, or not experiencing real stimuli if I tell you not to sense them. There are hardly any hypnotic phenomena you can't experience at least fairly well, and most extremely well, at this depth. At *30* and beyond your mind is very quiet and still when I'm not directing your attention to something, and you probably don't hear anything except my voice or other sounds I might direct your attention to.

You have reached at least 30 in earlier sessions, and it is a sufficient depth to be able to learn all the skills needed in this experiment, but it is very likely that you will go deeper than 30 in these studies.

By the time you have reached a depth of *40* or greater you have reached a *very* deep hypnotic state in which your mind is perfectly still and at peace if I'm not directing your attention to something. Whatever I do suggest to you at this depth and beyond is *perfectly real,* a total, real, all-absorbing experience at the time, as real as anything in life. You can experience *anything* I suggest at 40 and beyond.

I'm not going to define the depths beyond this, for little is known about them; if you go deeper than 40, and I hope you do, I'll ask you about the experiences that go with these greater depths so we may learn more about deep hypnosis.[10]

Remember now that increasing numbers up from zero indicate an increasing degree of hypnotic depth, from the starting point of ordinary wakefulness up to a state in which you can experience anything in hypnosis with complete realism. Your quick answers whenever I ask, "State?" will be my guide to the depth of your hypnotic state, and help me guide you more effectively. Always call out the *first* number that pops into your mind loudly and clearly. Whenever I ask, "State?" a number on the scale will instantly come into mind and you call it out.

I'll go over the various points that describe the scale again.

These instructions for the scale are usually read to the subject after he is hypnotized, and he is asked whether he comprehends them. Also, the instructions are briefly reread to the subject every half-dozen hypnotic sessions or so to refresh his memory of them.

10. In some earlier work (Tart, 1966a) with the North Carolina scale, 50 was defined as a state so profound that the subject's mind became sluggish, but this definition was dropped here.

The overall procedure in working with subjects in my laboratory on a prolonged basis is to treat them as explorers or colleagues working with the investigators, rather than as subjects who are being manipulated for purposes alien to them.

My overall impressions of results with the Extended North Carolina Scale have convinced me that it is the most useful measure of hypnotic depth I have seen. The only published data on this so far have been presented in the context of a study on responses to posthypnotic suggestion to dream about specified topics (Tart & Dick, 1970). In this study, 13 highly hypnotizable subjects were given a posthypnotic suggestion to dream about one or another of two stimulus narratives in their stage 1 REM dreams of the night. The size of the posthypnotic effect was measured by the number of stimulus elements appearing in the manifest dream content. Although the subjects were all highly hypnotizable (scored at least 10 of a possible 12, SHSS:C), there are still sufficient variation in reports on the Extended North Carolina Scale to warrant correlating these depth reports with subsequent posthypnotic dream performance.

Several ways of carrying out this correlation across subjects were possible, producing correlations which ranged from a low of .11 to a high of .51, the latter significant at the 10 per cent, 1-tailed level. Such correlations assumed that the subjects measured depth in a comparable manner, but this is not necessarily a good assumption; that is, a given subject may be measuring his depth consistently, but once he gets beyond the range commonly defined for all subjects he may not do so in exactly the same fashion as other subjects. More conservative tests, assuming only that each subject is consistent in his own measuring, shows that the posthypnotic dream effect was more than twice as large on a subject's night with a higher state report compared with his night with a lower one $(p < .025$, 1-tailed). As noted, this does not really indicate the potentiality of the scale because the use of subjects who were all extremely hypnotizable greatly restricts the range and automatically reduces correlation coefficients.

Some potentialities of the Extended North Carolina Scale, as well as some intriguing phenomena of deep hypnosis and data on the question of when deep hypnosis becomes another SoC will be illustrated by the data of a single subject. Other subjects have shown similar patterns, but these will not be referred to as this material is not yet completely analyzed.

William: Deep Hypnosis and Beyond

William, a 20-year-old male college student, is extremely intelligent, academically successful, and well adjusted. His only previous experience with hypnosis was some brief work with a psychiatrist cousin to teach him how to relax. In a screening session with the HGSHS, he scored 11 out of a possible 12. On a questionnaire he reported that he almost always recalled dreaming, that such dreaming was very vivid and elaborate, and that he had kept a dream diary at times in the past. William reported that he had sleep talked rather frequently as a child but did so only occasionally now. He had never sleepwalked. On individual testing with SHSS:C, he scored 12 out of a possible 12. He then had two training sessions designed to explore and maximize his hypnotic responsiveness in various areas, described elsewhere (Tart & Dick, 1970). In the first of these special training sessions, he was taught the Extended North Carolina Scale. He then took Forms I and II of the Stanford Profile Scale of Hypnotic Susceptibility (Weitzenhoffer & Hilgard, 1963) and scored 26 and 27 on Forms I and II, respectively, out of a possible maximum of 27 on each.

Over the course of the next eight months, William participated in a variety of experiments in my laboratory, which served to further increase his hypnotic experience and make him well adapted to functioning in the laboratory setting; he had ten sessions of training for operant control of the EEG alpha rhythm (Tart, 1969b), four experimental sessions in various aspects of hypnosis, and eight evening sessions in which he was hypnotized and given posthypnotic suggestions to carry out in his subsequent sleep in the laboratory, such as dreaming about a suggested topic (Tart & Dick, 1970), incorporating auditory stimuli into his dreams, and talking during his sleep. Thus, by the time William participated in the deep hypnosis experiment to be described here, he was familiar with the lab and had been hypnotized there 18 times. The deepest depth report given in any of these sessions was 60, and he usually gave reports between 40 and 50.

In the experimental session to be reported upon, it was explained to William that the purpose of the session was to find out what hypnosis meant to him personally. Specifically, he was informally interviewed for about an hour asking him what he usually experienced under hypnosis, other than his reactions to specifically suggested phenomena, and, if possible, what depth level, according to the Extended North Carolina Scale, he was at when he experienced these particular things. I then hypnotized him and at each 10-point interval on a depth continuum I would ask William to remain at that depth and describe whatever it was he was experiencing. No particular probing was done here other than for phenomena already mentioned by William; the emphasis was on his individual hypnotic experience. William also agreed to attempt to go much deeper than he ever had gone before.

The session was quite rewarding. Although William had never gone beyond 60 before, he went to 90, reporting at 10-point intervals on the Extended North Carolina Scale, and also briefly went from 90 to 130. These values beyond 40 had not, of course, been defined by the experimenter: They were the result of his own definition. Or, according to William's report, they were simply numbers that came to his mind when he was asked for his state. Despite repeated questioning by me and despite the fact that the subject was quite verbal and extremely good at describing his experiences, his only comment on how he measured his hypnotic depth was that when I asked him for a state report a number popped into his mind, he said it, and that was it. He had no idea how these numbers were generated, nor did he "understand" them, but he assumed they meant something since he had been told in the original Extended North Carolina Scale instructions that they would.

The results of both his preinduction interview about his general experience of hypnosis and the particular hypnotic session have been condensed into the graph shown in Figure 14.6.

William felt that his particular experience during this exploration was typical of his general experience with hypnosis. Various phenomena are plotted, each with its own ordinate of intensity. Circles indicate reports obtained during this particular hypnotic session, triangles are reports obtained during the interview preceding this session about all his hypnotic experiences to date. Every phenomenon was not assessed on every 10-point interval on the depth scale, so curves are shown as dotted where data points are missing. Discussion of this scale will indicate some of the phenomena of extremely deep hypnotic states and illustrate some of the theoretically possible relationships of effects to hypnotic depth discussed in the introductory section.

The first effect, "physical relaxation," is not plotted beyond 20. According to William his relaxation increases markedly as he is hypnotized, and quickly reaches a value of extremely relaxed. However, he reports that after a depth of 50 it does not make sense to ask him about physical relaxation because he's no longer identified with his body; his body is "just a thing, something I've left behind." One does not rate the relaxation of things.

The second experiential effect is of a "blackness" of the visual field. His visual field becomes quite black and formless as he goes into hypnosis. Nevertheless, it continues to become somehow blacker,[11] this being a roughly linear increase up to about 60. At this point he says the field continues to become blacker as he goes deeper, but it is in some sense "filled," that is, there is a sense that there is some kind of form(s) filling his visual field even though he is not perceiving any particular forms. Beyond 60 he is not particularly aware of any visual sensation unless his attention is drawn to it by the experimenter.

The third effect, a feeling of "peacefulness," also increases linearly from the beginning of the hypnotic state through approximately 60. William reports that he is extremely peaceful at this point. Beyond 60, he says that peacefulness is not a meaningful concept, as was the case with physical relaxation. As will be seen in the later plots of William's identity, there is no longer a self to be peaceful or not peaceful beyond this point.

---

11. William insists that this progression is not going from gray to darker gray to black, because his visual field is black to begin with, even though it gets "blacker." He recognizes the paradoxicalness of this statement, but considers it the best description he can give.

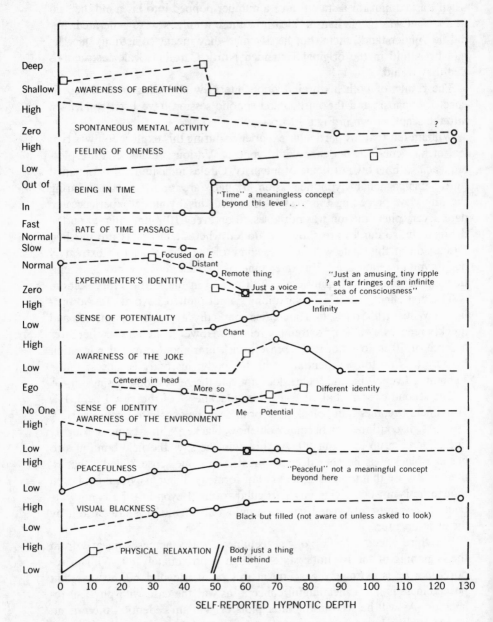

FIGURE 14.6. *Self-report of hypnotic experience (from Tart, 1970b).*

The fourth plotted effect is William's degree of "awareness of his environment," primarily the small sounds in the experimental room and the temperature and air currents in it. His awareness of the environment falls off rapidly and roughly linearly, and at about 50 reaches a point where he reports that he is not at all aware of the environment (with the exception of the hypnotist's voice). His awareness of the environment then stays at zero throughout the rest of the plotted continuum.

The fifth effect, labeled "sense of identity," is a little more complex. In the light stages of hypnosis William is fully aware of his ordinary identity and body image, but as he reaches a depth of about 30 he reports that his identity is "more centered in his head," that is, that his identity is dominated by feelings of his head and his mind. This feeling continues to increase, plotted as a decrease of his ordinary identity, and then his ordinary identity continues to decrease until around 80 or 90 he feels that his ordinary identity is completely in abeyance: "William" no longer exists. On the other hand, starting from about 50 he begins to sense another identity and this continually increases up through about 80, the last point plotted for this phenomenon. This identity is one of *potential*—he doesn't feel identified as any specific person or thing but only as the steadily increasing *potential to be anything or anyone*.

The sixth phenomena, labeled "awareness of the joke," is even more difficult to explain. This phenomenon manifests at about 50, reaches a maximum at about 70, then fades in intensity and is completely gone at 90. The "joke" is that the William should engage in strange activities like deep hypnosis, meditation, or taking drugs in order to alter his SoC; some "higher" aspect of his self is amused by all this activity, and William himself becomes aware of this amusement. Most people who have had several psychedelic drug sessions will recognize this as an effect that often occurs as the drug is beginning to take hold.

The next effect, labeled "sense of potentiality," starts off at a zero level but at around 50 first manifests itself as an awareness of some sort of chant or humming sound that is identified with the feeling that more and more experience is potentially available.[12] The specific form of the chant is lost but this sense of potentiality increases linearly from this point, until around 80 William feels that an infinite range of experience is potentially available, so this phenomenon levels off.

The eighth effect, "experimenter's identity," at first increases as the subject goes down to about 30 in hypnosis; that is, he becomes more and more aware of the experimenter. The experimenter then seems to become more and more distant and remote, and finally the experimenter possesses no identity, he is just a voice, and at the very deep levels he is "just an amus-

12. The chant William reported may be related to the Hindu concept of the sacred syllable Om, supposedly a basic sound of the Universe that a man can "hear" as mind becomes more universally attuned (Danielou, 1966).

ing, tiny ripple at the far fringes of an infinite sea of consciousness." There
is a slight discrepancy at 50 between William's actual experience and his estimate of what he generally experienced.

The ninth effect, "rate of time passage," indicates that William feels time
passing more and more slowly in a linear fashion as he goes down to about
40. This effect is no longer plotted for, as the next effect, "being in time,"
shows, William feels that time very suddenly ceases to be a meaningful concept for him: at 50 he is no longer in time, his experiences are somehow
timeless, they do not have a duration or a place, an order in the scheme of
things.[13]

The next effect, labeled "feeling of oneness," increases linearly throughout the depth range plotted. Here William reports feeling more and more at
one with the universe, although he does not ordinarily feel this. The effect is
plotted as being very low in his ordinary waking state.

The next effect is "spontaneous mental activity," that is, how much conscious mental activity goes on that is not related to specific suggestions by the
hypnotist to do something or to experience something. In the ordinary waking state this is quite high: An old Hindu metaphor describes the ordinary
mind as being like a sexually aroused and drunken monkey, constantly hopping about and chattering. This spontaneous mental activity goes steadily
down until it reaches an essentially zero level at about 90 and stays there
through the rest of the depth range plotted. Such a decrease in spontaneous
mental activity for hypnosis has also been reported elsewhere (Tart,
1966b).

The final effect plotted is William's "awareness of his own breathing." He
feels that his breathing tends to become steadily deeper as he becomes more
deeply hypnotized, but at 50 there is a very sudden change in his perceived
breathing: It becomes extremely shallow, almost imperceptable, and stays
that way through the rest of the hypnotic state. It is not known whether an
objective measure of respiration would show any changes at this point; William did not actually stop breathing.

Considering the above phenomena as a report of a well-trained observer,
we may make a number of comments. First it should be clear that William
has an exceptional ability for hypnosis; he appears to have gone far deeper
than the usual range of phenomena conventionally labeled "deep hypnosis."
As the extended North Carolina scale was defined for him, 30 was the level
ordinarily defined as deep hypnosis (amnesia, postive and negative hallucinations as defining phenomena), and 40 would be the approximate limit reported by many of the very highly hypnotizable subjects I have worked with
in the laboratory. Yet William reported a maximum depth of 130 which, if
one assumes reasonable validity and linearity for the scale, may be one of

13. Priestley (1964) discusses such experiences of being in and out of time quite
    well.

the deepest hypnotic states on record. This ability to go so deep may partially stem from his previous experience with meditation and psychedelic drugs. Further, William was exceptionally verbal and able to describe his experiences well. In the past, Erickson's (1952) exceptionally good subjects have reached a "stuporous" state, which may have reflected an inability to conceptualize and verbalize their experiences. Thus William's hypnotic experiences are illustrative of a potential range of hypnotic phenomena, but are not typical.

Second, the postulated nonlinearity and noncontinuity of possible effects (and subsystem operation, insofar as effects may be taken as indicators of subsystem operation) is apparent in William's data. In the ordinary range of light to deep hypnosis (roughly 0–40), most effects are linear, but "experimenter's identity" is curvilinear and "physical relaxation" is noncontinuous, that is, it becomes a meaningless variable half way through this range. Considering the entire depth range plotted, some effects show step functions ("awareness of breathing," "being in time"), rapid increases and decreases from zero ("awareness of the joke"), plateauing after an initial linear increase or decrease ("experimenter's identity," "sense of potentiality," "awareness of the environment," "visual blackness"), or disappearance by becoming meaningless ("peacefulness," "physical relaxation"). If, in the course of investigation, one used the intensity of *one* phenomenon as an index of hypnotic depth, very confusing results would be obtained if it were not linear and continuous, so the value of a multiphenomenal approach is apparent.

Third, the large number of step changes or fairly rapid changes in the 50 to 70 range raise the question, in view of the definition of SoCs at the beginning of this paper, of whether we are still dealing with "deep hypnosis" beyond the depth of approximately 70. These rapid changes might represent a transition from the gestalt configuration we call hypnosis to a new configuration, a new SoC. At its maximum level (assuming that the 70–130 range represents depth continuum for the new SoC), we have a state with the following phenomenological characteristics: (1) no awareness of the physical body; (2) no awareness of any discrete "thing" or sensation, but only awareness of a flux of potentiality; (3) no awareness of the real world environment, with the one exception of the (depersonalized) voice of the experimenter as "an amusing tiny ripple at the far fringes of an infinite sea of consciousness"; (4) being byond, outside of time; and (5) the identity "William" totally in abeyance, and identity being simply potentiality.

SoCs of this type have not been dealt with in Western scientific literature on hypnosis to any great extent, but sound similar to Eastern descriptions of consciousness of the Void, an SoC in which time, space, and ego are supposedly transcended, leaving pure awareness of the primal nothingness from which all manifested creation comes (Govinda, 1960; Phillips, 1963). Writers who have described the Void insist that the experience is ineffable and cannot be described in words, so the above description and comparison with William's experience is rough, to say the least. Thus William's data are not only of interest in terms of hypnotic depth and the transition from one SoC to another, but raise the possibility of using hypnotic states to induce and/or model mystical states.[14]

Finally, William's data illustrate some of the practical aspects of studying the depth of an SoC, particularly hypnosis, discussed at the beginning of this paper. Using the individual subject as a unit, a set of interrelationships of various phenomena with respect to hypnotic depth has been found; self-reported depth has ordered observed phenomena in a useful and theoretically important manner. Further research, to be reported in a future publication, will study this same sort of procedure in other subjects, repeat sessions with some subjects to study consistency, and make initial intersubject comparisons to determine which depth-phenomenology relationships are general and which represent idiosyncratic qualities of subjects. General relationships of phenomena with depth may be found and/or several classes of subjects may be found and/or it may be more appropriate to talk about several SoCs that have all been indiscriminately termed "hypnosis" in the past.

Finally, it should be stressed that the case of William has been presented to illustrate *potential* of self-reporting of hypnotic depth. The effects of subtle factors in the writer's laboratory, demand characteristics, and William's uniqueness must be assessed in the course of replication and extension of this work by others to solidly establish how much of this potential holds up and becomes practically and theoretically useful.

General Comments on Self-report Scales of Hypnotic Depth

A primary question of the studies reported in this chapter has been how well self-report scales of hypnotic depth actually measure the depth dimension of the hypnotic state. This is both a theoretical and an empirical question. Given the theoretical orientation presented earlier, the Long Stanford Scale and the Extended North Carolina Scale illustrate the theoretical complexities predicted and suggest strong potential, but the important question of the construct validity of these scales must await further theoretical specification and investigation. We shall primarily consider the empirical usefulness of the Long Stanford Scale in the remainder of this paper.

Certain assumptions must be made. One must assume that there is (are) a dimension(s) of depth or profundity of the hypnotic state, that a given subject may move along such dimension(s) from time to time, and that there are experiential correlates of position on each dimension that a subject can consciously perceive or unconsciously react to and report. That is, for a

14. Aaronson (1969) has reported direct hypnotic induction of the Void experience through specific suggestion.

given subject at a given position on the depth continuum there must be either steady state experiences or experiences in response to specific suggestions that the subject may use to judge his depth. Further, one must assume some commonality of the depth dimension across subjects in order to have a scale that is useful for persons other than the individual for whom it was developed, that is, one must assume that there is a great deal in common to the experience we label "hypnosis" across subjects.

Given these assumptions about the nature of a self-report scale, we may then consider the question of its validity. Specifically, it is a question of *construct* validity. Hypnotic depth, as defined here, is a complex dimension that has no *direct* correlate—there is no *particular* phenomenon or behavior the magnitude of which may be seen as directly reflecting hypnotic depth. We would expect all of our various measures (depth reports, SHSS:C behavioral, SHSS:C experiential, and Field's Inventory) to be related to hypnotic depth, but none of them to be equivalent to it. Thus depth reports should correlate highly with all these other hypnotic measures, but not perfectly.[15]

This is what was found: for SHSS:C behavioral, SHSS:C experiential, and Field's Inventory, the correlations with mean depth report were .74, .77, and .66, respectively. There is no doubt that depth reports are reflecting one or more significant dimensions of hypnotic behavior and experience, even if we cannot specify precisely what these dimensions are at present.

Assuming that reports with the Long Stanford Scale are probably as valid a measure of hypnotic depth as behavioral measures in terms of present knowledge, there are a number of advantages to adopting self-report measures as *the* measure of depth as opposed to conventional behavioral measures. First, it takes little time to teach the subject how to use the self-report scale. Second, it takes only seconds to get a report, and asking for these reports does not seem to disturb the subject. Third, ascertaining depth by behavioral measures at any given moment involves giving several suggestibility tests of varying degrees of difficulty. Judging by present data, the subject's depth might very well change in the time taken to administer these tests. Further, if one starts with tests that are too easy one risks boring the subject and taking a long time to find his response ceiling, while if one starts with tests that are too hard the consequent failure experiences might discourage the subject and/or decrease his depth.

Let us consider *how* the subjects manage to measure their depth of hypnosis—how do they come up with the numbers they report? The cognitive bases on which they must measure would be: previous knowledge of hypnotic phenomena, which Shor (1964a) has shown to be rather good in a college student population; knowledge of hypnosis gained in actual experi-

---

15. Indeed for some of the phenomena found in William's data, correlations would be negative or, if depth reports were compared to curvilinear or step functions while (erroneously) assuming linearity, zero.

mental participation; and the instructions, both explicit and implicit, for scaling. Given this, it is interesting to note that with less conscious cognitive activity involved in the measuring and reporting process (Instant), there were stronger relationships to the other measures of hypnotic performance, although these did not reach acceptable levels of statistical significance. LeCron's (1953) theory that the answers in the Instant condition come directly from the "subconscious" is much too complex to test experimentally at present, but it is clear that the Instant condition instructions favor an intuitive rather than a cognitive type of response.

One might expect that the subject's reactions to suggestibility test items would be the primary determinants of the subject's depth reports, such that the better he reacted, the higher a depth he would report, regardless of whether the depth reports were generated intuitively or cognitively. The data suggest, however, that this may not be too important a factor, for three reasons. First, only 21 per cent of the replies to the question of how the subjects scaled depth specifically mentioned reaction to the last item; rather, perceived changes in body experience were the most frequently mentioned (32 per cent) criteria. Second, the depth report obtained just *before* a suggestibility test item was highly predictive of passing or failing, as described earlier. Third, the depth report following the induction procedure, but before the subject could react to any suggestibility test items, was also highly correlated with other measures of hypnosis. Many subjects also mentioned experiences, unrelated to specific suggestions, which increased or decreased in intensity with their depth and which were used for measuring.[16] While reactions to passing and failing an item are a factor in measuring depth, the depth reports are not merely a trivial reflection of passing or failing items.[17]

Given that depth reports reflect the dimension of hypnotic depth, the present findings have an important implication for studies of "waking" suggestibility in comparison to hypnotic suggestibility. The high and medium susceptible subjects tended to show increases in their self-reports of hypnotic depth through the course of the suggestibility testing, indicating that the suggestibility test items may also function as deepening procedures. If so, it is possible that suggestibility test items given under "waking" conditions could function as hypnotic induction procedures for highly susceptible subjects; this finding has been reported earlier (Hilgard & Tart, 1966). Thus the simple procedure of *not* administering an induction in order to define the "waking suggestibility" group is misleading, because the group may well contain a

16. One subject, for example, reported "seeing" a pale green light permeating the experiential space in which he existed during hypnosis; when the light became more intense he gave reports of being deeper.
17. We might also note that the subjects' criterion for passing and failing test items might not be the same as the experimenter's. This was one reason for developing the experiential scoring of Form C. The higher relationships between self-reports and SHSS:C experiential support this notion.

few deeply hypnotized subjects before the testing is finished. Conversely, defining a group as "hypnotized" simply because the experimenter has gone through a traditional hypnotic induction procedure is also fallacious, as many subjects will not become hypnotized.

The present data also suggest that a new degree of precision in studies of hypnosis is possible. In many past studies of particular hypnotic phenomena, it is likely that the depth of hypnosis varied from subject to subject, or within the same subject from one repetition to the next, in an unknown manner. This would result in high variability of results that could obscure important relationships. If depth reports are used, the subject could be kept at the same relative depth level for each evocation of the phenomenon under study, thus eliminating a major source of variability.

Another possible practical use of depth reports is in studies attempting to maximize the hypnotic responsiveness of individual subjects: If a depth report indicated the subject was probably not deep enough to experience a suggested phenomenon well, his depth could be deepened before the phenomenon was suggested; thus a failure experience that might have adverse effects could be avoided. Similarly, the depth report could be used to tell how well the subject responded to particular deepening techniques. Other uses will undoubtedly be suggested by future work.

In conclusion, while the present data indicate practical usefulness for self-reports of hypnotic depth, they must serve primarily as a stimulus to more research if our theoretical understanding of the nature of hypnotic depth is to advance. We need wide scale explorations to answer the following sorts of questions: (1) What are the general experiential, behavioral, and physiological phenomena of hypnosis? (2) How are these related to the particular structure (demands and expectations) imposed in each laboratory, such that we can partial out these demands? (3) Is there a general phenomenology of the hypnotic state across subjects after these demands are partialled out, or are there several SoCs inadvertently mixed under the label "hypnosis"? (4) What is the relationship for individual subjects between self-reported hypnotic depth and various phenomena, and what is the interrelationship of the various phenomena? (5) How do various subjects actually carry out self-scaling of depth, and how is this affected by the structure imposed in each laboratory? (6) Is there a general interrelationship of phenomena and self-report measurement across subjects, or are there several varieties or several SoCs involved? (7) How do the possibilities of multidimensionality of depth (Shor, 1962) fit in?

It is hoped that the present material serves to illustrate the possibility of investigating these questions.

IV

Individual Researches within Specific Areas

Peter B. Field *is a Clinical Research Psychologist, VA Hospital, Brooklyn, Director of Research at the Morton Prince Clinic of the Institute for Research in Hypnosis, and in private practice. He received his doctorate from Harvard University in 1961. After a year as Director of Research at the Puerto Rico Institute of Psychiatry, he became a postdoctoral fellow at the Studies in Hypnosis Project, Massachusetts Mental Health Center and Harvard Medical School. In 1964 he became a research psychologist with the VA Hospital in Brooklyn. After obtaining training in clinical applications of hypnosis at the Morton Prince Clinic, he became its Director of Research in 1968. His research interests include hypnosis, psychotherapy, culture and personality, and alcoholism. He is a coauthor of* Personality and Persuasibility *with Irving L. Janis, Carl I. Hovland, and others.*

Field *interprets hypnotic communication from the standpoint of humanistic psychology, and presents empirical data in support of his position. He rejects the mechanistic viewpoint equating hypnosis with the uncritical acceptance of implanted ideas. Instead he feels that hypnotic communication can best be understood within the same framework as literature, drama, music, and art. The hypnotist utilities imagery, emotional impact, receptivity without analysis, dramatic tension, direct experience, informality, and spontaneity—modes of communication shared with the humanities and the arts. Field uses this framework to interpret a linguistic content analysis of the hypnotic induction, which he contrasts with a parallel analysis of formal and informal speech outside the hypnotic situation. He finds that the hypnotist uses vivid, concrete, redundant, personal, and intimate language, with lessened emphasis upon static abstract conceptualization and categorization.*

15

Humanistic Aspects of Hypnotic Communication

PETER B. FIELD

Several features of the traditional hypnotic induction seem unusual when considered from the standpoint of psycholinguistics or communications. For example, the hypnotist may use redundancy, rhythm, counting, silences, and intonation. He may use gestures and touch the subject. He may use concrete, clear, and vivid imagery, but also may use purposeful confusion. Sometimes he will slur his speech as if drowsy, and sometimes he will use a ritualistic singsong. Occasionally he will speak dramatically and theatrically, with force and conviction. At other times he will be gentle, soft, and intimate. After the trance is established, the hypnotist may seem to enter the subject's world of illusion by speaking to hallucinated figures or, during age regression, addressing the subject as if he were a child.

Some of this is well understood. The goal of the hypnotist is to build a relationship of trust and confidence, to help the subject relax physically and psychologically, and to lull the subject into a half-waking, half-sleep state. At the same time, some of the details of the process are not completely understood, and the theoretical framework to describe it is not unified or worked out in sufficient detail. The objective of this chapter is to consider hypnotic communication from a humanistic viewpoint, and to present some empirical data that seem to support this theoretical approach.

Few previous contributions have attempted to treat the language of the hypnotist from a consistent and unified theoretical position, but there are some notable exceptions. Erickson (1944) and Erickson, Haley, and Weakland (1959) have provided penetrating and detailed analyses of the formu-

The author thanks Erika Fromm, Ronald E. Shor, David McNeill, and Robert D. Palmer for helpful comments, and F. H. Kleinsinger, Pearl Schwartz, Gregory Schlitz, and Carol Wolitzky for research assistance.

lation of hypnotic speech, extending to minute details of wording. Erickson (in Haley, 1967) has originated many ingenious communication techniques, including pantomine, confusion, interspersal, and other specialized induction methods. Haley (1958, 1963) has treated hypnotic communication from an interactional standpoint, emphasizing the double-bind aspects of the hypnotist's language. In analyzing subject-hypnotist interaction patterns (Field, 1964), I reported that the hypnotist not only gave more suggestions, but also agreed more than the subject did, asked more questions, gave fewer opinions and less information, and so on. Troffer and Tart (1964) characterized the hypnotist's voice as "relaxed, somnolent, solicitous, convinced, dramatic, insistent, coaxing, breathy, sing-song, deeper, slower, soothing, sibilant, softer, droning, descriptive rather than commanding, and as having a sense of hushed intimacy" (p. 1330). Hunt (1969) found that both the hypnotist's and the subject's voices usually slowed down during hypnosis.

One of the most clear-cut aspects of the hypnotist's speech is that he is forming a deep, close relationship. This is indicated by the "hushed intimacy" reported by Troffer and Tart, by clinical experience, and by the emphasis on forming rapport in the literature on hypnotic induction. Gill and Brenman (1959) even report evidence for fantasies of fusion with the hypnotist, and discuss the identification with the hypnotist and incorporation of him by the subject. Two other features of hypnosis support the hypothesis that the hypnotist is establishing a close and intimate relationship, although it is a limited, controlled, and reversible intimacy. One feature is the invitation to suspend controls and defenses, which is only possible in the context of a trusting relationship. The other is the extreme relaxation, reminiscent of the relaxation, comfort, and security that accompanies a close relationship.

Intimacy, suspension of defenses, and the relaxation of tension between individuals are also goals of the newer humanistic movements within psychology. These movements include sensitivity training, with its emphasis on trust, openness, honesty. They include sensory awareness, psychodrama, Gestalt therapy, and encounter groups emphasizing spontaneity and intimacy. These movements do not seek to cure the sick, but to make healthy people healthier, to help realize potentialities. The humanistic movement in psychology accepts organismic, Gestalt, phenomenological, and existential viewpoints (Maslow, 1962).

Humanism as a coherent intellectual force is far more than a rejection of mechanistic and orthodox psychologies. It is a commitment to the values underlying the humanities and the arts, as well as the sciences. For example, the humanities and the arts value imagination, illusion, drama, and fantasy. In contrast to technological and mechanistic movements, the humanities and the arts value myth over reality, idealism over materialism, feeling over thinking, intuition over analysis. Creativity and originality are valued more than certainty. Merely classical or academic values are subordinated to humane concerns. The humanities and the arts do not communicate or reach understanding through detached objectivity, but through identification, participation, and emotional relatedness.

What has this to do with hypnotic communication? It is well known that hypnosis involves nonrational, emotional aspects, that there is an art to giving suggestions, and that the hypnotist could not be mistaken for a detached transmitter of a logical analysis. Moreover, there is already available an extended and persuasive comparison of hypnosis to one of the humanistic arts —the theater. In many publications Sarbin has presented a role-taking theory of hypnosis that points out analogies between an actor and a hypnotized subject, and between the hypnotist and a stage director (Sarbin and Andersen, 1967). Obviously there are some important similarities between the hypnotized subject who "becomes" a child and the actor who merges with his role. However, I would like to consider the possibility that there may be equally striking analogies between hypnotic communication and the imaginative, myth-creating processes found in the other humanities and arts. The hypnotist is not only a stage director, but also a painter who communicates through vivid images; a creative writer, who holds his readers spellbound; a musician, who communicates through intonation, rhythm, and timbre; and a poet, who induces feeling through creative and evocative use of words. It is no accident that works of art that create emotional impact are called "hypnotic" or "fascinating." In fact, the same process of absorption is induced by both the hypnotist and by any artist whose works create interest or a sense of immediacy.

Some aspects of hypnotic communication become clearer in this perspective. The relaxation of the touch taboo during hypnosis means that the hypnotist is communicating emotionally, is touching the subject in the metaphorical sense of the term. He is having impact upon the subject, touching his emotions, and affecting him, as a work of art touches us. The hypnotist's gestures perhaps grow out of this relaxation of the touch taboo. They signify emotional impact, not mere logical communication.

The musical aspects of hypnotic communication are another point of comparison between one of the arts and hypnosis. The singsong, lyrical quality of the hypnotist's language means that he is not communicating mere facts, but is touching the subject at another level. In primitive tribes, music, rhythmic chanting, drums, and so on, are used to induce hypnosis (Gill & Brenman, 1959). Music is wordless communication. A person can listen to music closely, become absorbed in it, and lose himself in it, without the need to treat it logically, to analyze it, to be practical or realistic about it. This receptivity without analysis is one of the hypnotist's goals. Shor (1960) has used absorption in music and art as one of the indices of susceptibility to trancelike experiences in everyday life.

Josephine Hilgard (1970, and in E. R. Hilgard, 1965b) has presented a great deal of evidence concerning the importance of imaginative involvement in the personality of hypnotizable subjects. She has found that the hyp-

notizable person is "capable of deep involvement in one or more imagina-
tive-feeling areas of experience—reading a novel, listening to music, having
an aesthetic experience of nature, or engaging in absorbing adventures of
body or mind" (1970, pp. 4–5). Her research shows that hypnotizability is
related to individual differences in absorption in such humanistic pursuits as
the dramatic arts, externally-directed fantasy, religion, exploration, and
emotional response to nature. She also reports a relationship between hypnotizability and choice of major among her college-student subjects. The humanities majors were the most susceptible, social science majors next, and
science and engineering students the least hypnotizable. The rigorous verbal,
mathematical, and logical reasoning among science students may not be
compatible with absorption in unrealistic or unconventional fantasy. Similarly, Coe (1964) found that drama students were more hypnotizable than
science students, and Shor (1970) has noted similarities between hypnosis
and absorption in imaginative literature. Apparently there is a close relationship between hypnotic susceptibility and the processes of imaginative
fantasy, aesthetic involvement, and capacity for absorption in dramatic imagery.

Another aspect of artistic and humanistic structuring of the hypnotic communication is the focus upon the subjective effect, and the progressive,
gradual building toward it. For example, on the Stanford Hypnotic Susceptibility Scale (Weitzenhoffer & Hilgard, 1959), some effort is made to convince the subject that he did in fact experience each phenomenon. On the
Hands Moving (Together) item, the hypnotist brings the subject's hands together rapidly to demonstrate how much they had already moved together
involuntarily. Plainly, subjective effect is an important issue in hypnosis,
just as it is in the humanities. If a novel has no subjective effect or impact, it
will not be read. Subjective experience is also an important issue for humanistic psychology, since it provides an intuitive insight into private and intimate feelings, and since it provides an alternative to mechanistic features of
behaviorism. The progressive building up to a subjective effect can also be
seen within the Stanford scale. On all items, suggestions are repeated with
variations in wording until the effect is ready for testing. This is similar to
the progressive building of tension within a motion picture, and to the presentation and re-presentation of a theme in music.

The term "suggestion" has two meanings, one of which casts light on
some of the problems of hypnotic communication. Its more familiar technical meaning is the transmission of influence or ideas, and their uncritical acceptance. Since this could be compared to molding plastic in a machine, it
may be called the mechanistic meaning of suggestion. It implies a passive recipient, a suspension of reason, and the implantation of an idea. But suggestion also has a second meaning, as Young (1931) pointed out long ago.
This is suggestion as indirection, hinting, or intimating. The hypnotist does
not communicate ideas prosaically, but presents them indirectly, in images,

or while the subject's attention is distracted. This, of course, is precisely the kind of communication seen in the humanities and the arts. A playwright does not say a person is bad; he shows his actions and lets the audience respond appropriately. An artist does not need to explain or to argue; he communicates by presenting concrete images. This indirect communication may be called the humanistic aspect of suggestion. It is prominent in hypnotic communication. Instead of asking a person directly to do something, the hypnotist asks him to let it happen involuntarily, or to imagine that it is happening, and to find that it then does happen.

From the standpoint of putting across a specific formal message, suggestion is indirect. But from the standpoint of emotional impact and access to primitive, nonrational modes of thinking, suggestion can be very direct. The reason for this is that suggestion uses imagery and symbolism, and seeks to circumvent the logical apparatus. As a result, suggestion at its best is very vivid, immediate, and concrete. As a case in point, George Grosz's drawings do not constitute a formal psychological analysis of pre-Hitler Germany, and from this purely logical standpoint they are indirect. But when considered in terms of emotional impact, vividness of imagery, and immediacy, they are very direct indeed. Similarly, the hypnotic suggestion to hallucinate an ideal self is indirect from the standpoint of a logical analysis of a person's strengths and weaknesses, but it gives a very direct and concrete representation of a self-concept.

The mechanistic view of suggestion is overintellectual. It sees hypnotic communication as a transmission of ideas from the hypnotist to the subject, whereas the humanistic viewpoint emphasizes the transactional, mutual aspects of communication. Mechanistic suggestion stamps in ideas, but humanistic suggestion hints, intimates, and sketches. The mechanistic viewpoint downgrades the higher mental processes, since it emphasizes uncritical acceptance. As a result, much of the older literature confused hypnotizability and gullibility. If suggestion is uncritical acceptance of ideas, then hypnosis is just a special case of persuasion. But if hypnosis is more allied to creative imagination, then the principles of the theater, the arts, and the humanities are better candidates for explaining hypnosis.

Another error of the overintellectual mechanistic viewpoint is the implication of disordered, erratic thinking by the hypnotized subject. If "uncritical acceptance" is the basis for hypnosis, then the subject is credulous, is reasoning illogically, is responding to prestige, fails to evaluate evidence, and responds on faith. But the humanistic viewpoint interprets the same facts differently. The subject is not deluded, but imaginative. He has not lost contact with reality, but is playfully restructuring it. As Gill and Brenman (1959) point out, he is not showing pathological regression, but an ego-syntonic regression. He is not irrational, but intuitive.

The hypnotized subject is not a malfunctioning logician or a scientist manqué, but a humanist, an artist. He is responding to themes, impressions, harmony. He is feeling spontaneously and emotionally. Humanistic and artistic concepts may help to understand these processes. This does not mean abandoning hardheaded thinking, but it is possible to be too tough-minded as well as too tender-minded. Humanistic and artistic issues that might be relevant include the tension between variety and thematic unification, the rise and fall of dramatic suspense, absorption of interest, and preparation for one effect with another effect. One practical example may help to illustrate these points. The mechanistic approach to suggestion would emphasize repetitious implanting, while the humanistic approach might emphasize the interweaving of two or more suggestions, the introduction of a theme and the later return to it, or the modification of suggestions by feedback from the subject. These ideas owe much to Erickson (1952), especially to his distinction between ritualistic and individualized induction methods, which is closely related to the distinction between mechanistic and humanistic suggestion.

Linguistic Aspects of Hypnotic Inductions

One convenient means of applying these concepts to concrete data is to compare hypnotic and nonhypnotic language. If mechanistic and humanistic processes can be distinguished within hypnosis, the contrast should be even sharper between hypnotic language and ordinary communication. Speech in the waking state is not designed to induce relaxation, drowsiness, or a special state of consciousness. It is concerned with practical reality, not with fantasy or imagination. It is designed to communicate opinions, thoughts, feelings, but not to build a structure of illusion. If the distinction between mechanistic and humanistic communication is meaningful, it should be observable in a content analysis of speech.

Two analyses were prepared, one comparing a sample of hypnotic language with formal speech, the other comparing the hypnotic sample with informal conversation. The first comparison was made with instructions to subjects in psychological experiments, while the second comparison used interviews with college students and hospitalized patients. Instructions to subjects in psychological experiments were chosen as a comparison for convenience, and also because the clear logic and critical awareness of these communications should contrast sharply with the structure of the hypnotic induction. Although this comparison has advantages, it also has some obvious disadvantages. For example, instructions to subjects in experiments are often highly formal and technical. Therefore a more informal, conversational comparison was also needed.

Ten published hypnotic inductions were chosen to provide a wide range of authors and methods. The inductions chosen were: Blum (1961, p. 213), Chiasson (1964, p. 366), Corley (1965, p. 35), Erickson (1964b, p. 190), Hershman (in Erickson, Hershman, & Secter, 1961, p. 140), Kroger (1963,

p. 64), Scott (1960, p. 34), Secter (1960, p. 79), Weitzenhoffer and Hilgard (1962, p. 8), and Wolberg (1948, p. 117). Three of the 10 inductions were designed for experimentation, and the remainder were primarily clinical. A sample of 100 consecutive words was chosen from the beginning of each induction, and a count of the grammatical class of each word was made. Introductory material was not scored, so that the induction proper of the Stanford scale was judged to begin at its second paragraph. A comparison sample of 10 instructions to subjects was scored in the same way from articles in the *Journal of Personality and Social Psychology,* 1966, 3, beginning on pages 290, 308, 341, 351, 354, 509, 519, and 624. Using an *N* of 20, Mann-Whitney tests were applied to the pooled ranks of the grammatical classes.

For the second analysis, each word of the hypnotic inductions was alphabetized and compared with word frequencies in spoken English, converted to a baseline frequency of words per thousand. The second analysis used the data of Howes (1966), based on 250,000 words drawn from 50 nondirective interviews of 5,000 words each, conducted with 20 college sophomores and 21 hospitalized patients. Because Howes pooled his data, the word frequencies he reports are not independent, and statistical tests are inappropriate. A difference in frequency of 3.9 words or more per thousand was arbitrarily chosen as the criterion for distinguishing important differences from less relevant ones.

Results and Discussion

Table 15.1 compares the grammatical classification of the hypnotic inductions and the nonhypnotic psychological instructions. Four word classes appeared significantly less often in the hypnotic than in the nonhypnotic communications: nouns, adjectives, articles, and prepositions. These categories obviously belong together for interpretation, since articles and adjectives modify nouns, and since prepositions take nouns as objects. The first finding, then, is that substantives and their modifiers are reduced in hypnotic communications. This may merely reflect the formality and technical language of the experimenter, but it may also cast some light upon hypnosis.

Nouns are subjects and objects, the initiators and recipients of action. In the psychological experiments they tended to be abstract concepts (such as "behavior," "decisions," "substances," "areas," "minutes") or environmental objects ("button," "shock," "machine," "inventory"). This suggests that instructions in psychological experiments are centered around action upon objects in the environment to achieve specifiable goals, while this practical, reality-oriented interaction is less important during hypnosis. The semantic content of the hypnotic induction implicitly suggests a detachment of attention from the environment, even when it does not explicitly say so. This detachment from practical, everyday reality is also a characteristic of the hu-

TABLE 15.1   Percentage distribution of words sampled from 10 hypnotic
            inductions and 10 nonhypnotic instructions

Hypnosis has:	Hypnotic Inductions	Nonhypnotic Instructions	Significance of Difference (Mann-Whitney)
1. Fewer nouns	14	20	.01
2. Fewer adjectives	6	13	.001
3. Fewer articles	4	9	.01
4. Fewer prepositions	7	10	.05
5. More second-person pronouns	6	3	.05
6. More second-person possessive adjectives	5	2	.05
7. More contractions	1	0	.05
8. More third-person pronouns	2	1	.05
9. More conjunctions	10	6	.05
10. More intransitive verbs	11	8	.10
11. More adverbs	14	7	.001
12. Others*	19	21	—
Total	99	100	

* No significant difference (greater than .10) for: demonstrative, indefinite, and first-person pronouns, first- and third-person possessive adjectives, reflexive, transitive, and auxiliary verbs, and "to" as infinitive. Because of rounding errors, column 1 does not add to 100 per cent.

manities and the arts, which are a respite from the utilitarian necessities and adaptations of everyday life. The emphasis on abstract concepts in the psychological instructions contrasts with the simplicity and concreteness of the hypnotic induction. The humanities and the arts share the hypnotist's concern with vivid, concrete representation, rather than intellectual analysis.

Adjectives and articles describe, limit, and qualify nouns. The hypnotist places little emphasis upon classification and categorization, as would be expected from his lessened use of abstract nouns. The hypnotist is not providing an intellectual analysis, but a direct experience. In addition, description of the environment or the presentation of abstract concepts would alert the subject to these aspects of reality. The hypnotist does not wish to alert his subject, nor to direct his attention to the current situation. Instead, he tries to reduce vigilance and to direct attention inward. Similarly, the lessened importance of prepositions in hypnotic inductions indicates the lessened emphasis upon relationships between abstract concepts, and by implication, the greater stress upon concrete sensations and behavior in hypnosis.

The lessened importance of action upon the environment in hypnotic language is also suggested by the tendency $(p < .10)$ for hypnotic inductions to have more intransitive verbs than nonhypnotic language employs. This finding suggests that the hypnotist encourages nonspecific action, behavior without a clear-cut and understandable objective. The hypnotist tries to blur the subject of action as well as the object of action: hypnotic behavior happens by itself, spontaneously, not with a deliberate decision. The hypnotized person does not make his hand rise, it just happens. The hand is moving without a clear-cut objective, spontaneously and impulsively.

A similar interpretation could explain the greater number of third-person pronouns in hypnotic inductions. This chiefly reflects the use of "it" as an indefinite nominative or object, as in "it always helps" or "take it easy." The hypnotist wishes to avoid specifying both the subject and object of action, and one way to do so is to use indefinite, global terminology. This lack of precision and specification has broader implications as well. The hypnotist wants to absorb the subject's attention, but not his critical thinking. He wants to communicate, but to avoid the focus of attention and awareness. This helps to explain some of the peculiarities of hypnotic communication, such as high-redundancy content and the low frequency of opinions and information. This may also be one factor in the success of some of the indirect induction techniques invented by Erickson, such as the confusion technique.

Hypnotic speech is closely focused about the experiences of the subject, as shown by the greater use of "you" and "your" (second-person pronoun and possessive adjective). The hypnotist's speech is totally oriented about the person he is hypnotizing. This implies that the subject's attention is withdrawn from the environment into himself, his inner experiences, his body, his person. Hypnosis is more a personalized relationship than a distant, detached psychological experiment. This immediacy and direct contact is also a primary quality of the humanities and the arts. The linguistic evidence questions the hypothesis that the hypnotized subject forgets everything but the hypnotist. Instead, the hypnotist forgets everything but his subject, while the subject is absorbed in a world of imagination. The hypnotist does not want the subject to give him direct attention, and instead tries to communicate below the level of conscious awareness.

Hypnotic inductions have more adverbs than the instructions to subjects do. Adverbs qualify action, indicating how and when an action is taking place. In other words, the hypnotic induction is generating behavior, not presenting concepts or environmental objects. Words in this category include not only behavior modifiers, but also terms such as "just" and "now," which provide highly general, nonspecific behavior cues. The immediacy of the humanistic perspective is found in the hypnotic induction, which shapes behavior as it takes place rather than telling subjects what to do later on. The high adverb count emphasizes the ongoing flow of experience and behavior in hypnosis, and contrasts it with the job orientation of the standard psychological experiment.

The greater number of conjunctions in the hypnotic induction also indicates this ongoing flow of experience and behavior. The hypnotist does not break up or punctuate his speech. Instead he generates an ongoing, continuous flow of words. Rather than a differentiated analysis, he presents an endless stream of ideas. This is a very simple form of syntactical structure. Hypnotic language tends to use fewer terms implying complex logical relationships, such as prepositions, while using more terms implying very simple logical relationships, such as conjunctions. The hypnotist is not really reasoning with his subject—he is presenting successive images. Instead of an articulated, integrated statement, the hypnotist generates ideas that are connected chiefly by simple conjunctions. The hypnotist is not building a logical structure, he is placing ideas side by side, as if stringing beads.

Another form of simple conjunction between words is seen in the greater number of contractions in the hypnotic inductions. The contractions imply the informality and intimacy of the hypnotic process, and contrast it with the formality and stiffness of the typical instruction to the subject. A contraction means that two words have been joined into one. Perhaps the same merging principle may be operating at the cognitive level as well as the linguistic level. In other words, ideas also may be joined together in unconventional ways during hypnosis, as if the traditional separation between them has been modified.

This analysis of grammatical categories suggests that the hypnotist has exchanged precision for impact. The hypnotist loses the advantages of clearcut abstract expression, but he gains something very important in its place. By relinquishing conventional abstract expressions he gains emotional and personal impact, and deepens the relationship.

The findings so far suggest that hypnotic language is simpler and more redundant than the control communication, but more direct evidence is needed. One way to check this point is to count the number of monosyllabic words in the two samples. This analysis showed that the 10 hypnotic inductions had more monosyllabic words (a median of 77 per cent) than the instructions to subjects (67 per cent). The difference between the two samples is significant at the .02 level by a Mann-Whitney test. The difference is not large, since the language of the nonhypnotic instructions was also not very complicated, but it is consistent. Words in hypnotic communications do tend to be short and simple.

Another supplementary analysis checked the redundancy of the hypnotic communications. This analysis made use of "cloze procedure" (Taylor, 1953). This technique requires judges to guess words that have been deleted from a text, thereby providing a measure of the redundancy or the contextual constraint. The more errors the judges make, the less redundant the text, and the more information it contains. Every fifth word was removed from the hypnotic and nonhypnotic texts, and the 20 texts were submitted in random order to seven judges (six psychologists and a research assistant).

The results indicated that the hypnotic inductions were more redundant, as expected, than the nonhypnotic instructions. More errors were made in guessing words deleted from the nonhypnotic text ($p < .001$, by a t test for correlated means). Once again, the difference between the two samples was quite small. The median error rate was 36.5 per cent for the hypnotic inductions and 41 per cent for the nonhypnotic instructions. Since each judge consistently made more errors in judging the nonhypnotic instructions, the very small difference proved to be highly significant statistically. The hypnotic inductions do seem to have a slightly greater redundancy and therefore a smaller information content than the control communications. The hypnotist is probably doing a good deal of nonverbal communication, through tone of voice, pauses, gestures, facial expression, and so forth, to substitute for the lowered information content in his speech. The hypnotist uses redundant, simplified language to circumvent the logical, conventional categories of thought. The hypnotist relies on connotation and evocation rather than denotation.

Table 15.2 shows a comparison of word frequencies in spoken English and in hypnotic inductions. This table shows all words that appeared at least once in the 1,000-word hypnotic sample, and which differed by at least 3.9 per thousand in frequency from words in spoken English. This new comparison generally confirms the findings of the first sample. Strikingly confirmed is the greater prevalence of "you" and "your" in the hypnotic induction. Spoken English, on the other hand, shows a greater number of other per-

TABLE 15.2 Hypnotic inductions versus spoken English: Words showing differences in frequency of 3.9 or more per 1,000

Word	Frequency per 1,000		Word	Frequency per 1,000	
	hypnotic inductions	spoken English		hypnotic inductions	spoken English
a, an*	13	26	is	13	7
and	44	38	just	11	5
are	18	3	keep	5	0.6
as	17	4	know*	4	10
attention	4	< 0.1	my*	2	6
be	9	5	now	7	3
can	9	3	on	13	7
chair	7	0.1	relax	8	< 0.1
comfortably	4	< 0.1	sit	5	0.3
eyes	6	< 0.1	target	4	< 0.1
feel	7	0.5	the*	28	40
fingers	4	< 0.1	they*	3	15
hand	7	0.3	thighs	6	< 0.1
hands	10	0.1	to	33	25
harder	4	< 0.1	very	7	2
how	6	1	we*	3	8
I*	13	40	will	22	1
if	9	4	you	64	19
in*	12	17	your	52	2

* Words with lower frequencies in hypnotic inductions than in spoken English.

sonal pronouns ("I," "we," and "they"), and a personal possessive adjective ("my"). These personal references were understandably not frequent in either the hypnotic inductions nor in the instructions to subjects in psychological experiments. They reconfirm the centering of the hypnotist's language exclusively about the subject, and the lessened references to the hypnotist's own opinions. This confirms the findings of interaction process analysis (Field, 1964).

This analysis also confirms the decreased frequency of articles in hypnosis, the increased frequency of adverbs such as "just," "now," "how," "very," and "as," and the increased use of the conjunction "and." No very clear indication is provided on whether there is a decreased frequency of nouns, adjectives, and prepositions. It is quite possible that high frequencies of these parts of speech are characteristic of the formal language of the psychological experiment. In other words, the previous finding of the low frequencies of nouns in hypnotic speech may in part reflect the informality of the hypnotist's speech in contrast to the formality of the language of the experiment. On the other hand, the low frequency of articles, which are closely linked to nouns, was confirmed in this second analysis.

The second analysis suggests that the nouns that are elevated in hypnotic speech are concrete nouns, referring to parts of the body, or else to the restricted parts of the environment that the hypnotist wishes the subject to be aware of ("chair" or "target" for eye fixation). The elevation of nouns for parts of the body indicates that the subject's attention is being withdrawn from the environment into his own body. At the same time, however, linguistic reference to parts of the body is a symbolic means of touching the body. This indicates the closeness and intimacy of hypnotic communication. Concrete nouns may be elevated in hypnosis, while the more abstract nouns and their modifiers are lowered, as the first analysis showed. This analysis also indicates that some prepositions dealing with location ("on" and "to") may be elevated in hypnosis, providing a more exact formulation of the previous finding that prepositions were lowered in hypnosis. Probably prepositions dealing with location are increased in hypnosis, whereas prepositions dealing with more abstract, conceptual relationships ("for," "from," "of") are decreased.

The analysis suggests that the hypnotist uses far more concrete terminology and less abstract formulation than generally appear in spoken English. This is also supported by the diminished frequency of the word "know" and the increased frequency of the word "feel" in hypnosis. Obviously, intellectual language declines in hypnosis and emotional, feeling language increases. The increased frequency of "are," "is," "be," and "will" may confirm the tendency toward more intransitive verbs as found in the first analysis. In addition to general classes of words that distinguish hypnotic speech from conversational discourse, there may be certain specific key words that are especially characteristic of hypnosis, such as "relax."

Summary

Hypnotic communication was compared to communication in the humanities and the arts. Points in common include use of nonverbal communication, vividness and concreteness of language, immediacy of communication, intimacy and closeness, rejection of abstract argumentation, and the primacy of the subjective experience. This viewpoint was illustrated by comparing linguistic classifications of hypnotic inductions with instructions to subjects in psychological experiments and with spoken English. These comparisons indicated that hypnotic language had fewer terms dealing with classification, categorization, abstract relationship, and abstract conceptualization, while it had more terms describing behavior, more terms linking other terms, more redundancy and monosyllabic words, and more terms centered around the person being hypnotized.

Doris Gruenewald *is a Senior Clinical Psychologist at the Psychosomatic and Psychiatric Institute for Research and Training at Michael Reese Hospital. She received her Ph.D. in psychology from the University of Chicago and has maintained her affiliation with that institution as a Research Associate. Her major interest is the development and application of psychotherapeutic principles with emphasis on a holistic approach, in which hypnosis plays an important part. She has been involved in hypnosis research with a psychophysiological and ego-psychological orientation and has contributed to the psychology of the borderline condition.*

Mark I. Oberlander *is a Senior Research Associate at the Institute for Juvenile Research in Chicago. He received his Ph.D. in clinical psychology from the University of Chicago in 1967, following which he assumed his current position. Since 1968, he has also held the position of Research Associate in the Department of Psychology at the University of Chicago, where he is involved in collaborative research with Erika Fromm and Doris Gruenewald. Current interests and research activities are in the areas of cognitive and personality development, with particular emphasis in the area of creativity. Dr. Oberlander is also in private practice where he makes extensive use of hypnotic techniques in the conduct of individual psychotherapy.*

Gruenewald, Fromm, and Oberlander *review developments in psychoanalytic ego psychology that have led to the theory that hypnosis is a form of adaptive regression. In adaptive regression the ego initiates, controls, and terminates regression by temporarily losing contact with reality for the purpose of gaining improved mastery over inner experiences. Those who view hypnosis as adaptive regression hypothesize that in hypnosis a regressed subsystem of the ego is placed in the service of the overall ego; this includes development of a special transference relationship to the hypnotist. The authors describe a study they have carried out, which derives from this theoretical viewpoint. Its purpose was to test the hypothesis that hypnosis is an adaptive regression.*

16

Hypnosis and Adaptive Regression: An Ego-Psychological Inquiry

DORIS GRUENEWALD, ERIKA FROMM, AND
MARK I. OBERLANDER

As the accumulated lore surrounding hypnosis is gradually swept away, it becomes increasingly evident that many of the phenomena and experiences historically attributed to hypnosis are products of a variety of factors not intrinsically bound up with it. Yet hypnosis persists, as a facet of consciousness as well as an area of scientific investigation that reaches across disciplines and theoretical orientations, each however pursuing its goal apart from the rest.

Psychoanalytic ego psychology has been concerned with hypnosis, admittedly outside its mainstream but enough to leave its mark on hypnosis research and theory. There has been a growing tendency within this theoretical orientation to regard hypnosis as a regression in the service of the ego or as an adaptive regression. This point of view has stimulated a line of research that demands further exploration, notwithstanding the pitfalls that still beset it. Our investigations (Fromm, Oberlander, & Gruenewald, 1970; Oberlander, Gruenewald, & Fromm, 1970) provide a representative example; their main features will be presented later in this chapter. The assumption that hypnosis is an adaptive regression has ego-psychological antecedents, the most salient of which will first be reviewed.

The research project described in this chapter was supported in part by a grant from The Psychiatric Training and Research Fund of the Illinois Department of Mental Health (Project # 17-303) and in the part by the Social Science Divisional Research Fund of The University of Chicago.

The Concept of Adaptive Regression

In the development of psychoanalysis the meaning of regression underwent a series of changes. In early psychoanalytic theory, regression referred to a global return to an earlier mode of functioning determined by infantile drives and specific fixation points in libidinal development. According to the topographic model, regression was defined as the tendency of the organism to shift from a "higher" to a "lower" mental system under conditions of stress and conflict (Freud, 1900). In hypnosis, the ego was assumed to be rendered nonfunctional. Hypnosis was discontinued as a treatment modality precisely because its "greatest triumph" was also its greatest fault; it unearthed unconscious material that was forced on the ego and retained only so long as the relationship with the hypnosis-inducing therapist remained intact (A. Freud, 1936).

Subsequent formulation of the structural model (Freud, 1923), with its tripartite division of the mental apparatus into id, ego, and superego, provided the groundwork for an ego-psychological conception of hypnosis. Of particular importance was the emphasis placed on the intersystemic relations of the ego and on its intrasystemic function of regulating the interplay of its own subordinate agencies.

Following the adoption of the structural model (Freud, 1923), there was a steady progression of formal thought regarding the structure and functions of the ego and, concomitantly, the meaning of regression. Among the numerous contributions to psychoanalytic ego psychology, the writings of Hartmann (1939), Kris (1934), and Rapaport (1953, 1958) are of paramount importance, especially in so far as they provide the conceptual ground for the subsequently presented theory of hypnosis as an adaptive regression (Gill & Brenman, 1959).

In *The Ego and the Id,* Freud (1923) postulated that the ego developed as a surface organ of perception that partially enveloped the id. Building on this theory, Hartmann (1939) was the first psychoanalytic writer to state unequivocally that both id and ego, as psychological structures, emerged from an undifferentiated matrix, and that certain functions, defined as belonging to the ego (such as sensory and basic protective mechanisms), were present at birth in at least rudimentary form. Hartmann saw these functions as biologically predetermined, innate structures independent of the instincts and their vicissitudes.

Given an "average expectable environment," the full development of these "apparatuses of primary autonomy" and their automatized efficiency depend only on the physical maturation of the organism. Although they serve to gratify drive demands and may be drawn into conflict, the primarily autonomous ego apparatuses belong in a "conflict-free sphere of the ego" and do not lose their characteristic independence except under extreme conditions. Other ego functions (such as thought and secondary defense mechanisms), according to Hartmann, have their roots in the instinctual drive organization and are created out of conflict and experience. In the course of development, these ego apparatuses undergo a "change of function," which brings with it structuralization and, ultimately, relative independence from their instinctual origins (compare Allport's "functional autonomy of motives," Allport, 1937). While the apparatuses of primary autonomy have independent, noninstinctual energy sources, the apparatuses of secondary autonomy depend for their maintenance and stability on the ego's ability to "neutralize" drive energy available to it from the id and to use this "neutral" (de-instinctualized) energy for the establishment of more or less permanent countercathexes against instinctual forces. To the extent that such countercathexes are maintained, the secondarily autonomous apparatuses also function outside of conflict. Although they are more vulnerable to instinctual vicissitudes, they too result in relatively stable structures.

Thus, the autonomy of both the primary and secondary ego apparatuses is always relative. So long as the developmental stages follow the direction of growth and independence, Hartmann speaks of a "progressive adaptation." However, like A. Freud (1936), who recognized the egosyntonic function of fantasy—by definition a regressive phenomenon—Hartmann (1939, 1964) acknowledges the possibility of successful adaptation achieved by way of regression. He thus distinguishes between "progressive" and "regressive" adaptation.

Regressive adaptation is in some respects identical with Kris's (1934) "regression in the service of the ego," described as the capacity of the ego to initiate and terminate libidinal and structural regression for the purpose of gaining improved mastery. Subject to voluntary control, this process is particularly evident in the enjoyment of art and humor and plays a significant role in certain phases of creative activity. It consists of an ego-regulated modification and relaxation of defensive barriers, so that earlier modes of perception and cognition are reactivated, and normally repressed affects, memories, and primitive components of experience can rise into conscious awareness. The mental content emerging from repression tends to possess qualities characteristic of primary-process thought and imagery. But in contrast to uncontrolled, pathological regression—where the ego stands by helplessly or is totally paralyzed vis-à-vis the involuntary breakthrough of such material—the mental content associated with regression in the service of the ego is assimilated and constructively utilized. The ego remains in control and, having relinquished its countercathexes for a goal-directed purpose, can reinstitute its usual organization at will.

Kris's treatment of regression, being chiefly concerned with artistic creativity, is somewhat narrower in scope, but it spells out the bipolarity of regression and its potential for enlarging the span of the ego.

As stated by Hartmann, the building of permanent psychological structures depends on the automatization of functions, that is, their becoming independent from the id's influence under stable developmental conditions.

Rapaport (1958) expands this line of thought in drawing the logical conclusion that the ego is relatively autonomous not only in relation to the id but also in relation to the environment. Both autonomies are considered relative in that disruption of either may result in a decrease of autonomy, and interference with one can affect both. The interrelationship of the autonomies is complex: relative autonomy from the id is predicated on the existence of the constitutionally given apparatuses of primary autonomy and on the automatized structures of secondary autonomy in so far as they have become independent of their instinctual origins; relative autonomy from the environment in turn is ultimately guaranteed by the very presence of the drives and their regulating influence on the ego in its relations with the outer world.

Whereas the ego was conceived in early psychoanalytic theory as little more than a mediator between the drives and the external environment, it now was considered a structure in its own right, with motivations and purposes unique to itself and with the capacity to resist, modify, and control the demands of both agencies.

The entire topic of the relative autonomies is intimately related to the still largely unsolved problem of ego activity and ego passivity. Rapaport (1967) specifies ego activity as one of the "parameters of the relative autonomy of the ego" [p. 566], defined as the capacity to control drive demand, delay drive discharge, guide thought towards discovering a suitable object, and institute appropriate behavior for drive gratification; or, in the absence of proper conditions for engaging in overt behavior, to set aside, suppress, or sublimate instinctual needs. Ego passivity, in contrast, is defined as "helplessness in the face of drive demands" [p. 555]. Appropriate action through ego channels may be blocked either because the ego is overwhelmed and its executive apparatus put in the service of indiscriminate drive discharge, or, as in the case of developmental arrest, because the necessary structures are lacking.

Behavior, however, is not to be taken as the criterion for ego activity or passivity for the reason that behavioral activity may reflect ego passivity or even ego paralysis, and behavioral passivity may in certain instances be associated with a high level of ego activity (see also Fromm, 1970; Schafer, 1968a). Rapaport acknowledges that his schematic presentation does not do justice to the complex interplay between activity and passivity, nor take account of the hierarchical layering of structures which themselves are not static but subject to the shifting of varyingly prepotent physiological and psychological states.

Schafer (1968a) takes issue with Rapaport, suggesting that the theoretical pursuit of activity and passivity may merely lead into a blind alley. Witness, for instance, the paradox of "passive mastery" during the narcissistic stage, in which the ego has as yet not become fully differentiated from the initial id-ego matrix. Mastery implies activity, in spite of the fact that the infant, viewed in his total life situation, is helpless vis-à-vis the environment, that is, passive. Witness also the postulate of "omnipotence" in the narcissistic stage, which again implies activity. As words, "activity" and "passivity" are too closely associated with their popular meaning, and as scientific terms they seem to be so inextricably enmeshed that Schafer finds them meaningless as explanatory concepts.

In spite of such conceptual difficulties, we believe that the terms "activity" and "passivity" may still serve a useful purpose if they are explicitly defined as bipolar continua. At one end of the activity pole one would find continual reinforcement of defensive barriers against instinctual forces in excess of a normal or optimal level. This process would be likely to lead to ego constriction, if not to overt pathology. If such constriction took on pathological dimensions, regression, in the event that it occurred, would tend to be of the involuntary kind resulting in temporary ego passivity. At the other end of the activity pole, the ego would use its synthetic function for the integration of instinctual forces, and thus be capable of adaptive regression. This too would involve temporary passivity, however by choice, not necessity. But again there is the paradox of "passive activity" and "active passivity," an impasse that cannot be resolved here. (See also Bachrach, 1968).

In Rapaport's scheme, activity and passivity refer to prevailing states of the total ego. Yet, "ego" is no longer considered a unitary entity, but rather a congeries of more or less cohesive structures, each with relatively discrete though interrelated functions, of which some are likely to be more active and some more passive at any given time. It therefore is somewhat misleading to speak of pathological regression as indicating ego passivity and of adaptive regression as indicating ego activity. The function under scrutiny must be identified and the conditions under which either prevails specified. One would then be in a better position to differentiate ego-controlled from uncontrolled regression in relation to the ego segment under investigation (cf. Schafer, 1968b).

Summing up, regression, as one of the ego's defensive and integrative mechanisms, serves the goal of adaptation to internal and external conditions with varying degrees of success. Adaptive as well as pathological regression may spread over a wide area or be limited to a small segment. In any event, it is rarely found in isolation, and it is more common to see elements of both.

Criteria for identifying adaptive regression as opposed to regression proper include the ability to seek out and initiate regressive experiences and to call a halt to them without help if conditions are judged to be no longer safe, with immediate and complete reinstatement of the usual psychic organization (Gill & Brenman, 1959). This is more likely to occur if there is flexibility and strength rather than rigidity and weakness.

The Concept of Adaptive Regression in Hypnosis

Although references to the regressive aspects of hypnosis are scattered throughout the early psychoanalytic literature, it was Schilder (1926) who first formulated what may be regarded a forerunner of the hypnosis-as-a-daptive-regression theory. Directly relevant to the present discussion is Schilder's viewpoint that only a part of the ego becomes involved in hypnosis and that "a considerable portion of the personality maintains its normal relations with the outside world" [p. 96]. Schilder assigns a central position to that portion, stating that it "may assume various attitudes toward the hypnotized portions" [p. 76], such as varying degrees of consent to participate or to remain in the role of a spectator. The central ego's active participation in the hypnotic procedures comes about through the transference relationship with the hypnotist and involves a quality of trance called "psychic depth." The greater the "psychic depth," the more the central ego's reality orientation is mediated through the person of or the relationship with the hypnotist. If the central ego functions more in the role of observer, the phenomena of hypnotic behavior may be elicited but tend to have a relatively mechanical quality.

In Schilder's formulation, the notion that the ego controls hypnotic regression is clearly implied. His ideas form a large part of the background for the theory of hypnosis as an adaptive regression promulgated by Gill and Brenman (1959).

Based on many years of clinical psychoanalytic research in hypnosis, Gill and Brenman's (1959) theory coordinates virtually all existing ego-psychological concepts. It leans heavily on the theoretical developments regarding the origin and autonomy of the ego that have been presented in the first part of this chapter. It furthermore attempts to reconcile such apparently conflicting directions as the traditional sensorimotor approach of experimental psychology and the strong emphasis on transference factors of psychoanalytic psychology.

In lieu of Schilder's central ego, a concept more in keeping with structural theory is envisaged, namely an overall ego relatively autonomous in relation to id and environment and in control of its apparatuses. Induction of hypnosis represents an attack on the apparatuses—a sensorimotor disorientation that eventuates in their partial de-automatization—and simultaneously the offer of a regressive (transference) relationship. In a successful induction, made possible by the overall ego's acquiescing and temporarily relinquishing control of its apparatuses to the hypnotist, the normally prevailing cathectic-countercathectic balance is upset and a regressive restructuring takes place. However, instead of regression occurring in the overall ego, as in regression proper, a subsystem of the ego is triggered into action, which searches for motivational patterns in accord with the regressed id-ego-superego derivatives to which it gains access. The shifting of energy distributions involves libidinal and attention cathexes. In the established hypnotic state, the subsystem becomes reorganized into a temporarily stable structure that not only regains partial control of the (re-automatized) apparatuses but also is put into the service of the overall ego. The basic structure of the overall ego remains unchanged, although the psychological space it occupies diminishes in proportion to the extent or dimensions it allows the regressed subsystem. The overall ego never loses contact with reality.

The forgoing is a brief recapitulation of the central point of Gill and Brenman's metapsychological theory of hypnosis. Moving from a descriptive base of observational data through increasingly abstract conceptualizations to the final theoretical statement, Gill and Brenman (1959) conclude that hypnosis is a regression in the service of the ego. However, they give due weight to instances where the observed facts are at variance with the theory: in some cases, for example, regression gets out of hand and invades the overall ego; also, a satisfactory hypnotic state with the hallmarks of adaptive regression may be obtained in persons whose ego can in no sense be regarded strong and flexible.

Gill and Brenman's theory is a well-reasoned, internally cohesive, intrasystemic view of the ego in relation to hypnosis, stated with the conviction of scientists committed deeply to their chosen task. Nevertheless, the exceptions duly noted by them are not accounted for in the theory. In spite of the fact that it was built from an observational basis, the data seem to have been fitted into preexisting psychoanalytic theory.

Gill and Brenman offer their theory as an ad hoc statement. An empirical study generated by the theory will now be described.

The Research Project

The expressed purpose of the research was to examine the hypothesis of hypnosis as adaptive regression. Terms used in psychoanalysis and in hypnosis can rarely be defined without resorting to equally undefined parallels. Consequently, some of the research variables and concepts were more stringently defined, in terms of operations performed, than others, which were simply used in their consensually validated form.

Hypnosis was accepted as a given, operationally defined by the controlled administration of standard induction procedures (Fromm & Weingarten, 1965; Weitzenhoffer & Hilgard, 1959, 1962), by the number of scale items passed, and to a small extent by the subjects' individual experience, reported by way of a subjective scale of depth similar to that of LeCron and Bordeaux (1947). Situational variables were controlled by counterbalanced experimental conditions, randomized assignment of subjects to experimental conditions, and use of four experimenters, two of whom were uninformed with regard to the purpose of the experiment. No attempt was made to control either the role of the hypnotist as perceived by the subject or the transference aspects of the hypnotic relationship, for which in any case no effective method of measurement exists.

With regard to regression, however, the situation was more favorable, as a recently developed system for scoring Rorschach responses made a quantitative evaluation of regressive processes possible (Holt, 1963, 1967; Holt & Havel, 1960).[1]

ADAPTIVE REGRESSION IN THE HOLT SYSTEM

In the standard Rorschach testing situation, the subject projects form and meaning onto objectively content-free inkblots and translates into verbal expression whatever imagery and thought are stimulated in him. Responses may be relatively free of or relatively loaded with mental representations of drive derivatives characteristic of primary process thought. The system provides for quantitative assessment of primary process intrusions and the manner in which such intrusions are handled by secondary process operations.

Holt (1963) considers primary process a hypothetical construct not accessible to direct observation. But if treated as an intervening variable, its products may be inferred from observable verbal behavior and scored according to form and content. Concurrent with or subsequent to the expression of primary process mentation, secondary process thinking and defensive and coping functions of the ego are also operative; they are similarly inferred from the responses and scored according to their form, content, and structure.

The Holt system for scoring Rorschach responses thus applies within limits of operational definitions of primary and secondary processes. Primary process is manifested by intrusions into verbal responses of primitive, drive-determined content; condensations, fragmentation, and loose or fluid associations; syncretic or autistic logic and logical contradictions; disregard of reality; and peculiarities of perceptual and linguistic organization. Secondary process is inferred from adherence to the demands of reality and rationality; purposefully organized thinking; minimal intrusion of primitive, drive-determined material; and automatic processing of such material into socially acceptable form. The distinction between the two types of perceptual-cognitive operations is rarely as clear as implied by these characteristics; individual responses ordinarily are interactive products of both.

In the Holt system all responses are first scored with regard to their form level, which provides an initial indicator of the subject's reality orientation and ability to match internal object representations with perceived form. Each response is then inspected to determine nature and extent of primary process manifestations, which, if present, are scored according to drive content, formal thought structure, and defenses that are simultaneously or sequentially operative. The end product of the scoring process is a numerical value, the Adaptive Regression score, which reflects the individual's capacity for constructive integration of primary process material. This score has positive and negative values. The larger it is, the deeper the regression is assumed to be; whether adaptive or maladaptive is judged by the positive or

1. For a selective review of the literature on adaptive regression and Holt's Rorschach scoring system see Fromm, Oberlander, and Gruenewald, 1970.

negative value of the score, by type, content, and intensity of primary-process products, by mode and manner of defensive operations, and by recovery from any evident loss of secondary process control within or across responses.

THE EXPERIMENT

Since the Holt Rorschach scoring system offers a relatively objective measure of regression, the study was designed to investigate those ego functions directly involved in taking the Rorschach test, viz., perception and cognition, and to evaluate regressive processes in and out of hypnosis on the basis of obtained scores. Design, methodology, and statistical analysis of results have been fully reported in two publications (Fromm, Oberlander, & Gruenewald, 1970; Oberlander, Gruenewald, & Fromm, 1970) and will be presented here only in summary.

Three dimensions of perceptual-cognitive functions and their implications for adaptive regression were examined in the normal waking state and in hypnosis for levels, that is, degree and kind of primary process manifestations and defenses; variability, that is, fluctuations in degree and kind of primary process manifestations and defenses; and content and structure of thought processes; each as expressed on the Rorschach test and scored according to Holt's system.

The test was administered in counterbalanced order (waking-hypnosis and hypnosis-waking) to 32 subjects selected from a volunteer student population who demonstrated good or excellent hypnotizability on a modified version (Fromm & Weingarten, 1965) of Form A of the Stanford Hypnotic Susceptibility Scale (SHSS; Weitzenhoffer & Hilgard, 1959). Each subject received two hypnosis training sessions prior to the hypnotic condition. Differences in personal style were controlled inasmuch as each subject went through both conditions with the same examiner and served as his own control. For the hypnotic experimental condition, Form C of the SHSS (Weitzenhoffer & Hilgard, 1962) was used as the induction technique.

It was hypothesized that perceptual-cognitive functions would change in the hypnotic condition in the direction of adaptive regression as measured by the Adaptive Regression score of the Holt system. Specific predictions were that incidence and variability of primary process manifestations would increase in hypnosis, and that defensive and coping functions would yield scores at least equal to but probably greater than the waking scores. Regarding content and structure of thought processes, it was hoped that the results of the experiment would permit the development of criteria for differentiating the two states.

Results

The data was analyzed in three phrases. The first set of analyses was concerned with the main question couched in the experimental hypothesis, namely, whether the hypothesis that hypnosis was an adaptive regression was tenable. The second set of analyses was instituted as a check on doubtful or equivocal results of the first and dealt with such issues as sex and adjustment differences in relation to adaptive versus maladaptive regression. The third set of analyses was addressed to the question whether a comparison of waking and trance Rorschach responses would sufficiently differentiate thought processes in both conditions to establish predictive criteria for each.

The first set of analyses indicated clearly that elements of primary process mentation intruded with greater frequency in the hypnosis condition ($p <$ .01). The order in which the hypnosis and waking conditions were administered had some influence on the extent of primary process intrusions, with direction varying across the four experimenters ($p < .05$). However, analysis of Adaptive Regression scores did not yield significant results. This phase in the evaluation of results supported the hypothesis of regressive influences in hypnosis but failed to distinguish adaptive from maladaptive regression.

In the second set of analyses, the Rorschach records were scored according to the Klopfer method (Klopfer et al., 1954) and dichotomized according to sex (male-female) and psychological adjustment ("more adjusted" and "less adjusted"). The increased frequency of primary process intrusions in the hypnosis condition was again highly significant ($p < .01$). Further, both the adjustment and sex factors were significantly associated with such intrusions and, moreover, with the variability of defensive and coping functions ($p < .05$) and with the variability of Adaptive Regression scores (for adjustment, $p < .01$; for the adjustment/sex interaction, $p < .05$). Thus, subjects who on the basis of their rescored Rorschach protocols were placed in the "less adjusted" category produced considerably more primary process material than the "more adjusted" subjects. With regard to sex differences, the "more adjusted" male subjects produced records with relatively less primary process material than the "more adjusted" female subjects, a trend that was reversed in that the "less adjusted" male subjects produced considerably more primary process material than the "less adjusted" female subjects.

Although, contrary to the hypothesis, the level of defensive and coping functions was slightly lower in hypnosis than in the waking state for both groups, there was a trend (not statistically significant) toward improved reality testing in hypnosis for the "less adjusted" male subjects and toward the opposite for the "less adjusted" female subjects. In general, the Adaptive Regression scores of the "more adjusted" male subjects were significantly greater than those of the "less adjusted" male subjects, while the "more adjusted" female subjects' Adaptive Regression scores were somewhat lower than those of the "less adjusted" female subjects.

For the third phase of analysis, the 84 substantive scoring categories thought to be most indicative of regression were tabulated and subjected to a comparison between the waking and hypnosis conditions. Of the 84 categories, 13 yielded significant differences in thought content and organization, and 26 categories indicated significantly greater variance in the hypnosis condition. Out of 22 content scoring categories, 15 were found to be more frequent in hypnosis as compared to waking Rorschach protocols—a difference that is significant at the .04 level. Similarly, 25 of 37 formal scoring categories were found to be more frequent in hypnosis protocols *(p <* .006). Those differences offer suggestive evidence regarding the nature of the primary processes expressed in hypnotic thought.

Subjecting the control and defense scoring categories to similar scrutiny suggested that at the .05 level of significance, hypnosis protocols were more frequently indicative of defensive functioning. However, when the defense and control categories were divided into adaptive versus maladaptive operations, a more coherent picture emerged. There was no difference between experimental conditions in the relative deployment of adaptive processes, whereas the frequency of maladaptive defenses was significantly greater in hypnosis protocols *(p <* .02).

Discussion

The study makes only a modest contribution to the problem posed at the outset. Nevertheless, the findings summarized above were corroborated by a research group at Yale University.[2] They lend themselves to a tentative interpretation of regressive phenomena not only within the limits of this research project, but also, somewhat more speculatively, in the ego-psychological approach to hypnosis.

The Rorschach situation as such may be defined as inviting regression because it requires the production of visual imagery, itself considered a mode of primary process functioning (Holt & Havel, 1960). Almost any kind of latent ideational content may be evoked when a Rorschach card is presented, but normally the subject scans a variety of memory images to find one or more that best fit the vaguely structured blot. In the process of perceiving and simultaneously translating perception into verbal form, defenses against the emergence of drive-determined thoughts are operating. Consequently, the distance from the primary process idea presumed to underlie an overt response shows the degree of neutralization, counter-cathectic strength, and hypercathexis of secondary process thinking.

In the experiment, the regressive element inherent in the Rorschach test was enhanced in the hypnosis condition, as manifested by a general increase in responses influenced by primary process. Interview material, obtained from all subjects to elicit their hypotheses concerning the experiment, showed that they were not aware of a demand to "regress." The increased

2. Sidney Blatt, personal communication, 1971.

production of primary process responses thus did not appear to be a function of the subjects' expectations. Although it was to some extent associated with the sequence in which the experimental conditions were administered, it held up whether the hypnosis condition preceded or followed the waking condition. It therefore was assumed to be a function of hypnosis.

On closer examination however, this interpretation is open to question. As stated earlier, the triggering into action of an ego subsystem results in the overall ego's relinquishing to the hypnotist control of its apparatuses, the subsystem's gaining control of the apparatuses in the process of becoming a temporarily stable structure, and the subsystem's search for new motivational patterns. Exposure to the Rorschach immediately following hypnosis induction, when the stabilization of the subsystem is presumably in progress, presents the subject with a ready-made motivational pattern whose implementation depends on perceptual-cognitive functions as they come under the sway of the subsystem. If, as was the case in the experiment, the person presenting the Rorschach is also the hypnotist, who is simultaneously offering a regressive transference relationship via hypnotic induction, another, potentially more powerful, ready-made motivational pattern is at hand. Determined partly by situational contingencies (such as the personality of the hypnotist), and partly by covert, unexplored, but relatively inevitable transference factors, this pattern is implemented according to the subject's dynamic style, as represented in the instinctual derivatives and attention cathexes to which the subsystem gains access. The experimenter, not in his role as hypnotist but rather as a specific person who has acquired increased stimulus value during hypnosis induction, may to some extent control the transference relationship by his attitudes; that is, he may subtly encourage or discourage its development and intensity. Yet, he cannot prevent its formation in a transference-prone individual, whose critical functions and testing of background reality have been at least partially given over to the hypnotist by the overall ego. The demand for regression is implicit even if not consciously recognized by either party. Hence, the increase in regressive Rorschach responses in the hypnosis condition may be interpreted as a function of the transference aspects in hypnosis but not as a function of hypnosis per se.

Support for this interpretation is implied in a previous investigation (Gruenewald & Fromm, 1967), in which subjects were given a Rorschach and an intelligence test under hypnosis, with the tests administered by a person other than the hypnotist. In the absence of the regression-facilitating hypnotic transference relationship with the examiner, no discernible regression took place in comparison with the subjects' waking-state baseline performance. It appears then that in the context of the subsystem's postulated access to id-ego-superego derivatives, the objective nature of the task and the motivational quality of the hypnotic relationship determine which part of the triad becomes dominant.

The gross division of overall ego and ego subsystem may be considered a regression if so defined, but it is questionable if regression in that sense is the same as the stipulated regression within the subsystem. While an association of hypnosis with regression in terms of the formation of a subsystem is upheld, a cause and effect relationship within the subsystem can be established only if experimental control of the hypnotist variable in a similar experiment should replicate the results obtained with regard to primary process manifestations.

The crucial question—Is hypnosis an adaptive regression?—is however at least tentatively answered by the finding that the direction of regression split along the adjustment-maladjustment axis.

It had been predicted that improved ego control would manifest itself in a quantitative increase and qualitative shift of the defensive and coping operations that accompanied the readier expression of primary process ideation in hypnosis. Contrary to the prediction, the results indicated a general, though nonsignificant, quantitative reduction of scores pertaining to defense and coping categories. The qualitative shift consisted in greater variability of these scores for the "more adjusted" and in decreased variability for the "less adjusted" subjects.

The quantitative reduction of defense and coping scores can be accounted for on the ground that hypnosis entails a constriction and attenuation of the perception of reality. For the duration of the hypnosis, the overall ego relinquishes a major or minor part of its normal awareness and processing of background information to the hypnotist. The deeper the hypnosis, the broader the subsystem's access to the apparatuses of perception, memory, judgment, and so forth. The activity of the subsystem increases as the overall ego becomes more passive. However, the amount of outside information available to the subsystem is diminished, being derived both from the overall ego and from the hypnotist. While input from within may become more extensive and more intensive, its processing is not controlled by the overall ego's constant checking of reality that takes place in the waking state. The amount of defense activity commensurate with the perceptual range of the overall ego is therefore diminished.

An increase in variability of defense and coping scores had been predicted as an indicator of loosened defenses and adaptive regression for all subjects. However, the second set of analyses disclosed that the loosening of defenses was not uniformly adaptive. Only the "more adjusted" subjects engaged in predominantly flexible and far-ranging ego activity in the hypnosis condition, with a preponderance of higher level coping mechanisms. The "less adjusted" subjects, in contrast, tended to become more constricted and to rely in greater part on maladaptive defenses. In the case of the "less adjusted" male subjects, a trend toward a slightly improved reality orientation appeared (as indicated by their form level scores). Although this trend may be interpreted as an ego-syntonic adaptation to the immediate situation and perhaps as an enduring personality trait, it scarcely fits the criteria stipulated for adaptive regression. Instead of comfortably accepting hypnosis, the "less adjusted" male subjects seemed to defend themselves against its potentially disorganizing influence by clinging to realistic features and intellectual functioning.

In the aggregate, the subjects' formal thought processes manifested more regression in hypnosis than in the waking state. But in relation to adaptive regression, the frequency of adaptive defenses did not exceed that of the waking condition, while maladaptive defenses were significantly more frequent in hypnosis.

In summary, the outcome of the investigation indicates facilitation of access to primary process ideation and differences in the organization of thought processes in hypnosis. The effects of increased accessibility and the degree of primary process expression appear to be a function of each individual's structural and dynamic characteristics and level of psychological adjustment. Moreover, situational and interpersonal variables cannot be neglected in evaluating the outcome.

We conclude that adaptive regression can take place in hypnosis but does not thereby become a function of hypnosis per se, and that the equation of hypnosis with adaptive regression is not tenable in its present form.

Conclusion

We will end this chapter with a few remarks that sum up our thinking as it relates to general issues pertaining to psychoanalytically-oriented hypnosis research.

It is our opinion that psychoanalytic theory offers the most comprehensive hypotheses for the functioning of the human mind and that much fruitful research can be generated from that basis. Nevertheless, there is an urgent need to rethink its concepts in a form that can bridge the gap between theoretical statement and operational definition.

Many efforts directed to that end are already under way, and the contemporary ferment in psychoanalytic thought has already left its mark. For instance, dissatisfaction with the ambiguities in the concept of "primary process" has resulted in critical papers that extend Freud's theory (cf. Gill, 1967; Holt, 1967). Rapaport (1958, 1967) and Schafer (1958, 1968a, 1968b) have significantly contributed to the extension of the theory of intrasystemic structural development and of ego activity and passivity. A recent paper by Fromm (1970) adds clarification to the latter. Holt's (1963) Rorschach scoring system for adaptive regression constitutes an important link between theory and research.

We have touched upon conceptual and linguistic difficulties inherent in psychoanalytic concepts. At the same time, we find cogency in Gill and Brenman's (1959) intrasystemic view of the ego in hypnosis. Sterba

(1934), following Freud's postulate of an observing ego, suggested a separation of the observing and experiencing parts of the ego in psychoanalysis, a notion equally applicable to hypnosis (Fromm, 1965). Bellak (1955) expresses a similar view, stated in terms of the "self-excluding function of the ego." This formulation has apparently not been taken up in the literature, but it deserves further exploration as it seems to have implications for the activity-passivity problem as well as for the concept of regression as now used. A reexamination of regression would certainly be in order. For example, are the ideational factors subsumed under "primary process" always regressive? Might they not in some instances (such as creativity and intuition) represent functions that mature and become autonomous in their own right? Such functions may be associated with and appropriate to different levels of ego processes under different conditions, without recourse to the concept of regression.

The account we have given of the research project should leave no doubt that, whether one espouses a "state" or "process" theory of hypnosis, any definitive statement concerning hypnosis is at best premature. There no longer is room for parochialism or reductionism in hypnosis research. A broader and more consistent joining of efforts across disciplines and theoretical orientations would be extraordinarily useful for the future of hypnosis research.

Ernest R. Hilgard *is an Emeritus Professor of Psychology at Stanford University, still actively engaged in research and teaching. He received his Ph.D. from Yale in 1930 and taught there until 1933, when he moved to Stanford, where he has been ever since, except for an interruption for service in Washington during World War II. His research activity has covered such fields as the experimental study of learning in animals and man, social influences upon level of aspiration, and problem solving. During the last decade and a half he has headed an active team doing research on hypnosis and human motivation. His books include* Theories of Learning, Introduction to Psychology, *and* Hypnotic Susceptibility *(also issued in a shorter paperback form as* The Experience of Hypnosis). *He is a past president of the American Psychological Association, and recently served as president of the Division of Psychological Hypnosis.*

David Nowlis *is a consultant for NASA and the Garrett Corporation, Los Angeles. He received his doctorate from Harvard University in 1965. He has been on the faculty at Claremont Men's College, Bryn Mawr College, and Stanford University. Most recently he has been working in the Virgin Islands and in Los Angeles on evaluation of those environmental parameters which affect the quality of life in isolated habitats such as space stations and the undersea marine research station Tektite II. He has coedited with E. C. Wortz the proceedings from the First National Symposium on Habitability.*

Hilgard and Nowlis *shift away in this exploratory study from the older question of whether hypnotic dreams are the same or different than night dreams. Conceding that they are different, they ask instead to what extent and in what ways the contents of hypnotic and night dreams overlap and diverge. Hypnotic dreams are compared with previous content analyses of night dreams. Hypnotic dreams are found to be shorter and have fewer characters. The kinds of characters are different and more psychedeliclike distortions are found in the hypnotic dreams. This exploratory study is just one representative offshoot from Hilgard's active research program (summarized in Hilgard, 1965). The research was supported by the National Institute of Mental Health, Grant MH-3859.*

17

The Contents of Hypnotic Dreams and Night Dreams: An Exercise in Method

ERNEST R. HILGARD AND DAVID P. NOWLIS

Hypnotic dreams are not identical with night dreams, but it is also true that many night dreams do not fit the stereotype of what a true dream should be like. Some night dreams are very short, some have little dramatic quality, distortion may be absent, the dreamer may know that he is dreaming, and so on. In comparing hypnotic dreams and night dreams it is therefore unlikely that there will be some entirely clear answer to the question: Is the hypnotic dream the same or different from a night dream? The answer will doubtless be that they overlap, but perhaps some important differences may be discovered.

The problem of comparing hypnotic dreams and night dreams is an old one, enhanced first by the considerable emphasis upon dreams in the work of Freud, and, second, by the new interest in sleep and dreams occasioned by new physiological methods, including EEGs and rapid eye movements (REMs). Others have reviewed the literature thoroughly. Moss's (1967) book includes not only his own discussions but reprints of the more important articles appearing up to that time. Among these is the review by Tart (1965a) in which the methodological problems are thoroughly discussed. In the past there was some polarization of opinions, as by Brenman (1949), who argued for a difference between hypnotic and night dreams, and by Mazer (1951), who took the opposite view. Authors of 20 of the 34 studies reviewed by Tart felt it desirable to make some comparisons between hyp-

Modified from a paper given at the meeting of the Society for Experimental and Clinical Hypnosis, Chicago, Illinois, November, 1968. The continued support of the National Institute of Mental Health, Grant MH-3859, is gratefully acknowledged.

notic dreams and night dreams; of these 20, only 10 favored some equation between the two kinds of dreams, 4 denied the similarity, and 6 felt that the evidence was insufficient to state firm conclusions.

The empirical material in the present study is a by-product of routine testing of subjects by hypnotic susceptibility scales in which hypnotic dreams are suggested under two conditions, one in which the suggestion included the statement that the dream will tell something about hypnosis, the other in which this statement was lacking. Hence there is this modest degree of differential motivation toward content.

The methodological purpose of the investigation was to see how best to use content analysis in comparing night dreams and hypnotic dreams, a suggestion deriving from Domhoff (1964), who proposed the use of some of Hall's work on content analysis of thousands of night dreams (for example, Hall and Van de Castle, 1966). Content analysis is not a simple tool; decisions have to be made regarding what kinds of "tokens" to count, and how much effort should be made to analyze (and count) symbolic distortions. Even among those committed to psychoanalytic theory there are disagreements concerning the nature of dreaming (for example, French and Fromm, 1964). As a starting point we decided to do what we could with categories deriving from Hall and Van de Castle, in order to compare our hypnotic dream sample with their night dream sample. We did not, however, feel it necessary to confine ourselves to these comparisons, and have made use of some comparisons with Perry (1964). The main methodological purpose is served, however, by attempting to use a content analysis with hypnotic dreams that will permit comparison with the large available collection of night dreams.

Procedure

We have collected a great many dreams within hypnosis in the course of administering the Stanford Hypnotic Susceptibility Scales, Form C, and the Profile Scales (Weitzenhoffer & Hilgard, 1962, 1967). The subjects, often inexperienced in either hypnosis or dream recall, received the following instructions on Form C:

We are very much interested in finding out what hypnosis and being hypnotized means to people. One of the best ways of finding out is through the dreams that people have while they are hypnotized. Some people dream directly about the meaning of hypnosis, while others dream about this meaning in an indirect way, symbolically, by dreaming about something which does not seem outwardly to be related to hypnosis, but may very well be. Now neither you nor I know what sort of a dream you are going to have, but I am going to allow you to rest for a little while and you are going to have a dream . . . a real dream . . . just the kind you have when you are asleep at night. When I stop talking to you very shortly, you will begin to dream.

You will have a dream about hypnosis. You will dream about what hypnosis means . . . Now you are falling asleep . . . Deeper and deeper asleep . . . Very much like when you sleep at night . . . Soon you will be deep asleep, soundly asleep. As soon as I stop talking you will begin to dream. When I speak to you again you will stop dreaming, if you still happen to be dreaming, and you will listen to me just as you have been doing. If you stop dreaming before I speak to you again, you will remain pleasantly and deeply relaxed . . . Now sleep and dream . . . Deep asleep!

One or two minutes of silence followed. The hypnotist then broke the silence thus:

The dream is over; if you had a dream you can remember every detail of it clearly, very clearly. You do not feel particularly sleepy or different from the way you felt before I told you to fall asleep and to dream, and you continue to remain deeply hypnotized. Whatever you dreamed you can remember quite clearly, and I want you to describe it to me from the beginning. Now tell me about your dream, right from the beginning. (Weitzenhoffer & Hilgard, 1962, pp. 21–22)

Some two-fifths of our unselected university subjects reported dreams. However, just as in the case of night sleep, a subject capable of dreaming under hypnosis does not always produce a dream upon request. In one sample of subjects, 34 had a dream on at least one of two opportunities, but only 20 dreamed on both occasions; 6 subjects who dreamed on the first day failed to dream on the second, and 8 who failed to dream on the first day had a dream on the second day.

Comparison of Hypnotic Dreams with Night Dreams

How real are the dreams reported under these rather artificial circumstances? Tart (1966a) found that subjects, when asked about the quality of their hypnotic dreams, reported a range from thinking or daydreaming, through watching a film or TV, to being "in" the dream as in a vivid night dream. The report of being "in" the dream was given by 13 per cent of 54 subjects who reported only borderline hypnotic states; and by 26 per cent of 27 subjects who felt they had really been hypnotized. Furthermore, we attempted to relate the reality of hypnotic dreaming to the depth of trance as measured by the scores obtained on this hypnotic susceptibility scale, excluding the dream item. Less than one-tenth of those in the lower third of the susceptibility distribution who reported a dream indicated that it was of dreamlike quality, while of those in the highest third of susceptibility who reported a dream about one-third reported that their hypnotic dream was "like a night dream."

If dreams are selected from the reports of highly susceptible subjects, a substantial proportion are likely to be very similar to night dreams. It may be instructive to study the content of such dreams. However, before undertaking a comparison of hypnotic dreams with night dreams, it should be pointed out that we did not expect them to be exactly alike, although we expected some overlap. Some of the reasons why we believed that hypnotic dreams produced should *not* correspond precisely to night dreams, no matter how much they may resemble them, included:

1. The hypnotic subject is not really asleep, so that there is a background of critical awareness, which may alter the dream. Such waking dreams—not to be confused with ordinary daydreams—occasionally are reported outside hypnosis, but they are rare.

2. The subject knows that he is going to report his dream. Therefore some conscious censorship doubtless is active. For example, one would expect few overtly sexual dreams under these circumstances. The frame of reference was more nearly that of a TAT story, sensitive to the setting in which it was produced.

3. Time demands are placed upon the subject. He is told to "dream now," rather than to have a spontaneous dream occasioned by his own inner needs when they arise.

4. A topical set is created. Some of the instructions read suggested that the dream be about hypnosis. When this suggestion was given, it may very well have made some difference, as we shall see later.

5. The dream report itself is made within whatever hypnotic state the subject has achieved or believes himself to have achieved, and this may also color his report.

Thus if we failed to find *any* difference between the hypnotic dreams and night dreams we would suspect that our content analysis measures were insensitive.

Single dreams, obtained under hypnosis from 172 subjects in the upper fourth of scores on SHSS:C (scores of 8 and above) were coded (Table 17.1). Nearly two-thirds of these dreams resembled typical night dreams; the others were less convincing.

Lacking a sample of night dreams from the same subjects, we have turned to a sample of night dreams analyzed by Hall and Van de Castle (1966). This is a somewhat unsatisfactory procedure. Therefore we have interpreted

TABLE 17.1   Reality of reported hypnotic dream

Reality as Judged by Coder	Number	Per Cent
Subject involved, as in real night dream	109	63
Like watching movie or TV, with visual imagery	56	33
Like thinking or daydreaming	7	4
Total[a]	172	100

SOURCE: After Hall and Van de Castle, 1966.

a. Because there was one dream per subject the number of subjects equal the number of dreams. Those subjects not dreaming were eliminated from this study.

TABLE 17.2 Contrast between hypnotic dream and night dream samples

	Hypnotic Dreams (present study)		*Night Dreams* (Hall and Van de Castle)	
Subjects	College students		College students	
Dream background	Hypnosis		Sleep	
Occasion for dream	Suggested		Spontaneous	
Dream topic	"About hypnosis"		Spontaneous	
Dream report recorded	By experimenter		By subject	
Source of subjects	Classes (scored 8 or higher on SHSS:C)		Classes	
Dreams per subject	1		5	
	Male	*Female*	*Male*	*Female*
Number of subjects	91	81	100	100
Number of dreams	91	81	500	500
Words per dream (range)	15–123	13–238	50–300	50–300
Words per dream (mean)	52.0	57.8	unknown	unknown
Characters per dream	1.3	1.3	2.4	2.8

SOURCE: After Hall and Van de Castle, 1966.

the comparison as a methodological exercise, testing whether or not a code developed for night dreams would be applicable to hypnotic dreams, at least as a rough indicator of similarities and differences by which to guide further research efforts. To avoid overinterpretation of our findings we present some differences between our sample and that of Hall and Van de Castle in Table 17.2. Apart from the differences in the manner in which the dreams were obtained and recorded, we note to begin with that the hypnotic dreams were much shorter (averaging near the lower limit of the night dreams), and they had fewer characters in them.[1]

CHARACTERS IN DREAMS

We have followed Hall and Van de Castle in counting characters. The dreamer is not counted, and a crowd of an unspecified number of persons is counted as one person. "Characters" include nonhuman animals and creatures as well as persons.

The mean difference in number of characters per dream is accounted for by the rapid fall-off of more than two characters besides the dreamer in the hypnotic dream, and the frequent occurrence of two or more characters in the night dream (Table 17.3). In the hypnotic sample, the differences between the sexes were statistically insignificant. If we interpret the night dream sample as if there were 100 subjects in each sex group, the slightly larger num-

1. Recall instructions for Hall and Van de Castle subjects included the following: "Your report should contain, whenever possible, a description of the setting of the dream, whether it was familiar to you or not, a description of the people, their sex, age, and relationship to you, and of any animals that appeared in the dream" (p. 313).

TABLE 17.3   Number of characters per dream

Number of Characters	Hypnotic Dreams (present study)		Night Dreams (Hall and Van de Castle)	
	male	female	male	female
	per cent	per cent	per cent	per cent
0 (dreamer only)	31	32	6	3
1	30	28	24	19
2	25	25	30	24
3	10	10	20	25
4	4	4	12	14
5	0	1	4	7
6 and more	0	0	4	8
Total	100	100	100	100
	$(N = 91)^a$	$(N = 81)^a$	$(N = 500)^b$	$(N = 500)^b$

SOURCE: After Hall and Van de Castle, 1966.

a. One dream per S. Differences between sexes not significant.

b. Five dreams per person, hence 100 Ss in each group. t—test, using $N = 100$, each sex: $t = 2.00$, $df = 198$, $p = .05$.

ber of characters among the female subjects was significant by a t-test ($p = < .05$). The night dreams contained significantly more characters than the hypnotic dreams ($t = 6.5$, $p = .001$).

The kinds of characters found in the two types of dreams also differed, as shown in Table 17.4. While the classes with most members tended to be quite similar in hypnotic and night dreams, a few differences were rather striking. First, human characters contrast more sharply than all characters (Table 17.3) because of the prominence of nonhuman characters in the hypnotic dreams. Second, representations of the immediate family were less frequent in the hypnotic dreams, possibly because the office setting and the suggestion to dream about hypnosis may have depressed the number of personal family associations. Uncertainty, vagueness, and metamorphosis also characterized the hypnotic dreams; there would have been even more metamorphoses if the animal and insect figures in hypnotic dreams had been included in Table 17.4. Again, these results may be due in part to the instructions to dream about hypnosis. Thus careful experimentation would be required to determine which aspects of dreaming are influenced by instructions.

PREVALENCE OF DISTORTIONS

The most striking feature of the hypnotic dream was the amount of distortion. Perry (1964), working in Sutcliffe's group in Sydney, Australia, has prepared a procedure for content analysis of dream distortions. The norms that he has provided are quite limited, but they permit a preliminary comparison between the night dreams in his sleep laboratory and the hypnotic dreams in our experiment. Considering only the agreed-upon distortions among the 60 dreams of his 14 subjects (Perry, 1964, Table 3, pp. 22-24), we note that such distortions were found in 8 of the 60 dreams or 13 per cent, and distortion in *any* dream occurred in 6 of his 14 subjects or 43 per cent. The gap between the two percentages—13 per cent and 43 per cent—shows what discrepancies can arise from analyzing in terms of *dreams* or in terms of *subjects* when there is more than one dream per subject. We find in our sample that, with one dream per subject, 54 per cent showed some distortion within a hypnotically suggested dream.

In any case, the distortions found in the dreams in our study were more numerous than those reported in night dreams of the only comparable sample. This difference suggests the wisdom of taking a more intense look at the kinds of distortions we found. Some events in these hypnotic dreams could best be described as "unusual transformation," others as "distortions." They are summarized in Table 17.5.

Note that for this purpose the dream of each subject was assigned to one category only. Thus if a distortion of the self was prominent, the dream was not also classified as a distortion of size, even though some slight size change might have been involved. Likewise, if change in body size was the most prominent characteristic, the dream was not also classified as a distortion of the self. The categories we used are best illustrated by quotations from the recorded reports of the dreams.

TRANSFORMATIONS OF SELF

1. "I was anchored in a chair, and my body felt like cast iron. Then I felt like I was away from my body—looking at myself in the chair which was

TABLE 17.4   Human characters found in hypnotic dreams and in night dreams, and their relative frequencies

Human Characters in Dreams	Hypnotic Dreams (present study)	Night Dreams (Hall and Van de Castle)
	per cent of characters	*per cent of characters*
Immediate family	1	12
Relatives	—	4
Known Others	19	35
Prominent persons	2	1
Identified by occupation	15	12
Identified by ethnic group	4	2
Strangers	16	20
Uncertain, vague	31	13
Dead persons	1	< 0.5
Imaginary persons	2	< 0.5
Metamorphoses	9	1
Total, per cent	100[a]	100[b]

SOURCE: After Hall and Van de Castle, 1966.

a. Total of 163 characters from 172 dreams, one per person.
b. Total of 2,471 characters from 1,000 dreams, five per person.

TABLE 17.5   Unusual transformations and distortions in hypnotic dreams

Transformation or Distortion	Subjects in Which This Transformation is Prominent
	per cent
Transformations	
Self	11
Something else	16
Scene	15
Total transformations	42
Distortions	
Floating	5
Falling	4
Staircases	1
Size changes	2
Total distortions	12
No transformations or distortions	46
Total	100
	(N = 172)

SOURCE: After Hall and Van de Castle, 1966.

now on a high pinnacle in dark black in a cave. It was about two-thirds of the way up. The cave was rough black rock. And I was observing myself in the chair all the time."

2. "I was with a friend, talking, but I felt as though part of me was not there, that my other self was behind me. Only my face was moving in front of this person."

3. "I'm in a green room, looking over the shoulder of a guy in front of me, who turned out to be me!"

Duplication of the self occurred often enough to suggest the dissociative split between the observing ego and the participating ego so often reported by hypnotic subjects. Such self-duplications were not reported in the night dreams studied by Hall and Van de Castle. The transformations of the self in the forgoing statements all involved duplication of the self, but of course the transformations listed in Table 17.5 also included other less dramatic changes in which the self, while not duplicated, was notably different from normal.

TRANSFORMATIONS OF SOMETHING ELSE

1. "There was a little top, striped, and it was spinning by. All of a sudden it had legs and arms, and then there was a bicycle and a swell looking girl with frizzy hair."

2. "There was a room, with a big, black roll of cheese rolling down a ramp, then it stopped. It was huge like a big stone, and it grew, and I could see it."

3. "I was painting a picture of Charles de Gaulle, and he came out of the picture, and he was going to put me in the army."

4. "Then I saw Jerry, and her breath turned into a flashlight."

5. "There were some fish swimming that were purplish-blue, with yellow eyes. They were saying hello to some other fish. Then another fish came and swallowed up one of them. But his eyes became the eyes of the second fish."

TRANSFORMATIONS OF SCENE

1. "Then there was no well—trying to move in this sticky stuff—couldn't move very well and then I was in the middle of a pasture. All was free, I could move around. It was very beautiful there, yellow and green trees, and sunny there."

2. "First I saw a long black angle coming from the top with white stripes. Everything else was gray. Then I saw a corner of a house. It had scalloped shingles. The sun was shining a lot, but I couldn't see a lot. Then I saw a man floating with a paper face, like a pancake. First it was straight up, then sideways. It looked like my uncle, funny, only without a beard. Then it changed and looked like a stylized Lenin. Then a page came up—a girl. A page from the *Ladies' Home Journal,* I think.

3. "First I began to see a large purple area, upon which black images were superimposed. First there was a helicopter, then a plane that I was in, and it was crashing. Next I saw two male faces, both ominous. The purple area became a sea in which I was swimming, with black trees on either side. When I came out, there were snakes all around."

DISTORTIONS

Floating. "I felt light, and I was floating out of the building, hanging over the campus."

Falling. "The chair formed into a kind of bag—warm. I curled into the bag and started to fall, not a fast fall, but I could see things as they passed by me. My hands were cold with no way to get them warm. The fall took about 30 seconds, no, must have been longer—from quite a height. The bag took the shape of a big tear drop."

Staircases. "I was with a friend of mine and we were by this big tower, it had a special staircase inside. It was very dark. We decided to climb to the top. It took a long time. We got very tired, but when we got up there we could see for a long way, all over."

Size Changes. "I was sitting there in this chair, and you were there, sitting. The chair and I grew smaller, only I grew smaller faster. I could walk around in the seat of the chair, so I did. Your pencil got so big you had to rest it on your shoulder."

We do not wish to give the impression that all of the dreams were as dramatic as these. Actually, there were no unusual transformations or distortions in half of the dreams, and many others lacked the dramatic qualities of those just described. However, the dreams often did have a psychedelic quality, shown in part by the frequency of views or vistas (Table 17.6).

It may be that the frequent references to floating, falling, staircases, and vistas were part of the symbolic representation of hypnosis called for in the instructions. We did, of course, look for the direct representation of hypnosis or the hypnotist; and found such references to be somewhat fewer than the instructions might have been expected to produce (Table 17.7).

The contrast between direct and indirect representation can best be illustrated by quotations from the recorded dreams.

DIRECT REPRESENTATION

1. "I was watching a split screen, and on one side a hypnotist show with Pat Collins could be seen, and on the other half I imagined people who were hypnotized, young children. . . .They were trying to teach these children all sorts of functions in order to make supermen of them by educating them with hypnosis. They were trying to show that they could make people into anything using hypnosis."

2. "And then I saw Pluto hypnotizing Daisy Duck. And I saw the tack coming closer, and it was pulsating, and it seemed to be falling off into something else and there seemed to be a lot of color! Amazing!"

INDIRECT REPRESENTATION

1. "I am walking down a road in the country—a crossroad—I take the one to the left. A mountain is in the distance; it's snowy and there are trees.

TABLE 17.6   Views or vistas in hypnotic dreams

	Subjects Reporting Dreams With Views or Vistas
	per cent
View of	
Mountain, forest, sea	23
Cities or buildings	3
Planets, sun, void	4
Total views of	30
View from	
Mountains, cliffs, towers	1
As consequence of flying, ballooning, levitating	2
Total views from	3
No views or vistas	67
Total	100
	(N = 172)

SOURCE: After Hall and Van de Castle, 1966.

TABLE 17.7   Representation of the hypnotist or hypnosis in hypnotic dreams "about hypnosis"

Representation	Per Cent of Subjects Reporting Dreams
Direct	8
Indirect	25
None identifiable	67
Total	100
	(N = 172)

SOURCE: After Hall and Van de Castle, 1966.

I climb the mountain. It's steep with a beautiful lake at the top with rocks all around it. I sit on one of the rocks, lose my balance and fall head over heels down the bank into the lake. That's all." (Later the subject reported that the crossroad was hypnotism: He could go either way.) "The mountain was hypnosis—an accomplishment—falling down the hill was coming to the end of hypnosis."

2. "I dreamed of having my arm in a hole in a sphere and not being able to bend it, no matter how hard I tried."

3. "There was a little man inside of my head, and he was controlling my whole body."

THE EFFECT OF CHANGED INSTRUCTIONS

All the hypnotic dream material discussed so far had been dream under suggestion from Form C; only a single opportunity to dream had been given. Many of the subjects were brought back at a later time for two sessions of the Profile Scales. In Form I the subject is not instructed to dream specifically about hypnosis, while Form II repeats essentially the instructions of Form C. Accordingly, there was an opportunity to see whether there were changes in the dream content corresponding to the changes in instructions. This was an imperfect experiment because all subjects had been given Form C earlier, and all had had the profile scales in the same order. Therefore it should be considered as exploratory only. The results are summarized in Table 17.8. It was apparent that the dream did in fact represent hypnosis more frequently when subjects were instructed to dream about hypnosis than when the topic of the dream was unspecified, a difference significant at the .025 level. However, the representation was usually indirect, even when identifiable. Perhaps some sort of free association technique would have revealed that the nonscored dreams also contained hypnosis representation, but in even more disguised forms.

SENSORY REPRESENTATION

The nature of sensory or perceptual representation in dreams was also of interest. Dreams are said to be primarily visual, with auditory imagery being a close second. We have found that tactual representation lagged only slightly

TABLE 17.8   Representation of hypnosis or the hypnotist in dreams with and without suggestion that the dream will be about hypnosis (N = 24 subjects dreaming both times)

		SPS Form II: Told to Dream about Hypnosis		
		no representation of hypnosis or hypnotist	direct or indirect representation of hypnosis or hypnotist	total
SPS Form I: Not Told Specifically to Dream About	Direct or indirect representation of hypnosis or hypnotist	1	3	4
Hypnosis	No representation of hypnosis or hypnotist	11	9	20
	Total	12	12	24

SOURCE: After Hall and Van de Castle, 1966.

Chi Square = 4.9, p < .025. (One-tailed test for score changes, with Yates correction; see McNemar, 1969, p. 263.)

behind vision, possibly because we have called attention to bodily feelings by instructing the subject to sit quietly with eyes closed (Table 17.9).

Because there were often fleeting references to other senses, we scored only the predominant sense. This was vision in a large proportion of the cases, although some dreams stressed touch (or kinesthesis) and audition.

Implications for Further Research

This study has shown the feasibility of discovering differences between dream samples on the basis of content analyses such as those done by Hall and Van de Castle (1966) and by Perry (1964). We believe that some of

TABLE 17.9   Senses predominate in hypnotic dreams

Dominant Sense	Hypnotic Dreams
	per cent
Vision	56
Touch (including kinesthesis)	12
Audition	9
Taste	0
Smell	0
Not ascertained	23
Total	100
	(N = 172)

SOURCE: After Hall and Van de Castle, 1966.

our substantive findings are likely to hold up on further experimentation; but this study is justified less on the basis of its findings than for its role as a feasibility study. Among further needed research steps are:

1. Dream samples in sleep and under hypnosis should be obtained from the same subjects, under conditions as similar as possible except for the hypnosis. Ideally this would mean having the subject sleep nights in the laboratory and be aroused to report spontaneous nocturnal dreams when they occur. On other occasions he would be hypnotized in bed at the same hour of the night and told to report the hypnotic dream. While these conditions are both artificial, the comparison of night dreams and hypnotic dreams requires that the differences that arise should be the result of sleep or hypnosis, and not of differences in setting that had nothing to do directly with either state.

2. Various kinds of instructions can be used in the production of hypnotic dreams (see Table 17.8), but great care needs to be exercised to prevent interactions with prior dream experiences under hypnosis. The ideal experiment would require a common background of hypnotic experience prior to being asked to dream under hypnosis, and with reference to the very first hypnotic dream, the administration of one of several alternative sets of instructions. This procedure would have the disadvantage of lack of practice in dreaming under hypnosis, but the advantage of no contamination through prior practice.

3. A series of dreams from the same subject proved to be fruitful in dream research on the dreams of patients (French & Fromm, 1964), and it is possible that a long series of dreams from the same subject in trance might also be revealing. Our observations along this line are clinical and unsystematic (as are Sacerdote's, 1967a), but the possibility of fruitful results from the study of series of dreams of nonpatients in the laboratory is worth exploring.

Conclusions

1. Hypnotic dreams, even under the somewhat artificial laboratory conditions here described, have much in common with night dreams, although there had been many reasons to expect differences.

2. The more highly susceptible the subject, the more likely he is to dream under hypnosis, and the more likely it is that his dream will be like a night dream.

3. While comparative evidence is hard to come by, it appears that the Alice-in-Wonderland types of distortion are somewhat more frequent in hypnotic dreams than in night dreams. This deserves more careful study, using the same subjects for reports of night dreams, hypnotic dreams, and projective fantasies.

4. The instruction to dream about hypnosis does not produce many direct references to hypnosis, but appears to increase the number of indirect references. This may be one reason for the frequency of dream distortion in our sample.

5. Interpretations of hypnotically induced dreams should probably consider the dreams to be projective products falling somewhere in between TAT stories and night dreams.

Howard Shevrin *is a psychoanalyst and clinical psychologist on the staff of The Menninger Foundation. Since 1956 he has devoted half of his time to research on unconscious mental processes, having developed a special subliminal technique for investigating different types of thought organization. One part of this research, done in collaboration with Dr. Lawrence Stross, dealt with the nature of unconscious mental processes in hypnosis. More recently he has been investigating certain brain processes that he has found to accompany unconscious thinking. In his clinical work he has treated as well as diagnosed the full range of psychoanalytic problems to be encountered in an institution like The Menninger Foundation. In 1969 he was graduated from The Topeka Psychoanalytic Institute, having completed training as a research fellow of The American Psychoanalytic Association. From 1954 to 1956 he completed a two-year postdoctoral course in clinical psychology at The Menninger Foundation.*

Shevrin *is concerned with the unconscious emotional impact that hypnosis may have on experimental subjects. In postexperimental interviews he found that subjects consciously described their hypnotic experiences as comfortable and agreeable, but that Card 12M TAT protocols elicited negative and ambivalent unconscious attitudes toward the hypnotic experience. Subjects consciously had a strong wish to cooperate but unconsciously they wanted to submit and to be cared for. When the experience was over and the latter wishes were unfulfilled, unconscious feelings of anxiety, conflict, and angry disappointment were generated.*

18

The Wish to Cooperate and the Temptation to Submit: The Hypnotized Subject's Dilemma

HOWARD SHEVRIN

Through all of its long history, in a variety of guises and under diverse names, hypnosis has retained an air of mystery and a touch of the sinister. The word itself refuses to become shopworn because it is surrounded with so intense an aura of affect and implication. Yet for those who practice it I am sure it is experienced as an instrument—a means toward an end, whether the end is treatment or research. Often what is work to the specialist, however, seems like play or Faustian legerdemain to the layman. By the same token, it becomes easy for the practitioner, caught up in technical issues, to overlook the impact his instrument has upon others. This is certainly less true for the therapist than for the experimenter, who does not so much share goals with the subject as enlist his cooperation for the experimenter's ends, which rarely include the subject's enlightenment. In this paper I would like to describe my enlightenment as an experimenter concerning the impact of hypnosis on experimental subjects.

In recent years I have collaborated in a series of experiments (Stross & Shevrin, 1968) involving hypnosis that was intended to explore the nature of hypnosis as an altered state of consciousness. I was not the hypnotist. In one of these experiments I interviewed the subjects, all women, in order to learn from them how they experienced hypnosis and what effect hypnosis

An earlier version of this paper was presented as part of a symposium on hypnoanalysis, at the Annual Meeting of the Society for Clinical and Experimental Hypnosis, University of Chicago, Chicago, Illinois, November 23, 1968.

had on the various tasks they were asked to perform. At the end of each interview I asked them to make up a story to the so-called "hypnosis" card (12M) of the TAT. At that time the overriding purpose of the research was to see if hypnosis would augment the effects of subliminal stimulation. We learned that it did in some respects and not in others. My preoccupation in the interviews was to understand better how hypnosis might bring about this augmenting effect. Actually, the interviews were disappointing in this respect. As a result, like all good experimenters, I forgot about them.

Recently I reread the interviews for reasons that are unclear to me and was forcibly struck by something that had utterly eluded me before. Although subject after subject described in positive and even glowing terms how relaxing, pleasant, and agreeable the hypnotic experience was, allusions to much different feelings in the interviews and—most remarkably—in their TAT stories were in striking contrast to these accolades. I set about to study these interviews and stories and have been most troubled by what I found concerning the underlying attitudes of hypnotic subjects at the end of an experiment. From a clinical standpoint, the stories were those of angry, disappointed, and frightened women. The pleasant goodbyes masked the injury these women felt they had suffered.

I know that there has been a history of experimentation involving the use of the hypnosis card to pre- or post-dict hypnotizability (Levitt, Lubin, & Brady, 1962; Levitt & Lubin, 1963; Sector, 1961; Venture, Kransdorff, & Kline, 1956; R. W. White, 1937). However, only one study to my knowledge collected stories immediately following hypnosis (Sarason & Rosenzweig, 1942), and in this study little is reported about the findings other than to state that some stories were positive and others ambivalent. Of the 13 subjects in our experiment only one was clearly positive in her stories. Of all the subjects she was the only one who had a continuing relationship with the hypnotist. He had been instructing her in the use of hypnosis during childbirth. Of the other 12 subjects, 5 were strikingly negative in their stories and the remaining 7 told stories which, only by stretching the term, could be called ambivalent. Before illustrating the data, let me discuss the nature of the hypnotic induction and give a brief description of the experiment.

The Stanford Hypnotic Susceptibility Scale, Form A (Weitzenhoffer & Hilgard, 1959) was used. Subjects were considered hypnotized when they passed at least 7 of the 12 challenge items on the Stanford Scale. However, most of the subjects scored positively in all 12 items. In general, subjects were at least in medium trances, and some were in deep hypnotic states. In all cases, the subject had to be sufficiently hypnotized to carry out the complex experimental procedure and still not be disrupted subjectively or "awakened" by the procedure.

The subjects were all women in their middle to late twenties or early thirties. They were all volunteers who had been successfully hypnotized on at least one other occasion by the same hypnotist and who were distinguished by the readiness and completeness with which they entered the hypnotic state. I stress that, as a group, they were friendly, willing, and even dedicated.

The experiment itself lasted four sessions. The first and second sessions were on successive days; a week later the third and fourth sessions were again on successive days. In each session the subject was hypnotized. Under hypnosis the subject was asked to describe a briefly flashed picture, to provide descriptions of images, to free associate, and to recall night dreams. These responses were also obtained in the waking state. At the end of the second and fourth sessions, I interviewed the subjects. The subject was asked to follow the experimental procedure step by step and to describe how each task was experienced in hypnosis and in the waking state. After this had been completed the "hypnosis" card was administered.

I would like to cite three subjects' experiences in some detail and then discuss the questions raised by these accounts.

First Case Illustration

Miss S. was a young unmarried woman in her early twenties who was readily hypnotized and had passed all of the items in the Stanford Scale. When I asked her what it was like to become hypnotized she replied:

> Well, I just relaxed. I felt very heavy and limp. I kept having the feeling yesterday and today that part of the time, possibly, I could have just woke up, but yet I didn't." When she was asked what more she could tell me about her experience of feeling heavy and limp she said, "Well, I just feel like, in a way, a little bit drunk. I just really couldn't do very much. I'm just so completely relaxed. . . . It's just like nothing else really matters, except being relaxed and, well for instance, I think it's just like if I were supposed to—well, probably even get up and walk—it would be extremely difficult to get out of this chair. . . . It's just like I don't really have any control over my arms and my legs and my hands and they're just useless and I know that they're there but I can't do anything with them.

For this subject the difference between being hypnotized and being awake was epitomized in these terms: "I think when I was hypnotized. . . the pictures all seemed to be a little dark, a little on the gray side and then when I was awake, they were bright." She characterized coming out of hypnosis by describing things as being "brighter. . .it seems like there's more light in the room."

When I pressed her further to define this quality of darkness in hypnosis the subject was most revealing: "It seems like there's no sunshine. It's like. . .well, I think probably hypnosis would be like a rainy day and being fully awake is like sunshine. Things are just grayer, they're not quite as vivid, there's not as much detail and outline, more blurry."

Yet the subject denied that the affects associated with rainy days were the feelings she associated with hypnosis:

> Well, the things I think of in connection with rainy days, I don't feel in connection with hypnosis. Rain always makes me a little depressed. It's on a rainy day when I enjoy having someone around to chat with or to talk to. I think I probably need the security of knowing somebody cares more on a rainy day than I do on a sunshiny one. A rainy day to me is a good time to stay home and read or listen to music with somebody that you care a lot about, that appreciates these things. It can be very depressing. I love to ride in the rain and I like to go to sleep at night with rain. But rain has always been to me, perhaps that God was unhappy with the way we were doing things here and He was crying.

At this point in the interview I showed the subject the "hypnosis" card and asked her for a story which she described as follows:

> I think probably these two men know each other, but they're not good friends and for some unknown reason the man in the chair has gotten the other fellow to the place where he would cooperate and he could put him into hypnosis, but I don't think the man on the couch is wanting to cooperate and it also looks like he's in pain. The man in the chair looks very mean and cruel. I think they're in a rather shabby room. There's probably *not much light* [italics added]. I have a feeling the man in the chair is going to do something, either physically that would be harmful or he may wait until the near future to do something to upset the other man very much. [How does the other man feel?] I don't think he—he doesn't want to cooperate. He knows this man is evil but for some unknown reason there's just not much he can do about it. It's like he's trying to get out of a windstorm but he's just blowing in the breeze. [How do you mean?] He knows he's in the middle of this windstorm and he knows that for his own safety he should try and get out or get some place where he can take cover but for some reason he has just more or less given up. He is going this way and that way, not really putting forth much effort, but yet basically he knows he should but he doesn't want to, it's easier to give up.

Second Case Illustration

This subject was a young woman in her middle twenties who was readily hypnotized. She passed 10 out of the 12 Stanford Scale items. When I asked her what it was like to be hypnotized she replied, "It's just relaxing. You don't worry about anything, you just relax like there was nothing else going on. Like you were asleep. It's all like a dream. . . . I don't really think about anything. I listen to Dr. S's voice and I'm completely relaxed. I'm limp, my body is limp. I don't feel like moving, just staying like I am. There's no urge to move or anything, like I'm asleep. In fact, it's more relaxing than when I'm asleep. . .your hands go limp, feel heavier. . .it's better when I go to sleep because when I sleep, I toss and turn and [in trance] I just feel completely relaxed."

When she was asked what it was like to come out of hypnosis she replied, "I just wake up. It's really just like being asleep for awhile. I wake up, only I'm not drowsy after I wake up. I feel much better after I come out of it than I did before I go in. . . . I have what the doctor calls tension headaches and a lot of times I can come out here and I can go under hypnosis and when I come out, the headache is gone and it doesn't bother me. . .I had a very bad one yesterday and it wasn't completely gone when I left. It was better."

This subject had the experience in the experimental session of not being able to remember a dream in the waking state but being able to recall the dream in great detail once under hypnosis. She said, "As usual, I didn't remember the dream before I went under hypnosis but then I remembered it and it seems like I have some of the silliest dreams that I don't remember [sic]. If I have a dream about a certain problem or something, I always remember it the next day, but if I don't remember it, the dream seems silly." Thus, it would seem this patient consciously had an agreeable experience in hypnosis with some therapeutic benefit and was also able to see for herself how hypnosis can augment memory. To the TAT card, however, she told the following story:

> The man to me looks dead on the couch. The man sitting up above him seems to think he can make him wake up or make him do something. He's very confident, it looks like the man sitting in the chair is very confident that he can make this man see and see whatever he is doing and the man on the couch just doesn't have any worries. He is dead, it is a fact. He just died naturally. He had a heart attack or something. The guy in the chair seems to think that he's an exception. This guy is going to wake up and see him even though he doesn't anyone else. He seems more like the mad scientist or something. [Does the man lying down know the other person?] No, he doesn't know him at all and this is a mad scientist or something. He is a doctor that has been called in. The man is in a strange place. He is in a strange house and I think he was called from a small village community out in the country. He thinks he has all these powers and he doesn't at all. [I see. What's the outcome?] The man in the chair is defeated and the man doesn't see him and people in the village town or country around seem to think he's a mad scientist. No one has anything to do with him. They leave him alone.

Third Case Illustration

The subject was a housewife, in her early thirties. Like the other two she was readily hypnotized. She described hypnosis in these terms, "It wasn't like drifting off to sleep. I was noticing as I was going to sleep the other

night . . . I am not completely relaxed . . . I just fall asleep and there's a
period of not being relaxed, whereas in hypnosis I feel as if my whole body
is relaxed. . . . I feel extremely *passive*. I'm very willing to do whatever he
says except in certain things where my logic interferes. . .that there is a
general heaviness of the body in concentrating on what he is saying. . .not
being able to move unless being given directions to do so." She described
bodily sensations as "sort of a sinking feeling it's hard to describe. It's as if I
were more relaxed than at any other time."

She was resistant to telling a story to the hypnosis card at the end of the
fourth session. She said that she did not like the picture. When asked what
was the matter with it she replied:

> Well, it's the power of the hypnotist and the submission of the subject. Too
> much difference in the two. That's probably what a story would be about.
> [Could you make one up?] I've got to go get Billy [her son]. What time is it?
> [She is encouraged to tell a story.] Okay. This is a patient coming in and—for
> treatment—he's been rather uncooperative during the—without hypnosis—
> so hypnosis is being tried. I just never liked the expression on this man's
> face . . . he has a distorted expression.

At the end of the second session she told this story to the card:

> I see this as the first person being very strong, especially because of the
> position of his hands and extreme passivity of the person lying down. Ac-
> tually, it doesn't look like a doctor-patient relationship. It looks more like
> two men who are equal—not equals but where the man has complete control.
> I don't know what could lead up to this type of situation though . . . I really
> can't make a story up. I don't perceive it as a doctor-patient relationship, but
> I can't think of what would lead up to this situation.

Discussion

In the first illustration, the conscious reference to hypnotic darkness and the
comparison of hypnosis to a rainy day are characterized as pleasant and
agreeable, although the effort at denial wears thin. She must explicitly dissociate the depressive connotations of rain from the hypnotic experience itself.
However, in the TAT story, darkness is now associated with a shabby room
and the hypnotic experience is likened to a windstorm that forces her to sur-
render to its superior power.

In the second illustration, the agreeable hypnotic experience, which was
better than sleep and helped alleviate a tension headache, is in marked contrast to the dead person who cannot be brought back to life by the mad scientist whose grandiosity is thwarted by the dead subject. In one of her "silly
dreams" that she could only recall in hypnosis the subject dreamed about a
play she was in. It was a rehearsal at which the actors mouthed but could
not speak their lines out loud. In one of her associations to the dream she

recalled how the director had been angry with the cast about their performance. She was obediently fulfilling her hypnotic role by recalling a dream in hypnosis, but it was a dream in which she was depicting a form of passive resistance. This dream is brought to its logical conclusion in the TAT story: rather death than yield. Certainly, these extremes are indicative of much conflict and discomfort.

In the third illustration, the hypnotic passivity stressed by the subject was likened to a satisfying sense of relaxation; yet in both of her TAT stories she was in much open conflict about the issue of submission, and passivity in these stories is given a negative connotation.

In all three illustrations, the conscious experience of hypnosis as positive and agreeable is reversed in the TAT stories. For his idealization as hypnotist, the experimenter suffers demonization in the subject's unconscious. This kind of extreme shift in the experience of experimental subjects was all the more striking in view of the close proximity in time between the hypnotic state and the interview.

Of the 20 stories obtained from the subjects, only 3 could readily be rated as positive in content, while 11 were strikingly negative, and 6 could be described as ambivalent. The previous case illustrations provide 3 instances of negative stories.

In order to provide some basis for comparison, I selected 13 subjects, all women, of approximately the same age and background, who had participated in a nonhypnotic experiment. The "hypnosis" card was administered as part of the TAT, and the TAT as part of a battery of psychodiagnostic tests.

Of these 13 women, 5 gave stories that could be described as positive and only 1 gave an entirely negative story, while 7 gave ambivalent stories. The following story was told by a young woman in her early twenties and is typical of the positive themes told by this group of subjects:

> The man lying down has known for some time he must have an operation for cancer. It will be a very painful operation. And due to the nature of it, it has been decided he will undergo the operation under hypnosis. In order to prepare him for this he must be hypnotized many times—to assure that the hypnotic trance during the operation will be successful. At the present time he is being hypnotized. He's not afraid, but he's having difficulty relaxing as shown by one knee slightly raised. The doctor talks to him gently and slowly he goes under. Being under hypnosis the doctor gives several suggestions such as he can raise his leg and hold it for several seconds, that pin pricks don't hurt, etc. When awakened, he finds it's really true. During each successive try he becomes more and more confident. The operation is a success and with hypnotic suggestion he suffers little pain. Successful.

The stories to the "hypnosis" card told by highly cooperative, experienced hypnotic subjects, when compared to those of this group of nonhypnotized subjects, tended to be extremely negative in content and were often accompanied by some negative affect and difficulty in telling the story. The hypnotic experience, far from relaxing them as they would like to believe, had stirred deeper feelings and attitudes, which were manifesting themselves in these TAT stories.

I would like to suggest that it is not enough to cite the existence of ambivalent attitudes toward hypnosis in order to explain the contrast between the conscious experience of hypnosis and the projected feelings about hypnosis presented by these subjects. Certainly in telling a TAT story it is possible for most people—and in particular nonpatients—to defend against the emergence of strongly negative feelings and attitudes. This could be expected when there is such an obvious relationship between the content of the card and an immediately preceding experience. Hardly more than 15 minutes before the interview and story, the subject had been most successfully hypnotized. She was then handed a card, which all the subjects immediately interpreted as a scene depicting hypnosis. Thus far it was all conscious. Yet, a significant number of subjects chose to tell a bitterly negative story about hypnosis. I believe this is an instance where the message *is* the medium: these subjects wished to communicate something about their hypnotic experiences that they were unable to convey in any other way. In the interview, questions about hypnosis were too closely related to the hypnotic experience itself, and criticism would have been too direct and guilt-provoking. But with the slight yet significant distance offered by the TAT picture, a veritable outpouring of negative feeling was forthcoming. These women wished to convey in a way that could remain politely disguised that they were angered and disappointed about the hypnotic experience. They were as women scorned.

Obviously, there is a discrepancy between the conscious experience of hypnosis and the feelings and needs it awakened. The subject in an hypnotic experiment has a strong conscious wish to cooperate, but in addition I would like to suggest that the regressive impact of the hypnotic induction awakens an equally strong temptation to submit. I am not mainly referring to a sexual temptation but to the more infantile longing to be loved and cared for and to have one's troubles washed away. Once the experience is over and nothing of the kind has happened, frustration and anger are to be expected. But perhaps more important than this reaction itself, which is already part of a process of reconstitution, is the intense conflict and anxiety that must be present in the hypnotic state itself.

The position I am taking here is in contrast to one taken by Orne (1965a), who stressed that the "neutral experimental manner" of the hypnotist-investigator guarantees that no emotional untoward effects will occur. He stated "that the induction of hypnosis itself does not lead to untoward consequences if it is perceived as relatively episodic. . .if the subject does not expect to be changed in any way and does not perceive the procedure as directed personally toward him" (p. 228). I would like to suggest that the very nature of the hypnotic induction results in the subject experiencing the "procedure as directed personally toward him." Gill and Brenman (1961) have described at some length the intrinsic regressive influence of the hypnotic induction itself. They emphasized, in particular, the way in which an induction disrupts the individual's normal adaptation to inner and outer stimuli and temporarily transforms a relatively impersonal acquaintanceship into an intense relationship that invites transferences. Gill and Brenman described in terms quite at variance with Orne's cool assessment what the hypnotic subject experiences in an experiment:

> The hypnotic subject in any research usually has an air of expectation, if not eagerness, that goes far beyond his simple intellectual curiosity—an air which reflects the atmosphere created by the hypnotist. The unspoken communication on a surface level might be: "Abdicate your usual powers; put yourself in my hands and I will open some of your inner doors so that you may have a glimpse of what lies beyond them." On a deeper level, we have come to believe the appeal is to that universal infantile core which longs for such a wholesale abdication. There is from the beginning a kind of unconscious emotional barter. [p. 11].

What is "episodic" is the occasion, not its impact. Although Orne noted the fact that fewer than 5 per cent of hypnotic subjects develop symptoms, this in itself is not the major issue (although it might be of interest to find out how many subjects would volunteer to be hypnotized if they were told in advance that they stood a 1 in 20 chance of developing symptoms). We would anticipate on the basis of clinical evidence that for every person who develops a symptom quite a few more are deeply troubled and try to master the disturbance in other ways. My main point would be that the hypnotist-experimenter must exercise much greater *continuing* concern for his hypnotized subject than to observe for and inquire into symptoms.

I recognize that the data I have presented do not constitute a formal study. Other explanations need to be considered. The subjects were all hypnotized by the same hypnotist. Could the results be due to his particular personality or way of inducing hypnosis? Or, could this type of ambivalence be characteristic of good hypnotic subjects? Would these subjects have told the same kind of story before they were hypnotized as they told immediately afterwards? These questions can only be answered empirically. To answer them affirmatively at this point would be to close the door on the need for a more careful examination of the effects of hypnosis on experimental subjects. It might very well be worthwhile to conduct a study in which various means for assessing conscious and unconscious attitudes toward hypnosis were studied before and after hypnosis. In particular, it might be useful to have an experimenter other than the hypnotist interview subjects and to administer projective tests which can then be interpreted and rated independently.

Once having stated this, I would like to conclude by pointing to another and quite different implication of these observations for the experimental use of hypnosis. The induction of hypnosis does not merely affect part functions such as perception and memory, but alters the state of the ego, the level of drive activation, the mode of thought and, most important, object relations. As such, it is an important tool for investigating these very important processes. Stross and I (Stross & Shevrin, 1969) reviewed a number of experimental studies including our own from this point of view. Because of its great potential value for research, it is all the more important that the regressive impact of hypnosis be kept in the forefront of the experimenter's mind so that the knowledge he seeks should not result in distress for those from whom the knowledge is obtained and for whose ultimate benefit the knowledge is intended.

Summary

In clinical work the dialectic between what is consciously and unconsciously desired constitutes an important counterpoint. Conscious fears turn out to be unconscious wishes. The therapist is always alert to this possibility and is oriented to helping a patient uncover and understand this seemingly paradoxical relationship. But the hypnotized experimental subject is invited to cooperate in an impersonal scientific venture in which a highly demanding and regressive *personal* relationship will be introduced. Under these circumstances, the desire to cooperate, present in most intelligent laymen, may be strongly augmented by the unconscious temptation to submit. Conflict and anxiety may thus be intensified by the very act of hypnotizing subjects in experimental settings.

Data from clinical interviews conducted with hypnotized experimental subjects, including the "hypnosis" card of the TAT, suggest that subjects who consciously talk about the relaxed, comfortable aspect of hypnosis are prone to tell stories in which the Svengali aspects of the hypnotist are stressed. The muscular relaxation often described by hypnotized subjects may have the unconscious significance of submission both for the subjects and the hypnotist. It may be wise to assume that every hypnotized subject is in a state of conflict as compared with nonhypnotized subjects. Projective tests following experimental hypnotic sessions may reveal greater conflict and anxiety in hypnotized subjects as compared to nonhypnotized subjects. Conflict and anxiety may generate an angry, disappointed reaction, which is neither beneficial for the subject nor for the future of research on hypnosis.

Philip Zimbardo *is Professor of Psychology at Stanford University where he is director of the Social Psychology training program and Co-Director with Ernest R. Hilgard of the Hypnosis Research Center. His advanced degrees were received from Yale University (Ph.D., 1959), where he was trained in "hard" experimental psychology (by Neal Miller, Frank Beach, and Fred Sheffield) as well as in "soft" social-cognitive psychology (by Carl Hovland and A. R. Cohen among others). His experience with hypnosis began when he assisted Milton Rosenberg with his study of affective-cognitive changes in attitudes induced by way of hypnosis. He took formal training in hypnosis at the Morton Prince Clinic for Hypnotherapy and advanced training under Paul Sacerdote. He is himself a "good hypnotic subject," and believes that extensive training is necessary to achieve a condition of deep hypnosis. He has coauthored* Psychology and Life, (8th ed.), Influencing Attitudes and Changing Behavior, Canvassing for Peace, *and has edited* The Cognitive Control of Motivation.

Christina Maslach *is an Assistant Professor of Psychology at the University of California at Berkeley. She received her Ph.D. from Stanford University in 1971. She has collaborated on a book with Philip Zimbardo and Ebbe B. Ebbesen,* Influencing Attitudes and Changing Behavior. *Her research interests include the dynamics of individuation and deindividuation, the effect of unexplained arousal, and the use of hypnosis in autonomic control.*

Gary Marshall *received his Ph.D. in 1972 from Stanford University, where he was associated with the Laboratory of Hypnosis Research. His research interests include the behavioral and physiological significance of imagery, an information-processing approach to hypnotic phenomena, and the internal-external and voluntary-involuntary controls of phenomenological reality.*

Zimbardo, Maslach, and Marshall *present three exploratory studies in which hypnosis is used as a tool for studying cognitive control over psychological and bodily functions. The first study deals with the cognitive control of skin temperature by hypnotic suggestions. They found that hypnotic subjects were able to produce different skin temperature in their two hands while waking control subjects could not. The second study deals with hypnotic time distortions. The subjective changes in time perception were behaviorally indexed by a special time-based operant reinforcement schedule requiring continuous adjustment. The third experiment was a partial replication of the 1962 Schachter and Singer study on the emotional labeling of unexplained drug-induced physiological arousal. It was found that hypnosis was effective in inducing arousal symptoms as well as amnesia for the cause of the arousal. However, this unexplained arousal always resulted in negative emotional states, regardless of whether the available cues in the situation were positive or negative.*

19

Hypnosis and the Psychology of Cognitive and Behavioral Control

PHILIP ZIMBARDO, CHRISTINA MASLACH, AND
GARY MARSHALL

"You do what you like. Or is it possible you have ever
not done what you liked—or even, maybe, what
you didn't like? What somebody else liked, in short?
Hark ye, my friend, that might be a pleasant change
for you, to divide up the willing and the doing and
stop tackling both jobs at once. Division of labour,
sistema american, sa! For instance, suppose you
were to show your tongue to this select and honourable
audience here—your whole tongue, right down to
the roots?"
"No, I won't," said the youth, hostilely. "Sticking
out your tongue shows a bad bringing-up."
"Nothing of the sort," retorted Cipolla. "You would
only be doing it. With all due respect to your
bringing-up, I suggest that before I count ten, you will
perform a right turn and stick out your tongue at the
company here further than you knew yourself
that you could stick it out."
He gazed at the youth, and his piercing eyes seemed
to sink deeper into their sockets. "Uno!" said he.
He had let his riding-whip slide down his arm and
made it whistle once through the air. The boy faced
about and put out his tongue so long, so extendedly,
that you would see it was the very uttermost in tongue
which he had to offer. Then turned back, stony-faced
to his former position.
Mario and the Magician, THOMAS MANN

These studies were financially supported by ONR research grant N00014-67-A-
0112-0041 to Professor P. Zimbardo, supplemented by funds from NIMH grant
03859-09 to Professor E. R. Hilgard.

If man cannot control himself, his environment, and to some extent the reactions of others, he lives with the threat of being overwhelmed by a mind rebelling, a body refusing to obey, a world extracting exorbitant "protection money" to allow him merely to survive, and a community being indifferent or hostile to his needs. Man's central pursuit, therefore, is knowledge of what factors control him and his destiny, and how he can gain a measure of control over them.

Hypnosis is a process in which the issues of control become salient, since it enables new forms of control to be created and old forms to be suspended or destroyed. As we read the tale of *Mario and the Magician* we are almost convinced that we could not be made so easily to act against our will—but not completely so. This element of doubt is precisely what has made hypnosis one of the most fascinating and frightening psychological experiences. Could the mere utterance of a few words by another person exert such powerful control over *your* behavior? You want to believe not, and in fact, many people live with the illusion of the dominance of their personal control over situational control.

Typically we center the locus of causality for our own behavior within ourselves, preferring to believe in our invulnerability to most situational forces, especially nonphysical, psychological ones. Milgram's (1963) research on blind obedience to authority helps shatter this myth. The subtle forces that operate in interpersonal situations can override the motives or values of the individual so much so that he continually follows instructions to harm a stranger, all the while protesting that he can not continue to obey. Inducing a majority of people to inflict pain upon a fellow man appears to require only the legitimization of this antisocial behavior by an authority figure in a white laboratory coat operating under the sanctions of "science."

However, looked at from a different perspective, if words can alter experience and modify behavior, if hypnosis somehow potentiates this effect, and if these words can be incorporated into auto-suggestion, then individuals have at their command a way to introduce control where they thought none was possible, or to countermand controls that apparently compel determined reactions.

In our view, the most fundamental characterization of hypnosis is that it is a unique state of consciousness developed through training experiences (either informally in life situations or formally via induction training programs). Various properties of the state permit alterations in the attribution of causality such that, for example, a physically intense shock does not produce pain, sniffing ammonia does not cause an aversive withdrawal response, or a psychedelic experience is generated without drugs—all through appropriate verbal suggestions. The hypnotic subject comes to believe that he or she can control perception, learning, memory, physiology, and other processes, making them independent of extrinsic stimulus control. In addition, such people will accept as a valid representation of reality their inability to control functions normally subjugated to personal, inner domination, such as moving one's finger, opening one's eyelids, or saying one's own name.

As social psychologists, we are primarily interested in the basic questions underlying the control of human behavior across a number of theoretically and practically relevant situations. We see hypnosis as a valuable methodological tool for the social psychologist to use in manipulating levels of reality, converting hypothetical constructs into operationally sound independent variables, and in creating a psychological state that facilitates genuine involvement by the subject in experimental procedures. As students of hypnosis, we are also concerned with understanding the control mechanisms it engages, with the processes whereby words, thoughts, images, physiological reactions, and behavioral actions are translated from one action code to another, and with helping to demonstrate the validity of the changes induced through hypnosis.

The research reported in this chapter represents a preliminary attempt to integrate our basic interest in cognitive and behavioral control processes with our interest in hypnosis as a method and as an independent area of inquiry.

Previous research has established the influence that cognitive variables (such as choice, justification, and dissonance) can exert on biological and psychological motives (Zimbardo, 1969). The first of our studies extends this interest in cognitive control to an attempt at controlling an autonomic function—skin temperature—by means of hypnotic suggestions.

The second study reported reflects our conviction that one of the most potent yet least recognized variables controlling behavior is time, or our temporal sense. The aspect of time that will be considered is temporal awareness (Lehmann, 1967). We are studying this aspect of time experimentally in terms of the awareness of the rate at which events occur, what might be called the tempo of life. Intervention in man's normal perception of clock time may have far-reaching consequences for changing pathological conditions and deficient performances that depend upon rate of functioning. This study employs the rather precise index of behavior modification provided by operant conditioning recording techniques.

A now classic study by Schachter and Singer (1962) demonstrated the importance of environmental-cognitive cues in determining the nature (and labeling) of emotions experienced under conditions of drug-induced physiological arousal. Subjects ignorant of the true source of their arousal were likely to act either in a "euphoric" manner or to become "angry" contingent upon the emotional behavior of another person (an experimental confederate). We had hoped to replicate this finding of the "plasticity" of emotional experience and to extend their findings by using hypnosis in place of the epinephrine injections for inducing the central state of unexplained arousal. However, our observations and data forced us to expand our focus to recognize, as of even greater importance, the pervasive role of unexplained arousal in creating emotional pathology.

Before describing each of these studies individually, we should mention briefly their common features of subject selection and formal hypnotic training. All subjects were undergraduates at Stanford University, recruited through the introductory psychology course. They participated in our training program and in the experiments voluntarily, being paid for each hour of participation. The subjects were selected from among the high scorers on a modified version of the Harvard Group Scale of Hypnotic Susceptibility (HGSHS, Shor & Orne, 1962), and randomly assigned to training or no-training groups. The no-training groups for some of the studies were divided into a group instructed to simulate hypnosis and a control group given the same task instructions without hypnosis or simulation suggestions. Both males and females were used in every group in each of the four studies, their data being combined in the absence of any statistically significant differences between them.

The hypnotic training, which averaged about 10 hours per subject, was conducted in small groups varying in size from two to eight per session. The group procedure is a standard part of our training approach because of its efficiency, because subjects usually find it more reassuring especially early in training, and because it allows the hypnotist to bring to bear additional social forces upon the occasional subject who is recalcitrant, "slow," or not confident in his or her ability to experience hypnosis. Our training is permissive in orientation, stressing the subject's choice to follow each suggestion, and directed toward getting the subject to achieve self-hypnosis (compare Zimbardo, Rapaport, & Baron, 1969). It also attempts to be personal, to establish a relationship of trust and mutual respect between hypnotist and subjects.

Many different induction techniques are used over the course of training (during which time the subjects were exposed to all three of us in our capacity as hypnotists). However, common to the verbal and nonverbal techniques was the development of a state of very deep relaxation. The training program sampled a wide variety of hypnotic experiences and included as a criterion test the successful completion of posthypnotic suggestions with accompanying amnesia, as well as increased ischemic pain tolerance (a measure developed by John Lenox, 1970a).

Control of Complex Skin Temperature

Maintenance of a relatively constant level of body temperature is a vital physiological function in man. It is so efficient and automatic that we become aware of the process only when pathological internal conditions cause us to react with fever or chills and when extremes of environmental conditions markedly alter the skin temperature of our limbs. To what extent can such a basic regulatory function be brought under volitional control?

In 1938, the Russian scientist A. R. Luria performed an interesting experiment that bears directly upon this question. He had been studying the remarkable mental feats of a man who appeared to have eidetic imagery. Apparently, his subject not only had "photographic memory," but could induce such vivid visual images that they exerted a profound influence on his behavior. When he was instructed to modify the skin temperature in his hands, it took only several minutes before he had made one hand hotter than it had been by two degrees, while the other became colder by one and a half degrees. These changes were attributed by the subject to the "reality" of his visual images: "I saw myself put my right hand on a hot stove. . .Oi, was it hot! So, naturally, the temperature of my hand increased. But I was holding a piece of ice in my left hand. I could see it there and began to squeeze it. And, of course, my hand got colder" (Luria, 1968, pp. 140–41).

Is such a phenomenon replicable with "normal" individuals not born with the remarkably developed eidetic ability of this man? We were led to believe so on the basis of converging research findings coming from three rather different sources: visceral learning, cognitive control of motivation, and hypnosis.

Neal Miller and his associates at The Rockefeller University (1969a, b) have recently demonstrated that the control over skeletal muscle responses through operant conditioning procedures can be extended to responses of the glands and viscera. Their work has generated the powerful conclusion that any discriminable response that is emitted by any part of the body can be learned if its occurrence is followed by reinforcement. "Learning" here refers to the change in frequency of making a specific response (such as cardiac acceleration or deceleration, or glandular secretion) when that change has as its consequence electrical stimulation in the pleasure center of the animal's hypothalamus. Miller believes that such results "force us to the radical reorientation of thinking of glandular visceral behavior, which ordinarily is concealed inside the body, in exactly the same way as we think of the externally more easily observable skeletal behavior" (Miller, 1969b, p. 11).

As mentioned earlier, Zimbardo and his colleagues (1969) have demonstrated that biological drives, as well as social motives, may be brought under the control of cognitive variables such as choice and justification. Subjects modified the impact of a host of drive stimuli at subjective, behavioral, and physiological levels, in the process of resolving an "irrational," dissonant commitment (such as not to eat when hungry, or to expose oneself to a noxious stimulus without adequate justification for doing so).

It appeared to us that hypnosis: (a) is a state in which the effects of cognitive processes on bodily functioning are amplified; (b) enables the subject to perceive the locus of causality for mind and body control as more internally centered and volitional; (c) is often accompanied by a heightened sense of visual imagery; and (d) can lead to intensive concentration and elimination of distractions. For these reasons, it should be possible for well-trained hypnotic subjects to gain control over regulation of their own skin temperature without either external reinforcement or even external feedback. There have been a few scattered attempts to control temperature through hypnosis or other methods (Chapman, Goodell, & Wolff, 1959; Green, Green, & Walters, 1970; McDowell, 1963). However, they have often lacked adequate controls and tend to focus on a single aspect of temperature modification, such as unidirectional changes.

Our present study was exploratory in nature and attempted to demonstrate that hypnotic subjects would be able to achieve simultaneous alteration of skin temperature in opposite directions in their two hands, while waking control subjects would not. The response of one hand getting hotter than normal, while the other gets colder, was chosen in order to rule out any simple notion of activation or prior learning, and to control for any naturally occuring changes in skin temperature, such as cold hands gradually warming up over time.

METHOD

Three of our trained hypnotic subjects were tested in a specially designed room in the Laboratory of Dermatology Research at the Stanford Medical Center. The ambient temperature in this room was automatically regulated to maintain a constant level. Ten thermocouples of copper constantin were taped to identical sites on the ventral surface of the two hands and forearms of the subjects. Both room and skin temperatures were continuously monitored by a Honeywell recording system, which printed them out directly in degrees centigrade. The subjects lay on beds with their arms resting comfortably at their sides and with open palms extended upward in exactly the same position. This posture was maintained throughout the session, and there was no overt body movement.

The instructions, which were delivered over an intercom, began with approximately 10 minutes of hypnotic induction. After the subjects were deeply hypnotized (according to their self-reports), they were asked to focus attention on their hands. They were then told to make an arbitrarily selected hand hotter, and the other colder, than normal. They were also given suggestions of several images that could be useful in producing this effect, and were encouraged to generate personal imagery and commands that might be necessary to achieve the desired result. Typically, the subject lay in silence for the duration of the testing session (which averaged about 10 minutes). The final instruction was to normalize the temperature in both hands by returning it to the initial baseline level.

Each of the subjects participated in two or three such sessions. In addition, one of the subjects (Zimbardo) completed two sessions utilizing autohypnosis. Communication between him and the experimenter occurred only to demarcate the various procedural stages being experienced.

Six waking control subjects also participated in each of two experimental sessions. The procedure was identical to that employed with the hypnotic subjects, except that they were not given any prior hypnotic training or the hypnotic induction during the experiment. The control group consisted of three male and three female undergraduate paid volunteers from the introductory psychology course at Stanford University. The hypnotized subjects, other than the senior author, were coeds drawn from the same population. All of the subjects were, of course, aware that the purpose of the research was to assess whether skin temperature could be altered through verbal instructions and imagery.

RESULTS

All of the hypnotic subjects demonstrated the ability to significantly alter localized skin temperature. Large differences (as much as 4° C.) between identical skin sites on opposite hands appeared within two minutes of the verbal suggestion, were maintained for the entire testing period, and then

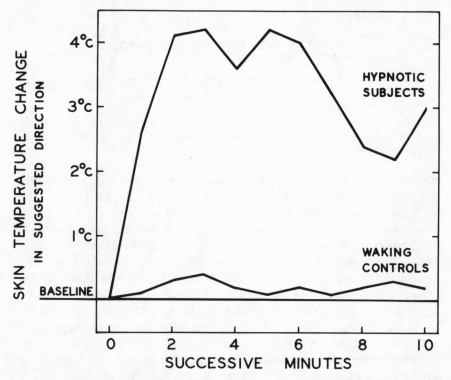

FIGURE 19.1. *Mean algebraic sum of bilateral skin temperature differences. ("Successful" directional changes in each hand were weighted positively, while changes which were opposite to the suggested direction were weighted negatively.)*

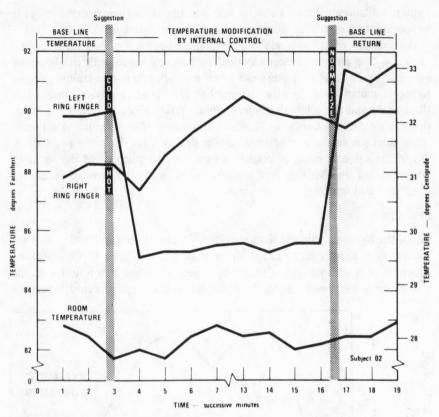

FIGURE 19.2. *Simultaneous modification of skin temperature in opposite directions in the right and left hands (omitted minutes 8–12 are no different from the rest of the modification period).*

were rapidly eliminated upon the suggestion to normalize skin temperature. Temperature decreases in the "cold" hand were generally much larger than the increases in the "hot" hand, the largest decrease being 7°C., while the largest increase was 2°C. In contrast, none of the waking control subjects were able to achieve such divergent changes in the temperature of their hands. The magnitude of the consistent changes produced by the hypnotic subjects was considerably greater than the slight fluctuations shown by the controls. The between-group differences illustrated in Figure 19.1 are highly reliable beyond the .001 level of significance ($t = 14.27$, $df = 7$).

When we examine the individual patterns of reaction in the hypnotized subjects, it becomes even more apparent that they were able to exert a considerable degree of control over the temperature of their two hands. The subject's data shown in Figure 19.2 reveal how, following the suggestion to make her left hand colder and right hand hotter (opposite to their relative baseline position), she rapidly "drove" them in the appropriate directions.

After maintaining the separation for more than 10 minutes, she reestablished the initial baseline difference as soon as she was given the instruction to normalize her skin temperature. Since there was no overlap in the temperature distributions of the two hands, the obtained differences from minute 4 to minute 16 were extremely significant ($p < .001$, within-subject $t = 20.18$, $df = 12$).

All of the hypnotic subjects reported great difficulty in performing this task due to the intensive concentration, extreme dissociation, and novel experience involved. Two of the subjects could not achieve a separation between the temperature of their two hands on the first day of testing, although they could vary both in conjunction. From analysis of the pattern of temperature changes and introspective reports, it appears that three different cognitive strategies were used to achieve these effects. The most frequent one was "unequal parallel shifts"—the temperature in the two hands increased or decreased in a similar direction, but at a faster rate in one of the two hands. A "holding and spreading" approach was used to focus most attention on changing the temperature of one hand and, once changed, to hold it steady while driving the temperature in the other hand away. The technique that appeared to be most difficult, but was effectively used for at least several minutes during each testing session, was "simultaneous divergence." Here the two hands seemed to act independently, with the arbitrarily chosen one getting hotter than normal, and the other becoming colder than normal.

Different types of imagery were generated by the subjects during the sessions in order to help produce the desired effect. Some of the imagery involved realistic experiences, such as having one hand in a bucket of ice water while the other was under a heat lamp. Other imagery had a more symbolic or fantasy quality: the "hot" hand was getting red with anger over something the "cold" hand did, and the "cold" hand was getting white with fear over this angry reaction. However, it seems that at times the most dramatic divergences in skin temperature were produced by imageless commands given independently to each hand: "You become hot, you become cold". All of the waking control subjects reported trying hard to meet the experimental demand, and generating assorted imagery for that purpose. Several even believed they had done so effectively, although as we noted the largest divergence was but a fraction of a degree.

Although we are not yet in a position to characterize the physiological mechanisms responsible for the control of skin temperature that we have shown, we believe that the role of hypnosis in the process is quite understandable. The research by Miller on visceral learning has stressed the important function served by curare in paralyzing the skeletal musculature of the animals. At first, this methodological control was thought to be necessary only to rule out possible influences of skeletal muscle responding on glandular and visceral responding. However, it now appears that curarizing the subjects may serve a more basic function: "It is possible that curare may help to maintain a constant stimulus situation and/or to shift the animal's attention from distracting skeletal activities to the relevant visceral ones" (Miller, 1969b, p. 19).

We would argue that the effects of hypnosis are analagous to those of curare, since hypnosis provides a set of training conditions that permit a greater than normal degree of generalized relaxation, removal of distracting stimuli, and enhanced concentration upon a given, relevant dimension. Hypnotic training may also aid in the control of experiential, behavioral, and physiological processes by increasing the subject's confidence in his ability to exert such control and by altering consciousness to the point that words and images can be more readily translated into a code language to which he is physiologically responsive.

While we feel this research demonstrates the fine degree of control it is possible for people to exert over one aspect of their autonomic nervous system, it is, nevertheless, a pilot study. The findings need to be replicated, additional measures must be introduced to discover how the instructional input yields the temperature difference output, and variations in type of feedback, imagery, and extent of practice should be incorporated into subsequent work.

To us, the significance of research in this area is less in understanding how hypnosis per se operates, but rather how human beings "naturally" learn to induce ulcers, tachycardia, excessive and uncontrolled sweating, and other forms of psychosomatic illness. Miller's work suggests that the intervention and modification of such reactions follow principles of operant conditioning. Our work adds the possibility that the sources of reinforcement in both producing and changing psychosomatic symptomatology may be cognitive in nature. Therapeutic control may thus be best achieved by combining the precision of reinforcement contingencies with the power of a more pervasive cognitive approach to dealing with such mind-body interactions.

Hypnotic Modification of Time Awareness or Tempo

To understand better the influence that time exerts on behavior and human thought, psychologists have begun to study the effects upon the subjective experience of time in response to psychedelic drugs, variations in stimulus sequencing, and stimulus "overload" (see Ornstein, 1970). But a more direct technique of interfering with the naturally occurring experience of time is provided by hypnosis. Aldous Huxley's fictional description in his book *Island* (1962) extols the potential benefits of distorting time through hypnotic suggestion.

> And it's in very deep trance—and only in very deep trance—that a person can be taught how to distort time. . . . One starts by learning how to ex-

perience twenty seconds as ten minutes, a minute as half an hour. In deep trance, it's really very easy. You listen to the teacher's suggestions and you sit there quietly for a long, long time. Two full hours—you'd be ready to take your oath on it. When you've been brought back, you look at your watch. Your experience of two hours was telescoped into exactly four minutes of clock time. . . . For example . . . here's a mathematical problem. In your normal state it might take you the best part of half an hour to solve. But now you distort time to the point where one minute is subjectively the equivalent of thirty minutes. Then you set to work on the problem. Thirty subjective minutes later it's solved. But thirty subjective minutes are one clock minute. . . . You can imagine what happens when somebody with a genius IQ is also capable of time distortion. The results are fantastic. (Pp. 210–11)

Cooper and Erickson (1950) have attempted to manipulate time awareness, or tempo, in much the manner described by Huxley. Hypnotic subjects were told that they would have a certain number of minutes of "special" time in which to execute some task. In actual clock time, they were given only several seconds, but many of the subjects reported experiencing the appropriate amount of time, indicating that those periods of time were filled at a phenomenological level with many activities. However, again only subjective data were used, and studies that have measured performance increments have generally yielded negative findings (Barber & Calverley, 1964g; Casey, 1966; Edmonston & Erbeck, 1967). The inherent difficulty of demonstrating that the subject is "really" experiencing time distortion by using performance increments is pointed up by Fischer (1967), who notes that it is possible to have "increased data content" with "*no* proportional increase in data processing and/or data reduction" (p. 451).

Before Aldous Huxley's vision of an improved educational technology based upon controlled modification of time awareness can be realized, it is necessary to demonstrate that more than subjective experience is being changed by such procedures. If time is perceived as existing in a new relationship to the occurrence of certain events, then behavioral measures that are sensitive to *rate of responding* should reveal this altered perception.

If a reinforcing stimulus event is contingent upon the rate at which a given response is emitted, then altering the time base should affect frequency of responding. In a situation where two responses per second (2/1) are required to generate a given stimulus event, then if perception of the time base were altered, frequency of response should change correspondingly. If one second of objective, or "clock" time were subjectively experienced as two seconds, for example, then the individual should emit twice as many responses as previously (4/1) in attempting to maintain the same stimulus event.

Since the electronic relay circuits involved in such an apparatus operate on real time parameters, a person operating on a subjective time dimension that was out of synchrony with real time would not be able to obtain or maintain the reinforcing state.

Since many of the consequences of our behavior are a function of the rate at which we perform certain classes of responses, modification of time awareness—speeding up or slowing down of perceived tempo—should have a profound effect on our adjustment to important environmental contingencies that depend upon our rate of responding.

In the research to be described, we attempted to modify one aspect of man's internal time machine, his awareness of tempo, or rate of movement of time, by means of hypnotic suggestion. The assumed changes in internal processes were measured "by analyzing the frequency, duration, and degree of their interference with a more easily measured process" (Lindsley, 1957, p. 1290). That more easily measured process was the rate of emission of a simple operant response, pressing a telegraph key. The operant response in turn, was part of a unique schedule of reinforcement—conjugate reinforcement—developed by Ogden Lindsley. Traditional reinforcement schedules are essentially "episodic"; trials are discrete events in which the subject works, obtains a reinforcement, consumes it, then resumes responding. The conjugate schedule more nearly approximates a dynamic interaction between behavior and the environment: changes in behavior change some part of the environment, while these stimulus changes feed back on the subject's behavior to maintain, intensify or reduce it.

For example, in the process of tuning in a favorite TV program that is out of focus, one turns a fine tuning dial until the desired level of clarity is reached, then stops fiddling with the controls and sits back to enjoy the program. But suppose TV sets were constructed so that once the image one wanted were clear (the reinforcing state of affairs), one had to continue to respond in order to keep it that way. Suppose a person had to learn to press a lever at a given rate (presses/unit time) to control the clarity of the stimulus. Pressing too fast or too slow would adversely affect stimulus presentation, and such changes in the stimulus would be cues to him that his rate of response was not appropriate. If the reinforcing state of affairs were desirable, he would learn to optimize the function relating how much work he would put out continuously for how much stimulus clarity he would find necessary. In fact, it would then be possible to measure just how desirable the reinforcement was in terms of this function.

Many interpersonal situations can be characterized as feedback loops of the kind illustrated in a conjugate reinforcement schedule. Our behavior changes some aspect of another person, and our perception of these changes (for example, degree of attentiveness to what we are saying) feeds back to maintain our behavior (if the attentiveness is appropriate), intensify it (if boredom begins to show), or reduce it (if the reaction is too intense). In a responsive environment behavior is modulated according to feedback from changes in a target stimulus, and must remain in a state of continual modulation as long as the target stimulus continues to change. Thus while behavior is under stimulus control, the stimulus is under behavioral control, and the relationship between them is established according to some temporal function relating response to reinforcement.

Zimbardo, Ebbesen, and Fraser (1971) have developed an apparatus and technique that uses the rate of emission of a simple external response (key pressing) as an objective index of subjective states. They have demonstrated the validity of this approach to assessing preferences and attitudes as well as the impact of social and physical stimuli on behavior. In the present study, we have used this same approach to evaluate the impact of induced time distortion on behavior in a situation where behavior is related to stimulus feedback as a function of a (time-based) rate of responding.

METHOD

Three groups of subjects were used for this study—hypnosis *(N = 12),* simulators *(N = 6),* and instructed controls (N = 12). During the experiment proper, the procedure was identical for each subject; the experimenter who delivered the instructions (via an intercom to a subject in an adjacent acoustic chamber) did not know to which of the three treatment conditions the subject had been randomly assigned. Thus all subjects were given the same tempo modification instructions. Prior to the first operant trial, however, one group of subjects, who had been extensively trained in hypnosis, was given an hypnotic induction by a second experimenter. The simulation group was told to simulate the reactions of an hypnotic subject and to behave as if they were hypnotized throughout the study. The control group was given no prior instructions.

All subjects were trained to press a key at different rates in order to maintain illumination of one or another target light in a stimulus array. The first of five trials (each of 2 minutes duration) established a comfortable operant rate of responding during which the subject learned that the onset and offset of the lights was under the control of rate of key pressing. The remaining four trials were divided into baseline periods and experimental periods. On one of the baseline trials, the subject was instructed merely to keep the red light on as long as possible, which required responding at the rate of three presses per second. On the other baseline trial, the task was to keep a blue light illuminated, requiring a faster rate of six presses per second. Pressing at a slower or faster rate than required by the target stimulus lighted a light other than the reinforced colored light. The subjects knew they could satisfy the task demand by pressing faster or slower in order to reach the appropriate level and then maintaining a consistent rate.

Interspersed between the baseline trials and the experimental trials were the instructions designed to modify temporal awareness. Subjects were told about the difference between clock time and subjective time, and then were given instructions designed to modify temporal awareness. Before one of the experimental trials, each subject was told to experience time as slowing down "so that a second will seem like a minute, and a minute will seem like an hour. You will experience time slowing down now, getting slower and slower. When you have done this and your experience of time has changed, signal me [the experimenter] that the change has taken place." Before the other experimental trial, each subject was told that time was speeding up "so that an hour will seem like a minute, a minute will seem like a second. You will experience time speeding up now, getting faster and faster."

Between the two tempo modification instructions, subjects were told to normalize their experience of time. Half the subjects were given the instructions to slow time down before being told to speed it up, while for the others the sequence was reversed. During the experimental trials, neither the target light nor the stimulus array were illuminated. It was the task of the subjects therefore to press at the same rate they had used previously, "a rate which would be sufficient to keep the target light on *if* the lights were on."

A cumulative recorder provided an on-going display of the subject's rate of responding and also a record of when the target rate was reached. An Esterline-Angus event recorder indicated the sequence and duration of which light level was being activated. A series of timers recorded the total time each light level was locked in by the relay circuitry (dependent, of course, upon the subject's rate of response). The two major dependent variables to be reported are: the percentage of total time available that key pressing rate corresponded to the rates associated with the target lights, and the number of times that responding deviated from the target level to an off-target level.

RESULTS

In order to simplify presentation of the mass of data and multiple comparisons made possible by the research design we have used, some data will be combined across conditions (which are not of primary interest).

The data offer strong support for the conclusion that the subjective experience of time awareness can be experimentally modified, and that this change has measurable consequences in behavior. The modification of subjective time sense (within a relatively brief procedure) would appear to require the concentration, imaginative involvement, and suspension of usual

TABLE 19.1   Per cent of time on target (for each 2-minute period)

Treatment	baseline (A)	Slow tempo	change	baseline (B)	Fast tempo	change
Hypnosis						
(N = 6)	74	36	−38	68	28	−40
Simulation						
(N = 3)	86	77	− 9	69	66	− 3
Control						
(N = 9)	78	66	−12	71	60	−11

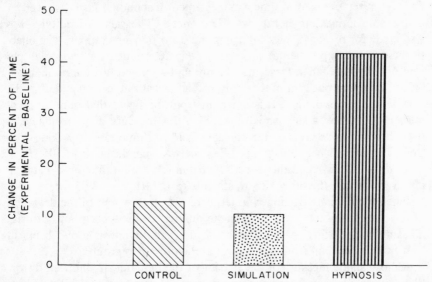

FIGURE 19.3. ´ *Mean per cent of time responding at off-target rates in direction of distortion suggestion.*

modes of analytical thinking that characterize the hypnotic experience. Only those subjects previously trained in hypnosis and in a state of hypnotic relaxation and concentration were able to translate the verbal suggestion of asynchronicity between clock time and personal time into "reality." On each of the variety of ways of analyzing the data from this experiment, the operant behavior of the hypnosis group was significantly different from that of other nonhypnotized subjects given the same time distortion suggestions, regardless of whether they were simulators or merely instructed waking controls. This conclusion is based on an analysis of change scores from a baseline level of responding to a postsuggestion level of responding. The specific nature of these induced changes is given in the following set of analyses.

Subjects in the three treatment conditions were generally equivalent in their baseline performance, pressing at a slow rate to keep one target light lighted, or at a fast rate required to maintain the other light. Following the time distortion manipulation, all groups were off target more than they had been during the baseline period. However, only the mean change for the hypnosis group was significant $(p < .01, t = 6.46, df = 5)$. The overall between-group differences in per cent of time on target (noted in Table 19.1) were significant $(p < .05, F = 4.44, df = 2, 15)$, as was the nearly four-fold difference between the hypnosis group and the other two $(p < .01, t = 3.22, df = 18)$.

A similar pattern emerges when we examine the measure of per cent of time responding at an off-target level in the specific direction suggested by the distortion instructions (reported in Figure 19.3). For each of the baseline levels, the per cent of time a subject spent responding faster, slower, or at the appropriate target rate was determined. The same trichotomy was also made for response rates following the distortion suggestions. The effectiveness of the experimental suggestions was determined by comparing per cent of time faster than target rate before and after the fast-tempo manipulation, as well as per cent of time slower than target rate before and after the slow-tempo manipulation. It is apparent from the figure that only the hypnosis group shows a substantial change on this measure of performance—over three times as great as the change of either simulators or waking controls. The overall between-group difference was significant $(p < .05, F = 4.26, df = 2, 15)$, and this effect is attributable to the difference between the hypnosis and the other two treatments $(p < .01, t = 3.05, df = 18)$.

When the data are examined in terms of the mean extent of the deviation of the tempo suggested, once again the differences between groups are significant $(p < .025, F = 5.20, df = 2, 15)$, the hypnosis group being at least twice as deviant from target level as the other two groups.

A more subtle measure of the efficacy of the hypnotically induced distortion of time awareness focuses upon patterns of response variability. In attempting to meet the experimental demand of maintaining a given operant rate of response during the baseline period, subjects would learn how to zero in on the target rate by pressing faster when a lower level light was on, and pressing slower when a higher level light was on. The number of shifts from one response level to another was recorded on the event recorder for each baseline and experimental period. If the subjects' instruction to press at the baseline target rate was more potent than the time distortion manipulation, then variations, or level shifts, should occur around the target level (for example, from level 2 to 3 or 3 to 4, or 4 to 3, etc., for target level 3). However, for those subjects for whom time had really "slowed down or speeded up," the target rate would have been shifted and thus *variability* in responding should be around this new target rather than around the original target rate. The prediction is thus that total variance will remain constant, but there will be a shift in the response distribution for the hypnotized subjects to off-initial target levels.

We have seen that subjects in the hypnosis group were more off target than those in the other groups. But in addition, their performance showed greater variation around off-target levels than around target levels (for example, from level 2 to 1, or 4 to 5 for target level 3). Table 19.2 shows that the total variation in shifts from one target level to another is equally greater for all groups in the experimental periods than in the baseline periods. This is to be expected without the extrinsic feedback provided by the illuminated target light. The simulation and control groups apparently had developed a relatively accurate sense of the appropriate target rate, but were unable to experience the tempo modification as well, since when they were off target

TABLE 19.2 Patterns of response variability (mean number of shifts to and away from target level compared to shifts within off-target levels, subtracted from baseline shifts)

Treatment	Total Variation	Variation Around Target Level	Variation Around Off-Target Levels
Hypnosis	+17.8	−13.2	+31.0
Simulation	+16.3	+18.0	− 1.7
Control	+19.0	+19.2	− 0.2

they were more likely to change their rate to return to the target level than to move to a more distant level. They show no greater variation around off-target levels during the experimental than the baseline periods. In sharp contrast, as predicted, the hypnosis group seemed to be responding to their new sense of time awareness, shifting less around the target level and very much more around the more remote levels. The hypnosis group differs significantly from both of the others on the measure of variation around the target $(p < .05, F = 4.85, df = 1, 15)$, and even more so in variation around off-target levels $(p < .001, F = 20.15, df = 1, 15)$.

Interviews with the subjects revealed that those in the simulation and instructed control groups tried to react *as if* time were speeding up or slowing down, but the demand to try to reproduce the previously appropriate level exerted a greater influence upon them. The subjects given the same time distortion instructions under hypnosis were apparently able to experience a change in time awareness. This changed perspective introduced an asynchrony between subjective time and the task-relevant clock time that in turn exerted a controlling influence on their behavior. Thus, they could not adequately relate (via rate of response behavior) to an environment programmed by objective time parameters.

Two different phenomenal experiences were reported by these subjects. For some, their time-distorted behavior seemed to be different; they found themselves responding faster or slower than they had previously, although not trying to do so consciously. For others, they were not aware of physically moving their key-pressing finger faster or slower, but the time between responses seemed to become either very long (slow tempo) or very short (fast tempo).

It seems to us that the combination provided by the power of hypnotic intervention in experience and the objective precision of the operant conditioning methodology has been effective in demonstrating the validity of inducing changes in time awareness. Our next step is to extend this approach to behaviors that are of more practical significance to the individual, such as problem solving, anxiety reduction, and perhaps affecting heart rate by changing awareness of the rate at which events occur.

Unexplained Arousal: Emotional "Plasticity" or
Emotional Pathology?

The experimental investigation of emotion has been given considerable impetus by the research of Schachter and Singer (1962), which specified the interacting components of emotional states as physiological arousal and an appropriate cognitive explanation of this arousal. They demonstrated that in the absence of an explanation for an arousal state, subjects will search the immediate environment for cognitive cues that can be used to make sense of and to label the arousal. Thus, starting with a common level of physiological activation, one subject will experience "anger" and another "euphoria," depending upon elements of the situation in which the activation occurs. These investigators used injections of epinephrine to induce the symptoms of arousal, and then either did or did not inform the subjects of this cause for their arousal.

In general, informed but aroused subjects did not react emotionally to the experimental situation, nor did unaroused subjects given placebo injections. However, uninformed arousal subjects tended to label their state as "happy" after exposure to a confederate who had acted euphoric, but as "angry" when the confederate acted angry.

Such a finding has a variety of interesting implications. It links physiological processes to social psychology via cognitive search and labeling operations; it encourages an experimental-analytical approach in studying emotion and emotional development; it underscores the learned modifiability, or situationally-determined, "plasticity" of emotion; and finally, from our point of view, a major consequence of this research is the suggestion that emotional pathology may be understood as a "successful yet unsuccessful" attempt by the individual to explain feelings of unexplained arousal or discontinuities in experience and behavior.

For these reasons, it seems obvious that independent replication of the Schachter and Singer study is necessary before we can accept the validity of its conclusions and extend them. Surprisingly, a review of the literature reveals no published attempts to do so. This may be due to the methodological complexity of the experiment, involving as it does a team of a medical doctor, observers, and a trained confederate for each subject. In addition, there is reluctance by many psychologists, and by college committees who pass on the use of human subjects, to sanction use of drugs in research with students.

Aside from the basic independent validation required to establish the acceptability of any conclusion, closer examination of the procedure and pattern of results of this study raises questions that can only be answered empirically. Briefly, some of these problems center around the action of epinephrine, the manipulation of the causal attribution for the arousal, the programmed activity of the confederate, some of the measures used, and weak or inconsistent between-treatment differences.

To illustrate some of these issues, it can be noted that the high level dosage used (0.5 cc.) would have a sudden, powerful onset usually within two minutes of the injection. Since little has occurred in the experiment between this experience and the always salient experience of receiving an injection, it is likely that the two events will be perceived as related. The experimenter attempted to break this causal link by simply instructing the subjects that the injection of an alleged vitamin supplement would have no side effects or effects different from those experienced. This explanation would seem to be weak relative to the more obvious temporal contiguity of unusual stimulus event and unusual personal reaction. Indeed, some subjects are reported to have made this association despite the instructions, and others may have also, but not reported doing so. Such a possibility helps account for the weak between-group effects found on some measures, which in part required an internal analysis of the data to yield statistical significance. Epinephrine also has a variable decay function for different individuals, so that for some it may wear off rapidly—before the confederate is in full-blown anger or euphoria—or slowly for others. With the only measure of arousal being pulse rate, taken after the entire session, and confounded by the subject's imitative activity of the confederate, one could not assess the on-going course of the physiological arousal.

The activity of the confederates was selected to represent the extremes of an emotion continuum, anger versus euphoria, but appears rather to represent a common point of agitation on an activity dimension and "bizarreness" or unusualness on a situational-expectation dimension. Would the same conclusion hold for passive emotions such as sorrow and joy? Perhaps not, if the mechanism for labeling is the association of one's internally agitated state with the comparably agitated behavior of the confederate. Then too, the question is raised of the less standardized interaction between confederate and subject in the euphoria than in the anger condition, since the former involved greater interaction with and participation by the subject. It also follows that direct participation by the subject in "emotional activity" may be what produces the experience and labeling of emotion through self-observation, and not a cognitive appraisal of the confederate's mood as a likely explanation for one's arousal.

Finally, it should be pointed out that there was no reported assessment by the subject of the confederate's mood, and more importantly, the major dependent measure is a relative index of emotion obtained by subtracting self-ratings of anger from happiness. In some experimental conditions, subjects are described as reacting with the emotion of anger, when in fact they are only less happy than other subjects. Obviously, emotions are scaled relatively, but there is also a categorical aspect of emotions; an experience of mild anger is not functionally equivalent to one of slight happiness.

In attempting to reproduce the previous results, while modifying the procedure to improve upon some of its questionable features and perhaps strengthen the basic manipulation of not having an explanation for one's arousal, we took advantage of the utility of hypnosis.

Orne (1967) has pointed out what is both a defining characteristic of hypnosis and the key to using hypnosis as a method for studying the phenomenon of unexplained arousal and discontinuities in experience and behavior:

> What is impressive about the hypnotized subject's behavior is that he appears capable of ignoring reality, responding instead to a reality constructed in part by the hypnotist's words. In addition, he may have amnesia for the experience and may manifest the effects of hypnosis at a much later time in response to predetermined cues. Again, what impresses one about the posthypnotic suggestion is not so much that the subject carries out the behavior, but that he does not appear cognizant of the reason for doing so. (P. 210)

Thus, it should be possible to produce marked physiological changes hypnotically (as shown by Crasilneck and Hall, 1959, and Sarbin, 1956) as well as posthypnotically, and also to induce amnesia for the cause of these changes. The use of hypnosis in place of epinephrine even allows for a better degree of experimental control over the nature of the onset of the arousal. The arousal symptoms can be hypnotically conditioned to a specific situational cue, and introduced at the appropriate time during the procedure. In addition to this major methodological change, we included several other modifications: physiological recording of GSR and heart rate to assess the hypnotically induced arousal; ratings of the confederate's mood; a more standardized, more believable set of activities engaged in by the confederate in both anger and happy conditions, and a battery of emotion scales.

It was expected that these changes would strengthen the treatment differences found by Schachter and Singer, and provide a more viable methodology for further exploration of the dynamics of emotional experience.

METHOD

The experimental session was divided into two parts. The purpose of Part I was to establish an arousal response to a particular cue and to demonstrate, through physiological recording, that this arousal involved actual physiological changes. In Part II, this arousal response was either elicited or not in the presence of a confederate who was behaving happily or angrily. Several dependent measures than assessed whether the arousal was interpreted in terms of the emotion displayed by the confederate. A summary diagram of the experimental procedure is shown in Figure 19.4.

Thirty-six subjects were used in this study (21 males and 15 females from the introductory psychology subject pool). Twenty-four received hypnotic training, while 12 did not. Half of the hypnosis group was not given the cue for arousal during Part II of the experiment, while the other half,

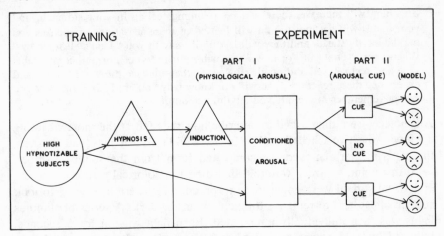

FIGURE 19.4. *Summary diagram of experiment.*

and all controls, did receive the cue. Each of these groups was divided into subgroups of 6 subjects who were then exposed to a (same sex) confederate acting happy or angry.

Part I: Physiological arousal

When each subject arrived for this study, he or she was greeted by one of the experimenters and asked to sign a "subject sheet," indicating voluntary participation in the experiment. The signature of the confederate was already on the sheet (as though he or she had arrived previously). The subject was told that the "other subject" was in the acoustic chamber, having his physiological responses recorded. He was then ushered past this room, where he could see the other experimenter busily engrossed with the recording machine. The first experimenter took him to another room and asked him to fill out a brief questionnaire. Soon after the subject completed this task, the second experimenter brought in the confederate and asked him to fill out a questionnaire. She then told the subject that it was his turn to be recorded and took him back to the acoustic chamber.

After recording electrodes were applied to the subject's arms, he was told to lean back comfortably in his chair and to follow the instructions that he would hear over the intercom. For the remainder of the period in the sound chamber, the subject's heart rate and GSR responses were continuously recorded on an Offner Type R Dynograph. The instructions were prerecorded on tape and thus were identical for all subjects.

The instructions began with a brief introduction followed by an hypnotic induction for the hypnosis subjects (this was eliminated for the unhypnotized group). All subjects then heard the following instructions:

In this session, the following reactions will occur whenever you see the word "start." When you see the word "start," your heart will beat faster, your breathing will increase, there will be a sinking feeling in your stomach, and your hands will get moist. You will feel all of these sensations as soon as you see the word "start," and they will last until I say to you "That's all for now." When I say, "That's all for now," you will return to your normal, comfortable state and feel relaxed and good. However, when you see the word "start" and experience these reactions, you will not know why you are feeling the way you are, or remember my telling you anything about it.

All subjects were then asked to describe how they felt at the moment, using a Mood-Adjective Checklist (V. Nowlis, 1963). When they had finished, the experimenter removed the completed form from the sound chamber.

At this point, subjects were told that their physiological responses to several visual stimuli were going to be recorded. They were instructed to look straight ahead and to remain sitting quietly in the dark. A series of stimulus lights was then individually illuminated. Each light was on for 5 seconds, followed by a 25-second period of darkness (this period was extended to 85-seconds for the last cue light). The first light was a red one, the second a white one, the third was labeled "stop," and the cue "start" was given as the fourth signal. At the end of the last darkness period, the subject was instructed to fill out a second Mood-Adjective Checklist, describing his feelings at that moment.

The subject was then given the cue for the disappearance of any symptoms he was experiencing and for the return to his normal physiological state and a relaxed psychological state. The suggestion about the symptoms and the word "start" (as well as the amnesia for it) was repeated, and hypnotic subjects were brought out of their hypnotic state. This concluded Part I; the electrodes were removed and the subject was brought out of the sound chamber.

Part II: Emotional cues

The experimenter took the subject back to the first room where the confederate was waiting. As they entered the room, the confederate asked the experimenter if they were going to begin the next part of the study. The experimenter than introduced the subject and the confederate to each other, and asked them to sit down at a table, which, though divided in half by a wooden partition, still enabled them to easily see each other. Before each of them was a memory drum, a learning test sheet, a folder containing bogus test materials (TAT pictures, a color-word test, pieces of a puzzle, and so forth), and some pencils. The experimenters were able to observe the subject and the confederate through a two-way mirror. An intercom system allowed the experimenters to give prerecorded instructions and to monitor the verbal interaction.

A learning task was then introduced in order to have a nonobvious way of presenting the arousal cue without either the confederate or observer being aware of the manipulation. Two 15-word lists were presented on the memory drum with a recall test after each one. The final word on the second list was either the arousal word "start" or a neutral word "speedy." Half of the hypnotic subjects got the arousal cue, the others the neutral cue. Thus with training, conditioning, and posthypnotic expectations in the two groups held constant, we could better assess the effects of the arousal cue on the behavior of the hypnotized subjects.

After the subject and the confederate had finished the recall test, they were told that the next part of the experiment would take a few minutes to be set up. It was suggested that they look through the materials in the folder while waiting for the next part to begin. They were then left alone for 4 minutes. During this period, the confederate went through a prearranged series of either "angry" behavior or "happy" behavior.

The confederate's behavior followed the same pattern in both the angry and happy conditions, although the content was different. During the first minute, he worked with the folder materials and made a few comments to himself about them, while in the second minute period he talked a little more about the experiment, school, and so on. During the third minute, he directed some questions at the subject, and during the fourth minute, he finished working with the materials and "accidentally" dropped them on the floor. In both conditions, his mood was mild at first, and then became more intense over time.

Thus, the "angry" confederate began by expressing some annoyance with the experiment and fumbling around with the folder materials. Gradually, his irritation began to build up, and he became more agitated (for example, scribbling on the pictures, crumpling up sheets of paper, moving back and forth in his chair). By the fourth minute, he had become quite angry and cursed when his folder "accidentally" spilled all over the floor. In the happy condition, the confederate began by expressing interest in the folder materials and by humming a tune to himself. Gradually, he began to laugh and joke about the experiment and to clown around with the materials (for example, drawing a mustache on a picture, making an airplane or hat out of the pieces of the puzzle). By the fourth minute, he was very happy and exuberant, and laughed loudly when the folder "accidentally" spilled on the floor.

At the end of the 4-minute period, one of the experimenters entered the room and asked the confederate to leave and go to another room for the next part of the experiment. The subject was told that another experimenter would join him in a minute, but before that, he should complete several questionnaires. One of these focused on the subject's present emotional feelings and physiological state, while the other assessed his reaction to the confederate. When this was completed, the experimenter entered and gave the cue for the disappearance of the physiological symptoms. All subjects were then questioned about their reactions to various aspects of the study. Those in the arousal condition were made to relax and were returned to the normal, unaroused, preexperimental condition. All subjects were asked not to talk about the experiment and were later given an elaborate debriefing session when the study was completed.

Summary of design

This study is a 2 x 2 factorial design (two levels of arousal and two levels of confederate emotion) with the addition of two unhypnotized groups. Six subjects were run in each of the six cells. In terms of the Schachter and Singer model, the experimental conditions of most interest are the two aroused groups, in which the subjects were both physiologically aroused and exposed to a happy or angry person. The arousal was produced by a combination of two factors: training in hypnosis and an arousal stimulus. The other experimental conditions lacked either one or the other of these two factors and thus represent two different types of control groups. The unaroused subjects received the identical treatment as the aroused condition except that they were not given the arousal stimulus. Similarly, the control condition was identical to the aroused groups except that these subjects had not been hypnotized.

RESULTS

Presentation of the results will be organized around five issues: (1) effectiveness of the physiological arousal manipulation; (2) evaluation of the confederate's mood; (3) behavioral differences between treatments; (4) experienced emotional differences between treatments; and (5) attribution of arousal and emotion.

Overview of results

In general, it can be said that the use of hypnotic training and the conditioning procedure utilized did produce a strong, persistent level of physiological arousal. Hypnotized subjects given an amnesia suggestion for the cause of their arousal were unaware of why they felt as they did. Differences between the angry and the happy confederate were perceived veridically by subjects in all conditions. These differences in the model's behavior were reflected in differences in the subjects' overt behavior. A happy model elicited far more prosocial behavior than an angry model, and more observation on the part of the subject. However, despite all of these apparently ideal conditions for replicating the finding of emotional plasticity, such a result did not occur. Aroused subjects reacted negatively across a range of self-reported items of emotion regardless of whether they had been exposed to the angry or to the happy model. Control subjects, not experiencing a comparable state of unexplained arousal, either did not react with emotion, or reacted positively.

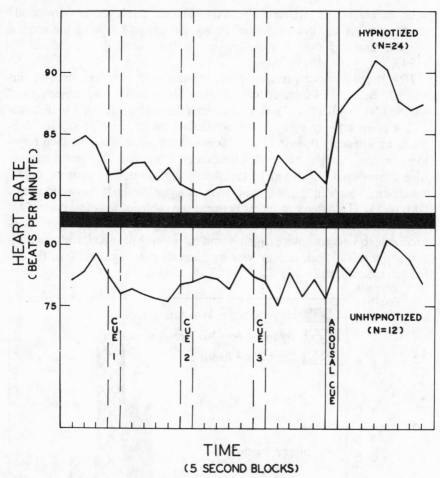

FIGURE 19.5. *Mean changes in heart rate to irrelevant and hypnotically conditioned stimuli.*

Physiological arousal

The physiological data from the first part of the experiment clearly show that the hypnotized subjects experienced a state of arousal upon seeing the word "start." In contrast, the unhypnotized subjects did not demonstrate such extreme physiological changes, even though they heard the identical instructions. Figure 19.5 shows the pattern of mean changes in heart rate for both groups. The difference between the highest heart rate recorded after the arousal stimulus and the highest heart rate following the three neutral stimuli is significantly greater for hypnotic subjects than for nonhypnotic ones ($p < .001$, $t = 5.16$, $df = 23$). Analysis of GSR responses also reveals differences in arousal. Hypnotic subjects displayed a significantly greater number of GSR responses during the minute following the arousal stimulus than did the unhypnotized group *(p < .05, F = 5.36, df = 1/34)*.

How did the subjects feel emotionally while they were experiencing this arousal? Before and immediately after the arousal stimulus, subjects filled out the Mood-Adjective Checklist, in which they rated each of 44 adjectives on a 4-point scale (ranging from "not feeling this emotion at all" to "definitely experiencing this emotion"). Some of the adjectives described negative emotions (such as "angry," "clutched up," "insecure"); some were positive ("overjoyed," "pleased," "warmhearted"); some were active ("bold," "energetic," "defiant"); and some were passive ("calm," "concentrating," "drowsy"). The difference scores between the subjects' pre- and postratings indicate the shift in mood that resulted from the physiological arousal. Hypnotic subjects became more negative and active in their mood, and less positive and passive. Their ratings were significantly more extreme than the unhypnotized subjects *(p < .001, F = 17.15, df = 1/34)*.

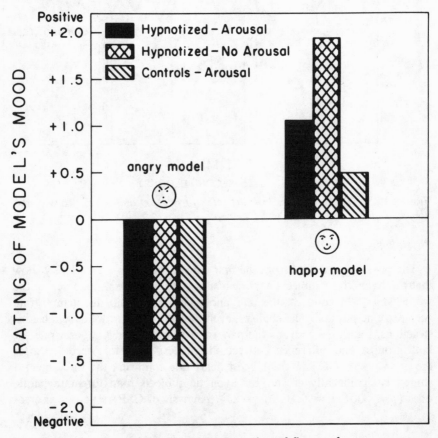

FIGURE 19.6.   *Perception of model's mood.*

Because hypnotic subjects responded physiologically to the arousal stimulus in the acoustic sound chamber, it was assumed that they would respond in the same way if they saw this stimulus during the learning task. Unfortunately, because we lacked telemetry equipment, it was not possible to record the subjects' physiological responses while they were with the confederate, and thus check on the validity of this assumption. However, two indirect measures of arousal were used. One indication of the success of the arousal manipulation comes from an analysis of the type of errors made on the recall test. Although there were no between-group differences in overall performance, the aroused-hypnotized subjects made more errors of omission than of commission while this pattern was reversed for subjects in the other two groups. It would be predicted that a subject performing under the distracting influence of intense arousal would be less able to search his memory for words which may have been on the list and come up with commission errors by recalling "new" words. Rather, it is likely he will write down only the words he has stored in readily accessible memory and stop—leading to more errors of omission. The difference in the ratio of commissions to omissions for the hypnotic versus the other two groups approaches significance $(p < .10, F = 3.33, df = 1/34)$.

On a second measure, which was taken as part of the last series of questionnaires, subjects reported which of a battery of physiological symptoms they were experiencing. From 92 to 100 per cent of the aroused subjects reported experiencing each of the four suggested symptoms, while only 26 to 52 per cent of the unaroused subjects reported having any one of the set of symptoms. The difference between proportions for each of the four symptoms computed separately is beyond the .001 level.

Perception of confederate

To check on the effectiveness of the confederate manipulation, subjects were asked to make ratings of the confederate. On scale items that described the confederate's mood (for example, angry—peaceful), subjects in the happy condition evaluated the confederate's mood as positive, while angry subjects reported it as negative. As seen in Figure 19.6, the difference between the two groups is extremely significant $(p < .001, F = 68.58, df = 1/32)$, which testifies to the success of this manipulation. The remaining scale items focused on the subject's personal evaluation of the confederate (for example, rude—polite). Subjects in the angry condition were more negative in their evaluation than subjects in the happy condition $(p < .025, F = 6.61, df = 1/32)$.

Overt "emotional" behavior

The overt behavior of the subjects varied as a function of the confederate's mood. As shown in Table 19.3, subjects who were with the happy confederate exhibited a significantly higher amount of positive social behaviors than did subjects who were with the angry confederate. This was true for

TABLE 19.3   Mean number of prosocial behaviors

	Verbal		
Confederate's Mood	aroused	Arousal Condition unaroused	control
Happy	4.42	4.33	2.50
Angry	.67	.42	.92

	Nonverbal		
Confederate's Mood	aroused	Arousal Condition unaroused	control
Happy	10.50	8.17	6.00
Angry	.83	.42	1.58

both verbal behaviors, such as agreeing with the confederate $(p < .001, F = 20.97, df = 1/30)$, and nonverbal behaviors, such as smiling, nodding one's head, and so forth $(p < .001, F = 44.80, df = 1/30)$. Furthermore, subjects in the aroused condition spent more time looking at the confederate when he was happy than when he was angry $(p < .025, F = 9.90, df = 1/10)$.

Reported "emotional" experience

Although the confederate's mood had an effect on subjects' overt behavior, it did not exert the expected influence on their reported emotional state. Rather, their felt emotion was a function of whether they were or were not experiencing unexplained arousal. Two of the questionnaire items on emotion were the identical ones used by Schachter and Singer, which asked subjects to rate on a 5-point scale just how happy and how angry they were. Following their procedure, an analysis of the difference scores (happy—angry) shows that both of the aroused conditions were experiencing a more negative emotional state than the conditions experiencing no arousal $(p < .01, F = 8.13, df = 1/32)$. Analyses of both the happy and the angry ratings separately provide even stronger evidence of the difference in emotional reactions between the aroused groups and the other groups without arousal. Aroused subjects were significantly more angry $(p < .005, F = 12.89, df = 1/32)$ and less happy $(p < .001, F = 16.34, df = 1/32)$ than the subjects in the unaroused and control groups. In all cases, there was no difference in patterns of emotion between subjects exposed to the happy and to the angry confederate, which indicates the lack of social/emotional influence these models had on the subjects.

The questionnaire also included a series of 7-point scale items on emotional feelings, such as happy—sad, anxious—calm, and so forth. The subjects' mean ratings on these 8 combined emotion items is shown in Figure 19.7. Aroused subjects reported a generally negative emotional state, which was significantly different from the emotional ratings of the unaroused and control groups $(p < .001, F = 25.88, df = 1/32)$. While the unaroused groups rated themselves as feeling a positive emotional state (the mean of 6.08 is different from zero at the .05 level, $t = 2.321$, $df = 11$), the control groups were neutral in their emotions; their scores did not differ significantly from zero. Apparently, the unaroused subjects were responding to the posthypnotic suggestion that they would feel relaxed and good when they came out of hypnosis, while the waking control subjects were unable to repond similarly to that same suggestion. The positive feelings of the unaroused group make even more dramatic the negative reaction of the aroused subjects, who had also received the same posthypnotic suggestion. Again there was no difference between the pattern of emotion ratings displayed by the aroused subjects in the happy condition and those in the angry condition.

Subjects were also asked to describe previous situations in which they had felt as they now did. These open-ended responses were rated by judges who were blind to both the purpose of the experiment and the condition of the subject. Aroused subjects described situations that were more negative (for example, waiting to take an exam, waiting to see the dentist, hearing bad

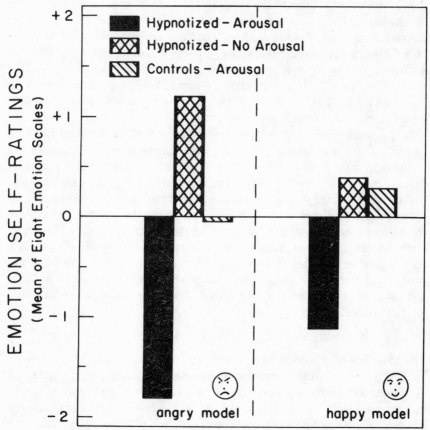

FIGURE 19.7. *Mean self-ratings on eight emotion scales.*

news, and so forth) than those described by subjects in both nonarousal conditions $(p < .001, F = 21.84, df = 1/30)$. Subjects who were not aroused described more passive situations than did the aroused group, and this was more true of the happy condition than of the angry condition $(p < .025, F = 6.44, df = 1/30)$.

Attribution of causality

In another questionnaire item, subjects were asked if they knew why they felt as they did and, if so, to state the reason. These responses were also scored by blind judges. One of these scores reflected the degree of similarity between the subject's stated reason for his feelings and the reasons given by the confederate for his emotional state (for example, "I'm very upset because I also don't like this experiment"). A significant interaction was found $(p < .025, F = 8.25, df = 1/30)$, in which the aroused subjects (who were experiencing a negative emotional state) were more similar to the confederate when he was angry than when he was happy. On the other hand, the two conditions with no arousal (who reported positive or neutral emotions) were more similar to the confederate when he was happy than when he was angry. The judges also rated the extent to which the subject said his emotional state was the *result* of the confederate's behavior (for example, "I'm feeling upset because that other guy was bothering me and getting on my nerves"). The analysis again reveals a significant interaction $(p < .001, F = 11.06, df = 2/16)$; subjects were more likely to attribute their emotion to the confederate's behavior when they were aroused than when they were not, but only in the angry condition.

It is possible that the posthypnotic suggestion had the effect of blocking any search for an explanation of the experienced arousal. This does not seem to be the case since 67 per cent of the arousal subjects did state they thought they knew why they felt as they did. However, in no case was their stated reason related to the experimentally induced cause. In the unaroused hypnotic group 50 per cent of the subjects stated they knew the cause of their current feelings, while 67 per cent of the controls also did. Thus there is no difference between groups in the likelihood that subjects will generate an explanation for their experienced state. The important difference appears to be that this state is a more negative one for the aroused subjects and the explanations they propose do not adequately explain or reduce their level of arousal.

CONCLUSION AND DISCUSSION

The following conclusions seem warranted by the available data. Hypnosis is effective in eliciting a specific syndrome of measurable physiological symptoms and in creating amnesia as to its cause. Emotional reaction can be differentiated into overt, behavioral, and subjective, experiential components, which in this study were not correlated. Subjects can laugh at the joke of a confederate but still be upset by their arousal state, or conversely, show distressed concern over the anger of a confederate, yet personally feel good. This finding, in fact, removes a source of ambiguity from interpretation of the data from experiments such as these. The experience of emotion appears to be more than self-labeling, which follows from observing oneself overtly acting in a particular "emotional" way. In addition, subjects can clearly separate their evaluation of another person's mood from their own. Aroused subjects made comments such as, "She was a very nice, bouncy, and talkative person, but I just don't feel bouncy and talkative right now."

The failure to find the "plasticity" effect of Schachter and Singer (1962) requires that we try a more direct replication of their study. In one of our studies (just begun), we will administer epinephrine and recreate their original procedure as closely as possible. We hope to discover, through a systematic program of replication, the variables that are responsible for the results they obtained. One of our studies will administer epinephrine to hypnotized subjects, while instructing them that they will feel whatever they happen to be feeling whenever a particular cue is presented (in the posthypnotic, test situation). Thus, we bring the onset of arousal under more precise experimental control without adding the questionable aspect of verbally providing the set of symptoms the subjects should be feeling—the symptoms thus remain partly their own private experience.

Most exciting to us is the possibility that *unexplained arousal* is the key to emotional pathology. If the need to explain discontinuities in behavior and experience leads to a cognitive search of the external and/or internal environment, then failure to come up with adequate causal explanation makes one's behavior "irrational." If it also appears that others in the same situation are not reacting similarly, then one's behavior becomes not "normal." To be different from others, to behave idiosyncratically and not know why, are the basic elements in our cultural definition of madness. We are in the process of developing a general model that we believe will explain the development of particular types of defensive mechanisms as well as neurotic and psychotic symptomatology. Such pathology is viewed as the end products of what begins as a rational search for understanding chronic, unexplained arousal. It may be that the Schachter-Singer model holds for the *development* of the emotional labeling process, but that by the time we become adults the experience of a marked discontinuity in state is always perceived negatively, and the search for an explanation is thus biased and motivated by the concern that failure to come up with an adequate explanation has pathological consequences in terms of loss of self-control. And it often does.

Conclusions

The studies reported in this chpter represent only a preliminary attempt to use hypnosis as a means to explore a variety of basic psychological phenomena.

We have been interested in the general problem of specifying the conditions that affect the degree of actual and perceived control an individual has over his internal as well as external environments. Autonomic functions can now be shown to be amenable to special procedures that bring them under stimulus, feedback, and cognitive controls. Such knowledge can then be used to intervene in pathological cases involving "learned" malfunctioning of the glands and viscera.

Hypnosis seems to be a powerful tool to investigate the role of temporal factors in the control of thought and action. Although we have only reported one study that manipulated the dimension of tempo, in other research underway we are uncovering fascinating consequences of varying temporal perspective. By putting hypnotic subjects in a condition of "expanded present," we have been able to study the release of behaviors and experiences characteristic of the psychedelic "trip" as well as a readiness for emotional contagion in a group of such subjects. Our interest in temporal control is also shown in our current attempt to develop a new type of therapy (Temporal Reconstruction Therapy), in which the reality of the present is substituted for the "reality" of the past in the memory of the hypnotically age-regressed subject or patient. In cases where the person would respond positively to current life conditions, but cannot because of a burden of traumatic memories (of being unloved, ugly, a failure, fat, etc., as a child), these real or imagined past events will be directly altered through suggestions to be the way the subject would have wanted them to be.

Our interest in the social, cognitive, and physiological determinants of emotion has been increasingly directed toward a concern for the development of emotional pathology. We assume that basic to many states is the initial experience of a discontinuity in behavior or strong physiological arousal —without an appropriate explanation to account for these events.

We hope to develop a model of madness that has as its major operating premise a *Catch 22* bind: Normal people engaged in the rational process of searching for a causal explanation for their inappropriate affect and responses may develop types of explanations that their society agrees are typical of those who are neurotic or psychotic. Hypnosis represents a unique approach for creating unexplained arousal and experiential discontinuities and then studying how both the individual and his "therapist" try to impose order and reason on this unacceptable condition.

Thus, the reader may see that although the three experiments reported here have apparently little in common, in effect they represent several aspects of the broad problem of how psychology can be better used to increase man's potential for control and to minimize the degree to which he is subject to the constraints of his physiology, the dictates of time, and the flux of his emotions.

We are encouraged enough by the overall pattern of significant findings to recommend that psychologists consider hypnosis as a valuable addition to their set of research tools. By doing so, they may gain in being better able to study certain complex problems such as those described here, as well as more traditional ones related to memory and learning. In turn, the study of hypnosis will also gain by having new research-oriented blood infused into its substance. We anticipate that the next decade will see this reciprocal relationship flourish to the mutual benefit of both hypnosis and psychology.

V

Anticipations for Future Research

Erika Fromm *is Professor of Psychology at the University of Chicago. She received her Ph.D. at the age of 23 from the University of Frankfurt, Germany, working under Max Wertheimer on Gestalt laws of perception. She became a research associate for a year in the Department of Psychiatry at the University of Amsterdam, Holland, and then established the first Psychology Laboratory in a State Hospital in that country. During that time her interest became centered on psychoanalytic theory and projective techniques. She emigrated to the United States with her husband in 1938, spent several years raising her family, took more training in psychoanalytic child therapy, and became a research associate at the Chicago Institute for Psychoanalysis. She served on the faculties of the University of Illinois Medical School and Northwestern University Medical School. Her research interests expanded to ego psychology, dream interpretation, psychoanalytic approaches to artistic creativity, and to hypnosis. In 1961 she joined the Department of Psychology at the University of Chicago. She is author of* Intelligence: A Dynamic Approach *with Lenore Hartman and* Dream Interpretation: A New Approach *with Thomas M. French. Dr. Fromm is currently President of the American Board of Psychological Hypnosis, President-Elect of Division 30 (Psychological Hypnosis) of the American Psychological Association, and Vice-President of the Society for Clinical and Experimental Hypnosis. She has been the Clinical Editor of the* International Journal for Clinical and Experimental Hypnosis *since 1969.*

Fromm *reports on a survey she conducted on future trends in hypnosis research. Questionnaires were sent to all members of the three professional hypnosis societies in this country who might conceivably be engaged in hypnosis research. Each recipient was asked to describe hypnosis research he had in progress, research he was planning to execute in the future, promising studies being planned by other investigators, and important additional research he would like to see done either by himself or by others. A content analysis was made of the responses, and frequencies were tallied. The result of this analysis was taken as a reflection of areas of attention and coming interest. On the basis of these findings, tentative predictions about future research trends are offered.*

20

Quo Vadis Hypnosis? Predictions of Future Trends in Hypnosis Research

ERIKA FROMM

In the Spring of 1970 questionnaires were mailed to those members of the Society of Clinical and Experimental Hypnosis and of the American Society of Clinical Hypnosis known to have an active involvement in research, and to all members of the recently founded Division on Psychological Hypnosis of the American Psychological Association. Of the 500 questionnaires mailed, 161, or 32 per cent, were returned. The questionnaire asked the respondent to describe the hypnosis research he had in progress, research he was planning to execute in the future, promising studies currently being planned by other investigators, and important additional research he would like to see done either by himself or by others.

The 295 research topics named were described at different levels of generality, with much complex overlapping. Despite these complexities a content analysis has here been made.

The questionnaire responses could be readily subdivided into two major categories. The first is what I call the "growing edges" in the study of hypnosis; the second is the more traditional continuation of existing lines of research. Under the first category can be placed nine subcategories: (1) the nature of hypnosis, (2) hypnosis as a subjective experience, (3) preconscious and unconscious processes, (4) self-hypnosis, (5) subject characteristics, (6) the personality of the hypnotist, (7) social psychology of hypnosis research, (8) new clinical applications of hypnosis, and (9) studies on the correspondences and differences between clinical and experimental hypnosis.

Three subcategories have been placed under the second category: (1) experimental hypnosis, (2) clinical research, and (3) educational applications of hypnosis. Frequencies are given in Table 20.1. The rest of this chapter discusses these questionnaire findings in greater detail as a way of prophesying future research trends in hypnosis.

TABLE 20.1   Frequency of responses to the hypnosis research questionnaire.

	Research		
	in pro-gress	pro-jected	needed
A. THE GROWING EDGES OF THE FIELD			
I. *The Nature of Hypnosis*	6		3
II. *Hypnosis as a Subjective Experience:*			
1. Phenomenology	5	2	2
2. Altered states of consciousness			
a. Measure: the subject's own reports	1		
b. Attempts to measure objectively the subjective experience (e.g., in analgesia)	1		
3. Modeling other altered states of consciousness with hypnosis	3	2	2
III. *Preconscious and Unconscious Processes*			
1. Differentiating fact and artifact with regard to hypnosis by means of differences in characteristics of cognitive processes	3		
2. Creativity and other regressions in the service of the ego	3	1	
3. Dreams: hypnotic and posthypnotic	2	9	1
4. The study of repression and other unconscious defenses by means of hypnosis	2	1	2
IV. *Self-hypnosis*	1	1	3
V. *Subject Characteristics*	9	3	2
VI. *The Personality of the Hypnotist*	1	1	3
VII. *Social Psychology of Hypnosis Research*	5		2
VIII. *New Clinical Applications of Hypnosis:*			
A. Integration of hypnotherapy with some of the recently developed psychotherapies:			2
1. Behavior modification	4	1	2
2. Desensitization	4	1	
3. Autogenic control techniques	1		
4. Self-actualization therapies	1	1	1
5. Group therapy with hypnosis	2	1	1
6. Hypnotic marathons	4	2	1
7. Art therapy	1	1	
8. Gestalt therapy			1
9. Existential therapy		1	
B. Hypnosis in the treatment of drug addiction	4	4	3

		Research		
		in pro-gress	*pro-jected*	*needed*
IX.	*Studies on the Correspondences and Differences Between Clinical and Experimental Hypnosis*	1		
B.	CONTINUATION OF ESTABLISHED RESEARCH LINES			
X.	*Experimental Hypnosis*			
	1. Hypnotizability studies	1	4	2
	2. Measures and methods of induction and deepening	3	1	1
	3. Neurophysiology	5	6	3
	4. The objective study of specific hypnotic phenomena and effects	13	4	5
XI.	*Clinical Research*			
	1. Theory and methods of hypnotherapy	9	2	2
	2. Application of hypnosis in hypnotherapy and hypno-analysis	26	25	22
	3. Outcome studies	2		2
XII.	*Educational Applications*	4	7	5
XIII.	*Miscellaneous*	6	3	7
	Totals:	132	84	80

A. Growing Edges

I. THE NATURE OF HYPNOSIS

A total of nine responses dealt with the nature of hypnosis. There appeared to be seven research questions of interest expressed in those responses:

- In what sense, if any, is hypnosis an altered state of consciousness?
- Is hypnosis no more than suggestibility?
- Can we isolate the necessary and sufficient variables for producing hypnosis?
- Is becoming hypnotized a skill that can be learned; that is, could everyone, with sufficient practice, learn to be deeply hypnotized?
- Does it require a basic talent to allow oneself temporarily to shed one's generalized reality orientation in order to allow primary process thought and imagery to come into awareness?
- To what extent is hypnosis a transference process?
- What differentiates hypnosis from the waking state and from sleep?

II. HYPNOSIS AS A SUBJECTIVE EXPERIENCE

Experiential aspects of hypnosis, although the most important aspects to the subject, have until recently tended to be ignored by the laboratory investigator seeking objectivity. Subjects, particularly after initial exposure to hypnosis, characteristically are eager to describe their subjective hypnotic experiences and usually are uninterested in their objective behavioral performance. With the advent of the new youth culture, with its emphasis on inner, highly personal experiences and altered states of awareness, there has been renewed interest by investigators in the phenomenology of hypnosis. Altogether there were 18 responses dealing with research on hypnosis as a subjective experience. These dealt with the phenomenology of ordinary and exceptionally deep hypnosis; the development of scales by which to quantify the experiential aspects of hypnosis; attempts to provide phenomenological characterizations of hypnotic experiences at different levels of depth, including the very deepest; and the exploration of variations in characteristics of hypnotic phenomena.

Two research projects are in progress that attempt to measure objectively the subjective experience of hypnosis as an altered state of consciousness. Several investigators expressed interest in the phenomenological similarities of hypnosis to drug-induced states and to "peak experiences." Seven respondents registered interest in comparing drug-induced and hypnotic altered states of consciousness.

III. PRECONSCIOUS AND UNCONSCIOUS PROCESSES

Since the classic studies in hysteria by Breuer and Freud, hypnosis has been widely considered to be a convenient method for the study of preconscious and unconscious processes. Our respondents showed a great deal of interest in undertaking studies on creativity, on hypnotic and posthypnotic dreams, and on repression, rationalizations, and other unconscious defenses. Of the 21 responses in these areas, 7 referred to projects in progress and 11 in prospect. Several studies of unconscious and preconscious defenses will include artificially induced conflicts and their solutions—a prime source for experimental investigation of the integrative and the defensive functions of the ego in *statu nascendi*.

Three respondents are engaged in research seeking differences in cognitive processes in the wake and hypnotic states. Indications are that cognitive processes in hypnosis contain evidence of more primary process manifestations, involve more adaptive use of introspection, and more fanciful elaboration of content and humor.

Four respondents are actively engaged in or are planning work on creativity in hypnosis, eleven on dreams. Three have research in progress or in prospect on the formation of unconscious defenses.

IV. SELF-HYPNOSIS

Little has been done in this research area. Our respondents reported only one project in progress and only one other in prospect.

Self-hypnosis has been used extensively in therapy, for controlling somatic pain and ameliorating psychological anguish. However, practically all hypnosis research has involved heterohypnosis. The assumption implicitly made is that heterohypnosis and autohypnosis are homologues; that we can teach autohypnosis by letting the patient recapitulate what he has experienced being hypnotized, including the fantasy of the transference object. There is, however, no direct research documentation of whether the experiential phenomena are indeed alike in the two instances—that is, whether the same abilities, ego functions, and substrata of personality are involved in both.

In heterohypnosis, the patient's or subject's ego, while listening to the hypnotist's patter, is often said to divide into an experiencing part and an observing part. With regard to self-hypnosis, where the subject gives the suggestions to himself, three major questions occur to me: To what extent does the ego in self-hypnosis split into three parts: instructing, observing, and experiencing functions (that is, the "Speaker," "Listener," and "Observer")? In what types of clinical cases is it indicated to teach self-hypnosis? What are the criteria for teaching self-hypnosis that should be used with reference to a normal population?

While only three of our respondents suggested that more research was needed on self-hypnosis, in my judgment there will be a great upsurge of scientific interest in it in the next decade. Once again, the youth movement and associated phenomena have focused interest on the development of the individual's inner potentialities and self-actualization, with special emphasis on subjective experiences. Scientific investigators will, it is thought, wish to study the problems and promise of self-hypnosis as well as of heterohypnosis.

V. SUBJECT CHARACTERISTICS

Subject characteristics not only influence hypnotizability, but also may be the source of variability in hypnotic performance. In particular the Stanford laboratory (E. R. Hilgard, 1965b; J. Hilgard, 1970) has shown great activity in relating hypnotic susceptibility to certain personality characteristics. Our respondents suggest that they will widen and extend this research in the future. Nine studies of subject characteristics are in process and three more are projected. These studies include: research into differences in personality characteristics between suggestible and nonsuggestible subjects; nosological studies by means of hypnotizability scores (for example, differentiating neurotic character disorders from primary psychopaths on the basis of their hypnotizability); conversely, in other studies, gender, state of emotional health (normality versus acute versus chronic schizophrenia), or very specific personality characteristics (such as sensitizers versus repressors) are used as independent variables to investigate differences in hypnotic performance.

In the clinical field, a variety of projects include specific studies such as a comparison of the personalities of patients who react well to surgery under hypnosis versus those who do not, and an inquiry into the dynamics of patients who resume smoking or overeating within six months after hypnotherapy, compared to those who remain abstinent. On the basis of the reports, the writer expects that hypnosis research will move into increasingly refined clinical differentiations of the personality characteristics of hypnotizable persons, and of types of patients who can profit lastingly from short-term hypnotherapy as opposed to those who cannot. The future research appears to be taking more cognizance of interpersonal variables and subject characteristics in the selection of experimental populations.

VI. THE PERSONALITY OF THE HYPNOTIST

Little research has been done concerning the personality of the hypnotist; only one such project is in process and one other is in the planning stage. However, three respondents urged further research in this area.

In the eighteenth and nineteenth centuries, hypnosis was flamboyant (Mesmer) or authoritarian (Charcot, Freud). The hypnotist was viewed as a powerful person who wished to subject others to his will for their own good. Since the end of World War II, hypnotists have generally come to practice a permissive kind of hypnosis. Obviously this new approach requires, at least in part, a different kind of personality or different varieties of personality as compared with the earlier approach.

As students of hypnosis become more sophisticated in establishing subject characteristics, they will also need to analyze the personality characteristics of the hypnotist. Thus one respondent plans to study what motivated the hypnotist to become a hypnotist. Another is exploring the extent to which prestige in the eyes of the patient may be a factor. However, prestige can hardly be the factor motivating the hypnosis researcher, since in many academic circles hypnosis has not yet gained full status as a legitimate field of research.

In my opinion, three types of studies are needed: studies tracing the career lines of well-known hypnosis researchers and hypnotherapists; studies based on interviews or questionnaires asking people in these fields what their conscious motivations have been for becoming and remaining hypnotists; and personality studies of the same groups of people, designed to tap their unconscious motivations and personality makeup.

VII. SOCIAL PSYCHOLOGY OF HYPNOSIS RESEARCH

One respondent urged that medicine's inertia in utilizing hypnosis as a method of treatment be explored. Another respondent reported research in progress on the "ivy-league effect" in hypnosis research, by which he meant that hypnosis research has tended to be looked upon askance by universities as if it were something mystic and not really worthy of scientific investigation. While such an attitude is still widespread, the fact that Hilgard at Stanford and Orne at the University of Pennsylvania have developed large laboratories for hypnosis research has given the field more prestige in the eyes of academia—a development that in itself might make an interesting topic for social psychological research.

It is also of interest to study the social atmosphere in which hypnosis research—or any kind of research for that matter—either flourishes or withers. Ethnic-cultural factors that contribute to hypnotic susceptibility also need to be studied, as one respondent urged. Moreover, we would not be surprised to find quantitative differences in hypnotizability between socioeconomic classes and races, perhaps depending on whether hypnotist and subject belong to the same class or race. We might also expect qualitative differences in what is experienced in hypnosis when comparing such diverse groups as college-bred suburban housewives and native Balinese religious dancers.

VIII. NEW CLINICAL APPLICATIONS OF HYPNOSIS

There were 133 responses with reference to clinical applications of hypnosis. Only those that deal with the "growing edges" of the field—44 research projects—will be discussed in this section. Of these, 21 are in progress and 12 are future projects; there were 11 suggestions concerning needed research in this area.

Integration of hypnotherapy with newer psychotherapies

The responses indicated that in the near future there will be many attempts to integrate hypnotherapy with some of the newer psychotherapies, such as behavior modification, desensitization, autogenic control techniques, and self-actualization therapies. Clinicians and researchers alike will try to find out whether these newer psychotherapies are more effective when the patient is in hypnosis or in the waking state.

Seven responses were concerned with studies of behavior modification, including comparisons between the waking and the hypnotic state; one study will deal with the relationship of Schutz's autogenic control techniques to the techniques of hypnosis, including similarities and differences. Desensitization techniques were the focus of five projects.

Mesmer, Liébeault, and other early hypnotherapists treated their patients in groups, but for nearly a century hypnotherapy has characteristically been practiced in a one-to-one situation. Currently, however, hypnotic group therapy is being vigorously developed. Three of the respondents are or soon will be doing studies in this area to compare the results of individual hypnotherapy or hypnoanalysis with those obtained by group hypnotherapy. Marathon hypnotherapy is also being tried. There were seven responses in this latter category.

Hypnosis in the treatment of drug addiction

The potential use of hypnosis in the exploration and treatment of the adolescent drug problem, mentioned earlier, is currently being studied by four respondents. Four more projects are being planned, and three other respondents emphasized the need for research in this area. Such studies can contribute to the understanding and treatment of addiction, perhaps making it possible for patients to experience, without danger, the relaxation and/or excitement they obtain from drugs. Such research could become of great clinical and social relevance. Studies will attempt to indicate whether hypnosis can be used as a substitute for drug taking, or help reduce stress in drug-withdrawal patients. The studies are also seen as likely to broaden the knowledge of the sensory and cognitive changes produced by hallucinogenic drugs.

IX. STUDIES ON THE CORRESPONDENCES AND DIFFERENCES BETWEEN CLINICAL AND EXPERIMENTAL HYPNOSIS

In the past, experimental researchers frequently tried to replicate findings of clinicians—and often failed. Whenever this happened, the clinicians were criticized for poor methodology and faulty observation. However, in the last few years, experimentalists as well as clinicians have come to realize that not all clinical data *can* be readily replicated in the laboratory; perhaps clinical and experimental situations have differing social characteristics that are likely to elicit different reactions from the hypnotized individual. Some workers have argued that a patient comes to his therapist with a set of expectations totally different from that of the curious student who comes to the hypnosis laboratory to participate in a new experience. It is possible, too, that a student who is paid a fee to participate in hypnosis experiments may react differently from one who wishes to experience hypnosis out of intellectual and/or emotion-loaded curiosity.

In my judgment, there has not been enough concern for the problem of similarities and differences between clinical and experimental hypnosis. Only one such study is in progress, and no projected ones were reported.

The problems in comparing clinical and experimental hypnosis involve the unwillingness of laboratory researchers to accept, as real, phenomena that may not be fully replicable in the traditional laboratory. While it is true that clinicians sometimes have been overly "credulous," the "skeptical" experimenter, with his emphasis on objectivity, can, it is felt, inhibit the occurrence of certain valid hypnotic phenomena.

B. Continuation of Established Research Lines

Our respondents reported that well-established lines of research will be continued. Sixty-three such projects are in progress, in contrast with 48 projects on the "growing edges." The same broad differences are also apparent in Table 20.1 with respect to studies in prospect and areas of needed research.

X. EXPERIMENTAL HYPNOSIS

Well-established lines of research in experimental hypnosis were found to cluster readily into three categories: hypnotizability, measures and methods of hypnotic induction, and the physiology of hypnosis.

Hypnotizability

In my view, an important task with reference to hypnotizability is the elaboration and measurement of multidimensional factors involved in hypnotic responsiveness. Research with Weitzenhoffer and Hilgard's Profile Scales (1967), and the development of a diagnostic measurement scale of Shor's three dimensions of hypnotic depth (1962), would seem highly relevant. All too often hypnotic depth is considered a univariate function.

Two of our respondents emphasized the need for future hypnotizability studies. One such study is in process and four others are projected. These studies include a longitudinal design for examining individual differences in hypnotic susceptibility and explorations of how such differences in susceptibility (as well as levels of hypnotizability) are modified from early childhood through old age. Earlier hypnotizability studies compared hypnotizability of given age groups, not through longitudinal development.

Measures and method of hypnotic induction

Another currently active field of established research is the study of procedures and measurement of hypnotic induction and deepening. Three projects are in process and a fourth is projected. Subjects of interest include rapid induction procedures, the effectiveness of induction and deepening procedures under various circumstances, and hypnotic induction profiles.

Physiology of hypnosis

Research on the physiology of hypnosis is continuing. Despite previous lack of success, a few researchers are looking for physiological or EEG indices that would prove the existence of hypnosis as a distinct state. Five projects are in progress, six are projected, and three respondents reported the need for further research in neurophysiology.

In my judgment, as interest in the subjective aspects of hypnosis increases —with increasing awareness that hypnosis is an altered state of consciousness and that the very essence of hypnosis is in the subject's subjective experience—the search for physiological and neuroelectric substrata of hypnosis as proof of the existence of a hypnotic state will fade into the background. Researchers will no longer feel as compelled to look intently for *objective* measures of the subjective experience.

A good many of our respondents are interested in the study of specific hypnotic phenomena and effects. There are 12 projects in process and 4 more projected; five other respondents stressed the need for more such studies.

Seven questions on typical hypnotic phenomena continue to intrigue investigators: (1) posthypnotic amnesia as a means of studying forgetting or repression; (2) time distortion; (3) hypnotic alterations of aspects of perception and conscious experience, particularly visual perception; (4) variables influencing hypnotically-induced anesthesia; (5) effects of hypnosis on reaction time when either alertness or sleepiness has been suggested during induction; (6) the tracking of eye movements with hypnotically-induced positive and negative hallucinations; and (7) the problems of hypnosis in relation to pain, including the placebo effect.

XI. CONTINUATION OF ESTABLISHED LINES OF CLINICAL RESEARCH

Much clinical research is currently being carried forward along established lines. Thirty-four projects were reported in process, 27 were in prospect, and 26 were listed as needed.

Application of hypnosis in hypnotherapy and hypnoanalysis

Studies continue to be made on the feasibility and use of hypnosis in psychotherapy and for the relief of somatic pain. Studies of hypnosis as used in hypnotherapy elicited a total of 73 responses: 26 projects are in progress, 25 are projected, and 22 needed projects were suggested. There is likely to be heavy research emphasis on the use of hypnosis in the psychotherapy of neuroses, character neuroses, and psychosomatic problems. There are also indications of more concerted attempts to treat psychoses, particularly schizophrenia and the borderline states.

Studies are currently in process on the use of hypnosis in such areas as anxiety, rage, asthma, stuttering, mental retardation, and sexual malfunctioning.

One project was reported on the therapeutic use of hypnosis in brain injury cases in connection with physical medicine and rehabilitation services in hospitals. There will also be studies of the effectiveness of hypnosis in treating habit disorders (smoking, overeating, alcoholism). In some of these studies simple hypnotic suggestions are to be compared with more dynamic hypnoanalytic techniques. Controlled case studies on pain reduction, notably in the treatment of carcinoma and as an auxiliary treatment for severe burns, are projected. Hypnosis in childbirth and hypnotic analgesia and anesthesia training will continue to be used and investigated. Psychological preparation for and recovery from surgery by means of hypnosis also will continue to be studied.

On a somewhat more theoretical level, there will be explorations of the possibility of producing artificial conflicts and artificial neuroses through posthypnotic suggestion. Two studies have been launched that will attempt to identify the necessary and sufficient conditions for the production of psychopathology. One area where hypnosis would seem to be the natural therapy of choice, but where so far it has not been used extensively, is in connection with sleep disorders; however, only one such study is now in process.

It has been apparent for some time that we need more studies on hypnotherapeutic method and theory. There appear to be seven key questions:

- What is the preferred hypnotherapeutic method in various types of cases?
- When should hypnoanalysis be the therapy of choice?
- When is direct versus indirect suggestion preferable?
- When should hypnotherapy be supportive rather than reconstructive?
- Does rehearsal in fantasy under hypnosis help patients to change maladaptive behavior and personality patterns?
- What about ego-integrative therapeutic methods versus uncovering methods?
- When do we most profitably speak to our patients in the language of the unconscious—in symbols—and when should we use rational, secondary-process speech?

There are 18 projects in process seeking answers to these questions and 10 more are projected. Eight suggestions for needed research in hypnotherapeutic theory and methods were also submitted.

XII. THE APPLICATION OF HYPNOSIS IN EDUCATION

The possible influence hypnosis can have on ameliorating educational problems continues to interest researchers. Four projects are in process, seven are projected, and five additional needed projects were mentioned. However, it is very doubtful that large-scale use will be made of their methods and findings in our school systems. The nineteenth century concept of the hypnotist as a manipulator of men, with no respect for the individual's wishes and defenses, is still too prevalent.

Researchers are, however, continuing to study the effects of hypnosis and different forms of hypnotherapy on concentration, reading speed, comprehension, and learning retention. Other studies are on the use of hypnosis in overcoming educational blocks and in stirring the academic underachiever to use his full potential.

Purpose and Prediction

The purpose of this chapter was to survey what researchers in the field say they are interested in pursuing or feel should be pursued. The survey polled all of the contributors to this volume as well as almost everyone who might conceivably be engaged in hypnosis research. As a large number of the persons polled are practitioners who are not actively interested in research, the 32 per cent return rate is felt to be a reasonable representation of current interests. While newcomers to the field, young investigators, and graduate students are underrepresented in the sample, their interests are hopefully given expression in the responses of their teachers, colleagues, and supervisors.

As an expression of research activity and interest this survey can be taken as an estimate or appraisal of future trends in hypnosis research. As a prophecy of the future, such an appraisal doubtless has many shortcomings. In balance, however, it seems to me that it stands as a more reasonable basis for prophesy than a reliance on my own hunches, hopes, and biases. In a sense each of the chapters in this volume carries with it a prediction of future research growth. This final chapter is merely an attempt to expand the inquiry to include all members of the research community. It seems to me a cogent appraisal, but only time will tell. At the very least, the survey may serve as a useful bench mark against which to compare actual research developments in the years ahead.

Bibliography

Aaronson, B. The hypnotic induction of the Void. Paper read at American Society for Clinical Hypnosis, San Francisco, October, 1969.

Ackerknecht, E. H. "Mesmerism" in primitive societies. *Ciba Symposia*, 1948, *9*, 826–831.

Agle, D. P., Ratnoff, O. D., & Wasman, M. Studies in autoerythrocyte sensitization: The induction of purpuric lesions by hypnotic suggestion *Psychosomatic Medicine*, 1967, *29*, 491–503.

Agosti, E., & Camerota, G. Some effects of hypnotic suggestion on respiratory function. *International Journal of Clinical and Experimental Hypnosis*, 1965, *13*, 149–156.

Ainsworth, Mary D. Problems of validation. In B. Klopfer, Mary D. Ainsworth, W. G. Klopfer, & R. R. Holt, *Developments in the Rorschach Technique. Vol. 1, Technique and Theory*. Yonkers, New York: World Book Co. 1954, pp. 405–500.

Akstein, D. The induction of hypnosis in the light of reflexology. *American Journal of Clinical Hypnosis*, 1965, *7*, 281–300.

Allison, J. Adaptive regression and intense religious experiences. *Journal of Nervous and Mental Disease*, 1967, *145*, 452–463.

Allport, G. W. *Personality: A Psychological Interpretation*. New York: Holt, 1937.

Allport, G. W., Vernon, P. E. & Lindzey, G. *Study of Values*. (Rev. ed.) Boston: Houghton Mifflin Company, 1951.

Amadeo, M., & Shagass, C. Eye movements, attention, and hypnosis. *Journal of Nervous and Mental Disease*, 1963, *136*, 139–145.

Anand, B. K., Chhina, G. S., & Singh, B. Some aspects of electro-encephalographic studies in yogis. *Electroencephalography and Clinical Neurophysiology*, 1961, *13*, 452–456. Reprinted in Tart, 1969a, pp. 503–506.

Andersen, M. L. Correlates of hypnotic performance: An historical and role-theoretical analysis. Unpublished doctoral dissertation, University of California, Berkeley, 1963.

587

Anderson, M. N. Hypnosis in anesthesia. *Journal of the Medical Association of the State of Alabama*, 1957, *27*, 121–125.

Andrew, Dorothy M., Paterson, D. G., & Longstaff, H. P. *Minnesota Clerical Test*. New York: The Psychological Corporation, 1933.

Antrobus, Judith S., & Antrobus, J. S. Discrimination of two sleep stages by human subjects. *Psychophysiology*, 1967, *4*, 48–55.

Antrobus, J. S., Antrobus, Judith S., & Singer, J. L. Eye movements accompanying daydreaming, visual imagery, and thought suppression. *Journal of Abnormal and Social Psychology*, 1964, *69*, 244–252.

Antrobus, J. S., Singer, J. L., & Greenberg, S. Studies in the stream of consciousness: Experimental enhancement and suppression of spontaneous cognitive processes. *Perceptual and Motor Skills*, 1966, *23*, 399–417.

Arkin, A. M., Hastey, J. M., & Reiser, M. F. Post-hypnotically stimulated sleeptalking. *Journal of Nervous and Mental Disease*, 1966, *142*, 293–309.

Arnold, Magda B. On the mechanism of suggestion and hypnosis. *Journal of Abnormal and Social Psychology*, 1946, *41*, 107–128.

Arnold, Magda B. Brain function in hypnosis. *International Journal of Clinical and Experimental Hypnosis*, 1959, *7*, 109–119.

Arons, H. *How to Routine an Ethical Hypnotic Lecture-Demonstration*. Irvington, N. J.: Power Publishers, 1961.

Ås, A. Non-hypnotic experiences related to hypnotizability in male and female college students. *Scandanavian Journal of Psychology*, 1962, *3*, 112–121.

Ås, A. Hypnotizability as a function of nonhypnotic experiences. *Journal of Abnormal and Social Psychology*, 1963, *66*, 142–150.

Ås, A., O'Hara, J. W., & Munger, M. P. The measurement of subjective experiences presumably related to hypnotic susceptibility. *Scandanavian Journal of Psychology*, 1962, *3*, 47–64.

Ås, A., & Østvold, S. Hypnosis as subjective experience. *Scandanavian Journal of Psychology*, 1968, *9*, 33–38.

Asch, S. E. *Social Psychology*. Englewood Cliffs, N. J.: Prentice-Hall, 1952.

Aschan, G., Finer, B. L., & Hagbarth, K. E. The influence of hypnotic suggestion on vestibular nystagmus. *Acta Oto-Laryngologica*, 1962, *55*, 97–110.

Ascher, L. M., & Barber, T. X. An attempted replication of the Parrish-Lundy-Leibowitz study on hypnotic age-regression. Harding, Mass.: The Medfield Foundation, 1968.

Aserinsky, E., & Kleitman, N. Regularly occurring periods of eye motility, and concomitant phenomena, during sleep. *Science*, 1953, *118*, 273–274.

Ashley, W. R., Harper, R. S., & Runyon, D. L. The perceived size of coins in normal and hypnotically induced economic states. *American Journal of Psychology*, 1951, *64*, 564–572.

August, R. V. *Hypnosis in Obstetrics*. New York: McGraw-Hill, 1961.

Austin, Margaret, Perry, C., Sutcliffe, J. P., & Yeomans, N. Can somnambulists successfully simulate hypnotic behavior without becoming entranced? *International Journal of Clinical and Experimental Hypnosis*, 1963, *11*, 175–186.

Bachrach, H. M. Adaptive regression, empathy and psychotherapy: Theory and research study. *Psychotherapy: Theory, Research and Practice*, 1968, *5*, 203–209.

Backus, P. S. An experimental note on hypnotic ablation of optokinetic nystagmus. *American Journal of Clinical Hypnosis*, 1962, *4*, 184–188.

Bailly, J. S., et al. *Rapport des commissaires chargés par le roi de l'examen du magnétisme animal*, 11 aôut 1784. Signed: Franklin (Chairman), Majault, Le

Roy, Sallin, Bailly (Reporter), d'Arcet, De Bory, Guillotin, Lavoisier. Paris: Imprim. royale, 1784. In A. Bertrand, *Du magnétisme animal*. (On animal magnetism). Paris: J. B. Baillière, 1826, pp. 67–147. English translation: *Animal magnetism. Report of Dr. (Benjamin) Franklin and other Commissioners, charged by the King of France with the examination of the animal magnetism as practiced in Paris. Translated from the French. With an historical outline of the "science", an abstract of the Report on magnetic experiments, made by a Committee of the Royal Academy of Medicine, in 1831; and Remarks on Col. Stone's Pamphlet*. Philadelphia: H. Perkins, 1837. Translation also published separately, Philadelphia, J. Johnson, 1785.

Bailly, J. S., et al. *Exposé des expériences qui ont été faites pour l'examen du magnétisme animal. Lû à l'Académie des Sciences, par M. Bailly, en son nom et au nom de Messrs. Franklin, Le Roy, De Bory, et Lavoisier, le 4 Septembre 1784*. (Experiences made during the examination of animal magnetism. Paper read at the French Academy of Sciences by Mr. Bailey in his own name and that of Franklin, Le Roy, De Bory and Lavoisier, Sept. 4, 1784.) Paris: Imprimerie royale, 1785.

Bailly, J. S., et al. *Rapport secret sur le memsérisme, ou magnétisme animal*. (Secret report on Mesmerism or Animal magnetism). Paris, 11 aôut 1784b. (Not published.) Signed: Franklin (Chairman), De Bory, Lavoisier, Bailly (Reporter), Majault, Sallin, d'Arcet, Guillotin, Le Roy. Reproduced in A. Bertrand. *Du magnétisme animal*. (On animal magnetism). Paris: J. B. Baillière, 1826, pp. 511–516. Reproduced in A Binet & C. Féré. *Animal Magnetism*. French original, 1887. English translation, New York: D. Appleton & Co., 1888, pp. 18–25.

Banister, H., & Zangwill, O. L. Experimentally induced visual paramnesia. *British Journal of Psychology*, 1941, *32*, 30–51.

Barbarin, C. de. *Système raisonné du magnétisme universel*. (A logical system of universal magnetism). Paris: Gastelier, 1786.

Barber, T. X. Comparison of suggestibility during "light sleep" and hypnosis. *Science*, 1956, *124*, 405.

Barber, T. X. Hypnosis as perceptual-cognitive restructuring: III. From somnambulism to autohypnosis. *Journal of Psychology*, 1957, *44*, 299–304.

Barber, T. X. The after images of "hallucinated" and "imagined" colors. *Journal of Abnormal and Social Psychology*, 1959, *59*, 136–139.

Barber, T. X. Toward a theory of pain: Relief of chronic pain by prefrontal leucotomy, opiates, placebos, and hypnosis. *Psychological Bulletin*, 1959, *56*, 430–460.

Barber, T. X. The necessary and sufficient conditions for hypnotic behavior. *American Journal of Clinical Hypnosis*, 1960, *3*, 31–42.

Barber, T. X. Experimental evidence for a theory of hypnotic behavior: II. Experimental controls in hypnotic age-regression. *International Journal of Clinical and Experimental Hypnosis*, 1961a, *9*, 181–193.

Barber, T. X. Physiological effects of "hypnosis". *Psychological Bulletin*, 1961b, *58*, 390–419.

Barber, T. X. Hypnotic age regression: A critical review. *Psychosomatic Medicine*, 1962a, *24*, 286–299.

Barber, T. X. Toward a theory of hypnosis: Posthypnotic behavior. *Archives of General Psychiatry*, 1962b, *7*, 321–342.

Barber, T. X. Experimental controls and the phenomena of "hypnosis": A critique of hypnotic research methodology. *Journal of Nervous and Mental Disease*, 1962c, *134*, 493–505.

Barber, T. X. Toward a theory of "hypnotic" behavior: The "hypnotically induced dream." *Journal of Nervous and Mental Disease,* 1962d, *135,* 206–221.

Barber T. X. The effects of "hypnosis" on pain: A critical review of experimental and clinical findings. *Psychosomatic Medicine,* 1963, *25,* 303–333.

Barber, T. X. "Hypnosis" as a causal variable in present-day psychology: A critical analysis. *Psychological Reports,* 1964a, *14,* 839–842.

Barber, T. X. Hypnotic "colorblindness," "blindness," and "deafness": (A review of research findings). *Diseases of the Nervous System,* 1964b, *25,* 529–538.

Barber, T. X. Toward a theory of "hypnotic" behavior: Positive visual and auditory hallucinations. *Psychological Record,* 1964c, *14,* 197–210.

Barber, T. X. Empirical evidence for a theory of "hypnotic" behavior. *Psychological Record,* 1964d, *14,* 457–467.

Barber, T. X. Measuring "hypnotic-like" suggestibility with and without "hypnotic induction"; psychometric properties, norms, and variables influencing response to the Barber Suggestibility Scale (BSS). *Psychological Reports,* 1965a, *16,* 809–844.

Barber, T. X. Physiological effects of "hypnotic suggestions": A critical review of recent research (1960–64). *Psychological Bulletin,* 1965b, *63,* 201–222.

Barber, T. X. Experimental analyses of "hypnotic" behavior: A review of recent empirical findings. *Journal of Abnormal Psychology,* 1965c, *70,* 132–154.

Barber, T. X. "Hypnotic" phenomena: A critique of experimental methods. In J. E. Gordon (Ed.), 1967, pp. 444–480.

Barber, T. X. An empirically-based formulation of hypnotism. *American Journal of Clinical Hypnosis,* 1969a, *12,* 100–130.

Barber, T. X. *Hypnosis: A Scientific Approach.* New York: Van Nostrand-Reinhold Co., 1969b.

Barber, T. X. *LSD, Marihuana, Yoga, and Hypnosis.* Chicago: Aldine Publishing Co., 1970a.

Barber, T. X. The phenomenology of ('hypnotic') suggestibility. Harding, Mass.: The Medfield Foundation, 1970b.

Barber, T. X., & Calverley, D. S. "Hypnotic behavior" as a function of task motivation. *Journal of Psychology,* 1962, *54,* 363–389.

Barber, T. X., & Calverley, D. S. "Hypnotic-like" suggestibility in children and adults. *Journal of Abnormal and Social Psychology,* 1963, *66,* 589–597.

Barber, T. X., & Calverley, D. S. The relative effectiveness of task motivating instructions and trance-induction procedure in the production of "hypnotic-like" behaviors. *Journal of Nervous and Mental Disease,* 1963, *137,* 107–116.

Barber, T. X., & Calverley, D. S. Effect of *E*'s tone of voice on "hypnotic-like" suggestibility. *Psychological Reports,* 1964a, *15,* 139–144.

Barber, T. X. & Calverley, D. S. Empirical evidence for a theory of "hypnotic" behavior: Effects of pretest instructions on response to primary suggestions. *Psychological Record,* 1964b, *14,* 457–467.

Barber, T. X., & Calverley, D. S. Experimental studies in "hypnotic" behavior: Suggested deafness evaluated by delayed auditory feedback. *British Journal of Psychology,* 1964c, *55,* 439–466.

Barber, T. X., & Calverley, D. S. The definition of the situation as a variable affecting "hypnotic-like" suggestibility. *Journal of Clinical Psychology,* 1964d, *20,* 438–440.

Barber, T. X., & Calverley, D. S. Toward a theory of hypnotic behavior: Effects on suggestibility of defining the situation as hypnosis and defining response to suggestions as easy. *Journal of Abnormal and Social Psychology,* 1964e, *68,* 585–592.

Barber, T. X., & Calverley, D. S. Toward a theory of "hypnotic" behavior: Enhancement of strength and endurance. *Canadian Journal of Psychology,* 1964f, *18,* 156–167.

Barber, T. X., & Calverley, D. S. Toward a theory of "hypnotic" behavior: An experimental study of "hypnotic time distortion". *Archives of General Psychiatry,* 1964g, *10,* 209–216.

Barber, T. X., & Calverley, D. S. Empirical evidence for a theory of hypnotic behavior: Effects on suggestibility of five variables typically included in hypnotic induction procedures. *Journal of Consulting Psychology,* 1965, *29,* 98–107.

Barber, T. X., & Calverley, D. S. Effects on recall of hypnotic induction, motivational suggestions, and suggested regression: A methodological and experimental analysis. *Journal of Abnormal Psychology,* 1966a, *71,* 169–180.

Barber, T. X., & Calverley, D. S. Toward a theory of "hypnotic" behavior: Experimental analyses of suggested amnesia. *Journal of Abnormal Psychology,* 1966b, *71,* 95–107.

Barber, T. X., & Calverley, D. S. Toward a theory of hypnotic behavior: Experimental evaluation of Hull's postulate that hypnotic susceptibility is a habit phenomenon. *Journal of Personality,* 1966c, *34,* 416–433.

Barber, T. X., & Calverley, D. S. Toward a theory of "hypnotic" behavior: Replication and extension of experiments by Barber and co-workers (1962–65) and Hilgard and Tart (1966). *International Journal of Clinical and Experimental Hypnosis,* 1968, *16,* 179–195.

Barber, T. X., & Calverley, D. S. Effects of hypnotic induction, suggestions of anesthesia, and distraction on subjective and physiological responses to pain. Paper presented at Eastern Psychological Association, Annual Meeting, Philadelphia, April, 1969a.

Barber, T. X., & Calverley, D. S. Multidimensional analysis of "hypnotic" behavior. *Journal of Abnormal Psychology,* 1969b, *74,* 209–220.

Barber, T. X., Chauncey, H. H., & Winer, R. A. Effect of hypnotic and non-hypnotic suggestions on paratid gland response to gustatory stimuli. *Psychosomatic Medicine,* 1964, *26,* 374–380.

Barber, T. X., & Coules, J. Electrical skin conductance and galvanic skin response during "hypnosis". *International Journal of Clinical and Experimental Hypnosis,* 1959, *7,* 79–92.

Barber, T. X., Dalal, A. S., & Calverley, D. S. The subjective reports of hypnotic subjects. *American Journal of Clinical Hypnosis,* 1968, *11,* 74–88.

Barber, T. X., & Glass, L. B. Significant factors in hypnotic behavior. *Journal of Abnormal and Social Psychology,* 1962, *64,* 222–228.

Barber, T. X., & Hahn, K. W., Jr. Physiological and subjective responses to pain producing stimulation under hypnotically-suggested and waking-imagined "analgesia." *Journal of Abnormal and Social Psychology,* 1962, *65,* 411–418.

Barber, T. X., & Hahn, K. W., Jr. Experimental studies in "hypnotic" behavior: Physiological and subjective effects of imagined pain. *Journal of Nervous and Mental Disease,* 1964, *139,* 416–425.

Barker, W., & Burgwin, S. Brain wave patterns during hypnosis, hypnotic sleep and normal sleep. *Archives of Neurology and Psychiatry,* 1949, *62,* 412–420.

Barnlund, D. C. *Interpersonal Communication: Survey and Studies.* Boston: Houghton Mifflin, 1968.

Barron, F. Threshold for the perception of human movement in inkblots. *Journal of Consulting Psychology,* 1955, *19,* 33–38.

Barron, F. The psychology of creativity. In F. Barron (Ed.), *New Directions in Psychology II.* New York: Holt, Rinehart & Winston, 1965.

Barron, F. *Creative Person and Creative Process*. New York: Holt, Rinehart and Winston, 1969.

Barry, H., Jr., MacKinnon, D. W., & Murray, H. A., Jr. Studies in personality: A. Hypnotizability as a personality trait and its typological relations. *Human Biology*, 1931, *3*, 1–36.

Bartlett, E. S., Faw, T. T., & Liebert, R. M. The effects of suggestions of alertness in hypnosis on pupillary response: Report on a single subject. *International Journal of Clinical and Experimental Hypnosis*, 1967, *15*, 189–192.

Baudouin, C. *Suggestion and Autosuggestion: A Psychological and Pedagogical Study Based upon the Investigations Made by the New Nancy School*. Translated from the French by E. Paul & C. Paul. New York: Dodd, Mead & Co., 1922.

Beck, E. C., & Barolin, G. S. Effect of hypnotic suggestions on evoked potentials. *Journal of Nervous and Mental Disease*, 1965, *140*, 154–161.

Beck, E. C., Dustman, R. E., & Beier, E. G. Hypnotic suggestions and visually evoked potentials. *Electroencephalography and Clinical Neurophysiology*, 1966, *20*, 397–400.

Beecher, H. K. *Measurement of Subjective Responses: Quantitative effects of drugs*. New York: Oxford University Press, 1959.

Beh, Helen C., & Barratt, P.E.H. Discrimination and conditioning during sleep as indicated by the electroencephalogram. *Science*, 1965, *147*, 1470–1471.

Bellak, L. An ego-psychological theory of hypnosis. *International Journal of Psycho-analysis*, 1955, *36*, 375–378.

Bellak, L. Creativity: Some random notes to a systematic consideration. *Journal of Projective Techniques*, 1958, *22*, 363–380.

Benedict, R. Anthropology and the abnormal. *Journal of General Psychology*, 1934, *10*, 59–82.

Bennett, J. H. *The Mesmeric Mania of 1851, with a Physiological Explanation of the Phenomena Produced*. Edinburgh: Sutherland & Knox; London: Simpkin, Marshall, & Co., and S. Highley, 1851.

Bennett, L. L., & Scott, N. E. The production of electrocardiographic abnormalities by suggestion under hypnosis: A case report. *American Practitioner*, 1949, *4*, 189–190.

Benussi, V. Zur experimentellen Grundlegung hypno-suggestiver Methoden psychischer Analyse. (The experimental basis of hypnosuggestive methods in psychological analysis). *Psychologische Forschung*, 1927, *9*, 197–274.

Benyamini, K. Experimental effects of hypnotically induced anxiety, arousal, and inhibition. Unpublished doctoral dissertation, University of Michigan, 1963.

Bergasse, N. *Considérations sur le magnétisme animal, ou sur la theorie au monde et des êtres organisés d'aprés les principles de M. Mesmer*. (Thoughts on animal magnetism or on the theory of the world and beings organized according to the principles of Mr. Mesmer.) La Haye, 1784.

Bergmann, M. S., Graham, H., & Leavitt, H. G. Rorschach exploration of consecutive hypnotic chronological age level regressions. *Psychosomatic Medicine*, 1947, *9*, 20–28.

Bergson, Henri, Simulation inconsciente dans l'état d'hypnotisme. (Unconscious simulation in the hypnotic state.) *Revue Philosophique*, 1886, *22*, 525–531.

Berman, R., Simonson, E., & Heron, W. Electrocardiographic effects associated with hypnotic suggestion in normal and coronary sclerotic individuals. *Journal of Applied Physiology*, 1954, *7*, 89–92.

Bernheim, H. M. *Hypnosis and Suggestion in Psychotherapy: A Treatise on the*

Nature and Uses of Hypnotism. French original of first part, 1884, second part, 1886; with a new preface, 1887. English translation by C. A. Herter, 1888. Reissued with an introduction by E. R. Hilgard, New Hyde Park, N. Y.: University Books, 1964.

Bernheim, H. *Suggestive Therapeutics: A Treatise on the Nature and Uses of Hypnotism*. C. A. Herter (Trans.) New York: G. P. Putnam's Sons, 1889.

Bernstein, M. *The Search for Bridey Murphy*. New York: Doubleday, 1956.

Bertini, M., Lewis, H. B., & Witkin, H. A. Some preliminary observations with an experimental procedure for the study of hypnagogic and related phenomena. *Archivivo di psicologia, Neurologia e Psichiatria*, 1964, *25*, 493–534.

Bertrand, A.J.F. *Traité du somnambulisme et des différentes modifications qu'il présente*. (Treatise on somnambulism and its various modifications). Paris: J. G. Dentu, 1823.

Bertrand, A. J. F. *Extase: De l'état d'extase considére comme une des causes des effets attrubués au magnétisme animal*. (Ecstasy: On the state of ecstasy which is considered to be one of the causes of the effects attributed to animal magnetism). Paris: Encyclopédie Progressive, No. 8, Béchet et Cie, et al., 1826a.

Bertrand, A. J. F. *Du magnétisme animal en France et des jugements qu'en ont portés les sociétés savantes; avec le texte des divers rapports faits en 1784 par les commissaires de L' Académie des Sciences, de la Faculté et de la Société Royale de Medécine, et une analyse de derniéres séances de l'Academie Royale de Medécine et du Rapport de M. Husson; suivi de considérations sur l'apparition de l'extase dans les traitements magnétiques. Seconde Partie: Du somnambulisme artificiel considéré comme une variété de l'exiase*. (On animal magnetism in France and the judgments of the scientific societies; with texts of the various reports made in 1784 by the commissioners of the Academy of Sciences, the Faculty of the Royal Society of Medicine and an analysis of the last sessions of the Royal Academy of Medicine and of the report of Mr. Husson; with added thoughts on the phenomenon of ecstasy in magnetic therapy. Part II: Artificial somnambulism conceived of as a variation of ecstasy). Paris: J. B. Ballière, 1826b.

Best, H. L., & Michaels, R. M. Living out "future" experience under hypnosis. *Science*, 1954, *120*, 1077.

Bettinghaus, E. P. *Persuasive Communication*. New York: Holt, Rinehart & Winston, 1968.

Betts, G. H. The distribution and functions of mental imagery. *Teachers College, Contributions to Education*, 1909, No. 26.

Binet, A., & Féré, C. *Animal Magnetism*. French Original, 1886. English translation, New York: D. Appleton-Century Co., 1888.

Bitterman, M. E., & Marcuse, F. L. Autonomic response in posthypnotic amnesia. *Journal of Experimental Psychology*, 1945, *35*, 248–252.

Black, S., & Friedman, M. Effects of emotion and pain on adrenocortical function investigated by hypnosis. *British Medical Journal*, 1968, *1*, 477–481.

Blake, H., & Gerard, R. W. Brain potentials during sleep. *American Journal of Physiology*, 1937, *119*, 692–703.

Blatt, S. J. Patterns of cardiac arousal during complex mental activity. *Journal of Abnormal and Social Psychology*, 1961, *63*, 272–282.

Blatt, S. J., Allison, J. & Feirstein, A. The capacity to cope with cognitive complexity. *Journal of Personality*, 1969, *37*, 269–288.

Blatt, S. J., & Stein, M. I. Efficiency in problem solving. *Journal of Psychology*, 1959, *48*, 193–213.

Bleuler, E. Psychology of hypnosis. *Münchener Medizinische Wochenschrift*, 1889, *36*, 76. Reproduced in A. Forel, 1907, pp. 315–320.

Bloch, B. Über die Heilung der Warzen durch Suggestion. *Klinische Wochenschrift*, 1927, *2*, 2271–2275; 2320–2325.

Blum, G. S. *The Blacky Pictures: A Technique for the Exploration of Personality Dynamics.* Ann Arbor, Michigan: Psychodynamic Instruments, 1950.

Blum, G. S. *A Model of the Mind: Explored by Hypnotically Controlled Experiments and Examined for its Psychodynamic Implications.* New York: John Wiley and Sons, 1961.

Blum, G. S. Hypnosis in psychodynamic research. In J. E. Gordon (Ed.), 1967, pp. 83–109.

Blum, G. S., Geiwitz, P. J., & Hauenstein, Louise S. Principles of cognitive reverberation. *Behavioral Science*, 1967, *12*, 275–288.

Blum, G. S., Geiwitz, P. J., & Stewart, C. G. Cognitive arousal: The evolution of a model. *Journal of Personality and Social Psychology*, 1967, *5*, 138–151.

Blum, G. S., & Graef, J. R. The detection over time of subjects simulating hpynosis. *International Journal of Clinical and Experimental Hypnosis*, 1971, *19*, 211–224.

Blum, G. S., Graef, J. R., & Hauenstein, Louise S. Effects of interference and cognitive arousal upon the processing of organized thought. *Journal of Abnormal Psychology*, 1968, *73*, 610–614.

Blum, G. S., Hauenstein, Louise S., & Graef, J. R. Studies in cognitive reverberation: Replications and extensions. *Behavioral Science*, 1968, *13*, 171–177.

Blum, G. S., & Wohl, B. M. An experimental analysis of the nature and operation of anxiety. *Journal of Abnormal Psychology*, 1971, *78*, 1–8.

Bobbitt, R. A. The repression hypothesis studied in a situation of hypnotically induced conflict. *Journal of Abnormal and Social Psychology*, 1958, *56*, 204–212.

Bogdonoff, M. D., Combs, J. J., Bryant, G. D., & Warren, J. V. Cardiovascular responses in experimentally induced alterations of affect. *Circulation*, 1959, *20*, 353–359.

Bonnefoy, J. B. *Analyse raisonée des rapports des commissaires charges par le roi de l'examen du magnétisme animal.* (A rational analysis of the reports of the commissioners who were charged by the King with the investigation of animal magnetism). (Not published). 1784.

Borelli, S. Psychische Einflüsse und reactive Hauterscheinungen. *Münchener Medizinische Wochenschrift*, 1953, *95*, 1078–1082.

Boring, E. G. *A History of Experimental Psychology.* Originally published, 1929, (2nd edition). New York: Appleton-Century-Crofts, 1950.

Boucher, R. G., & Hilgard, E. R. Volunteer bias in hypnotic experimentation. *American Journal of Clinical Hypnosis*, 1962, *5*, 49–51.

Bowers, K. S. Hypnotic behavior: The differentiation of trance and demand characteristic variables. *Journal of Abnormal Psychology*, 1966, *71*, 42–51.

Bowers, K. S. The effect of demands for honesty on reports of visual and auditory hallucinations. *International Journal of Clinical and Experimental Hypnosis*, 1967, *15*, 31–36.

Bowers, K. S. Hypnosis and creativity: A preliminary investigation. *International Journal of Clinical and Experimental Hypnosis*, 1968, *16*, 38–52.

Bowers, K. S. Creativity and hypnotic susceptibility. Paper presented at American Psychological Association, Washington, D. C., September 1969.

Bowers, K. S. Heart rate and GSR concommitants of vigilance and arousal. *Canadian Journal of Psychology*, 1971a, *25*, 175–183.

Bowers, K. S. Sex and susceptibility as moderator variables in the relationship of creativity and hypnotic susceptibility. *Journal of Abnormal Psychology,* 1971b, *78,* 93–100.

Bowers, K. S., & Keeling, K. R. Heart rate variability in creative functioning. *Psychological Reports,* 1971, *29,* 160–162.

Bowers, K. S., & Gilmore, J. B. Subjective report and credibility: An inquiry involving hypnotic hallucinations. *Journal of Abnormal Psychology,* 1969, *74,* 443–451.

Bowers, K. S., & van der Meulen, Sandra J. Effect of hypnotic susceptibility on creativity test performance. *Journal of Personality and Social Psychology,* 1970, *14,* 247–256.

Bowers, Patricia G. Effect of hypnosis and suggestions of reduced defensiveness on creativity test performance. *Journal of Personality,* 1967, *35,* 311–322.

Boyers, J. M., & Morgan, Arlene. The veridicality of posthypnotic amnesia. Hawthorne House Research Memorandum, Stanford University 1969.

Brady, J. P., & Levitt, E. E. Nystagmus as a criterion of hypnotically induced visual hallucinations. *Science,* 1964, *146,* 85–86.

Brady, J. P., & Levitt, E. E. Hypnotically induced visual hallucinations. *Psychosomatic Medicine,* 1966, *28,* 351–363.

Brady, J. P., Levitt, E. E., & Lubin, B. Expressed fear of hypnosis and volunteering behavior. *Journal of Nervous and Mental Disease,* 1961, *133,* 216–217.

Brady, J. P., & Rosner, B. S. Rapid eye movements in hypnotically induced dreams. *Journal of Nervous and Mental Disease,* 1966, *143,* 28–35.

Braginsky, B. M., Braginsky, D. D., & Ring, K. *Methods of Madness: The Mental Hospital as a Last Resort.* New York: Holt, Rinehart & Winston, 1969.

Braid, J. *Neurypnology: The Rationale of Nervous Sleep Considered in Relation with Animal Magnetism, Illustrated by Numerous Cases of its Successful Application in the Relief and Cure of Disease.* London: John Churchill, 1843. Edited version under title: *Braid on Hypnotism: Neurypnology. A new Edition Edited with an Introduction, Biographical and Bibliographical, Embodying the Author's Later Views and Further Evidence on the Subject.* Edited by A. E. Waite. London: George Redway, 1889. Reprinted as: *Braid on Hypnotism: The Beginnings of Modern Hypnosis.* New York: Julian Press, 1960.

Braid, J. *The Power of the Mind Over the Body: An Experimental Inquiry into the Nature and Cause of the Phenomena Attributed by Reichenbach and Others to a "New Imponderable".* London: John Churchill; Edinburgh: Adam and Charles Black, 1846. This pamphlet is a slightly revised reproduction of three papers published in the *Medical Times,* June 13, 20, & 23, 1846. This abridged account is found in A. E. Waite. Synopsis of counter-experiments undertaken by James Braid to illustrate his criticism of Reichenbach. Appendix III, 352–361, in J. Braid, 1889. Another abridged version, pp. 3–19; 31–36, is reprinted in W. Dennis, *Readings in the History of Psychology,* New York: Appleton-Century-Crofts, 1948, pp. 178–193.

Braid, J. Facts and observations as to the relative value of mesmeric and hypnotic coma, and ethereal narcotism, for the mitigation or entire prevention of pain during surgical operations. *Medical Times,* 1847, *15,* 381–382.

Braid, J. *Magic, Witchcraft, Animal Magnetism, Hypnotism, and Electrobiology: Being a Digest of the Latest Views of the Author on These Subjects.* Third edition, greatly enlarge, embracing observations of J. C. Colquhoun's "An History of magic, witchcraft, and animal magnetism". London: John Churchill, 1852.

Bramwell, J. M. James Braid: His work and writings. *Society for Psychical Research: Proceedings*, 1896–7a, *12*, Part 30, Supplement 127–166.

Bramwell, J. M. What is hypnotism? *Society for Psychical Research: Proceedings*, 1896–97b, *12*, Part 31, 204–258.

Bramwell, J. M. *Hypnotism: Its History, Practice and Theory*. London: Grant Richards, 1903. Reissued with new introduction. New York: Julian Press, 1956.

Branca, A. A., & Podolnick, E. E. Normal, hypnotically induced, and feigned anxiety as reflected in and detected by the MMPI. *Journal of Consulting Psychology*, 1961, *25*, 165–170.

Breuer, J., & Freud, S. (1893a). *Studies on Hysteria*. Newly translated from the German and edited by J. Strachey. With the collaboration of Anna Freud. (Earlier translation by A. A. Brill, 1936). New York: Basic Books, 1957.

Breuer, J., & Freud, S. Über den psychischen Mechanismus hysterischer Phenomene (On the psychical mechanisms of hysterical phenomena). *Neurologisches Zentralblatt*, 1893b, *1 and 2*, 4–10; 43–47. Translated by J. Rickman in *Collected Papers*, Vol. 1. London: The Hogarth Press, 1924.

Brenman, Margaret. The use of hypnotic techniques in a study of tension systems. In Margaret Brenman & M. M. Gill, 1947, pp. 195–253.

Brenman, Margaret. Dreams and hypnosis. *Psychoanalytic Quarterly*, 1949, *18*, 455–465.

Brenman, Margaret, & Gill, M. M. *Hypnotherapy: A Survey of the Literature*. With appended case reports and an experimental study. New York: International Universities Press, 1947.

Brickner, R. M., & Kubie, L. S. A miniature psychotic storm produced by a superego conflict over simple post-hypnotic suggestion. *Psychoanalytic Quarterly*, 1936, *5*, 467–487.

Bromberg, W. *The Mind of Man: A History of Psychotherapy and Psychoanalysis*. New York: Harper, 1959. (Originally published under title *Man Above Humanity: A History of Psychotherapy*. Philadelphia: Lippincott, 1954).

Brooks, L. R. The suppression of visualization by reading. *Quarterly Journal of Experimental Psychology*, 1967, *19*, 289–299.

Brooks, L. R. The internal representation of spatial and verbal information. Paper presented to Eastern Psychological Association, Washington, D.C., April, 1968.

Brown, Barbara B. Recognition of aspects of consciousness through association with EEG alpha activity represented by a light signal. *Psychophysiology*, 1970, *6*, 442–452.

Bruner, J. S., & Goodman, C. C. Value and need as organizing factors in perception. *Journal of Abnormal and Social Psychology*, 1947, *42*, 33–44.

Burchard, E. M. L. The evolution of psychoanalytic tasks and goals: A historical study of Freud's writings on technique. *Psychiatry*, 1958, *21*, 341–357.

Burdin, C., & Dubois, F. (d'Amiens). *Histoire académique du magnétisme animal: accompagnée de notes et de remarques critiques sur toutes les observations et expériences faites jusqu'a ce jour*. (Academic history of animal magnetism: with notes and critical remarks with regard to all observations and experiences made up to the present). Paris: J. B. Baillière, 1841.

Burr, C. W. The reflexes of early infancy. *British Journal of Children's Disease*, 1921, *18*, 152–153.

Bush, M., Hatcher, R., & Mayman, M. Reality attentiveness-inattentiveness and externalization-internalization in defensive style. *Journal of Consulting and Clinical Psychology*, 1969, *33*, 343–350.

Butler, B. The use of hypnosis in the care of the cancer patient. *Cancer,* 1954, *7,* 1–14.

Butler, J. M., & Rice, Laura N. Adience, self-actualization, and drive theory. In J. M. Wepman and R. W. Heine (Eds.) *Concepts of Personality.* Chicago: Aldine Publishing Company, 1963, pp. 79–110.

'Calostro,' *Entertaining with Hypnotism.* Closter, N. J.: Calostro Publications, 1949.

Cambareri, J. D. The effects of sensory isolation on suggestible and non-suggestible psychology graduate students. Unpublished doctoral dissertation, University of Utah, 1958. *Dissertation Abstracts,* 1959, *19,* 1813.

Campbell, H. J. *Correlative Physiology of the Nervous System.* London: Academic Press, 1965, pp. 212–246.

Cannon, W. B. "Voodoo" death. *American Anthropologist,* 1942, *44,* 169–181.

Cantril, H. Experiments in the wording of questions. *Public Opinion Quarterly,* 1940, *4,* 330–332.

Carlson, E. T. Charles Poyen brings mesmerism to America. *Journal of the History of Medicine and Allied Sciences,* 1960, *15,* 121–132.

Casey, G. A. Hypnotic time distortion and learning. *Dissertation Abstracts,* 1966, *27,* 2116–2117.

Chapman, L. F., Goodell, Helen, & Wolff, H. G. Increased inflammatory reaction induced by central nervous system activity. *Transactions of the Association of American Physicians,* 1959, *72,* 84–109.

Charcot, J. M. Essai d'une distinction nosographique des divers états compris sous le nom d'Hypnotisme. (Attempt to make a nosographic distinction of the different nervous states known under the name of Hypnotism). *Comptes rendus de l'Académie des Sciences,* 1882a, *44.* Summarized in A. Binet and C. S. Féré, 1887, pp. 154–163.

Charcot, J. M. Sur les divers états nerveux déterminés par l'hypnotisation chez les hystériques. *Comptes rendus hebdomadaires des séances de l'Académie des Sciences* (On different nervous states as they appear when hysterics are hypnotized. *Biweekly accounts of the meetings of the Academy of Sciences),* 1882b, *94,* 403–405.

Charcot, J. M. *Oeuvres complètes.* (Complete works) Paris: Aux Bureaux du Progrès Médical, 1886. 9 vols.

Charcot, J. M. The faith-cure. *New Review,* 1893, *8,* No. 44, 18–31.

Chase, W. W. An experiment in controlled nystagmus using hypnosis. *American Journal of Optometry,* 1963, *40,* 463–468.

Chaves, J. F. Hypnosis reconceptualized: An overview of Barber's theoretical and empirical work. *Psychological Reports,* 1968, *22,* 587–608.

Chertok, L. *Psychosomatic Methods in Painless Childbirth: History, Theory and Practice.* Foreward by R. G. Douglas. Translated from the 2nd French edition by D. Leigh. New York: Pergamon Press, 1959.

Chertok, L. Theory of hypnosis since 1889. *International Journal of Psychiatry,* 1967, *3,* 188–199.

Chertok, L. *Hypnosis.* Translated from an expanded version of the 3rd French edition in collaboration with the author by D. Graham. Oxford: Pergamon Press, 1966.

Chertok, L., & Kramarz, P. Hypnosis, sleep, and electro-encephalography. *Journal of Nervous and Mental Disease,* 1959, *128,* 227–238.

Chiasson, S. W. Hypnosis in postoperative urinary retention. *American Journal of Clinical Hypnosis,* 1964, *6,* 366–368.

Clarke, G. H. V. The charming of warts. *Journal of Investigative Dermatology*, 1965, *45*, 15–21.

Clemes, S. Repression and hypnotic amnesia. *Journal of Abnormal and Social Psychology*, 1964, *69*, 62–69.

Clynes, M., Kohn, M., & Lifshitz, K. Dynamics and spatial behavior of light evoked potentials, their modification under hypnosis, and on-line correlation in relation to rhythmic components. *Annals of the New York Academy of Science*, 1963, *112*, 468–509.

Cobb, J. C., Evans, F. J., Gustafson, L. A., O'Connell, D. N., Orne, M. T., & Shor, R. E. Specific motor response during sleep to sleep-administered meaningful suggestion: An exploratory investigation. *Perceptual and Motor Skills*, 1965, *20*, 629–636.

Cobb, J. C., & Shor, R. E. Development of techniques to maximize hypnotic responsiveness. Paper presented at the meeting of the Eastern Psychological Association, Philadelphia, April, 1964.

Coe, W. C. The heuristic value of role theory and hypnosis. Unpublished doctoral dissertation, University of California, (Berkeley), 1964.

Coe, W. C. Hypnosis as role enactment: The role demand variable. *American Journal of Clinical Hypnosis*, 1966, *8*, 189–191.

Coe, W. C., & Sarbin, T. R. An experimental demonstration of hypnosis as role enactment. *Journal of Abnormal Psychology*, 1966, *71*, 400–406.

Coe, W. C., & Sarbin, T. R. An alternative interpretation to the multiple composition of hypnotic scales: A single role-relevant skill. *Journal of Personality and Social Psychology*, 1971, *18*, 1–8.

Cogger, W. G., Jr., & Edmonston, W. E. Hypnosis and oral temperature: A reevaluation of experimental techniques. *International Journal of Clinical and Experimental Hypnosis*, (in press).

Collins, J. K. Muscular endurance in normal and hypnotic states: A study of suggested catalepsy. Honors thesis, Department of Psychology, University of Sydney, Australia, 1961.

Colquhoun, J. C. *Isis Revelata: An Inquiry into the Origin. Progress, and Present State of Animal Magnetism*. 3rd edition. Edinburgh: William Wilson, 1844, 2 volumes.

Conn, J. H. Historical aspects of scientific hypnosis. *Journal of Clinical and Experimental Hypnosis*, 1957, *5*, 17–24.

Conti, A. P. Heart rate conditioning in and out of hypnosis. Unpublished bachelor's thesis, Colgate University, 1968.

Cooper, L. F., & Erickson, M. H. Time distortion in hypnosis II. *Bulletin Georgetown University Medical Center*, 1950, *4*, 50–68.

Cooper, L. M. Spontaneous and suggested posthypnotic source amnesia. *International Journal of Clinical and Experimental Hypnosis*, 1966a, *14*, 180–193.

Cooper, L. M. What is hypnotic amnesia? Paper presented at meeting of American Psychological Association, New York, September, 1966.

Cooper, L. M. Expectations about hypnosis of college students who have not been hypnotized. Unpublished research, Brigham Young University, 1969.

Cooper, L. M. Hypnotic amnesia. (Chapter in this volume)

Cooper, L. M., & Harrison, R. V. Individual recall of serially presented motor tasks: Individual administration. Unpublished research, Brigham Young University, 1969.

Cooper, L. M., & Hoskovec, J. Hypnotic suggestions for learning during stage 1 REM sleep. Unpublished research, Brigham Young University, 1966.

Cooper, L. M., & London, P. Sex and hypnotic susceptibility in children. *International Journal of Clinical and Experimental Hypnosis*, 1966, *14*, 55–60.

Cooper, L. M., & Moore, Rosemarie K. Individual recall of serially presented motor tasks: Group presentations. Unpublished research, Brigham Young University, 1967.

Cooper, L. M., & Young, J. Hypnotic recall amnesia as a function of manipulated expectation. Unpublished research, Brigham Young University, 1971.

Coors, D. A determination of the density of post-hypnotic amnesia for the stylus maze. Thesis submitted for B.A. degree, University of Wisconsin, 1928.

Corley, J. B. Hypnosis and the anesthetist. *American Journal of Clinical Hypnosis*, 1965, *8*, 34–36.

Counts, R. M., & Mensh, I. N. Personality characteristics in hypnotically-induced hostility. *Journal of Clinical Psychology*, 1950, *6*, 325–330.

Coué, E. *Self-Mastery through Conscious Autosuggestion*. London: George Allen & Unwin, 1922.

Crasilneck, H. B., & Hall, J. A. Physiological changes associated with hypnosis: A review of the literature since 1948. *International Journal of Clinical and Experimental Hypnosis*, 1959, *7*, 9–50.

Crawley, E. *The Mystic Rose: A Study of Primitive Marriage and of Primitive Thought in its Bearing on Marriage*. Rev. by T. Besterman. London: Methuen & Co., Ltd., 1927.

Cronin, D. M., Spanos, N. P., & Barber, T. X. Augmenting hypnotic suggestibility by providing favorable information about hypnosis. *American Journal of Clinical Hypnosis*, 1971, *13*, 259–264.

Dalal, A. S. An empirical approach to hypnosis: An overview of Barber's work. *Archives of General Psychiatry*, 1966, *15*, 151–157.

Damaser, Esther C. An experimental study of long-term post-hypnotic suggestion. Unpublished doctoral dissertation, Harvard University, 1964.

Damaser, Esther C., Shor, R. E., & Orne, M. T. Physiological effects during hypnotically requested emotions. *Psychosomatic Medicine*, 1963, *25*, 334–343.

Danielou, A. The influence of sound phenomena on human consciousness. *Psychedelic Review*, 1966, *7*, 20–26.

Darnton, R. *Mesmerism and the End of the Enlightenment in France*. Cambridge, Mass.: Harvard University Press, 1968.

Darrow, C. W., Henry, E. C., Gill, M. M., & Brenman, Margaret. Inter-area electroencephalographic relationships affected by hypnosis: Preliminary report, *Electroencephalography and Clinical Neurophysiology*, 1950, *2*, 231–240.

Das, J. P. The Pavlovian theory of hypnosis: An evaluation. *Journal of Mental Science*, 1958a, *104*, 82–90.

Das, J. P. Conditioning and hypnosis. *Journal of Experimental Psychology*, 1958b, *56*, 110–113.

Davis, F. C. The functional significance of imagery differences. *Journal of Experimental Psychology*, 1932, *15*, 630–661.

Davis, L. W., & Husband, R. W. A study of hypnotic susceptibility in relation to personality traits. *Journal of Abnormal and Social Psychology*, 1931, *26*, 175–182.

Davis, R. C., & Kantor, J. R. Skin resistance during hypnotic states. *Journal of General Psychology*, 1935, *13*, 62–81.

Dawson, H. E., Jr. Concurrent conditioning of autonomic processes in humans. Unpublished doctoral dissertation, Indiana University, 1953. Cited by Shearn (1961).

Deckert, G. H., & West, L. J. Hypnosis and experimental psychopathology. *American Journal of Clinical Hypnosis,* 1963, *5,* 256–276.

Deckert, G. H., & West, L. J. The problem of hypnotizability: A review. *International Journal of Clinical and Experimental Hypnosis,* 1963, *11,* 205–235.

Deikman, A. J. Experimental meditation. *Journal of Nervous and Mental Disease,* 1963, *136,* 329–343. Reprinted in Tart, 1969a, pp. 199–218.

DeLeon, G. Conditioning the human heart with noise as the unconditioned stimulus. *Journal of Experimental Psychology,* 1964, *68,* 518–520.

Deleuze, J. P. F. *Histoire critique du magnétisme animal.* (Critical history of animal magnetism). Paris, 1819.

Deleuze, J. P. F. *Practical Instruction in Animal Magnetism: Part I.* French original 1825. Translated from the Paris edition by T. C. Hartshorn, with notes by the translator referring to cases in this country. Providence, R.I.: B. Cranston & Co., 1837.

Dellas, Marie, & Gaier, E. L. Identification of creativity: The individual. *Psychological Bulletin,* 1970, *73,* 55–73.

Dermen, D., & London, P. Correlates of hypnotic susceptibility. *Journal of Consulting Psychology,* 1965, *29,* 537–545.

Dessoir, M. *Bibliographie des modernen Hypnotismus.* (Bibliography of modern hypnotism). Berlin: Carl Dunckers Verlag, 1888.

Dessoir, M. *Erster Nachtrag zur Bibliographie des modernen Hypnotismus.* (First supplement to the bibliography of modern hypnotism). Berlin: Carl Dunckers Verlag, 1890.

Dittborn, J. M., & Aristeguieta, A. Expectation and spontaneous posthypnotic amnesia: An experimental note. *American Journal of Clinical Hypnosis,* 1962, *4,* 268–269.

Dittborn, J. M., Muñoz, L., & Aristeguieta, A. Facilitation of suggested sleep after repeated performances of the sleep suggestibility test. *International Journal of Clinical and Experimental Hypnosis,* 1963, *11,* 236–240.

Dittborn, J. M., & O'Connell, D. N. Behavioral sleep, physiological sleep, and hypnotizability. *International Journal of Clinical and Experimental Hypnosis,* 1967, *15,* 181–188.

Domhoff, B. Night dreams and hypnotic dreams: Is there evidence that they are different? *International Journal of Clinical and Experimental Hypnosis,* 1964, *12,* 159–168.

Dorcus, R. M., Brintnall, A. K., & Case, H. W. Control experiments and their relation to theories of hypnotism. *Journal of General Psychology,* 1941, *24,* 217–221.

Drever, J. *A Dictionary of Psychology.* Middlesex: Penguin Books, 1952.

Dudek, Stephanie Z. Suggestion and play therapy in the cure of warts in children: A pilot study. *Journal of Nervous and Mental Disease,* 1967, *145,* 37–42.

Dudek, Stephanie Z. M: An active energy system correlating Rorschach M with ease of creative expression. *Journal of Projective Techniques and Personality Assessment,* 1968a, *32,* 453–461.

Dudek, Stephanie Z. Regression and creativity: A comparison of the Rorschach records of successful vs. unsuccessful painters and writers. *Journal of Nervous and Mental Disease,* 1968b, *147,* 535–546.

Dudley, D. L., Holmes, T. H., Martin, C. J., & Ripley, H. S. Changes in respiration associated with hypnotically induced emotion, pain, and exercise. *Psychosomatic Medicine,* 1964, *26,* 46–57.

Dudley, D. L., Holmes, T. H., Martin, C. J., & Ripley, H. S. Hypnotically induced facsimile of pain. *Archives of General Psychiatry,* 1966, *15,* 198–204.

Dudley, D. L., Holmes, T. H., & Ripley, H. S. Hypnotically induced and suggested facsimile of head pain. *Journal of Nervous and Mental Disease*, 1967, *144*, 258–265.

Dulany, D. E., Jr. Hypotheses and habits in verbal "operant conditioning." *Journal of Abnormal and Social Psychology*, 1961, *63*, 251–263.

Dunbar, F. *Emotions and Bodily Changes*. 4th edition. New York: Columbia University Press, 1954.

Dynes, J. B. An experimental study of hypnotic anaesthesia. *Journal of Abnormal and Social Psychology*, 1932, *27*, 79–88.

Edmonston, W. E., Jr. Stimulus-Response theory of hypnosis. In J. E. Gordon, (Ed.), 1967, pp. 345–387.

Edmonston, W. E., Jr. Hypnosis and electrodermal responses. *American Journal of Clinical Hypnosis*, 1968, *11*, 16–25.

Edmonston, W. E., Jr., & Erbeck, J. R. Hypnotic time distortion: A note. *American Journal of Clinical Hypnosis*, 1967, *10*, 79–80.

Edmonston, W. E., Jr., & Pessin, M. Hypnosis as related to learning and electrodermal measures. *American Journal of Clinical Hypnosis*, 1966, *9*, 31–51.

Edmonston, W. E., Jr., & Robertson, T. G., Jr. A comparison of the effects of task motivational and hypnotic induction instructions on responsiveness to hypnotic suggestibility scales. *American Journal of Clinical Hypnosis*, 1967, *9*, 184–187.

Edwards, G. Post-hypnotic amnesia and post-hypnotic effect. *British Journal of Psychiatry*, 1965, *111*, 316–325.

Ehrlich, Elizabeth A. W. Effects of anxiety and pleasure on memory span. Unpublished doctoral dissertation, University of Michigan, 1965.

Eichhorn, R., & Tracktir, J. The relationship between anxiety, hypnotically induced emotions and gastric secretion. *Gastroenterology*, 1955a, *29*, 422–431.

Eichhorn, R., & Tracktir, J. The effect of hypnotically induced emotions upon gastric secretion. *Gastroenterology*, 1955b, *29*, 432–438.

Eichhorn, R., & Tracktir, J. The effect of hypnosis upon gastric secretion. *Gastroenterology*, 1955c, *29*, 417–421.

Eisenbud, J. The psychology of headache: A case studied experimentally. *Psychiatric Quarterly*, 1937, *11*, 592–619.

Eisenbud, J. A method for investigating the effect of repression on the somatic expression of emotion in vegetative functions: A preliminary report. *Psychosomatic Medicine*, 1939, *1*, 376–387.

Ellenberger, H. F. Charcot and the Salpêtrière School. *American Journal of Psychotherapy*, 1965a, *19*, 253–267.

Ellenberger, H. F. Mesmer and Puységur: From magnetism to hypnotism. *Psychoanalytic Review*, 1965b, *52*, 137–153.

Ellenberger, H. F. *The Discovery of the Unconscious: The History and Evolution of Dynamic Psychiatry*. New York: Basic Books, 1970.

Elliotson, J. *Numerous Cases of Surgical Operations without Pain in the Mesmeric State*. London: H. Baillière, 1843.

Elliotson, J. The London College of physicians and mesmerists (when it became Dr. Elliotson's turn to deliver the Harveian Oration). *Zoist*, 1848–49, *6*, No. 24 (Jan., 1849), 399–405.

Elliotson, J. *The Harveian Oration, Delivered before the Royal College of Physicians, London, June 27, 1846*. In Latin and with an English version and notes. London: H. Baillière, 1846.

Elson, C. de. *Observations sur le magnétisme animal*. (Observations on animal magnetism). London and Paris: Didot, Saugrain, & Clousier, 1780.

Elson, C. de. *Observations sur les deux rapports de MM. les Commissaires nommés par sa Majesté, pour l'examen du magnétisme animal.* (Observations on the two reports of the commissioners named by his Majesty to investigate animal magnetism). Paris: Clousier, 1784.

Engstrom, D. R. The enhancement of EEG alpha production and its effects on hypnotic susceptibility. Unpublished doctoral dissertation, University of Southern California, 1970.

Engstrom, D. R., London, P. and Hart, J. T. Increasing hypnotic susceptibility by EEG alpha training. Paper presented at the annual meeting of the American Psychological Association, Miami Beach, September, 1970.

Erle, R. A. The representation of temporal features of events in hypnotically induced dreams: An exploratory study. Unpublished Masters Thesis, Clark University, Mass., 1958.

Erickson, M. H. A study of clinical and experimental findings on hypnotic deafness: I. Clinical experimentation and findings. *Journal of General Psychology,* 1938a, *19,* 127–150.

Erickson, M. H. A study of clinical and experimental findings on hypnotic deafness: II. Experimental findings with a conditioned response technique. *Journal of General Psychology,* 1938b, *19,* 151–167.

Erickson, M. H. The applications of hypnosis to psychiatry. *Medical Record,* 1939a, *150,* 60–65.

Erickson, M. H. An experimental investigation of the possible anti-social use of hypnosis. *Psychiatry,* 1939b, *2,* 391–414.

Erickson, M. H. Hypnosis: A general review. *Diseases of the Nervous System,* 1941, *2,* 13–18.

Erickson, M. H. Hypnotic investigation of psychosomatic phenomena: Psychosomatic interrelationships studied by experimental hypnosis. *Psychosomatic Medicine,* 1943, *5,* 51–58.

Erickson, M. H. The method employed to formulate a complex story for the induction of an experimental neurosis in a hypnotic subject. *Journal of General Psychology,* 1944, *31,* 67–84. Reprinted in J. Haley (Ed.), 1967, pp. 312–325.

Erickson, M. H. Deep hypnosis and its induction. In L. M. LeCron (Ed.), *Experimental Hypnosis: A Symposium of Articles on Research.* New York: The Macmillan Co., 1952, pp. 70–112. Reprinted in J. Haley (Ed.), 1967, pp. 7–31.

Erickson, M. H. Hypnosis in painful terminal illness. *American Journal of Clinical Hypnosis,* 1958, *1,* 117–121.

Erickson, M. H. Historical note on the hand levitation and other ideomotor techniques. *American Journal of Clinical Hypnosis,* 1960, *3,* 196–199.

Erickson, M. H. Basic psychological problems in hypnosis research (and panel discussion). In G. H. Estabrooks (Ed.) *Hypnosis: Current Problems.* New York: Harper & Row, 1962, pp. 207–223, 238–272.

Erickson, M. H. Initial experiments investigating the nature of hypnosis. *American Journal of Clinical Hypnosis,* 1964a, *7,* 152–162.

Erickson, M. H. The confusion technique in hypnosis. *American Journal of Clinical Hypnosis,* 1964b, *6,* 183–207. Reprinted in J. Haley, (Ed.), 1967, pp. 130–157.

Erickson, M. H. Further experimental investigation of hypnosis: Hypnotic and nonhypnotic realities. *American Journal of Clinical Hypnosis,* 1967b, *10,* 87–135.

Erickson, M. H., & Brickner, R. M. Hypnotic investigation of psychosomatic phenomena. II. The development of aphasia-like reactions from hypnotically induced amnesias. *Psychosomatic Medicine,* 1943, *5,* 59–66.

Erickson, M. H., & Erickson, Elizabeth M. The hypnotic induction of hallucinatory color vision followed by pseudo-negative after-images. *Journal of Experimental Psychology*, 1938, *22*, 581–588.

Erickson, M. H., & Erickson, Elizabeth M. Concerning the nature and character of post-hypnotic behavior. *Journal of General Psychology*, 1941, *24*, 95–133.

Erickson, M. H., Haley, J., & Weakland, J. H. A transcript of a trance induction with commentary. *American Journal of Clinical Hypnosis*, 1959, *2*, 49–84. Reprinted in J. Haley, (Ed.), 1967, pp. 51–88.

Erickson, M. H., Hershman, S., & Secter, I.I. *The Practical Application of Medical and Dental Hypnosis*. New York: Julian Press, 1961.

Eriksen, C. W. Unconscious processes. In M. R. Jones (Ed.), *Nebraska Symposium on Motivation*. Lincoln, Nebraska: University of Nebraska Press, 1958. pp. 169–227.

Eriksen, C. W. (Ed.) *Behavior and Awareness: A Symposium of Research and Interpretation*. Durham, N.C.: Duke University Press, 1962.

Erikson, E. H. (1950) *Childhood and Society*. New York: W. W. Norton & Co., 1963, 2nd edition.

Esdaile, J. *Mesmerism in India and Its Practical Application in Surgery and Medicine*. London: Longman's, Green & Co., 1850. Reissued under title, *Hypnosis in Medicine and Surgery*. With introduction and supplementary reports on current applications by W. S. Kroger. New York: Julian Press, 1957.

Esdaile, J. *Natural and Mesmeric Clairvoyance, with the Practical Application of Mesmerism in Surgery and Medicine*. London: Baillière, 1852.

Estabrooks, G. H. The psychogalvanic reflex in hypnosis. *Journal of General Psychology*, 1930, *3*, 150–157.

Estabrooks, G. H. *Hypnotism*. New York: Dutton, 1943.

Evans, F. J. The structure of hypnosis: A factor analytic investigation. Unpublished doctoral dissertation, University of Sydney, Australia, 1965.

Evans, F. J. The case of the disappearing hypnotist. Paper read at American Psychological Association Convention, New York, September, 1966.

Evans, F. J. Suggestibility in the normal waking state. *Psychological Bulletin*, 1967, *67*, 114–129.

Evans, F. J. Recent trends in experimental hypnosis. *Behavioral Science*, 1968, *13*, 477–487.

Evans, F. J. Simultaneous changes in skin potential and subjective estimates of depth of hypnosis. Paper presented at the meeting of the Eastern Psychological Association, Atlantic City, April, 1970.

Evans, F. J. Contextual forgetting: A study of source amnesia. Paper presented at the meeting of the Eastern Psychological Association, New York, April, 1971.

Evans, F. J., Gustafson, L. A., O'Connell, D. N., Orne, M. T., & Shor, R. E. Response during sleep with intervening waking amnesia. *Science*, 1966, *152*, 666–667.

Evans, F. J., Gustafson, L. A., O'Connell, D. N., Orne, M. T., & Shor, R. E. Sleep-induced behavioral response: Relationship to susceptibility to hypnosis and laboratory sleep patterns. *Journal of Nervous and Mental Disease*, 1969, *148*, 467–476.

Evans, F. J., Gustafson, L. A., O'Connell, D. N., Orne, M. T., & Shor, R. E. Verbally induced behavioral responses during sleep. *Journal of Nervous and Mental Disease*, 1970, *150*, 171–187.

Evans, F. J., & Orchard, W. Sleep learning: The successful waking recall of material presented during sleep. Paper presented at the meeting of the Association for the Psychophysiological Study of Sleep. Boston, March 1969.

Evans, F. J., & Orne, M. T. Motivation, performance, and hypnosis. *International Journal of Clinical and Experimental Hypnosis*, 1965, *13*, 103–116.

Evans, F. J., Reich, L. H., & Orne, M. T. Optokinetic nystagmus, eye movements, and hypnotically induced hallucinations. *Journal of Nervous and Mental Disease*, 1972, *152*, 419–431.

Evans, F. J., & Thorn, Wendy A. F. Source amnesia after hypnosis. *American Psychologist*, 1963, *18*, 373. (Abstract)

Evans, F. J., & Thorn, Wendy A. F. Two types of posthypnotic amnesia: Recall amnesia and source amnesia. *International Journal of Clinical and Experimental Hypnosis*, 1966, *14*, 162–179.

Eysenck, H. J., & Furneaux, W. D. Primary and secondary suggestibility: An experimental and statistical study. *Journal of Experimental Psychology*, 1945, *35*, 485–503.

Fabrikant, M. B. Monetary equivalents of hypnotically induced degrees of pleasure. (In press.)

Faria, J. C. A. de. *De le cause du sommeil lucide ou étude de la nature de l'homme*. (On the cause of lucid sleep: a study on the nature of man). Second edition edited by D. G. Dalgado. Paris: Henri Jouve, 1906.

Fehr, F. S., & Stern, J. A. The effect of hypnosis on attention to relevant and irrelevant stimuli. *International Journal of Clinical and Experimental Hypnosis*, 1967, *15*, 134–143.

Feirstein, A. Personality correlates of tolerance for unrealistic experiences. *Journal of Consulting Psychology*, 1967, *31*, 387–395.

Ferster, C. B., Levitt, E. E., Zimmerman, J., & Brady, J. P. The measurement of hypnotic effects by operant-reinforcement techniques. *Psychological Record*, 1961, *11*, 427–430.

Field, P. B. Bales interaction analysis of hypnosis. *International Journal of Clinical and Experimental Hypnosis*, 1964, *12*, 88–98.

Field, P. B. An inventory scale of hypnotic depth. *International Journal of Clinical and Experimental Hypnosis*, 1965, *13*, 238–249.

Field, P. B. Some self-rating measures related to hypnotizability. *Perceptual and Motor Skills*, 1966, *23*, 1179–1187.

Field, P. B., Evans, F. J., & Orne, M. T. Order of difficulty of suggestions during hypnosis. *International Journal of Clinical and Experimental Hypnosis*, 1965, *13*, 183–192.

Field, P. B., & Palmer, R. D. Factor analysis: Hypnosis inventory. *International Journal of Clinical and Experimental Hypnosis*, 1969, *17*, 50–61.

Fischer, R. (Ed.) Interdisciplinary Perspectives of Time, *Annals of the New York Academy of Sciences*, 1967, *138*, 367–915.

Fisher, C. Psychoanalytic implications of recent research on sleep and dreaming: *Journal of the American Psychoanalytic Association*, 1965, *13*, 197–303.

Fisher, S. The role of expectancy in the performance of post-hypnotic behavior. *Journal of Abnormal and Social Psychology*, 1954, *49*, 503–507.

Fisher, S. An investigation of alleged conditioning phenomena under hypnosis. *Journal of Clinical and Experimental Hypnosis*, 1955, *3*, 71–103.

Fisher, S. Problems of interpretation and controls in hypnotic research. In G. H. Estabrooks (Ed.), *Hypnosis: Current Problems*. New York: Harper & Row, 1962, pp. 109–126.

Fisher, V. E., & Marrow, A. J. Experimental study of moods. *Character & Personality*, 1934, *2*, 202–208.

Fiss, H., Ellman, S. J., & Klein, G. S. Effects of interruption of rapid eye-movement sleep on fantasy in the waking state. *Psychophysiology*, 1968, *4*, 364. (Abstract)

Fitzgerald, E. T. Measurement of openness to experience: A study of regression in the service of the ego. *Journal of Personality and Social Psychology,* 1966, *4,* 655–663.

Flavell, J. H. *The Developmental Psychology of Jean Piaget.* Princeton, N. J.: D. Van Nostrand, 1963.

Ford, L. F., & Yeager, C. L. Changes in electroencephalogram in subjects under hypnosis. *Diseases of the Nervous System,* 1948, *9,* 190–192.

Forel, A. *Hypnotism or Suggestion and Psychotherapy: A Study of the Psychological, Psycho-physiological and Therapeutic Aspects of Hypnotism.* Translated from the 5th German edition by H. W. Armit, American edition, revised and corrected. New York: Rebman Co., 1907.

Foulkes, D. *The Psychology of Sleep.* New York: Charles Scribner's Sons, 1966.

Foulkes, D., & Vogel, G. Mental activity at sleep onset. *Journal of Abnormal Psychology,* 1965, *70,* 231–243.

Freedman, S. J., & Marks, Patricia A. Visual imagery produced by rhythmic photic stimulation: Personality correlates and phenomenology. *British Journal of Psychology,* 1965, *56,* 95–112.

French, T. M., & Fromm, Erika. *Dream Interpretation: A New Approach.* New York: Basic Books, 1964.

Fresacher, L. A way into the hypnotic state. *British Journal of Medical Hypnotism,* 1951, *3,* 12–13.

Freud, Anna. (1936). *The Ego and the Mechanisms of Defense.* New York: International Universities Press, 1946.

Freud, S. (1900). The interpretation of dreams. *Standard Edition,* J. Strachey, (Ed.), Vols. 4 & 5. London: The Hogarth Press, 1953.

Freud, S. *Introductary Lectures on Psycho-Analysis.* (Joan Riviere, Trans.) London: Allen & Unwin, 1922.

Freud, S. (1923). The ego and the id. *Standard Edition,* J. Stranchey, (Ed.), Vol. 19. London: The Hogarth Press, 1961.

Freud, S. (1925). *An Autobiographical Study.* Authorized translation for the 2nd edition by J. Strachey, 1946. New York: W. W. Norton, 1952.

Friedlander, J. W., & Sarbin, T. R. The depth of hypnosis. *Journal of Abnormal and Social Psychology,* 1938, *33,* 453–475.

Fromm, Erika. Hypnoanalysis: Theory and two case excerpts. *Psychotherapy: Theory, Research and Practice,* 1965, *2,* 127–133.

Fromm, Erika. Activity and passivity of the ego in hypnosis. Paper read at the 22nd Annual Convention of the Society for Clinical and Experimental Hypnosis, Philadelphia, October, 1970.

Fromm, Erika. Activity and passivity of the ego in hypnosis. *International Journal of Clinical and Experimental Hypnosis,* 1972, *20.*

Fromm, Erika, Oberlander, M. I., & Gruenewald, Doris. Perceptual and cognitive processes in different states of consciousness: The waking state and hypnosis—with implications for hypnotherapy. Paper presented at the Convention of American Psychological Association, Washington, D.C., September, 1969.

Fromm, Erika, Oberlander, M. I., & Gruenewald, Doris. Perceptual and cognitive processes in different states of consciousness: The waking state and hypnosis. *Journal of Projective Techniques and Personality Assessment,* 1970, *34,* 375–387.

Fromm, Erika, & Weingarten, F. Permissive modification of Weitzenhoffer & Hilgard's Stanford Hypnotic Susceptibility Scale, Form A. Unpublished Manuscript. University of Chicago, 1965.

Furneaux, W. D. The prediction of susceptibility to hypnosis. *Journal of Personality,* 1946, *14,* 281–294.

Galbraith, G. C., London, P., Leibovitz, M. P., Cooper, L. M., & Hart, J. T. EEG and hypnotic susceptibility, *Journal of Comparative and Physiological Psychology*, 1970, *72*, 125–131.

Galdston, I. Hypnosis and modern psychiatry. *Ciba Symposia*, 1948a, *9*, 845–856.

Galdston, I. Mesmer and animal magnetism. *Ciba Symposia*, 1948b, *9*, 832–837.

Gamble, K. R., & Kellner, H. Creative functioning and cognitive regression. *Journal of Personality and Social Psychology*, 1968, *9*, 266–271.

Ganong, W. F. *Review of Medical Physiology.* (3rd edition) Los Altos, California: Lange Medical Publications, 1967.

Gardner, R. W., Holzman, P. S., Klein, G. S., Linton, H. P., & Spence, D. P. Cognitive control: A study of individual consistencies in cognitive behavior. *Psychological Issues*, 1959, *1*, 1–186.

Geiwitz, P. J. Structure of boredom. *Journal of Personality and Social Psychology*, 1966, *3*, 592–600.

Germann, A. C. Hypnosis as related to the scientific detection of deception by polygraph examination: A pilot study. *International Journal of Clinical and Experimental Hypnosis*, 1961, *9*, 309–311.

Gheorghiu, V. Some peculiarities of posthypnotic source amnesia of information. In L. Chertok (Ed.), *Psychophysiological Mechanisms of Hypnosis.* New York: Springer-Verlag, 1969, pp. 112–122.

Ghiselin, B. *The Creative Process: A Symposium.* New York: New American Library, 1952.

Gibson, W. *The Boat.* Boston: Houghton Mifflin, 1953.

Gibson, W. B. *The Key to Hypnotism.* New York: Key Publishing Co., 1956.

Gidro-Frank, L., & Bowersbuch, M. K. A study of the plantar response in hypnotic age regression. *Journal of Nervous and Mental Disease*, 1948, *107*, 443–458.

Gidro-Frank, L., & Bull, N. Emotions induced and studied in hypnotic subjects: Part I: The method. *Journal of Nervous and Mental Disease*, 1950, *111*, 91–100.

Giles, E. A cross-validation study of the Pascal technique of hypnotic induction. *International Journal of Clinical and Experimental Hypnosis*, 1962, *10*, 101–108.

Gill, M. M. The primary process. In R. R. Holt, (Ed.), Motives and thought: Psychoanalytic essays in honor of David Rapaport. *Psychological Issues*, Monograph 18–19. New York: International Universities Press, 1967, pp. 260–298.

Gill, M. M., & Brenman, Margaret. *Hypnosis and Related States: Psychoanalytic Studies in Regression.* New York: International Universities Press, 1959.

Golann, S. E. Psychological study of creativity. *Psychological Bulletin*, 1963, *60*, 548–565.

Goldsmith, Margaret L. *Franz Anton Mesmer: The History of an Idea.* London: Arthur Barker; New York: Doubleday, Doran, 1934.

Goldstein, M. S., & Sipprelle, C. N. Hypnotically induced amnesia versus ablation of memory. *International Journal of Clinical and Experimental Hypnosis*, 1970, *18*, 211–216.

Gordon, J. E. Leading and following psychotherapeutic techniques with hypnotically induced repression and hostility. *Journal of Abnormal and Social Psychology*, 1957, *54*, 405–410.

Gordon, J. E. (Ed.) *Handbook of Clinical and Experimental Hypnosis.* New York: Macmillan, 1967.

Gordon, J. E. Hypnosis in research on psychotherapy. In J. E. Gordon (Ed.), 1967, pp. 148–202.

Gormley, W. J. *Medical Hypnosis: Historical Introduction to its Morality in the Light of Papal, Theological and Medical Teaching.* Washington, D.C.: The Catholic University of America Press, 1961.

Gorton, B. E. The physiology of hypnosis.—I. *Psychiatric Quarterly,* 1949, *23,* 317–343; The physiology of hypnosis—II. *Psychiatric Quarterly,* 1949, *23,* 457–485.

Gorton, B. E. Current problems of physiologic research in hypnosis. In G. H. Estabrooks (Ed.), *Hypnosis: Current Problems.* New York: Harper & Row, 1962, pp. 30–53.

Gottlieb, A. A., Gleser, Goldine C., & Gottschalk, L. A. Verbal and physiological responses to hypnotic suggestion of attitudes. *Psychosomatic Medicine,* 1967, *29,* 172–183.

Gough, H. G. The F minus K dissimulation index for the Minnesota Multiphasic Personality Inventory. *Journal of Consulting Psychology,* 1950, *14,* 408–413.

Gough, H. G. Identifying the creative man. *Journal of Value Engineering,* 1964, *2,* 5–12.

Govinda, A. B. *Foundations of Tibetan Mysticism.* New York: Dutton, 1960.

Graef, J. R. The influence of cognitive states on time estimation and subjective time rate. Unpublished doctoral dissertation, University of Michigan, 1969.

Graham, D. T., & Wolf, S. Pathogenesis of urticaria: Experimental study of life situations, emotions, and cutaneous vascular reactions. *Journal of the American Medical Association,* 1950, *143,* 1396–1402.

Graham, F. K., & Kunish, Nancy O. Physiological responses of unhypnotized subjects to attitude suggestions. *Psychosomatic Medicine,* 1965, *27,* 317–329.

Graham, K. R., & Patton, Ann. Retroactive inhibition, hypnosis and hypnotic amnesia. *International Journal of Clinical and Experimental Hypnosis,* 1968, *16,* 68–74.

Granda, A. M., & Hammack, J. T. Operant behavior during sleep. *Science,* 1961, *133,* 1485–1486.

Gravitz, M. A., & Forbes, M. E. Hypnosis and the conceptualization of a continuum of consciousness. *British Journal of Medical Hypnotism,* 1963, *15,* 21–25.

Gravitz, M. A., & Kramer, Mary F. A study of some factors associated with hypnotic-like experience. *American Journal of Clinical Hypnosis,* 1967, *10,* 48–51.

Gray, J. The effect of productivity on primary process and creativity. *Journal of Projective Techniques and Personality Assessment,* 1969, *33,* 213–218.

Green, E. E., Green, Alyce M., & Walters, E. D. Self-regulation of internal states. In J. Rose (Ed.), *Progress of Cybernetics: Proceedings of the First International Congress of Cybernetics, London, 1969.* London: Gordon & Breach Science Publishers, 1970.

Griffin, Dorothy P. Movement responses and creativity. *Journal of Consulting Psychology,* 1958, *22,* 134–136.

Grimm, F. M. von, & Diderot, D. Rapport des commissaires chargés par le roi de l'examen du magnétisme animal, 1784. (Report of the commissioners charged by the King with the investigation of animal magnetism). *Correspondance Littéraire*, Pt. 3, Vol. 3, Paris, 1813, pp. 10–20.

Grossberg, J. M., & Wilson, Helen K. Physiological changes accompanying the visualization of fearful and neutral situations. *Journal of Personality and Social Psychology*, 1968, *10*, 124–133.

Grosz, H. J. The relation of serum ascorbic acid level to adrenocortical secretion during experimentally induced emotional stress in human subjects. *Journal of Psychosomatic Research*, 1961, *5*, 253–262.

Grosz, H. J., & Levitt, E. E. The effects of hypnotically induced anxiety on the Manifest Anxiety Scale and the Barron Ego-strength Scale. *Journal of Abnormal and Social Psychology*, 1959, *59*, 281–283.

Gruenewald, Doris, & Fromm, Erika. Hypnosis, simulation and brain damage. *Journal of Abnormal Psychology*, 1967, *72*, 191–192.

Guilford, J. P. *Personality*. New York: McGraw-Hill, 1959.

Guilford, J. P. Some theoretical views of creativity. In H. Helson & W. Bevan (Eds.), *Contemporary Approaches to Psychology*. Princeton, New Jersey: D. Van Nostrand Company, 1967, 419–459.

Gurney, E. The stages of hypnotism. *Society for Psychical Research: Proceedings*, 1884, *2*, 61–72.

Hadfield, J. A. The influence of suggestion on body temperature. *Lancet*, 1920, *2*, 68–69.

Hahn, K. W., Jr., & Barber, T. X. Hallucinations with and without hypnotic induction: An extension of the Brady & Levitt study. Harding, Mass.: The Medfield Foundation, 1966.

Haim, E. Beitrag zur Frage der Sensibilität der Abdominalorgane. *Zentralblatt für Chirurgie*, 1908, *35*, 337–338.

Haley, J. An interactional explanation of hypnosis. *American Journal of Clinical Hypnosis*, 1958, *1*, 41–57.

Haley, J. *Strategies of Psychotherapy*. New York: Grune & Stratton, 1963.

Haley, J. (Ed.) *Advanced Techniques of Hypnosis and Therapy: Selected Papers of Milton H. Erickson, M. D.* New York: Grune & Stratton, 1967.

Hall, C. R. *Mesmerism: Its Rise, Progress, and Mysteries*. New York: Burgess, Stringer, & Co., 1845. First American edition. From *Lancet*, in serial, London, 1845, *1*, beginning pp. 112–118.

Hall, C. S., & Van de Castle, R. L. *The Content Analysis of Dreams*. New York: Appleton-Century-Crofts, 1966.

Hall, W. H., Herb, R. W., Brady, J. P., & Brooks, F. P. Gastric function during hypnosis and hypnotically-induced gastro-intestinal symptoms. *Journal of Psychosomatic Research*, 1967, *11*, 263–266.

Halliday, A. M., & Mason, A. A. Cortical evoked potentials during hypnotic anaesthesia. *Electroencephalography and Clinical Neuro-physiology*, 1964, *16*, 314.

Halper, C., Pivik, T., & Dement, W. An attempt to reduce the REM rebound following REM deprivation by the use of induced waking mentation. Paper presented at the meeting of the Association for the Psychophysiological Study of Sleep, Boston, March, 1969.

Hamel, I. A. A study and analysis of the conditioned reflex. *Psychological Monographs*, 1919, *27*, No. 118, 1–65.

Hammer, A. G., Evans, F. J., & Bartlett, Mary. Factors in hypnosis and suggestion. *Journal of Abnormal and Social Psychology*, 1963, *67*, 15–23.

Harano, K., Ogawa, K., & Naruse, G. A study of plethysmography and skin temperature during active concentration and autogenic exercise. In W. Luthe, (Ed.), *Autogenic Training*. New York: Grune & Stratton, 1965, pp. 55–58.

Harman, W. W., McKim, R. H., Mogar, R. E., Fadiman, J., & Stolaroff, M. J. Psychedelic agents in creative problem solving: A pilot study. *Psychological Reports*, 1966, *19*, 211–227. Reprinted in C. T. Tart, (Ed.), 1969, pp. 445–461.

Hart, E. *Hypnotism, Mesmerism, and the New Witchcraft*. New York: D. Appleton & Co., 1898.

Hartley, E. L., & Hartley, Ruth E. *Fundamentals of Social Psychology*. New York: Knopf, 1958.

Hartmann, H. (1939). *Ego Psychology and the Problem of Adaptation*. New York: International Universities Press, 1958.

Hartmann, H. *Essays on Ego Psychology: Selected Problems in Psychoanalytic Theory*. New York: International Universities Press, 1964.

Hartnett, J., Nowlis, D., & Svorad, D. Hypnotic susceptibility and EEG alpha: Three correlations. Hawthorne House Research Memorandum, No. 97, 1969.

Hatfield, Elaine C. The validity of the LeCron method of evaluating hypnotic depth. *International Journal of Clinical and Experimental Hypnosis*, 1961, *9*, 215–221.

Hauenstein, Louise S. Anger, salience and the appreciation of hostile humor. Unpublished doctoral dissertation, University of Michigan, 1970.

Hedegard, Sheila A. G. A molecular analysis of psychological defense mechanisms. Unpublished doctoral dissertation, University of Michigan, 1968.

Heidenhain, R. *Hypnotism or Animal Magnetism: Physiological Observations*. Translated from the 4th German edition by L. C. Wooldridge. With a preface by G. J. Romanes. London: K. Paul, Trench & Company, 1888.

Heimann, H., & Spoerri, T. Elektroencephalographische Untersuchungen an Hypnotisierten. *Monatsschrift für Psychiatrie und Neurologie*, 1953, *125*, 261–271.

Helfman (Damaser), Esther, Shor, R. E., & Orne, M. T. Requested emotions in the wake and the hypnotic states. Paper read at the Convention of the American Psychological Association, Chicago, September, 1960.

Helson, Ravenna. Generality of sex differences in creative style. *Journal of Personality*, 1968, *36*, 33–48.

Hepps, R. B., & Brady, J. P. Hypnotically induced tachycardia: An experiment with simulating controls. *Journal of Nervous and Mental Disease*, 1967, *145*, 131–137.

Hernández-Peón, R., & Donoso, M. Influence of attention and suggestion upon subcortical evoked electrical activity in the human brain. In L. van Bogaert & J. Radermecker (Eds.), *First International Congress of Neurological Sciences*. London: Pergamon Press, 1959, *3*, 385–386.

Heron, W. The pathology of boredom. *Scientific American*, 1957, *196*, 52–56.

Hersch, C. The cognitive functioning of the creative person: A developmental analysis. *Journal of Projective Techniques*, 1962, *26*, 193–200.

Hibler, F. W. An experimental investigation of negative after-images of hallucinated colors in hypnosis. *Journal of Experimental Psychology*, 1940, *27*, 45–57.

Hilgard, E. R. Impulsive versus realistic thinking: An examination of the distinction between primary and secondary processes in thought. *Psychological Bulletin*, 1962, *59*, 477–488.

Hilgard, E. R. The motivational relevance of hypnosis. In D. Levine (Ed.), *Ne-*

braska Symposium on Motivation. Lincoln, Nebraska: University of Nebraska Press, 1964, pp. 1–44.

Hilgard, E. R. Hypnosis. *Annual Review of Psychology,* 1965a, *16,* 157–180.

Hilgard, E. R. *Hypnotic Susceptibility.* New York: Harcourt, Brace & World Inc., 1965b.

Hilgard, E. R. Posthypnotic amnesia: Experiments and theory. *International Journal of Clinical and Experimental Hypnosis,* 1966, *14,* 104–111.

Hilgard, E. R. Individual differences in hypnotizability. In J. E. Gordon (Ed.), 1967, pp. 391–443.

Hilgard, E. R. Creativity: Slogan and substance. *The Centennial Review,* 1968, *12,* 40–58.

Hilgard, E. R. Altered states of awareness. *Journal of Nervous and Mental Disease,* 1969a, *149,* 68–79.

Hilgard, E. R. Experimental psychology and hypnosis. In L. Chertok (Ed.), *Psychophysiological Mechanisms of Hypnosis.* Berlin: Springer-Verlag, 1969b, pp. 123–138.

Hilgard, E. R. Pain as a puzzle for psychology and physiology. *American Psychologist,* 1969c, *24,* 103–113.

Hilgard, E. R., & Cooper, L. M. Spontaneous and suggested posthypnotic amnesia. *International Journal of Clinical and Experimental Hypnosis,* 1965, *13,* 261–273.

Hilgard, E. R., Cooper, L. M., Lenox, J., Morgan, Arlene H., & Voevodsky, J. The use of pain-state reports in the study of hypnotic analgesia to the pain of ice water. *Journal of Nervous and Mental Disease,* 1967, *144,* 506–513.

Hilgard, E. R., & Hommel, L. S. Selective amnesia for events within hypnosis in relation to repression. *Journal of Personality,* 1961, *29,* 205–216.

Hilgard, E. R., & Marquis, D. G. *Conditioning and Learning.* New York: Appleton-Century, 1940.

Hilgard, E. R., & Tart, C. T. Responsiveness to suggestions following waking and imagination instructions and following induction of hypnosis. *Journal of Abnormal Psychology,* 1966, *71,* 196–208.

Hilgard, E. R., Weitzenhoffer, A. M., Landes, J., & Moore, Rosemarie K. The distribution of susceptibility to hypnosis in a student population: A study using the Stanford Hypnotic Susceptibility Scale. *Psychological Monographs,* 1961, *75,* No. 8, 1–22.

Hilgard, Josephine R. *Personality and Hypnosis: A Study of Imaginative Involvement.* Chicago: University of Chicago Press, 1970.

Hill, H. E., Kornetsky, C. H., Flanary, H. G., & Wikler, A. Effects of anxiety and morphine on discrimination of intensities of painful stimuli. *Journal of Clinical Investigation,* 1952a, *31,* 473–480.

Hill, H. E., Kornetsky, C. H., Flanary, H. G., & Wikler, A. Studies on anxiety associated with anticipation of pain: I. Effects of morphine. *Archives of Neurology and Psychiatry,* 1952b, *67,* 612–619.

Hodge, J. R., & Wagner, E. E. The validity of hypnotically induced emotional states. *American Journal of Clinical Hypnosis,* 1964, *7,* 37–41.

Holt, R. R. Cognitive controls and primary processes. *Journal of Psychological Researches, Madras,* 1960, *4,* 105–112.

Holt, R. R. Manual for the scoring of primary process manifestations in Rorschach responses. (9th edition) New York: Research Center for Mental Health, New York University, 1963 (mimeographed).

Holt, R. R. Imagery: The return of the ostracized. *American Psychologist,* 1964, *19,* 254–264.

Holt, R. R. The development of the primary process: A structural view. In R. R. Holt, (Ed.), Motives and Thought: Psychoanalytic essays in honor of David Rapaport. *Psychological Issues,* Monograph 18/19. New York: International Universities Press, 1967, pp. 345–383.

Holt, R. R., & Havel, Joan. A method for assessing primary and secondary process in the Rorschach. In Maria A. Rickers-Ovsiankina (Ed.), *Rorschach Psychology.* New York: John Wiley & Sons, 1960, pp. 263–315.

Holtzman, W. H., Thorpe, J. S., Swartz, J. D., & Herron, E. W. *Inkblot Perception and Personality: Holtzman Inkblot Technique.* Austin: University of Texas Press, 1961.

Horowitz, M. J. Visual imagery and cognitive organization. *American Journal of Psychiatry,* 1967, *123,* 938–946.

Horowitz, M. J., Adams, J. E., & Rutkin, B. B. Visual imagery on brain stimulation. *Archives of General Psychiatry,* 1968, *19,* 469–486.

Hoskovec, J. Hypnopedia in the Soviet Union: A critical review of recent major experiments. *International Journal of Clinical and Experimental Hypnosis,* 1966, *14,* 308–315.

Howes, D. A Word count of spoken English. *Journal of Verbal Learning and Verbal Behavior,* 1966, *5,* 572–606.

Hull, C. L. Quantitative methods of investigating waking suggestion. *Journal of Abnormal and Social Psychology,* 1929, *24,* 153–169.

Hull, C. L. Quantitative methods of investigating hypnotic suggestion. Part I. *Journal of Abnormal and Social Psychology,* 1930, *25,* 200–223.

Hull, C. L. Quantitative methods of investigating hypnotic suggestion. Part II. *Journal of Abnormal and Social Psychology,* 1931, *25,* 390–417.

Hull, C. L. *Hypnosis and Suggestibility: An Experimental Approach.* New York: Appleton-Century-Crofts, 1933.

Hunt, J. McV. Intrinsic motivation and its role in psychological development. In D. Levine (Ed.), *Nebraska Symposium on Motivation.* Lincoln, Nebraska: University of Nebraska Press, 1965, pp. 189–282.

Hunt, Sonja M. The speech of the subject under hypnosis. *International Journal of Clinical and Experimental Hypnosis,* 1969, *17,* 209–216.

Huse, B. Does the hypnotic trance favor the recall of faint memories? *Journal of Experimental Psychology,* 1930, *13,* 519–529.

Husson, H. M., et al. *Report of the Experiments on Animal Magnetism, Made by a Committee of the Medical Section of the French Royal Academy of Sciences; Read at the Meeting of the 21st and 28th of June, 1831.* Signed: Bourdois de la Motte (President), Fourquier, Gueneau de Mussy, Guersent, Husson (Reporter), Itard, J. J. Leroux, Marc, Thillaye. English translation by J. C. Colquhoun, with an historical and explanatory introduction, and an appendix (on somnambulistic transposability of the senses). Edinburgh: Robert Cadell; London: Whittaker & Co., 1833. Also translated and preceded with an introduction by C. St. Poyen St. Sauveur. Boston: D. K. Hitchcock, 1836. Also abstracted translation in J. S. Bailly, et al., 1837, pp. 52–58.

Huston, P. E., Shakow, D., & Erickson, M. H. A study of hypnotically induced complexes by means of the Luria technique. *Journal of General Psychology,* 1934, *11,* 65–97.

Huxley, A. *Island.* New York: Harper & Row, 1962.

Huxley, A. *The Doors of Perception.* New York: Harper & Row, 1963.

Ikemi, Y., Akagi, M., Maeda, J., Fukumoto, T., Kawate, K., Hirakawa, K., Gondo, S., Nakagawa, T., Honda, T., Sakamoto, A., & Yasumatsu, A. Experimental studies on the psychosomatic disorders of the digestive system. *Proceedings of the World Congress on Gastroenterology*, 1959, 169–180.

Ikemi, Y., Akagi, M., Maeda, J., Fukumoto, T., Kawate, K., Hirakawa, K., Gondo, S., Nakagawa, T., Honda, T., Sakamoto, A., & Kumagai, M. Hypnotic experiments on the psychosomatic aspects of gastrointestinal disorders. *International Journal of Clinical and Experimental Hypnosis*, 1959, 7, 139–150.

Ikemi, Y., & Nakagawa, S. A psychosomatic study of contagious dermatitis. *Kyushu Journal of Medical Science*, 1962, 13, 335–352.

Imm, C. R. An exploration of repression through hypnotically implanted conflicts. Unpublished doctoral dissertation, Stanford University, 1965.

Jackson, P. W., & Messick, S. The person, the product and the response: Conceptual problems in the assessment of creativity. *Journal of Personality*, 1965, 33, 309–329.

Jacobson, A., & Kales, A. Somnambulism: All night EEG and related studies. In S. S. Kety, E. V. Evarts and H. L. Williams (Eds.) *Sleep and Altered States of Consciousness*. Proceedings of the Association for Research in Nervous and Mental Disease, Dec. 3 & 4, 1965. Baltimore: Williams & Wilkins, 1965, pp. 424–455.

Jacobson, E. Electrical measurements of neuromuscular states during mental activities: Imagination of movement involving skeletal muscle. *American Journal of Physiology*, 1930, 91, 567–608.

Jacobson, E. Electrophysiology of mental activities. *American Journal of Psychology*, 1932, 44, 677–694.

Jacobson, E. *Progressive Relaxation*. Chicago: University of Chicago Press, 1938.

Jacobson, E. Relaxation methods in labor: A critique of current techniques in natural childbirth. *American Journal of Obstetrics and Gynecology*, 1954, 67, 1035–1048.

James, W., & Carnochan, G. M. Report of the committee on hypnotism. *American Society for Psychical Research: Proceedings*, 1885–1889, 1, No. 2, 95–102.

Janet, P. *Psychological Healing: A Historical and Clinical Study*. French original, 1919. English translation by E. Paul & C. Paul. New York: The Macmillan Co., 1925. 2 vols.

Jenness, A. Hypnotism. In J. McV. Hunt (Ed.), *Personality and the Behavior Disorders*. New York: The Ronald Press, 1944, pp. 466–502.

Jenness, A. Somnambulism, imagery, and hypnotizability. Paper presented at the Convention of the American Psychological Association, Chicago, 1965.

Jenness, A., & Jorgensen, Ada P. Ratings of vividness of imagery in the waking state compared with reports of somnambulism. *American Journal of Psychology*, 1941, 54, 253–259.

Jenness, A., & Wible, C. L. Respiration and heart action in sleep and hypnosis. *Journal of General Psychology*, 1937, 16, 197–222.

Johner, C. H., & Perlman, H. B. Hypnosis and vestibular function. *Annals of Otology, Rhinology & Laryngology*, 1968, 77, 126–138.

Johnson, P. O., & Jackson, R. W. B. *Modern Statistical Methods: Descriptive and Inductive*. Chicago: Rand McNally, 1959.

Johnson, R. F. Q., Maher, B. A., & Barber, T. X. Artifact in the purported essence of hypnosis: An experimental and theoretical evaluation of trance logic. (In press.)

Jones, R. M. *Ego Synthesis in Dreams*. Cambridge: Schenkman, 1962.

Jussieu, A. L. de. *Rapport de l'un commissaire chargé par le roi de l'examen du magnétisme animal*. (Report of a commissioner charged by the King with the investigation of animal magnetism). *Paris, 12 septembre 1784.* Paris: Herissant, 1784. Reproduced in A. Bertrand, 1826, pp. 151–206.

Kales, A. (Ed.) *Sleep: Physiology and Pathology: A Symposium.* Philadelphia: J. B. Lippincott & Co., 1969.

Kamiya, J. Operant control of the EEG alpha rhythm and some of its reported effects on consciousness. In C. T. Tart (Ed.), *Altered States of Consciousness.* New York, Wiley, 1969a, pp. 509–517.

Kanfer, F. H., & Goldfoot, D. A. Self-control and tolerance of noxious stimulation. *Psychological Reports,* 1966, *18,* 79–85.

Kanzer, M. G. The therapeutic use of dreams induced by hypnotic suggestion. *Psychoanalytic Quarterly,* 1945, *14,* 313–335.

Kasamatsu, A., & Hirai, T. An electroencephelographic study on the Zen meditation (Zazen). *Folia Psychiatrica et Neurologica Japonica,* 1966, *20,* 315–336. Reprinted in C. T. Tart, (Ed.), 1969a, pp. 489–502.

Katzenstein, A. An empirical scatter analysis of electrobiological data in hypnotized patients. *American Journal of Clinical Hypnosis,* 1965, *7,* 320–324.

Kaufman, M. R. Hypnosis in psychotherapy today: Anachronism, fixation, regression, or valid modality? *Archives of General Psychiatry,* 1961, *4,* 30–39.

Kehoe, M., & Ironside, W. Studies on the experimental evocation of depressive responses using hypnosis: II. The influence of depressive responses upon the secretion of gastric acid. *Psychosomatic Medicine,* 1963, *25,* 403–419.

Kehoe, M., & Ironside, W. Studies on the experimental evocation of depressive responses using hypnosis: III. The secretory rate of total gastric acid with respect to various spontaneous experiences such as nausea, disgust, crying, and dyspnea. *Psychosomatic Medicine,* 1964, *26,* 224–249.

Kelsey, Denys E. R. Phantasies of birth and prenatal experiences recovered from patients undergoing hypnoanalysis. *Journal of Mental Science,* 1953, *99,* 216–223.

Kerner, J. Seeress of Prevorst. Translated from the German. In G. Bush, (Ed.), *Mesmer and Swedenborg: or, the Relation of the Developments of Mesmerism to the Doctrines and Disclosures of Swedenborg.* New York: John Allen, 1847. Appendix B.

Kesner, L. S. A comparison of the effectiveness of two psychotherapy techniques in the resolution of a posthypnotic conflict. *Journal of Clinical and Experimental Hypnosis,* 1954, *2,* 55–75.

Kety, S. S. Consciousness and the metabolism of the brain. In H. A. Abramson (Ed.), *Problems of Consciousness; Transactions of the Third Conference,* March 10 and 11, 1952, New York, New York: Josiah Macy, Jr. Foundation, 1952, pp. 11–73.

Kihlstrom, J. F., & Evans, F. J. Posthypnotic amnesia as disorganized retrieval. Proceedings of the Annual Convention of the American Psychological Association, 1971, *6,* 775–776.

Klein, D. B. The experimental production of dreams during hypnosis. *University of Texas Bulletin,* 1930, *3009,* 1–71.

Klein, G. S. Peremptory ideation: Structure and force in motivated ideas. In R. R. Holt (Ed.) *Motives and Thought: Psychoanalytic Essays in Honor of David Rapaport. Psychological Issues* (18/19), 1967, *5,* 80–128. New York: International Universities Press.

Kleitman, N. *Sleep and Wakefulness.* Chicago: University of Chicago Press, 1963.

Kline, M. V. Hypnosis and age progression: A case report. *Journal of Genetic Psychology,* 1951, *78,* 195–206.

Kline, M. V. *Freud and Hypnosis: The Interaction of Psychodynamics and Hypnosis*. New York: Julian Press, 1958.

Kline, M. V. Hypnotic amnesia in psychotherapy. *International Journal of Clinical and Experimental Hypnosis*, 1966, *14*, 112–120.

Kline, M. V. The production of antisocial behavior through hypnosis: New clinical data. Paper presented at the 22nd Annual Convention of the Society for Clinical and Experimental Hypnosis. Philadelphia, November, 1970.

Kline, M. V., Guze, H., & Haggerty, A. D. An experimental study of the nature of hypnotic deafness: Effects of delayed speech feed-back. *Journal of Clinical and Experimental Hypnosis*, 1954, *2*, 145–156.

Kline, M. V., & Linder, M. Psychodynamic factors in the experimental investigation of hypnotically induced emotions with particular reference to blood glucose measurements. *Journal of Psychology*, 1969, *71*, 21–25.

Klinger, B. I. Effect of peer model responsiveness and length of induction procedure on hypnotic responsiveness. *Journal of Abnormal Psychology*, 1970, *75*, 15–18.

Klopfer, B., Ainsworth, Mary D., Klopfer, W., & Holt, R. R. *Developments in the Rorschach Technique*. Yonkers, N. Y.: World Book Co., 1954.

Klopp, K. K. Production of local anesthesia using waking suggestion with the child patient. *International Journal of Clinical and Experimental Hypnosis*, 1961, *9*, 59–62.

Knowles, F. W. Hypnosis in amnesic states. A report of seven cases. *New Zealand Medical Journal*, 1964, *63*, 100–103.

Kolers, P. A. The illusion of movement. *Scientific American*, 1964, *211*, 98–106.

Kornetsky, C. Effects of anxiety and morphine on the anticipation and perception of painful radiant thermal stimuli. *Journal of Comparative Physiology and Psychology*, 1954, *47*, 130–132.

Korotkin, I. I., & Suslova, M. M. Investigation into higher nervous activity in subjects in the somnambulistic phase of hypnosis. *Zhurnal Vyssheĭ Nervnoĭ Deĭâtel'nosti*, 1951, *1*, 617–622. (Cited by Das, 1958a).

Korotkin, I. I., & Suslova, M. M. Investigation into the higher nervous activity in some somnambulistic phase of hypnosis during different depths of hypnotic sleep. *Fiziologicheskii Zhurnal*, 1953, *39*, 423–431. (Cited by Das, 1958a).

Korotkin, I. I., & Suslova, M. M. About some characteristics of the reciprocal influence of signal systems in hypnotic and posthypnotic states. *Zhurnal Vyssheĭ Nervnoĭ Deĭâtel'nosti*, 1955a, *5*, 511–519. (Read in abstract only.)

Korotkin, I. I., & Suslova, M. M. Materials for the investigation into the nervous mechanism of post-hypnotic suggestion with hysterics. *Zhurnal Vyssheĭ Nervnoĭ Deĭâtel'nosti*, 1955b, *5*, 697–707. (Read in abstract only.)

Korotkin, I. I., & Suslova, M. M. On the physiological mechanism of inhibitory action on stimuli inhibited by hypnotic suggestions. *Doklady Akademii Nauk, SSSR*, 1955c, *102*, 189–192. (Cited by Das, 1958a).

Korotkin, I. I., & Suslova, M. M. Changes in conditioned and unconditioned reflexes during suggestion states in hypnosis. In *The Central Nervous System and Human Behavior—Translations from the Russian Medical Literature*. Bethesda, Maryland: U.S. Department of Health, Education & Welfare, 1959, pp. 653–670.

Korotkin, I. I., & Suslova, M. M. Comparative effects of suggestion in the waking state and in hypnosis. *Pavlov Journal of Higher Nervous Activity*, 1960, *10*, 185–192.

Korotkin, I. I., & Suslova, M. M. An attempt to change the localization of conditioned inhibition by verbal suggestion in the state of hypnosis. *Zhurnal Vysshei Nervnoi Deiatel'nosti,* 1962, *12,* 778–787. (Read in abstract only.)

Kraines, S. H. Hypnosis: Physiologic inhibition and excitation. *Psychosomatics,* 1969, *10,* 36–41.

Kramer, E., & Tucker, G. R. Hypnotically suggested deafness and delayed auditory feedback. *International Journal of Clinical and Experimental Hypnosis,* 1967, *15,* 37–43.

Kratochvil, S. Sleep hypnosis and waking hypnosis. *International Journal of Clinical and Experimental Hypnosis,* 1970, *18,* 25–40.

Krippner, S. The psychedelic state, the hypnotic trance, and the creative act. In C. T. Tart (Ed.), 1969a, pp. 271–290.

Kris, E. (1934). *Psychoanalytic Explorations in Art.* New York: International Universities Press, 1952.

Kroger, W. S. Introduction and supplemental reports on hypnoanesthesia. In J. Esdaile, 1957.

Kroger, W. S. *Clinical and Experimental Hypnosis.* Philadelphia: J. B. Lippincott Co., 1963.

Kroger, W. S. Comprehensive management of obesity. *American Journal of Clinical Hypnosis,* 1970, *12,* 165–176.

Kroger, W. S., & Freed, S. C. The psychosomatic treatment of functional dysmenorrhea by hypnosis. *American Journal of Obstetrics and Gynecology,* 1943, *46,* 817–822.

Krojanker, R. J. Training of the unconscious by hypnodramatic re-enactment of dreams. *Group Psychotherapy,* 1962, *15,* 134–143.

Kubie, L. S. Hypnotism. *Archives of General Psychiatry,* 1961, *4,* 40–54.

Kuhn, T. S. *The Structure of Scientific Revolutions.* Chicago: University of Chicago Press, 1962.

Lacey, J. I. Psychophysiological approaches to the evaluation of psychotherapeutic process and outcome. In E. A. Rubenstein & M. B. Parloff (Eds.), *Research in Psychotherapy.* Washington, D. C.: National Publishing Company, 1959, pp. 160–208.

Lacey, J. I. Somatic response patterning and stress: Some revisions of activation theory. In M. H. Appley & R. Trumbull (Eds.), *Psychological Stress: Issues in Research.* New York: Appleton-Century-Crofts, 1967, pp. 14–37.

Lacey, J. I., Kagan, J., Lacey, Beatrice C., & Moss, H. A. The visceral level: Situational determinants and behavioral correlates of autonomic response patterns. In P. H. Knapp (Ed.), *Expressions of the Emotions in Man.* New York: International Universities Press, 1963, pp. 161–196.

Lafontaine, C. *L'art de magnétiser, ou le Magnétisme animal Considéré sous le point de vue théorique, pratique, et thérapeutique.* (The Art of Magnetizing), (3rd edition). Paris: G. Baillière, 1860.

Lane, Barbara M. A validation test of the Rorschach movement interpretations. *American Journal of Orthopsychiatry,* 1948, *18,* 292–296.

Laplanche, Jean, & Pontalis, J. B. Fantasy and the origins of sexuality. *International Journal of Psycho-analysis,* 1968, *49,* 1–18.

Larsen, S. Strategies for reducing phobic behavior. Doctoral dissertation, Stanford University, 1965.

LeBon, G. *The Crowd: A Study of the Popular Mind.* (French original, 1895.) London: T. F. Unwin, 1896.

LeBon, G. *Les opinions et les croyances.* Paris: Flammarion, 1911.

LeCron, L. M. A method of measuring the depth of hypnosis. *Journal of Clinical and Experimental Hypnosis*, 1953, *1*, 4–7.

LeCron, L. M. A study of age regression under hypnosis. In L. M. LeCron (Ed.), *Experimental Hypnosis: A Symposium of Articles on Research by Many of the World's Leading Authorities*. New York: The Macmillan Co., 1952, pp. 155–174.

LeCron, L. M., & Bordeaux, J. *Hypnotism Today*. New York: Grune & Stratton, 1947.

Lee-Teng, Evelyn. Trance-susceptibility, induction susceptibility, and acquiescence as factors in hypnotic performance. *Journal of Abnormal Psychology*, 1965, *70*, 383–389.

Leger, T. *Animal Magnetism or Psychodunamy*. New York: D. Appleton & Co., 1846.

Lehmann, H. E. Time and psychopathology. In R. Fischer (Ed.), 1967, pp. 798–821.

Lenox, J. R. A failure of hypnotic state to effect numerical task performance. Unpublished doctoral dissertation, Stanford University, 1970.

Lenox, J. R. Effect of hypnotic analgesia on verbal report and cardiovascular responses to ischemic pain. *Journal of Abnormal Psychology*, 1970, *75*, 199–206.

Leonard, J. R. An investigation of hypnotic age-regression. Unpublished doctoral dissertation, University of Kentucky, 1963.

Leriche, R. *The Surgery of Pain*. Baltimore: Williams & Wilkins, 1939.

Lerner, Barbara. Dream function reconsidered. *Journal of Abnormal Psychology*, 1967, *72*, 85–100.

Leuba, C. The use of hypnosis for controlling variables in psychological experiments. *Journal of Abnormal and Social Psychology*, 1941, *36*, 271–274.

Levine, K. N., Grassi, J. P., & Gerson, M. J. Hypnotically induced mood changes in the verbal and graphic Rorschach: A case study. *Rorschach Research Exchange*, 1943, *7*, 130–144.

Levine, M. Electrical skin resistance during hypnosis. *Archives of Neurology and Psychiatry*, 1930, *24*, 937–942.

Levitt, E. E. Some data from hypnosis experiments leading to speculations about individual differences in defenses against anxiety. Paper read at the International Congress on Hypnosis, New York, October, 1963.

Levitt, E. E. *The Psychology of Anxiety*. Indianapolis: Bobbs-Merrill Company, Inc., 1967.

Levitt, E. E., & Brady, J. P. Psychophysiology of hypnosis. In J. M. Schneck (Ed.), 1963a, pp. 314–362.

Levitt, E. E., den Breeijen, A., & Persky, H. The induction of clinical anxiety by means of a standardized hypnotic technique. *American Journal of Clinical Hypnosis*, 1960, *2*, 206–214.

Levitt, E. E., & Grosz, H. J. A comparison of quantifiable Rorschach anxiety indicators in hypnotically induced anxiety and normal states. *Journal of Consulting Psychology*, 1960, *24*, 31–34.

Levitt, E. E., Lubin, B., & Brady, J. P. On the use of TAT card 12M as an indicator of attitude toward hypnosis. *International Journal of Clinical and Experimental Hypnosis*, 1962, *10*, 145–150.

Levitt, E. E., & Lubin, B. TAT card "12MF" and hypnosis themes in females. *International Journal of Clinical and Experimental Hypnosis*, 1963, *11*, 241–244.

Levitt, E. E., & Persky, H. Experimental evidence for the validity of the IPAT Anxiety Scale. *Journal of Clinical Psychology*, 1962, *18*, 458–461.

Levitt, E. E., & Persky, H. Relation of Rorschach factors and plasma hydrocortisone level in hypnotically induced anxiety. *Psychosomatic Medicine*, 1960, *22*, 218–223.

Levitt, E. E., Persky, H., & Brady, J. P. *Hypnotic Induction of Anxiety: A Psychoendocrine Investigation*. Springfield, Ill.: Charles C. Thomas, 1964.

Levitt, E. E., Persky, H., Brady, J. P., Fitzgerald, J., & den Breeijen, A. Evidence for hypnotically induced amnesia as an analog of repression. *Journal of Nervous and Mental Disease*, 1961, *133*, 218–221.

Levitt, E. E., Persky, H., Brady, J. P., & Fitzgerald, J. A. The effect of hydrocortisone infusion on hypnotically induced anxiety. *Psychosomatic Medicine*, 1963, *25*, 158–161.

Lewis, D. *Quantitative Methods in Psychology*. New York: McGraw-Hill, 1960.

Lewis, D. J., & Adams, H. E. Retrograde amnesia from conditioned competing responses. *Science*, 1963, *141*, 516–517.

Lewis, J. H., & Sarbin, T. R. Studies in psychosomatics: I. The influence of hypnotic stimulation on gastric hunger contractions. *Psychosomatic Medicine*, 1943, *5*, 125–131.

Lewis, T. *The Blood Vessels of the Human Skin and their Responses*. London: Shaw & Sons, 1927.

Lewis, T. *Pain*. New York: Macmillan, 1942.

Liébeault, A. A. *Du sommeil et des états analogues considérés surtout au point de vue de l'action moral sur le physique.* (Of sleep and related states, conceived of from the viewpoint of the action of the psyche upon the soma). Paris: V. Masson, 1866. Vienna: F. Deuticke, 1892.

Liébeault, A. A. Anesthesie par suggestion. *Journal Magnetisme*, 1885, 64–67.

Liebert, R. M., Rubin, Norma, & Hilgard, E. R. The effects of suggestions of alertness in hypnosis on paired-associate learning. *Journal of Personality*, 1965, *33*, 605–612.

Live, C. The effects of practice in the trance upon learning in the normal waking state. Unpublished B. A. thesis, University of Wisconsin, 1929.

Lindauer, M. S. Imagery and sensory modality. *Perceptual and Motor Skills*, 1969, *29*, 203–215.

Lindsley, O. R. Operant behavior during sleep: A measure of depth of sleep. *Science*, 1957, *126*, 1290–1291.

Livshits, L. S. The investigation of the higher nervous activity of man in hypnosis in relation to chronic alcoholism. *Pavlov Journal of Higher Nervous Activity*, 1959, *9*, 745–753.

Lohr, Naomi E. Determinants of subjective uncertainty. Unpublished doctoral dissertation, University of Michigan, 1967.

London, P. Subject characteristics in hypnosis research: Part I. A survey of experience, interest, and opinion. *International Journal of Clinical and Experimental Hypnosis*, 1961, *9*, 151–161.

London, P. *The Children's Hypnotic Susceptibility Scale*. Palo Alto, California: Consulting Psychologist Press, 1963.

London, P. The psychophysiology of hypnotic susceptibility. Paper presented at the annual meeting of the American Psychological Association Convention, Washington, D.C., August, 1969.

London, P., & Cooper, L. M. Norms of hypnotic susceptibility in children. *Developmental Psychology*, 1969, *1*, 113–124.

London, P., Cooper, L. M., & Johnson, H. J. Subject characteristics in hypnosis research: II. Attitudes towards hypnosis, volunteer status, and personality measures. III. Some correlates of hypnotic susceptibility. *International Journal of Clinical and Experimental Hypnosis,* 1962, *10,* 13–21.

London, P., & Fuhrer, M. Hypnosis, motivation and performance. *Journal of Personality,* 1961, *29,* 321–333.

London, P., Hart, J. T., & Leibovitz, M. P. EEG alpha rhythms and susceptibility to hypnosis. *Nature,* 1968, *219,* 71–72.

London, P., Hart, J. T., Leibovitz, M. P., & McDevitt, R. A. The psychophysiology of hypnotic susceptibility. In L. Chertok (Ed.), *Psychophysiological Mechanisms of Hypnosis.* New York: Springer-Verlag, 1969, pp. 151–172.

London, P., & McDevitt, R. A. AMRL–TR–67–142 (W-P AF Base, Ohio: Aerospace Medical Research Laboratories, 1967).

Lonk, A. F. *"The Original" Complete Seventy-two Part Manual of Hypnosis and Psychotherapeutics, and also Mysteries of Time and Space.* (Revised 3rd edition). Palatine, Illinois: Adolph F. Lonk, 1947.

Loomis, A. L., Harvey, E. N., & Hobart, G. A. Brain potentials during hypnosis. *Science,* 1936, *83,* 239–241.

Lorge, I., with Curtiss, C. C. Prestige, suggestion and attitudes. *Journal of Social Psychology,* 1936, *7,* 386–402.

Lubin, B., Brady, J. P., & Levitt, E. E. A comparison of personality characteristics of volunteers and nonvolunteers for hypnosis experiments. *Journal of Clinical Psychology,* 1962, *18,* 341–343.

Ludwig, A. M. An historical survey of the early roots of mesmerism. *International Journal of Clinical and Experimental Hypnosis,* 1964, *12,* 205–217.

Ludwig, A. M. Altered states of consciousness. *Archives of General Psychiatry,* 1966, *15,* 225–234. Reprinted in C. T. Tart (Ed.), 1969a, pp. 9–22.

Lundholm, H. A hormic theory of hallucinations. *British Journal of Medical Psychology,* 1932, *11,* 269–282.

Luria, A. R. *The Nature of Human Conflicts.* New York: Liveright, 1932.

Luria, A. R. *The Mind of a Mnemonist: A little book about a vast memory.* New York: Basic Books, 1968.

Lustig, D. J. *You, Too, Can be a Hypnotist.* Philadelphia: Kanter's Magic Shop, 1956.

Luthe, W. (Ed.), *Autogenic Therapy: Vol. IV. Research and Theory.* New York: Grune & Stratton Inc., 1970.

Macchi, V., Card. *Encyclical letter on the abuses of magnetism, Holy Roman Inquisition.* Vatican, Rome, 1856. Original text in Latin quoted by G. Mabru, *Les Magnétiseurs jugés par eux mêmes; nouvelle enquête sur le magnétisme animal.* (The Magnetizers in their own judgment; a new research on animal magnetism). Paris: Mallet-Bachelier, 1858, Translated and with commentary in A. Binet & C. S. Féré, (Eds.), 1888, pp. 54–58.

Maccoby, Eleanor E. Sex differences in intellectual functioning. In Eleanor E. Maccoby (Ed.), *The Development of Sex Differences.* Stanford, Cal.: Stanford University Press, 1966, pp. 25–55.

Maccoby, Eleanor E., & Maccoby, N. The interview: A tool of social science. In G. Lindzey (Ed.), *Handbook of Social Psychology. Vol. 1. Theory and Method.* Cambridge, Mass.: Addison-Wesley Publishing Company, 1954, pp. 449–487.

Mackenzie, J. *Symptoms and their Interpretation.* London: Shaw & Sons, 1909.

Macvaugh, G. S. *Hypnosis Readiness Inventory: A Self-confidence developer in ability to hypnotize.* Chevy Chase, Md.: G. S. Macvaugh, 1969.

Maddi, S. R. Motivational aspects of creativity. *Journal of Personality*, 1965, *33*, 330–347.

Maiolo, A. T., Porro, G. B., & Granone, F. Cerebral hemodynamics and metabolism in hypnosis. *British Medical Journal*, 1969, *1*, 314–320.

Marcuse, F. L. (Ed.) *Hypnosis Throughout the World*. With a foreward by B. B. Raginsky. Springfield, Ill.: Charles C. Thomas Publishers, 1964.

Marenina, A. I. Further investigation of the dynamics of cerebral potentials in the various phases of hypnosis in man. *Fiziologicheskii Zhurnal SSSR imeni I. M. Sechenova*, 1955, *41*, 742–747.

Marks, R. W. *The Story of Hypnotism*. New York: Prentice-Hall, 1947.

Marmer, M. J. The role of hypnosis in anesthesiology. *Journal of the American Medical Association*, 1956, *162*, 441–443.

Marquis, D. G., & Hilgard, E. R. Conditioned lid responses to light in dogs after removal of the visual cortex. *Journal of Comparative Psychology*, 1936, *22*, 157–178.

Martin, I., & Grosz, H. J. Hypnotically induced emotions: Autonomic and skeletal muscle activity in patients with affective illnesses. *Archives of General Psychiatry*, 1964, *11*, 203–213.

Maslow, A. H. *Toward a Psychology of Being*. Princeton: Van Nostrand, 1962.

Maupin, E. W. Individual differences in response to a Zen meditation exercise. *Journal of Consulting Psychology*, 1965, *29*, 139–145. Reprinted in C. T. Tart (Ed.), 1969a, pp. 187–198.

May, J. R., & Edmonston, W. E., Jr. Hypnosis and a plethysmographic measure of two types of situational anxiety. *American Journal of Clinical Hypnosis*, 1966, *9*, 109–113.

Mayman, M., & Voth, H. M. Reality closeness, phantasy and autokinesis: A dimension of cognitive style. *Journal of Abnormal Psychology*, 1969, *74*, 635–641.

Mazer, M. An experimental study of the hypnotic dream. *Psychiatry*, 1951, *14*, 265–277.

McBain, W. N. Imagery and suggestibility: A test of the Arnold hypothesis. *Journal of Abnormal and Social Psychology*, 1954, *49*, 36–44.

McCally, M., & Barnard, G. W. Modification of the immersion diuresis by hypnotic suggestion. *Psychosomatic Medicine*, 1968, *30*, 287–297.

McCranie, E. J., & Crasilneck, H. B. The conditioned reflex in hypnotic age regression. *Journal of Clinical and Experimental Psychopathology*, 1955, *16*, 120–123.

McDonald, D. G. Conditional and unconditional autonomic responses during sleep. U.S. Navy Medical Neuropsychiatric Research Unit, San Diego, Cal. Report 65–28, Ad. 481520, January, 1966.

McDowell, M. Hypnosis in dermatology. In J. M. Schneck (Ed.), 1963a, pp. 122–142.

McGill, O. *The Encyclopedia of Stage Hypnotism*. Colon, Mich.: Abbott's Magic Novelty Co., 1947.

McGlashan, T. H., Evans, F. J., & Orne, M. T. The nature of hypnotic analgesia and placebo response to experimental pain. *Psychosomatic Medicine*, 1969, *31*, 227–246.

McGlothlin, W. H., Cohen, S., & McGlothlin, M. Personality and attitude changes in volunteer subjects following repeated administration of LSD. In J. Schlien (Ed.), *Research in Psychotherapy, Vol. III*. Washington, D.C.: American Psychological Association, 1968.

McGraw, M. B. Development of the plantar response in healthy infants. *American Journal of Diseases of Children*, 1941, *61*, 1215–1221.

McGuire, W. J. The nature of attitudes and attitude change. In G. Lindzey & E. Aronson (Eds.), *The Handbook of Social Psychology, III: The Individual in a Social Context.* (2nd edition). Reading, Mass.: Addison-Wesley Publishing Co., 1969, pp. 136–314.

McKellar, P. *Imagination and Thinking: A Psychological Analysis.* New York: Basic Books, 1957.

McNemar, Q. *Psychological Statistics* (4th edition). New York: Wiley, 1970.

McPeake, J. D. Hypnosis, suggestions, and psychosomatics. *Diseases of the Nervous System*, 1968, *29*, 536–544.

Meares, A. *Theories of hypnosis.* In J. M. Schneck (Ed.), 1963a, pp. 390–405.

Mednick, S. A., & Mednick, Martha T. *Examiners Manual: Remote Associates Test.* Boston: Houghton-Mifflin Company, 1967.

Meeker, W. B., & Barber, T. X. Toward an explanation of stage hypnosis. *Journal of Abnormal Psychology*, 1971, *77*, 61–70.

Melei, Janet P., & Hilgard, E. R. Attitudes toward hypnosis, self-predictions, and hypnotic susceptibility. *International Journal of Clinical and Experimental Hypnosis*, 1964, *12*, 99–108.

Mellenbruch, P. L. The validity of a personality inventory tested by hypnosis. *American Journal of Clinical Hypnosis*, 1962, *2*, 111–114.

Memmesheimer, A. M., & Eisenlohr, E. Untersuchungen über die Suggestivbehandlung der Warzen. *Dermatologische Zeitschrift*, 1931, *62*, 63–68.

Mendelsohn, G. A. Experiments on the psychoanalytic mechanism of isolation. Unpublished doctoral dissertation, University of Michigan, 1960.

Mendelsohn, G. A., & Griswold, Barbara B. Differential use of incidental stimuli in problem solving as a function of creativity. *Journal of Abnormal and Social Psychology*, 1964, *68*, 431–436.

Menzies, R. Further studies of conditioned vasomotor responses in human subjects. *Journal of Experimental Psychology*, 1941, *29*, 457–482.

Mesel, E., & Ledford, F. F., Jr. The electroencephalogram during hypnotic age regression (to infancy) in epileptic patients. *Archives of Neurology*, 1959, *1*, 516–521.

Mesmer, F. A. *Mémoire sur la découverte du Magnétisme Animal.* Geneva, 1774. With the *Précis historique écrite par M. Paradis en mars 1777.* Paris: Didot, 1779. English version: *Mesmerism by Doctor Mesmer: Dissertation on the discovery of Animal Magnetism, 1779.* Translated by V. R. Myers. Published with G. Frankau, *Introductory Monograph.* London: Macdonald, 1948. Abridged version of Myers' translation in J. Ehrenwald (Ed.), *From Medicine Man to Freud: An Anthology, Edited, with Notes.* New York: Dell Publishing Co., 1956, pp. 256–280. Second edition (Title): *Memoir of F. A. Mesmer, Doctor of Medicine, On His Discoveries, 1799,* translated by J. Eden, Mt. Vernon, N. Y.: Eden Press, 1957.

Mesmer, F. A. *Aphorismes de M. Mesmer: Dictés à l'assemblée de ses élèves, & dans lesquels on trouve ses principes, sa théorie & les moyens de magnétiser; le tout formant un corps de doctrine, devéloppé en trois cents quarantequatre paragraphes pour faciliter l'application des commentaries au magnétisme animal.* (Aphorisms of Mr. Mesmer: dictated to the assembly of his students & containing his principles, theories & methods of magnetizing; the whole forming a doctrine, developed in 344 paragraphs, that facilitates the discussion of animal magnetism). Recorded from spoken lectures, edited, and with notes by

C. de Veaumorel. (3rd edition, revised and expanded.) Paris: Bertrand, 1785. English version: *Maxims on Animal Magnetism.* Translated and with an introduction by J. Eden. Mt. Vernon, N. Y.: Eden Press, 1958.

Mesmer, F. A. *Mesmerismus oder System der Wechselwirkungen, Theorie und Anwendung des thierischen Magnetismus als die allgemeine Heilkunde zur Erhaltung des Menschen.* Herausgegeben von C. C. Wolfart. (Mesmerism or a system of reciprocal effects: The theory and application of animal magnetism as the general therapeutics for the preservation of mankind. Edited by C. C. Wolfart). Berlin: Rikolaischen, 1814.

Messerschmidt, R. A quantitative investigation of the alleged independent operation of conscious and subconscious processes. *Journal of Abnormal and Social Psychology,* 1927, *22,* 325–340.

Michael, Lois I. A factor analysis of mental imagery. *Dissertation Abstracts,* 1967, *27,* 3761.

Milgram, S. Behavioral study of obedience. *Journal of Abnormal and Social Psychology,* 1963, *67,* 371–378.

Miller, N. E. Learning of visceral and glandular responses. *Science,* 1969a, *163,* 434–445.

Miller, N. E. Autonomic learning: Clinical and physiological implications. Invited lecture at the XIX International Congress of Psychology, London, 1969b.

Mischel, W. *Personality and Assessment.* New York: Wiley, 1968.

Mitchell, J. F. Local anesthesia in general surgery. *Journal of the American Medical Association,* 1907, *49,* 198–201.

Mitchell, Mildred B. Retroactive inhibition and hypnosis. *Journal of General Psychology,* 1932, *7,* 343–359.

Moll, A. *Hypnotism.* German original, 1889. Translated by A. F. Hopkirk, from the 4th enlarged edition. London: Walter Scott, 1890. New York: Charles Scribner's Sons, 1898. Reissued under title: *The Study of Hypnosis: Historical, Clinical, and Experimental Research in the Techniques of Hypnotic Induction.* Introduction by J. H. Conn. New York: Julian Press, 1958.

Moore, Rosemarie K., & Lauer, Lillian W. Hypnotic susceptibility in middle childhood. *International Journal of Clinical and Experimental Hypnosis,* 1963, *11,* 167–174.

Moore, W. F. Effects of posthypnotic stimulation of hostility upon motivation. *American Journal of Clinical Hypnosis,* 1964, *7,* 130–135.

Morávek, M. Effect of suggested anaesthesia on motor activity. *Activitas Nervosa Superior,* 1968, *10,* 132–135.

Mordey, T. R. The relationship between certain motives and suggestibility. Unpublished Masters thesis, Roosevelt University, 1960.

Morgan, Arlene H., & Lam, D. The relationship of the Betts vividness of imagery questionnaire and hypnotic susceptibility: Failure to replicate. Unpublished paper, Hawthorne House Research Memorandum, 1969, No. 103.

Morris, G. O., & Singer, Margaret T. Sleep deprivation: The context of consciousness. *Journal of Nervous and Mental Disease,* 1966, *143,* 291–304.

Moss, C. S. Experimental paradigms for the hypnotic investigation of dream symbolism. *International Journal of Clinical and Experimental Hypnosis,* 1961, *9,* 105–117.

Moss, C. S. *The Hypnotic Investigation of Dreams.* New York: John Wiley & Sons, 1967.

Murphy, G. *Historical Introduction to Modern Psychology.* Revised edition. New York: Harcourt, Brace, 1949.

Myden, W. Interpretation and evaluation of certain personality characteristics involved in creative production. *Perceptual and Motor Skills*, 1959, *9*, 139–158.

Myers, F. W. H. Human personality in the light of hypnotic suggestion. *Society for Psychical Research: Proceedings*, 1886–87, *4*, 1–24.

Myers, F. W. H. The subliminal consciousness. *Society for Psychical Research: Proceedings*, 1891–92, *7*, 298–355.

Nace, E. P., & Orne, M. T. Fate of an uncompleted posthypnotic suggestion. *Journal of Abnormal Psychology*, 1970, *75*, 278–285.

Nachmansohn, M. Concerning experimentally produced dreams. In D. Rapaport (Ed.) *Organization and Pathology of Thought*, New York: Columbia Univ. Press, 1951, pp. 257–287.

Nagge, J. W. An experimental test of the theory of associative interference. *Journal of Experimental Psychology*, 1935, *18*, 663–682.

Naruse, G., & Obonai, T. Decomposition and fusion of mental images in the drowsy and post-hypnotic hallucinatory state. *Journal of Clinical and Experimental Hypnosis*, 1953, *1*, 23–41.

Neisser, U. *Cognitive Psychology*. New York: Appleton-Century-Crofts, 1967.

Neisser, U. Selective reading: A method for the study of visual attention. Paper presented at the symposium: Attention: Some growing points in recent research, XIX International Congress of Psychology, London, 1969.

Nelson, R. A. *A Complete Course in Stage Hypnotism*. Columbus, Ohio: Nelson Enterprises, 1965.

Nichols, D. C. A reconceptualization of the concept of hypnosis. In S. Lesse (Ed.), *An Evaluation of the Results of the Psychotherapies*. Springfield, Ill.: Charles C. Thomas, 1968, pp. 201–220.

Notterman, J. M., Schoenfeld, W. N., & Bersh, P. J. A comparison of three extinction procedures following heart rate conditioning. *Journal of Abnormal and Social Psychology*, 1952a, *47*, 674–677.

Notterman, J. M., Schoenfeld, W. N., & Bersh, P. J. Partial reinforcement and conditioned heart rate response in human subjects. *Science*, 1952b, *115*, 77–79.

Nowlis, D. P., & Rhead, J. C. Relation of eyes-closed resting EEG alpha activity to hypnotic susceptibility. *Perceptual and Motor Skills*, 1968, *27*, 1047–1050.

Nowlis, V. The concept of mood. In S. M. Farber & R. H. L. Wilson (Eds.), *Conflict and Creativity*. New York: McGraw-Hill, 1963, pp. 73–88.

Oberlander, M. I., Gruenewald, Doris, & Fromm, Erika. Content and structural characteristics of thought processes in hypnosis. Paper read at the Annual Convention of the American Psychological Association, Miami Beach, September, 1970.

O'Connell, D. N. An experimental comparison of hypnotic depth measured by self-ratings and by an objective scale. *International Journal of Clinical and Experimental Hypnosis*, 1964, *12*, 34–46.

O'Connell, D. N. Selective recall of hypnotic susceptibility items: Evidence for repression or enhancement? *International Journal of Clinical and Experimental Hypnosis*, 1966, *14*, 150–161.

O'Connell, D. N., Gustafson, L. A., Evans, F. J., Orne, M. T., & Shor, R. E. Can waking and Stage 1 sleep always be told apart by EEG criteria alone? Paper presented at the meeting of the Association for the Psychophysiological Study of Sleep, Washington, D.C., March, 1965.

O'Connell, D. N., & Orne, M. T. Bioelectric correlates of hypnosis: An experimental reevaluation. *Journal of Psychiatric Research*, 1962, *1*, 201–213.

O'Connell, D. N., & Orne, M. T. Endosomatic electrodermal correlates of hypnotic depth and susceptibility. *Journal of Psychiatric Research*, 1968, *6*, 1–12.

O'Connell, D. N., Shor, R. E., & Orne, M. T. Hypnotic age regression: An empirical and methodological analysis. *Journal of Abnormal Psychology Monograph*, 1970, *76*, (3, Pt. 2).

Orne, M. T. The mechanisms of hypnotic age regression: An experimental study. *Journal of Abnormal and Social Psychology*, 1951, *46*, 213–225.

Orne, M. T. The nature of hypnosis: Artifact and essence. *Journal of Abnormal and Social Psychology*, 1959, *58*, 277–299.

Orne, M. T. The potential uses of hypnosis in interrogation. In A. D. Biderman & H. Zimmer (Eds.), *The Manipulation of Human Behavior*. New York: John Wiley & Sons, 1961, pp. 169–215.

Orne, M. T. Antisocial behavior and hypnosis: Problems of control and validation in empirical studies. In G. H. Estabrooks (Ed.), *Hypnosis: Current Problems*. New York: Harper & Row, 1962a, pp. 137–192.

Orne, M. T. On the social psychology of the psychological experiment: With particular reference to demand characteristics and their implications. *American Psychologist*, 1962b, *17*, 776–783.

Orne, M. T. Hypnotically induced hallucinations. In L. J. West (Ed.), *Hallucinations*. New York: Grune & Stratton, 1962c, pp. 211–219.

Orne, M. T. Undesirable effects of hypnosis: The determinants and management. *International Journal of Clinical and Experimental Hypnosis*, 1965a, *13*, 226–237.

Orne, M. T. Demand characteristics and their implications for real life: The importance of quasi-controls. Paper presented at the American Psychological Association Convention, Chicago, September, 1965b.

Orne, M. T. On the mechanisms of posthypnotic amnesia. *International Journal of Clinical and Experimental Hypnosis*, 1966a, *14*, 121–134.

Orne, M. T. Hypnosis, motivation and compliance. *American Journal of Psychiatry*, 1966b, *122*, 721–726.

Orne, M. T. What must a satisfactory theory of hypnosis explain? *International Journal of Psychiatry*, 1967, *3*, 206–211.

Orne, M. T. Demand characteristics and the concept of quasi-controls. In R. Rosenthal & R. L. Rosnow (Eds.), *Artifact in Behavioral Research*. New York: Academic Press, 1969, pp. 143–179.

Orne, M. T. Hypnosis, motivation and the ecological validity of the psychological experiment. In W. J. Arnold & M. M. Page (Eds.), *Nebraska Symposium on Motivation*. Lincoln, Nebraska: University of Nebraska Press, 1970, pp. 187–265.

Orne, M. T., & Evans, F. J. Social control in the psychological experiment: Antisocial behavior and hypnosis. *Journal of Personality and Social Psychology*, 1965, *1*, 189–200.

Orne, M. T., & Evans, F. J. Inadvertent termination of hypnosis with hypnotized and simulating subjects. *International Journal of Clinical and Experimental Hypnosis*, 1966, *14*, 61–78.

Orne, M. T., & O'Connell, D. N. Diagnostic ratings of hypnotizability. *International Journal of Clinical and Experimental Hypnosis*. 1967, *15*, 125–133.

Orne, M. T., Sheehan, P. W., & Evans, F. J. Occurrence of posthypnotic behavior outside the experimental setting. *Journal of Personality and Social Psychology*, 1968, *9*, 189–196.

Ornstein, R. E. *On the Experience of Time*. Baltimore: Penguin Books, 1970.

Orzeck, A. Z. Multiple self concepts as affected by non-hypnotic assumed mood states. Paper read at the 5th Annual Scientific Meeting of the American Society of Clinical Hypnosis, 1962.

Osborn, Anne G., Bunker, J. P., Cooper, L. M., Frank, G. S., & Hilgard, E. R. Effects of thiopental sedation on learning and memory. *Science*, 1967, *157*, 574–576.

Oswald, I. *Sleeping and Waking: Physiology and Psychology*. Amsterdam: American Elsevier, 1962.

Otto, H. A. *Explorations in Human Potentialities*. Springfield, Ill.: Charles C. Thomas, 1966.

Palmer, R. D., & Field, P. B. Visual imagery and susceptibility to hypnosis. *Journal of Consulting and Clinical Psychology*, 1968, *32*, 456–461.

Parrish, M., Lundy, R. M., & Leibowitz, H. W. Effect of hypnotic age regression on the magnitude of the Ponzo and Poggendorff illusions. *Journal of Abnormal Psychology*, 1969, *74*, 693–698.

Paskewitz, D. A., & Orne, M. T. The effect of cognitive tasks on the feedback control of alpha activity. Paper presented at the meeting of the Society for Psychophysiological Research, New Orleans, November, 1970.

Patten, E. F. Does post-hypnotic amnesia apply to practice effects? *Journal of General Psychology*, 1932, *7*, 196–201.

Pattie, F. A., Jr. The production of blisters by hypnotic suggestion: A review. *Journal of Abnormal and Social Psychology*, 1941, *36*, 62–72.

Pattie, F. A., Jr. The effect of hypnotically induced hostility on Rorschach responses. *Journal of Clinical Psychology*, 1954, *10*, 161–164.

Pattie, F. A., Jr. Methods of induction, susceptibility of subjects, and criteria of hypnosis. In R. M. Dorcus (Ed.), *Hypnosis and its Therapeutic Applications*. New York: McGraw-Hill, 1956a, ch. 2.

Pattie, F. A., Jr. Mesmer's medical dissertation and its debt to Mead's De Imperio Solis ac Lunae. *Journal of the History of Medicine and Allied Sciences*, 1956b, *11*, 275–287.

Pattie, F. A., Jr. American contributions to the science of hypnosis. In L. Kuhn & S. Russo (Eds.), *Modern Hypnosis*. Hollywood, Cal.: Wilshire, 1958.

Pattie, F. A., Jr. A brief history of hypnotism. In J. E. Gordon (Ed.), 1967, pp. 10–43.

Paul, G. L. The production of blisters by hypnotic suggestion: Another look. *Psychosomatic Medicine*, 1963, *25*, 233–244.

Pavlov, I. P. The identity of inhibition with sleep and hypnosis. *Scientific Monthly*, 1923, *17*, 603–608.

Pavlov, I. P. *Conditioned Reflexes*. London: Oxford University Press, 1927.

Pavlov, I. P. *Selected Works*. Edited by J. Gibbons under the supervision of Kh. S. Koshtoyants, Moscow: Foreign Languages Publishing House, 1955, pp. 345–368.

Pavlov, B. V., & Povorinskii, Iu. A. K voprosu o vzaimodeist vii pervoi i vtoroi signal nykh sistem v somnambulicheskoi faze gipnoza. *Zhurnal Vyssheĭ Nervnoĭ Deĭatel'nosti*, 1953, *3*, 381–391.(Cited in H.B.Crasilneck & J.A.Hall, 1959.)

Perkins, K. A. Repression, psychopathology, and drive representation: An experimental hypnotic investigation of the management of impulse inhibition. Unpublished doctoral dissertation, Michigan State University, 1965.

Perky, C. W. An experimental study of imagination. *American Journal of Psychology*, 1910, *21*, 422–452.

Perry, C. W. Content analysis of dream reports. In J. P. Sutcliffe, (Ed.), *The Relation of Imagery and Fantasy to Hypnosis*. (Progress report on N.I.M.H.

Project M–3950.) Sydney, Australia: Department of Psychology, The University of Sydney, 1964, pp. 1–46.

Perry, C. W. An investigation of the relationship between proneness to fantasy and susceptibility to hypnosis. Unpublished doctoral dissertation, University of Sydney, Sydney, Australia, 1965.

Perry, C. W., Evans, F. J., O'Connell, D. N., Orne, M. T., & Orne, Emily C. Behavioral response to verbal stimuli administered and tested during REM sleep: A further investigation. Philadelphia, Pa.: Institute of the Pennsylvania Hospital, 1972.

Persky, H., Grosz, H. J., Norton, J. A., & McMurtry, Mildred. Effect of hypnotically-induced anxiety on the plasma hydrocortisone level of normal subjects. *Journal of Clinical Endocrinology and Metabolism, 1959, 19,* 700–710.

Pessin, M., Plapp, J. N., & Stern, J. A. Effects of hypnosis induction and attention direction on electrodermal responses. *American Journal of Clinical Hypnosis,* 1968, *10,* 198–206.

Pfungst, O. *Clever Hans (The Horse of Mr. von Osten).* [Re-issue of 1911 ed.] (R. Rosenthal, Ed.) New York: Holt, Rinehart & Winston, Inc., 1965.

Phillips, B. (Ed.) *The Essentials of Zen Buddhism: An Anthology of the Writings of Daisetz T. Suzuki.* London: Rider & Co., 1963, pp. 31–32.

Phillips, L., Kaden, S., & Waldman, M. Rorschach indices of developmental level. *Journal of Genetic Psychology, 1959, 94,* 267–285.

Pine, F., & Holt, R. R. Creativity and primary process: A study of adaptive regression. *Journal of Abnormal and Social Psychology, 1960, 61,* 370–379.

Piotrowski, Z. A. A Rorschach compendium; revised and enlarged. In J. A. Brussel et al. (Eds.), *A Rorschach Training Manual.* Utica, N.Y.: State Hospitals Press, 1950.

Plapp, J. M. *Hypnosis, Conditioning, and Physiological Responses.* Ann Arbor, Mich.: University Microfilms, 1967.

Plapp, J. M., & Edmonston, W. E., Jr. Extinction of a conditioned motor response following hypnosis. *Journal of Abnormal and Social Psychology, 1965, 70,* 378–382.

Platonov, K. I. (Ed.) *The Word as a Physiological and Therapeutic Factor: Problems of theory and practice of psychotherapy on the basis of the theory of I. P. Pavlov.* Translated from 2nd Russian edition (1955) by D. A. Myshne. Moscow: Foreign Languages Publishing House, 1959.

Podmore, F. *Mesmerism and Christian Science: A Short History of Mental Healing.* London and Philadelphia: G. W. Jacobs & Co., 1909.

Poe, D. C. The effects of hypnotically hallucinated practice of a motor and a cognitive task. *Dissertation Abstracts,* 1967, *27,* 2899.

Poe, E. A. *The Philosophy of Animal Magnetism, by a Gentleman of Philadelphia: Together with the System of Manipulating Adopted to Produce Ecstacy and Somnambulism—The Effects and the Rationale.* With an essay on Poe by J. Jackson attributing authorship to Poe. Philadelphia: Patterson & White, 1928. Originally published anonymously and without essay. Philadelphia: Merrihew & Gunn, 1837.

Poissonnier, P. I., et al. *Rapport des commissaires de la Société Royale de Médecine, nommés par le roi, pour faire l'examen du magnétisme animal. Paris, 16 aout 1748.* (Report of the commissioners of the Royal Medical Society named by the King to examine animal magnetism. Paris, Aug. 16, 1784). Signed: Poissonnier, Caille, Mauduyt, Andry. Reproduced in A. Bertrand, (Ed.), 1826b, pp. 482–510.

Priestley, J. B. *Man and Time*. Garden City, New York: Doubleday, 1964.

Prince, M. (1905). *The Dissociation of a Personality: A Biographical Study in Abnormal Psychology*. New York: Longmans, Green & Co., 1920.

Prince, R. (Ed.) *Trance and Possession States*. Proceedings of the Second Annual Conference, R. M. Bucke Memorial Society, 4–6 March, 1966. Montreal, Canada: R. M. Bucke Memorial Society, 1968.

Propping, K. Zur Frage der Sensibilität der Bauchhöhle. *Beiträge zur klinischen Chirurgie*, 1909, *63*, 690–710.

Pruesse, M. G. Repressers, sensitizers, and hypnotically induced hostility. Unpublished doctoral dissertation, University of Waterloo, Waterloo, Ontario, Canada, 1967.

Puységur, A. M. Marquis de. Letter (on the discovery of artificial somnambulism) to a member of the Société de Harmonie. March 8, 1784a. Reproduced in A. Teste, (Ed.), *Practical Manual of Animal Magnetism*. Translated from the second French edition by D. Spillan. London: H. Baillière, 1843, pp. 17–19.

Puységur, A. M. Marquis de. *Mémoires pour servir à l'histoire et à l'éstablissement du magnétisme animal*. (Remembrances which may serve to establish animal magnetism and its history). Third edition. Paris: J. G. Dentu, 1820. (First edition, 1784b; second edition, Cellot, 1809.)

Puységur, A. M. Marquis de. *Du magnétisme animal, considéré dans ses rapports avec diverses branches de la Physique générale*, avec *Extrait de ma Correspondance sur le magnétisme animal*. (Animal magnetism and its relation to various branches of general physics; with an extract of my correspondence on animal magnetism). Paris: Desenne (Cellot), 1807.

Puységur, A. M. Marquis de. *Recherches, expériences et observations physiologiques sur l'homme dans l'état de somnambulisme naturel, et dans le somnambulisme provoqué par l'acte magnétique*. (Physiologic investigations, experiences, and observations on man in the natural and in the magnetic state of somnambulism). Paris: J. G. Dentu, 1811.

Puységur, A. M. Marquis de. *An Essay of Instruction on Animal Magnetism: Translated from the French of the Marquis de Puységur, together with various extracts upon the subject, and notes*. Translated and edited by J. King. New York: J. C. Kelley, 1837.

Quay, H. C. Emotions in hypnotic dreams: A quantitative investigation. Unpublished Masters thesis, Florida State University, 1952.

Rand, B. (Ed.) Bibliography of philosophy, psychology and cognate subjects: G. Psychology: i. Hypnotism and suggestion. In J. M. Baldwin (Ed.), *Dictionary of Philosophy and Psychology*. Vol 3, Part II. New York and London: Macmillan, 1925, pp. 1059–1067.

Rapaport, D. (Ed.) *Organization and Pathology of Thought*. New York: Columbia University Press, 1951.

Rapaport, D. (1953). Some metapsychological considerations concerning activity and passivity. In M. M. Gill (Ed.), *The Collected Papers of David Rapaport*. New York: Basic Books, 1967, pp. 530–568.

Rapaport, D. The theory of ego autonomy: A generalization. *Bulletin of the Menninger Clinic*, 1958, *22*, 13–35. Reproduced in M. M. Gill (Ed.), *The Collected Papers of David Rapaport*. New York: Basic Books, 1967, pp. 722–744.

Ravitz, L. J. Electrometric correlates of the hypnotic state. *Science*, 1950, *112*, 341–351.

Ravitz, L. J. Standing potential correlates of hypnosis and narcosis. *AMA Archives of Neurology and Psychiatry*, 1951a, *65*, 413–436.

Ravitz, L. J. The use of D.C. measurements in psychiatry. *Neuropsychiatry*, 1951b, *1*, 3–12.

Rechtschaffen, A., & Kales, A. (Eds.) *A Manual of Standardized Terminology, Techniques and Scoring System for Sleep Stages of Human Subjects*. Washington, D.C.: National Institutes of Health Publication No. 204, U.S. Government Printing Office, 1968, Public Health Service.

Reich, L. H. Optokinetic nystagmus during hypnotic hallucinations. Paper presented at Eastern Psychological Association, Annual Meeting, Atlantic City, April 1970.

Reichenbach, C. Baron von. *Researches on Magnetism, Electricity, Heat, Light, Crystallization and Chemism, in their Relations to the Vital Force*. From the German with preface and notes by J. Ashburner. London, 1850.

Reid, A. F., & Curtsinger, G. Physiological changes associated with hypnosis: The effect of hypnosis on temperature. *International Journal of Clinical and Experimental Hypnosis*, 1968, *16*, 111–119.

Reiff, R., & Scheerer, M. *Memory and Hypnotic Age Regression: Developmental Aspects of Cognitive Function Explored through Hypnosis*. New York: International Universities Press, 1959.

Renner, Vivian. Effects of modification of cognitive style on creative behavior. *Journal of Personality and Social Psychology*, 1970, *14*, 257–262.

Reyher, J. Posthypnotic stimulation of hypnotically induced conflict in relation to psychosomatic reactions and psychopathology. *Psychosomatic Medicine*, 1961a, *23*, 384–391.

Reyher, J. Posthypnotic stimulation of hypnotically induced conflict in relation to antisocial behavior. *Journal of Social Therapy*, 1961b, *7*, 92–97.

Reyher, J. A paradigm for determining the clinical relevance of hypnotically induced psychopathology. *Psychological Bulletin*, 1962, *59*, 344–352.

Reyher, J. Brain mechanisms, intrapsychic processes and behavior: A theory of hypnosis and psychopathology. *American Journal of Clinical Hypnosis*, 1964, *7*, 107–119.

Reyher, J. Hypnosis in research on psychopathology. In J. E. Gordon (Ed.), 1967, pp. 110–147.

Reyher, J. Posthypnotic conflict as related to psychopathology. Paper read at the Convention of the American Psychological Association, Washington, D.C., September, 1969a.

Reyher, J. Comment on "Artificial induction of posthypnotic conflict". *Journal of Abnormal Psychology*, 1969b, *74*, 420–422.

Rhoades, C. D., & Edmonston, W. E., Jr. Personality correlates of hypnotizability: A study using the Harvard Group Scale of Hypnotic Susceptibility, the 16-PF and the IPAT. *American Journal of Clinical Hypnosis*, 1969, *11*, 228–233.

Richardson, A. *Mental Imagery*. New York: Springer Publishing Company, Inc., 1969.

Richet, C. The simulation of somnambulism. *Lancet*, 1881, *1*, 8–9, 51–52.

Richman, D. N. A critique of two recent theories of hypnosis: The psychoanalytic theory of Gill and Brenman contrasted with the behavioral theory of Barber. *Psychiatric Quarterly*, 1965, *39*, 278–292.

Riecken, H. W. A program for research on experiments in social psychology. In N. F. Washburne (Ed.), *Decisions, Values and Groups*. Vol. 2. New York: Pergamon Press, 1962, pp. 25–41.

Roberts, D. R. An electrophysiological theory of hypnosis. *International Journal of Clinical and Experimental Hypnosis,* 1960, *8,* 43–55.

Roberts, Mary J. Attention and cognitive controls as related to individual differences in hypnotic susceptibility. *Dissertation Abstracts,* 1965, *25,* 4261.

Rosen, G. John Elliotson, Physician and hypnotist. *Bulletin of the History of Medicine,* 1936, *4,* 600–603.

Rosen, G. Mesmerism and surgery: A strange chapter in the history of anesthesia. *Journal of the History of Medicine and Allied Sciences,* 1946, *1,* 527–550.

Rosen, G. From mesmerism to hypnotism. *Ciba Symposium,* 1948, *9,* 838–844.

Rosen, G. History of medical hypnosis: From animal magnetism to medical hypnosis. In J. M. Schneck (Ed.), 1963a, pp. 3–28.

Rosenhan, D. L. Hypnosis and personality: A moderator variable analysis. In L. Chertok (Ed.), *Psychophysiological Mechanisms of Hypnosis.* New York: Springer-Verlag, 1969, pp. 193–198.

Rosenhan, D. L., & Tomkins, S. S. On preference for hypnosis and hypnotizability. *International Journal of Clinical and Experimental Hypnosis,* 1964, *12,* 109–114.

Rosenthal, B. G., & Mele, H. The validity of hypnotically induced color hallucinations. *Journal of Abnormal and Social Psychology,* 1952, *47,* 700–704.

Rossi, A. M., Furhman, A., & Solomon, P. Arousal levels and thought processes during sensory deprivation. *Journal of Abnormal Psychology,* 1967, *72,* 166–173.

Rossi, A. M., Sturrock, J. B., & Solomon, P. Suggested effects on reported imagery in sensory deprivation. *Perceptual and Motor Skills,* 1963, *16,* 39–45.

Rorschach, H. *Psychodiagnostics* (4th edition). Berne: Verlag Hans Huber, 1949.

Rowland, L. W. Will hypnotized persons try to harm themselves or others? *Journal of Abnormal and Social Psychology,* 1939, *34,* 114–117.

Rubenstein, R., & Newman, R. The living out of "future" experiences under hypnosis. *Science,* 1954, *119,* 472–473.

Rubin, F. (Ed.) *Current Research in Hypnopaedia.* New York: American Elsevier Publishing Co., 1968.

Rugg, H. *Imagination.* New York: Harper & Row, 1963.

Ryle, G. *The Concept of Mind.* London: William Brendon, 1955.

Sacerdote, P. *Induced Dreams.* New York: Vantage Press, 1967.

Sacerdote, P. On the psycho-biological effects of hypnosis. *American Journal of Clinical Hypnosis,* 1967, *10,* 10–14.

Sachar, E. J., Fishman, J. R., & Mason, J. W. The influence of the hypnotic trance on plasma 17-hydroxycorticosteriod concentration. *Psychosomatic Medicine,* 1964, *26,* 635–636. (Abstract)

Sachar, E. J., Cobb, J. C., & Shor, R. E. Plasma cortisol changes during hypnotic trance: Relation to depth of hypnosis. *Archives of General Psychiatry,* 1966, *14,* 482–490.

Sachs, L. B., & Anderson, W. L. Modification of hypnotic susceptibility. *International Journal of Clinical and Experimental Hypnosis,* 1967, *15,* 172–180.

Sampimon, R. L. H., & Woodruff, M. F. A. Some observations concerning the use of hypnosis as a substitute for anesthesia. *Medical Journal of Australia,* 1946, *1,* 393–395.

Sanders, R. S., & Reyher, J. Sensory deprivation and the enhancement of hypnotic susceptibility. *Journal of Abnormal Psychology,* 1969, *74,* 375–381.

Sarason, S., & Rosenzweig, S. An experimental study of the triadic hypothesis: Reaction to frustration, ego-defense and hypnotizability: II. Thematic apperception approach. *Character and Personality,* 1942, *11,* 150–165.

Sarbin, T. R. Contributions to role-taking theory: I. Hypnotic behavior. *Psychological Review,* 1950, *57,* 255–270.

Sarbin, T. R. Role theory. In G. Lindzey (Ed.), *Handbook of Social Psychology, I. Theory and Method.* Cambridge: Addison-Wesley Publishing Co., 1954, pp. 223–258.

Sarbin, T. R. Physiological effects of hypnotic stimulation. In R. M. Dorcus, (Ed.), *Hypnosis and its Therapeutic Applications.* New York: McGraw-Hill, 1956, pp. 1–57.

Sarbin, T. R. Attempts to understand hypnotic phenomena. In L. Postman (Ed.), *Psychology in the Making: Histories of selected research problems.* New York: Knopf, 1962, pp. 745–785.

Sarbin, T. R. Role theoretical interpretation of psychological change. In P. Worchel & D. Byrne (Eds.), *Personality Change.* New York: Wiley, 1964, pp. 176–219.

Sarbin, T. R. The concept of hallucination. *Journal of Personality,* 1967, *35,* 359–380.

Sarbin, T. R., & Andersen, M. L. Base-rate expectancies and perceptual alterations in hypnosis. *British Journal of Social and Clinical Psychology,* 1963, *2,* 112–121.

Sarbin, T. R., & Andersen. M. L. Role-theoretical analysis of hypnotic behavior. In J. Gordon (Ed.), 1967, pp. 319–344.

Sarbin, T. R., & Coe, W. C. *Hypnotic Behavior: The Psychology of Influence Communication.* New York: Holt, Rinehart & Winston, (in press).

Sarbin, T. R., & Kroger, R. O. On Wundt's theory of hypnosis. *International Journal of Clinical and Experimental Hypnosis,* 1963, *11,* 245–259.

Scantlebury, R. E., Frick, H. L., & Patterson, T. L. The effect of normal and hypnotically induced dreams on the gastric hunger movements of man. *Journal of Applied Psychology,* 1942, *26,* 682–691.

Scantlebury, R. E., & Patterson, T. L. Hunger motility in a hypnotised subject. *Quarterly Journal of Experimental Physiology,* 1940, *30,* 347–358.

Schachtel, E. G. On memory and childhood amnesia. *Psychiatry,* 1947, *10,* 1–26.

Schachtel, E. G. Projection and its relation to character attitudes and creativity in the kinesthetic responses: Contributions to an understanding of Rorschach's test, IV. *Psychiatry,* 1950, *13,* 69–100.

Schachtel, E. G. *Metamorphosis: On the Development of Affect, Perception, Attention, and Memory.* New York: Basic Books, 1959.

Schachter, S., & Singer, J. E. Cognitive, social and physiological determinants of emotional state. *Psychological Review,* 1962, *69,* 379–399.

Schafer, R. Regression in the service of the ego: The relevance of a psychoanalytic concept for personality assessment. In G. Lindzey (Ed.), *Assessment of Human Motives.* New York: Holt, Rinehart & Winston, 1958, pp. 119–148.

Schafer, R. On the theoretical and technical conceptualization of activity and passivity. *Psychoanalytic Quarterly,* 1968a, *37,* 173–198.

Schafer, R. *Aspects of Internalization.* New York: International Universities Press, 1968b.

Scheibe, K. E., Gray, A. L., & Keim, C. S. Hypnotically induced deafness and delayed auditory feedback: A comparison of real and simulating subjects. *International Journal of Clinical and Experimental Hypnosis,* 1968, *16,* 158–164.

Schiff, S. K., Bunney, W. E., & Freedman, D. X. A study of ocular movements in hypnotically induced dreams. *Journal of Nervous and Mental Disease,* 1961, *133,* 59–68.

Schilder, P. F., & Kauders, O. *Hypnosis*. Translated from the German by S. Rothenberg. Nervous and Mental Disease Monographs Series, 1927, No. 46. Reissued in P. F. Schilder, *The Nature of Hypnosis*. New translation by Gerda Corvin. New York: International Universities Press, 1956, pp. 43–184.

Schneck, J. M. The school of the Hospital de la Charité in the history of hypnosis. *Journal of the History of Medicine and Allied Sciences*, 1952, *7*, 271–279.

Schneck, J. M. An experimental study of hypnotically induced auditory hallucinations. *Journal of Clinical and Experimental Hypnosis*, 1954a, *2*, 163–170.

Schneck, J. M. Countertransference in Freud's rejection of hypnosis. *American Journal of Psychiatry*, 1954b, *110*, 928–931.

Schneck, J. M. Robert Browning and mesmerism. *Bulletin of the Medical Library Association*, October, 1956, *44*, 443–451.

Schneck, J. M. Relationships between hypnotist-audience and hypnotist-subject interaction. *Journal of Clinical and Experimental Hypnosis*, 1958, *6*, 171–181.

Schneck, J. M. The history of electrotherapy and its correlation with Mesmer's animal magnetism. *American Journal of Psychiatry*, 1959, *116*, 463–464.

Schneck, J. M. Charcot and hypnosis. *Journal of the American Medical Association*, 1961a, *176* (1), 157–158.

Schneck, J. M. Jean-Martin Charcot and the history of experimental hypnosis. *Journal of the History of Medicine and Allied Sciences*, 1961b, *16*, 297–305.

Schneck, J. M. (1953). *Hypnosis in Modern Medicine*. Springfield, Ill.: C. C. Thomas, third edition, 1963a.

Schneck, J. M. Clinical and experimental aspects of hypnotic dreams. In M. V. Kline (Ed.), *Clinical Correlations of Experimental Hypnosis*. Springfield, Ill.: C. C. Thomas, 1963b, pp. 75–100.

Schneck, J. M. History of medical hypnosis: Additions and elaborations, 1963c. In J. M. Schneck (Ed.), 1963a. (l.c. 1953), pp. 406–421.

Schonbar, Rosalea A. Temporal and emotional factors in the selective recall of dreams. *Journal of Consulting Psychology*, 1961, *25*, 67–73.

Schrenck-Notzing, A. F. Ein experimenteller und kritischer Beitrage zur Frage der suggestiven Hervorrufung circumscripter vasomotoischer Veränderungen auf der äusseren Haut. *Zeitschrift für Hypnotismus*, 1896, *4*, 209–228.

Schroetter, K. Experimental dreams. In D. Rapaport (Ed.) *Organization and Pathology of Thought*. New York: Columbia Univ. Press. 1951, pp. 234–248.

Schultz, J. H. Ueber selbsttätige (autogene) Umstellungen der Wärmestrahlung der menschlichen Haut im Autosuggestiven Training. *Deutsche Medizinische Wochenschrift*, 1926, *14*, 571–572.

Schultz, J. H. *Das Autogene Training*. Stuttgart: Georg Thieme Verlag, 1932.

Schwarz, B. E., Bickford, R. G., & Rasmussen, W. C. Hypnotic phenomena, including hypnotically activated seizures, studied with the electroencephalogram. *Journal of Nervous and Mental Disease*, 1955, *122*, 564–574.

Scott, H. D. Hypnosis and the conditioned reflex. *Journal of General Psychology*, 1930, *4*, 113–130.

Scott, M. J. *Hypnosis in Skin and Allergic Diseases*. Springfield, Ill.: C. C. Thomas, 1960.

Sears, R. R. An experimental study of hypnotic anesthesia. *Journal of Experimental Psychology*, 1932, *15*, 1–22.

Secord, P. F., & Blackman, C. W. *Social Psychology*. New York: McGraw-Hill, 1964.

Sector, I. I. An investigation of hypnotizability as a function of attitude toward hypnosis. *American Journal of Clinical Hypnosis*, 1960, *3*, 75–89.

Secter, I. I. TAT card 12M as a predictor of hypnotizability. *American Journal of Clinical Hypnosis,* 1961, *3,* 179–184.

Segal, S. J. Patterns of response to thirst in an imaging task (Perky technique) as a function of cognitive style. *Journal of Personality,* 1968, *36,* 574–588.

Segal, S. J., & Nathan, S. The Perky effect: Incorporation of an external stimulus into an imagery experience under placebo and control conditions. *Perceptual and Motor Skills,* 1964, *18,* 385–395.

Sernan, J. M. A. *Doutes d'un Privincial proposés à Messieurs les Médecins-Commissaires chargés par le roi de l'examen du Magnétisme Animal.* (Doubts of a man from the provinces, proposed to the medical commissioners charged by the King with the investigation of animal magnetism). Lyon, 1784.

Shearn, D. Does the heart learn? *Psychological Bulletin,* 1961, *58,* 452–458.

Sheehan, P. W. Accuracy and vividness of visual images. *Perceptual and Motor Skills,* 1966a, *23,* 391–398.

Sheehan, P. W. Functional similarity of imaging to perceiving: Individual differences in vividness of imagery. *Perceptual and Motor Skills,* 1966b, *23,* 1011–1033. (Monograph Supplement 6–V23).

Sheehan, P. W. A shortened form of Betts' Questionnaire Upon Mental Imagery. *Journal of Clinical Psychology,* 1967a, *23,* 386–389.

Sheehan, P. W. Reliability of a short test of imagery. *Perceptual and Motor Skills,* 1967b, *25,* 744.

Sheehan, P. W. Visual imagery and the organizational properties of perceived stimuli. *British Journal of Psychology,* 1967c, *58,* 247–252.

Sheehan, P. W. Artificial induction of posthypnotic conflict. *Journal of Abnormal Psychology,* 1969, *74,* 16–25.

Sheehan, P. W. An explication of the real-simulating model: A reply to Reyher's comment on "Artificial induction of posthypnotic conflict." *International Journal of Clinical and Experimental Hypnosis,* 1971, *19,* 46–51.

Sheehan, P. W., & Orne, M. T. Some comments on the nature of posthypnotic behavior. *Journal of Nervous and Mental Disease,* 1968, *146,* 209–220.

Shor, R. E. Hypnosis and the concept of the generalized reality-orientation. *American Journal of Psychotherapy,* 1959, *13,* 582–602. Reprinted in Tart, 1969a, pp. 233–250.

Shor, R. E. The frequency of naturally occurring 'hypnotic-like' experiences in the normal college population. *International Journal of Clinical and Experimental Hypnosis,* 1960, *8,* 151–163.

Shor, R. E. Three dimensions of hypnotic depth. *International Journal of Clinical and Experimental Hypnosis,* 1962, *10,* 23–38. Reprinted in Tart, 1969a, pp. 251–262.

Shor, R. E. The accuracy of estimating the relative difficulty of typical hypnotic phenomena. *International Journal of Clinical and Experimental Hypnosis,* 1964a, *12,* 191–201.

Shor, R. E. A note on shock tolerances of real and simulating hypnotic subjects. *International Journal of Clinical and Experimental Hypnosis,* 1964b, *12,* 258–262.

Shor, R. E. Physiological effects of painful stimulation during hypnotic analgesia. In J. E. Gordon (Ed.), 1967, pp. 511–549.

Shor, R. E. Periodical literature on hypnotism and mesmerism. *American Journal of Clinical Hypnosis,* 1968, *10,* 265–266.

Shor, R. E. The three-factor theory of hypnosis as applied to the book-reading fantasy and to the concept of suggestion. *International Journal of Clinical and Experimental Hypnosis,* 1970, *18,* 89–98.

Shor, R. E., & Orne, Emily C. *The Harvard Group Scale of Hypnotic Susceptibility, Form A.* Palo Alto, Calif.: Consulting Psychologists Press, 1962.

Shor, R. E., & Orne, M. T. (Eds.) *The Nature of Hypnosis: Selected Basic Readings.* New York: Holt, Rinehart & Winston, 1965.

Shor, R. E., Orne, M. T., & O'Connell, D. N. Validation and cross-validation of a scale of self-reported personal experiences which predicts hypnotizability. *Journal of Psychology,* 1962, *53,* 55–75.

Shor, R. E., Orne, M. T., & O'Connell, D. N. Psychological correlates of plateau hypnotizability in a special volunteer sample. *Journal of Personality and Social Psychology,* 1966, *3,* 80–95.

Sidis, B. *The Psychology of Suggestion.* With an introduction by W. James. New York: D. Appleton-Century Co., 1898.

Sidis, B. An inquiry into the nature of hallucinations. I. *Psychological Review,* 1904a, *11,* 15–29.

Sidis, B. An inquiry into the nature of hallucination. II. *Psychological Review,* 1904b, *11,* 104–137.

Sidis, B. Are there hypnotic hallucinations? *Psychological Review,* 1906, *13,* 239–257.

Silverman, J. A. Paradigm for the study of altered states of consciousness. *British Journal of Psychiatry,* 1968, *114,* 1201–1218.

Simon, C. W., & Emmons, W. H. EEG, consciousness, and sleep. *Science,* 1956, *124,* 1066–1069.

Sinclair-Gieben, A. H. C., & Chalmers, D. Evaluation of treatment of warts by hypnosis. *Lancet,* 1959, *2,* 480–482.

Singer, J. L. *Daydreaming: An Introduction to the Experimental Study of Inner Experience.* New York: Random House, 1966.

Singer, J. L., & Antrobus, J. S. Eye movements during fantasies: Imagining and suppressing fantasies. *Archives of General Psychiatry,* 1965, *12,* 71–76.

Solomons, L. M., & Stein, Gertrude. Normal motor automatism. *Psychological Review,* 1896, *3,* 492–512.

Solovey, Galina, & Milechnin, A. Concerning the nature of hypnotic phenomena. *Journal of Clinical and Experimental Hypnosis,* 1957, *5,* 67–76.

Sommerschield, H. Posthypnotic conflict, repression and psychopathology. Unpublished doctoral dissertation, Michigan State University, 1965.

Spanos, N. P. Barber's reconceptualization of hypnosis: An evaluation of criticisms. *Journal of Experimental Research in Personality,* 1970, *4,* 241–258.

Spanos, N. P. Goal-directed fantasy and the performance of hypnotic test suggestions. *Psychiatry,* 1971, *34,* 86–96.

Spanos, N. P., & Barber, T. X. "Hypnotic" experiences as inferred from subjective reports: Auditory and visual hallucinations. *Journal of Experimental Research in Personality,* 1968, *3,* 136–150.

Spanos, N. P., & Barber, T. X. A second attempted replication of the Parrish-Lundy-Leibowitz study on hypnotic age-regression. Harding, Mass.: The Medfield Foundation, 1969.

Spanos, N. P., & Barber, T. X. Cognitive activity during "hypnotic" suggestibility: Goal-directed fantasy and the experience of non-volition. *Journal of Personality,* (in press).

Spanos, N. P., Barber, T. X., & Lang, G. Effects of hypnotic induction, suggestions of analgesia, and demands for honesty on subjective reports of pain. Department of Sociology, Boston University, 1969.

Spanos, N. P., & Chaves, J. F. Hypnosis research: A methodological critique of two alternative paradigms. *American Journal of Clinical Hypnosis,* 1970, *13,* 108–127.

Stankler, L. A critical assessment of the cure of warts by suggestion. *Practitioner*, 1967, *198*, 690–694.

Stein, M. I. Creativity. In E. F. Borgatta & W. W. Lambert (Eds.), *Handbook of Personality Theory and Research.* Chicago: Rand McNally & Company, 1968, pp. 900–942.

Stein, M. I., & Meer, B. Perceptual organization in a study of creativity. *Journal of Psychology*, 1954, *37*, 39–43.

Sterba, R. The fate of the ego in analytic therapy. *International Journal of Psychoanalysis*, 1934, *15*, 117–126.

Stern, J. A., Edmonston, W., Ulett, G. A., & Levitsky, A. Electrodermal measures in experimental amnesia. *Journal of Abnormal and Social Psychology*, 1963, *67*, 397–401.

Stern, J. A., Winokur, G., Graham, D. T., & Graham, F. K. Alterations in physiological measures during experimentally induced attitudes. *Journal of Psychosomatic Research*, 1961, *5*, 73–82.

Stevenson, D. R., Stoyva, J., & Beach, H. D. Retroactive inhibition and hypnosis. *Bulletin of the Maritime Psychological Association*, 1962, *11*, 11–15.

Stoyva, J. M. Posthypnotically suggested dreams and the sleep cycle. *Archives of General Psychiatry*, 1965, *12*, 287–294.

Strickler, C. B. A quantitative study of post-hypnotic amnesia. *Journal of Abnormal and Social Psychology*, 1929, *24*, 108–119.

Stroop, J. R. Studies of interference in serial verbal reaction. *Journal of Experimental Psychology*, 1935, *18*, 643–672.

Strosberg, I. M., & Vics, I. I. Physiologic changes in the eye during hypnosis. *American Journal of Clinical Hypnosis*, 1962, *4*, 264–267.

Stross, L., & Shevrin, H. Differences in thought organization between hypnosis and the waking state: An experimental approach. *Bulletin of the Menninger Clinic*, 1962, *26*, 237–247.

Stross, L., & Shevrin, H. A comparison of dream recall in wakefulness and hypnosis. *International Journal of Clinical and Experimental Hypnosis*, 1967, *15*, 63–71.

Stross, L., & Shevrin, H. Thought organization in hypnosis and the waking state: The effects of subliminal stimulation in different states of consciousness. *Journal of Nervous and Mental Disease*, 1968, *147*, 272–288.

Stross, L., & Shevrin, H. Hypnosis as a method for investigating unconscious thought processes: A review of research. *Journal of the American Psychoanalytic Association*, 1969, *17*, 100–135.

Stukát, K. G. *Suggestibility: A Factorial and Experimental Analysis.* Stockholm: Almqvist & Wiksell, 1958.

Sturrock, J. B. Objective assessment of hypnotic amnesia. Paper read at meeting of the Eastern Psychological Association, New York, April, 1966. (Cited in Barber, 1969b.)

Sulzberger, M. B., & Wolf, J. The treatment of warts by suggestion. *Medical Record*, 1934, *140*, 552–556.

Sutcliffe, J. P. Hypnoticbehaviour:Fantasy or simulation? Unpublished doctoral dissertation, University of Sydney, Sydney, Australia, 1958.

Sutcliffe, J. P. "Credulous" and "skeptical" views of hypnotic phenomena: A review of certain evidence and methodology. *International Journal of Clinical and Experimental Hypnosis*, 1960, *8*, 73–101.

Sutcliffe, J. P. "Credulous" and "skeptical" views of hypnotic phenomena: Experiments in esthesia, hallucination, and delusion. *Journal of Abnormal and Social Psychology*, 1961, *62*, 189–200.

Sutcliffe, J. P., Perry, C. W., & Sheehan, P. W. The relation of some aspects of imagery and fantasy to hypnotizability. *Journal of Abnormal Psychology,* 1970, *76,* 279–287.

Sweetland, A. Hypnotic neuroses: Hypochondriasis and depression. *Journal of General Psychology,* 1948, *39,* 91–105.

Szasz, T. S. Psychoanalysis and suggestion: An historical and logical analysis. *Comprehensive Psychiatry,* 1963, *4,* 271–280.

Tarde, G. (1890) *Les Lois de L'imitation, Etude Socioligique* (The laws of imitation: a sociological study). Paris: Alcan, 1907.

Tart, C. T. Hypnotic depth and basal skin resistance. *International Journal of Clinical and Experimental Hypnosis,* 1963, *11,* 81–92.

Tart, C. T. A comparison of suggested dreams occurring in hypnosis and sleep. *International Journal of Clinical and Experimental Hypnosis,* 1964, *12,* 263–289.

Tart, C. T. The hypnotic dream: Methodological problems and a review of the literature. *Psychological Bulletin,* 1965a, *63,* 87–99.

Tart, C. T. Toward the experimental control of dreaming: A review of the literature. *Psychological Bulletin,* 1965b, *64,* 81–91.

Tart, C. T. Types of hypnotic dreams and their relation to hypnotic depth. *Journal of Abnormal Psychology,* 1966a, *71,* 377–382.

Tart, C. T. Thought and imagery in the hypnotic state: Psychophysiological correlates. Paper presented at the meeting of the American Psychological Association, New York, 1966b.

Tart, C. T. Psychedelic experiences associated with a novel hypnotic procedure, mutual hypnosis. *American Journal of Clinical Hypnosis,* 1967, *10,* 65–78.

Tart, C. T. (Ed.) *Altered States of Consciousness:* A Book of Readings. New York: John Wiley & Sons, 1969a.

Tart, C. T. Three studies of EEG alpha feedback. *Biofeedback Society Proceedings,* 1969b, Santa Monica, Part III, 14–19.

Tart, C. T. Waking from sleep at a preselected time. *Journal of the American Society of Psychosomatic Dentistry and Medicine,* 1970a, *17,* 3–16.

Tart, C. T. Self-report scales of hypnotic depth. *International Journal of Clinical and Experimental Hypnosis,* 1970b, *18,* 105–125.

Tart, C. T. Transpersonal potentialities of deep hypnosis. *Journal of Transpersonal Psychology,* 1970c, *2,* 33.

Tart, C. T. Scoring the experience of hypnosis. In preparation.

Tart, C. T., & Dick, Lois. Conscious control of dreaming: I. The posthypnotic dream. *Journal of Abnormal Psychology,* 1970, *76,* 304–315.

Tart, C. T., & Hilgard, E. R. Responsiveness to suggestions under "hypnosis" and "waking-imagination" conditions: A methodological observation. *International Journal of Clinical and Experimental Hypnosis,* 1966, *14,* 247–256.

Takahashi, R. An experimental examination of the dissociation hypothesis in hypnosis. *Journal of Clinical and Experimental Hypnosis,* 1958, *6,* 139–151.

Taylor, W. L. "Cloze procedure": A new tool for measuring readability. *Journalism Quarterly,* 1953, *30,* 415–433.

Thorn, Wendy A. F. A study of the correlates of dissociation as measured by hypnotic amnesia. Unpublished B.A. (Hons.) thesis, Department of Psychology, University of Sydney, 1960.

Thorne, D. E. Amnesia and hypnosis. *International Journal of Clinical and Experimental Hypnosis,* 1969, *17,* 225–241.

Timney, B. N., & Barber, T.X. Hypnotic induction and oral temperature. *International Journal of Clinical and Experimental Hypnosis,* 1969, *17,* 121–132.

Tinterow, M. M. (Ed.) *Foundations of Hypnosis: From Mesmer to Freud.* Springfield, Ill.: Charles C. Thomas, 1970.

Tourney, G. The use of the hypnotically-induced complex in psychosomatic research. *Psychiatric Research Reports,* 1956, *3,* 74–76.

Tracy, D. F. *How to Use Hypnosis.* New York: Sterling Publishing Co., 1952.

Trent, J. C. Surgical anesthesia, 1846–1946. *Journal of the History of Medicine and Allied Sciences,* 1946, *1,* 505–514.

Troffer, Suzanne A., & Tart, C. T. Experimenter bias in hypnotist performance. *Science,* 1964, *145,* 1330–1331.

True, R. M. Experimental control in hypnotic age regression states. *Science,* 1949, *110,* 583–584.

True, R. M., & Stephenson, C. W. Controlled experiments correlating electroencephalogram, pulse, and plantar reflexes with hypnotic age regression and induced emotional states. *Personality,* 1951, *1,* 252–263.

Tryk, H. E. Assessment in the study of creativity. In P. McReynolds (Ed.), *Advances in Psychological Assessment, Vol. I.* Palo Alto, Cal.: Science and Behavior Books, Inc., 1968, pp. 34–54.

Tsinkin, A. Blood pressure in hypnosis (experimental investigation). *Psychoneurological Institute, Ukraine,* 1930a, *14.* (Cited by Platonov, 1959.)

Tsinkin, A. Pulse and respiration during normal waking and hypnosis (experimental investigation). *Psychoneurological Institute, Ukraine,* 1930b,14. (Cited by Platonov, 1959.)

Ullman, M. Herpes simplex and second degree burn induced under hypnosis. *American Journal of Psychiatry,* 1947, *103,* 828–830.

Ullman, M. The adaptive significance of the dream. *Journal of Nervous and Mental Disease,* 1959, *129,* 144–149.

Ullman, M., & Dudek, Stephanie. On the psyche and warts: II. Hypnotic suggestion and warts. *Psychosomatic Medicine,* 1960, *22,* 68–76.

Underwood, H. W. The validity of hypnotically induced visual hallucinations. *Journal of Abnormal and Social Psychology,* 1960, *61,* 39–46.

Van den Berg, J. H. An existential explanation of the guided daydream in psychotherapy. *Review of Existential Psychology and Psychiatry,* 1962, *2,* 5–35.

Vandenbergh, R. L., Sussman, K. E., & Titus, C. C. Effects of hypnotically induced acute emotional stress on carbohydrate and lipid metabolism in patients with diabetes mellitus. *Psychosomatic Medicine,* 1966, *28,* 382–390.

Vanderhoof, Ellen, & Clancy, J. Peripheral blood flow as an indicator of emotional reaction. *Journal of Applied Physiology,* 1962, *17,* 67–70.

Van der Walde, P. H. Interpretation of hypnosis in terms of ego psychology. *Archives of General Psychiatry,* 1965, *12,* 438–447.

Veenstra, G. J. The effectiveness of posthypnotically aroused anger in producing psychopathology. Unpublished master's thesis, Michigan State University, 1969.

Ventur, P., Kransdorff, M., & Kline, M. V. A differential study of emotional attitudes toward hypnosis with card 12M of the Thematic Apperception Test. *British Journal of Medical Hypnosis,* 1956, *8,* 5–16.

Vogel, G., Foulkes, D., & Trosman, H. Ego functions and dreaming during sleep onset. *Archives of General Psychiatry,* 1966, *14,* 238–248. Reprinted in C. T. Tart (Ed.), 1969a, pp. 75–92.

Vollmer, H. Treatment of warts by suggestion. *Psychosomatic Medicine,* 1946, *8,* 138–142.

Wagner, E. E., & Hodge, J. R. Transformation of Rorschach content under two hypnotic trance levels. *Journal of Projective Techniques and Personality Assessment,* 1968, *32,* 433–449.

Wallach, M. A., & Kogan, N. A new look at the creativity-intelligence distinction. *Journal of Personality*, 1965, *33*, 348–369.

Watkins, J. G. *Hypnotherapy of War Neuroses*. New York: Ronald Press, 1949.

Watkins, J. G. Symposium on posthypnotic amnesia: Discussion. *International Journal of Clinical and Experimental Hypnosis*, 1966, *14*, 139–149.

Watson, R. I. *The Great Psychologists: From Aristotle to Freud*. Third edition. Philadelphia: Lippincott, 1971.

Wegner, Norma, & Zeaman, D. Strength of Cardiac conditioned responses with varying unconditioned stimulus durations. *Psychological Review*, 1958, *65*, 238–241.

Weinberg, H. Evidence suggesting the acquisition of a simple discrimination during sleep. *Canadian Journal of Psychology*, 1966, *20*, 1–11.

Weinstein, E., Abrams, S., & Gibbons, D. The validity of the polygraph with hypnotically induced repression and guilt. *American Journal of Psychiatry*, 1970, *126*, 1159–1162.

Weitzenhoffer, A. M. *Hypnotism: An Objective Study in Suggestibility*. New York: John Wiley & Sons, 1953.

Weitzenhoffer, A. M. *General Techniques of Hypnotism*. New York: Grune & Stratton, 1957a.

Weitzenhoffer, A. M. Posthypnotic behavior and the recall of the hypnotic suggestion. *Journal of Clinical and Experimental Hypnosis*, 1957b, *5*, 41–58.

Weitzenhoffer, A. M. Hypnosis and eye movements. I. Preliminary report on a possible slow eye movement correlate of hypnosis. *American Journal of Clinical Hypnosis*, 1969, *11*, 221–227.

Weitzenhoffer, A. M. & Hilgard, E. R. *Stanford Hypnotic Susceptibility Scale, Forms A and B*. Palo Alto, Calif.: Consulting Psychologists Press, 1959.

Weitzenhoffer, A. M. & Hilgard, E. R. *Stanford Hypnotic Susceptibility Scale, Form C*. Palo Alto, Calif.: Consulting Psychologists Press, 1962.

Weitzenhoffer, A. M., & Hilgard, E. R. *Revised Stanford Profile Scales of Hypnotic Susceptibility, Forms I and II*. Palo Alto, Calif.: Consulting Psychologists Press, 1967.

Wells, W. R. The extent and duration of post-hypnotic amnesia. *Journal of Psychology*, 1940, *9*, 137–151.

Welsh, G. S. An anxiety index and an internalization ratio for the MMPI. *Journal of Consulting Psychology*, 1952, *16*, 65–72.

Welsh, G. S., & Barron, F. *Barron-Welsh Art Scale*. Palo Alto, Calif.: Consulting Psychologists Press, 1963.

West, L. J. Psychophysiology of hypnosis. *Journal of the American Medical Association*, 1960, *172*, 672–675.

White, B. J., Alter, R. D., Snow, M. E., & Thorne, D. E. Use of instructions and hypnosis to minimize anchor effects. *Journal of Experimental Psychology*, 1968, *77*, 415–421.

White, M. M. The physical and mental traits of individuals susceptible to hypnosis. *Journal of Abnormal and Social Psychology*, 1930, *25*, 293–298.

White, R. W. Prediction of hypnotic susceptibility from a knowledge of subject's attitude. *Journal of Psychology*, 1937, *3*, 265–277.

White, R. W. A preface to the theory of hypnotism. *Journal of Abnormal and Social Psychology*, 1941, *36*, 477–505.

Whitehorn, J. C., Lundholm, Helge, Fox, E. L., & Benedict, F. G. The metabolic rate in "hypnotic sleep". *New England Journal of Medicine*. 1932, *206*, 777–781.

Whitehorn, J. C., Lundholm, Helge, & Gardner, G. E. The metabolic rate in emotional moods induced by suggestion in hypnosis. *American Journal of Psychiatry*, 1930, *9*, 661–666.

Whytt, R. *Essay on the Vital and Other Involuntary Motions of Animals*. Edinburgh: John Balfour, 1763. Cited in F. Fearing, *Reflex Action: A Study in the History of Physiological Psychology*. New York: Hafner Publishing Co., 1964.

Wible, C. L., & Jenness, A. Electrocardiograms during sleep and hypnosis. *Journal of Psychology*. 1936, *1*, 235–245.

Wickramasekera, I. The effects of sensory restriction on susceptibility to hypnosis: A hypothesis, some preliminary data, and theoretical speculation. *International Journal of Clinical and Experimental Hypnosis*, 1969, *17*, 217–224.

Wild, Cynthia. Creativity and adaptive regression. *Journal of Personality and Social Psychology*, 1965, *2*, 161–169.

Williams, G. W. Hypnosis in perspective. In L. M. LeCron (Ed.), *Experimental Hypnosis: A Symposium of Research*. New York: The Macmillan Company, 1952, pp. 4–21.

Williams, G. W. Clark L. Hull and his work on hypnosis. *Journal of Clinical and Experimental Hypnosis*, 1953, *1*, 1–3.

Williams, G. W. Difficulty in dehypnotizing. *Journal of Clinical and Experimental Hypnosis*, 1953, *1*, 3–12.

Williams, H. L., Morlock, H. C., Jr., & Morlock, Jean V. Instrumental behavior during sleep. *Psychophysiology*, 1966, *2*, 208–216.

Williamsen, J. A., Johnson, H. J., & Eriksen, C. W. Some characteristics of posthypnotic amnesia. *Journal of Abnormal Psychology*, 1965, *70*, 123–131.

Wilson, D. L. The role of confirmation of expectancies in hypnotic induction. Unpublished doctoral dissertation, University of North Carolina, 1967.

Wiseman, R. J. The Rorschach as a stimulus for hypnotic dreams: A study of unconscious processes. Unpublished doctoral dissertation, Michigan State University, 1962.

Wiseman, R. J., & Reyher, J. A procedure utilizing dreams for deepening the hypnotic trance. *American Journal of Clinical Hypnosis*, 1962, *5*, 105–110.

Witkin, H. A. Influencing dream content. In M. Kramer (Ed.), *Dream Psychology and the New Biology of Dreaming*. Springfield, Ill.: Charles C. Thomas Publishers, 1969, pp. 285–359.

Wolberg, L. R. *Hypnoanalysis*. New York: Grune & Stratton, 1945.

Wolberg, L. R. *Medical Hypnosis*. New York: Grune & Stratton, 1948, 2 vols.

Wolff, L. V. The response to plantar stimulation in infancy. *American Journal of Diseases of Children*, 1930, *39*, 1176–1185.

Woodworth, R. S. *Experimental Psychology*. London: Methuen & Co., 1939.

Wright, M. E. Symposium on posthypnotic amnesia: Discussion. *International Journal of Clinical and Experimental Hypnosis*, 1966, *14*, 135–138.

Wright, Nancy A., & Zubek, J. P. Relationship between perceptual deprivation tolerance and adequacy of defenses as measured by the Rorschach. *Journal of Abnormal Psychology*, 1969, *74*, 615–617.

Wundt, W. M. *Hypnotismus und Suggestion* (Hypnotism and Suggestion). Leipzig: Engelmann, 1892.

Wydenbruck, Nora P. von. *Doctor Mesmer: An Historical Study*. London: John Westhouse, 1947.

Yates, A. J. Simulation and hypnotic age regression. *International Journal of Clinical and Experimental Hypnosis*, 1960, *8*, 243–249.

Yanovski, A. G. Hypnosis as a research tool in cardiology. In G. H. Estabrooks, ed., Hypnosis: current problems. New York: Harper & Row, 1962, pp. 76–108.

Yanovski, A., & Curtis, G. C. Hypnosis and stress. *American Journal of Clinical Hypnosis*, 1968, *10*, 149–156.

Young, J., & Cooper, L. M. Hypnotic recall amnesia as a function of expectation. Unpublished research, Brigham Young University, 1970.

Young, J., & Cooper, L. M. The manifestation posthypnotic recall amnesia of those who expect it and those who do not. Unpublished research, Brigham Young University, 1970.

Young, P. C. An experimental study of mental and physical functions in the normal and hypnotic state. *American Journal of Psychology*, 1925, *36*, 214–232. (Based upon doctoral dissertation under W. McDougall, Harvard University, 1923).

Young, P. C. Is rapport an essential characteristic of hypnosis? *Journal of Abnormal and Social Psychology*, 1927, *22*, 130–139.

Young, P. C. Suggestion as indirection. *Journal of Abnormal and Social Psychology*, 1931, *26*, 69–90.

Young, P. C. Hypnotic regression—fact or artifact? *Journal of Abnormal and Social Psychology*, 1940, *35*, 273–278.

Young, P. C. Antisocial uses of hypnosis. In. L. M. LeCron (Ed.), *Experimental Hypnosis*. New York: The Macmillan Co., 1952, pp. 376–409.

Zamansky, H. S., Scharf, B., & Brightbill, R. The effect of expectancy for hypnosis on prehypnotic performance. *Journal of Personality*, 1964, *32*, 236–248.

Zeaman, D., Deane, G., & Wegner, Norma. Amplitude and latency characteristics of the conditioned heart response. *Journal of Psychology*, 1954, *38*, 235–250.

Zeaman, D., & Wegner, Norma. The role of drive reduction in the classical conditioning of an autonomically mediated response. *Journal of Experimental Psychology*, 1954, *48*, 349–354.

Zilboorg, G., & Henry, G. W. *A History of Medical Psychology*. New York: W. W. Norton & Co., 1941.

Zimbardo, P. G. *The Cognitive Control of Motivation: The Consequences of Choice and Dissonance*. Glenview, Ill.: Scott, Foresman & Co., 1969.

Zimbardo, P. G., Ebbesen, E. B., & Fraser, S. C. The objective measurement of subjective states. *Journal of Personality and Social Psychology*, (in press).

Zimbardo, P. G., Rapaport, C., & Baron, J. Pain control by hypnotic induction of motivational states. In P. G. Zimbardo (Ed.), 1969, pp. 136–152.

Zuckerman, M. Perceptual isolation as a stress situation: A review. *Archives of General Psychiatry*, 1964, *11*, 255–276.

Zuckerman, M., Persky, H., Link, Katherine E., & Basu, G. K. Experimental and subject factors determining responses to sensory deprivation, social isolation, and confinement. *Journal of Abnormal Psychology*, 1968, *73*, 183–194.

Zung, W. W. K., & Wilson, W. P. Response to auditory stimulation during sleep: Discrimination and arousal as studied with electroencephalography. *Archives of General Psychiatry*, 1961, *4*, 548–552.

Zweig, S. *Mental Healers: Franz Anton Mesmer, Mary Baker Eddy, Sigmund Freud*. German original 1931. Translated by E. Paul & C. Paul. New York: Garden City Publishing Co., Inc., 1932.

Author Index

Aaronson, B., 474
Abdulhusein, S. D., 247
Abrams, S., 109
Ackerknecht, E. H., 16
Adams, J. E., 298
Agle, D. P., 111
Ainsworth, Mary D., 109
Akstein, D., 349
Allison, J., 263, 280, 281
Allport, G. W., 497
Amadeo, M., 63, 202–205, 272–273
Anand, B. K., 259
Andersen, M. L., 119, 147, 180, 210, 387, 483
Anderson, M. N., 141
Anderson, W. L., 175–176
Andrew, Dorothy M., 284
Antrobus, Judith S., 63, 272, 274
Antrobus, J. S., 63, 272, 274, 278, 280, 294, 309
Aristeguieta, A., 65, 231
Arkin, A. M., 64
Arnold, Magda B., 170–171, 214, 295, 301, 305, 349
Arons, H., 133
Ås, A., 256, 260, 282, 287–289, 306
Asch, S. E., 405
Aschan, G., 207
Ascher, L. M., 145

Aserinsky, E., 49, 61, 202
Ashley, W. R., 98
August, R. V., 143
Austin, Margaret J., 408

Bachrach, H. M., 499
Backus, P. S., 206–207
Bailly, J. S., 21
Banister, H., 223
Barbarin, C. de, 21
Bakan, P., 362
Barber, T. X., 40, 52, 61, 66, 85, 90, 101, 103–106, 119, 122, 123, 125, 127–128, 133–134, 139, 141–146, 148–151, 155–159, 162–163, 165–166, 168, 172–177, 179–180, 182, 187–190, 193, 195, 209, 220–221, 224, 226–229, 241, 244–247, 255–256, 293–296, 303–304, 360, 311–312, 314, 334, 387, 424, 549
Barker, W., 51, 199
Barnard, G. W., 191
Barnlund, D. C., 181
Barolin, G. S., 198
Baron, J., 542
Barratt, P. E. H., 48, 65
Barron, F., 264, 267–268, 279, 286
Barry, H., Jr., 35, 221
Bartlett, E. S., 207
Bartlett, Mary, 51

639

Subject Index